Teaching Mathematics for the 21st Century

Methods and Activities for Grades 6–12

Second Edition

Linda Huetinck

California State University at Northridge

Sara N. Munshin

Los Angeles Unified School District

PEARSON

Merrill
Prentice Hall

Upper Saddle River, New Jersey
Columbus, Ohio

Library of Congress Cataloging in Publication Data

Huetinck, Linda.
  Teaching mathematics for the 21st century: methods and activities for grades 6-12 /
Linda Huetinck, Sara N. Munshin.— 2nd ed.
      p. cm.
  Includes bibliographical references and index.
  ISBN 0-13-048833-X
  1. Mathematics—Study and teaching (Middle school) 2. Mathematics—Study and
teaching (Secondary) I. Title: Teaching mathematics for the twenty-first century. II.
Munshin, Sara N. III. Title.

QA11.2H84 2004
510'.71'2—dc21

2002045463

Vice President and Executive Publisher: Jeffery W. Johnston
Senior Editor: Linda Ashe Montgomery
Editorial Assistant: Laura J. Weaver
Production Editor: Linda Hillis Bayma
Text Design and Production Coordination: Elm Street Publishing Services, Inc.
Design Coordinator: Diane C. Lorenzo
Cover Designer: Jeff Vanik
Cover Image: Corbis
Production Manager: Pamela D. Bennett
Director of Marketing: Ann Castel Davis
Marketing Manager: Darcy Betts Prybella
Marketing Coordinator: Tyra Poole

This book was set by Carlisle Communications, Ltd. It was printed and bound by
Phoenix Book Tech. The cover was printed by Phoenix Color Corp.

Pearson Education Ltd.
Pearson Education Singapore Pte. Ltd.
Pearson Education Canada, Ltd.
Pearson Education–Japan
Pearson Education Australia Pty. Limited
Pearson Education North Asia Ltd.
Pearson Educación de Mexico, S.A. de C.V.
Pearson Education Malaysia Pte. Ltd.

10 9 8 7 6 5 4 3 2 1
ISBN: 0-13-048833-X

We would like to dedicate this book to our husbands,
John Huetinck and Sid Munshin.
Without their love and continual support,
this book would not have been possible.

Educator Learning Center:
An Invaluable Online Resource

Merrill Education and the Association for Supervision and Curriculum Development (ASCD) invite you to take advantage of a new online resource, one that provides access to the top research and proven strategies associated with ASCD and Merrill—the Educator Learning Center. At **www.EducatorLearningCenter.com** you will find resources that will enhance your students' understanding of course topics and of current educational issues, in addition to being invaluable for further research.

How the Educator Learning Center will help your students become better teachers

With the combined resources of Merrill Education and ASCD, you and your students will find a wealth of tools and materials to better prepare them for the classroom.

Research

- More than 600 articles from the ASCD journal *Educational Leadership* discuss everyday issues faced by practicing teachers.
- A direct link on the site to Research Navigator™ gives students access to many of the leading education journals, as well as extensive content detailing the research process.
- Excerpts from Merrill Education texts give your students insights on important topics of instructional methods, diverse populations, assessment, classroom management, technology, and refining classroom practice.

Classroom Practice

- Hundreds of lesson plans and teaching strategies are categorized by content area and age range.
- Case studies and classroom video footage provide virtual field experience for student reflection.
- Computer simulations and other electronic tools keep your students abreast of today's classrooms and current technologies.

Look into the value of Educator Learning Center yourself

Preview the value of this educational environment by visiting **www.EducatorLearningCenter.com** and clicking on "Demo." For a free 4-month subscription to the Educator Learning Center in conjunction with this text, simply contact your Merrill/Prentice Hall sales representative.

Preface

"It's time to let the secret out: Mathematics is not primarily a matter of plugging numbers into formulas and performing rote computations. It is a way of thinking and questioning that may be unfamiliar to many of us, but is available to almost all of us." So states John Allen Paulos in *A Mathematician Reads the Newspaper* (New York: Anchor Books, 1996).

This second edition of *Teaching Mathematics for the 21st Century* is intended to help you let the secret out—to open up to your students the wonderful discoveries and challenges of the pattern-making and problem-solving aspects of a subject you may already find fascinating. If you think back to those mathematics teachers who surely inspired you to want to emulate their enthusiasm, clarity, and reasoning ability, we believe you can see that they, too, opened doors to your understanding of content beyond the procedures. The beauty and elegance of mathematics, as well as the need to apply mathematics to become an informed citizen of our democracy, must be imparted to today's students. This can be a big challenge when these students bring into your classroom a mind-set with a more limited (and to them, boring) perspective of mathematics.

This book came out of our experiences in middle- and high-school classrooms, as well as our extensive work with pre- and in-service teachers. Not only have we provided mathematics teachers with many forms of professional development but we have also visited the classrooms of hundreds of teachers in many different types of communities and been inspired by observing situations where mathematical understanding is clearly a goal that is being realized. We call the kind of teaching that goes on in these classrooms "*Standards*-based," referring to the *Standards* documents produced by the National Council of Teachers of Mathematics (NCTM), the most recent of which is the *Principles and Standards for School Mathematics* (PSSM, 2000). All mathematics teachers can implement *Standards*-based instruction in their classrooms, and all students can benefit from this experience.

We trust that the assistance provided through this book and through your pre-service and in-service classes will help you enjoy a career that is person-ally and professionally satisfying. And we hope that mathematical thinking will become a common part of your students' lives.

ORGANIZATION OF THE TEXT

Teaching Mathematics for the 21st Century contains twelve chapters organized into three overall parts. The first five chapters provide both theoretical and practical suggestions concerning what you should know and consider before you "step on the stage" of your first classroom. Chapters 6 through 10 discuss the ongoing realities of the classroom—planning and fine-tuning daily lessons, managing classrooms where discourse is valued, assessing and evaluating students, and dealing with issues of equity as they affect the classroom. The final two chapters look to your future as a member of a professional community, both in how you relate to constituents outside of education and how you avail yourself of ongoing professional growth activities as a lifelong learner. Within each part, the chapters are independent and can be studied in any order.

Part I: Prior to Entering the Classroom

Chapter 1, "History and Introduction to Mathematics Education Reform," provides extensive background about the history and development of the significant concepts leading to the current reform. The chapter details methods of teaching mathematics throughout the last half of the 20th century. We discuss research in cooperative learning and offer practical suggestions for implementing cooperative learning, one of the common activities in contemporary teaching practice. The mathematical focus of the activities in this chapter is logic.

Chapter 2, "Learning, Motivation, and Basic Management Skills," begins by discussing the main learning theories and models of intelligence that underlie the educational psychology behind reform in mathematics education. The section on motivation introduces some main concepts of the topic. Aspects of motivation are interwoven with the selection of activities and instructional design throughout the book. The second half of the chapter is devoted to decisions related to management skills teachers need before the first day of class. Examples and problems center on probability. Different approaches to probability tasks illustrate different theories of learning. Motivation and management issues also come into play with this content area, since probability tasks most often involve hands-on activities.

Chapter 3, "Concrete to Abstract With Tools, Manipulatives, Computer Programs, and Calculators," introduces a variety of methods to increase the preservice teacher's tool kit of teaching ideas. An effective way to explore this chapter is with a series of stations using the different manipulatives and calculators in a round-robin laboratory setting. Groups of students spend a given time at each station to become familiar with the available manipulative, and then they rotate to the next station. If class sets are available, lessons and activities using the MIRA, patty paper, and graphing calculators can be done more easily with the entire class working simultaneously on the same exercise in cooperative groups. Of course, the computer activities can be supplemented according to the computer software available at your site. The unifying topics for this chapter consist of the foundational concepts of arithmetic, geometry, and algebra. Secondary teachers need to understand the concept development approach to mathematics both as a preferred way of introducing new topics and as an approach to intervention.

Chapter 4, "*Standards*-Based Curricula With Sample Lessons," provides an opportunity to explore elements of different reform curricula, including sample materials from some programs. The chapter contrasts and compares segments of instructional sequences within some exemplary middle- and high-school programs. The emphasis is on data analysis activities incorporating methods of data collection (including the use of probeware) and ways to analyze data. What better content to link with reform materials than data analysis, since it effectively meshes the Technology Principle with the Representation and Communication Standards of the PSSM?

Chapter 5, "Geometry and Algebra Redefined?" explores the current development of these areas of mathematics and illustrates effective ways to integrate them. Algebra and geometry activities in the chapter provide the vehicle for this discussion.

Part II: Teaching and Learning in the Classroom

The second part of the text begins with Chapter 6, "Planning Instruction." This chapter starts with an overview of the teacher's community and school culture. Next, a discussion of semester, unit, and daily planning gives examples for each stage in the planning process. The chapter highlights different strategies for effective lessons based on the materials to be studied. The examples and problems in this chapter focus on matrices and their applications, as that topic lends itself to many different grade levels and applications.

Chapter 7, "Promoting Communication in the Classroom," presents a view of discipline as an integral part of instruction and classroom communication. We offer practical suggestions for promoting discourse, encouraging communication through student writing, and building a community of learners. Illustrations and problems are drawn from the discrete mathematics topics of graph theory and group theory, both of which lend themselves well to various types of classroom communication.

In Chapter 8, "Assessing Individual Student Performance," we introduce formative assessment and summative assessment (evaluation). The discussion includes basic test design and grade determination, topics of great concern to beginning teachers. Activities involving patterns in mathematics illustrate the importance of assessing students' mathematical reasoning in a *Standards*-based classroom.

The topic of Chapter 9, "Student Equity," is complex and broad. This chapter serves only as an introduction to some of the equity issues facing teachers. The prevailing issue throughout the chapter is how to make mathematics accessible to all students. A discussion of the effects of tracking is followed by considerations of effective ways to help multicultural/multiethnic students, females, gifted/talented students, and students with mild learning difficulties to be successful in mathematics. The mathematical emphasis of this chapter is nonstandard problems that are rich in content yet open to a variety of solution approaches.

Chapter 10, "Focus on Performance Assessment," extends the discussion of assessment in Chapter 8 by exploring the use of performance tasks and rubric scoring. In our experience, the area of assessment has grown so complex, with alternative methods unfamiliar to student teachers, that it is best to approach assessment in two different chapters with time between to absorb this broad and very important aspect of *Standards*-based teaching. The role of externally mandated assessments also is presented. The chapter also touches on uses of the Internet by mathematics students and their families. Investigations in applied mathematics and modeling allow students to practice writing solutions that are assessed by rubrics.

Part III: Ongoing Development

The third part of this text opens with Chapter 11, "Communicating With Parents and Community." This chapter demonstrates effective ways to interact with parents, the school community, and other mathematics students. Topics include managing back-to-school nights, parent conferences, family mathematics nights, and entry into mathematics contests. The mathematical content comprises number sense, estimation, and measurement, all of which are mathematical tasks that can be connected to real-life experiences.

Chapter 12, "Professional Growth," encourages students to be lifelong learners of the profession of teaching. This chapter discusses the topic of evaluation by supervisors, which is of paramount concern to the beginning teacher. Certification through the National Board for Professional Teaching Standards is described as a goal of exemplary teachers. The mathematical focus of lessons written and shared by experienced teacher leaders is on post-core topics in discrete mathematics, trigonometry, and pre-calculus.

FEATURES INCLUDED IN THE TEXT

This book is suitable for both undergraduate and graduate courses for teachers of mathematics, as well as for in-service enrichment courses. It may also be used for classes for supplementary credential programs and for retraining persons from other careers who are becoming teachers. We selected mathematical material and pedagogy of great richness, anticipating that this text not only will be useful to undergraduate and graduate methods students and professors, but also will continue to be a resource to teachers throughout their career.

To support those objectives, *Teaching Mathematics for the 21st Century* includes a variety of features:

- Many chapters contain vignettes taken from actual classroom experiences.
- Exemplary teachers have contributed their philosophies on different issues and materials that work in their classrooms.

- The problems, investigations, and instructional sequences in every chapter have been classroom tested with secondary-level students. They demonstrate the wide range of activities to be found in today's mathematics curricula.
- Additional activities at the end of each chapter provide mathematics exercises to use along with or in place of those integrated in the chapters.
- In the back of the book, "Activity Notes to the Teacher for Selected Problems" helps teachers implement the content and methods found in the activities, sample lessons, and instructional sequences of each chapter.
- An annotated list of recommended resources is given at the end of each chapter.
- An extensive list of references combined for all the chapters appears at the end of the book.

NEW TO THIS EDITION

This second edition has been extensively reworked to update materials and make the format of the activities more accessible. A number of these enhancements merit special notice:

- Throughout the text, we apply the NCTM's *Principles and Standards of School Mathematics*. Chapters quote the core principles and main ideas of the PSSM where appropriate. Each of the activities, sample lessons, and instructional sequences indicates the relevant standard, so both pre-service and in-service teachers can see how they might apply these standards in the classroom.
- Activities, lessons, and instructional sequences are interactive. An improved format allows greater ease of use with secondary-level students. These significant elements of the text encourage involvement in *Standards*-based quality mathematics in every chapter. In each chapter's introduction, an "About the Activities for This Chapter" section describes how the mathematical lessons work with the discussion material of the text and with each other to build power in mathematical thinking. The integration of activities and discussion topics helps teachers apply educational theory to actual mathematics lessons.
- For additional interactive opportunities, a Companion Website (http://www.prenhall.com/huetinck) includes links to other helpful resources on the Internet. When you see the Website icon, additional information about this topic can be accessed on our Website.

- A variety of Instructional Resources have been added to the end of each chapter. Many of these are recent books and articles in *The Mathematics Teacher* and *Teaching Middle School Mathematics* published since the first edition of this text.

ACKNOWLEDGMENTS

This book would not have been possible without the following people:

- Our students, who have taught us to make mathematics more relevant;
- Classroom teacher colleagues, who have demonstrated the type of teaching we advocate and who have shared their teaching ideas with us;
- Other professional colleagues at the university and in consulting capacities, who have given us excellent feedback and sources of information to include to make this book more complete and accurate.

A few mathematics teachers we have worked with deserve special thanks, as they have made particular contributions to the book: Kathy Blackwood, Venice High School, Los Angeles Unified School District (LAUSD) (ret.); Jack Bloom, Porter Middle School, LAUSD; Bob Drake, Local District H, LAUSD; Beverly Gleason, Santa Monica High School, Santa Monica–Malibu Unified School District; Kathy Layton, Beverly Hills High School, Beverly Hills Unified School District (ret.); Christine LeBeau, Quartz Hill High School, Antelope Valley (CA) Union High School District; Suzanne Lewis, Frost Middle School, LAUSD; Scott Malloy, Brea-Olinda (CA) High School; Yvonne Mojica, Verdugo Hills High School, LAUSD; Sal Quesada, Roosevelt High School, LAUSD; Richard

Sisley, Polytechnic High School, Pasadena; Tom Walters, Mathematics Diagnostic Testing Program, University of California, Los Angeles; and Jane Wortman, Beverly Hills High School.

Thanks to Shirley Gray, California State University, Los Angeles; John F. Moelter, retired high-school teacher; and Janet Trentacosta, editor of the *ComMuniCator*, the journal of the California Mathematics Council, for their permission to use the materials they developed. The following California State University–Northridge professors provided collaborative assistance: Beverly Cabello and Barnabas Hughes.

The following reviewers were both encouraging and specific in giving directions for improvements of the draft manuscripts of this edition and the first edition: Ed Dickey, University of South Carolina; Judith Wells, University of Southern Indiana; and Steven W. Ziebarth, Western Michigan University.

We truly appreciate the Merrill/Prentice Hall editors with whom we have worked. Brad Potthoff listened to our original concept of the book at the NCTM annual meeting in San Diego in the mid-1990s and thought we could make a contribution to the field we love (mathematics teaching). He gave us good advice during the years it took to make the ideas a reality. The editor of the second edition, Linda Montgomery, helped us address major concerns we had about the original format. We hope you agree that this new edition is even more teacher-friendly.

Many thanks to these individuals and to the unnamed students and colleagues who continue to hold standards of practical relevance and good mathematics before us in this endeavor.

Linda Huetinck
Sara N. Munshin

Discover the Companion Website Accompanying This Book

The Prentice Hall Companion Website: A Virtual Learning Environment

Technology is a constantly growing and changing aspect of our field that is creating a need for content and resources. To address this emerging need, Prentice Hall has developed an online learning environment for students and professors alike—Companion Websites—to support our textbooks.

In creating a Companion Website, our goal is to build on and enhance what the textbook already offers. For this reason, the content for each user-friendly website is organized by chapter and provides the professor and student with a variety of meaningful resources.

For the Professor—

Every Companion Website integrates **Syllabus Manager**™, an online syllabus creation and management utility.

- **Syllabus Manager**™ provides you, the instructor, with an easy, step-by-step process to create and revise syllabi, with direct links into the Companion Website and other online content without having to learn HTML.

- Students may log on to your syllabus during any study session. All they need to know is the web address for the Companion Website and the password you've assigned to your syllabus.

- After you have created a syllabus using **Syllabus Manager**™, students may enter the syllabus for their course section from any point in the Companion Website.

- Clicking on a date, the student is shown the list of activities for the assignment. The activities for each assignment are linked directly to actual content, saving time for students.

- Adding assignments consists of clicking on the desired due date, then filling in the details of the assignment—name of the assignment, instructions, and whether it is a one-time or repeating assignment.

- In addition, links to other activities can be created easily. If the activity is online, a URL can be entered in the space provided, and it will be linked automatically in the final syllabus.

- Your completed syllabus is hosted on our servers, allowing convenient updates from any computer on the Internet. Changes you make to your syllabus are immediately available to your students at their next log on.

Common Companion Website features for students include:

For the Student—

- **Chapter Topics**—Outline key concepts from the text.

- **Interactive Self-quizzes**—Complete with hints and automatic grading that provide immediate feedback for students.

  After students submit their answers for the interactive self-quizzes, the Companion Website **Results Reporter** computes a percentage grade, provides a graphic representation of how many questions were answered correctly and incorrectly, and gives a question-by-question analysis of the quiz. Students are given the option to send their quiz to up to four email addresses (professor, teaching assistant, study partner, etc.).

- **Web Destinations**—Links to www sites that relate to chapter content.

- **Message Board**—Virtual bulletin board to post or respond to questions or comments from a national audience.

To take advantage of the many available resources, please visit the *Teaching Mathematics for the 21st Century: Methods and Activities for Grades 6–12,* Second Edition, Companion Website at

www.prenhall.com/huetinck

Contents

PART II TEACHING AND LEARNING IN THE CLASSROOM 195

CHAPTER 7

Promoting Communication in the Classroom 239

CHAPTER 8

Assessing Individual Student Performance 301

CHAPTER 9

Student Equity 339

PART III ONGOING DEVELOPMENT 415

List of Activities

If the title of the activity is not self-explanatory, the relevant mathematical topic is listed beneath the title. Necessary or optional equipment, such as manipulatives, calculators, or computer programs, is indicated in italic type after the title. An asterisk before an activity indicates that it is on the Companion Website for this book.

Chapter 11: Communicating With Parents and Community

Mathematical Focus: Number Sense, Estimation, and Measurement

Chapter 12: Professional Growth

Mathematical Focus: Post-Core Topics

NOTE: Every effort has been made to provide accurate and current Internet information in this book. However, the Internet and information posted on it are constantly changing, so it is inevitable that some of the Internet addresses listed in this text-book will change.

PART

I

Prior to Entering the Classroom

This book is about teaching secondary mathematics, and it is intended for all of us who strive to become better at what we do. Although we selected resources from many places in development of the book, materials from the National Council of Teachers of Mathematics (NCTM) play a prominent role. In particular, the 2000 publication of the NCTM document, *Principles and Standards for School Mathematics* (PSSM), provides the underlying philosophy of this text as it very appropriately leads us into the 21st century. Thus, whenever you see "*Standards*" mentioned, it is that document and its predecessors that are being used as referents.

Part I includes areas that beginning teachers should be concerned with before they enter the classroom. Chapter 1 begins with a review of mathematics education in the United States during the past 50 years, emphasizing the impact on the average classroom. Chapter 2 summarizes the research on various aspects of learning theory, connecting these ideas to motivation and classroom management issues. Appropriate use of the broad range of tools available for modern classrooms, including manipulatives and electronic technology, is discussed in Chapter 3, with sample lessons using a number of those tools. Chapter 4 presents examples of instructional sequences from a sampling of the curricula developed in responses to the NCTM *Standards*. Part I concludes with a modern perspective of algebra and geometry in Chapter 5.

History and Introduction to Mathematics Education Reform

The National Council of Teachers of Mathematics, a prime force in mathematics education during the last half century, refined its reform efforts and led mathematics education into the 21st century with the 2000 publication of the document, *Principles and Standards for School Mathematics* (PSSM). We will continue to refer to that research-based document as well as teacher material based on that document throughout this book. The Companion Website for this book has a link to NCTM where PSSM can be downloaded. That document builds on other documents referenced in this first chapter.

This chapter serves two purposes. First, it presents an overview of mathematics education in the United States in the previous 50 years, with an introduction to specific aspects of *Standards*-based mathematics prevalent in the 1990s. Many of those aspects will be revisited in later chapters at much greater depth. Second, it emphasizes one of the teaching strategies used in *Standards*-based classrooms—cooperative learning. As in all chapters, one mathematical content area is highlighted and several classroom-tested activities are provided.

ABOUT THE ACTIVITIES FOR THIS CHAPTER

The content focus of the first chapter is logic because logical reasoning underlies all mathematics. Some of the activities in this chapter deal directly with the language of logic and deductive reasoning. Also, mathematical reasoning permeates the activities you will be using throughout the book. The activities in Chapter 1 that do not have logic as a content focus are designed to show specific aspects of cooperative group work in the secondary mathematics classroom. Following the guidelines established in this chapter is necessary for successfully implementing the group activities in the remainder of the book.

In Activity 1.1, each student in a group of four receives different parts of a geometric puzzle and must communicate silently with the other members of the group in order to solve the puzzle. A similar structure occurs in Activity 1.2, and here the content is deductive logic, with Venn diagrams a tool for solving the problem. Activity 1.3 has students use the think-pair-share strategy to develop responses to the prompts. The vocabulary of logic is applied to various geometric shapes here. Park Beautification (Activity 1.4) is an example of a structured group project where different students are assigned different roles within the project. It also includes an example of group self-assessment. Activity 1.5 provides another example of a cooperative activity. Each student in a group of four first builds a rectangle that satisfies the description given on a clue. Students then build a common rectangle that satisfies all four clues.

The additional activities in Chapter 1 use deductive logic in different settings. Rainbow Logic (Activity 1.6) is a game students can play at home with family members. Condo Neighbors and No Homework (Activities 1.7 and 1.8) illustrate the use of charts to eliminate nonsolutions of different levels of logic problems. Activity 1.9, the final one in this chapter, is modified from a *Standards*-based high school textbook. Throughout this book, you will have many more opportunities to try problems taken from *Standards*-based programs.

A BRIEF HISTORY OF SCHOOL MATHEMATICS

Mathematics reform has been a topic of concern in the United States for many decades. In the 1927 National Council of Teachers of Mathematics (NCTM) Yearbook, *Curriculum Problems in Teaching Mathematics*,

Barber relates that junior high school mathematics does not make sense to students because they are simply memorizing procedures without understanding the practical applications of mathematical tools. Today, more than 75 years later, mathematics reformers continue to examine ways to make mathematics more relevant to young people. At the outset, however, we want to emphasize that any changes in curriculum, instruction, and assessment should never become the goal; rather, they are means to the overarching goal of increased student learning of quality mathematics.

It is inappropriate to use the image of a pendulum swing as a metaphor for recurring pressures to bring about higher mathematics achievement through various, and sometimes conflicting, means. Even though there are identifiable phases of change, Cuban (1990) shows that the two-dimensional notion of returning to a baseline each time a new educational "fad" is widely adopted and then rejected is simply not accurate. Instead, he asserts that "most of the reforms get implemented in word rather than deed, especially in classrooms" (p. 7). That is, teachers adapt materials and procedures and continue to make daily classroom decisions based on their own knowledge, skill, and beliefs. They make changes based on what they see working in their classrooms and what their students' comfort level allows. Teachers tend to continue to use proven materials and methods, regardless of new research, directives, and curricula. Or, as another researcher (Osborne, 1992) puts it, "The new expectations have contained the old expectations rather than replaced them" (p. 21).

The need for all students to leave high school well prepared for the 21st century, whether they continue their education at a college or university or enter the workforce immediately after leaving high school, drives the current reform. By either route, the changing workplace requires all citizens to be lifelong learners. Indeed, all students should have tools for self-directed learning, effective cooperative efforts, and technology to access and analyze information. English and bilingual learners, students with physical handicaps, and students with learning disabilities all are included in the vision of the reform in mathematics. To the largest extent possible, *each* student should have not only the opportunity but also additional support, as appropriate, to successfully complete at least 2 years of the high school mathematics curriculum (algebra and geometry or 2 years in integrated coursework).

Traditional Approach

There are two main components to what was considered an effective and efficient approach to education in the United States, and which is referred to by most mathematics educators as the traditional approach. The first component is teaching by telling, that is, by the teacher presenting information and the students thereby assimilating the information. The second component of the traditional approach is the practice of assigning students to different groups, based on some form of achievement information, to receive qualitatively different content.

The combined effects of ability tracking and overreliance on the lecture method have resulted in huge numbers of our students graduating from high school without the necessary background for success in college or even the basic numeracy skills for good citizenship and workforce competency, according to standardized assessment instruments. With an ever more diverse student population and an increasingly sophisticated technological world, something had to be done. Even with increased college entrance requirements in mathematics, very few students continued to enroll in, let alone complete, mathematically intensive college majors. In the mid-1980s, almost half of the students receiving doctoral degrees in mathematics from American universities were not Americans (National Research Council, 1985). The National Science Foundation reported in a study that, of students entering universities in 1989 as mathematics majors, more than half had changed that major before graduation—the largest switch of any content area. Of perhaps even more concern, however, was the lack of qualified workers for technology-intensive industry (Johnson et al., 1987).

We will review some of the factors leading to the current situation in mathematics education. We begin with the "new math" era of the late 1950s. We then consider societal pressures toward increased equity and the development of student-centered classrooms. Finally, we discuss the issues surrounding the "back-to-basics" movement of the 1970s and continue from there to the current situation.

"New Math"

How was the "new math" reform movement of the 1960s different from today's attempts to improve mathematics outcomes for students? (Documentation for the following analysis can be found in the referenced sources. The following description includes examples from the authors' personal experiences, since we both were involved in educational structures from the late 1950s to the present.) The impetus for the "new math" was the successful launch of *Sputnik,* the Soviet satellite, in 1957. In the United States, there was concern that we were so far behind the Soviet Union, our Cold War enemy, that our national security was in danger. In response, a spate of federal funds became available to improve the mathematics, science, and foreign language competence of our schoolchildren. University mathematicians, with an eye to developing future mathematicians, identified the necessity of having some students understand the structural underpinnings of mathematics as the basis for their future work in mathematics. These mathematicians intended to "jump-start" the young people who demonstrated a talent for mathematics and better prepare them for the rigors of university mathematics programs. Their strategy was to introduce topics into the school mathematics curriculum that lent themselves to the development of mathematical reasoning and proof.

Two components of the "New Math," as translated into the elementary and secondary textbooks that appeared at the time, were set theory (including set notation) and the structural properties of mathematics (commutativity, associativity, closure, etc.). Sometimes structural properties were developed through the study of number systems other than the Hindu-Arabic base-10 system. These topics often were presented abstractly in textbooks, not connected to any practical applications. For example, in typical eighth-grade texts of that era, integer addition was introduced by giving a set of principles, such as the commutative, associative, and distributive principles, that could be extended from the whole number system to the integers, and later to the set of rational numbers. Algebra texts continued this approach with particular emphasis on additive and multiplicative inverses and their applications to equation solving.

Society's Concerns With New Math   Many elementary teachers, already insecure in their own mathematical knowledge, failed to fully understand or appreciate the mathematical implications of the structural approach, however. Indeed, many had difficulty connecting skill in calculation that they were familiar with and the abstract underpinnings promoted in materials grounded in the new approach. Exacerbating their lack of content knowledge was the fact that insufficient professional development was provided to support the change.

Likewise, support materials for teachers and students did not take parents into account. Worksheets on abstract reasoning were sent home, instead of worksheets on calculations. The result was a tremendous amount of parental confusion and consternation. In short, most parents had no understanding of what their children were learning and its relationship to their conception of arithmetic. The complaints came, for example, that students could identify the associative property underlying multiplication and addition but were not able to get correct answers on standard arithmetic exercises. As a consequence, most elementary programs based on the "new math" were discontinued.

The overall response in the mathematics community, however, was not to do away with "new math" altogether. Almost all current era textbooks continue to include lessons emphasizing concepts of fundamental importance to student understanding and appreciation of mathematics. Thus, various sorting activities still appear in elementary textbooks, with or without set notation. Sets are used in algebra (solution sets, for example) and in probability (sample space). Learning multiplication facts is made simpler by knowing that the operation is commutative, whether the term is introduced or not. In fact, an astonishment to students working with matrices, a topic now occurring in some ninth-grade materials, is that matrix multiplication, in general, is not commutative.

Continuing Influence of New Math   At the high-school level, one of the most popular series of algebra textbooks, commonly known as Dolciani, in reference to one of the major authors, was published in 1970 with the title *Modern Algebra: Structure and Method, Books 1 and 2.* The two major authors of these books, as well as the editorial adviser, were involved with the School Mathematics Study Group (SMSG), an outgrowth of the reform movement of the 1960s. Sets and mathematical structure, as indicated in the title, play a major role throughout the curriculum. Many iterations later, even after the death of Mary Dolciani, those textbooks remain among the most widely used in the United States. So in that sense, the "new math" did not go away. Rather, it was adapted to enhance and extend the skills-based algebra textbooks that were commonly used before that time.

Societal Pressures Toward Increased Equity

In addition to the curricular changes influenced by *Sputnik,* other changes in school mathematics came about in response to social issues. Even though these issues were not directly connected to "new math," they occurred during the same time period and often compounded and confused the public about the direction of mathematics education.

Student Accessibility   Those concerned with equity and access (the civil rights movement was very strong during the 1960s) questioned the fact that some children were never even exposed to higher

mathematics topics because of differentiated curricula that essentially prevented them from ever being in a college preparatory class. We now recognize that content originally seen as appropriate only for mathematically "gifted" students can be made accessible to all. Also, textbooks at all levels should present challenging material to students, and all students should have the opportunity to learn higher level mathematics.

The notion of a basal mathematics curriculum for all students at the middle-school level was proposed during this time but not implemented in most parts of the United States. Most secondary mathematics classrooms continued to track students according to perceived ability. When we were teaching junior high school in the 1970s, students still were tracked into three different mathematics groups (with placement based on reading scores!), each with its own textbook (easy, medium, hard). Some attempts were made at that time to address equity concerns since none of the texts was solely computational. All had some vestiges of the structural approach, but still there was a marked difference in the level and presentation of the material. During high school, students could take up to 3 years of mathematics in which arithmetic skills were practiced again and again through unending series of worksheets or programmed texts.

Gender Equity   Another social change of the 1970s that influenced education was the women's movement. It was evident that changes were needed due to gender-related inequities within mathematics and science education. Indeed, the need for some of those changes evolved as a result of the changing roles of women within the society. In the 1950s, it still was the norm for the man in the family to work outside the home and the woman— even if she held a university degree—to stay home and care for the children and the needs of the household. During the 1970s the right of women to pursue intellectual and professional opportunities was asserted. Within a short time, economic realities and the desire of families to maintain a given standard of living made it more necessary for women to work outside the home, regardless of past role expectations.

At this time, male students in U.S. high schools enrolled in more mathematics courses, persisted more in those courses, and aspired to mathematics-intensive careers at a much greater rate than did female students. Those careers generally commanded higher salaries than careers requiring less mathematics. Thus, women who were not well prepared in mathematics were shut out of many lucrative career opportunities. In response to this discrepancy, research identified effective teaching strategies for female mathematics students. Projects such as EQUALS at the Lawrence Hall of Science in Berkeley, California, were funded to provide professional development for teachers to acquaint them with issues, materials, and methods pertinent to gender-related attitudes about mathematics.

Today, issues around gender and mathematics persist, with controversy over the benefits of single-sex secondary mathematics classes still in the news. Another gender-related issue has to do with mathematics scores on high-stakes tests such as the Preliminary Scholastic Achievement Test (PSAT) and the Scholastic Achievement Test (SAT). Over the previous 30 or more years, male scores in mathematics have been around 50 points higher, on average, than female scores. The bases for persistent gaps in SAT mathematics scores favoring males have long been debated. Because scores have been shown to be positively correlated to the number of mathematics classes taken, and males generally take more mathematics classes than females, their higher scores could be partly explained by course-taking patterns. In addition, more women overall took the tests, and their socioeconomic range, especially on the low end, was larger than that of male test takers, according to one Educational Testing Service representative (Rigol, 1990). Thus, socioeconomic differences might contribute to some of the variation in achievement. Equity issues such as these, paired with an increasingly diverse student population, laid the groundwork for a significantly different approach to mathematics reform in the 1990s than was introduced in the 1960s and 1970s.

Student-Centered Classrooms

During the 1970s, research on children's learning began to inform mathematics classrooms, especially those at the elementary level. Piaget's work on developmental stages of learning was incorporated into elementary teaching training. Professional development efforts were funded from many sources to enhance the mathematics content knowledge and pedagogical skills of elementary teachers. The elementary teachers who participated in these various summer institutes learned ways to teach mathematics to young children that were compatible with the children's developmental levels. Manipulatives were encouraged to assist students in understanding mathematical concepts through experiences leading from the concrete through the representational to the abstract.

Again, although these programs were of short duration, the strategy did not disappear; teachers who found the methods successful in their classrooms continued to use them and advocate for them, even into retirement. In general, research on developmental stages in mathematics learning has been an area of educational psychology that continues to grow and inform the mathematics reforms of today's classrooms.

Open classrooms and alternative schools also sprang forth in the 1970s. These programs were child-centered, with a philosophy of learning based on encouragement and extensions provided by the teacher on a somewhat individualized basis. The open classroom theory called for considerable structure and follow-through by the teacher informed by the interests of the child. A talented teacher who understood the importance of cognitive guideposts for the students could have marvelous results, as was true in the kindergarten classroom of co-author Sara Munshin's students. However, there were some unfortunate situations in which there were no consequences for lack of achievement, and as a result, students were allowed to proceed, seemingly with no accountability for their learning outcomes. Accountability for student learning is an important feature of today's mathematics educational reform. All persons concerned with mathematics education must keep the primary goals in clear view—to have every student become mathematically powerful, that is, able to understand and use mathematics in his or her professional and everyday life.

Back to Basics and Beyond

The "back-to-basics" movement came into prominence in the late 1970s, partly as a reaction to the fear that open classrooms resulted in nebulous student outcomes, and partly in response to the concerns expressed by business and industry that high-school diplomas did not ensure that newly graduated employees possessed necessary skill levels. Textbooks reflecting this movement consisted mostly of computational exercises, although other topics, such as probability, were placed as chapter "extras" or near the end of the books. These textbook series inevitably began with computational review. Basal mathematics textbooks became commonplace in middle schools during this time, with heterogeneous groupings at the seventh grade and differentiation occurring in eighth grade. The more able eighth-graders were placed into algebra instead of using the standard eighth-grade textbook. Before this time, algebra was considered a ninth-grade course for the able students.

Concomitant with the back-to-basics movement was the implementation of state and district minimum competency testing requirements, in addition to course completion requirements for high school graduation. As reported by Catterall (1987), about half of the states at that time required that each student pass a minimum proficiency test before she received a diploma, regardless of courses completed and credits earned.

The NCTM came forth with its "Agenda for the 80s" (1980) in part as a response to the back-to-basics movement. Standardized test results across the United States showed mathematics educators as well as the public that students' computational competency alone was not sufficient to equip them to use the mathematics in real-world and academic situations dependent upon mathematical reasoning. Basic skills, although important, were useless unless students could apply these skills in problem-solving situations. Students needed to experience problems that were realistic and designed to give them the experience of "doing" mathematics as mathematicians, scientists, and others in the workplace would. Real-life problems usually are not as neatly tied to specific mathematical procedures as typical textbook word problems. Exploration of possible approaches, starting over again when a particular approach is found to be fruitless, consulting with others on strategies, and checking results within the context of the given situation and practical constraints all are part of how mathematics is used outside the classroom. These kinds of problem-solving experiences, mathematics educators believed, need to be part of school mathematics.

The work of George Polya on the heuristics of problem solving was a frequent referent. Polya spent many years as a professor of mathematics at Stanford University in Palo Alto, California. In the second volume of *Mathematical Discovery* (1967), he lays out a typical thinking process of a mathematical problem solver. Beginning with understanding what is to be found by solving the problem, continuing through the process of expressing the problem in mathematical language, calling upon the mathematical tools and knowledge relevant to the problem (this is frequently a recursive process), selecting and using those that lead to a solution, and continually assessing one's own progress, Polya stresses reasoning as a key to doing mathematics. His "Ten Commandments for Teachers" are reprinted in Figure 1.1. Polya's influence on the inclusion of problem solving in school mathematics is evident to this day.

Figure 1.1
Polya's Ten Commandments for Teachers

1. Be interested in your subject.
2. Know your subject.
3. Know about the ways of learning: The best way to learn anything is to discover it yourself.
4. Try to read the faces of your students, try to see their expectations and difficulties, put yourself in their place.
5. Give them not only information, but "know-how," attitudes of mind, the habit of methodical work.
6. Let them learn guessing.
7. Let them learn proving.
8. Look out for such features of the problem at hand as may be useful in solving the problems to come—try to disclose the general pattern that lies behind the present concrete situation.
9. Do not give away your whole secret at once—let the students guess before you tell it—let them find out by themselves as much as is feasible.
10. Suggest it, do not force it down their throats.

Source: Polya, George (1967). *Mathematical Discovery: On Understanding, Learning, and Teaching Problem Solving.* New York: John Wiley & Sons, Inc.

Set 1.1   *Discussion Questions*

Questions with an asterisk appear in the Message Board section of the Companion Website at ***http://www.prenhall.com/huetinck.*** Go to Chapter 1 and click on the Message Board to find and respond to the question.

1. In what ways does increasing high-school graduation requirements to three years of college preparatory mathematics for all students, as recommended in the NCTM *Standards,* address the goal of mathematical power for all students? What concerns are there about increasing graduation requirements in mathematics?

2. What efforts do you see being made to avoid the mistakes made by the advocates of "new math" as *Standards*-based instruction is implemented currently?

*3. According to the authors, it is not appropriate to use the image of a pendulum swing as a metaphor for classroom implementation of changes that occur periodically in mathematics education. From your own experience as a student (and as a teacher, if relevant), tell whether you agree or disagree and why.

The Last Decade of the Millennium

Shortly after NCTM's "Agenda for the 80s" was distributed, the publication *A Nation at Risk* (1983) sounded a clarion call for increased attention to improving educational outcomes in the United States. The greatest threat to our society was not from outside our boundaries. Instead, the threat posed by huge numbers of young people deficient in the educational tools needed to work and function in our society boded for economic disaster. Improving educational outcomes for *all* students became the rallying cry for the next wave of reform. Thus, the mathematics reforms beginning in the 1980s were a response to poor achievement in mathematics by far too many students.

Background of the 1990s *Standards* Movement/Reform Literature

It was during this time that the first NCTM document, *Curriculum and Evaluation Standards for School Mathematics* (1989), was developed. As contrasted to the university-based and -driven "new math," input and feedback were elicited from a diverse constituency of those affected by mathematics education: the business community, parent groups, teacher groups, and university mathematicians. Draft copies of the document were widely circulated, and feedback was encouraged and considered in the development of the published document. Thus, from the onset, a broad consensus was developed. Another marked difference from the "new math" was that the curriculum reforms were always intended to be accessible to every student. At the high-school level, this was reinforced by a follow-up booklet to the *Curriculum and Evaluation Standards,* entitled *The Core Curriculum.* A radical shift from the tracking policies and assumptions prevalent in the United States during most of the century was proposed. A core set of expectations for *all* students was delineated, and at the high-school level, an "extended core" of material for those intending mathematics-intensive college and career goals was proposed. Those core learnings included a full range of mathematical topics, including algebra, geometry, probability, and statistics. The *Standards* also stressed changes in the delivery of instruction, calling on contemporary research in teaching and learning (to be addressed in detail in later chapters in this text).

The development of a national consensus was reinforced by the publication of several other like-minded documents by the Mathematical Sciences Education Board of the National Research Council.

They included: *Everybody Counts—A Report to the Nation on the Future of Mathematics Education* (1989), *Reshaping School Mathematics: A Philosophy and Framework for Curriculum* (1990), *Counting on You—Actions Supporting Mathematics Teaching Standards* (1991), and *Moving Beyond Myths: Revitalizing Undergraduate Mathematics* (1991). These documents espouse a consistent philosophy of learning and teaching mathematics, from preschool through college. Mathematics as a content area is growing and evolving, regarded as a set of tools for dealing with the tangible world and for developing ways of thinking logically and creatively. Learning theory also has evolved, ranging from behavioral models emphasizing observable behavior to cognitive models that deal more directly with the learning process and use contemporary knowledge about how the brain works. Students bring to formal schooling a wide range of abilities, beliefs, and experiences that can be called upon, as appropriate, to enhance and ensure mathematical understanding. Likewise, teaching involves a complex set of competencies in content knowledge, pedagogy, and interpersonal skills, all of which continue to grow with professional development and interaction with colleagues. The basic skills for the 21st century include problem solving, critical thinking, and methods for analyzing data as a basis for making informed decisions.

Go to Web Destinations for Chapter 1 at **http://www.prenhall.com/huetinck** to find links to NCTM standards documents.

NCTM Teaching Standards   The next in NCTM's triumvirate of standards documents was the *Professional Standards for Teaching Mathematics* (1991). This document addressed changes in the classroom environment necessary to accomplish the achievement outcomes advocated in the previous document. In addition, it addressed professional development, both pre- and in-service, and the teacher evaluation process, stressing collaborative models and self-evaluation. Particularly pertinent to this course is the fourth standard as stated here:

Standard 4: Knowing Mathematical Pedagogy
   The pre-service and continuing education of teachers of mathematics should develop teachers' knowledge of and ability to use and evaluate

- instructional materials and resources, including technology;
- ways to represent mathematics concepts and procedures;
- instructional strategies and classroom organizational models;

- ways to promote discourse and foster a sense of mathematical community;
- means for assessing student understanding of mathematics. (p. 151)

NCTM Assessment Standards The final document, the *Assessment Standards for School Mathematics,* was published in 1995. A summary of the purposes of assessment set forth in that document is given later in this book. At this point, only the six Mathematics Assessment Standards are summarized:

- The Mathematics Standard (p. 11): assessment should reflect the mathematics that all students need to know and be able to do.
- The Learning Standard (p. 13): assessment should enhance mathematics learning.
- The Equity Standard (p. 15): assessment should promote equity.
- The Openness Standard (p. 17): assessment should be an open process.
- The Inferences Standard (p. 19): assessment should promote valid inferences about mathematics learning.
- The Coherence Standard (p. 21): assessment should be a coherent process.

The NCTM *Standards* were revised, and a draft of the updated version was distributed in fall 1998. The revision process again included input from a broad range of constituencies. The three original *Standards* volumes were combined into one document that is more compact and avoids duplication, similar to the *National Science Education Standards* (1996) prepared by the National Research Council. The latest research supporting the NCTM goals were drawn upon and used in the revisions. The basic goals have not changed: A quality mathematics education is desirable and is possible for every child.

Changing Teacher Beliefs and Attitudes

These *Standards* and related documents addressed and challenged some commonly held teacher beliefs about mathematics and learning. Dossey (1992) describes two fundamentally different views of mathematics. The reform documents portray mathematics as "a dynamic, growing field of study," whereas "other conceptions of the subject define mathematics as a static discipline, with a known set of concepts, principles, and skills" (p. 39). The way one views mathematics, he finds, has a major influence on one's teaching approach. Either a teacher is establishing environments to promote the development of mathematical thinking and connections in students, or a teacher is seeking for the best way to impart previously established knowledge to students.

Smith (1996) suggests that teacher efficacy is reinforced by the belief that mathematics can best be

conveyed to students through telling. Teaching a clearly defined set of objectives with easily measured outcomes based on computational and procedural remembering makes sense because it is unambiguous to the teacher. When this approach is used, however, students may come to view mathematics as meaningless memorization, quickly to be forgotten. They also may become experts in giving the teacher back what they perceive the teacher wants, without seeing any relevance of the mathematics to their lives, present and future, except as a hurdle to be cleared by doing well on tests that lead to college entrance. On the other hand, classrooms in which students are actively involved in mathematical tasks that have many approaches and possible alternative outcomes may produce insecurity on the part of teachers, including those who recognize the benefits of such approaches. Even well-intentioned teachers may not know how to implement practices that they did not experience as students. That is why professional development that includes ongoing opportunities for teachers to share classroom experiences and work together to implement new methods is considered a necessary element of *Standards*-based mathematics classrooms.

Indeed, today's teachers may feel insecure dealing with mathematical topics in their students' textbooks that they have not experienced in teacher preparation programs. The discrete mathematics topic of networks is but one example of content not previously experienced even by mathematics majors. For this reason, professional development for teachers of mathematics must always include both content and pedagogy. In contrast to the 1970s, many opportunities for such development exist today through district workshops, university courses, professional conferences, and summer institutes for teachers to increase their content knowledge and pedagogical skills and to form professional networks. Other chapters of the text will discuss these opportunities in more detail.

TODAY'S STANDARDS-BASED CLASSROOMS

What can the visitor to a reform-based secondary mathematics classroom in the United States at the onset of the 21st century expect to see that is different from a typical secondary mathematics classroom of 50 years before? What changes might be observed in a classroom based on the NCTM *Standards*? The remainder of this chapter presents some research and suggestions in response to these questions and then focuses specifically on cooperative learning in the classroom. This strategy is one of many used by teachers in *Standards*-based classrooms (other strategies will be examined in subsequent chapters). We begin with the cooperative learning strategy because it is widely implemented currently in exemplary secondary mathematics classrooms. Because cooperative learning is so dependent upon communication and logical reasoning, cooperative activities, of necessity, depend on students' logical thinking in order to be successfully completed. Some of these activities are presented in the text that follows.

Research on Typical Secondary Mathematics Classes

Every 10 years, data on the typical U.S. mathematics classroom are gathered in international studies. For the Second International Mathematics Study (SIMS), done at the end of the 1981–82 school year, approximately 7,000 eighth-graders from about 600 randomly selected classrooms in public and private schools were tested, as well as 5,000 high-school seniors enrolled in advanced mathematics and others from a similar random sample of classrooms. *The Underachieving Curriculum* summarized and analyzed the SIMS results (McKnight, 1987). Here are some of the findings regarding instruction in the sample of classrooms surveyed for that study:

"Mathematics instruction in the U.S. is clearly textbook-driven." (p. 75)

"At the eighth-grade level, instruction appeared to be dominated by abstract and symbolic representations of content." (p. 79)

". . . the single strategy most frequently emphasized by teachers was presenting and demonstrating procedures or stating definitions and properties—what has been characterized as 'tell and show' approaches." (p. 81)

The Third International Mathematics and Science Study (TIMSS) results for eighth-grade mathematics and science were released in 1996, along with additional research funded by the U.S. Department of Education and carried out by James Stigler of UCLA. Stigler's videotape project shows examples of typical eighth-grade mathematics lessons being presented in American, Japanese, and German schools. These studies show that, despite a few significant exceptions, not a lot has changed in American classrooms regarding the delivery of instruction.

Go to Web Destinations for Chapter 1 at **http://www.prenhall.com/huetinck** to find links to TIMSS.

The U.S. curriculum largely consists of a series of topics to be covered in a year, determined mainly by the chosen textbook. Although "mastery" is a goal in most classrooms, the tension between covering the textbook and allowing adequate time for students to develop their understanding and retention of mathematical concepts creates conflicts within individual teachers and among faculty. According to TIMSS, the number of topics students are expected to cover in any given year in the United States is much greater than in comparison countries. An implication of this situation is students' difficulty in developing mastery, even of skills, since short-term retention is a logical outcome of trying to cover a plethora of topics without adequate time for deeper understanding.

One of the ways this shallow coverage is played out in the typical traditional curriculum is by going over number operations again and again, from grade to grade. The same content may be repeated for up to 8 years in American textbooks; in international comparison studies, content may be repeated in textbooks 3 years. At the same time, concept development seldom is given sufficient consideration in U.S. mathematics classrooms. Conceptual understanding involves language and connections and occurs over time, not in a single lesson. For example, the concept of proportionality, key to middle-school mathematics, should be developed by seeing that proportions model many different situations in which a constant rate of change is assumed. Having students learn to solve proportional equations by cross multiplying, for example, does not ensure their ability to understand and apply the concept in new situations.

Thanks to the efforts of the NCTM and other state and national efforts, in some secondary mathematics classrooms we now have in practice teaching innovations intended to provide greater opportunity for student understanding of mathematics. These research-based innovations are consistent with the teaching practices recommended in the NCTM *Professional Standards for Teaching Mathematics* as well as other reform documents. They include:

- students working in groups for at least part of the class period;
- students working on long-range projects and/or investigations;
- students having ready access to manipulatives and calculators;
- students presenting problem solutions to the class, with feedback;
- students writing reports that present their reasoning process when approaching a problem, including false starts;
- students participating in ongoing assessment activities, including self-assessment.

Reconceptualizing the Nature of Mathematics

Mathematics as a given set of rules to be learned, although common, is but one perception of the content area. Another perception, that of mathematics as invented by humans through inductive and deductive processes; more nearly fits how mathematicians work.

This second perception is becoming more prevalent as the basis of content and instruction in today's schools. Student-centered investigations and discovery lessons are included in exemplary instructional materials. Textbooks and supplemental materials contain new topics, such as fractals, that are contemporary inventions, thereby allowing students to see mathematics as a growing, living body of knowledge and not simply facts or algorithms to be assimilated.

When technology is incorporated as part of an investigation, additional opportunities occur for unique discoveries. An article about a high-school student who used dynamical geometry software to suggest a theorem for partitioning triangles appeared in the May 1996 issue of *Mathematics Teacher* (Watanabe, Hanson, and Nowosielski, 1996). That student was able to share his conjecture with college mathematicians, who then entered into a professional dialogue about possible approaches to a deductive proof of the student's conjecture. Such occurrences are not uncommon, as today's students are given tools to use in exploring and recording information, whether technology-generated or from other sources in their world.

Applying Research From Cognitive Psychology

Behavioral psychology, of which B. F. Skinner probably was the best-known proponent, provided the basis for the learning theory behind classroom instruction for the past several decades. This theory of learning extended findings about the behavior of rats in mazes to human learning. Just as rats could improve their efficiency in navigating the maze, people could modify their responses to given situations through practice. Behaviorism lent itself naturally to rote-learning methods. "Behavioral objectives" became the basis of teaching and testing. For example, a typical objective from this era is "90% of the students will be able to score 80% or higher on a test involving addition of unlike fractions." Being able to perform calculations with sufficient speed and accuracy was equated with mathematical knowledge, and in many people's minds, it still is. Whether conceptual understanding had occurred and whether students exhibited the ability to use mathematical tools to solve nonroutine problems was seldom questioned or assessed, partly because educators had no tools with which to measure less-objective student outcomes.

Cognitive psychology, on the other hand, concerns how children connect mathematics with their world in order to make sense out of both. It assumes that young people bring knowledge and experience to the classroom that they can use when presented with a problem rich in content and with many possible solution approaches. This theory suggests that students, through grappling with such problems and seeing that many paths can be taken in arriving at a satisfactory solution to the problem, develop better understanding of mathematical concepts and processes and greater confidence in their ability to apply them to new situations. The theoretical groundwork for developing new ways of assessing students' conceptual understanding and problem-solving ability was laid along with this view of how people learn.

Manipulatives and technology as tools for concept development are key elements of *Standards*-based classrooms. Later in this text we will discuss more specifics regarding the effective uses of these tools. For now, we acknowledge that concept development lessons incorporating manipulative activities and inquiry, when well designed, take time in order for deep understanding to occur. Taking the time to adequately develop the concept should not be seen as a negative, however. Taking time for students to make the concept their own decreases the time needed in the future to reteach and reinforce the learning. Similar to Japanese curricula, as reported in TIMSS, *Standards*-based curricula allow sufficient time for key grade-level concepts so that students fully comprehend them.

A teacher who is knowledgeable about the benefits of cognitive approaches to learning will include problem-solving activities regularly as part of instruction and assessment. Cooperative group problem-solving activities or group projects are visible components of today's exemplary classrooms. Problem-solving activities also are effective for students for whom English is a second language, with appropriate support such as written translations, visual diagrams, oral summaries, explanations in their native language, and the use of other techniques known to make the problems comprehensible to English learners.

Incorporating Technology

All high-school mathematics students should have access to graphing technology (usually on a calculator), spreadsheets, and dynamic geometry tools (Geometer's Sketchpad,® Cabri, etc.). Technology makes some traditional topics less important, others more important, and new topics possible. Discrete mathematics naturally lends itself to calculator technology. For example, iteration is so simple on most scientific calculators that even middle-school students can observe number patterns that grow in regular ways and begin to grasp the concepts of divergence and convergence through generalizing the patterns.

Transformational geometry and the relationship between the algebraic form of a function and the appearance of its graph can now be a regular part of first-year algebra. As the functional approach to algebra is developed in subsequent years and tied to data analysis, students will be better able to connect the various representations of functions (data tables, graphs, and equations). The capability of technology to represent three-dimensional graphs more rapidly and accurately than those drawn by hand opens the door to greater understanding by more secondary mathematics students of complex space shapes and their characteristics. In the recent past, those kinds of representations were difficult to produce and seldom addressed until calculus was well under way. Now high-school students regularly work with 3-D shapes in computer labs, on some calculators, and even via computer-assisted design (CAD) in tech-prep labs. The mathematics made possible by technology must be made available to all students.

Access to the Internet is a part of every student's future. Beyond navigating the World Wide Web, how can students incorporate its capabilities into their learning of mathematics? Data can be collected from all over the world to use for simple or sophisticated analyses. The results of mathematical explorations can be shared with students in distant classrooms. Teachers and students can hold discussions, via e-mail, of challenging mathematical problems and ways to approach solving them. Enrichment topics can be explored via the research capabilities of this technology. Teachers can upload and download lessons and get ideas for applications problems from information posted about weather, space exploration, medicine, sports, and myriad other topics. Technology has changed our daily lives in many ways and it will change schooling, as well.

Preparing Students for the Workplace

Students who are intending to pursue non-college-based careers can no longer be penalized by having inadequate mathematics backgrounds. According to the Secretary's Commission on Achieving Necessary Skills (SCANS) report, published by the U.S. Department of Labor in 1990, the workplace needs workers with the skills listed in Figure 1.2.

Figure 1.2
Preparing Students for the Workplace

1. Basic Skills
Reading: locates, understands, and interprets written information in prose and in documents such as manuals, graphs, and schedules
Writing: communicates thoughts, ideas, information, and messages in writing; creates documents such as letters, directions manuals, reports, graphs, and flowcharts
Arithmetic, mathematics: performs basic computations and approaches practical problems by choosing appropriately from a variety of mathematical techniques
Listening: receives, attends to, interprets, and responds to verbal messages and other cues
Speaking: organizes ideas and communicates orally

2. Thinking Skills
Creative thinking: generates new ideas
Decision making: specifies goals and constraints, generates alternatives, considers risks, and evaluates and chooses the best alternative
Problem solving: recognizes problems and devises and implements plans of action
Visualizing: organizes and processes symbols, pictures, graphs, objects, and other information
Knowing how to learn: uses efficient learning techniques to acquire and apply new knowledge and skills
Reasoning: discovers a rule or principle underlying the relationship between two or more objects and applies it when solving a problem

3. Personal Qualities
Responsibility: exerts a high level of effort and perseveres toward goal attainment
Self-esteem: believes in own self-worth and maintains a positive view of self
Sociability: demonstrates understanding, friendliness, adaptability, empathy, and politeness in group setting
Self-management: assesses self accurately, sets personal goals, monitors progress, and exhibits self-control
Integrity/honesty: chooses ethical courses of action

Source: "Secretary's Commission on Achieving Necessary Skills (SCANS)," U.S. Department of Labor, 1990.

Evaluating Effectiveness

Are students learning more mathematics as a result of changes in curriculum and instruction? How do we know? The complexity of answering such questions is quite daunting. Yet, most mathematics educators seem to agree on the importance of multiple forms of assessment and the need to relate them to the purposes of those assessments. Various types of assessment are needed to allow students the opportunity to demonstrate what mathematics they know and how they can apply their mathematical knowledge in different settings. For assessment related to grades, students in *Standards*-based classrooms complete projects, make oral and written presentations, and use technology to support and/or verify solutions in addition to taking pencil-and-paper tests. All of these activities and others, such as group observations, are included as elements of a grade. Assessment also can be used by the teachers to inform instruction. Checklists of group participation, questioning techniques to elicit student thinking, and reading student journal entries are but a few of the ways assessment might be carried out.

Even the "high stakes" tests are modifying multiple-choice formats to include other formats that provide different opportunities for students to demonstrate their mathematical understanding. For example, the Scholastic Achievement Test (SAT) allows calculators and includes sections that are not multiple-choice. Free-response items on Advanced Placement calculus exams require students to apply their mathematical skills and communicate their methods. The use of criterion-referenced, performance-based, as well as norm-referenced tests for school, district, and state evaluation is becoming much more common.

Set 1.2   *Discussion Questions*

Questions with an asterisk appear in the Message Board section of the Companion Website at *http://www.prenhall.com/huetinck.* Go to Chapter 1 and click on the Message Board to find and respond to the question.

*1. Discuss your view of mathematics and how it influences your teaching approach. What might cause your view to change?

2. The five major shifts referenced in the NCTM *Professional Standards* (1991, p. 3) will be modeled in this text. They are:

   - toward classrooms as mathematical communities;
   - toward logic and mathematical evidence as verification;
   - toward mathematical reasoning;
   - toward conjecturing, inventing, and problem solving;
   - toward connecting mathematics, its ideas, and its applications.

   Why are these changes recommended? What barriers might there be to implementing them?

3. What features would you expect to find in a *Standards*-based mathematics textbook for middle school? for high school?

4. Identify three key mathematical concepts (not skills) that all students should be able to master in the first year of the high-school curriculum. Why are these important?

COOPERATIVE LEARNING IN SECONDARY MATHEMATICS

Cooperative learning is a relatively recent addition to the mathematics classroom. It is highlighted here because it has become common practice in many classrooms in which exemplary curricula include it as a regular feature. Its techniques can be used to move any curriculum from a traditional format to one that is more student-centered. There is considerable research on the effectiveness of cooperative learning groups for promoting student learning in mathematics, especially in problem solving, a major goal of the reform.

The positive relationship between retention of mathematical concepts and student involvement in the learning process has been shown in many research studies (Davidson & Kroll, 1991; Dees, 1991; Duren & Cherrington, 1992). Having students work together on problem-solving activities that are structured to foster both individual responsibility for the mathematical learning and cooperative behaviors is key. Student collaboration as one of several modes of learning is recommended in all current reform documents.

Classroom Benefits

Cooperative learning delivers benefits to students and teachers alike.

Benefits to Students   Cooperative learning enhances students' knowledge and attitudes in several ways:

- Concepts and problem-solving approaches are clarified and extended by students needing to communicate them to one another.
- Confidence is built through oral presentations and written discussion of procedures and processes involved in doing the mathematics.
- Critical thinking is developed by seeing and analyzing a variety of approaches to a given problem situation.
- Appreciation of and respect for other ways of thinking and learning are enhanced.
- Positive attitudes about mathematics and the mathematics classroom are fostered.

Benefits to Teachers   Cooperative learning can improve teachers' effectiveness and even make teaching easier:

- Responsibility for learning is placed more in the domain of the learner than in a lecture-driven setting.

- The teacher has the opportunity, through listening to student interactions, to assess understanding at all stages of a unit, rather than only at the culmination.
- The paperwork load is decreased through judicious use of selected assignment collection and group grades.
- Different student academic strengths and learning modalities are recognized and drawn upon as they are manifested during the group process.
- Students' explanations in their own words and style rather than in the words of the teacher's vernacular enhance the content understanding of both the speaker and the listener.

Considerations for Setting Up Cooperative Groups

Considerable planning is needed when using groups. Simply having students sit together and work is seldom an effective way to accomplish learning goals. The teacher, students, and materials must be prepared ahead of time. At the onset, identify the learning goal or outcome and make it clear to the students. Otherwise, they may see the activity as a time to relax and play rather than as an opportunity to increase their knowledge and ability to work with others to solve problems. Robert Slavin (1988), an acknowledged expert in the field of cooperative learning, states two essential conditions for maximizing achievement with cooperative learning: (1) have a group goal that is important to the students, and (2) maintain individual accountability for the learning objective(s).

In promoting positive interdependence, consider the following items:

- Clearly define a common goal for the entire group.
- Assign different roles and responsibilities to each member of the group, determined either by the teacher or by the group.
- Allot resources so that they must be shared. For example, one set of manipulatives is to be shared among a group of four students.
- Divide the information to be used among the group members. (Some of the sample activities that follow this section are specifically structured to give each student a unique part of the information needed to solve the problem. An alternative that can be used with a standard complex word problem is to copy it and cut the sentences apart so that each student receives a single part of the problem.)
- Require a single product of the group—a poster, written report, physical model, etc.

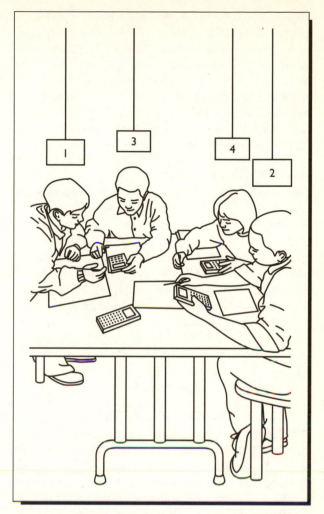

Hanging numbers designate each group's seats and can also be used to randomly select a person from each group to present a problem solution.

- Establish a firm time limit for the completion of projects, and occasionally for completing specific portions of a project.
- Grade a project for meeting the criteria of the activity, rather than grading the efforts of individual students.

This implies a group grade, which sometimes is an effective way of eliciting total participation of group members.

As part of their classroom repertoire, teachers need to be able to know and use techniques for placing students in small groups, develop lessons that maximize the participation of group members, monitor group progress, and assess group outcomes. Entire books have been written about various cooperative learning techniques, some of which are exclusively devoted to applications of this technique within a mathematics classroom.

There are two basic philosophies for placing students in groups. The first is a highly structured approach in which each group of four is set up by the teacher prior to class. These groups of four consist of one high-achieving student, one low-achieving student, and two middle-achieving students. The intent is to assure a heterogeneous mixture in each group. Some teachers find this structure helpful and use it almost exclusively. Others feel that the teacher selection based on perceived achievement in fact reinforces student perceptions of themselves as good in math or not good in math, especially if the high achiever tends to become the group leader, with the other students less willing to suggest alternative approaches to a problem if they believe a "smarter" person has the best approach. This concern can be addressed partly by careful assignment of group roles and by group self-assessments that allow members to state whether they felt able to participate freely and share their ideas without their being devalued.

Research on the benefits of these configurations of cooperative learning groups to various types of students is varied. Webb (1980), in a study investigating group interaction and mathematical errors of 11th-grade students working individually and in four-person heterogeneous-ability groups, found that for high-ability students, the group condition seemed to be detrimental to learning new (algorithmic) material but advantageous for performance on previously learned material. Middle-ability students were at an advantage for learning new material but somewhat set back on applying previously learned information. For low-ability students, group work was beneficial for both kinds of material. A more recent study (Qin, Johnson, and Johnson, 1995), which used a meta-analysis of 46 studies, found that members of cooperative teams consistently outperformed individuals competing with each other on four types of problem-solving activities.

The alternative approach to the teacher-determined groups is random selection. When groups are formed through random selection, such as drawing a card from a deck and working with others who drew cards of the same value, students realize that they are not placed in the group according to any set of criteria. A possible disadvantage, however, is that groups may result that contain an overabundance of one type of achiever. This could result in the group's being unable to stay on task, complete the task, or work effectively. A possible antidote to this issue is to change groups every 4 to 6 weeks. On the other hand, students who might not take the lead in a group containing supposedly brighter students might have greater opportunity to assert their leadership skills to make the group productive in a randomly selected group. Any student can help the group persist, model collaboration, or suggest nonstandard approaches to a problem.

Little research exists addressing the benefits of random heterogeneous grouping compared to selected mixed groups regarding comparative achievement. Slavin (1980) does point to other types of positive outcomes of heterogeneous groups, such as positive race relations, improvement in student self-esteem, and mutual concern among students. Of course, there is no guarantee that any group selection method works all of the time.

Regardless of the method of group selection used, the teacher must plan where those groups are going to be placed in the classroom. If students are going to move individual desks back and forth between rows and groups, where are the individuals in a group to be seated in order to facilitate those changes quickly and quietly? In rooms equipped with tables, how are the tables to be arranged so that everyone can see the teacher during whole-class instruction?

In addition, teachers should establish guidelines for groups working together. One guideline, for example, is to ask the teacher for assistance only when every person in the group is certain that he or she does not understand some aspect of the problem. Guidelines concerning courtesy and listening to one another also are important. Finally, once students are in new groups, they need to begin with some socializing activities. The following activities—Activity 1.1, Cooperative Geometry, and Activity 1.2, Basketball and Volleyball Players—are particularly effective when initiating cooperative grouping in a classroom. Another simple collaborative activity is to ask group members to get acquainted by finding one characteristic they all have in common.

The best guideline for managing cooperative groups is common sense. If two students have a personality clash to the extent that it is preventing progress on the mathematics, the conflict must be addressed. Teachers should be very wary of allowing students to change groups because of social reasons, however. Once an open door is provided, all students will want to work only with their friends. Instead, the teacher can begin by stressing the real-life necessity of working cooperatively with people in the workplace who might not be friends outside of work. Intervention strategies such as having all members of the group write about their perceptions of the situation along with possible solutions might be helpful. Likewise, if some groups are too social, they need to be reminded of the detrimental effects of such behavior on their goal. As a final resort, individuals may need either to work alone or to be placed by the teacher in a different group to maintain overall harmony in the classroom.

In urban situations, outside affiliations (gang membership, etc.) could result in students not wanting to work together. If the school has established norms that insist upon respect within its walls, administrators and counselors can be enlisted to help teachers deal with potentially uncomfortable situations. It is both desirable and possible, based on SM's experience in a barrio high school, that these outside affiliations be set aside in the classroom and that students gain tolerance and respect for one another by working together toward a common goal.

Some classroom activities are not appropriate for group work. Listening and taking notes, working on exercise sets, and developing written explanations of a mathematical process are examples of activities that suggest individual work in a large group setting. Activities that do lend themselves to group work include those (1) requiring different tasks to divide among members of the group such as gathering data, analyzing data, and writing an explanation of the process; (2) allowing multiple solution approaches and representations so that students can share different perspectives; and (3) stressing sufficiently complex information to stimulate student discussion as to the key elements of the problem and various strategies for dealing with the problem.

Teacher Actions During Cooperative Group Activities

Monitoring and encouraging group progress toward the desired goal is the primary activity of the teacher. She also can note different approaches to the given problem/situation with the idea of having students share their strategies at a later point in the activity. In addition, questioning techniques to keep students focused are very helpful. Some suggestions from the NCTM *Professional Standards* (1991, p. 3) for helping students work together are as follows:

"What do others think about what Jamie said?"
"Does anyone have the same answer but a different way to explain it?"
"Would you ask the rest of the class that question?"
"Can you convince the rest of us that your suggestion makes sense?"

The teacher's role during group activities involves a lot of walking around, listening, and moving quickly from group to group. Using a simple checklist, note such group dynamics as listening to one another, supporting other team members, keeping the group

FOR TEACHERS

Activity 1.1 Cooperative Geometry

Mathematical Content:
Spatial relationships, congruence (PSSM Geometry Standard for Grades 6–8)

Materials Needed:
One envelope per group
One set of four squares per group

Directions: Divide students into groups of four. Prior to the activity, cut the squares for each group. Cut the pieces along the bold lines, and paper-clip together the pieces of each square that have the same letter of the alphabet. Hence, there are three *A* pieces clipped together, three *B* pieces, three *C* pieces, and three *D* pieces. Provide the following directions for each student group.

"When you get your envelope, there will be a paper-clipped set of three pieces of paper for each person in your group. Work together so that each person can form a square using three puzzle pieces. You may *not* talk to each other. To exchange pieces, you must give a piece directly to a particular group member. No one may take a piece from another person."

At the end of the activity, have students clip the pieces back together and replace them in the envelope before continuing with another cooperative activity such as Activity 1.2.

Questions to Ask: Use the following questions to debrief student groups at the end of the activity. You may place them on the chalkboard or on an overhead transparency.

1. How did you feel about not being allowed to talk?
2. What were some problems your group had in completing the puzzle?
3. What did you learn from this activity?

Extensions: Have students use any congruent square as the unit of 1 area measure and tell what fractional part each of the small pieces is of that unit.

Have students determine the angle measure of each small piece that forms the squares, assuming right angles and congruent lengths for all completed squares.

FOR STUDENTS

Activity 1.1
Cooperative Geometry

Directions: You will need one copy of this page for each group of four students. Cut each square into three pieces as indicated, clip the pieces together by letter and place each set of letters in a small envelope. One student will get all three A pieces, one will get all the B's, and so on.

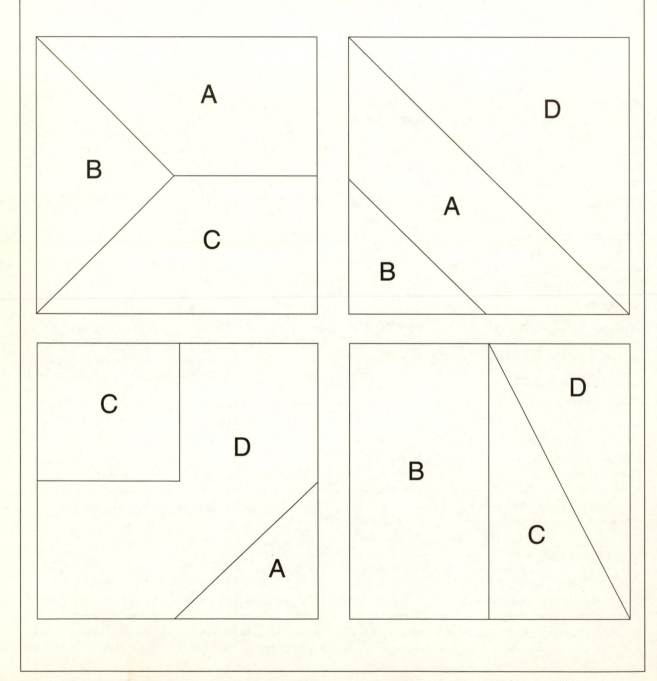

Source: Adapted from *OFF & RUNNING,* published by EQUALS, Lawrence Hall of Science, Berkeley, CA 94720. © Regents, University of California at Berkeley.

F O R   T E A C H E R S

Activity 1.2 Basketball and Volleyball Players

Mathematical Content:
Logic of sets with intersections; Venn diagrams (PSSM Reasoning and Proof Standard for Grades 6–8).

Materials Needed:
One set of the six clues given below, cut up, for each group of four students; envelopes for each group, containing six clues.

Directions: Give each group of four to six students an envelope containing the six clues and two labels. Know that the bottom two clues are not necessary to solve the problem, but can be used to verify the reasoning. Provide the following directions or glue the student directions on the outside of each group envelope.

"Each person is responsible for sharing her clue with teammates and for listening as the other clues are read. You may use any previously learned strategies to help you solve the problem. (*Hint:* Venn diagrams might be helpful.) When you believe you have completed the problem, be able to explain how you know your solution is correct."

At the end of the activity, have students replace the clues and labels in their envelope.

Questions to Ask:
1. Which clue was the most helpful?
2. What strategies did your group use to solve the problem?
3. What kind of Venn diagram best illustrates this problem? Why?
4. What numbers from the problem fit into what parts of the Venn diagram?

Extension: Have students create their own Venn diagram and story, then write clues to give to another group to solve.

F O R   S T U D E N T S

Activity 1.2
Basketball and Volleyball Players

Directions: Each person in the group must take responsibility for at least one clue given to your group. Each group member reads his or her clue(s) to the other members of the group and considers *how* or *if* it helps the group solve the problem. Explain why.

BASKETBALL AND VOLLEYBALL	
Some basketball players also play volleyball. Some volleyball players also play basketball. How many play each sport?	There are a total of 23 basketball and volleyball players. How many play each sport?
Five basketball players are also volleyball players. How many play each sport?	Ten volleyball players are not basketball players. How many play each sport?
1/3 of the volleyball players are also basketball players. How many play each sport?	The ratio of those who only play basketball to those who only play volleyball is 4:5. How many play each sport?

Figure 1.3
Cooperative Behavior Checklist (+ and – marks are used to indicate quality of participation)

	Student	On-task	Listening	Supporting	Comments
Team 1	A				
	B				
	C				
	D				
Team 2	A				
	B				
	C				
	D				

Continue for the number of groups in the classroom.

on task, etc. A sample checklist is shown in Figure 1.3. The letters for each team could refer either to specific task responsibilities or to seating locations within the group. For example, if the group was randomly selected by drawing cards, the letters C, D, H, and S could be used to represent the suits (clubs, diamonds, hearts, and spades), especially if the seating was consistent among groups.

Models of Cooperative Group Lessons

Several forms of cooperative group models have been identified and researched. The following list describes several models, along with their key components and the intended academic outcomes:

1. *Think-pair-share.* This is one of the concept development structures identified in Kagan (1992).

F O R   T E A C H E R S

Activity 1.3 All, Some, or None

Mathematical Content:
Logic, geometry (PSSM Reasoning and Proof Standard for Grades 6–8)

Materials Needed:
One copy of the worksheet per student; a transparency of the worksheet.

Directions: Working with the entire class, elicit responses for box (a). Possible correct responses are: (1) All of the shapes are squares. (2) Some of the shapes have sides larger than a centimeter. (3) None of the shapes contains an obtuse angle. Accept all mathematically accurate responses, and write them on chalkboard or overhead in complete sentences for students to refer to while continuing. Provide the following directions, using a think-pair-share model:

"You will be given 5 minutes (or more) to write as many correct responses as you can to the ad-

ditional boxes on the worksheet. When I give the signal, you and a partner will each share your responses for 2 minutes. The two of you will have an additional 10 minutes to complete as many responses as you can together."

Questions to Ask: Use the following questions to debrief at the end of the activity:
1. Which box was the most challenging for you?
2. Who has at least one response that you think is correct for box (g)?
3. Where might you go to find other words to use on this worksheet?
4. Give the response that your team is proudest of.

Extension: Have students create additional All, Some, None problems with other mathematical content (algebra, number theory, etc.).

This model lends itself to nonroutine problem solving in which students are given opportunities to apply mathematical reasoning and draw upon a variety of mathematical tools to deal with open-ended situations. Even though students may be seated in groups of four, the emphasis here is one-on-one interaction. This form of cooperative grouping also has the advantage of being most likely to elicit maximum participation from all members of a class, as each person has the opportunity to be both a listener and a problem solver. The teacher first presents a problem or poses a question that each individual is to think (and frequently write) about silently. Then each member of the pair is given a set amount of time, usually 1–2 minutes, to discuss her response with the other member of the pair. Next, additional sharing can occur with groups of four or with the entire class. This process can be used along with other cooperative methods and has the advantage of individual accountability in a relatively safe setting—limiting one's sharing to just one other person. Activity 1.3 lends itself to a think-pair-share approach.

FOR STUDENTS

Activity 1.3
All, Some, or None

Directions: Write three statements about the geometric properties of the figures in each group. One statement should give a characteristic *all* of the figures have, one should give a characteristic *some* have, and one should give a characteristic *none* of them have. Try to do this without repeating a characteristic.

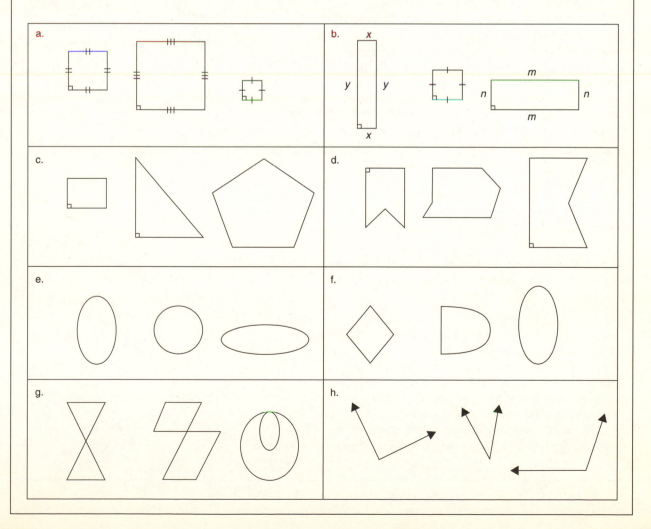

2. *Team learning.* Place students in heterogeneous groups, usually with three to five members, by a variety of methods, including randomization. The activity is designed to give each member of the team a different task or role that contributes to the completion of the assignment. Assessment frequently includes group self-assessment concerning the solution of the given problem and the contribution of each member to the group goal. Activity 1.4, Park Beautification Project, although not specifically dealing with the content of logic, is shared here as an example of a team project with the major features of this model.

F O R T E A C H E R S

Activity 1.4 Park Beautification Project

Mathematical Content:
Scale drawing, problem solving (PSSM Problem Solving Standard for Grades 6–8).

Materials Needed:
Graph paper, large 2-foot by 3-foot grid paper, colored markers, rulers, calculators, directions packet for each group, and evaluation for each individual after the project is completed.

Directions: This project is designed to be done in groups of four, although modifications can be made for other group sizes. It is expected to take more than one class period to complete. Daily benchmarks can be given, and those who do not complete them must do so outside of class time. For example, a completed budget sheet can be due at the end of the first class period, a scale drawing by the end of the second period, the large drawing and presentation plan by the end of the third period, and the presentations made the fourth period.

Questions to Ask:
1. What was the hardest part of preparing the budget sheet?
2. How do you think budgets are decided when projects are developed in real life?
3. How did the group decide where to place the items in the park?
4. What information did you use to estimate the size of items in the park?
5. What is your most important "selling point" for having your park selected as the best?
6. What would you do to improve your project?

Extensions: Find an actual site in the community, and develop plans for beautifying it. Include research on cost of items needed to complete the project, assuming labor is donated.

F O R S T U D E N T S

Activity 1.4
Park Beautification Project (page 1 of 3)

A vacant area in our community is going to be made into a park, and $20,000 has been set aside to develop it. The people of the community have volunteered to do the work. They want a park that uses energy and resources well. The park should be suitable for people of all ages. It should be a safe place. It should be attractive. Include in your park one hill, one large tree, and one small tree, all of which are free. Any other items in your park must be paid for. The park is to be 200 feet by 300 feet, which is about as long as a football field and a little wider.

Our class will design the park. We will be working in groups of four. The best group design will be submitted to the community council.

The project will be given a group grade, with each person in the group receiving the same points, except for absentees. The total possible is 50 points. Points will be based upon the following:

a design which is safe and can be used by all ages;

an accurate budget;

the attractiveness of the final plan;

the presentation of the final plan.

FOR STUDENTS

Activity 1.4
Park Beautification Project (page 2 of 3)

Directions: The teacher will assign you to groups. Within the group, each person should have a role. Decide who will have each role before you continue with the tasks for the project.

1. The *engineer* is responsible for the overall design and safety.

   Name_____

2. The *accountant* keeps track of the budget.

   Name_____

3. The *PR person* is in charge of presenting the group's proposal to the entire class.

   Name_____

4. The *draftsperson* is in charge of drawing the final plan.

   Name_____

Steps to complete the project:

1. Fill in the Budget Sheet.

   a. Decide what items from the Budget Sheet you want to have in your park. You do not have to use all of them. If you want an item that is not listed, check with the teacher.

   b. Find the total cost of what you want, and be sure it is less than $20,000.

PARK BEAUTIFICATION PROJECT BUDGET SHEET

COST OF MATERIALS AND EQUIPMENT

Item	Cost	Unit	Quantity	Total Cost
Brick paving on 1″ flat sand	$8.80	1 sq. ft.		
Rope (exercise)	$300	18′		
Sand	$1	1 cu. ft.		
Stepping stones	$5	Each		
Plants and shrubs	Varies			
Trash barrels (30 gal. galvanized)	$110.00	Each		
Bench (6′ aluminum with back)	$245.00	Each		
Chain link fencing (6′ high)	$82.50	10 running ft.		
Asphalt pavement (3″ thick)	$3.50	1 sq. ft.		
4′ picnic table with 2 benches	$350	Each		
Drinking fountain—2 bubblers	$1350	Each		
Playground equipment	Varies			
10′ bike rack with 14 spaces	$515	1 rack		
Barbeque, single	$175	Each		
8′ street light (400 watts)	$2,100	Each		
Bathroom (pair, 12′ × 40′)	$125,000	With utilities		
Stage (20′ square, 8″ high)	$300	Each		
Permanent bleachers	$112	Seat		
Backstop, baseball	$3,800	Each		
			Total Cost: $_____	

Price Sources: Playworld Systems Park and Playground Sourcebook, 2001; PW (Patterson-Williams) Athletic Company Catalog, 2001; Wabash Valley 2001 Plastisol Coated Furniture Catalog.

F O R   S T U D E N T S

Activity 1.4
Park Beautification Project (page 3 of 3)

2. Make a scale drawing of the park.

   a. Decide the length represented by a segment on the graph paper. Draw in the hill, large tree, and small tree on the graph paper.

   b. Cut the larger items out of pieces of paper, to scale, and decide where they would fit in the park. Move them around until the group agrees and then paste them down. Draw in the other features.

3. Work on the final design and class presentation.

   a. Discuss any special features you want to emphasize and how to do so.

   b. Draw the park on a large piece of paper, provided by the teacher, using markers to draw in all of its features. Make it attractive, as you will be showing it to the entire class.

   c. Plan your oral presentation. How would you "sell" your park to the members of the community? Think of ways to convince your classmates that your park is the best one in the class.

4. Give a group presentation to the class. Include the cost, the features, and any special ideas you have. The winning group will receive a special bonus.

Assess This Activity: After the presentation is complete, answer the questions below on a separate piece of paper, and give it to the teacher. Be sure to put your name on the paper you turn in.

  1. About the activity

   a. What did you like about this project?

   b. How would you change the project if it were done again?

  2. About your group

Write the names of your group members on your paper. Include your own name. Write by each name the number that you feel describes that person's participation in the project.

	Team Members	Excellent	Good	Fair	Poor	None
1.		1	2	3	4	5
2.		1	2	3	4	5
3.		1	2	3	4	5
4.		1	2	3	4	5
5.		1	2	3	4	5

Please add any comments that you would like to about your group.

Be sure your name and the date are at the top of your paper.

3. *Random selection.* This variation of team learning is specifically intended to promote mastery of specific skills. Groups of four students cooperate to work practice exercises with the idea that anyone in the group could be called upon at random by the teacher to work out or hand in the problem(s). The entire group is graded on the accuracy of that individual's processes and answers. The random selection is sometimes done with a spinner divided into four equal sections, with each section having a number or symbol based upon the counting-off system. For example, if a deck of cards is used to group students with the same number or face card, then the four sections of the spinner could be labeled as clubs, diamonds, hearts, and spades. The teacher then calls only on the randomly selected student from each group to respond or turn in the paper for her group.

4. *Collaborative learning.* Students work together, in small groups, on a common task. For example, they correct homework together at the beginning of a class period, providing help as needed within the group. While this method has positive management implications for the teacher, who can complete attendance and other tasks while students are working together, individual accountability is decreased. Because of the potential for weaker students obtaining only cursory understanding by essentially copying what stronger students have done, this method is less conducive to retention of concepts (see Webb, 1992).

Groupwork Follow-Through and Assessment

An article appearing in the November 1992 issue of NCTM *Mathematics Teacher* (Kroll, Masingila, & Mau) suggests one way of combining points for group outcomes and individual efforts in problem-solving investigations. This plan assumes that the groundwork described above is already in place and that the classroom groups have some experience working together and writing out solutions to problems. A class norm is that students work together toward the goal of each member understanding the mathematics involved in solving the problem.

An analytic scoring scheme for the group outcome consists of points for understanding the problem, planning a solution, and completing/checking the solution (see Figure 1.4). The group is given a numerical score for its solution of the assigned problem. Then, individuals must, on their own, answer questions about their group's solution and solve extensions of the given problem. A second score is given to each individual. Thus, all of the students in a given group would receive the same score based on their group's effort, but group members could potentially receive different scores on their individual efforts. One way of arriving at points for a grade would be to add the two scores. Another would be to average the individual scores and add the average to the group score, thereby resulting in the same score for each member of the group. Activity 1.5 is an example of cooperative problem solving to which a scoring rubric such as the one described in Figure 1.4 might be applied.

Figure 1.4
Analytic Scoring Scale*

Understanding the problem	0: Complete misunderstanding of the problem
	3: Misunderstanding or misinterpreting part of the problem
	6: Complete understanding of the problem
Planning a solution	0: No attempt or totally inappropriate plan
	3: Partially correct plan based on part of the problem's being interpreted correctly
	6: Plan that leads or could have led to a correct solution if implemented properly
Getting an answer	0: No answer or wrong answer based on an inappropriate plan
	1: Copying error, computational error, or partial answer for a problem with multiple answers
	2: Incorrect answer following from an incorrect plan that was implemented properly
	3: Correct answer and correct label for the answer

Source: Kroll, D. L., Masingila, J. O., & Mau, S. T. (1992). "Grading Cooperative Problem Solving," *Mathematics Teacher, 85*(8), pp. 619–627. Reprinted by permission. Reston, VA: National Council of Teachers of Mathematics.
*Adapted from Charles, Lester, and O'Daffer (1987, 30)

FOR TEACHERS

Activity 1.5 Build a Rectangle

Mathematical Content:
Perimeter and area of rectangles, problem solving (PSSM Middle School Standards for Geometry and Problem Solving)

Materials Needed:
Centimeter graph paper (one quarter of a standard piece per student plus one additional page per group), one problem page per group, one pair of scissors per group if the group is to separate the clues, a grid to use on the overhead projector

Directions: Divide students into groups of four. Provide the following directions for each student group.

"When you get your direction sheet, cut the clues apart so that each person has one part. Each person reads his or her clue and draws a rectangle that satisfies that clue on a small piece of graph paper. Check with a partner to see if the rectangle is a correct solution to the clue. After all four members of your group have a correct rectangle, work together to make a fifth triangle that satisfies all four clues. It could happen that one of the original rectangles could also be a solution to the group rectangle."

Questions to Ask: This activity works well when one triangle at a time is discussed after the activity is completed. Questions could include the following:

1. Give some solutions to Clue 1. How do you know that those answers satisfy that clue?
2. What has to be true of at least one side of the rectangle built to satisfy Clue 2? (It has to be a multiple of 5; it has to end in 5.) Give some solutions.
3. Give some solutions to Clue 3. What do all rectangles built to satisfy this clue have in common?
4. What are some solutions to Clue 4? Do any of these solutions also satisfy another clue?
5. Could I have a volunteer from one group draw the group's solution on the overhead grid? Explain how that solution satisfies all the clues. (Continue with other groups with different solutions.)

Extensions: Create your own Build a Rectangle puzzle.

Source: Adapted with permission from Marcy Cook.

Set 1.3 *Discussion Questions*

 Questions with an asterisk appear in the Message Board section of the Companion Website at *http://www.prenhall.com/huetinck.* Go to Chapter 1 and click on the Message Board to find and respond to the question.

1. What are some benefits of cooperative learning for the teacher? for the student?
2. What are some things to consider in order to maximize students' mathematical learning during a cooperative learning lesson?
*3. List some concerns you have about using cooperative learning in a secondary mathematics classroom and some strategies for dealing with them.

LOGIC—CONTENT AREA OR TOOL?

Some attention usually is given to the formal structure of deductive logic in traditional geometry textbooks. Prior to that, however, students can develop some understanding of the ideas and vocabulary of deductive reasoning. The mathematical use and understanding of words relating to logic should be a part of the curriculum. Activity 1.3, "All, Some, or None," found earlier in this chapter, has students use the words *all, some,* and *none* in a geometry setting.

The mathematical uses of the connective words *and* and *or* also are very important in mathematics, as is the word *not.* In a typical first-year algebra course, for example, students use these words in their mathematical sense when developing solutions of inequalities, particularly inequalities containing absolute values. In today's technology-intensive environments, many students come to a mathematics classroom having an informal sense of the logical use of *and* and *or,* since they are part of Boolean logic—the basis for computer circuitry and many of the games developed for computers.

Venn diagrams with overlapping areas are useful for representing logical relationships. Elementary students frequently participate in sorting activities using cords for Venn diagrams and realia such as buttons, shoes, and shells to place in the various areas of the Venn diagrams so that the relationships may be identified verbally. Attribute blocks also are used for sorting activities, reinforcing geometric vocabulary as well as the logic behind the sorting.

FOR STUDENTS

Activity 1.5
Build a Rectangle

Directions: When you get your direction sheet, cut the clues apart so that each person has one part. Each person reads his or her clue and draws a rectangle that satisfies that clue on a small piece of graph paper. Check with a partner to see if the rectangle is a correct solution to the clue. After all four members of your group have a correct rectangle, work together to make a fifth triangle that satisfies all four clues. It could happen that one of the original rectangles could also be a solution to the group rectangle.

1. Form a rectangle that could be divided into three equal squares by two lines only.

2. Form a rectangle with an area that is a multiple of 5 square units and less than 90 square units.

3. Form a rectangle with perimeter equal to a number that is divisible by 10.

4. Form a rectangle with the width less than 1/2 the length.

Inductive Versus Deductive Reasoning

The following discussion on inductive and deductive reasoning is adapted from a workshop presented by Morris L. Costor, April 1997, at the NCTM Annual Meeting in Minneapolis, Minnesota:

Inductive reasoning is a process of observing data, recognizing patterns, and making predictions based on your observations. The predictions you make from your observations are called *conjectures*.

■ Example 1: Students are asked to explore the midsegments of a triangle, using dynamic geometry technology. (A midsegment is a line segment connecting the midpoints of two sides of a triangle.) Based on the measurement taken of the resulting line segments, as compared to the sides of the original triangle, students conjecture that the length of a midsegment is always half the length of the third side.

A conjecture based on many observations may or may not be true. It takes only one counterexample to show that a conjecture is not always true.

Figure 1.5
Model of Technology Use

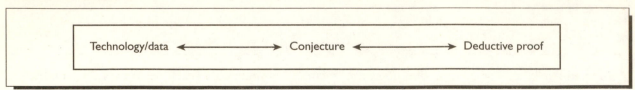

- Example 2: A production-control supervisor noticed that during the first 3 hours of a production day the number of cars coming off the assembly line doubled each hour: 10 cars the first hour, 20 the second hour, and 40 the third. What is your conjecture for the fourth hour? Would your conjecture change if you knew the maximum production rate was 60 cars per hour? What could explain the rate of change the first 3 hours?

Because often it is impossible to examine all the data for a situation, inductive reasoning can leave us with a sense of uncertainty in our conjectures. To ease this uncertainty, we turn to another form of reasoning.

Deductive reasoning is a process that starts with statements that are considered true and shows that other statements logically follow from them.

- Example 3: Referring back to example 1, students would need to prove that the midsegments of a triangle are always equal to one half the opposite side of the triangle by going back to definitions of midpoints, previously developed theorems, and definitions pertinent to the situation, and developing logical sequence of reasoning, with justification, to prove the conjecture to be true for all cases. Even if no counterexample can be found, mathematicians do not accept a theorem as true without deductive proof.

Inductive and deductive reasoning are totally different. Inductive reasoning is based on examining trends in data to develop conjectures. Deductive reasoning is based on logically ordering statements of fact to produce conclusions.

The use of technology in the classroom provides many opportunities for exploration, conjecture, refinement, and substantiation of a proposition, using both inductive and deductive methods, as described previously. The model in Figure 1.5 represents this interaction (Hirschhorn & Thompson, 1996, p. 138). Technology allows students to gather visual and numerical data that may lead them to formulate conjectures. Deciding whether conjectures are true motivates students to discuss proof and decide on

the evidence required to convince themselves and others of their results. In searching for a proof, students might find counterexamples that lead to new conjectures or that might extend and hone their original conjectures. Eventually, students learn to move in both directions when examining mathematical "truth."

Summary

This chapter presented the mathematics reforms of the 21st century in the historical context of American school mathematics of the past 50 years. Elements of the national reform efforts that culminated in the 1989 publication of the National Council of Teachers of Mathematics' *Curriculum and Evaluation Standards for School Mathematics* were described. They included remnants of the "new math," research on mathematics teaching and learning, and the role of technology in the K–12 classroom.

The pedagogical focus was cooperative learning, as research efforts on this approach go back at least a decade and are often related to another major thrust of current mathematics education—success for all students.

The content focus was logic, because of its relationship to the kinds of activities that are appropriate for group work and its historical role in the development of mathematics as an academic discipline.

The stage was now set for you to explore in more detail ways you can implement the *Principles and Standards for School Mathematics* (2000), NCTM's guiding document for school mathematics of the new century, as you continue through this textbook.

ASSIGNMENTS

1. Interview a nonmathematics major about (a) her perceptions of mathematics and (b) whether she enjoyed mathematics classes in high school and why. Write a summary of the interview.

2. Talk with a secondary mathematics teacher who uses cooperative groups in the classroom and ask her to respond to the following issues:

   - promoting more equitable student achievement through cooperative learning;

   - initiating, designing, and selecting cooperative group activities;

   - developing norms for group participation;

   - monitoring and assessing group progress;

   - determining when to use cooperative activities.

   Bring a written copy of the teacher's response to class.

INSTRUCTIONAL RESOURCES

Curcio, F. R. (1999). Dispelling myths about reform in school mathematics. *Mathematics Teaching in the Middle School, 4*(5), 282–284.

This article helps to clarify some key issues facing *Standards*-based mathematics reforms, with ample references to support the author's conclusions.

Erickson, T. (1989). *Get it Together: Math Problems for Groups, Grades 4–12:* EQUALS Program. Berkeley, CA: Lawrence Hall of Science.

These group activities are written in a wide range of topics and levels of difficulty. Six clue cards per problem promote group cooperation, since each member has information needed for the solution.

Erickson, T. (1996). *United We Solve: Math Problems for Groups, Grades 5–10*. Oakland, CA: eeps media.

More than 100 problems for groups of students, keyed to NCTM *Standards* and to middle-grades *Standards*-based curricula.

Pagni, D. L., & Shultz, H. S. (1999). Card logic. *Mathematics Teaching in the Middle School, 5*(2), 74–77.

This article describes an activity where students follow certain sorting rules to arrive at a set of 16 cards arranged in alphabetical order. Several solution strategies are given.

Stenmark, J. K., Thompson, V., & Cossey, R. (1986). *Family Math/Matematica para la Familia*. Berkeley, CA: Lawrence Hall of Science.

Skill- and concept-reinforcing mathematics activities that can be done at home with readily available household materials comprise this book. The activities are coded for primary, upper-elementary, and middle-school students.

ADDITIONAL ACTIVITIES

Activity 1.6 Rainbow Logic
Activity 1.7 Condo Neighbors
Activity 1.8 No Homework
Activity 1.9 Four Bags of Gold

These activities all rely on deductive reasoning. Often, students' reasoning is unconscious, so thoughtful debriefing of solution processes allows students to verbalize their reasoning and connect the language of logic to their solutions. The if . . . then . . . structure and the process of elimination used in these activities are important to problem solving in general.

F O R   T E A C H E R S

Activity 1.6 Rainbow Logic

Mathematical Content:
Deductive logic, spatial relationships (PSSM Middle School Standards for Geometry/Reasoning and Proof)

Materials Needed:
Grids—3-by-3-inch and 4-by-4-inch (you may use 1-inch grid paper and have students draw the borders); 1-by-1-inch colored squares in red, green, blue, and yellow. For classroom demonstrations, overhead transparency grids and clear plastic squares in the four colors could also be used.

Directions: Even though this game is designed to be learned at a family math workshop and subsequently played at home by a parent and child, a preview could be done in class.

Questions to Ask: Use the following questions to debrief with a partner or with class members after the game is over.

1. Does it matter whether the first question is about a row or a column?

2. What is a good strategy for the second question?

3. What is the smallest number of questions needed to be sure you have determined the secret 3-by-3 grid? Explain.

4. How do you keep track of your guesses?

Extensions: After students are comfortable with the 3-by-3 grid, have them play the game on a larger square grid with more colors. In each case, there must be an equal number of squares for each color.

	Column A	Column B	Column C
Row 1			
Row 2			
Row 3			

Source: Reprinted with permission from *Family Math,* published by EQUALS, Lawrence Hall of Science, Berkeley, CA 94720. Regents, University of California at Berkeley.

FOR STUDENTS

Activity 1.6
Rainbow Logic

Directions: The object of the game is for the second player to determine the arrangement of colored squares on a hidden grid made by the first player in as few turns as possible. Start with a 3-by-3-inch grid and three squares each of three colors. The first player arranges her nine squares on a grid that the other player cannot see, following the rule that every square of one color must be connected to another square of that color by at least one full side. The second player should have a blank 3-by-3-inch grid and three squares each of three colors to use during the game.

Example: Suppose the leader creates the following secret grid:

	Column A	Column B	Column C
Row 1	Red	Yellow	Yellow
Row 2	Red	Red	Yellow
Row 3	Green	Green	Green

Note that a red square in row 1, column A and another in row 2, column B would not be legal according to the rules of the game unless the third red were in either row 1, column B or in row 2, column A.

Player 2 can only ask for the colors in a row or a column. Player 1 gives the colors, but not necessarily in the order they appear in the secret grid.

For example, if player 2 asks for Column B, the response could be red, green, yellow. Player 2 must then decide what other row or column would give her more information to determine the correct placement of the colors. *Note:* It may be helpful for the leader to record the answers she gives in order to review the strategy after the game is over. This occurs when player 2 determines the exact location of all 9 squares on the secret grid. The object is to do this with the fewest possible questions.

F O R   T E A C H E R S

Activity 1.7 Condo Neighbors

Mathematical Content:
Deductive logic (PSSM Reasoning and Proof Standard for Grades 6–8)

Materials Needed:
See grid provided with the activity. Chips for each student in two colors—one for false and one for
true.

Directions: This could be a sample problem for all problems of this type. An elimination process is used
to determine the solution. For example, since Jonquil can't be the radio announcer, a "false" chip can be
placed on the grid in that location. As soon as one occupation is determined, a "true" chip is placed there
and "false" chips in the other locations.

Questions to Ask: Have students explain their reasoning for eliminating answers.

Extensions: See Internet sources or game books for other problems of this type. Activity 1.8 is a considerably more complicated logic problem.

F O R   S T U D E N T S

Activity 1.7
Condo Neighbors

Directions: Read the following information, and see if you can figure out who is who.

Anita, Becky, and Jonquil live next door to each other. Becky has the middle condo. They work as a
chemist, a radio announcer, and a doctor. The radio announcer feeds Jonquil's cat when she goes away
for the weekend. The chemist taps on Anita's wall when her CD player is too loud. From the clues given
find the occupation of each woman.

	Anita	Becky	Jonquil
Chemist			
Radio Announcer			
Doctor			

FOR TEACHERS

Activity 1.8 No Homework

Mathematical Content:
Deductive logic (PSSM Reasoning and Proof Standard for Grades 6–8)

Materials Needed:
"No Homework" activity directions with grid

Directions: Students may work in pairs.

Questions to Ask: The following questions are examples of those that could be asked when students get stuck.
1. Which person do you know the most about? Which clues provided that information?
2. When you have eliminated three of the five possibilities, what can you do next? (Assume one possible solution and pursue it to see if it fits the other clues. If it does not, it is likely that the other one is the correct one.)

Note: This one is very challenging!

FOR STUDENTS

Activity 1.8
No Homework (page 1 of 2)

Directions: Read the following facts, and see if you and your partner can solve this problem.

Because of their good grades, Francisco and four of his friends, each taking a different summer school class, earned the right to skip their homework on a different day of the week (Monday through Friday). From the clues, determine the first and last name of each student, the day each did not do homework, and the summer school class each person is taking.
1. The person who skipped Monday's homework assignment and the person enrolled in the social studies class are the young man whose last name is Hicks and the student whose last name is Gamboa, not necessarily in that order.
2. Lamont is neither the boy who skipped the Friday homework assignment nor the boy whose last name is Blatt.
3. Candace's last name is not Fong.
4. Lila decided not to do her homework the day before the student who is enrolled in the English class, who decided not to do homework the day before the student whose last name is Hicks.
5. Of Ernie and the student who is enrolled in the French class, one's last name is Fong and the other's last name is Blatt, not necessarily in that order.
6. The student who skipped homework on Wednesday and the student who is enrolled in the math class are surnamed Hicks and McNeil, not necessarily in that order.

F O R   S T U D E N T S

Activity 1.8
No Homework (page 2 of 2)

		CHART FOR NO HOMEWORK														
		Last Name					Day					Class				
		Blatt	Fong	Gamboa	Hicks	McNeil	Monday	Tuesday	Wednesday	Thursday	Friday	English	French	Math	Science	Social Studies
Student	Candace															
	Ernie															
	Francisco															
	Lila															
	Lamont															
Class	English															
	French															
	Math															
	Science															
	Social Studies															
Day	Monday															
	Tuesday															
	Wednesday															
	Thursday															
	Friday															

FOR TEACHERS

Activity 1.9 Eight Bags of Gold

Mathematical Content:
Deductive logic (PSSM Reasoning and Proof Standard for Grades 6–8)

Materials Needed:
The problem statement, a pan balance, and weights (optional)

Directions: This is a typical *Interactive Mathematics Project* problem of the week (POW). (See Chapter 4 for a more complete description of this high-school curriculum, which was designated "promising" by the U.S. Department of Education.) A POW is generally given to students on a Monday and due the following Monday. Each day during the week, students, grouped in fours, may be given a few minutes to share ideas about the problem. The solution is written up individually, with the process described in the student's own words, along with diagrams made by the student and extensions suggested by the student. Even when they don't find a final solution, students turn in evidence of approaches they have tried and explanations of why they know a particular approach does not work.

Questions to Ask: The first day of the POW, most questions are directed at understanding the problem. Since fair amounts of reading and vocabulary are involved, strategies to assist students in their comprehension and/or techniques for students whose native language is not English would be appropriate at this stage.

The subsequent days, students may be asked to briefly share insights or approaches they are considering. The day the POW is submitted, one or more students, randomly selected, present a portion of the solution to the entire class. Classmates may ask constructive questions after the presentation is complete, facilitated by the teacher.

Extensions: These are created by the students themselves. They may include easier problems appropriate for younger students.

FOR STUDENTS

Activity 1.9
Eight Bags of Gold

Directions: Read the story and follow the directions to solve.

Once upon a time there was a very economical king who gathered up all the gold in his land and put it into eight bags. He made sure that each bag weighed exactly the same amount.

The king then chose the eight people in the country whom he trusted the most. He gave a bag of gold to each of them to keep safe for him. On special occasions the king asked them to bring the bags back so he could look at them. (He liked looking at gold, even though he didn't like spending it.)

One day the king heard from a foreign trader that someone from the king's country had given the trader some gold in exchange for some merchandise. The trader couldn't describe the person who had given her the gold, but she knew that it was someone from the king's country. Since the king owned all of the gold in his country, it was obvious that one of the eight people he trusted was cheating him.

The only scale in the country was a pan balance. This scale wouldn't tell how much something weighed, but it could compare two things and indicate which was heavier and which was lighter.

The person whose bag was lighter than the others would clearly be the cheat. So the king asked the eight trusted people to bring their bags of gold to him.

Being very economical, the king wanted to use the pan balance as few times as possible. He thought he might have to use it three times in order to be sure which bag was lighter than the rest. His court mathematician thought that it could be done in fewer weighings. What do you think?

To solve this question, follow these steps.

1. Develop a scheme for comparing bags that will always find the light one.
2. Explain how you can be sure your scheme will always work.
3. Explain how you know that there is no scheme with fewer weighings that will work.

Note: Each comparison counts as a new weighing, even if some of the bags are the same as on the previous comparison.

Write-Up:

Problem Statement: In your own words, write what the problem is you are trying to solve.
Process: Describe how you found your answer and how you convinced yourself that your method works in all situations. If you think your answer is the best possible, describe how you came to that conclusion.
Solution: Describe your solution to the king's problem as clearly as possible. Then write a proof that your method will work in every situation. If you think that the king cannot find the lighter bag in fewer than three weighings, prove it.
Extensions: Make up a similar problem to this problem. The new problem could be easier or harder, but it should involve the same solution strategy.
Evaluation: Say whether this problem was too easy, extremely challenging, or just about right for you, and why.

Source: Fendel, Dan, et. al. (1997). *Interactive Mathematics Program,* Key Curriculum Press, 1150 65th Street, Emeryville, CA 94608, 1-800-995-MATH. Reprinted with permission.

CHAPTER 2

Learning, Motivation, and Basic Management Skills

Beginning teachers and principals of beginning teachers consistently name successful classroom management techniques as essential to exemplary teaching; these effective techniques must be grounded in a thorough understanding of how students learn and are motivated. The previous chapter dealt with the nature of mathematics and the related belief structures of teachers who successfully implement the reform recommendations of the NCTM *Standards* documents in their classrooms. This chapter expands your foundation knowledge to include educational learning theory and motivation.

We recognize that the topics discussed in this chapter may be taught more extensively in courses required in a credential program, such as educational psychology and classroom management. Therefore, the topics will be briefly described herein, serving as a review for students who have already completed those courses and as a brief introduction for students who may not yet have been presented with this information. A discussion of theories of educational psychology is very important for understanding that one basis of the reform in mathematics education is founded in our increasing knowledge of how students learn. The discussions in this chapter are enhanced with examples and applications pertinent to mathematics education, with particular attention given to those theories and techniques most applicable to current mathematics educational innovations. For continuity of content, activities are based on the mathematical topic of probability.

ABOUT THE ACTIVITIES FOR THIS CHAPTER

The content focus of this chapter is probability, for four main reasons. First, the activities highlight different ways of applying the teacher's understanding of student learning as related to the major theories of educational psychology. Knowing students is the basic theme of this chapter. Second, probability comes at the beginning of this text because all too often this significant subject is at the end of most secondary level texts, and classes seldom finish the book. There is an increasing emphasis on improving our students' standing on international studies as compared with students in other First World countries. The subject of probability has gained in importance since most other countries begin the study of that subject in elementary school. For the same reason, many statewide exams have also begun including test items on probability. Third, probability is certainly an important topic to understand as students move into making complex decisions now required of adults in our modern society. Lastly, students enjoy probability and are intrinsically interested in probability, which makes teaching it a pleasure. They understand the concept of fairness and are seldom reluctant to voice an opinion of whether or not a game is fair. However, sometimes their intuition is accurate, and sometimes it is not. This basic understanding of fairness can be used as a foundation for developing methods of probing probability with mathematical analysis. Thus students see the benefits of using mathematics in proving or disproving their intuitive concepts.

The probability activities were selected to include a variety of solution methods that are not easily reduced to textbook equations. Some of the problems are counterintuitive. The first three activities involve the Game Show. This is a novel problem because new information is supplied by the game show host in the midst of the situation, which complicates the solution. Each of the Game Show Activities (2.1, 2.2, and 2.3) illustrates one of the three different ways the problem can be approached, using each of three different ways of applying constructivism, which is detailed in the reading. Also, the method of solving the Game Show Problem can be based upon the students' level of sophistication and

problem-solving ability. Activities 2.5, 2.6, 2.7, and 2.10 are based on whether or not the situation is fair, and these activities present an increasing level of difficulty. Activity 2.6 is an excellent review problem that includes a number of different ways of calculating probability. Activity 2.7 and 2.9 are problems in geometric probability. Activity 2.7 relies on a ratio of areas, and Activity 2.9 is more abstract. It requires students to consider possible points on a given line segment to form a triangle with a second line segment of one-half the length of the first. Activity 2.8 provides an opportunity for students to explore a simulation and then compare theoretical values with experimental data.

When reading this chapter, take breaks to try out the activities. Think of ways you learn and approach the problems and reflect on how your students would do these problems. Place yourself in the role of the student, and try to see the problem as he would. Then put yourself in the role of the teacher deciding how to present probability, and plan the activities best suited for your students. What level of background understanding would be necessary for certain activities? What activities would be appropriate for students of different ages? How would you prepare students for the simulations or discovery situations? Note that Activity 2.4 is the only one in this chapter that is not based on probability. However, this activity, The Blindfold and the Puzzle, belongs in this chapter because it illustrates the roles of the students and teacher working together to create a community of learners based in sound educational psychology.

LEARNING THEORIES

Schools of educational psychology have differing views of two elements fundamental to a theory of learning. It is accepted that we cannot directly observe thinking processes. For example, as you work through a problem in front of the class, John may be looking straight at you, even taking notes, but you cannot know whether he is paying attention or whether the explanation you are giving is increasing his mathematical understanding. You can observe only that he is writing and that his eyes are directed toward you. Some educational psychologists prefer to base their understanding on this kind of observable behavior, while others prefer to focus on the working of the mind, even though such information must be found indirectly.

A second area in which educators differ concerns the definition of the nature of learning. Educators agree that learning is change, but they disagree on whether the change is primarily in behavior or in mental associations.

Currently there are four main theories of learning: behaviorism, social cognitive theory, information-processing theory, and constructivism. The last of these is the predominant theoretical orientation for the reform in mathematics education. However, each of the theories of learning applies in some teaching setting, so a teacher needs to develop an understanding of all of them. The following paragraphs briefly outline the main features of the four theories and their specific contributions to mathematics education.

In addition to the four main theories of learning, this chapter includes additional components of learning theory. Knowledge of the work of Piaget and Vygotsky contribute to an understanding of the foundation of constructivism, the pedagogical perspective underlying the reform in mathematics education advocated by literature from the National Council of Mathematics Teachers and the Mathematics Association of America. This chapter discusses constructivism, in the paradigm of schema theory, from three different perspectives. The appropriateness of each depends on the way the teacher applies the theory to classroom activities. Following these discussions is a brief introduction to theories of multiple intelligences and to differences in learning styles.

Behaviorism

In an effort to introduce scientific rigor into their field, psychologists at the turn of the century began the study of observable behavior and related environments instead of focusing solely on what is happening "inside" the human being during learning. This perspective, known as behaviorism and widely embraced by psychologists for the first half of the 20th century, considered learning to be a change of behavior. Behaviorists studied the learning of many species of animals, in addition to humans, with the expectation that examining animals with simpler brains and nervous systems than those of humans could serve to illuminate characteristics of human behavior.

Behaviorists consider a young child's mind to be a blank slate. They maintain that environmental factors develop that child into an adult individual with unique ways of behaving. A person receives two types of conditioning from his environment: classical and operant. For classical conditioning to take place, there must be a specific outside stimulus that elicits a certain response. In a learning sequence, the response initially is an unconditioned, automatic, involuntary one. Ivan Pavlov observed, for example, that a dog salivated in response to having meat powder placed in its mouth. Then a light was flashed at the same time the dog was given meat powder. After a number of trials, the dogs began to salivate at the flashing light when the meat was not present, having become conditioned to a response (Pavlov, 1928). Sometimes, the conditioning period may be very short, as with a child who develops a fear of all dogs after being bitten by only one dog. By analogy to his animal experiments, Pavlov hoped to illuminate the origin and development of some forms of human psychosis (Gantt, "Introduction" in Pavlov, 1941). In recent years this pairing of two stimuli—that of the unconditioned and the conditioned responses—has been reinterpreted due to increased understanding of the associations underlying Pavlovian conditioning. Modern thinking characterizes conditioning as the learning from exposure to relations between events in an environment (Rescorla, 1988). Pavlovian conditioning has a role in education as a model for modifying behavior through experience.

Operant conditioning with focus on the emitted response is important in human learning. Operant conditioning differs from classical conditioning in that the response must come *before* the stimulus, thus, in opposite order to the stimuli followed by the response found in classical conditioning. B. F. Skinner, a noted researcher in the field, studied the basic principle of operant conditioning. A reinforced stimulus, called a reinforcer, is more than likely to occur again (Skinner, 1954, 1968). Another important contrast between classical and operant conditioning is that the response usually is voluntary in operant conditioning, i.e., under the control of the individual. After the initial response is made, the teacher can provide either positive or negative reinforcement, either of which may produce increased or decreased frequency of a response since the response depends on the individual affected. Productive behaviors such as knowing the multiplication tables may be encouraged because of the reward of positive teacher and parental attention. Or students may utilize disruptive behaviors to get teacher and parental attention, since some young people will consider even negative attention to be rewarding. This example illustrates the common knowledge of teachers and parents that stimuli reinforce differently for different individuals.

Behavior Modification An important application of behaviorism to education today is behavior modification. Behavior can be modified by manipulation of the environment and adjustment of the consequences of the behavior toward achieving the desired behavior (Michael & Meyerson, 1962). Experienced teachers know that the classroom arrangement may affect student deportment. The sections on basic management skills at the end of this chapter give a number of suggestions for room arrangement that minimizes possible interference to instruction and encourages a good learning environment.

The giving of tokens for achievement is another example of behaviorism at work in the classroom. Although some teachers may feel that secondary-level students do not appreciate "gold stars," such is not always the case. When new ninth-graders enrolled in his high-school geometry class, a colleague began a "Smiling Face Club," consisting of putting students' names on the board for earning A grades on papers. Soon his older geometry students heard of the practice and asked to be included. To his surprise, when these same students took Trigonometry/Math Analysis as juniors and seniors, they again requested "Club" membership. The students did not work only for the recognition, but they did enjoy receiving it.

Programmed Instruction   Programmed instruction is a behaviorist methodology still in evidence in some less sophisticated computer software providing instruction in mathematics. It was advocated and promoted by Skinner and Pressey in the 1960s (Skinner, 1968; Pressey, 1963). Utilizing teaching machines to increase the immediate reinforcement to students and thereby increase the efficiency of education was an important aspect of their work. The basic premise of programmed mathematics programs is that if the learning tasks are divided into small segments in a linear sequence, the students will be reinforced or corrected at each step so that misconceptions will not develop. In general, the early printed materials were arranged so that the student was tested at the end of each skill—for example, multiplication of 3-digit numbers by 2-digit numbers—and allowed to move to the next unit only after showing mastery of the operation by correctly answering a given number of like problems on a quiz.

Most programmed instruction of the 1950s and 1960s was aimed at general skill development in basic arithmetic. One of the authors (LH) once taught this type of course, which required students to proceed through 454 packets in up to 3 years of general mathematics. An advantage was that students could proceed at their own pace, a benefit close to Skinner's heart. The disadvantage was that students seemed more intent on gathering points by completing a nearly endless supply of worksheets than on understanding mathematical concepts. Some current computer programs that drill on a quick response to random arithmetic problems and reward correct answers by sending up a rocket or adding a boxcar to a train on the screen are other examples of this type of instruction.

There is now evidence that information is retained much better if it is organized into schemas, and that rote learning is not an efficient method of permanent learning. Rather, facts should be purposefully connected through instructional activities.

Certain aspects of the behavioral learning theory are quite appropriate today. For example, when we reward students for achievement, we encourage them to further success; misbehavior decreases when the teacher moves from giving attention based on less desired behavior to reinforcing/rewarding desired behavior.

Even contemporary behaviorists are finding that the mind cannot be treated as a black box, however. Student thinking processes must enter into consideration. Pressey, himself a proponent of programmed instruction, realized its difficulties, saying that children gradually develop understanding of a number system as Piaget has described, "not by so crude a rote process as the accretion of bits of learning stuck on by reinforcement, but by progressive processes of cognitive integration and clarification" (1963, p. 2). He concludes that the learning of meaningful information is largely unique to humans.

Set 2.1   *Discussion Questions*

Questions with an asterisk appear in the Message Board section of the Companion Website at *http://www.prenhall.com/huetinck*. Go to Chapter 2 and click on the Message Board to find and respond to the question.

1. Discuss in a small group the different types of behaviorist methods you have observed in the classroom (at any level) and how well these methods seemed to work.
2. How have the behaviorists changed their thinking in the past century?
3. Is it possible that positive reinforcement in the form of effusive praise may sometimes be less than effective in the classroom? For example, what about the student who is not praised?
4. Is it positive reinforcement to seat students in order of highest to lowest scores attained on the last unit exam? Consider all students.
*5. What rote memorization do you believe is absolutely essential in learning mathematics? Consider the broad range of students you may have.

Social Cognitive Theory

Social cognitive theory was originally called observation learning theory due to its main assertion that much can be learned from observing others. The theory differs from behaviorism by defining learning as change of mental associations and in emphasizing cognitive processes rather than observable behavior. Goal setting and related control over behavior and environmental conditions also distinguish it from behaviorism. Some distinctive features of social cognitive theory are that humans have the complex capacity to use symbols to represent events, and that people do not simply react to events but "select, organize and transform the stimuli that impinge upon them" (Bandura, 1977, p. vii).

According to the social cognitive theoretical framework for analyzing human thought and behavior initiated by Bandura, a model of observational learning includes four processes (1977, 1986):

1. *Attentional.* Students will attend to role models who exhibit competence, prestige, gender-appropriate behavior, and behavior that the observer believes will assist in attaining their goals. To learn from observation, students must pay attention to and accurately perceive the significant features of the model. Students may not see the idealized straight line teachers see on a graphing calculator. For example, we have asked students to draw the graph for $Y = 2X + 3$ from the graphing calculator and received a fine stair-step figure exactly as viewed on the screen. Students new to the graphing calculator must be told that the discrete pixels composing the screen distort the figure from a single straight line; they need to attend to the overall shape of the graph and not to draw in each tiny zigzag.

2. *Retention.* For future learning to be affected, the behavior must be retained. The response patterns are represented as memory in symbolic form, primarily either image or verbal. When learning becomes highly correlated, a name will evoke an image and vice versa. For example, graphing calculators with the dual nature of symbolic and graphical representation of a function can build an integrated understanding. The knowledgeable student will "picture" a parabola opening downward with a maximum above the x-axis when given the equation $Y = -2X^2 + 4$. In addition, practice is a memory aid when done in short segments over time.

3. *Motor reproduction.* Learning involves translating symbolic representation into appropriate actions, but the correct action rarely is attained at first. Errors in the execution of an action are cues for corrective action until the novice thinker advances to become more expert in approach. Motor reproduction is not only kinesthetic activity but also mental activity. For example, in the mathematical classroom community, students in cooperative groups can provide each other feedback as different approaches are attempted while solving a problem of some complexity. The teacher monitors the group process and gives guidance when appropriate to assist productive actions.

4. *Motivational.* "Social learning theory distinguishes between requisition and performance because people do not enact everything they learn" (Bandura, 1977, p. 28). Humans emulate behaviors that they observe are effective for others in order to attain ends that they themselves desire. There may be a variety of reasons an observer does not successfully match the actions of a model, such as not observing all the relevant activities, not recalling the modeled events, or not having the physical ability to perform the actions. As a result of the concept that a learner decides what to observe (i.e., what to learn), Bandura added and developed motivational theory based on goal-oriented behavior. He believed we could self-reinforce for learning new behaviors. This is in contrast to the behaviorists, who focused on external reinforcement.

Expansion into Cognitive Development   Other social cognitive researchers expanded the theory into intellectual development. Rosenthal and Zimmerman state that Bandura's work "showed the pervasiveness of social modeling, that it could teach without overt practice or direct incentives" (1978, p. xi). They cited massive databases in the cognitive sphere to advance their analysis in educational psychology. Social cognitive theory researchers explored ways to provide novice learners with the tools to improve their performance so they could be fully informed participants in their learning. Teaching strategies for students to learn from texts helped them learn to learn (Brown, Campione & Day, 1981); training underachieving students to use methods to monitor their progress improved their achievement in arithmetic (Stevenson & Fantuzzo, 1986); and praising students for working hard for past achievement resulted in more rapid progress in learning subtraction than imploring them to work harder in the future (Schunk, 1982). We know from experience that we do learn a great deal by interacting socially with others. This theory interprets vicarious and observational learning in the social setting.

As in behaviorism, social cognitive theory promotes the idea that consequences of behavior influence resultant learning but differ due to emphasis on mental activities under control of the learner. Social cognitive theory does not detail the characteristics of mental processes that lead to acquisition of knowledge, as does information processing theory.

Vignette 2.1   Modeling Behavior

Teacher: Today we are going to learn how to enter data into a graphing calculator. Everyone get out your calculators, turn them on, and then press the key marked STAT. On the board is the list of numbers to enter.

Student: Where is the STAT key?

Teacher: The STAT key is in the second row below the graphing window and the third column from the left. If you do not see the table like this one on the graphing calculator overhead, raise your hand, and I will assist you. If you already have numbers in the tables, raise your hand, and I will help you clear them.

(Teacher moves around the room, helping students and asking the more knowledgeable students to assist others.)

Teacher: Enter the numbers one at a time, remembering to press the ENTER key after each number. Be sure to double-check each value.

Although the NCTM *Standards* recommend a student-centered or discovery approach, in this case modeling is far more efficient than discovery or asking the students to read the manual. Most of us have had the experience of being stumped in computer usage and being assisted by only a few words from a more experienced user, even after unsuccessfully consulting the computer manual. Of course, students should be encouraged to explore and discover relationships with the calculator as soon as they are somewhat familiar with its keyboard.

Set 2.2   Discussion Questions

Questions with an asterisk appear in the Message Board section of the Companion Website at *http://www.prenhall.com/huetinck.* Go to Chapter 2 and click on the Message Board to find and respond to the question.

1. What ideas from social cognitive theory will you take into the classroom and why?
2. In terms of the four processes of observational learning, explain why several students may be attentive to the same lesson but gain entirely different understandings of the concepts modeled.

3. In addition to the example of calculator usage given in this section, what other types of mathematics lessons are most effectively modeled?
*4. How can an understanding of the social relationships among students and their peers assist you during instruction?

Information-Processing Theory

According to information-processing theory, learning is a significant change in mental processes and in considering those internal learning processes. But information-processing theory goes further than either behaviorism or social cognitive theory in examining how humans attain, remember, and organize information. Theorists in this field believe students are active in their learning processes by choosing the elements of their environment that they will process and by imposing their own meaning from their previous experiences. Thus, due to different previous learning situations and differing degrees of attention to the presentation at hand, students presented with seemingly identical learning situations will learn different things. These educational psychologists draw inferences about cognitive processes by observing students' behavior and recognizing that, because only humans have the facility for verbal communication, our ways of learning differ from those of other species.

Four terms commonly used in basic computer models are useful in laying the foundation of information-processing theory:

- *Storage*—the acquisition of knowledge. Teachers must consider what methods are the most effective for assisting students in committing new information to memory.
- *Encoding*—the manner in which the information is stored. A computer may simply store information as binary—on or off bits—but the human mind does not store information in total. We may store information as a visual picture or change a verbal description to a visual form. Most frequently, we store the general idea, so we may not even make the effort to encode certain specifics, especially if they are not of interest.
- *Retrieval*—the recall of information.
- *Control processes*—guide the flow of information throughout the whole system.

For ease of discussion, we will consider a simplified description in which the human memory has three main components (which may or may not be separate levels). The memory components are: (1) the sensory register, (2) working, or short-term, memory, and (3) long-term memory. The sensory register holds input in more or less unencoded form. You receive input through ears, eyes, and touch. Although the sensory register has the capacity to take in a lot of information, the information stored in this register does not last longer than perhaps 1 to 3 seconds. Working, or short-term, memory can be considered a temporary holding bin for new information while it is being processed. Information at this stage probably lasts only 5 to 20 seconds. Long-term memory is the component of the human memory system that holds information for a relatively long time. Long-term memory appears to have unlimited capacity, is of long duration—especially compared to the other two components—and, most importantly, is a rich network of interconnected information interacting with information previously stored there. This information is said to be stored in schemas, which are bodies organized around overarching principles (Ormrod, 1995).

Teachers who use information processing theory approaches to learning must assist students in developing schemas. It is helpful to think of a schema as an interconnected map of individual concepts. As students gain in expertise, the map increases in complexity as the interconnections and the number of concepts increase in complexity. Teachers can ask questions to lead the students to understanding, as illustrated in Vignette 2.2.

Vignette 2.2   Developing a Schema

Teacher: OK, open your books to page 7 and silently read the instructions. (*pause*) Can anybody tell me what the assignment is?

Karen: We are supposed to fill in the blanks and find the rule for how the In-Out machine works.

Teacher: Karen, can you give me an example of what you're saying?

Karen: Well, I don't know how to explain it in words, but I think I can do it.

Teacher: Can anybody help her? (*silence*) Well, imagine a change machine. What happens when you deposit a dollar? What usually comes out?

Students: Quarters.

Teacher: What do you think is happening inside the machine?

Kevin: The machine divides the dollar into quarters.

Theresa: No, I think it multiplies it to quarters.

Teacher: What do you think, Jannel?

Jannel: I don't know. I think it does both. It gives you 4 quarters back, so it is multiplying it, but it is dividing it because 1 quarter is less than a dollar.

Teacher: What happens if you deposit 2 dollars? How many quarters do you get?

Othon: I know, Miss P. It gives you 8 quarters back, and if you deposit 3 dollars, it gives you back 12 quarters, and if you deposit 4 dollars, it gives you 16.

Theresa: See, I told you it is multiplying the dollar bills by 4.

Teacher: So how can I write that in words?

Stan: You can multiply x times 4 and get y.

Teacher: Where did you get the x and y?

Stan: The "In" in the machines is the x, and the y is the "Out" all the time.

Teacher: Are you sure? Can I use a and b instead?

Theresa: (pause) I think it really doesn't matter.

Teacher: OK, your job as a team is to come up with rules for the In-Out machines. I'll be walking around the room answering questions.

Constructivism

Constructivism is a cognitive learning theory that has come from both social cognitive theory and information learning theory. "Learning mathematics requires construction, not passive reception, and to know mathematics requires constructive work with mathematical objects in a mathematics community" (Davis, Maher, & Noddings, 1990, p. 2). The work by Davis and colleagues, *Constructivist Views on the Teaching and Learning of Mathematics: Monograph 4* (NCTM, 1990), was 5 years in development by outstanding researchers, theorists, and mathematics educators whose goal was to propose practical ways to improve the teaching and learning of mathematics. In 1985, when this group began, *constructivism* was a word hardly even heard, and unfortunately it has since become a buzzword that means many different things to different people. The view of constructivism endorsed by *Monograph 4,* in agreement with the NCTM *Standards* (1989) and the National Research Council's *Everybody Counts* (1989), will be the basis for our discussion. They actively endorse the constructivist approach to mathematics education defined in a number of reform documents. "Mathematical learning should be viewed as both a process of active individual construction and a process of enculturation into the mathematical practices of wider society" (Cobb, 1994, p. 13).

Constructivism is a pedagogical perspective with historical roots. Neisser describes its central assertion, "that seeing, hearing, and remembering are all acts of construction, which may make more or less use of stimulus information, depending on circumstances" (1967, p. 8, as quoted by Noddings in Davis, Maher, & Noddings, 1990). Richard Skemp, a British mathematician and psychologist, states two basic principles of the learning of mathematics:

(1) Concepts of a higher order than those which a person already has cannot be communicated to him by a definition, but only by arranging for him to encounter a suitable collection of examples. (2) Since in mathematics these examples are almost invariably other

concepts, it must first be ensured that these are already formed in the mind of the learner. (1971, p. 32)

Skemp recommends finding suitable examples for a concept that are alike in the elements to be abstracted and different in ways that are not significant. *Schema* is the general psychology term for related groupings of concepts, and the study of structures of concepts interrelated in a variety of ways is an important aspect of mathematics. These schema integrate existing knowledge and are necessary mental tools for subsequent attainment of knowledge. He relates a study of remembering symbols associated with words that indicates that "schematically learnt material was not only better learnt, but better retained" (p. 42). Von Glaserfeld (1987) says "perceiving, from a constructivist point of view, is always an active making rather than a passive receiving . . ." (p. 217, as quoted on p. 8 by Noddings in Davis, Maher, & Noddings, 1990).

The roots of constructivism in the learning of science go back further in time, and early research in the field is instructive, even for those not teaching science. Piaget, who provided the psychological basis for science education, believed that children are naturally curious about their world and are active learners trying to make sense of it. They organize their information in basic units or schemas. As long as children can assimilate new experiences into their schema or frameworks of ideas, they are in a comfortable state of equilibrium. However, if children explore new ideas that do not fit into their existing schemas, they will feel mental discomfort that requires a replacing or enlarging of their schemas to again attain equilibrium. Duckworth, the translator for Piaget at conferences, states, "You cannot further understanding in a child simply by talking to him" (p. 173, 1964) and quotes Piaget directly, "The goal of education is . . . to create the possibilities for the child to invent and discover" (p. 174, 1964). In these elements of his theory Piaget was a constructivist. Although some modern cognitive scientists do not consider Piaget to be a constructivist because of some parts of his theory, especially that development from naive to expert thinking is roughly age dependent and attained in stages, he was instrumental in developing the ideas of mental constructs.

Vygotsky's Work In addition to Piaget's perspective, the work of Vygotsky is critical to an understanding of constructivism. Vygotsky worked in Russia during the 1920s and 1930s, but his writings were not widely known by Americans until his works were translated into English and published a number of years after his death. The first published book, *Thought and Language* (1962), related Vygotsky's theories about how thought and language are interrelated for the young child. The second book published, *Mind and Society* (1978), illuminated his ideas that important developmental interactions occur when a competent adult assists a child to accomplish tasks that the child cannot do independently. These tasks are said to be in the child's zone of proximal development. The teaching adult provides a scaffold to interact with the student to provide the necessary support to enable the student to succeed in an activity. A scaffold can be simple as providing leading questions to enable the student to see the steps required to work a word problem.

The constructivist approach to teaching requires establishing a community of mathematics learners:

> When one applies constructivism to the issue of teaching, one must reject the assumption that one can simply pass on information to a set of learners and expect that understanding will result. Communication is a far more complex process than this. When teaching concepts, as a form of communication, the teacher must form an adequate model of the students' ways of viewing an idea and s/he then must assist the student in restructuring those views to be more adequate from the students' and from the teacher's perspective. (Confrey, 1990, p. 109)

Teachers and students work together to enable students to deepen their understanding of mathematics.

Three Types of Constructivism Researchers suggest that there are three different types of constructivists, based on the teacher's methodology: endogenous, exogenous, and dialectical. The teacher who uses student-driven exploration and/or inquiry based largely on Piagetian theory is said to be an endogenous constructivist. This mathematics teacher allows students to build on previous information about mathematics in an inquiry lesson designed to lead students to work out new concepts and relationships. A second teacher operates as an exogenous constructivist, favoring modeling and explanation reflected in the social cognitive learning theory and information processing theories. A third teacher, differing from the first two, may be a dialectical constructivist, emphasizing scaffolding for the child. He will depend less on discovery lessons and more on coaching students as they work. This teacher acts as a guide using the work of Vygotsky (Muthukrishna & Borkowski, 1996, pp. 60–65, edited by Carr). In practice, teachers do and should change their tactics as the curriculum and classroom environment require, even though their basic beliefs about the nature of teaching and learning mathematics may result in the preference of one style over another.

Figure 2.1
Four Views of Learning

	Behavioral	Exogenous Constructivism	Endogenous Constructivism	Dialectical Constructivism/ Situated Learning
	Skinner	**J. Anderson**	**Piaget**	**Vygotsky**
Knowledge	Fixed body of knowledge to acquire	Fixed body of knowledge to acquire	Changing body of knowledge, individually constructed in social world	Socially constructed knowledge
	Stimulated from outside	Stimulated from outside	Built on what learner brings	Built on what participants contribute, construct together
		Prior knowledge influences how information is processed		
Learning	Acquisition of facts, skills, concepts	Acquisition of facts, skills, concepts, and strategies	Active construction, restructuring prior knowledge	Collaborative construction of socially defined knowledge and values
	Occurs through drill, guided practice	Occurs through the effective application of strategies	Occurs through multiple opportunities and diverse processes to connect to what is already known	Occurs through socially constructed opportunities
Teaching	Transmission	Transmission	Challenge, guide thinking toward more complete understanding	Co-construct knowledge with students
	Presentation (telling)	Guide students toward more "accurate" and complete knowledge		
Role of Teacher	Manager, supervisor	Teach and model effective strategies	Facilitator, guide	Facilitator, guide
				Co-participant
	Correct wrong answers	Correct misconceptions	Listen for student's current conceptions, ideas, thinking	Co-construct different interpretation of knowledge; listen to socially constructed conceptions
Role of Peers	Not usually considered	Not necessary but can influence information processing	Not necessary but can stimulate thinking, raise questions	Ordinary part of process of knowledge construction
Role of Student	Passive reception of information	Active processor of information, strategy user	Active construction (within mind)	Active co-construction with others and self
	Active listener, direction follower	Organizer and reorganizer of information	Active thinker, explainer, interpreter, questioner	Active thinker, explainer, interpreter, questioner
		Rememberer		Active social participator

Note: There are variations within each of these views of learning that differ in emphasis. There is also an overlap in constructive views.
Source: Adapted by permission of the author from Hermine H. Marshall. *Reconceptualizing Learning for Restructured Schools*. Paper presented at the Annual Meeting of the American Educational Research Association, April, 1992.

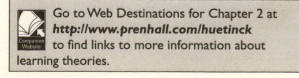

Go to Web Destinations for Chapter 2 at *http://www.prenhall.com/huetinck* to find links to more information about learning theories.

The Game Show Problem, for example, can be approached in a variety of ways. In the three activities that follow, the Game Show Problem, which is difficult for most mathematics students, is used as a basis with three different pedagogical methods: (1) endogenous—

an open-ended discovery lesson with a spinner in which the students compare experimental outcomes to develop a solution; (2) exogenous—modeled practice of tree diagrams by the teacher to solve relatively simple problems so that students can then apply the principles to the more complex Game Show Problem; and (3) dialectical—using a teacher-guided scaffold beginning with a card problem to lead into the Game Show Problem. Solutions to these three activities appear in the Notes to the Teacher at the end of the text.

The Game Show Problem

Imagine you are a contestant on a game show. You can select one of three doors. Behind one door is a new car; behind each of the other two doors is a goat. Of course, you wish to open the door to win the car. You put your hand on one of the doorknobs, but before you open it, the game show host opens a door revealing a goat. [The teacher should act this out in front of the class.] Given this, should you switch to select the other door, or should you open the one you chose first? Does it matter? The first two solutions to this problem are adapted from the article "Monte's Dilemma: Should You Stick or Switch?" by Shaughnessy and Dick (1991).

 Go to Web Destinations for Chapter 2 at **http://www.prenhall.com/huetinck** to find more information on the Game Show.

Vignette 2.3   Discovery with a Number Cube

The students are analyzing several chips and six-sided cube games in an eighth-grade math class. Carlos is the extrovert, so the teacher decided to play the class against Carlos, because if you have Carlos's attention, you have everyone's attention.

Teacher: OK, we will begin the game now. Carlos is going to throw the number cube. Remember, if it is an even number, Carlos gets one point. If it is an odd number, we get one point. Before we begin, who do you think will win?

Carlos: I will.

Teacher: Why?

Carlos: Because I know.

Teacher: That's not a good reason. You have to tell us why you actually believe you are going to win. Look, there are more of us than you. I think we are going to win because it is 33 against 1. Think about your reasons before you answer. Someone tell me who

you think will win and why. Does Carlos have a better probability to win or do we?

Yvonne: I think we both will win because we have the same numbers.

Teacher: What numbers?

Yvonne: Carlos can win with the two, four, and six, and we win with the one, three, and five. We both win with three numbers.

Teacher: What does that say about the probabilities?

Yvonne: They are equal.

Teacher: What are they?

Yvonne: Three out of six for Carlos and three out of six for us.

Teacher: OK, now let's play. Throw the die.

(Carlos throws 16 times, as the teacher records.)

Teacher: How many even and how many odd results did we get?

Various Students: Nine even, and seven odd.

Carlos: I won. I told you so.

A discussion follows, calculating the probability found in the trials and indicating that the game had experimental results that are seldom exactly the same as theoretical results.

F O R   T E A C H E R S

Activity 2.1 Game Show: A Discovery Simulation With a Spinner (Endogenous)

Mathematical Content:
Probability (PSSM Data Analysis and Probability Standard for Grades 6–8 and 9–12)

Materials Needed:
Spinner; a copy of the figure shown in the activity (one per group of four)

Directions: Before approaching the discovery activity, students will need some prior experience with simulations and probability of simpler problems. Employ a lesson similar to that in Vignette 2.3. Another possibility is an activity such as 2.5, which introduces the spinner and probability.

Read the Game Show Problem to the students, and display the problem for all to read. Be certain they understand it by acting out the opening of three imaginary doors. Students follow the instructions given on the following page.

F O R   S T U D E N T S

Activity 2.1
Game Show: A Discovery Simulation With a Spinner

The Game Show Problem can be modeled by using a spinner on a clear plastic base over the figure shown:

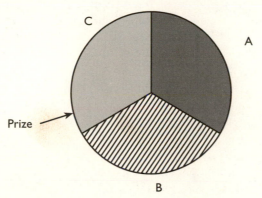

Directions: Turn the spinner. The prize is always behind Door C in this simulation. First you will switch 20 times from where the spinner lands, and then you spin another 20 times without switching. Record whether you win or lose for each of the 40 turns. Remember that the game host always opens a door with the goat.

Example of one trial: The spinner lands on Door C. The game host opens either Door B or Door A. For the first 20 times, you must switch, so you switch to Door A if the host picked Door B and to Door B if the host picked Door A. You lose either way. In case you were doing the last 20 trials where you do not switch, you would stay and win if the spinner landed on Door C. When you are through with the 40 trials, record your results on the overhead transparency.

Before beginning, write down your prediction of the best strategy.

Switching		Not Switching	
Number of Wins	Number of Losses	Number of Wins	Number of Losses

Total the numbers for all the groups in the class.

1. How many times did we switch-and-win compared with the number of times we won but did not switch?
2. Which appears to be the best strategy?
3. Explain.

Source: Shaughnessy, J. M., & Dick, T. (1991). Monty's dilemma: Should you stick or switch? *The Mathematics Teacher, 84,* 252–256. Reprinted with permission.

F O R   T E A C H E R S

Activity 2.2 Game Show: Drawing Tree Diagrams (Exogenous)

Mathematical Content:
Probability (PSSM Data Analysis and Probability
   Standard for Grades 6–8 and 9–12)

Materials Needed:
Tree diagram models

Directions: Model how to make a tree diagram
with a simple example of tossing two coins. Read
the Game Show Problem to the students, and be
certain that they understand the situation. The
first two examples of making tree diagrams for
three coins and for number cubes lead into the
tree diagram for the Game Show Problem. The
page below can be copied to put on an overhead
projector transparency.

F O R   S T U D E N T S

Activity 2.2
Game Show: Drawing Tree Diagrams

Directions: Read the following paragraph about a game show. Then do the Student Activities to learn
how to solve the Game Show Problem.

   Imagine you are a contestant on a game show. You can select one of three doors. Behind one door
is a new car; behind each of the other two doors is a goat. Of course, you wish to open the door to win
the car. You put your hand on one of the doorknobs, but before you open it, the game show host opens
a door revealing a goat. Given this, should you switch to select the other door, or should you open the
one you chose first? Does it matter?

Student Activities:

1. If we toss three coins, what is the probability of getting three heads in a row? Make a tree diagram
   illustrating your answer.

2. If we throw two number cubes, what is the probability of getting a total of 7? Make a tree diagram
   illustrating your answer.

3. Make a tree diagram illustrating your answer for the Game Show Problem.

Source: Shaughnessy, J. M., & Dick, T. (1991). Monty's dilemma: Should you stick or switch? *The Mathematics Teacher, 84,* 252–256.
Reprinted with permission.

FOR TEACHERS

Activity 2.3 Game Show: Calculate Probability (Dialectical/Scaffolding)

Mathematical Content:
Probability (PSSM Data Analysis and Probability Standard for Grades 6–8 and 9–12)

Materials Needed:
Handout and one deck of cards for all class demonstration.

Directions: Assist the student as they progress through the activities preliminary to the Game Show Problem. Since not all students may have had experience in playing cards, show a deck of cards to the class as you read through the definition with them at the beginning of the problem. The playing card lead activity is simpler than the Game Show Problem but should get students to thinking about how the removal of choices changes probability. Be certain that the students understand the Game Show situation before beginning the handout.

FOR STUDENTS

Activity 2.3
Game Show: Calculate Probability (page 1 of 2)

Directions: Work through the problem below in the order presented to prepare to work the Game Show Problem.

A regular deck of cards has 52 cards with 13 spades (black), 13 clubs (black), 13 hearts (red), and 13 diamonds (red). You play a game with a friend in which you win if you draw a spade. First your friend asks you to select a card from the complete deck, which is turned face down.

1. What is the probability of selecting a spade? Explain your calculation.

Next your friend offers to take all the hearts out of the deck and let you draw from the new deck.

2. Should you accept your friend's offer to draw from the reduced deck instead of the original deck? Explain.

F O R   S T U D E N T S

Activity 2.3
Game Show: Calculate Probability (page 2 of 2)

The Game Show Problem: Imagine you are a contestant on a game show. You can select one of three doors. Behind one door is a new car; behind each of the other two doors is a goat. Of course, you wish to open the door to win the car. You put your hand on one of the doorknobs, but before you open it, the game show host opens a door revealing a goat. Given this, should you switch to select the other door, or should you open the one you chose first? Does it matter?

Make a sketch of the three doors and prizes to assist your reasoning that the game host always opens a door with a goat behind it.

1. What is the probability of winning the car if you stick with your original choice? Explain.

2. If you *must* switch, how many doors can you select that will allow you to win? Explain.

3. What is the probability of winning the car if you *must* switch? Explain.

4. What is the best strategy? Explain.

Source: Shaughnessy, J. M., & Dick, T. (1991). Monty's dilemma: Should you stick or switch? *The Mathematics Teacher, 84,* 252–256. Reprinted with permission.

Set 2.3 Discussion Questions

 Questions with an asterisk appear in the Message Board section of the Companion Website at *http://www.prenhall.com/huetinck.* Go to Chapter 2 and click on the Message Board to find and respond to the question.

1. In reading the chapter thus far, reflect on how you are relating the material to your preexisting schemas. Are you using images or silent words to process the material?
2. In what ways are each of the three main theories of learning related to your personal methods of learning?
3. What are some ways you can relate new mathematical information to your students' existing schemas for better retention?
*4. Reread the three activities using the Game Show Problem. Do you feel one method might be more effective for younger students and another for more mathematically sophisticated students? Explain.
5. With which constructivist approach would you be more comfortable—endogenous, exogenous, or scaffold? Does your answer depend on the considered ability level of your students and on the concepts to be learned? Why or why not?

OTHER WAYS TO VIEW LEARNING

In addition to the four main education psychological theories described above, other educational psychologists have devised alternative views of student learning through discussion of multiple intelligences and preferred learning styles. Curriculum has been developed specifically to captivate and motivate students who may access learning in individually different ways.

Multiple Intelligences

A number of researchers in educational psychology have come to defend the concept of multiple intelligences as opposed to identifying one intelligent quotient. Thus teachers must be aware that it is not accurate to think of students as being "smart" or "not smart"; students with high performance in one area may not have high performance in another. The debate continues on the number of distinct intelligences and the definitions of those intelligences. Sternberg (1994) defines three, and Guilford (1967) defines as

many as 180 intelligences. The number is not important, but rather the seminal idea is that we must not categorize students according to ability on a narrow set of criteria. The theory of multiple intelligences which has received the most attention from practitioners is that of Howard Gardner (1983). Therefore, we describe his theory here as an example.

A phrase appearing throughout the *Standards* is "mathematics for all students." We must understand ways to interest students who differ in abilities. A relevant theory, the theory of multiple intelligences developed by Howard Gardner, came from a psychobiological perspective along two lines of research that he has pursued for some years. One is the development of gifted and normal young persons. The other is research of individuals who have had brain damage that affects their cognitive abilities. He defines intelligence as a set of skills that enables an individual to "resolve genuine problems or difficulties that he or she encounters and, when appropriate, to create an effective product . . . thereby laying the groundwork for the acquisition of new knowledge." (1983, p. 60)

Although Howard Gardner states that there cannot be any one irrefutable set of intelligences, nevertheless he has a stringent set of criteria for selecting the seven he has chosen. The seven are each briefly outlined below:

- Linguistic intelligence is involved in four main aspects of linguistic knowledge, which are the ability to use words to convince others, to use words as a mnemonic device, to use words to explain concepts, and to use words to reflect upon language.
- Musical intelligence deals with musical composition, the basic elements of music (pitch, rhythm, and tone), and the power to evoke an emotional response.
- Logical-mathematical development is outlined by Piaget as proceeding from sensorimotor interaction with the real world, to concrete, to formal operations. Gardner agrees with Piaget in large part, but finds it well documented that this domain is "less regular, lock-step and stagelike than Piaget" envisioned (1983, p. 134). Scientists as well as mathematicians deal primarily with a world of "pattern making" that requires an interlocking set of logical capabilities.
- Spatial intelligence is orienting oneself to differing views of an object, achieving a painting with tension, balance, and good composition, and seeing similarities in seemingly disparate forms.
- Bodily-kinesthetic intelligence is demonstrated by persons who have outstanding control over their own body motions, such as athletes and actors, or

persons who can masterfully manipulate objects, such as musicians, surgeons, or craftspersons.

- Intrapersonal intelligence requires access of one's own feelings and the ability to draw upon these feelings to guide one's own behavior. This type of personal intelligence is basically inwardly directed.
- Interpersonal intelligence is outward toward other persons. This is the ability to read and move others.

Although there may be some overlap such that the intelligences are not completely independent of one another, Gardner cites extensive and broad research to support his choice of these seven divisions (Gardner, 1983). In recent interviews Gardner has suggested that he is considering adding an eighth intelligence, Naturalist, described as the ability to recognize patterns in the environment as for example species of animals and plants and to productively utilize the information (Gardner, 1995).

The term *intelligence* is used purposely to denote an innate propensity, but whether an ability develops does depend on culture and experiences. Gardner notes that testing and even our formal schooling primarily lie in the two fields of linguistic and logical-mathematical intelligence. This may also be a cultural issue. He says "logical-mathematical intelligence has been of singular importance in the history of the West, and its importance shows no sign of diminishing" (1983, p. 167). He finds the logical-mathematical skill to be one way of thinking that is neither superior nor inferior to any other in the sets of intelligences. "Each intelligence has its own ordering mechanisms, and the way that an intelligence performs its ordering reflects its own principles and its own preferred media" (1983, p. 169).

A primary goal of the NCTM *Standards* is to help all students develop mathematical power. The theory of multiple intelligences (MI) can provide teachers with a perspective to invent methods of teaching mathematics to appeal to students with differing capabilities. If you wish to use this theory as an element in designing lessons, we suggest reading further on the subject. Gardner (1995) discusses myths concerning his theory and some elements of current practice that purport to embody his theory but do not. The 1994 Yearbook of the Association for Supervisors and Curriculum Development, *Multiple Intelligences in the Classroom*, includes many suggestions for teachers to introduce MI theory in curriculum, teaching strategies, classroom environment, and assessment (Armstrong, 1994). Teachers should not expect to find a set number of alternative approaches reflecting different intelligences, but should strive for multiple representations when they assist a range of students to make

sense of the mathematical concept under study. The inclusion of mathematical manipulatives, communication about mathematics, use of group work, and connections to other disciplines are a few of the different avenues teachers can employ to help students tap into their unique strengths to learn mathematics.

Learning Styles

An individual's learning style is the preferred way to use one's abilities. Much of the initial work in the field was done by psychologists developing effective team building for business management. Many theories of styles have been published (Gregorc, 1985; Kiersey & Bates, 1984; Rideout & Richardson, 1989). The Myers-Briggs Type Indicator is a popular personality inventory that has been simplified and adapted for use in education.

The foundational belief in attention to learning styles is that if teachers understand their preferred learning styles and those of their students, they will be able to adjust their curriculum and teaching methods to accommodate students with different learning styles. "By keying teaching and assessment techniques to the diverse ways people think and learn, teachers will be surprised at how much smarter their students get" (Sternberg, 1994, pp. 36–40).

Kiersey simplifies the 16 Myers-Briggs Type Indicator (MBTI) types into four groups. The MBTI uses two categories, labeled N for intuitive and S for sensing, based on the preferred mode of processing information—either by senses (S), which includes about 76% of the population, or by intuition (N), which includes about 24% of the population. Then each of these types is paired with either perception (P) or judging (J), which are basic differences in ways persons approach problem solving. Judging types like to have issues clarified, desire an agenda, and work toward closure. In contrast, perceiving types like openness, flexibility, and as much information as possible. They resist being tied to a schedule. It is particularly interesting that the Myers-Briggs styles in these four categories for the general student population differ greatly from the Myers-Briggs styles for the population of K–12 teachers. The conforming person SJ (sensing-judgmental) comprises 38% of the general population, in contrast to 56% of the teaching population. It does appear that the traditional school setting favors the learning style of this type of individual. The greatest mismatch in the traditional school setting is with the SP person, who learns through sensory activity and may be criticized by the judging person as aimless and indecisive due to his preference for the perceiving mode of problem solving. SP types make up 38% of the general population and only 2% of the teaching population (Rockinger, 1980).

These differences in learning styles are of particular interest in mathematics because of the wide variations in approach to problem-solving activities by different personality types. Campbell and Davis suggest we can improve learning by considering psychological type in designing activities involving critical thinking skills. They view the dichotomy of judging and perceiving as central to differences in students' orientation to learning. Problems designed to elicit a variety of approaches allow students to access the learning task using their preferred style (1988).

As part of a classroom research project, a group of four exemplary secondary-level teachers administered a personality profile test similar to the Myers-Briggs, the Kiersey Temperament Sorter (Kiersey & Bates, 1984). They focused on the judging versus the perceiving learning styles in problem solving. Approximately half of the population is one style and half the other, according to the research based on the Kiersey Temperament Sorter. The teacher researchers found a 50% split for the two types in the low-level classes such as pre-algebra, but the percentage of judging types increased as the level of mathematics increased. For example, students in second-year algebra were 75% judging, and 80% of the pre-calculus class were judging types. The obvious question is whether methods of teaching mathematics are inhibiting the progress of students who are perceiving types (Mussack, 1996). It would be of considerable interest to administer the Kiersey Temperament Sorter to accomplished research mathematicians. Would they be more likely to be high in perceiving or in judging characteristics? It would appear that the openness and flexible problem-solving styles of a perceiving individual might be helpful to a researcher on the edge of accepted theory who is moving into new territories. Yet, according to this study, this personality type is less likely to persist in taking higher mathematics. In view of our effort to teach mathematics for all students, these thoughts are especially intriguing.

Set 2.4   Discussion Questions

1. How does Gardner's definition of intelligence differ from others you have studied or formed through experience?
2. How are the seven intelligences related? How do they differ?
3. In what ways can you ensure that students with different learning styles can be successful in your classroom?

MOTIVATION

We have all watched a young child walk a low wall, climb a tree, or learn to ride a bike and then heard him proclaim proudly, "I did it." It is this joy of accomplishment that we would like to capture in the intellectual domain of doing mathematics. We must not underestimate the desire of young people to grow in skill, understanding, and control over their lives. As mathematics teachers, we hope to instill an internal motivation in our students to become mathematically powerful.

To understand motivation, it is necessary to examine the achievement goals that move the student to work well independently or contribute in a group activity, to persist on challenging problems, to begin work when expected, to work until the end of the period, to exhibit interest in the task at hand, and to try to achieve mathematical understanding even when an immediate award is not apparent. There are two approaches that relate to positive task orientation. These are intrinsic and extrinsic goals. With an intrinsic goal the student is striving to develop new skills, increase understanding, and improve achievement. With an extrinsic goal the student is trying to perform well with respect to other students, and in order to impress others, may even try to do better with less effort. Thus, the extrinsically motivated student views learning as a way to outperform classmates for ego gratification. Research indicates that intrinsic learning is associated with taking risks, persisting on a task, and selecting challenging tasks. Further, studies show that mastery goals motivate students to become actively involved in their learning. In contrast, extrinsic goals are associated with reluctance to lose face and therefore may elicit failure avoidance demonstrated by reluctance to even begin a task (Muthukrishna & Borkowski, 1996).

Students' goals are related to their beliefs about the reasons for success. Students with intrinsic goals attribute academic success to effort and persistence. These task-oriented students tend to believe that excellence is a result of their attempts to understand and integrate their knowledge. On the other hand, students with extrinsic goals tend to believe that innate ability and, perhaps, even second-guessing the teacher lead to success. The student with intrinsic goals is inwardly motivated, whereas the student with extrinsic goals is motivated by external conditions. In constructivist classrooms, students learn to "discover ways to solve problems if they make the effort to think about them and work hard to understand them. These classroom practices foster task orientation and enhance beliefs that success in mathematics depends on attempts to make sense out of the subject matter" (Muthukrishna & Borkowski, 1996, p. 69).

Three main elements central in developing a classroom environment to motivate students are learning tasks, teacher beliefs, and students beliefs—all of which frequently are intertwined. These elements are discussed in reference to the new goals for students outlined in the *Standards* (NCTM, 1989, pp. 5–6).

Developing Confidence

One goal for students is "that they become confident in their ability to do mathematics" (NCTM, 1989, p. 5). Students are more likely to be intrinsically motivated if they believe they can successfully achieve the assigned task. Although many persons might enjoy running, swimming, or rowing, few of us endeavor to enter a triathlon because we know that our talents are not equal to the task. All too often, students are given a remedial task that was difficult for them in the past, so they quickly recognize the situation and act out their frustration by conducting avoidance behaviors rather than face defeat again. If your students need to learn material they did not master at an appropriate earlier age try to embody the mathematics concept in a method that is new to them. This might include introducing a game or contest situation. Encouragement that the task will not be difficult accelerates the learning situation because the teacher indicates belief in their success.

This assumes that the task is possible for the majority of the class. Allow students to work individually or in groups so you have time to assist those who need you in a one-on-one situation. Experience with different students and different courses will enable you to judge accurately the ability levels of your students, which, in turn, will give you clues of how to best structure a lesson that leads to increasing student confidence and achievement.

Intrinsic Motivation

When students are actively involved in their learning, they become intrinsically motivated. The classroom must be a place in which interesting problems are regularly explored using important mathematical ideas, by giving students the opportunity "to explore, conjecture, and reason logically . . . to use a variety of mathematical methods effectively to solve nonroutine problems" (NCTM, 1989, p. 5). Teaching mathematics in this way reflects three other goals of the *Standards*, that students "become mathematical problem solvers" who "learn to communicate

mathematically" and "learn to reason mathematically" (1989, p. 5). This requires teaching mathematics for understanding instead of providing clear instructions to follow an algorithm. Skemp (1971) wrote, "How effective intrinsic motivation is for learning mathematics can be something which many teachers do not yet appreciate. Until this intrinsic motivation is better comprehended and put to work, mathematics will remain for many a subject to be endured, not enjoyed, and dropped as soon as the necessary exam results have been achieved" (p. 135). It is this view of mathematics leading to extrinsic goals that the constructivist classroom seeks to overcome.

Students learn to communicate mathematics in a variety of settings and through varied means; including cooperative groups, class presentations, portfolios, and written, full-sentence descriptions of problem-solving methods. Chapters on assessment of student progress must include these issues because students realize that we test what we value. To assess nonroutine problems may necessitate variance from the common 90%+ for an A, 80%+ for B, etc., since original problems are much more difficult to solve than skill-oriented problems. Assessment sections found later in this text consider all these issues in detail. Learning to communicate mathematically also includes correctly using the symbols, operations, and terms of mathematics. "This is best accomplished in problem situations in which the use of the language of mathematics becomes natural" (NCTM. 1989, p. 5).

Research indicates that a sense of control of one's life promotes intrinsic motivation. In addition to being actively involved in learning, students should be given problems that can be solved by different methods. They can then choose the method that makes the most sense to them. For example, geometry teachers find that some students prefer to use the familiar two-column proof, while others prefer to use paragraph proofs or flow proofs. Open-ended problems may have several right answers, depending upon assumptions made by the students, in which case, the thoughtfulness of the answer is judged in addition to its numerical value. In the constructivist classroom, the student assumes greater responsibility for learning than in the traditional classroom, since the teacher is not the sole source of knowledge and understanding. The purpose is not to achieve the answer desired by the teacher, but to integrate information into one's own expanding mathematical understanding.

The fifth NCTM goal for students to "learn to reason mathematically" (NCTM, 1989, p. 5) includes making conjectures, testing them, discussing them mathematically, and building new conjectures on previous structures. Reasoning is of greater importance than finding a right answer. Although skill building is important, students can become so involved in the operations that they miss the overarching themes and connections. Many of our tools in mathematics such as calculators and computers can assist students in appreciating the big picture because the important concepts do not so easily get lost in numerical details. When students begin to build connections, they are developing the ability to reason mathematically.

As discussed in the previous paragraphs, students' beliefs about their ability to do mathematics is important to motivation, but of equal if not greater importance to reform is the necessity of a match between the students' beliefs about what it means to do mathematics and the classroom culture. The student who is accustomed to asking the teacher for the right answer may get frustrated when the constructivist teacher answers the question with a question formulated to help the student think through the problem. The student who believes that using manipulatives is play will not make the effort to connect the hands-on experience to the mathematical abstraction, a key step in using the activity to advance mathematical thinking. The *Standards* recommend a guiding role for the teacher instead of giving explicit instructions about how to solve problems. If students have come to expect mathematics to be quickly working a number of similar problems based on a set of rules, at first they may not value activities designed to assist them in making discoveries in activities that take longer. As one student in a school initiating reform curriculum complained to me, the observer, "The problem with XXX program is that you have to stop and really think." In our experience after what may be an initial frustration with a new methodology, students soon come to use the freedom to explore and find excitement in mathematics as a problem-solving activity with constructivist learning.

Research Conclusions

Kloosterman (1996) reports on a study in which he taught two classes of youngsters to solve nonroutine problems. To encourage the students to think for themselves, he refused to tell them whether their answers were correct. Soon some students refused to work, presumably because he was not doing what a teacher should do. However, after a while the students adapted and began to work very diligently to double-check their problems to ensure correctness. He lists the following beliefs about learning mathematics that are necessary to consider and debate:

- "Mathematics is computation." For students to be willing to persist on nonroutine problems, they must not believe that the hallmark of a good mathematician is to perform computations quickly, but rather to have an appreciation of the benefit of the ability to attack and solve problems new to their experience, even when it takes time to work one problem.
- "Mathematics requires proof." For students to become comfortable with making conjectures, they must go beyond the concept of mathematics as simply structured, deductive proof and instead perceive it as requiring mathematical justification.
- "Mathematics is useful." For students to recognize the application of mathematical procedures in solving real-world problems, they must perceive numerical operations as tools, not as goals in themselves.
- "Mathematics topics are integrated." For students to try a variety of approaches to problem solving, they must envision an integration of mathematical concepts and processes instead of a series of unrelated topics, each with its own solution method.
- "Mathematics consists of clearly defined problems." For students to learn to estimate and make reasonable assumptions, they cannot expect all mathematical problems to include only exactly what is needed in the problem (pp. 135–137).

A group of exemplary high-school teachers conducted action research by alternatively teaching units with either direct instruction or guided discovery methodology to examine students' preferences and beliefs about learning mathematics. The teachers had been trained in constructivist techniques in an extensive 3-year professional development program. Three of the teachers primarily taught the innovative curriculum, Interactive Mathematics Project (IMP). A fourth teacher who had previously taught this curriculum began a new position in a very traditional school with traditional mathematics curriculum. The teachers collaborated to rewrite the IMP materials into directed instruction format and the traditional curriculum into discovery lessons. They varied the order of presentation methods of several units of coursework and surveyed the students to find their preferences in modes of instruction. Half of the students had a strong preference for guided discovery, one fourth had no preference, and one fourth preferred direct instruction. The statistically significant results showed that students were more likely to feel positive about their mathematics class and more likely to rate themselves highly on their mathematics ability when taught by guided discovery. These results held when either gender, grade level, course grade, or previous curriculum experience were considered. A majority of students enjoyed some teaching and learning with each pedagogy, i.e., they liked variety. The students had remarkably mature thoughts on the research. One said, "The teachers should decide which method to use based on the concepts in the curriculum" (Callis, 1997, p. 57).

Holmes gives three suggestions to help students internalize mathematical learning goals. First, use cooperative learning arrangements. "Group problem solving helps learners develop problem-solving skills" (1990, p. 104). Students can plan and execute data analysis projects, prepare bulletin boards, and present concepts collectively. Second, emphasize the value of mathematics. Students experience mathematics as a reasonable way to approach the solution of practical problems and thereby develop a favorable view of the discipline. Third, ask open questions. Require students to defend and reflect upon their answers. Students should be encouraged to challenge each other's assumptions.

During our teaching experiences in constructivist classrooms in quite different educational settings, we found the secondary-level students very interested in knowing why we chose to teach in this mode. From time to time we would briefly explain basic beliefs of the characteristics of the subject and beliefs about effective learning that led to curricular decisions. The students were very receptive of these ideas. Some students, especially the high achievers, were nervous at first. It seemed they felt it a little unfair that the "learning game" had changed. They knew how to "win" in the competitive, teacher-dominated classroom and were not sure they would still succeed with the constructivist culture. This uncertainty always passed within a few weeks, however. A student may half jokingly say, "Please just give me the answer!" when you answer his question with a question. Try responding by smiling and saying "I wouldn't insult your intelligence that way, but I will give you a clue if you choose."

Students are motivated to model behavior that leads to outcomes they value. Mathematics students ask, "When are we going to use this?" A poster of this name, speakers from the community, or videos such as "Futures" by Jamie Escalente—real-life hero of the film *Stand and Deliver*, help motivate students by presenting role models attesting to the importance of problem solving and skills in the world of work. However, mathematics is not only a means to an occupation but a worthy human-made universe to explore for its own sake. Sometimes I (LH) would answer, "It doesn't matter. We learn it because it is so beautiful to see how everything fits together." I got a few strange looks in response, but the students did think about what I said.

Incorporating contexts from students' personal experiences adds interest to the course of study. In the affective domain, teachers must model respect for students to lay the foundation for a community of learning in which contributions of all class members are honored. Knowing that a teacher is interested in them as human beings can motivate students to continue to persist even when outside pressures might distract them. Enthusiastic teachers who display a love and knowledge of mathematics, have expectations of student success, and utilize wide-ranging problem-solving techniques are those who motivate students to achieve academic excellence.

Activity 2.4 is a delightful way to introduce students to the concept of being responsible for their learning. In the exercise, both the instructor giving directions and the assembler of the puzzle must do their part to achieve the desired goal. In exactly the same manner, the teacher and students must be motivated to do their part in the learning process.

Set 2.5   Discussion Questions

 Questions with an asterisk appear in the Message Board section of the Companion Website at ***http://www.prenhall.com/huetinck.*** Go to Chapter 2 and click on the Message Board to find and respond to the question.

1. To what extent does motivation come through the curriculum, activities, etc.?
2. Why do you think the students in the study cited above preferred the guided discovery approach over the lecture method?
3. How can we strive to make mathematics intrinsically motivating for our students?
*4. Mathematics is applicable to solving real-world problems, is an interesting human-made universe, and has boundaries expanding by research. How can you motivate students to appreciate these components of mathematics?

BASIC MANAGEMENT SKILLS

Your beliefs in the efficacy of certain learning and motivation theories in given situations are put into effect through the ways you manage your classroom. Certainly, arranging desks in parallel rows and columns elicits the expectation of teacher-directed lecture. A constructivist classroom is set up

FOR TEACHERS

Activity 2.4 A Blindfold and a Puzzle

Mathematical Content:
Communication (PSSM Communication Standard for Grades 6–8 and 9–12)

Materials Needed:
A scarf for a blindfold and a wooden or cardboard puzzle of 6–9 pieces for ages 3–5 per group

Introduction: We heard about the following exercise from visiting with a teacher at lunch at a conference. She always does this exercise with her students the first day of class to initiate a discussion of the elements of successful instruction. After the exercise with your students, reflect on the experience asking yourself questions such as, In what ways is this exercise similar to assisting a student in developing a schema? In what ways it is easier than assisting a student to develop a mathematical schema? What other elements of instruction and learning does this activity illustrate?

Directions: Divide the students into groups of three. Explain the rules as follows:

Each member of the group has a different role: instructor, assembler, and observer. A blindfolded person assembles the puzzle according to the directions of the instructor. The instructor may give only verbal instructions and may not touch a puzzle piece or touch the person assembling the puzzle. The third person is the observer, who makes sure the other two group members follow the rules and notes instructions that assist or hinder the process of putting the puzzle together. Let the students decide how to distribute their roles.

When the students have decided upon their roles and the blindfolds are securely in place, pass out one puzzle to each group. The observer may assist only if a piece is very close to fitting but won't quite go in.

Try the exercise again with the participants exchanging roles.

Questions to Ask:
1. How does this exercise demonstrate the complementary roles of teacher and learner?
2. As the blindfolded person, did you find the instructions easy to follow? Could the instructions such as "up," "down," "turn right," and "turn left" have been clarified?
3. As the instructor, how was it sometimes difficult to verbalize helpful instructions?
4. Does it assist the process for the instructor to begin with the overview of a description of the completed picture?

differently and anticipates more student interaction. Before the students arrive, you must make a number of decisions concerning room arrangement, ways of establishing expectations of student behavior, and general class organization. These decisions reflect your attitudes toward best practices, as well as consideration of the practical measures necessary in managing a successful learning environment.

Room Arrangement

Review the room arrangement and be certain the environment encourages active student involvement. An inviting space exhibiting student work projects the information that interesting and important activities take place here. A flexible but ordered classroom provides structure but invites all to participate as a community of learners.

Look over your classroom and make a mental map of the activities the students will do. Two primary considerations in planning room arrangement are (1) ways to focus the students' attention and (2) ways to have the maximum number of students' desks readily accessible for your assistance. Following are a number of elements for a well-functioning classroom:

Overhead Projector The overhead projector provides a natural focus for teaching. You can put a problem of the week, a warm-up problem, answers to homework, or instructions for an investigation on the screen to initiate a smooth beginning of class. Students can start working immediately while you record attendance, check homework, check absence slips, or simply greet students. This practice also allows you to view the students face-to-face while providing written information. Further, it promotes classroom control because you can see all the students. Also, secondary-level students readily show it when they are confused, and it is important to read their body language.

In some rooms, the lighting may be too bright in front of the projector screen for all to see it clearly. You can begin the year by removing the bulbs from the offensive lights, accompanied by a taped note to the custodians requesting them not to replace the bulbs. Other rooms may have separate controls for different areas of lighting. Window curtains, blinds, and open doors all contribute to changes in light level. Try out the room arrangement by sitting in different seats to be certain that every student can see all areas of the screen. If not all areas are visible from every seat, either move the screen or mask out the partial view areas on the overhead projector so you will remember not to write there.

Relatively inexpensive light-emitting diode (LED) panels allowing projection of the calculator screen greatly enhance teaching with calculators. Many teachers find it useful to have two overhead projectors. One is for the calculator screen, and the other is for written instructions either on the calculator keys to be used or on the mathematics being investigated. Different students can operate one projector while the teacher writes on the other, or students can present in groups by assuming different responsibilities.

Prepared transparency slides can allow efficient use of class time under certain conditions. Prepared slides reduce the time necessary to draw figures. Students can individually write on slides their different approaches to solving a problem for sharing with the class. Cooperative groups can effectively share their information from investigations or projects on transparency slides. We do not recommend, however, that teachers write out solutions to all problems on slides before class and uncover them periodically, as some lecturers do. Rather, teachers should demonstrate their procedures as they think, so students can experience expert reasoning processes in real time.

Desks Room arrangements to consider should allow you easy access to most of the students. Do not cut yourself off by staying behind a podium or front desk. Different student desk arrangements should be used for different types of activities. Consider some of the following seating configurations:

- U-shaped or horseshoe-shaped arrangements (see Figure 2.2) for whole-class instruction allow the overhead projector or calculator/computer display to be viewed by all students. You can

Figure 2.2
U-Shaped Arrangement

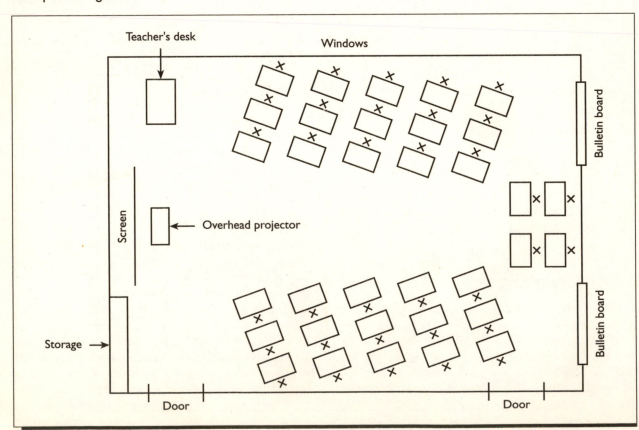

move easily among the students to assist while the significant material is displayed at the front.

- A circle promotes discussion on mathematical topics and problem solving. This seminar arrangement somewhat neutralizes your authority. It encourages students to talk directly to each other instead of requiring the teacher to be the hub of conversation. This is an excellent arrangement for either underachieving or accelerated students who are working in medium-sized groups for remediation or enrichment.
- Three or four desks together allow students to work in the space where the desks join and to see each other. When students work in groups, it may be helpful to have tags for the different group numbers hanging from the ceiling to remind students how to group their desks. We have found that if a beginning teacher always uses groups of students facing each other as in a foursome, the students may not attend to the teacher's instructions when necessary. Therefore, have the students turn their desks toward each other for group activities only.
- A chevron arrangement is effective for game competitions used to add interest to the topic under study. It also works well for mathematical instruction when a large number of the students are excused for an activity or for reviewing material.
- Desks in straight rows are appropriate for a guest speaker, a video (on a large screen), or standardized testing. Rows can quickly move together in twos so students can think-pair-share ideas.
- Tables are becoming more prevalent in mathematics classrooms. The flat tops are particularly desirable if manipulatives are used often. I (SM) used a table arrangement that essentially had no single front of the room, so different presentation techniques using the overhead projector, student work on the chalkboard, and information on the white board could be used as students turned their orientation. (See Figure 2.3.) On days in which individual tests were given, tables were moved apart so that all students faced the same direction.

Avoiding Disruptions   Think of the optimum placement for tardy sign-in, wastebasket, and pencil sharpener. To avoid interrupting class for a tardy student, keep a sheet on a clipboard placed on a

Figure 2.3
Tables Arrangement

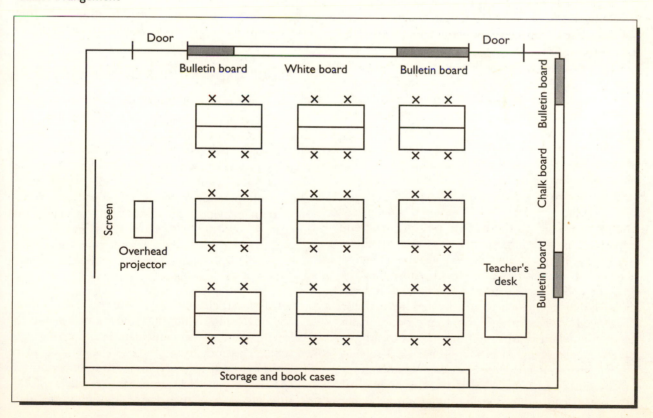

high stool near the door to the room. The sheet has columns for name, date, and period. Later, when the class is working on a problem, you can attend to the tardy. (A student might occasionally sign in as Superman, but it will be rare, and you will be able to figure out which student was tardy.)

If you allow students to use the pencil sharpener or wastebasket without permission during class, as most high-school teachers do, you do not want the associated activity to interfere with the learning situation. Put these items at the back of the room.

Teacher's Items   Establish your space to keep personal items or materials with limited student access, such as the roll book. This can be a desk at the back, bookcases in a corner, or a set of file cabinets. Use organizers to facilitate collection and safekeeping of student assignments. Spend the minimum amount of class time in this area so you are not cut off from your students.

Classroom Supplies   Decide how and where materials should be kept and how they should be handled. Use organizers or shelf labels for maintaining order and to ease distribution of equipment. You do not want to waste class time searching for rulers or a certain manipulative. Inexpensive plastic containers or see-through zipper-locking plastic bags are useful in this regard. Some teachers set containers of materials out at each desk or set of desks for student use. Others save a central location to which one person from each group can come to pick up materials as needed.

Think of other teaching devices planned to facilitate classroom organization. If your students take and analyze data over a period of time, chart paper may be useful. Some teachers use a specially designed holder with calculator-size pockets to hang on the wall for easy student access to calculators. Students are each given a number and can pick up their assigned calculator at the beginning of the period and return it at the end of the period.

Energy Savers   Consider ways to preserve your energy. Dealing with large numbers of young people is exciting but can also be exhausting. Effective teachers seldom sit down in class because they realize the need to move among the students and see the majority of the class at all times to monitor progress. However, a high stool to use occasionally as a perch when instructing from the overhead can be an energy saver. Also, it took me (LH) several years to realize that the presence of a box of tissues on my desk was directly related to the number of my colds because the sneezing students unwittingly spread germs over my work space. Save your energy by allowing students to assist in monitoring details such as collecting homework, redistributing papers (not tests), and so on. Many teachers find they are allergic to chalk dust. If you are, use chart paper, ask for a white board, and be sure to get projectors as needed. Is a microphone available if you begin to get a scratchy throat?

Decor   After you have considered the functioning of the room, make it attractive. Leave room for displays of student work. Posters add color. If you should get an unattractive room, the more posters the better. It takes little artistic ability to put colorful borders inside bulletin boards with cut-out letters indicating the content on each board, such as announcements, assignments, school rules, student expectations, or cartoons.

Room Sharing   If your assignment requires moving from one room to the next, your need for organization will be even greater. Insist on some storage space in each room and an overhead projector in each room. Ask for a cart to move and store the materials that must travel and a "home base" in which to keep personal items. Take the time to interface with the other teachers sharing the same rooms so misunderstandings about room usage do not develop. Be assured that administrators and department chairpersons realize the difficulty of sharing rooms, and seek their assistance when needed.

Teacher Expectations of Students

Envision just how you expect the students to operate within your classroom. You will need to ask questions of your department chairperson to know what resources you do or do not have available. The courses you teach, the levels of students in those courses, and your curriculum will affect your choices of operating methods. The specifics of classroom management during classroom instruction are intricately involved with curriculum and are discussed in detail in another chapter. As an introduction to basic management skills, however, consider your answers to the following questions:

- What class behavior will you expect, and when and how will you introduce the topic? Will you allow the students to participate in discussing and setting classroom expectations? The simplest plan is to begin with school rules and add expectations specific to your classroom. Most teachers inform students of these rules in writing on the first day of class or simply refer them to the school expectations that often are posted in each classroom. In a community building classroom you may wish to give students time to consider, develop, and write up expected classroom behavior. We used the same set of expectations in all our classes but informed students differently, depending on the course and the level of the students. Because non-college-intended students may be more forgetful of the rules, we requested that each student write them out and keep a handwritten copy in his notebook. Thus, there can be no doubt that each student knows the rules. College-intended students may need a brief rule review. In addition to school rules, these two expectations may be sufficient: (1) everyone is treated with respect in this room, and (2) everyone participates in working on mathematics in this room. Some schools, especially middle schools, require teachers to send home for parent or guardian signature a form with the course description as well as a page listing rules. This does require the necessary bookkeeping to be certain all forms are returned. Do not request that the rule page be returned with parent signature, however, unless you will do whatever is necessary to enforce the rules. Classroom expectations may be posted on a bulletin board for easy reference.

- How will you handle students who come to class without materials, i.e., no paper, pencil, or text? Of course, students should be prepared, but if they are not it is far better to provide materials than to allow them to miss the learning experience. For writing material, students can use the backs of old handouts or even papers from the wastebasket if they cannot borrow from a friend. The teacher can provide "loaner" pencils for collateral (keys, belt, or coin—nothing of great value). Let students share texts unless one student begins to abuse the privilege, in which case additional action must be taken. Loaner paper rulers and protractors can be made by photocopying clear plastic rulers and protractors.

- Will you assign homework over the weekend? over a holiday? or the night after a test? Be familiar with your school's policies suggesting amounts of homework at different grade levels for different types of classes. Will you allow time to start the homework in class? There is wide divergence of opinion among experienced teachers on this point. Some teachers believe students should always begin the homework in class to become confident to finish it at home. Other teachers require students to have classwork relating to the homework, but will not give the homework assignment until the end of the period to encourage students to work completely through the period.

- Will you provide assignments on paper, the overhead projector, or on the board? What will be the frequency of distribution of assignments such as daily, weekly, or by the unit? Some schools limit the amount of photocopying available, and even if there is no limit, you do not want to be stuck by the reprographic machine. On the other hand, providing written assignments saves class time spent in copying them down. Further, dealing with absences may be eased because a student has the written assignment for reference even if he did not attend class. Some teachers have students take turns maintaining class assignments and notes in a notebook for reference by students who have been absent. Generally, it is best practice to give assignments daily or in short lists to non-college-intended students because a lengthy assignment page may be daunting to them. Upper-level students bound for college may wish to have the assignment for a whole unit so they can work ahead if they have complex schedules. However, they should realize that assignments are likely to change because the teacher will adjust according to the students' understanding of the concepts as they are taught.

- How will you manage recordkeeping? A seating chart for each class slipped inside a clear plastic sheet protector is a quick way to record attendance each period. Mark on the plastic and enter the absences in the roll book at the end of the day. The marks can include not only attendance but also participation. Wipe the sheets clean for use the next day. Does your school allow computer grade sheets to be the official record? Most do, but some schools still require grades to be hand-entered in a standard gradebook as the official record. Find out your schools' standard marking scheme for excused absences, unexcused absences, tardies, and cuts. Will you have grades and attendance in the same book? Is there a standard computer program you can use for this purpose? Assessment is such a complex subject, it is addressed in detail in two later chapters.

- Will you have a teaching assistant, school aide, school service student, or access to photocopying services? Will you have a personal computer? If any of these assists are available, think of the ways you would like these resources to be utilized to facilitate your teaching situation.

Daily Organization

Figure 2.4 shows the many elements of a daily lesson plan. The most important segments are those in the classroom titled INTO, THROUGH, and BEYOND. The INTO (sometimes called a SET) is designed to signal a change from the beginning exercises to the new material that will be discussed this day or for the main activity of the lesson. This short interlude also gets the students ready—set to explore further—and serves to elicit student participation in the lesson to come. The THROUGH encompasses the main ideas for the class which are either an extension of previous work or a beginning of completely new concepts. The BEYOND provides the student with the opportunity to more fully comprehend the main lesson through additional activi-

ties that strengthen learning. Note that the teacher also has additional obligations before and after teaching the mathematics during the class period.

The many options with each segment of the day's class allow myriad variations within this framework. Middle-school students will need to change activities more frequently than older students due to their shorter attention spans. Thus, the *or* suggestions may become *and* suggestions. A number of high schools are adopting block scheduling in which students meet for class for up to 2-hour periods, but fewer than five times a week. This schedule organization will necessitate greater variety in the daily plan, with discussion, individual seat work, and group work all occurring within one class period.

Before we get to the specifics of lesson planning in Chapter 7, you will be introduced to a variety of

Figure 2.4
Daily Organization

Before Class at Home
>   Semester plan, weekly plans, daily plans, write assessments

Before Class at School
>   Create pleasant and informative room environment.
>   Daily agenda/unit assignments on bulletin board or transparency
>   As needed: Stand at door and greet students and check for supplies

During Class
>   Beginning: Warm-up
>   OR   Stamp, collect homework and/or discuss homework
>   OR   Problem of the week
>   OR   Return papers
>   (Be sure students are occupied with meaningful work while you attend to bookkeeping tasks such as recording attendance.)
>   Main lesson:

Main Elements of Lesson
>   Into
>   Through   new material (discovery, model, or scaffold)
>   OR   problem solving/applications
>   OR   assessment
>   OR   enrichment/extension
>   OR   long-range problem
>   OR   project
>   OR   investigation/experiment (may take a series of days)
>   (Methods include using activity, manipulative, calculator, computer, found materials, and writing exercises using a variety of pedagogies such as questioning techniques, cooperative groups, chalk talk, student presentations, think-pair-share, etc.)
>   Beyond   finish classwork
>   OR   begin homework
>   OR   write in journal
>   straighten the room
>   Grades 6–8: Dismiss by groups or by class when ready

After Class
>   Assess student work—homework, quizzes, exams, notebooks, journal entries, problem of the week, etc.
>   Recordkeeping—attendance, grades, progress reports, assignments for makeup

manipulative and computer tools in Chapter 3 and innovative curriculum and various types of effective classroom groupings in Chapter 4, along with different ways to organize the class, including whole class instruction, small group instruction, think-pair-share, chalk talk, and students as presenters and as tutors. Chapter 5 presents basic assessment practices. These chapters explore the rich possibilities available for building a mathematically powerful learning environment as you begin to make choices matching teaching methodology to mathematical concepts and as you build a repertoire of variations in instruction.

Set 2.6   *Discussion Questions*

Questions with an asterisk appear in the Message Board section of the Companion Website at **http://www.prenhall.com/huetinck.** Go to Chapter 2 and click on the Message Board to find and respond to the question.

1. What management techniques could you employ to best allow for different learning styles when you have 30 or more students a period for five or six periods a day?
*2. Discuss your answers to the questions posed in the section titled "Teacher Expectations of Students."

Summary

Chapter 2 provides an overview of educational psychology and basic management skills. These two aspects of teaching are interlinked because to teach effectively, you must know your students and use the methodology appropriate to their learning modes and your teaching style. Experienced teachers use different teaching styles depending upon student needs.

Basic management skills include arranging the learning environment, being clear about your expectations of students, using thoughtful curriculum organization, and utilizing your school's resources. All of these skills develop from an understanding of yourself, your school's culture, and your students. Management is connected to everything you do in the classroom, including materials used, selection of teaching tools, methods of assessment, and daily communication in the classroom. Thus, management is involved in all of the following chapters of this text.

Throughout the rest of your teaching career, these topics will evolve as you gain experience with different students, expand your use of teaching tools, and diversify your teaching practices.

ASSIGNMENTS

1. The easiest element of the daily lesson plan for teachers-in-training to verbally practice is the INTO segment. The INTO has two purposes: (a) to provide an attention-getting break from the opening activities such as review of homework and the main new material and (b) to lead into the main presentation of the day's lesson. It can be a cartoon, a brief reference to the history of mathematics, or an application of interest to the students. Plan for no more than 2 to 4 minutes, and actively involve the students. Of course, the INTO cannot assume understanding of the concepts to be presented in the lesson that is to follow, but it is related to those concepts. Conduct an INTO for a group of secondary level mathematics students or for your colleagues taking the role of secondary level students.

2. Describe the steps of a lesson for the following problem: What is the probability of a couple having one girl if they have two children? Write three approaches to the problem including a discovery simulation, a modeling lesson, and a

scaffolding lesson. These lessons can use mathematical methods similar to the examples for the Game Show Problem.

3. Students frequently explore the sum on two number cubes, numbered 1 through 6 on each side. Describe the steps of a lesson exploring probability based on the difference of the numbers on two number cubes.

4. Geometric probability is an area of probability that is not often illustrated for secondary-level students. Make up a dart board game and associated rules that are fair for the contestant and another game that is not. Use any interesting teaching approach with secondary level students and reflect on the lesson. Was it appropriate for the grade level and knowledge background for the students? How might you improve the game to use it again? (See the geometric probability problem in the additional activities for possible ideas, or *Geometric Probability*, a volume in the NCTM Series, *New Topics for Secondary School Mathematics*.)

INSTRUCTIONAL RESOURCES

Department of Mathematics and Computer Science, North Carolina School of Science and Mathematics. (1988). *Geometric probability* (*New topics for secondary school mathematics series*). Reston, VA: National Council of Teachers of Mathematics.

This volume contains a number of interesting problems, including the triangle problem, fairground problem, random sum problem, and geometric probability applications to geology.

Gnandesikan, M., Scheaffer, R. L., & Swift, J. (1987). *The art and techniques of simulation*. Palo Alto, CA: Dale Seymour Publications.

Thirty applications are organized into four units that cover the basic concepts of statistics and probability using data and active experiments. The student's edition and separate teacher's edition are third in a series published jointly by the American Statistical Association and NCTM with support from the National Science Foundation.

Lawrence, A. (1999). From the Giver of the twenty-one balloons: Explorations with probability. *Mathematics Teaching in the Middle School, 4,* 504–509.

The authors develop probability lessons from two volumes of children's literature. The informative article discusses all aspects of a lesson including initial warm-up, activity sheets, experiments, and sample student responses.

Mikusa, M. G., & Lewellen, H. (1999). Now here is that authority on mathematics reform, Dr. Constructivist! *Mathematics Teacher, 92,* 158–163.

The authors invented Dr. Constructivist, who answers teachers' concern about using constructivist approaches in the classroom with the light touch reminiscent of Dear Abby columns. They are a delight to read and excellent to discuss with your colleagues.

Newman, C. M., Obremski, T. E., & Scheaffer, R. L. (1987). *Exploring probability* (*Quantitative literacy series*). Palo Alto, CA: Dale Seymour Publications.

Forty-three activities are designed to provide a working knowledge of elementary probability using counting skill and knowledge of fractions. The student's edition and separate teacher's edition are second in a series published jointly by the American Statistical Association and NCTM with support from the National Science Foundation.

Shaughnessy, J. M., & Dick, T. (1991). Monty's dilemma: Should you stick or switch? *Mathematics Teacher, 91,* 252–256.

The instructional approaches of simulation and tree diagrams are thoroughly explained for the Game Show Problem.

Shulte, A. P., & Choate, S. A. (1977). *What are my chances?* Mountain View, CA: Creative Publications.

Seventy-seven activities begin with counting skills and extend to permutations and combinations. Teacher's notes are provided and permission is given to duplicate the materials for the students of the teacher for whom they are purchased.

Shulte, A. P., & Smart, J. (1981). *Teaching statistics and probability*. Yearbook of the National Council of Teachers of Mathematics.

This book has a wealth of information including reasons for teaching statistics and probability, samples of existing courses, classroom activities for K–12, ideas for teaching and learning specific topics, applications, and using computers.

ADDITIONAL ACTIVITIES—PROBABILITY

Activity 2.5	Odd or Even?
Activity 2.6	A Fair Deal for the Carrier
Activity 2.7	A Fair Dart Game?
Activity 2.8	Probable Triangles
Activity 2.9	The Triangle Problem
Activity 2.10	Mix and Match

Considering whether games are fair is an excellent way to begin the study of probability. Students immediately are interested and understand what fairness means. The first three activities deal with the fairness of games.

F O R   T E A C H E R S

Activity 2.5 Odd or Even?

Mathematical Content:
Probability (PSSM Data Analysis and Probability Standard for Grades 6–8 and 9–12)

Materials Needed:
Paper/pencil—clear plastic spinners are optional

Directions: Students seem to be able to understand whether or not a game is fair without much explanation. This activity can be entirely a paper-and-pencil activity or used in conjunction with spinners. If clear plastic spinners are available, students may play the game in pairs by placing the center of the spinner over the center of the diagram. Ask each group of students to enter their data on a common chart on either an overhead transparency or on large chart paper. Lead the discussion to summarize the data from the whole class and determine how close the experimental data are to the theoretical probabilities.

Extension: Ask students to design a similar game that is fair. Ask them to design a game where one player has twice as much probability to win as the other.

F O R   S T U D E N T S

Activity 2.5
Odd or Even?

Directions: Read through the problem below. Discuss your thoughts with another classmate. Then respond to the two comments in the list below.

Michiko and Patricia are going to play a spinner game. These are the rules:

1. When it is a player's turn, she spins both spinners.
2. Then she adds the two numbers that the arrows point to.
3. If the sum is odd (1, 3, 5, . . .), Michiko wins, even if it was not her turn.
4. If the sum is even (0, 2, 4, . . .), Patricia wins, even if it was not her turn.

Patricia tries a test spin, first. Here is what she spins:

The sum from the first spin is 3, because 3 + 0 = 3. Michiko wins.
Michiko says, "I like this game. I have a better chance to win it than you do."
Patricia says, "No, I have a better chance to win it than you do."

1. Use mathematics to decide which girl is right.
2. Write a note to both girls, explaining how you know who has the better chance of winning.

Source: *Great Tasks and More!!,* National Council of Supervisors of Mathematics, 1996.

F O R T E A C H E R S

Activity 2.6 A Fair Deal for the Carrier?

Mathematical Content:
Probability (PSSM Data Analysis and Probability Standard for Grades 6–8 and 9–12)

Materials Needed:
Paper/pencil; dice and coins (optional)

Directions: To work this multipart problem, students will need prior experience working with probabilities of throwing dice and tossing coins. A Fair Deal? is a homework problem in the Game of Pig Unit from the *Interactive Mathematics Project Year 1*. This problem is an excellent review to connect different methods of calculating probability. Ask students to explain and defend their methods of solution, which may vary considerably. Some students will simply compare each situation to the $5 per week, while others may calculate the probability for each of the schemes. Depending upon the knowledge base of your students, you may request that they use one of these general methods or the other.

F O R S T U D E N T S

Activity 2.6
A Fair Deal for the Carrier?

Directions: In each of the following situations, the customer would ordinarily pay $5 per week for newspapers. Instead, the customer offers a different plan. You, the paper carrier, have to decide which of these schemes of chance would give you a better-than-fair deal over the long run. Explain how you arrive at your decisions.

1. The customer will place 1 five-dollar bill and 3 one-dollar bills in a bag. You will draw out 2 bills.

2. The customer will place 1 five-dollar bill and 2 one-dollar bills in a bag. You will draw out 2 bills.

3. You will toss three coins. If two or more land heads, you get $9. Otherwise, you get $1.

4. You will toss three coins. If all three land the same (that is, all heads or all tails), you get $15. Otherwise, you get $1.

5. You roll a pair of dice. If the sum is exactly 7, you get $20. Otherwise you get $2.

6. Each week, 1 twenty-dollar bill and 4 one-dollar bills are placed in an empty bag. You pick 1 bill.

Source: *"Interactive Mathematics Program Year I,"* published by Key Curriculum Press, 1150 65th Street, Emeryville, CA 94608, 1-800-995-MATH. Reprinted with permission.

F O R   T E A C H E R S

Activity 2.7 A Fair Dart Game?

Mathematical Content:
Geometric probability (PSSM Data Analysis and Probability Standard for Grades 6–8 and 9–12)

Materials Needed:
Paper/pencil

Directions: Geometric probability is all too often left out of the curriculum; however, students are familiar with it through carnival games. If students do not understand how to approach this problem without instruction, begin with allowing students to throw darts at games of their design. Assume that only the darts that hit the board count and that it is equally likely that the dart hit any one spot.

Questions to Ask:
1. How do you know whether or not the game is equally fair for board owner and dart thrower?
2. What is a mathematical strategy to check if the game is fair?
3. Must we consider the entire board, or are there symmetries that can be used to simplify the problem?

F O R   S T U D E N T S

Activity 2.7
A Fair Dart Game?

Directions: You throw darts at this game board. Assume the darts can randomly hit any spot on the board. You win if the dart hits in a dark area, and the game owner wins if the dart lands on a light space.

Is the game fair?

Extension: Consider a common carnival game of throwing a coin on a field of saucers. In what ways are the situations similar? In what ways are the situations different?

F O R   S T U D E N T S

FOR TEACHERS

Activity 2.8 Probable Triangles

Mathematical Content:
Probability, permutations, and combinations (PSSM Data Analysis and Probability Standard for Grades 6–8 and 9–12)

Materials Needed:
Number cubes, rulers, and 1 package of thin spaghetti

Directions: In Part I students will explore what combinations of lengths of 1, 2, 3, 4, 5, and 6 will result in a triangle. Before preceding to the next part, pull the class together to discuss their findings. Students should understand the sum of the shorter sides of the triangle must be greater than the longest side to be able to form a triangle.

For Part II, form 12 groups, and assign each group the task of examining one column of the Possible Arrangements Chart. For each set of numbers, the students will decide whether the arrangement is "not a triangle, E, I, or S." The two groups with the same column provide a check. Then tally the class data for the totals of each of the four cases for All Possible Arrangements.

In Part III the students will throw three number cubes and record whether the numbers indicated on the number cube are "not a triangle, E, I, or S." Tally all the class experimental data. Help the students calculate the experimental percentage of the four cases and the theoretical percentage from the chart. Lead the discussion of why the experimental percentages and theoretical probabilities do not match. Students can explore combinations in the extension of the activity.

FOR STUDENTS

Activity 2.8
Probable Triangles (page 1 of 2)

Directions: In each part, read the task, answer the questions and perform the mathematics as requested.

Part I: Take several pieces of thin spaghetti and break them into three lengths each of 1 inch, 2 inches, 3 inches, 4 inches, 5 inches, and 6 inches. Discard the extra pieces. Roll three number cubes, and match the number on the cubes with the lengths of spaghetti. Record the lengths of the three sides and whether it is possible to make a triangle with those three lengths. Repeat about 6 times.

Compare your results with the data from other members of your group.

Make a hypothesis: When will three lengths form a triangle? Explain.

Part II: How many possible different arrangements are there for outcomes when the three number cubes are tossed? Explain your calculation.

Look at the list of possible arrangements provided by your teacher. Using your pieces of spaghetti or your hypothesis from Part I, determine whether an arrangement is:

— not a triangle
E an equilateral triangle with all three sides the same.
I an isosceles triangle with two equal sides
S a scalene triangle with all sides of different length.

Calculate the percentage for each case: not a triangle, an equilateral triangle, an isosceles triangle, or a scalene triangle for All Possible Arrangements.

F O R   S T U D E N T S

Activity 2.8
Probable Triangles (page 2 of 2)

Part III: Throw the number cubes 20 times and record your data. Record whether the lengths given by the number cubes are: not a triangle, an equilateral triangle, an isosceles triangle, or a scalene triangle. Combine your data with the whole class, and calculate the percentage for each case. Compare the theoretical percentage found in Part II with this experimental percentage.

Extension: There are 56 unique sets of the numbers on the three number cubes when order is not considered. These are called combinations. Calculate this number. (*Hint:* Consider the problem to be of three parts: (1) combinations with all three numbers different; (2) combinations with two numbers the same; and (3) combinations with all three numbers the same.)

All Possible Arrangements for Three Number Cubes

111 ____	211 ____	311 ____	411 ____	511 ____	611 ____
112 ____	212 ____	312 ____	412 ____	512 ____	612 ____
113 ____	213 ____	313 ____	413 ____	513 ____	613 ____
114 ____	214 ____	314 ____	414 ____	514 ____	614 ____
115 ____	215 ____	315 ____	415 ____	515 ____	615 ____
116 ____	216 ____	316 ____	416 ____	516 ____	616 ____
121 ____	221 ____	321 ____	421 ____	521 ____	621 ____
122 ____	222 ____	322 ____	422 ____	522 ____	622 ____
123 ____	223 ____	323 ____	423 ____	523 ____	623 ____
124 ____	224 ____	324 ____	424 ____	524 ____	624 ____
125 ____	225 ____	325 ____	425 ____	525 ____	625 ____
126 ____	226 ____	326 ____	426 ____	526 ____	626 ____
131 ____	231 ____	331 ____	431 ____	531 ____	631 ____
132 ____	232 ____	332 ____	432 ____	532 ____	632 ____
133 ____	233 ____	333 ____	433 ____	533 ____	633 ____
134 ____	234 ____	334 ____	434 ____	534 ____	634 ____
135 ____	235 ____	335 ____	435 ____	535 ____	635 ____
136 ____	236 ____	336 ____	436 ____	536 ____	636 ____
141 ____	241 ____	341 ____	441 ____	541 ____	641 ____
142 ____	242 ____	342 ____	442 ____	542 ____	642 ____
143 ____	243 ____	343 ____	443 ____	543 ____	643 ____
144 ____	244 ____	344 ____	444 ____	544 ____	644 ____
145 ____	245 ____	345 ____	445 ____	545 ____	645 ____
146 ____	246 ____	346 ____	446 ____	546 ____	646 ____
151 ____	251 ____	351 ____	451 ____	551 ____	651 ____
152 ____	252 ____	352 ____	452 ____	552 ____	652 ____
153 ____	253 ____	353 ____	453 ____	553 ____	653 ____
154 ____	254 ____	354 ____	454 ____	554 ____	654 ____
155 ____	255 ____	355 ____	455 ____	555 ____	655 ____
156 ____	256 ____	356 ____	456 ____	556 ____	656 ____
161 ____	261 ____	361 ____	461 ____	561 ____	661 ____
162 ____	262 ____	362 ____	462 ____	562 ____	662 ____
163 ____	263 ____	363 ____	463 ____	563 ____	663 ____
164 ____	264 ____	364 ____	464 ____	564 ____	664 ____
165 ____	265 ____	365 ____	465 ____	565 ____	665 ____
166 ____	266 ____	366 ____	466 ____	566 ____	666 ____

FOR TEACHERS

Activity 2.9 The Triangle Problem

Mathematical Content:
Geometric probability, inequalities (PSSM Data Analysis and Probability Standard for Grades 9–12)

Materials Needed:
One meter stick per group (or a 1-meter length of paper marked in centimeters)

Directions: Before this exercise, students should understand that a triangle can be formed only if the sum of the shortest two sides is longer than the third side of the triangle. If students are not as familiar with the metric system as you would wish, they will benefit by making their own one-meter paper "stick" using short metric rulers. "Paper rulers" can be made directly by photocopying a real ruler.

    The problem begins with two sticks, one of which is twice the length of the other. The student worksheet leads the students to answer the question, "What is the probability that a random break in the longest stick will give two lengths that can form a triangle with another stick that is one half as long?"

Extensions: For extensions on this problem, go to Web Destinations for Chapter 2 at *http://www.prenhall.com/huetinck.*

FOR STUDENTS

Activity 2.9
The Triangle Problem

Directions: You are given two sticks, one of which is twice as long as the other. Through this exercise you will be able to answer the following problem:

"Two sticks are given, with one stick that is twice as long as the other. What is the probability that a random break anywhere in the longest stick will result in segments so that the two pieces form a triangle with another stick that is half as long as the original stick?"

1. Consider the meter stick to be a line of length AB. With your eyes closed, randomly pick a point X somewhere on the meter stick. Record this point to the nearest 10 cm mark. Thus AX (from end A to X) will be one side of the triangle and XB (from the point X to the other end) will be another side of the triangle. The second stick, CD, has the length $AB/2$.

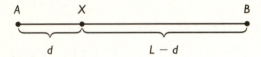 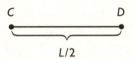

   Can a triangle be formed with these two sides and a 50 cm length? Try this experiment 10 different times.

2. What is required for the lengths AX and BX to be able to form a triangle with CD?

3. What are the positions of X on the meter stick so that a triangle may be formed with AX, BX, and CD?

4. Write the inequality that expresses the relationship you found in Part 3.

5. Rewrite the inequality in generalized terms for any two sticks such as AB and CD where CD has one-half the length of AB.

Source: Adapted from *The Triangle Problem, Geometry Probability* (p. 6), NCTM.

FOR TEACHERS

Activity 2.10 Mix and Match

Mathematical Content:
Probability (PSSM Data Analysis and Probability Standard for Grades 6–8 and 9–12)

Materials Needed:
Two items of one color and three items of a different color (chips, paper squares, marbles, etc.); a sack or an envelope

Directions: This is an excellent exercise in probability because students can use at least three different methods of solving the problem, depending upon their prior knowledge and ability level.

Activity 2.10
Mix and Match

Directions: Consider the following two games:

GAME 1

Two items of one color and two items of another color are placed in a sack or envelope. Without looking, a player draws out two of these. Regardless of who draws, Player A wins if they are the same color, and Player B wins if they do not match. The players take turns drawing (after replacement from previous draw). Is this game fair?

GAME 2

One item of one color and three items of another color are placed in a sack or envelope. Without looking, a player draws out two of these. Regardless of who draws, Player A wins if they are the same color, and Player B wins if they do not match. The players take turns drawing (after replacement from previous draw). Is this game fair?

1. What do you hypothesize about the fairness of Game 1 and Game 2? Does a certain player have an advantage in either game? Explain.

2. Play each game 10 times. Make a chart for wins of Player A and Player B for each of the games. Add your data to the chart for the class.

Game 1	Player A Wins	Player B Wins	Game 2	Player A Wins	Player B Wins

3. What is the experimental probability for a match in Game 1, according to the data of your class?

4. What is the experimental probability for a match in Game 2, according to the data of your class?

5. How could you calculate the mathematical probability for each game? Explain your method(s).

6. Which games(s) are fair?

CHAPTER 3

Concrete to Abstract With Tools, Manipulatives, Computer Programs, and Calculators

I n the past decade mathematics teachers have enthusiastically welcomed the great increase in the number of items contained in their teaching toolkits. We no longer rely solely on chalk and chalkboard to engage students in learning mathematics. The *Professional Standards for Teaching Mathematics* states:

> In order to establish discourse that is focused on exploring mathematical ideas, not just on reporting correct answers, the means of mathematical communication and approaches to mathematical reasoning must

be broad and varied. Teachers must value and encourage the use of a variety of tools rather than placing excessive emphasis on conventional mathematics symbols. . . . Teachers should also help students learn to use calculators, computers, and other technological devices as tools for mathematical discourse. Given the range of mathematical tools available, teachers should often allow and encourage students to select the means they find most useful for working on or discussing a particular mathematical problem. At other times, in order to develop students' repertoire of mathematical tools, teachers may specify the means students are to use. (NCTM, 1991, p. 52)

Descriptions and activities for the exemplary use of technology—broadly defined as manipulatives, calculators, and computers—are the subjects of this chapter. However, these are only a potential path to mathematical communication and understanding and must be closely linked with a meaningful curriculum. Also, these technologies must be integrated with either written or verbal communication about mathematics and supplemented by assessment to serve students most effectively. (Discussion concerning emerging curriculum and the related topics of communication and assessment are addressed in subsequent chapters.) The focus of this chapter is to help develop a working knowledge of ways to assist students in using handheld tools and computer worlds to access abstract mathematical concepts.

The set of topics selected for this chapter can be no more than a sampling of the many manipulatives, computer programs, and calculators available for students in grades 6 through 12. We hope that readers will recognize the breadth of possibilities for teaching with technology, but we do not want to overwhelm teachers with lists of tools. We have never seen a definition of a mathematical manipulative; however, we employ the common usage which is that of objects that can be handled or touched by students. Unless stated otherwise in the text or teacher information at the beginning of an activity with manipulatives, it is assumed that students are using the manipulatives individually or in small groups so that each student can facilitate learning through kinesthetics. Students learn most effectively with calculators when each has one to use at school and at home, but monetary restraints may require classroom sets or sharing in small groups. The same can be said for learning through computers. However, as is pointed out later in the chapter, computers, calculators, and manipulatives can be quite effective in facilitating understanding when an appropriate display device is used in a whole-class dialogue with the teacher.

ABOUT THE ACTIVITIES FOR THIS CHAPTER

For mathematical continuity of content, activities in this chapter focus on foundation concepts in arithmetic, geometry, and algebra. The text is interspersed with exercises that serve as examples for specific lessons. Lessons are placed in the sections that discuss the equipment needed for the activities.

The equipment showcased in the activities are those in common usage in up to date secondary level mathematics classrooms. Manipulatives can be purchased or cheaply made. For example, sheets for algebra tiles can be copied on heavy paper so that each student can cut out her own set for easy access as needed. Also, manipulatives can be as simple as folded paper. The graphing calculators and four-function calculators ever present now in mathematics classrooms lend themselves well to discoveries for students, whereas in the past, calculators were commonly used for checking answers. The use of dynamic geometry programs encourages students to make and test conjectures instead of memorizing theorems.

As you read the text, stop to try the activities as a student would, or if possible, use them with groups of students in grades 6 through 12. Remember what it was like for you to learn these lesson concepts for the first time. Of course, you now have visual images of geometric and algebraic relationships in your mind that naïve learners have yet to formulate. As a learner of mathematics, you might have been able to progress more quickly from concrete to abstract thought than many other first-time learners. Nobel laureate Richard Feynman said that the essence of being an exemplary teacher is to remember what it was like before you knew the idea.

In using these activities with grades 6–12 students, observe carefully how different students choose to use the manipulatives. Check often for understanding to ensure that students are using the equipment to assist their advancement to the general abstraction under investigation, allowing for differing paths to learning and differing rates of increasing expert thinking.

After working through an activity as a student, change to the perspective of a teacher. Ask yourself questions such as these: Where is the most effective place to fit this activity in the curriculum? As an introduction? As part of a review to connect ideas? Throughout the chapter to accumulate understanding? What prior understanding is necessary to assist students to use the activity as a discovery? What concluding discussion or activities will I conduct to be certain that students have internalized the instruction intended through technology? Since the students learned with technology, is it appropriate to assess knowledge with the same technology?

Again from the perspective of a teacher, look at the sources of the activities. They were selected to display the wealth of supplementary materials available to the teacher in designing a curriculum best suited for her students. The sources are various NCTM materials, journal articles, books of activities, software companies, and conference presentations by teachers. None of the sources are published texts. (Those are the sources for activities in the next chapter.) As you advance as a professional, be aware of the rich materials to find with your colleagues in settings for teacher enhancement for both your growth in mathematical understanding and to add excitement for your students' learning.

MANIPULATIVES

A manipulative is an object that students can handle and move to address mathematical concepts through visual and kinesthetic senses. According to educational psychology, some students are kinesthetic learners, so touching objects may be especially effective for them. Further, research indicates that all learners can benefit from manipulatives. Suydam and Higgins (1977), after reviewing a number of studies, concluded that elementary-level students who used manipulatives scored significantly higher in achievement. Ashlock maintained that students learn patterns of errors because they move too quickly into abstraction when they still need practice with concrete objects (Driscoll, 1981). Hunting (quoted in Suydam and Higgins, 1977) advocated the use of physical materials in teaching fractions due to his finding of a lack of understanding of equivalent fractions for fourth-, sixth-, and eighth-grade students. Manipulatives have moved from the elementary school to the middle school and are now frequently employed at the high-school level as the supporting innovative curriculum is being developed.

From Concrete to Abstract With Manipulatives

There is a long history of support for the practice of advancing students' mathematical understanding by moving from concrete experiences to abstract thinking. The abstraction of symbolic representation assists us in making deep connections in mathematics and even enables us to follow logical thinking into uncharted territories to expand the field of mathematics. However, the sophistication necessary for understanding abstract representations and the facile use of symbolic mathematics is not easily gained. This passage from concrete to abstract thinking has been described as "not so much a bridge as the entire journey" (Driscoll, 1981, p. 11). Even as late as middle school, many students find their understanding of abstraction grounded in their perceptions of the real world. Piaget's research indicated that symbolic representations have meanings for students as old as 12 only if they are closely tied to concrete representations (Driscoll, 1981).

Educational researchers Piaget, Skemp, and the van Hieles concluded that students proceed through learning stages. Manipulatives are significant aids to learning in all four of Piaget's stages, which he identifies as sensormotor, preoperational, concrete operational, and formal operational. In contrast, Skemp recognizes two levels of development: students at the second level of mental associations build on the first level, which is based in physical activities (Kennedy, 1986). In the 1950s Dutch educators Dina van Hiele-Geldof and Pierre van Hiele became concerned with secondary level students' difficulties in learning geometry. They studied how students learn geometry and identified five levels of instructional experiences through which students pass to reach the highest level of ability to establish rigorous theorems. These levels, known as the van Hiele levels, ask students to use visual, verbal, drawing, logical, and applied skills as they pass through five levels: recognition, analysis, ordering, deduction, and rigor. Students must master large portions of prior levels before attaining proficiency at advanced levels (Hoffer, 1981). There is no single route or rate to abstraction, but research has shown that manipulatives can be important to students taking this journey (Driscoll, 1981).

Using Manipulatives

The most significant influence on the successful use of manipulatives is the quality of teacher-conducted instruction in their use. The objects or representations themselves cannot teach. Just as a first-time user of the graphing calculator may not "see" a straight line for a linear equation (i.e., she sees the fine zigzag instead), a student may become distracted by manipulative color or shapes that are extraneous to the mathematical concept under study.

Further, facility with manipulatives does not guarantee understanding. Lessons with manipulatives must be carefully designed to advance students' thinking from "naive" to "expert." Thus, teachers must consider a number of issues in using manipulatives to make mathematics more accessible for students.

For example, before employing manipulatives, a teacher must avoid some assumptions. Clements and McMillen (1996) warn us of three. First, do not assume that the images you see when using manipulatives are identical to those seen by your students. You approach the activity from an expert position and can easily appreciate the connections between the concrete object(s) and the appropriate abstraction(s). In contrast, students come from a naive perspective. Their use of a specific manipulative may or may not lead them to the abstraction. Second, do not assume when students maneuver objects in specified ways that the expected mental associations automatically follow. For example, Gravemeijer, an educational researcher, found that students' patterns of thinking following manipulations on an abacus did not necessarily follow those patterns intended by the teachers. Third, realize that manipulatives can be used in a rote manner. Students may blindly follow a set of rules with manipulatives without really understanding the underlying ideas, just as they might do with symbolic algorithms. The effective use of manipulatives requires your thoughtful consideration, with manipulative use as a means—not an end—to developing students' thinking with your guidance (Clements & McMillen, 1996).

The following suggestions outline some considerations for effective and appropriate use of manipulatives:

- Select manipulatives that the *students* will use. Although this may seem an obvious suggestion, all too often teachers resort to carrying out demonstrations rather than supplying students with manipulatives due, perhaps, to a lack of time or lack of money for adequate sets of materials. The benefits of manipulatives are reduced if students cannot handle and move the objects themselves. If cost is a concern, consider using the kinds of manipulatives that can be made, laminated in plastic, and reused for many years.

- Select manipulatives that allow multiple applications. As you will see in the following examples, some manipulatives can be used for differing concepts and with students of different levels. Thus, you can use them throughout the year in various classes for students within a broad spectrum of ability. Manipulatives serving a number of purposes enable students to be creative in their applications in a variety of conceptual settings and help you stretch your materials budget. Also, when students are familiar with a manipulative, they know how to handle the objects and need less time for exploration. Further, when manipulatives can be used in a variety of ways, fewer are needed, and thus the problem of adequate and convenient storage is lessened.

- At the beginning of the year impress upon students the importance of proper treatment of all classroom materials. Even if the materials consist of nothing more than 3-by-5-inch cards, time and money were invested to procure them. They must be handled with respect.

- Give general rules for using manipulatives, including when they can be used and where they will be stored. When introducing each new manipulative discuss its safe and considerate use. Be explicit in your instructions of how to put the equipment away.

- When using a manipulative new to your students, always allow exploration time. Usually, they are intrigued and wish to experiment with the objects. If you try to go directly to a structured lesson you will lose the students. Plan for "play" time and ask students to observe some properties of the manipulatives in their initial examination.

- In introducing a topic, use one specific manipulative. After thoroughly working with the one representation, you may then allow students to try other concrete representations, especially if they suggest them. However, do not overwhelm students with a number of different representations at the early stages of development of a concept.

- Do encourage students to use manipulatives when they feel it would assist their learning. It is good practice to have manipulatives available to students upon request. Having a variety of manipulatives available allows students to select the representations most helpful to them. The practice of calling upon different manipulatives is particularly effective after the introduction of a concept, while students are extending their knowledge of the area of study.

- Remember that students advance at different rates. Some students might choose to use manipulatives long after other students prefer to move quickly to pictorial or symbolic representations. Students should not be required to use manipulatives if they can develop other methods of achieving understanding. Pictorial and symbolic representations can be less cumbersome than physical objects, especially for students with good visualization skills.

- Be certain that all students have an opportunity to manipulate the objects. If one set of materials is given to a cooperative group, structure the activity so that all students are physically involved. This may be done by requiring a different exercise by each member of the group. To the same end, you might assure equity by incorporating an evaluation into the activity by randomly selecting one student in each group to demonstrate the group's ability either to you or to the class.

- Consider the appropriateness of the manipulative to the age of the students. Unfortunately, some excellent materials for practice with core concepts are decorated with cute pictures that may turn off high-school students. I (SM) was amazed at how much more readily my high-school students took to secondary multilink cubes colored only white, black, and gray than to the more colorful multilink cubes used at the elementary school, although the same concepts could be developed by either type. Introduce any manipulative activity by indicating the important underlying mathematics so that students perceive it is a worthy exercise, regardless of their grade level or ability level.
- Organize the manipulatives in transparent bags, appropriately sized boxes, or containers that are easy to take out and put away neatly.

Bloomer and Carlson (1993) give the following excellent advice:

We don't allow students to say "I don't get it," but have them say, "I don't *quite* get it yet." This creates an expectation and trust in the students that they will understand the materials. They know

- it will be presented in several ways, with several different manipulatives;
- it's all right if they don't understand well at first;
- they can use the manipulative for as long as they feel a need; and
- they have a teacher, each other, and their previous experience to draw on for help.

Their comfort and confidence levels increase, and the amount of math anxiety decreases. (p. 5)

A complaint from some teachers is that they have no time to use manipulatives because they have so much material "to cover." If you feel the pressure to "cover" the text, ask yourself, "Who is covering the material?" All too frequently it is the teacher and not the students. Since you already know the mathematics, it makes no sense to "cover" the material without instilling student understanding. Although at first it may seem that manipulatives are too time consuming, remember the Chinese adage. "I hear, and I forget. I see, and I remember. I do, and I understand." For many students, *doing* requires making concrete ties to their real-world experiences and

the doing is enhanced by manipulatives. Teachers find that as concepts become more difficult, students familiar with procedures using manipulatives often get new skills as a "free ride" (Bohan, 1990). Bloomer and Carlson (1993) say:

Time is short. Manipulative and inquiry lessons take longer, both initially and because you need to include the connecting stage. You may fear you will never cover the curriculum or that students will not have the written skills to pass the required tests. Halfway through the year, you may start to get that familiar feeling of panic. We know it happens because we've been there.

An interesting thing happens.... Because (students) often see advanced lessons as requiring not new skills but logical extensions of what they have already learned, they begin to grasp concepts more quickly. Therefore, subsequent skill acquisition occurs at a much faster pace. (pp. 3–4)

In the next section of this chapter, common uses of some popular manipulatives are illustrated. All of the manipulatives described can be purchased, and most can be made. Certainly, the examples are by no means exhaustive of the many types of manipulatives now available. New manipulative applications developed and advanced by exemplary teachers are regularly presented in the journals of the NCTM. Further, at conferences you will also find many great ideas for using manipulatives. With experience you will invent manipulatives and explore new ways of using them. The following section simply offers a beginning.

Set 3.1   *Discussion Questions*

 Questions with an asterisk appear in the Message Board section of the Companion Website at *http://www.prenhall.com/huetinck.* Go to Chapter 3 and click on the Message Board to find and respond to the question.

*1. What teacher behaviors maximize the effective use of manipulatives in the classroom?

2. Is it possible for students to become too dependent upon manipulatives? Explain.

Fraction Stacks, Pattern Blocks, Fraction Bars, and Cuisenaire Rods

Fraction stacks, pattern blocks, fraction bars, fraction circles, and Cuisenaire rods are different manipulatives helpful in instruction with fractions. (These manipulatives also are effective in other mathematical contexts. For example, pattern blocks

Figure 3.1
Fraction Stacks

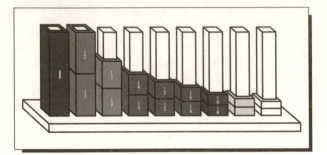

are used in Chapter 5 to develop intuitive understanding of angle measurement.) Even teachers of high-school upper-level courses frequently find that students still have difficulties with fractions. A thorough introduction to fractions and review of the basic operations with manipulatives can go far to address this common deficiency.

The fraction stacks shown in Figure 3.1 have movable segments on each tower marked with the fraction of the whole that each piece represents. By examination, students can see how the given divisions of the tower height result in the given fractions. By moving the pieces to determine how different combinations of fractions add to a whole, students can explore equivalent fractions.

Pattern blocks come in six shapes, and the shapes usually are colored. These shapes and associated colors are triangle (green), parallelogram (blue), trapezoid (red), hexagon (yellow), rhombus (tan), and square (orange). In this activity, students move from the concepts to the symbolism in adding fractions with unlike denominators.

Cuisenaire rods and fraction bars can be used for multiplying and dividing fractions. Cuisenaire rods are different-colored unsegmented bars representing lengths 1 through 10. The one cube is one cubic centimeter, the two is twice as long, and so on, as shown in Figure 3.2. Fraction bars, as the name implies, are fractions of a given rectangular area divided into bars. Teachers sometimes have students make their own fraction bars, but students may get frustrated working with them because edges may not match precisely; that is, four pieces each representing 1/8 may not line up to exactly equal one piece representing 1/2. In Activity 3.2, homemade fraction bars are used to divide fractions. Students can cut out their own set from a published template that is reproduced on stiff paper.

Figure 3.2
Cuisenaire Rods

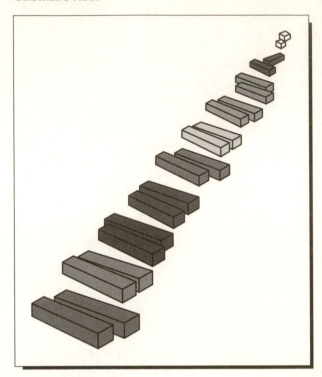

F O R   T E A C H E R S

Activity 3.1 Pattern Block Addition of Fractions with Unlike Denominators

Mathematical Content:
Patterns, fractions, conjectures (PSSM Number and Operations Standard for Grades 6–8)

Materials Needed:
Pattern blocks and worksheet with outline

Directions: This exercise gives insight into addition of fractions with different denominators using four of the six pattern blocks. Note that the fraction problems add to less than 1. Adding fractions with a sum between 1 and 2 is a simple extension to test for understanding.

FOR STUDENTS

Activity 3.1
Pattern Block Addition of Fractions with Unlike Denominators

Directions: Four pattern blocks are pictured and named in Figure A below. Look at the pattern block shapes, then answer the questions and work the problems by using the shapes.

Figure A: Pattern Blocks

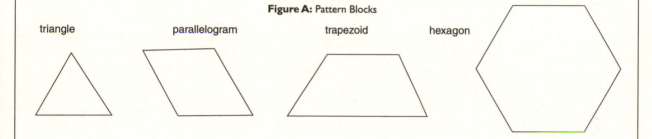

triangle   parallelogram   trapezoid   hexagon

1. Imagine that the shape in Figure B is the floor plan of a house of the future. If you had carpet in the shapes as shown in Figure A, how many of each type of pattern block will cover Figure B? It is permissible to cut a carpet piece. Write your answer in the blank provided.

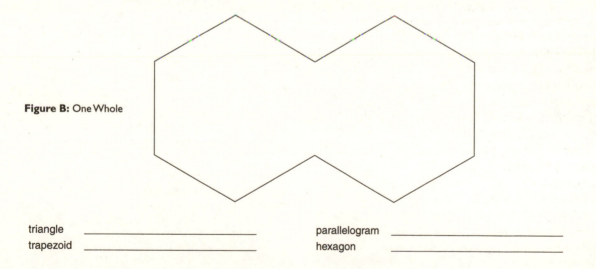

Figure B: One Whole

triangle _____   parallelogram _____

trapezoid _____   hexagon _____

2. By covering Figure B with different combinations of pattern blocks, add the following fractions. Make a picture to show how you covered the outline. Describe in words or pictures the method you used.

     a. 1/2 + 1/4

     b. 2/3 + 1/6

     c. 3/12 + 1/3

     d. 3/4 + 1/6

FOR TEACHERS

Activity 3.2 Divide a Fraction by a Fraction

Mathematical Content:
Patterns, fractions (PSSM Number and Operations Standard for Grades 6–8)

Time:
1+ periods

Materials Needed:
Fraction bars (directions in Manipulative Information section) or Cuisenaire® rods

Anticipatory Set:
Use *fraction bars* or *Cuisenaire® rods.*

Have students find $2 ÷ ¼$, *how many fourths are contained in 2*. Then lay out 2 wholes, and find how many fourths it takes to cover them. (8) There are 8 fourths in 2. Repeat with $2 ÷ ½$ (4).

Pose this problem: I have two cakes, and I divide each into eighths. How many people can I serve? (16) How do I write this as a math problem? Have students use the fraction bars to solve the problem. $(2 ÷ ⅛ = 16)$.

Explain that now there is only half of a cake left. How many people can you serve—how many eighths are left? The problem will be written as $½ ÷ ⅛$. How can they solve it?

Procedure 1:
To develop the concept of dividing a fraction by a fraction

Use *fraction bars or Cuisenaire® rods* and *paper*.

Continue the problem from the Anticipatory Set: $½ ÷ ⅛$. Have students lay out their whole bar and find the $½$. Say: We have to find out how many eighths *are contained in* the $½$ bar.

Students place eighths over the $½$ bar and find 4 eighths are in $½$.

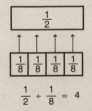

$$\frac{1}{2} ÷ \frac{1}{8} = 4$$

Repeat the procedure with $⁸⁄₁₆ ÷ ¼$ (2) and $⅝ ÷ ²⁄₁₆$ (6). Emphasize finding how many groups of a certain size *are contained in* the original fraction.

Students use the bars to find the answers. They chart their results, looking for patterns.

Continue the practice, giving problems with mixed numbers as well: $1¾ ÷ ⅜$ (6).

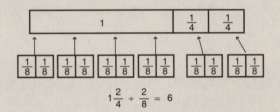

$$1\frac{2}{4} ÷ \frac{2}{8} = 6$$

Write the mixed numbers as improper fractions so that their chart entries will be consistent.

Ask: Do you see any patterns in your charts?

Some students may see that they can invert and multiply. Most should notice that they are coming out with answers larger than one.

Remind students that they know how to divide a whole number like three by a fraction.

Ask: What do you have to do to the whole number before you invert the divisor and multiply?

Students respond: Change it to that number over one, like $³⁄₁$.

We've been using bars to divide fractions by fractions. Is $³⁄₁$ a fraction? (yes) Do you think we could use this technique with a smaller fraction like $¾$?

Now move to the stage at which students write as well as use the bars. Have students use bars and write corresponding steps on paper as they work.

Students rewrite their division problems as multiplication problems to see whether the answers are the same.

Dictate problems for students to solve. After they become confident with the process, they can move to working the problem first on paper and then checking with their bars.

Colored Chips, Base-Ten Blocks, Balances, and Algebra Tiles

Colored chips, base-ten blocks, balances, and algebra tiles provide interesting ways to introduce algebra concepts.

Colored chips can be purchased such as plastic chips of two different colors, pieces of paper of two different colors, or even two different colors of beans. With this simple equipment you can teach addition and subtraction of signed integers much more easily than the traditional methods that relies on the definition of absolute value. One color of beans represents positive integers and the other color represents negative numbers, with each bean standing for one unit. This is the simple and cheap equipment used in Activity 3.3. Most teachers agree that this is one of the best ways to teach how to combine, although other methods must also be employed to teach the concept.

Base-ten blocks, illustrated in Figure 3.3, are primarily used to teach place value notation, but also can be used to show students that multiplying a two-digit number by a two-digit number is the same operation as multiplying an algebraic binomial by another binomial. As shown in Figure 3.4, two sheets of 10-by-10 blocks, six 1-by-10 blocks, and four 1-by-1 blocks can be regrouped to find the product. The procedure is to find the area of each smaller rectangle and add to get the total area representing the product. The only difference in multiplying algebraic binomials is that students may not

Figure 3.3
Base-Ten Blocks

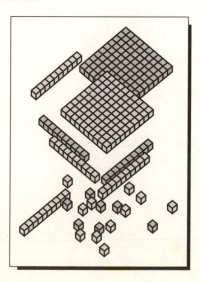

Figure 3.4
Multiplying Numbers

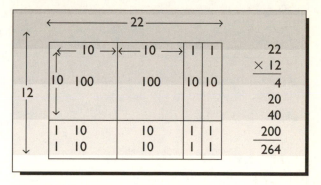

F O R   T E A C H E R S

Activity 3.3 Add and Subtract Positive and Negative Integers

Mathematical Content:
Addition and subtraction of positive and negative integers (PSSM Representation Standard for Grades 6–8 and 9–12)

Materials Needed:
Dark and light beans or chips or two different colors

Directions: It is necessary to begin with the explanation of additive identity (or the zero concept)—that an equal number of black beans and white beans equal 0. This is not a difficult idea for students to grasp, especially if it is related to owing money and being owed an equal amount of money.

The negative and positive signs within the parentheses refer to the color of the chips. The addition of subtraction sign between the two numbers refers to adding or taking away the prescribed number of chips. In time this will make more sense to the students than changing the second sign when subtracting.

When the students get to problem 4 *do not* tell or suggest that they add sets of zeros (equal numbers of the two color objects). This is why it is essential to have a separate area for extra pieces and for the work space. When students can view the extra pieces, they can figure out what to do. Let students have the fun of this discovery.

F O R   S T U D E N T S

Activity 3.3
Add and Subtract Positive and Negative Integers

Directions: Solve Problems 2 and 3, using the method illustrated in Problem 1.

1. −4 + (−5)

Solution: ●●●● + ●●●●● = −9

2. +4 − (+2) =

3. −7 − (−4) =

4. 15 + (−8) =

5. +3 − (+5) =

6. +5 − (−9) =

7. 22 − (+7) =

EXTRA PIECES

WORK SPACE

Figure 3.5
Arithmetic and Algebraic Examples

$(20 + 2)(10 + 2)$	$(x + 3)(x + 5)$
20 + 2	x + 3
10 + 2	x + 5
40 + 4	5x + 15
200 + 20	$x^2 + 3x$
200 + 60 + 4 = 264	$x^2 + 8x + 15$

Figure 3.6
Balancing Equations

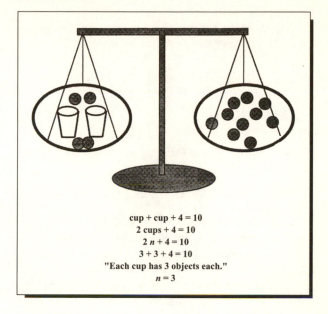

cup + cup + 4 = 10
2 cups + 4 = 10
2 n + 4 = 10
3 + 3 + 4 = 10
"Each cup has 3 objects each."
n = 3

readily recognize the like terms that can be combined and unlike terms that cannot. Figure 3.5 illustrates that multiplying arithmetic and algebraic expressions is the same operation. Build upon arithmetic knowledge in teaching algebra.

Teaching families of concepts increases students' knowledge of the nature of mathematics. Thus, students do not need to be taught the FOIL method (multiply First terms. Outside terms, Inside terms and Last terms). They already know the procedure for multiplication, and it can be extended to multiplication between polynomials of any number of terms. Some texts still have separate sections of the chapter for multiplying a binomial by a monomial, a trinomial by a monomial, and a trinomial by a binomial. However, such an organization falsely leads students to believe that there are different methods for multiplying, depending on the number of terms. Teaching multiplication by the method illustrated above neatly illuminates the single procedure behind multiplication: to multiply each term in the first set of parentheses by each term in the second and combine where possible.

Students can use cups and chips to represent the two sides of an equation that must balance, or they may actually set objects on a mathematical balance to discover how to balance equations. Even simple balances made for the science class are difficult to use for this mathematical lesson, though, because they are too sensitive to appear completely balanced unless the objects are carefully placed in the center of each pan and the balance is adjusted frequently. Some "balances" do not actually move but only simulate a balance; however, these are little better than using cups and chips and are much more expensive. A mathematical balance that works well for this type of activity is made by ETA of Vernon Hills, Illinois. Figure 3.6 shows how students can use paper cups and chips to balance equations. If funds are tight, this is an instance in which it would be appropriate for the teacher to have one balance

at the front of the classroom for demonstration. For example, conceal a number of washers (or weights) in a paper cup (which is so light its mass can be ignored) and place it on one side of the balance. Then show the students that an equal number of washers are needed on the other side for balance. The concept of a variable is difficult, and this method of introduction is effective. Other problems with more variables can be modeled in a manner similar to the example in Figure 3.6.

Algebra tiles are useful manipulatives for a number of algebraic operations: adding and subtracting polynomials, multiplying and dividing polynomials, factoring trinomials, and solving equations by completing the square. The ability for multiple applications makes this manipulative particularly attractive.

Algebra tiles can be purchased or cut from the inexpensive colored plastic sheets used for needlepoint. The plastic needlepoint squares are cut apart with an exacto knife, losing one row for each cut. The only difficulty with these tiles is that the smallest—1-by-1 squares—are very small and easily lost. Again, some activity books include outlines of models that can be copied and laminated with plastic for long-term use.

Begin simply, by representing multiplication with the unit algebra tiles. Ask students how many different rectangles they can make with an area of 12 tiles, to emphasize the concepts of factors and of area. Then ask students how many rectangles are possible with 7 tiles, to reinforce the concept of prime numbers. After dealing with integers, then move to representations of polynomials using the models shown in Figure 3.7. Addition, subtraction, and multiplication of polynomials can follow. Require students to explain their thinking processes and indicate their understanding by recording different methods, for example, pictorial or symbolic representations.

To factor with algebra tiles, the given terms must be arranged into a rectangular array. The factors are then modeled by the expressions across the top and down the side of the array, as shown in Figure 3.8. Try Activity 3.4 by arranging tiles in a square to mathematically complete the square of a quadratic.

Vignette 3.1   A Teacher-Made Manipulative

Materials: squares made from cardboard and graph paper

Mathematical Content: multiplying numbers and binomials

The Lesson: I reminded the class of the concept of area and instructed them to find the area of the first rectangle on the activity page, to generalize a formula, and to apply it to the second rectangle on the page. We then discussed the results. We noted that the area of a region was the sum of the areas of its constituent parts. The students then found the area of each small rectan-

gle in the second set of problems and summed them to find the area of the total rectangle. They also set up the formula for finding the area of the total rectangle as length times width. The class noted that the two approaches are equivalent. The students then worked the third set of problems. Their assignment was to construct their own rectangles and to find their total area by either method.

Reflection: The pretest given the day before showed only two students from last year's class had remembered how to multiply simple binomials. The same short quiz given at the end of the period indicated that three-fourths of the class now understood. This lesson helped to concretize what appeared to most of the class to be meaningless symbols before the lesson.

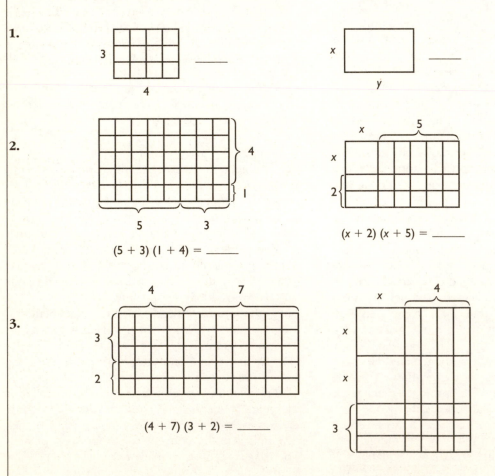

1.

2.   (5 + 3) (1 + 4) = _____

(x + 2) (x + 5) = _____

3.   (4 + 7) (3 + 2) = _____

(2x + 3) (x + 4) = _____

Figure 3.7
Algebra Tile Models

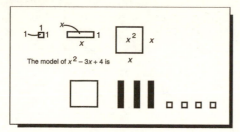

Source: *Algebra Tiles for the Overhead Projector,* Cuisenaire Company of America, pp. 10, 28–29 (Howden, 1985).

Vignette 3.2   Algebra Tiles

Mathematical Content: To visualize the factoring of general quadratic trinomials as dimensions of manipulatives representing area.

Materials: Algebra tiles

The Lesson: Two previous lessons on the addition and subtraction of polynomials and the multiplication of binomials squared introduced students to the visual advantage of representing variable expressions with tiles.

In this example they were asked to determine the factors of a general quadratic trinomial by taking the array of tiles "one x^2 tile, five x tiles, and six unit tiles," rearranging them to form a rectangle if possible and reading the dimensions of the rectangle directly from its linear edges.

What Happened: I expected to see the students discover the "model" arrangement found in books with the x^2 tile in one corner and other tiles filling in the rectangle on the two interior sides. One of the first volunteers at the overhead gave the unsettling but artistic solution as follows:

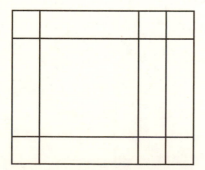

Deciding this arrangement legitimately portrayed the factors of the general quadratic trinomial, in this case $x + 2$ and $x + 3$, the class eagerly took on a second exercise, $2x^2 + 11x + 12$, which yielded similar satisfying results. Additional appropriate problems were assigned for both multiplication and factoring.

Figure 3.8
Algebra Tile Solution

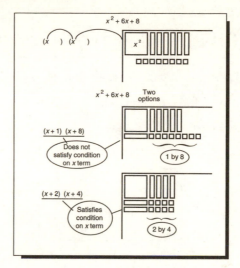

Reflection: Thoroughly engaged in solving the puzzle aspect of the exercise, the students seemed to enjoy the color and concreteness of the tiles themselves, as well as the conceptual connection with algebraic factoring patterns learned earlier. Follow-up of these activities will include reflection on the value of using this modeling tool at the individual level.

F O R   T E A C H E R S

Activity 3.4 Completing the Square with Algebra Tiles

Mathematical Content:
Algebraic equations (PSSM Representational Standard for Grades 9–12)

Materials Needed:
Algebra tiles or graph paper

Directions: This activity can follow students' practice in factoring with algebra tiles. The object is to find the number of tiles necessary to complete a square. Note that these examples do not deal with negatives, which can be modeled differently depending upon the specific system of algebra tiles you use. The Algebra Lab Gear system requires making a second layer of tiles when dealing with negative x values. These problems are left for you to explore in the multitude of materials available for algebra tiles.

F O R   S T U D E N T S

Activity 3.4
Completing the Square with Algebra Tiles

Directions: Solve Problems 2 and 3, using the method illustrated in Problem 1.

1. Model for the equation $x^2 + 8x = 9$

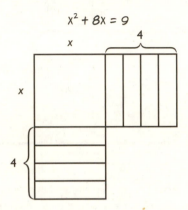

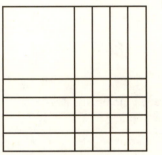

Complete the square geometrically by adding 16 units.

This drawing represents the following equation:
$$x^2 + 8x + 16 = 9 + 16$$
$$x^2 + 8x + 16 = 25$$
The length of each edge of the square gives the equation,
$$x + 4 = 5$$
$$\text{so } x = 1$$

Solve the equations and show your method pictorially.

2. $x^2 + 6x = 16$

3. $x^2 + 14x = 72$

4. Discuss the answers to these questions:

    a. Ordinarily, how many square roots does a number have?

    b. How many answers do these problems have? Explain.

5. al-Khwarizmi had another method for completing the square. It is similar to the one you have just done, but is not entirely identical. Your task is to figure out his method from the following equation and the figure. (*Hint:* Visualize the dotted square. Add the pieces of the total and set equal to the length times the width of the complete square.)

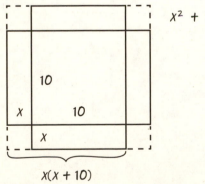

$$x^2 + 10x = 39$$

Source: Contributed by Dr. Barnabas Hughes, Professor Emeritus at California State University, Northridge.

Mirrors, MIRAs, Patty Paper, and Geoboards

Mirrors, MIRAs, patty paper, and geoboards are especially useful in visualizing geometry concepts, although they can be used in other contexts as well.

Mirrors are an excellent method to use in exploring symmetry. Small glass mirrors can be obtained from hobby shops. For safety, the backs and edges should be covered with masking tape. Stiff mylar mirrors can be purchased relatively cheaply and will last for a number of years. (Remember to take off the protecting clear plastic film for a good reflection.) Although mirrors may have limited use, they are nonetheless a valuable addition to a teacher's mathematics toolbox because they are familiar, cheap, and easy to store. They may be used in the classroom in a variety of interesting ways. For example, provide each student with a mirror and have her draw the capital letters of the alphabet on a sheet of paper. Develop a Venn diagram indicating the letters of the alphabet that have a vertical line of symmetry, a horizontal line of symmetry, both horizontal and vertical lines of symmetry, and no axis of symmetry. The position of the letter K in the Venn diagram may be debated since, if it is drawn as typed, it does not have an axis of symmetry. The way some students handwrite the letter does allow one axis of symmetry, however.

A MIRA enables students to accurately construct geometric figures because of its beveled edge, which allows a line to be drawn in the middle of the reflecting surface. The bevel is placed down on the tabletop on the edge facing the student. With a sharp pencil, beginning geometry students will find simple constructions much easier using a MIRA than a ruler and a compass. (Of course, they must have experience with these tools, as well.)

Figure 3.9 illustrates the bisection of a line segment with a MIRA. The student draws a line segment, marking each end with a dot that is easily visible. Viewing from the left of the figure, with the beveled edge down on the tabletop and toward the student, she lines the reflected red part of the segment with the real segment to the left of the MIRA. The MIRA is moved until the dot of the red reflected part of the line segment is superimposed on the dot on the left end of the drawn segment. The line drawn along the MIRA is the perpendicular bisector of the segment.

Patty paper, the 4-inch-by-4-inch papers used between hamburger patties at fast food restaurants, can be purchased in boxes of 500 or 1,000 sheets at

Figure 3.9
Finding the Perpendicular Bisector of a Segment

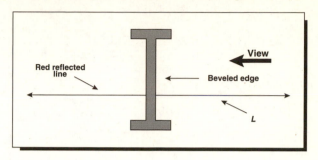

Figure 3.10
Bisecting an Angle with Patty Paper

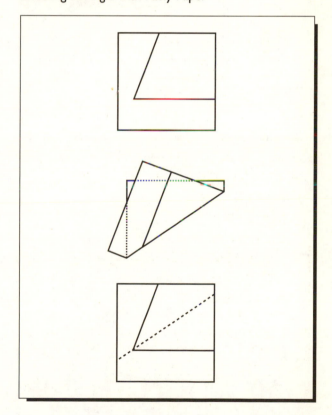

restaurant stores very cheaply. Figure 3.10 shows the steps followed to bisect an angle with patty paper. Accurate figures are easy to make if care is taken to make hard creases.

Geoboards are of several different types, including those with arrays of 5-by-5 pegs, 11-by-11 pegs, and circles of pegs. The 11-by-11 peg boards are most useful at the secondary level because the 10-by-10 spaces are helpful in exploring percent, and

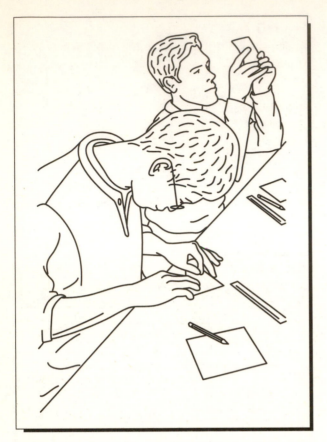

Students hold geometric figures drawn on patty paper to the light in order to align parts of the figures.

Students explore area and perimeter of right triangles through the use of geoboards.

decimals. The larger number of pegs enables students to find relationships between perimeter and area of figures of relatively larger unit sizes. Also, the smaller distance between the pegs is not difficult for students in the 6th through 12th grades to manage. Try Activity 3.5 using either 11-by-11 geoboard or dot paper.

 Go to Web Destinations for Chapter 3 at
http://www.prenhall.com/huetinck
to find links to resources for manipulatives.

Set 3.2   Discussion Questions

 Questions with an asterisk appear in the Message Board section of the Companion Website at ***http://www.prenhall.com/huetinck.*** Go to Chapter 3 and click on the Message Board to find and respond to the question.

1. What are the main issues teachers should consider in using manipulatives to make mathematics more accessible to students?
2. Make a table with a list of common manipulatives and the specific concepts they can illuminate.
*3. How do you encourage students who do not achieve in a conceptual area and feel that manipulatives are "too much trouble" to continue their use until the students thoroughly understand the concept?
4. Some educators (Baroody, 1993) have suggested that number sticks are better than Cuisenaire rods for teaching arithmetic concepts. Number sticks are constructed from interlocking blocks, with the number of blocks directly relating to the number represented. Since the Cuisenaire rods are unsegmented rods that must be compared to a code of length or of color, the number represented by the rod is not as obvious as it is with the segmented sticks. Brody believes that the rods do not model a youngsters' concept of number, which is a collection of discrete objects. This and associated research cautions teachers to consider whether a given manipulative always provides the intended link between a concrete model and symbolic representation. As a teacher, what can you do to assess your students' mathematical perceptions when they are working with manipulatives?

F O R   T E A C H E R S

Activity 3.5 More About Area, Perimeter, and Right Triangles

Mathematical Content:
Patterns, area, making conjectures (PSSM
   Geometry Standard for Grades 6–8 and 9–12)

Materials Needed:
Geoboards (11 × 11 pegs) and elastic bands or
   dot paper

Directions: Students explore patterns of different right triangles. Dot paper can also be used for
the exercise.

F O R   S T U D E N T S

Activity 3.5
More About Area, Perimeter, and Right Triangles

PAIRS EXPLORE

Directions: Work with your partner and one geoboard. Solve each problem on the geoboard. Record
your solutions.

1. Make triangle *A* shown below. Build squares on each leg and the hypotenuse of the triangle as
   shown. Record the areas in a table like this one:

Triangle	Area of leg 1 square	Area of leg 2 square	Area of hypotenuse square	Area of triangle

2. Make triangles *B* and *C*. Make a square on each leg and the hypotenuse of both triangles. Record
   the areas for these triangles in the table.

PAIRS SHARE

Share your solutions. Be sure everyone agrees that each solution is correct.
   Put your heads together to talk about the following questions. Be ready to share your answers with
the class.

- What kinds of patterns do you see in the table?
- How do the squares relate to each other? How do you think this relates to the sides of the triangle?

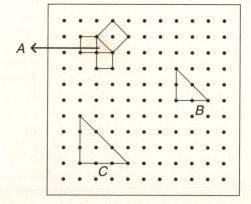

Source: Reprinted from *Junior High Cooperative Problem Solving With Geoboards*. © 1991 Creative Publications.

COMPUTER SOFTWARE

In the past decade computer software has become faster, as well as more imaginative, colorful, motivating, and user friendly. The "rapid-fire" or "drill and kill" programs are supplemented by software that gives students freedom to construct and dynamically change geometric figures, to perform algebraic manipulations, and to take notes on their processes. Students can move drawings of manipulatives on the computer screen with the aid of a mouse. Geometer's Sketchpad and CABRI, preceded by the Geometric Supposer series and joined by Geometry Toolkit for middle school, can be used to stimulate students to make conjectures regularly in geometry. Due to the proliferation of mathematics software, only a fraction of available software can be illustrated in this text. Algebraic manipulation software such as DERIVE, IBM Mathematics Toolkit, and Mathematica will not be showcased in this text because their use is not yet common in secondary-level schools. (Chapter 12 includes a lesson with the graphing calculator, which uses a program like DERIVE.) We fully realize that the line between computer and calculator is entirely arbitrary, since graphing calculators can rightly be considered handheld computers.

Kaput (1992) compares the task of describing computer technology in mathematics education to the task of a geologist in describing a newly active volcano. All is rapidly evolving before our eyes, with forces acting in different directions. We can only guess at what the future will bring. We would add, however, we cannot let the changing scene be an excuse for "analysis paralysis"—waiting for the latest word before becoming involved. Experience with current technology leads to expertise with the newest developments. Schools are only beginning to tap the teaching potential of computers in ways that do not mimic textbook instruction. We highly recommend *Technology and Mathematics Education* by Kaput for its discussion of greater depth on the history of technology in mathematics education and its summary of the state of affairs at the time it was written, as well as its review of the classical research on the subject. Only in the last few years have we begun to improve on the conditions lamented by Kaput. Now we are procuring greater numbers of computers, developing more imaginative software and supporting curricula, and providing teacher in-service and pre-service opportunities. Further, most districts have at least begun implementation of support services to ease logistics difficulties for the classroom teacher. These support services include centralized policies and location for making and storing program copies, repair services, and the hiring of personnel to staff computer labs.

From Concrete to Abstract With Computer Microworlds

In the discussion of manipulatives earlier in the chapter, we skipped over the complex question "What is concrete?" so that we could include computer microworlds in the dialogue at this juncture. The admonitions from Clements and McMillen (1996) about assumptions to avoid when using manipulatives are based on an attempt to answer this question. They define the word *concrete* from its root, to grow together. As in a concrete sidewalk, separate particles are combined to form an interconnected mass. Researchers analyzing studies of both manipulatives lessons and comparable computer lessons come to no conclusions about which environment is more concrete to students, that is, which is the best means to interconnected mathematical ideas. Constructs are in the mind, and manipulated physical objects, drawn pictorial representations, or computer figures moved by a computer mouse all may provide pathways from experience to symbolic representation. After examining a number of computer programs we will return to this discussion to compare characteristics of certain software with those of manipulatives.

Software Emulating Manipulatives

A number of programs provide movement of pictorial manipulatives on a computer. We selected a few relatively new software pieces for examination: the three in the *Hands-On Math Series I, II,* and *III, The Balancing Act,* and *Geometry Toolkit* (Ventura Systems). All of these programs are aimed at students up to the eighth grade, but they can be extended to older students.

Hands-On Math Volumes I, II, and *III* emphasize active learning using a computer in a manipulative approach to mathematics. Each manual comprises two sections: the first half is a teacher's guide explaining program features and ideas for instructional strategies and the second half is a set of reproducible activity sheets arranged in order by the manipulative device. *Hands-On Math* encourages students to discuss, share, and creatively explore mathematics. Some lessons in *Volume I* incorporate tangrams (seven simple shapes of different-sized triangles, one square, and one parallelogram that can fit together to make a square) to learn addition of fractions and geometric reflections; a geoboard playground with activities for area, perimeter, and Pick's formula; and number bars that can be used to

Figure 3.11
Balancing Act

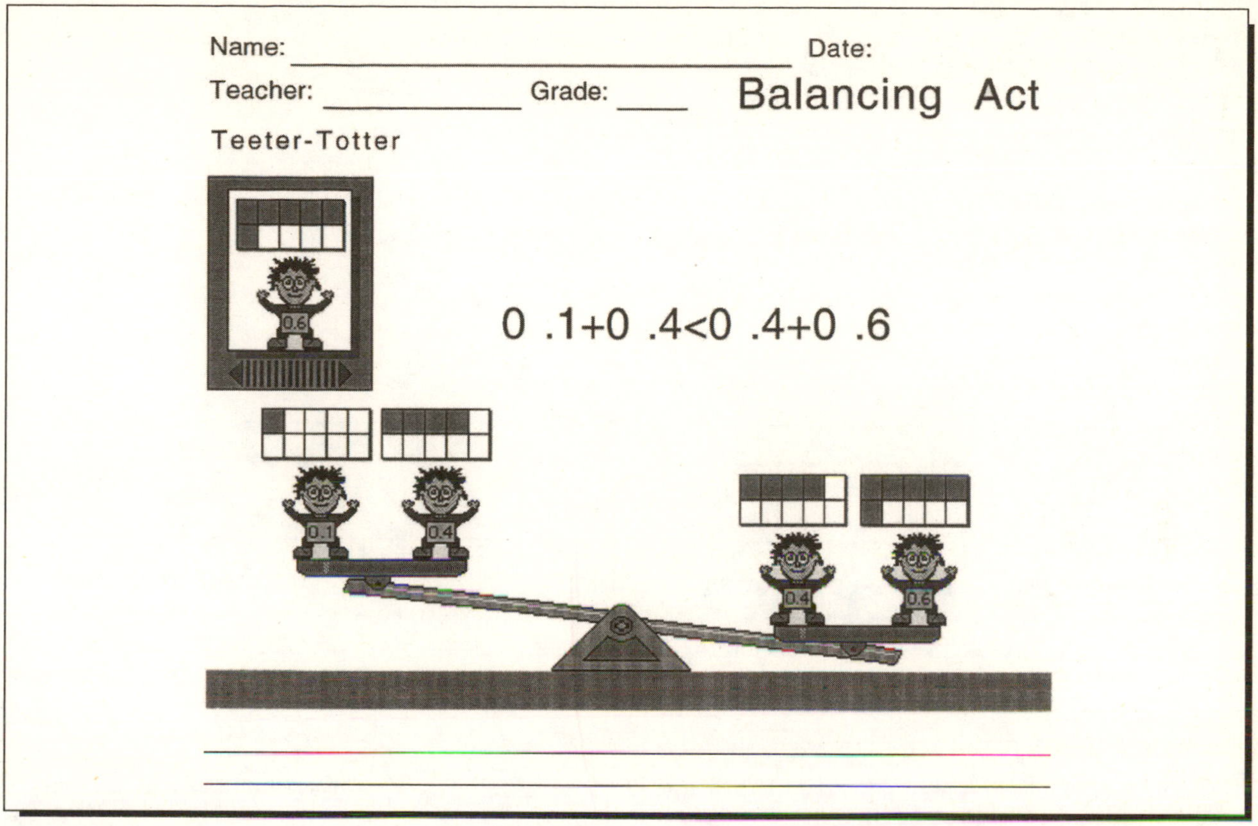

multiply fractions and to find the least common multiple and the greatest common factor. *Volume II* has five playgrounds: two-color counters, color tiles, mirrors, attribute blocks, and base-10 blocks. *Volume III* includes six playgrounds: hundreds chart, graph center, number balance, dominoes, line design, and fraction sticks.

Students using *The Balancing Act* can balance equations with three different tools: a teeter-totter, a number balance, or a scale. Interesting algebra activities include testing the commutative property and associative properties with a balance. The written

activities are intended as a starting point, and the software design enables much more complicated problems than those illustrated in the teacher's guide. Students may move ball-juggling figures to make one side of the teeter-totter go down, or use figures balancing balloons representing integers of opposite signs to investigate adding and subtracting directed numbers. As shown in Figure 3.11, students may compare fractions in pie shape forms or bar forms. Display of the accompanying equation can be either activated or deactivated. One activity from this software is given as Activity 3.6.

FOR TEACHERS

Activity 3.6 Greatest Common Factor

Mathematical Content:
Patterns, greatest common factor (PSSM Number and Operations Standard for Grades 6–8 and 9–12).

Materials Needed:
Software and Cuisenaire rods (optional for reinforcement)

Directions: The students move rods of different lengths on the screen to find the GCF for randomly selected numbers.

F O R   S T U D E N T S

Activity 3.6
Greatest Common Factor

Name_____   Date_____

Directions: The Greatest Common Factor (GCF) is the largest number that is a factor of two other numbers. Here is a method using number bars that will find the GCF for 12 and 8.

The factors of 12 are 6, 4, 3, 2, and 1. The factors of 8 are 4, 2, and 1. The largest number that is common to both sets of factors is 4.

Use the Number Bars Playground to find the GCF for 12 and 15. Color the grid to show your work.

Use number bars to find the GCF for these numbers:

1. 6 and 8 _____	**6.** 12 and 16 _____	**11.** 14 and 21 _____
2. 4 and 8 _____	**7.** 8 and 14 _____	**12.** 15 and 18 _____
3. 5 and 20 _____	**8.** 12 and 15 _____	**13.** 20 and 12 _____
4. 25 and 15 _____	**9.** 4 and 16 _____	**14.** 10 and 15 _____
5. 16 and 8 _____	**10.** 3 and 15 _____	**15.** 6 and 4 _____

Source: Adapted with permission from *Hands-On Math,* Vol. 1, Ventura Educational Systems, p. 23. © 1988–1995 Ventura Educational Systems.

Let us now return to the discussion contrasting manipulatives and computer microworlds that simulate manipulatives. Mathematical ideas are made real by their connections within meaningful contexts (Clements & McMillen, 1996). Computer depictions of manipulatives may be as meaningful or real as the manipulatives themselves. There are reasons that computer simulations of manipulatives may be easier to manage than manipulative models. The following discussion of some of these reasons is based partly on Clements and McMillen and partly on our experiences in teaching with technology:

■ Computers offer flexibility of presentation so students can select the most individually meaningful representation. For example, in the *HandsOn* geoboard environment students can choose 25-peg or 100-peg boards. In the *Geometry Toolkit,* students can number the pegs or use a coordinate system to locate pegs. *The Balancing Act* provides three balancing environments for similar but parallel representations of equations.

■ Computers can quickly print out or store figures and or notes. In most of the computer environments discussed, the students can split the viewing screen to use a notepad for recording comments next to the figure under examination. These notes can be printed to give the teacher written feedback on student understanding.

■ Computers enable students to quickly explore many varied examples to come to a generalization about the underlying characteristics of mathematical entities. For example, in Activity 3.6, students can try a variety of cases to develop a conjecture about finding the greatest common factor.

■ Computers can present a more dependable environment than manipulatives in some cases. For example, as noted earlier in the chapter, balances frequently do not balance when they should, due to friction or lack of frequent adjustment. The computer equivalents always work as expected.

■ The logistics of computer environments may be easier to manage than manipulatives: computer pictorials cannot be lost and do not need storage space or careful handling (computer "elastic bands" do not break).

■ Color and sound are motivating to students, although the teacher may wish to turn sound off for obvious reasons. Color can assist in understanding. For example, ask students to find the number of squares on a 5-by-5-peg geoboard. This is a simplified version of the Checkerboard Problem, a nonstandard problem found in the additional activities section of Chapter 9. It is easier to keep track of the different-size squares with colored computer bands than with a large number of elastic bands needed on an actual geoboard.

■ Research indicates that students are more aware of their processes when commanding the computer to make movements than when simply moving forms by hand, where movements may not be intellectually noted. Students may not formalize translations and reflections with hands-on modeling. After telling the computer what to do, however, they are more apt to fully describe these motions (Clements & McMillen, 1996).

■ Most computer programs provide exemplary scaffolding by giving progressive levels of problems and challenge environments that enable students to proceed at an individual rate.

The admonitions in using modeling computer environments are the same as with manipulatives. Teachers still must ensure that students internalize connections and actively participate in their learning. Provide adequate discussion and reflection time for students to construct concepts from their exercises. Although computers have been widely used in many fields for years, only in the past decade has there been a proliferation of classroom resources of computer programs that approach mathematical ideas in ways profoundly different from print methods. Therefore, there is little research in this area to guide teachers. Furthermore, the recent explosion in the use of technology in mathematics education probably will not allow research to advise practice for some years. Thus, teachers must monitor student progress, reflect on practice, and confer with colleagues to decide what is most effective for their students.

Vignette 3.3 Teaching Geometry with Computers

Technology: Geometric Supposer—*Triangles* software; 8 Macintosh computers

Mathematical Content: congruence theorems of triangles

The Lesson: I made copies of activity sheets provided with the software and distributed them to each student as she entered the lab. I guided the students through instructions for turning on the computer and starting the program (previously loaded on the hard disk). The content dealt specifically with side-angle-side and angle-side-angle problems.

Reflection: One period has 34 students, so as many as five students had to share one computer. Still, they managed to cooperate well under the crowded conditions (the lab is approximately one third to one fourth the size of a regular classroom).

Now I regularly schedule after-school hours (for extra credit) for individual exploration. I have written a set of worksheet explorations designed to introduce students to various features of the *Geometric Supposer* while reinforcing theorems presented in the regular classroom.

I find that my energy and interest in teaching Geometry have been renewed, and I think the introduction of technology into the curriculum has revolutionized my priorities concerning teaching methods and questioning techniques. I find I relate many of my lecture/ presentations to some of the activities the students experienced in the lab.

Dynamical Geometry

Geometry, in particular, has been greatly affected by computer software. Logo was developed in the 1960s by Feurzeig and Papert, who provided a link between a manipulative—a mechanical turtle that moved on the floor—and a computer representation of the direction and magnitude of that movement. The first uses were aimed at encouraging young students to explore a mathematical universe. Elementary programming skills as well as complex logic can be taught with the Logo program. So many research studies and activity articles have been written on Logo that we refer you to the rich body of published work. The Geometric Supposer series, begun in the mid-1980s, switched the focus of geometry class from proofs to conjecture building as students could construct and explore many different theorems. The CABRI system, developed in France, allowed animation wherein a construction can be adjusted by dragging figures. In addition, users can record their steps in a construction, called a macro. Presently, CABRI is a feature on the TI-92 handheld computer and, as such, probably will gain in popularity since each student can now have immediate hands-on access for a relatively low cost. The Geometer's Sketchpad (GSP) currently is the most popular of geometric software due to its ease of use, dynamical qualities, and rich and varied supplementary materials.

The best way to become familiar with the main elements of the Geometer's Sketchpad is to "play" with constructing figures to gain ease in drawing and manipulating them. Figure 3.12, Quick Reference, illustrates the program's main capabilities. After opening the program, pull down the "File" menu to get a "New Sketch." The blank drawing screen will appear with the tools down the side and the menus across the top. The user's guide in the software materials includes 14 tours and details to familiarize you with the main features of making a sketch, or visual geometric drawing. The power of the program is that you can move carefully constructed geometric figures dynamically, by "pulling" with the mouse, to illustrate geometric principles.

Geometer's Sketchpad makes two kinds of documents: the sketch that is the geometric drawing and the script that is a record of the commands used to construct the sketch. Using GSP 3.0, to make a script begin with both a "New Sketch" and a "New Script" on the computer screen, click Record on the script and the computer will make a list of the steps you make while drawing the figure. (Note: "Script" in GSP 3.0 has been replaced by "custom tools" in the newer 4.0 version. The 4.0 version automatically makes the list of steps of a drawing). Saving these two types of documents gives you, the teacher, a variety of modes for investigating geometry in the classroom. Best practice is to have access to a computer laboratory where students can have hands-on experience with dynamic geometry. Teaching Geometry with the Geometer's Sketchpad, in the program materials, includes a number of classroom-ready investigations. If your students do not have the facility or sophistication to make the figures, however, you can provide the sketches for them to explore. If you have only one computer without an overhead projector, groups of students can take turns using the computer while the rest of the class does constructions with standard geometry tools. With one computer and a projection device, you can conduct a whole group discussion using the script to construct the figure step-by-step using the program as a presentation tool.

These ideas only touch on the plentiful possibilities for dynamic geometry software to be found in the literature and in books of classroom-ready materials. Note that Activity 3.7 includes teacher directions with step-by-step instructions, followed by an illustration of the completed figure and the accompanying script.

We would like to comment on several characteristics of the GSP program. The accompanying script can be rerun in step play or fast play to reconstruct the geometric figure, similar to a macro for CABRI. However, note that the Point on Object can appear anywhere on the selected element, so, for some figures, elements will need to be moved to certain regions to end with the desired figure. The secret for a good construction is to make a figure that holds together under prescribed movement but is not too stiff to be dynamic. If you simply use the segment tool to draw Segment m instead of selecting Seg-

Figure 3.12
Quick Reference

Quick Reference
For Windows® and Macintosh®
Version 4.0

About Document Windows

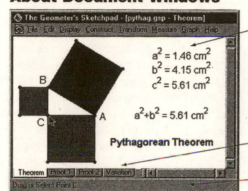

Sketch Plane. Draw new objects here using the **Point, Compass, Straightedge,** and **Text** tools. Drag objects to explore relationships using the **Selection Arrow** tool. Select objects and use menus to reformat or measure them, or to construct new objects defined by selected objects.

Page Tabs. In multi-page documents, use tabs to switch pages. (To add new pages, choose **File | Document Options**.)

Status Line. Describes current selections or tool action.

About the Toolbox

Selection Arrow and **Translate** tool: Click on objects in sketch to select them. Drag objects to move (**Translate**) them. (Press icon to pull out **Translate, Rotate,** and **Dilate** arrows.)

Point tool: Click in blank sketch area to create an independent point. Or click on object to create a point on that object.

Compass (Circle) tool: Press mouse button to create center, drag to create circle, release to create radius control point. Center and radius points can be independent points or points on objects.

Straightedge (Segment) tool: Press to create first endpoint, drag to create segment, release to create second endpoint. (Press icon to pull out **Segment, Ray,** and **Line** tools.)

Text tool: Double-click in blank area to create caption. Click on object to display or hide label. Drag label to reposition. Double-click on label, measure, or caption to edit or change style.

Custom tools: Press icon to display commands for creating new tools, and a list of all available custom tools. Choose custom tool from list to use in sketch. (See **Custom Tools**.)

Selecting Objects

Many menu commands require that you first select objects in your sketch to act upon. Commands that are gray are unavailable. Make unavailable commands available by first selecting their necessary objects.

To select one or more objects	Click each unselected object with **Selection Arrow**.
To select objects with selection rectangle	Click in blank sketch area with **Selection Arrow**; drag to define rectangular selection area; release to select all objects in, or partially in, selection rectangle.
To deselect one or more objects from group	Click each selected object with **Selection Arrow**.
To deselect all objects	Click in blank sketch area with **Selection Arrow**.

Source: *The Geometer's Sketchpad*, Key Curriculum Press, 1150 65th Street, Emeryville, CA 94608, 1-800-995-MATH. Reprinted with permission.

ment under the Construct Menu, the segment may not be attached to Segment *j* and Line *k*. Then the figure will come apart when moved. Note that Points *A, B,* and *C* are givens for the script. If we had used these points in later construction, the figure would not have as many possible dynamic points.

Teachers find that students need the experience of construction with conventional tools before advancing to the computer; otherwise, the students do not fully appreciate the logic behind the computer. For example, high-school students familiar only with geometric software will be mystified that they cannot construct a perpendicular line when only a segment or line is selected. However, after thinking of their own constructions with straightedge and compass, they realize that to draw a perpendicular line they must choose not only a segment or line but also a point. Thus, GSP can reinforce geometric principles of construction encountered in traditional methods, but not fully internalized.

Many supplementary materials exist to use with the GSP. The Geometer's Sketchpad program includes a book of teaching notes and sample activities. In addition, five books are available with 100 to 300 pages each of add-on modules with reproducible blackline masters of activities, including *Geometry through the Circle, Pythagoras Plugged In, Exploring Conic Sections, Perspective Drawing,* and *Exploring Trigonometry.* There are two new add-on

modules for middle school: *Geometry Activities* and *Shape Makers*. GSP activities are keyed to the *Discovering Geometry* textbook, and the transformations, including dilations, are closely related to approaches in the University of Chicago series of textbooks. Of course, the investigations can illuminate many geometric principles found in all geometry books and integrated mathematics texts.

It is important to use the most efficient tool for the learning task. Sometimes, this may be a very simple method without computers. For example, with GSP you can draw a triangle, measure each of the angles, and use the GSP calculator to find the total measure of the three angles. Then, as you move a vertex, the sum stays the same as the angles change their measures. However, a simpler and much cheaper demonstration is for each student to cut out a triangle, tear each vertex off the triangle, place the three original vertices together, and show that the sum is a straight line for all the different triangles. A lesson plan that requires students to use GSP to draw polygons and measure and sum the exterior angles is another example of using a sledgehammer to drive a tack.

 Go to Web Destinations for Chapter 3 at **http://www.prenhall.com/huetinck** to find links to calculator resources.

FOR TEACHERS

Activity 3.7 Dynamic Geometry to Compare Areas

Mathematical Content:
Areas of triangle and parallelogram, ratio (PSSM Standard Geometry for Grades 6–8 and 9–12)

Materials Needed:
Geometer's Sketchpad software 4.0 and appropriate computer

Directions: The instructions assume some familiarity with the use of Geometer's Sketchpad, although no expertise is necessary. The next page illustrates the desired figure and its custom tool (script) for your reference. Do not show it to the students before their exploration.

If you have only one computer and a display device, you can initiate an interesting whole class

discussion by asking the students to tell you what each step should be. To do this, draw the figure ahead of time, "Select all" under the Edit menu. Then with the select tool move to the bottom tool on the left and "Create new tool." This is a custom tool, similar to the script used in the GSP 3.0. Provide a name for the custom tool (script). Delete the figure to keep the list of commands on the screen. Cover the list of commands so the student see only the blank page. Place three highlighted points on the screen for the Givens. Then you can move through the script one step at a time using the Next Step button on the lower left. Before you get to the measurements, ask the students to write a hypothesis about the ratio of the areas.

FOR STUDENTS

Activity 3.7
Dynamic Geometry to Compare Areas (page 1 of 2)

Directions: With the figure of a parallelogram and a triangle, you will be able to find the relation-ship between the areas of the two shapes. When you have finished making the drawing, drag differ-ent parts of the figure to see the dynamic effects of Geometer's Sketchpad. In the directions below, an underlined word such as *Construct* indicates a menu name at the top of the screen. A word in quotes such as "Segment" is found under the menu by clicking on the menu and dragging down to the menu item wanted. To select, always return to click on the select tool; then click on the command or drawing part you want. Keep a figure selected by holding the shift key when it is made or using the select tool to click on it.

1. Construct a parallelogram with these steps:

   a. With the point tool, highlight two points with one slightly below and to the side of the other (*A* and *B*).

   b. Under the Construct menu, select "Segment" to join the 2 points (segment *j*).

   c. Select the point tool and place another point (*C*) below the segment *j*.

   d. Highlight segment *j* and point *C*. Under the *Construct* menu select "Parallel line" (*k*).

   e. Highlight *A* and *C*. Under the Construct menu, select "Segment" (*l*).

   f. Highlight point *B* and segment *l*. Under the Construct menu, select "Parallel line" (*m*).

   g. Highlight line *k* and line *m*. Under the Construct menu, select "Intersection" (*D*).

   h. Highlight points *A, B, D,* and *C* in that order. Under the Construct menu, select "Quadrilateral In-terior." With the interior selected (see crosshatch design), go under Display and "Color" to select a light color such as yellow.

2. Construct the triangle inside the parallelogram with these steps:

   a. Highlight segment *j*. Under the Construct menu select "Point on segment" (*E*).

   b. Highlight *D, E,* and *C* in that order. Under the Construct menu select "Triangle interior." With the interior of just the triangle selected select a dark color such as blue under *Display* and "Color."

F O R   S T U D E N T S

Activity 3.7
Dynamic Geometry to Compare Areas (page 2 of 2)

3. Measure the areas and compare the areas by the following steps:

   a. Highlight the yellow area. Under the Measure menu select "Area." Click with the select tool on the white area of the page to deselect the Area *ABDC*. Measure the blue area in the same way.

   b. Highlight both area measures. Under the Measure menu select "Calculator."

   c. Click Values on the New Calculation small screen. Drag to Area *ABDC*, click on the divide sign, drag under Values to Area *DEC*, then click OK. This gives you the calculated ratio of the areas.

4. Deselect all on the screen. With the mouse grab different parts of the figure and watch what happens.

5. Answer the following questions:

   a. What happens when you move the bottom line?

   b. What happens to the ratios of the areas when you move Point *A, B,* or *C*?

   c. What happens when you move Point D?

   d. What conjecture can you make about the relative areas of the triangle and the parallelogram?

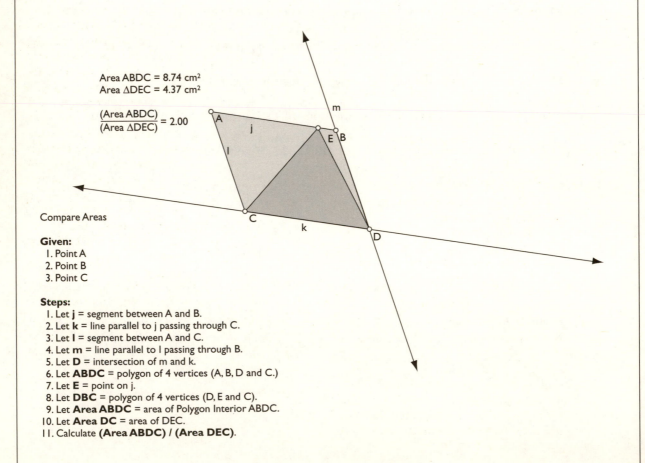

Area ABDC = 8.74 cm²
Area △DEC = 4.37 cm²

$$\frac{(\text{Area } ABDC)}{(\text{Area } \triangle DEC)} = 2.00$$

Compare Areas

Given:
  1. Point A
  2. Point B
  3. Point C

Steps:
  1. Let **j** = segment between A and B.
  2. Let **k** = line parallel to j passing through C.
  3. Let **l** = segment between A and C.
  4. Let **m** = line parallel to l passing through B.
  5. Let **D** = intersection of m and k.
  6. Let **ABDC** = polygon of 4 vertices (A, B, D and C.)
  7. Let **E** = point on j.
  8. Let **DBC** = polygon of 4 vertices (D, E and C).
  9. Let **Area ABDC** = area of Polygon Interior ABDC.
  10. Let **Area DC** = area of DEC.
  11. Calculate **(Area ABDC) / (Area DEC)**.

From the Editor's Desk:

Using the "What If" Machine

by Janet Trentacosta

Recently I attended a conference and was fortunate enough to attend a session presided by Dorothy Strong, Mathematics Supervisor for Chicago Public Schools. During the session on implementing the NCTM *Curriculum and Evaluation Standards,* a question regarding the use of calculators in classrooms surfaced. As part of her response, Dorothy made the statement: "Maybe we should stop calling these instruments 'calculators' and start calling them 'what if' machines."

I couldn't help thinking about what she said and the implications this new name would have for our classrooms. Instead of simply using these machines to find the answers to computation problems, we would be making full use of this technology to develop mathematically powerful students at every grade level. As the 1992 California *Mathematics Framework* states (p. 57): "Technology, properly used, opens mathematical vistas not previously available. For instance, in mathematics programs that are empowering, students can use microworlds to construct and test strategies ... Empowering programs make full use of technology without diluting in any way a student's responsibility for thinking and reasoning."

Often times we only think about computers as providing unlimited opportunities to explore and test conjectures. However, calculators are definitely less expensive and much more accessible to all students. Even graphing calculators have come within the price range of most schools and provide many of the functions that were once reserved for expensive computers.

But the true power of these "what if" machines comes in exploring and trying to explain what is happening. For example, primary students might be asked what would happen if they started with a number such as 6 and then added 2 to it, then added 2 to that answer, and continued to add 2 to each answer from then on. They could be asked to describe any patterns they found. Another what if question could then be: What if the first number were a different number, such as 7?

Upper elementary students can be introduced to negative numbers through such activities as: What happens if we start counting backwards from 15. What is the smallest number we can get? By using the "what if" machine and repeated subtraction ($15 - 1 = = = \ldots$), students find out that there are numbers less than 0. They can then try to explain what these numbers are.

Middle school students can use the "what if" machine to explore properties of exponents and can also explore patterns in digits when given numbers are raised to various powers. They can explore what happens to the mean and median of a set of numbers if, for example, each number is doubled or if a constant is added to each number in the set. The possibilities for exploration are endless and are limited only by the imagination of the students.

High school students now have a whole new world open to them with the availability of graphing calculators, oops, I mean graphing "what if" machines. Instead of spending endless class periods plotting points and trying to draw graphs, they can now use their "what if" machine, input an equation, graph it, and then ask: What if I change a number here or a sign there? What will the new graph look like and how does it compare with the previous graph?

I totally agree with Dorothy Strong's idea that we look upon these calculating machines as something much more powerful. They are truly machines that allow us to make conjectures, explore patterns and relationships, and test hypotheses. If all of us tried to use our "what if" machines in these ways, we would certainly be doing our part to providing a mathematically powerful program for all of our students.

Thank you, Dorothy, for your wonderful insight!

For those of you who wish to submit articles or activities for publication in the *ComMuniCator,* there is information given inside the back cover. However, there is now another way people can reach me.

My office has now come into the technological age and can be accessed through Internet. If you wish to contact me through the Internet network, my address is: jtrentac @ ec.sdcs.k12.ca.us. I hope some of you will take advantage of this opportunity to contact me and share ideas and information.

Source: Trentacosta, J. (1993). Using the what-if machine. *CMC ComMuniCator,* California Mathematics Council, *18*(2), 2. Reprinted with permission.

CALCULATORS

Calculators are useful for checking calculations, avoiding laborious and time-consuming calculations, matching estimations, and other quick pencil methods. Here, however, we will focus on calculators as "what if" machines that use technology to open vistas that cannot be approached by previously available methods. Calculators, or handheld computers, can empower students to use microworlds to construct and test hypotheses. The following article, "Using the 'What If' Machine," was written by the editor of the California Mathematics Council journal (Trentacosta, 1993). Like any good idea in education, the idea has caught on and traveled. Activity 3.8 illustrates how even an unsophisticated calculator can be used as a "what if" machine.

Go to Web Destinations for Chapter 3 at
http://www.prenhall.com/huetinck
to find links to several prominent software sources.

FOR TEACHERS

Activity 3.8 The Terminators

Mathematical Content:
Fractions, terminating and repeating decimals, fractions (PSSM Number and Operation Standard for
  Grades 6–8 and 9–12)

Materials:
Four-function calculator and activity page

Directions: This is an example of using a calculator as a "what if" machine. What happens if fractions are changed to decimals and the resulting patterns are explored? The following activity is enhanced by the calculator because students can focus on number theory and not on tedious manual long division.

Activity 3.8
The Terminators

Directions: Fractions to explore:

1/2   1/3   3/4   5/6   3/8   5/8   1/7   5/7   1/10   3/25   1/11   9/16   8/15   1/9   7/9   5/12   3/20   6/7

With a calculator, find the decimal equivalent for each of the given fractions. Write the repeating decimals in the left column of the Recording Chart and the Terminating Decimals in the right column.

RECORDING CHART

Repeating Decimals	Terminating Decimals
ex. 5/6 = .833	ex: 1/2 = .5

Check with your partner for agreement on column placement.

1. What do you notice about the fractions in the left column?

   What do you notice about the fractions in the right column?

2. How are the fractions in the left column different from those in the right column?

3. Write the prime factorization of the denominators and note the conjecture you find.

4. Test your conjecture with different fractions.

5. Compare your conjecture with another pair of students. Discuss your findings.

6. Present your findings to the class.

CLASSROOM CHANGES WITH TECHNOLOGY

A number of research studies note changes in the traditional roles of teacher and students in technologically rich classrooms. The *Standards* recommend a change in teacher role to that of a "guide on the side" rather than "the sage on the stage." Fraser, et al. (1991) liken the microcomputer to a teaching assistant—a personality with an independent presence in the classroom. From the teacher's perspective, this teaching assistant must display flexibility to fit with the teacher's style and intentions. From the student's perspective, the microcomputer is regarded not as another teacher but as a microworld with an unknown system to explore. The microcomputer can assume some tasks that generally were carried out by the teacher, permitting the teacher to shift naturally from the traditional role to an advisory role. For example, the computer assumed the roles as task setter and management at certain times so these functions did not always rest on the teacher. This can free the teacher to spend more time in developing higher-level learning activities. Dunham (1991) found that students exhibited a wider variety of roles when using graphing calculators. They were less passive, worked in groups more, and consulted the technology for problem solving. The teachers were managers as well as consultants and spent less time explaining and functioning as task masters.

An extensive meta-analysis of 79 research reports assessing the effects of calculators found all grade- and ability-level students possessed a better attitude toward mathematics when using calculators and better self-concepts than students not using calculators (Hembree & Dessart, 1986). Achievement was related to demonstrations of skills, including acquisition, retention, and transfer. The paper-and-pencil skills of the students were equal to those of control groups. The same was true of medium-ability students, except for grade 4. Some conclusions of the study are as follows: calculators can be especially important in improving the average students' basic paper-and-pencil skills and problem-solving ability, the use of calculators in assessment produces much higher achievement, and improved problem- solving performance is related to improved computation and process selection. They recommend that students use calculators in all grades K–12 and that students in grades 5 and above should use calculators during all problem-solving activities, including testing.

An interesting study conducted by an experienced group of teachers investigated the attitudes of students toward graphing calculators in a variety of classrooms of differing levels in three high schools. All of these teachers had participated in a project emphasizing computer visualization and had used graphing calculators in the classroom on a nearly daily basis. They found that the less experienced mathematics students appreciated the calculator more than the students in higher-level mathematics classes. Specifically, they found that the beginning algebra students believed the calculators assisted their learning of mathematics concepts, but the calculus students did not generally agree with this idea.

Bert K. Waits and Franklin Demanna have been pioneers in the use of technology in mathematics education and are the founders of the Calculator Project, which has involved thousands of teachers in in-service programs with graphing calculators. The following paragraph is from a preprint of their 1994 article, "What Have We Learned in Ten Years?":

> The fact is that we know the mathematics curriculum today must change because of technology. Mathematics is alive and changing and technology is part of that change. Appropriate use of technology promotes better mathematics teaching and learning. Our friend, Tom Romberg (Professor of Mathematics Education at the University of Wisconsin and a leader of the *Standards* working groups), says we are teaching 13th-century arithmetic, 18th-century analysis, and B.C. geometry in our schools today. He is correct! We *must* start teaching modern, applicable mathematics. We *must* use technology to help students *do* mathematics.

Set 3.3   Discussion Questions

Questions with an asterisk appear in the Message Board section of the Companion Website at *http://www.prenhall.com/huetinck.* Go to Chapter 3 and click on the Message Board to find and respond to the question.

1. How would you plan to use GSP with students: switch after beginning with traditional construction tools; at the same time as using traditional tools: or only after completing/mastering constructions with traditional tools?

2. Our goal is to have students involved in their learning due to intrinsic motivation. To what extent can calculators and/or manipulatives be intrinsically motivating?

*3. Are the arithmetic, algebra, and geometry we teach today outmoded by the topics now accessible through technology, or have we simply acquired new methods of teaching the traditional concepts? Defend your position.

4. Which curricular or conceptual areas do you expect will change in the future due to easy access to technology? Which will not change?

Summary

Manipulatives, calculators, and computers extends the teachers' abilities to reach all students by varying the pace, giving necessary reinforcement, and providing a variety of ways for students with different learning abilities and styles to access mathematical knowledge. "Perhaps the most exciting potential of technology is its effect on increasing the amount of time that can be devoted to developing conceptual understandings and reasoning processes that lie at the heart of mathematical problem solving. Spreadsheets permit students to explore situations without excessive algebraic manipulation. Calculators and computers remove the onerous and time-consuming manipulative aspects of an investigation. Graphing utilities and instructional software like the Geometric Supposer or Geometer's Sketchpad enable students to visualize relationships readily and to test ideas quickly." (NCTM. 1996, p.9).

Chapter 3 builds on the main concepts in Chapters 1 and 2, forming a bridge to Chapter 4. Chapter 2 discussed our expanding knowledge of how students learn. This knowledge and acknowledgment of how society has changed stimulated the move to the *Standards*-based classrooms discussed in Chapter 1. Chapter 4 features innovative *Standards*-based curricula that incorporate the methodology and tools of the previous chapters. By weaving these elements together, we have developed increasingly exciting ways to teach and learn mathematics.

ASSIGNMENTS

1. What would be an effective way for you to approach an irate parent who opposes the use of calculators in your classroom? Outline the points you would make with specific mathematical examples of ways a calculator can enhance conceptual understanding.

2. Peruse a catalog or browse a store specializing in teaching supplies to become aware of the instructional resources available for use in your classroom.

3. Consider a topic in geometry and plan how you would teach it with access to Geometer's Sketchpad and with differing computer facilities: one computer only; one computer and one display device; and a computer lab with enough computers for each student.

INSTRUCTIONAL RESOURCES

Resources abound for manipulative, computer software, and calculator use. We chose these references either because they complement the examples given in this text or are especially imaginative.

Arithmetic Teacher (1986, February).
The entire issue is devoted to manipulatives with good classroom suggestions for the teacher, discussions of research, and illumination of curricular issues.

Bloomer, A. M., & Carlson, P. A. T. (1993). *Activity math, using manipulatives in the classroom*. Menlo Park, CA: Addison-Wesley.
Eighty-three lessons with anticipatory sets and up to 7 procedures per lesson provide classroom-ready instruction using a wide variety of manipulatives. The material is aimed at middle school and remedial high school classes. In addition the lessons are related to the *Standards* and a scope and sequence are provided. A very useful appendix includes reproducible pages for teacher-made manipulatives.

Bradley, E. H. (1997). Is algebra in the cards? *Mathematics Teaching in the Middle School, 2(6),* 398–403.
Playing cards is a fun manipulative addition to algebra. This well-written article includes an algebra trick, assists to motivating students, examples of eighth-grade student work, and suggestions for further study through a rich activity.

Brown, A. R. (1999). Geometry's giant leap. *Mathematics Teacher, 92(9),* 816–819.

> This teacher reports on the success of his students' geometry projects using the dynamic geometry software of the TI-92 calculator. The discussion includes a list of project titles and a discussion of the impact the dynamic geometry software had on the geometry curriculum.

Dwyer, M., and Pfiefer, R. E. (1999). Exploring hyperbolic geometry with the Geometer's Sketchpad. *Mathematics Teacher, 92(7),* 632–637.

> The authors present constructions in hyperbolic geometry as "an intriguing introduction to the Pointcare model of hyperbolic geometry." Step-by-step instructions are provided, as well as reference to the Swarthmore website and Geometer's Sketchpad script tools used in the constructions.

Dyke, F. V. (1995). A concrete approach to mathematical induction. *Mathematics Teacher, 88(4),* 302–306, 314–318.

> This well-detailed set of activities uses graph paper and interlocking cubes to construct models to teach the difficult topic of mathematical induction. It is aimed at geometry students in grade 10 through grade 12.

Geometer's Sketchpad [Computer software]. Berkeley, CA: Key Curriculum Press.

> Student versions are available as well as teacher and/or school site copies. The notebook that comes with the software has excellent teaching ideas for applying this user-friendly software.

Hoffer, A. (1981). Geometry is more than proof. *Mathematics Teacher, 74(1),* 11–18.

> The van Hiele levels are succinctly described. This article gives a reasonable argument for teaching geometry as more than proof, with reference to research and experience.

Kinach, B. (1993). Solving linear equations physically. In C. R. Hirsch & R. A. Laing (Eds.), *Activities for Active Learning and Teaching—Selections from the "Mathematics Teacher."* Reston, VA: National Council of Teachers of Mathematics.

> The activities provide opportunities for students to solve linear equations by physical and pictorial models. Only common supplies of scissors, tagboard, and cardboard are required (published September 1985 in MT).

Laycock, M., & Schadler, R. A. (1973). *Algebra in the Concrete.* Hayward, CA: Activity Resources Co., Inc.

> Multibase blocks and a variety of manipulatives are combined with many pictures to illustrate solving problems in sequences, building algebraic expressions, factoring trinomials, and solving linear equations and simultaneous equations.

Lipp, A. (2000). Cubic polynomials. *Mathematics Teacher, 93(9),* 788–792.

> This interesting topic for able high school students is approached through graphing calculators and software capable of drawing 3D perspectives.

Lutkin, D. (1996). The incredible three-by-five card! *Mathematics Teacher, 89(2),* 96–98.

> The author explores "much mathematics embedded in this well-known card." Activities include partitioning, labeling, measuring, cutting, and positioning to find angular and triangular relationships and derivation of the Pythagorean Theorem.

National Council of Teachers of Mathematics. (1996). *A core curriculum, addenda series, grades 9–12.* Weston, VA: NCTM.

Schultz, J. E. and Waters, M. S. (2000). Why representations? *Mathematics Teacher, 93(6),* 448–453.

> This fine article discusses manipulative, graphing calculators, and computer use in terms of the Representation Standard of NCTM's *Principles and Standards for School Mathematics (2001).*

Thompson, A. D. and Sproule, S. L. (2000). Deciding when to use calculators. *Mathematics Teaching in the Middle School 6(2),* 126–129.

> The authors present a framework for a rationale to assist you in deciding when and how to use calculators in the classroom.

Turik, D., and Blum, D. (1993). Ladders and saws. *Mathematics Teacher, 86(6),* 510–513.

> With the simple manipulative of a triangle cut of stiff paper, students draw a pattern of ladders and saws to illustrate many relationships between angles and lines. The exercise has been around for years, and this is a particularly good write-up of the activity. Students can keep the figure they draw and refer to it many different times in the geometry curriculum, so the activity has a "long life."

Various authors. Technology Tips. *Mathematics Teacher.*

> Many issues of the journal have excellent short articles with hints of how to effectively use technology in teaching certain concepts.

Ventura Educational Systems, P.O. BOX 425. Grover Beach, CA 93483, (800) 473–7383.

> A number of pieces of software assist students in visualizing foundational concepts in algebra, geometry, and statistics through the manipulative approach in a computer microworld.

Walter, M. I. (1995, fifth printing). *Boxes, squares, and other things: A teacher's guide for a unit in informal geometry*. Reston, VA: National Council of Teachers of Mathematics.

   Well-paced, logically ordered, and interesting informal geometry activities with constructivist

teacher scripts, problems, and extensions are aimed at middle-school students, but would be beneficial in many higher-level classes. The mathematics involved in this unit are congruence, symmetry, geometric transformations, and groups.

ADDITIONAL ACTIVITIES

Activity 3.9	Beginning Algebra Parametrics on the Graphing Calculator
Activity 3.10	Similarities and Differences in Properties of Different Families of Functions
Activities 3.11 and 3.12	Exploring Exponential Functions with Paper Folding, and The Ozone Layer
Activity 3.13	The Pythagorean Theorem with Geometer's Sketchpad

These activities use a variety of calculators or handheld computers to explore foundational concepts in algebra and geometry.

FOR TEACHERS

Activity 3.9 Beginning Algebra Parametrics on the Graphing Calculator

Mathematical Content:
Slope and transformations of a figure and of a line (PSSM Algebra Standard for Grades 9–12)

Materials Needed:
Graphing calculator

Directions: Parametric equations on the graphing calculator automatically separate the *X*-coordinates from the *Y*-coordinates so students can more easily understand how changes in either coordinate affects a figure. Also, parametric equations allow a segment to be produced instead of a line, which has some visual advantages.

FOR STUDENTS

Activity 3.9
Beginning Algebra Parametrics on the Graphing Calculator
(page 1 of 2)

Directions: Parametrics emphasize the independence of the X- and Y-coordinates and allow a segment to be graphed instead of a complete line. Thus the graphing calculator illustrates the effects of transformations. When working in parametric mode the equations for X and Y are expressed in terms of a third variable, T. The calculator window is set for the values of T to be substituted into the X and Y equations as well as the range and domain.

PARAMETRIC EQUATIONS OF LINES AND SLOPE

Given Points A and B, let one "step" be the respective moves in each of the x and y directions to get from Point A to Point B. That is, x-step $= X_B - X_A$ and y step $= Y_B - Y_A$. Then the parametric equations of line segment AB are:

$$X_{TI} = X_A + T^* (x \text{ step})$$

and

$$Y_{TI} = Y_A + T^* (y \text{ step})$$

1. Enter the equations $X_{TI} = 0 + T^*(2)$ and $Y_{TI} = 0 + T^*3$ with window: $T_{min} = 0$, $T_{max} = 1$, $T_{step} = 1$; $X_{min} = -1$, $X_{max} = 10$, $X_{scl} = 1$; $Y_{min} = -1$, $Y_{max} = 10$, $Y_{scl} = 1$ [hereafter abbreviated as $T(0, 1, 1)$; $X(-1, 10, 1)$; $Y(-1, 10, 1)$]

Before pressing the graph key, sketch your expectation of the graph.

   a. Does the graph meet your expectation? Why or why not?

   b. What is the slope of this line? How is the slope related to the equations for X and Y?

   c. Experiment with different equations for X and Y by changing the number multiplying T.

Record your explorations including a sketch and the equations used. If you must change the window for X and Y, also record the window settings for each different line. What happens to the line segment when you change the number multiplying T? Explain.

   d. For the original equation set T_{max} 5 = 2. What happens to the line segment?

   e. Is this what you expected? Explain why or why not.

TRANSFORMATIONS

2. Change the initial number in the X equation to another value.

Before pressing the graph key, sketch your expectation of the graph.

   a. What does this do to the graph?

   b. What do you expect to happen when you change the initial number in the Y equation? Explain.

   c. Experiment with different initial numbers for X and Y. Record your explorations, including a sketch and the equations used. If you must change the window for X and Y, also record the window settings for each different line. What happens to the line segment when you change the initial number? Explain.

FOR STUDENTS

Activity 3.9
Beginning Algebra Parametrics on the Graphing Calculator (page 2 of 2)

3. We will now enter two different line segments to compare them. You must enter $X_{2T} = 2X_{1T}$. To do this, press the $Y=$ key and arrow down to the X_{2T} line, enter a 2 and then press the key Y-VARS, move to Parametric (2), select X_{1T} by pressing ENTER. [Now you get $X_{2T} = 2X_{1T}$]

   Still in the $Y=$ window, arrow down to Y_{2T}, press Y-VARS, select Parametric (2), arrow down to Y_{1T} (2), press ENTER. [Now you have $Y_{2T} = Y_{1T}$]

Before pressing the graph key, sketch your expectation of the graphs.

  a. Was the graph what you expected? Why or why not?

  b. Change the initial value of the X equation to change the graphs. Record your observations by sketching the graphs and writing the associated equations. How does changing this number affect the graph?

  c. Change the number multiplying T. How does this change the graphs?

Piece Wise Functions:

4. Enter the following:
   $X_{1T} = -2 + T$
   $Y_{1T} = 2 - 4T$
   $X_{2T} = -1 + T$
   $Y_{2T} = -2 + T$
   $X_{3T} = 0 + T$
   $Y_{3T} = -1 - T$
   $X_{4T} = 1 + T$
   $Y_{4T} = -2 + 4T$
   with window: $T(0, 1, 1)$; $X(-5, 5, 1)$; $Y(-5, 5, 1)$

Before pressing the graph key, sketch your expectation of the graphs.

  a. Explain the resulting graph.

  b. Experiment with changing the figure.

Extension

5. Enter the following:
   $X_{1T} = -1 - T$
   $Y_{1T} = -2 + 4T^2$
   $X_{2T} = -1 + T$
   $Y_{2T} = -2 + T^2$
   $X_{3T} = 1 - T$
   $Y_{3T} = -2 + T^2$
   $X_{4T} = 1 + T$
   $Y_{4T} = -2 + 4T^2$

   with window: T (0, 1, .1; note decimal); $X(-3, 3, 1)$; $Y(-3, 3, 1)$

Explain the graph.

Source: Adapted from a presentation by Jane Wortman, California Mathematics Council, South Conference, Palm Springs, California, November 1997.

F O R   T E A C H E R S

Activity 3.10 Similarities and Differences in Properties of Different Families of Functions

Mathematical Content:
Functions (PSSM Algebra Standard for Grades 9–12)

Materials Needed:
Graphing calculator

Directions: This is an excellent exercise for students to explore different functions before beginning to study functions, or it can work equally well to assist students to make connections between the different functions they have studied previously.

F O R   S T U D E N T S

Activity 3.10
Similarities and Differences in Properties of Different Families of Functions (page 1 of 2)

Directions: Use the following set of test functions to compare and contrast properties of linear, exponential, quadratic, higher-degree-polynomial, and rational functions. Make notes about the tables and graphs related to your test functions. Record your observations in the chart below. Enlist computing aid as needed when constructing tables of values and function graphs.

Linear	Exponential	Quadratic	Higher-Degree Polynomial	Rational
$f(x) = 2x + 3$	$g(x) = 3^x$	$h(x) = x^2 + 10x + 4$	$k(x) = 0.5x^3 - 6x$	$m(x) = 8/x$
$f(x) = -2x + 3$	$g(x) = (0.3)^x$	$h(x) = -x^2 + 10x + 4$	$k(x) = -0.5x^3 + 6x$	$m(x) = 8/x^2$

FOR STUDENTS

Activity 3.10
Similarities and Differences in Properties of Different Families of Functions (page 2 of 2)

SUMMARY OF OBSERVATIONS

Function Form	Rate of Change[a]	Symmetry Feature[b]	No. of Max/ Min Values[c]	Special Features[d]
$f(x) = mx + b$				
$f(x) = a^x$ (exponential)				
$f(x) = ax^2 + bx + c$ (quadratic)				
$f(x) = ax^3 + bx^2 + cx + d$ (cubic)				
$f(x) = ax^4 + bx^3 + cx^2 + dx + e$ (quartic)				
$f(x) = \frac{a}{x}$				
$f(x) = \frac{a}{x^2}$				
$f(x) = \frac{a}{x^3}$				
$f(x) = \frac{a}{x^4}$				

[a] Variable (increasing or decreasing) or constant

[b] Symmetry about the vertical axis, about the origin, or about a vertical line that is not the vertical axis

[c] None, one, two, and so on

[d] Mention features that make this family different from any others in the table.

Source: *Algebra in a Technological World, Addenda Series, Grades 9–12*, pp. 80–81. National Council of Teachers of Mathematics (1996), Reston, VA. Reprinted with permission.

FOR TEACHERS

Activities 3.11 and 3.12   Exploring Exponential Functions with Paper Folding and the Ozone Layer

Mathematical Content:
Exponential relationships (PSSM Algebra Standard for Grades 6–8 and 9–12)

Materials Needed:
Graphing calculator

Directions: This is an example of using a very simple manipulative—folded paper. The first activity of folding paper leads into the application problem of the ozone layer. The second activity follows with more exploration of exponential relationships.

FOR STUDENTS

Activity 3.11
Exploring Exponential Functions: Paper Folding

Directions: Take a single sheet of paper. When you fold it in half, you have two sections of paper. If you fold the sheet in half again, you will have four sections, and so on. The diagram below illustrates the process.

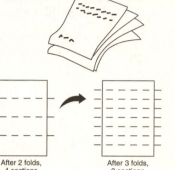

| After 0 folds, 1 section | After 1 fold, 2 sections | After 2 folds, 4 sections | After 3 folds, 8 sections |

1. Complete the table below, which gives the number of sections $S(n)$ as a function of the number of folds n.

Number of folds (n)	0	1	2	3	4	5	6
Number of sections S(n)	1	2	4	8			

By observing the table, and thinking about the action of continually folding a sheet of paper in half, we can work out a rule for $S(n)$ in terms of n.

Number of sections after 0 folds $= S(0) = 1$

Number of sections after 1 fold $= S(1) = S(0) \times 2 = 1 \times 2 = 1 \times 2^1$

Number of sections after 2 folds $=$ ___ $=$ _____ $=$ ___ $=$ _____

Number of sections after 3 folds $=$ ___ $=$ _____ $=$ ___ $=$ _____

$\vdots$

Number of sections after n folds $=$ ___ $=$ _____ $=$ ___ $= 1 \times 2^n = 2^n$

The function rule $S(n) = 2^n$ is an example of an exponential function. The independent variable n is the power or exponent and the constant 2 is the base. In general, exponential functions have the independent variable in the exponent.

Note: If we substitute $n = 0$ into the rule $S(n) = 2^n$, the rule gives $S(0) = 2^0$. Since we know that $S(0) = 1$, this means that $2^0 = 1$. In general, if a is not equal to zero, we get $a^0 = 1$.

Using your graphing utility, enter and plot the graph of the function $S(n)$. You may need to experiment with the viewing window to get a good picture.

2. **a.** From the graph, how many sections would there be after you had made 10 folds?
   b. Check your answer with your calculator.

3. **a.** From the graph, how many folds will give 8192 sections?
   b. Check your answer with the calculator.

4. Find $S(3.2)$.
   Explain why substituting 3.2 in the rule for $S(n)$ does not make sense.

Source: *Graphic Algebra, Explorations with a Graphing Calculator,* Key Curriculum Press, 1150 65th Street, Emeryville, CA 94608, 1-800-995-MATH. Reprinted with permission.

FOR STUDENTS

Activity 3.12
Exploring Exponential Functions: The Ozone Layer (page 1 of 2)

Directions: Read the following information about the earth's ozone layer. Then solve the problems about changes in the ozone layer.

In 1995, the ozone layer was approximately 50 kilometers deep. According to some scientific reports, 1% of the ozone layer is being destroyed each year. This means that in each year the depth is 99% of what it was the previous year.

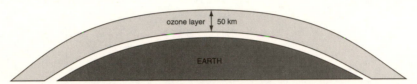

1. Complete the following information relating to the thickness of the ozone layer.

   Let t be the number of years that have elapsed since 1995 and $W(t)$ be the width of the ozone layer.

   Ozone thickness after 0 years = $W(0) = 50$

   Ozone thickness after 1 year = $W(1) = 50 \times 0.99$ = $50\,(0.99)^1$ km

   Ozone thickness after 2 years = $W(2) =$ _____ = _____ km

   Ozone thickness after 3 years = ____ = _____ = _____ km

   $\vdots$ $\vdots$ $\vdots$ $\vdots$

   Ozone thickness after t years = $W(t)$ = _____ = _____ km

Note: Again this function is an exponential function with t as the exponent and the constant 0.99 is the base. Unlike the example on paper folding, the exponent t can take any positive value (not just a whole number value).

Using your graphing utility, enter and plot the graph of the function $W(t)$. You may need to experiment with the viewing window to get a good picture. Use the graph to help you answer the following questions.

2. **a.** Estimate the thickness of the ozone layer at the start of July 1997, when $t = 2\frac{1}{2}$ years.

   b. Check your answer with your calculator.

3. **a.** During which year will the ozone layer be half of its 1995 thickness?

   b. During which year will the ozone layer be a quarter of its 1995 thickness?

   c. During which year will the ozone layer be an eighth of its 1995 thickness?

   d. Write a simple statement about the time taken for half of the remaining thickness to disappear.

4. If the thickness of the ozone layer drops to 100 meters, it will have effectively disappeared. Predict when the ozone layer will have effectively disappeared.

FOR STUDENTS

Activity 3.12
Exploring Exponential Functions: The Ozone Layer (page 2 of 2)

5. Complete the table below.

Number of years since 1995 (t)	0	10	20	30
Thickness of ozone layer (W(t)) in km	50			

Note: If your graphing utility can create a table of values, you could use this feature here. Use the values in this table to help you answer question 6.

6. a. To find the percentage decrease in the thickness of the ozone layer in the first 10-year period, complete the following statement.

$$\% \text{ change} = \frac{\text{new thickness} - \text{previous thickness}}{\text{previous thickness}} \times 100\%$$

$$= \frac{W(10) - W(0)}{W(0)} \times 100\%$$

$$= \underline{\hspace{2cm}} \%$$

So there is a percentage decrease of _____%.

b. To find the percentage decrease in the width of the ozone layer over the second 10-year period, complete the following statement.

$$\% \text{ change} = \frac{\text{new thickness} - \text{previous thickness}}{\text{previous thickness}} \times 100\%$$

$$= \frac{W(20) - W(10)}{W(10)} \times 100\%$$

$$= \underline{\hspace{2cm}} \%$$

So there is a percentage decrease of _____%.

c. To find the percentage decrease in the width of the ozone layer in the third 10-year period, complete the following statement.

$$\% \text{ change} = \frac{\text{new thickness} - \text{previous thickness}}{\text{previous thickness}} \times 100\%$$

$$= \frac{W(30) - W(20)}{W(20)} \times 100\%$$

$$= \underline{\hspace{2cm}} \%$$

So there is a percentage decrease of _____ %.

d. Write a simple statement relating the percentage decrease in the thickness of the ozone layer to the number of 10-year periods that have elapsed.

7. If the ozone layer loses 1% each year, why does it lose less than 10% in 10 years?

Source: *Graphic Algebra, Explorations with a Graphing Calculator,* Key Curriculum Press, 1150 65th Street, Emeryville, CA 94608, 1-800-995-MATH. Reprinted with permission.

FOR TEACHERS

Activity 3.13 The Pythagorean Theorem with Geometer's Sketchpad

Mathematical Content:
Pythagorean theorem (PSSM Geometry Standard for Grades 6–8 and 9–12)

Materials Needed:
Geometer's Sketchpad software

Directions: Students make a script for a right triangle. They then make another script for a square on one side. This script is used to draw a square on all sides. The same procedure is then used for a hexagon. More advanced students may extend the exercise to make any figure on one side of the right triangle and then rotate it and dialate it to the other two sides. Then have students "grab" one point on the triangle to move the figure for different right triangles. This exploration exploits the dynamic properties of GSP. They will be surprised that any shape correctly scaled on the three sides will follow the Pythagorean theorem (generally stated only in terms of squares).

FOR STUDENTS

Activity 3.13
The Pythagorean Theorem with Geometer's Sketchpad

Directions:

1. Construct a right triangle, and measure the areas of the rectangles on each side. Then compare the area of the rectangle on the longest side with sum of the areas of the rectangles on the other two sides. What do you find?

2. Move the triangle so that the right angle changes measure. What do you find?

3. Construct other polygons on the three sides of a right triangle. Compare the same areas as in part 1.

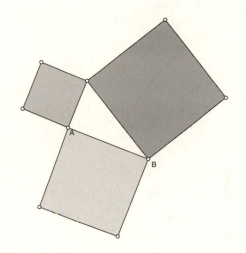

One possible solution:

Area(Polygon 1) = 1.54 square inches

Area(Polygon 2) = 0.21 square inches

Area(Polygon 3) = 1.33 square inches

Area(Polygon 2) + Area(Polygon 3) = 1.54 square inches

Area(Polygon 4) = 4.01 square inches

Area(Polygon 6) = 0.55 square inches

Area(Polygon 5) = 3.45 square inches

Area(Polygon 5) + Area(Polygon 6) = 4.01 square inches

Area(Polygon 7) = 0.67 square inches

Area(Polygon 8) = 0.09 square inches

Area(Polygon 9) = 0.58 square inches

Area(Polygon 8) + Area(Polygon 9) = 0.67 square inches

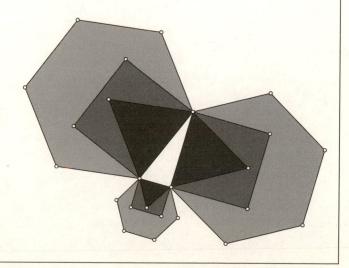

Source: *Pythagoras Plugged In,* Key Curriculum Press, 1150 65th Street, Emeryville, CA 94608, 1-800-995-MATH. Reprinted with permission.

CHAPTER

4

Standards-Based Curricula
With Sample Lessons

T his chapter focuses on new developments in secondary mathematics curricula. Many of these programs began as curriculum development projects funded by the National Science Foundation (NSF) to provide exemplars of *Standards*-based materials for use in middle school and high school. Some of these projects received funding at the state level through the federal Eisenhower Program for improving mathematics and science education. Some programs were originally developed by commercial publishers, and most of the NSF projects are now available through commercial sources after the initial development, piloting, and revision occurred under NSF auspices. The one exception is the College Preparatory Mathematics program, which is operated by a nonprofit organization. Additional *Standards*-driven curricula beyond those described in the body of this chapter are listed in the Additional Annotated Model Curricula at the end of the chapter. All of these *Standards*-based curricula are intended to be appropriate for all students. As such, they include a variety of types of teaching strategies, lesson presentations, and activities intended to meet the needs of students in heterogeneous classrooms.

ABOUT THE INSTRUCTIONAL SEQUENCES FOR THIS CHAPTER

Examples of "Instructional Sequences" taken directly from or based on *Standards*,-based programs are provided so that you can compare what is asked of students in these programs with what is asked of students in traditional curricula. In this chapter the term *Instructional Sequence* is used to distinguish the classroom experiences contained in the *Standards*-based programs from the typical "lesson-a-day" format of most traditional American textbooks. These instructional sequences include activities as components of broader instructional objectives such as conceptual understanding and ability to apply the mathematical skills and concepts within mathematical and real-world contexts. Other aspects of exemplary curricula, such as the use of Problems of the Week and group projects, will be dealt with in later chapters. All of the *Standards*-based curricula of this chapter incorporate teaching suggestions intended to provide access to the content for students with a broad range of learning styles and previous mathematical experiences.

Data Analysis

The instructional sequences illustrate the content thread of data analysis as it is presented in samples of exemplary secondary mathematics curricula based on the *Principles and Standards for School Mathematics*. Data analysis represents an approach to mathematics content that naturally incorporates technology and requires students to reason and communicate what they can infer about data and what considerations need to be made, given the context of the situation generating the data. The designation "instructional sequence" indicates that the design of these materials goes beyond a set of activities. Rather, the sequence of activities and questions has been honed to bring about deeper understanding of the underlying mathematics.

Instructional Sequences 4.1–4.4 are based on actual pages of *Standards*-based curricula. We start with two middle-school sequences that explore linear relationships with and without graphing calculators. We then move to the high-school curriculum, showing the growth in complexity of the mathematics students learn as they use *Standards*-based materials at that level. The fourth sequence deals with nonlinear data. The remaining activities use probeware-generated data or tables of previously collected information as bases for analysis. Functions representing the data include sinusoidal curves, inverse functions, and exponential functions.

STANDARDS-BASED CURRICULA IN SECONDARY MATHEMATICS

A report that appeared in *The Arithmetic Teacher* in 1987 is generally referred to as the Flanders Report. In studying the content of the seventh- and eighth-grade textbooks commonly in use at that time, Flanders found that close to 70% of the material in these books was rehashed from previous grades, with number and computation topics predominating. In comparison, in the ninth grade, when students encountered algebra for the first time, the material in their text was typically 80% new material. Since algebra was well documented at that time as the "gatekeeper" course for college attendance, rethinking the content of middle-school curriculum was considered both as a way of improving students' success in the high-school college-preparatory classes and as a tool to promote equity. Failure in algebra was disproportionately large in certain ethnic groups in the United States, notably African-Americans, Latinos, and Native Americans. Overall, students in the traditional high-school mathematics sequence (Algebra I, Geometry, Algebra II) had an attrition rate such that only around 5% of students nationally passed the AP calculus exam. Even more significant was the number of students who did not qualify for university admission because of deficiencies in mathematics.

Curriculum Development Background

The NCTM *Curriculum and Evaluation Standards* (1989) document, in its call for a common core curriculum for all secondary students, resulted in the development of curricular materials that maintained a high level of mathematics content and included presentations and teaching strategies to allow greater access to the content by a wide range of students. A number of new curricular programs addressing these criteria are now being taught nationwide. All of these programs strive to deepen the mathematical content by including the major strands of mathematics each year as students progress through the sequence of courses. To deal with inclusion issues, lesson designs include a variety of teaching strategies to involve students more actively in doing and explaining quality mathematics. Alternative assessment approaches also are built into the programs. Common features of these new curricula include:

- involving current classroom teachers in the development and piloting of lessons and units;
- requiring in some cases, and strongly recommending in all cases, teacher training as part of curriculum implementation;
- revisiting key concepts each year of the program and developing them in greater and greater depth (sometimes called *spiraling*);
- connecting different content strands (algebra, geometry, statistics, etc.) each year of the program;
- building in a variety of pedagogical techniques to the presentation of concepts, including hands-on activities and appropriate use of technology;
- emphasizing student involvement through group work, projects, and written and oral presentation;
- using a variety of assessment techniques such as performance tasks, long-term projects, and oral presentations, as well as standard pencil-and-paper tests;
- evaluating academic outcomes with diverse student populations over time, especially with NSF-funded programs.

Before the complete curricular programs were available, exemplary units, sometimes called *replacement units,* were available for teachers to try in their classrooms as a way of seeing how students reacted to them without making a major commitment to change the entire curriculum. At the middle-school level, five such units were published under the auspices of the Middle Grades Mathematics Project (MGMP), a precursor to the Connected Mathematics Project. Middle schools with which we are familiar worked as departments to incorporate these units into their curriculum. They determined which of the units would be used at a specific grade level (sixth, seventh, eighth) so that students would not repeat units in subsequent years with different teachers. At the high-school level, an example of a replacement unit is "Baker's Choice," a unit on linear programming adapted from the Interactive Mathematics Program.

The process of curriculum development and revision is ongoing, and many other programs are beginning to include aspects of the reform to varying degrees. Undoubtedly, other programs will continue to emerge that help students and teachers meet the goals of the *Standards.*

Three national centers are charged with providing services for National Science Foundation–funded curricula, one each for elementary, middle, and high school. The elementary center will not be referenced here. The source for middle-school services, the Show-Me Center, is located at the University of Missouri. Through it, interested groups may obtain information about the following middle-school curriculum projects:

Connected Mathematics Project
Mathematics in Context
MathScape
Middle Grades Math Thematics (STEM)

The COMPASS (Curricular Options in Mathematics for All Secondary Students) at Ithaca College in New York provides services for the following high-school projects:

Contemporary Mathematics in Context (Core-Plus
    Mathematics Project)
Interactive Mathematics Program
MATH Connections
Mathematics: Modeling Our World (ARISE)
SIMMS Integrated Mathematics: A Modeling
    Approach Using Technology

 For information about the Show-Me Center and COMPASS Websites, go to **http://www.prenhall.com/huetinck** and click on Web Destinations for Chapter 4.

The teacher's role in selecting, designing, and implementing curriculum, especially exemplary curriculum, is particularly significant because of the challenge of helping students go beyond remembering a series of steps or skills to recognize the connections among the mathematical topics. Each group of students brings a unique set of needs and competencies to the classroom, and the contemporary materials provide substantial assistance to the teacher who wants to make mathematics more meaningful for the broadest possible range of students by giving teachers alternative activities and strategies.

Data Analysis in Exemplary Programs

Exemplary secondary mathematics curricular programs place greater emphasis on statistics and data analysis than do traditional programs. As expressed in the NCTM booklet *Data Analysis and Statistics* (Burrill et al., 1992), the rationale for including such material is based on the perceived needs of students in an information-intensive future. Statistics has to do with making sense out of data, or seeing numbers associated with a context. Therefore, students must have opportunities to collect and organize data, to represent the data with visual displays and summary statistics, and to analyze the results. Teachers also report greater interest and involvement on the part of their students, particularly those who have not always been successful in traditional, computation-based mathematics, in problems and projects in which real data are collected and analyzed.

In the early 1980s, the American Statistical Association (ASA) and the NCTM worked together on the Quantitative Literacy Project, with additional funding from the National Science Foundation. That collaboration produced a set of supplemental units in statistics and probability to be used in classrooms in middle and high school. As technology with statistical features became available, more curriculum materials for Grades 6 to 12 came to include data analysis topics. Some high schools offered courses in statistics and probability as elective courses for students who had completed the 3-year high-school core sequence. In 1997, the first Advanced Placement (AP) Statistics exam was administered in high schools across the country. Students who pass this exam show that their knowledge of statistics is equivalent to that of students in an introductory college course in the subject. The increased incorporation of statistics in the secondary curriculum provides students with additional avenues for mathematical growth—particularly for students not pursuing mathematics-intensive careers requiring calculus. Social science majors, for example, generally are required to take at least one statistics class as part of their university program. Student awareness of statistics as a university major or as an essential component of related majors, such as actuarial science, increases with the inclusion of more statistics into the high-school curriculum.

Scheaffer (1990) distinguishes between what he calls exploratory data analysis and classical statistics. A data analysis approach, he asserts, is "easy, entertaining, and wide open to creativity; it is the way scientific investigation should begin." Students can collect, organize, and depict data from real-life situations. As their mathematical knowledge grows, they can propose more and more sophisticated mathematical models to describe the data and use the data for prediction. Classical statistics can then be used to confirm the initial findings through the use of assumptions, designs, and analytic tools. Scheaffer goes on to state that most of what a high-school graduate should know about statistics should come from the exploratory data analysis approach.

The study of statistics through exploratory data analysis reinforces other mathematical skills and concepts related to number sense, algebra, and probability. Mathematical modeling often combines function concepts from algebra with data analysis. Starting with bivariate data, the independent variable is identified, when possible. Using the visual representation of the data by a scatter plot, a line of best fit is proposed, either by informal, trial-and-error procedures or by the use of technology to "crunch" the data to make them fit a particular type of function. The analysis part of this type of function modeling has two aspects. One aspect is comparing the data and the actual situation with the mathematical model. Does the model make sense in terms of the context of the situation? If not, what are the discrepancies and their possible causes? Looking at intercepts and interpreting their real-life meaning is an example of this type of analysis. The other aspect of this type of function modeling is more mathematical and requires additional analysis. An examination of the residuals in a given model is one example of a more advanced technique that can be used to verify the probable validity of a model or to identify rationales for proposing different models.

The Instructional Sequences appearing later in this chapter are examples taken from exemplary curricula. They illustrate data analysis activities and approaches typical to the particular curriculum and represent the kind of work students are expected to do in exemplary curricula in general.

MODEL MIDDLE-SCHOOL PROGRAMS

If you can recall your middle-school mathematics experience, it is very likely that the lessons in your textbook were a two-page format. On the first page was a brief introduction, sometimes illustrated with drawings or photographs, and accompanied by several problems and solutions for the skill being taught that day. The second page consisted mainly of exercises mimicking the examples, possibly with a few word problems at the end of the assignment. Problem-solving activities included in those textbooks usually were described as optional within a lesson set, or as extras at the end of a chapter. As a consequence, problem solving was frequently given short shrift, or even ignored in favor of covering additional skills included in the book.

Given this experience, it should be no surprise that American students, when surveyed on national and international assessments, characterize mathematics as nothing more than a set of facts and procedures to memorize. As the textbook analysis included in the Third International Study of Science and Mathematics (TIMSS) showed, U.S. mathematics textbooks contain far more topics to be covered each year than are included in textbooks of other countries studied. Hence, the U.S. mathematics curriculum has been characterized as "a mile wide and an inch deep." Typical U.S. textbooks also repeat topics for many more years than do international counterparts.

General Description of the Programs

The exemplary programs described here are different from those in the TIMSS textbook analysis in that they do not include an extensive review of material covered in previous years. Rather, they present challenging but age-appropriate mathematics in ways that promote student engagement and understanding. These exemplary curricula start by providing coherent 3-year mathematics programs for Grades 6 through 8. They lay a solid foundation for algebra, geometry, and statistics while extending calculation skills and understanding to include rational numbers. The lessons are appropriate for the developmental needs of early adolescence. The strong mathematical backgrounds and positive attitudes about mathematics resulting from participation in these programs encourage students to continue in 3-year college preparatory programs in Grades 9 through 11 and to take advanced mathematics in the senior year of high school. These programs build students' algebraic, geometric, and statistical reasoning abilities, as well as extending number sense to accompany proportional reasoning and proficiency with rational numbers.

Further, middle-school programs based on the NCTM *Standards* take into account the unique needs and interests of young adolescents and help them connect mathematics to their world by including lessons that utilize mathematics in contextual situations that interest adolescents. They challenge students to deeper understanding of mathematics, allow for multiple representations of solutions, and bring in formal procedures only as students show comprehension of the concepts being presented. The end goal goes beyond procedural knowledge, which certainly is important, to the notion of mathematics as relevant and helpful for dealing with the concerns of everyday living as well as for development of logical reasoning.

Representative Programs

This chapter considers three representative programs in greater depth. Other programs are described in the annotated resource list at the end of the chapter.

The Connected Mathematics Project Developed at Michigan State University with funding from the NSF, the Connected Mathematics Project emphasizes

connections among the mathematical strands, between mathematics and other disciplines, between the teaching activities and interests of students, and between the preparation students have received in elementary school and the goals of the high-school core curriculum. It consists of eight units per grade level, each developed around a series of investigations that emphasize a major concept or cluster of concepts. The units use the following instructional design: Launch, Explore, Summarize, Apply/Extend. Thus, students in this program will not only learn the basics of solving equations, they will also understand and be able to apply mathematical concepts involving probability, numbers, statistics, measurement, geometry, and algebra.

Mathematics in Context Developed in Wisconsin and funded by the NSF, Mathematics in Context is a world-recognized and acclaimed curriculum from the Freudenthal Institute in the Netherlands, adapted for use in American schools in Grades 5 through 8. The philosophy of the program's 40 units is to present problem situations of interest to students as contexts from which to develop their mathematical competence and understanding. The four content strands of geometry, numbers, algebra, and statistics are developed throughout the 4 years of the curriculum. Support materials are provided for teachers. As with all of the model middle-school programs, students who successfully complete the Mathematics in Context program will enter the high-school college-preparatory mathematics program.

Seeing and Thinking Mathematically (MathScape) Developed by the Educational Development Center in Newton, Massachusetts, with funding from the NSF, the MathScape curriculum builds upon the central theme of mathematics in the human experience. Its focus is on helping students learn mathematical ways of seeing and thinking about their world. This program reflects the view that learning is a process of constructing one's own knowledge, and it emphasizes the importance of the social context (group work and discourse) of learning for middle-school students. The curriculum uses technology extensively by integrating computer simulations, exploratory environments, and calculators as tools. In addition, the project includes teachers' support, suggestions for student assessment, classroom implementation, and parent involvement.

An Unresolved Dilemma

In spite of the strengths of these curricula, an unresolved dilemma remains. The middle-school programs described here were specifically designed according to the unique developmental needs of students at those grade levels. Each program is based on a curriculum of quality mathematics that students can explore in depth during a coordinated 3-year sequence of learning. But for students to take calculus before graduating from high school, they may need to begin the high-school sequence in the eighth grade. At the time of this writing, each year fewer than 10% of high-school students graduating nationally received a passing score—where 5 is the highest possible—in calculus. Educators, politicians, and community members are pressuring school districts to increase the number of students enrolling in and successfully completing Advanced Placement (AP) Calculus during high school. They want students to begin their college-preparatory sequence in mathematics (Algebra 1 or a *Standards*-based high-school course 1) in the eighth grade.

Teachers of the exemplary middle-school programs report that the units are so rich in content that completion of the entire 3-year sequence will send students to high school well prepared to meet the challenges of a rigorous curriculum, even to the extent that successful students should begin the second year of college-preparatory mathematics in the ninth grade. Should this be the case, the importance of articulation between middle-school and high-school mathematics departments becomes even more critical. Will the receiving high schools provide a mathematics program that builds on the knowledge that students gained in comprehensive *Standards*-based middle-school programs, or will they insist on evidence of specific skill mastery before allowing students to move into the second-year course, usually geometry?

Set 4.1 Discussion Questions

 Questions with an asterisk appear in the Message Board section of the Companion Website at *http://www.prenhall.com/huetinck*. Go to Chapter 4 and click on the Message Board to find and respond to the question.

*1. Discuss the eighth-grade mathematics dilemma, giving the pros and cons of having all students begin college-preparatory mathematics (that is, a course that meets college entrance requirements) at this grade level. In your discussion, consider the educational and social implications of having different curricular choices for eighth-grade students, some college preparatory and some not.

2. Discuss the viability of having the successful completion of a 3-year comprehensive middle-school program qualify students to enter high school at ninth grade prepared to take Geometry or course 2 of a *Standards*-based program.

Another aspect of programs at the middle-school level is the frequent use of a "core" program in which students take mathematics and science from the same teacher during an extended block of time. The use of science contexts in many of the exemplary curricula described here makes it easy to combine them in a coring situation. The collection, depiction, and analysis of "real" data related to science is the most common way of coordinating mathematics and science. The statistics presented in the units we describe allow the middle-school student to carry the analysis to a deeper understanding than is typical at this age level.

Sample Middle-School Instructional Sequences

Mathematics in Context contains one unit each of data and statistics in Grades 5 through 7 and two units in Grade 8. The fifth-grade data unit has students creating and interpreting different standard graphs (bar and line graphs, pie charts, pictograms), describing data in tabular and graphical form, and using data and descriptive statistics as aids to argument. In the sixth-grade unit entitled "Dealing with Data," students are given a data set listing the heights of fathers and the corresponding heights of their adult sons. The goal of the unit is to make sense of the data set through the use of different statistical tools, including scatter plots, stem-and-leaf plots, histograms, and box-and-whisker plots. After depicting the data in these ways, students interpret them and draw inferences about possible relationships between the variables. Students learn how to calculate mean, median, and mode and to connect these measures to graphs of the data. Students also investigate the strengths and weaknesses of each measure of central tendency and type of graph. For example, which measure of central tendency—the mean, median, or mode—is most useful for the given situation? This instructional sequence prepares students for further statistics activities later in the curriculum, specifically in the seventh-grade unit, "Statistics and the Environment," and the eighth-grade units, "Insights Into Data" and "Digging Numbers." In the latter, students apply what they learned in previous grades to archaeological data.

Instructional Sequence 4.1 comes from the unit "Insights Into Data." This curriculum uses the term *section* to designate an instructional sequence. In Section D in this unit, for example, students grow bean sprouts for a week and use the data collected from that activity as the basis for their univariate statistical analyses. (Note the connection here of

FOR TEACHERS

Instructional Sequence 4.1 Egg Dimensions

Mathematical Content:
Describing linear relationships with equations; predicting (extrapolating) from a linear model (PSSM
  Data Analysis and Probability Standard for Grades 6–8, especially scatter plots and line of best fit)

Materials Needed:
Data sets, transparent grids and graph paper, graphing technology that finds line of best fit

Directions: Distribute to students tables that identify length and width of a variety of bird eggs. (See an
encyclopedia for data of this nature.) Request that students examine the mathematical relationship between smaller groups of the data to look for graphical and numeric patterns. The Warblers of Britain table
on the student page summarizes the relevant data for one type of bird. Students make a scatter plot of
the warbler data.

   Students work alone or in pairs. Depending on familiarity with the technology and other aspects of this
lesson, the activity may take one to two class periods.

Source: Reprinted with permission from the *Insights into Data,* student book in the Mathematics in Context program © Encyclopedia
Britannica Educational Corporation.

FOR STUDENTS

Instructional Sequence 4.1
Egg Dimensions (page 1 of 2)

Directions: Use the data about egg size in the Warblers of Britain table to solve the following problems.

Name	Egg Length (mm)	Egg Width (mm)
Black cup	19.6	14.7
Chiff Chaff	15.5	12.0
Firecrest	13.5	10.3
Garden warbler	20.1	14.8
Goldcrest	13.6	10.3
Grasshopper warbler	18.1	13.8
Lesser whitethrust	16.5	12.6
Reed warbler	18.3	13.6
Sedge warbler	17.7	13.1
White throat	18.1	13.8
Wood warbler	16.1	12.6

1. On your graph paper, make a scatter plot of the warbler data, putting egg length on the horizontal
   axis and egg width on the vertical axis. You may need to estimate the location of the point representing each type of egg. Number your axes carefully. Use a scale that allows the data to be spread
   over much of your graph paper.

2. Trace your scatter plot onto a transparency, and draw a straight line that seems to fit the data. Be
   ready to show your work to the class and tell why you drew the line where you did.

3. Explain how your line could be used to predict the dimensions of larger eggs.

4. Enter the data into your graphing technology, and have it make a scatter plot of the data.

5. You will now have the technology draw a line of best fit for the warbler data. Continue to work
   through Questions 6–9 on the assignment.

F O R   S T U D E N T S

Instructional Sequence 4.1
Egg Dimensions (page 2 of 2)

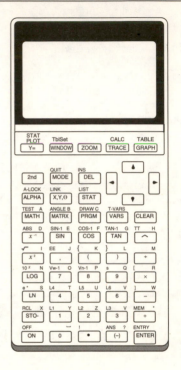

Statisticians often use a line called the **least-squares linear regression line** to predict data according to certain criteria. You can find the equation for this line by using a graphing calculator or computer software.

6. a. Find the equation of the least-squares linear regression line for the warbler eggs. Make a scatter plot on your calculator and graph the equation you found.

    b. Now use your new line to find the width of a warbler egg that is 16.5 mm long. How close is the prediction?

    c. Overall, how well does the least-squares linear regression line seem to predict?

There is another line that statisticians can use called the **median fit line.** This is a good line to use when there are outliers in the data.

7. a. Use your graphing calculator to find the equation of the median fit line, and graph the line in your scatter plot.

    b. How does the median fit line compare with the least-squares linear regression equation?

    c. Does the line seem to do a good job of predicting the width of the eggs?

8. a. Select one of the lines. What is the slope of the line? How can you find this number from the equation?

    b. How can you show this number in the graph?

    c. What does this tell you about the relationship between the length and the width of warbler eggs?

9. a. What does the other number in the equation represent on the graph?

    b. What does the number mean in terms of egg length and width?

Source: Reprinted with permission from the *Insights into Data* student book in the Mathematics in Context program. © Encyclopedia Britannica Educational Corporation.

life science/biology with mathematics.) In Section E, students examine different examples of bivariate data and learn to recognize positive correlations, negative correlations, and a lack of correlations. In Section F, the final section of the standard curriculum (although optional extensions are provided beyond this unit), the unit is simply entitled "Lines."

Another example of modeling in the middle-school curriculum is an instructional sequence from the Grade 8 unit, "Thinking With Mathematical Models," from the *Connected Mathematics Project*. The content map in Figure 4.1 shows how this unit

fits into the rest of the curriculum. In Grade 6, the unit on data has students gathering, organizing, analyzing, and making decisions based on data. Students in this program have been introduced to linearity in a Grade 7 module, "Moving Straight Ahead," in which they learn to express linear relationships in words, tables, graphs, and symbols. The Grade 8 unit from which Instructional Sequence 4.2 is taken is the first of the year, setting the stage for the development of various types of functions as models throughout the year. *Breaking Bridges* is the first investigation in this unit. The first student page of the investigation is provided on page 128.

Figure 4.1
General View of the CMP Curriculum

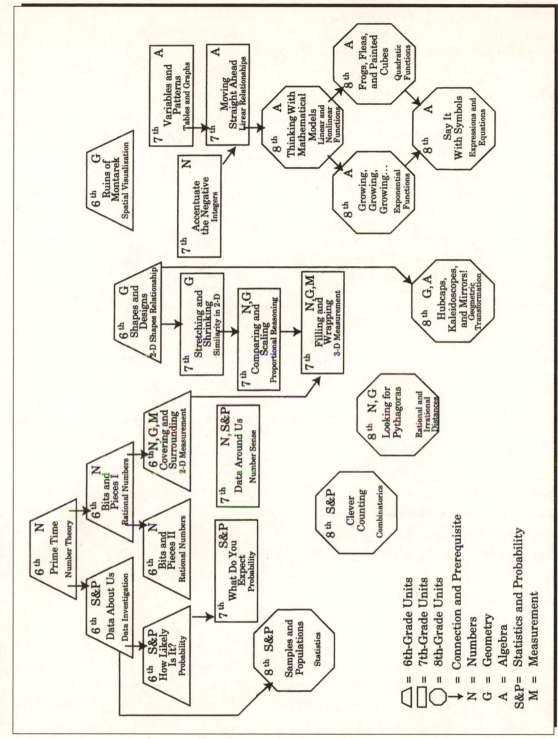

Source: From *Connected Mathematics Getting to Know Connected Mathematics* by Glenda Lappan, James T. Fey, William M. Fitzgerald, Susan N. Friel, & Elizabeth Defanis Phillips © 1996 by Michigan State University. Published by Prentice Hall. Used by permission of Pearson Education, Inc.

F O R   T E A C H E R S

Instructional Sequence 4.2 Breaking Bridges

Mathematical Content: Describing linear relationships with tables, graphs, and equations; predicting (extrapolating) from a linear model (PSSM Data Analysis and Probability Standard for Grades 6–8)

Materials Needed: Crosswise half sheets for 8½-by-11-inch copier paper, rulers, pennies, small paper cups, graph paper, graphing technology

Directions: Have students work in groups of three to four to complete the experiment.
1. Have students read the directions on pages 128 and 129. Demonstrate a bridge of thickness 1 and use it to set up a table with one column for the thickness and the other for the number of pennies needed to crumple the bridge. Remind students to have about 1 inch on either end of every bridge overlap each book and to place the cup consistently in the middle of every bridge.
2. Students conduct the experiment in their groups. They take notes on the procedure and record the data for the first 5 tables. Each group graphs its data as a scatter plot.
3. Using transparencies, have groups present their data table and graphs to the entire class. Discuss the linear nature of the graph and use it to predict the breaking point of bridges made with additional layers of paper, including half layers.

Extension: Have student enter their bridge data into a graphing calculator, graph the scatter plot, and have the calculator perform a linear regression to find a line of best fit. Compare the different linear equations produced in the groups.

Source: From *Connected Mathematics Thinking with Mathematical Models* by Glenda Lappan, James T. Fey, William M. Fitzgerald, Susan N. Friel, & Elizabeth Defanis Phillips © 2002 by Michigan State University. Published by Prentice Hall. Used by permission of Pearson Education, Inc.

F O R   S T U D E N T S

Instructional Sequence 4.2
Breaking Bridges (page 1 of 2)

Linear Models: Testing Paper Bridges
Most bridges are built with frames of steel beams. Steel is very strong, but if you put enough weight on any beam, it will bend or break. The amount of weight a beam can support is related to its thickness and design. To design a bridge, engineers need to understand these relationships thoroughly. Engineers often use scale models to test the strength of their bridge designs.

Directions: In this problem, you will do an experiment to test some of the principles involved in building bridges. Using the equipment listed, follow the procedure for building and testing paper bridges.

Equipment: Several 11-inch-by-4-inch strips of paper, two books of the same thickness, a small paper cup, and about 50 pennies

Procedure:
- Make a paper "bridge" by folding up 1 inch on each long side of one of the paper strips.

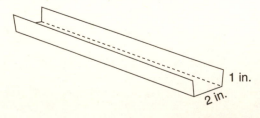

FOR STUDENTS

Instructional Sequence 4.2
Breaking Bridges (page 2 of 2)

- Suspend the bridge between the two books. The bridge should overlap each book by about 1 inch. Place the paper cup in the center of the bridge.
- Put pennies into the cup, one at a time, until the bridge crumples. Record the number of pennies you added to the cup. This number is the **breaking weight** of the bridge.

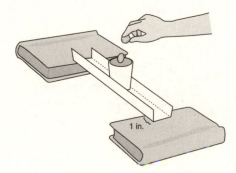

- Put two strips together to make a bridge of double thickness. Find the breaking weight for this bridge. Repeat this experiment to find breaking weights for bridges made from three, four, and five strips of paper.

1. Do the experiment described above to find breaking weights for bridges 1, 2, 3, 4, and 5 layers thick.

2. Make a table and a graph of your data.

3. Describe the pattern of change in the data. Then, use the pattern to predict the breaking weights for bridges 6 and 7 layers thick.

4. Suppose you could use half-layers of paper to build the bridges. What breaking weights would you predict for bridges 2.5 layers thick and 3.5 layers thick?

FOLLOW-UP

How would you expect your results to change if you used a stronger material, such as poster board or balsa wood, to make your bridges?

Source: From *Connected Mathematics Thinking with Mathematical Models* by Glenda Lappan, James T. Fey, William M. Fitzgerald, Susan N. Friel, & Elizabeth Defanis Phillips © 2002 by Michigan State University. Published by Prentice Hall. Used by permission of Pearson Education, Inc.

MODEL THREE-YEAR COLLEGE PREPARATORY PROGRAMS

General Description of the Programs

In the NCTM *Curriculum and Evaluation Standards* (1989) document, mathematics educators envisioned programs that would "encourage and enable students to value mathematics, gain confidence in their own mathematical ability, become mathematical problem solvers, communicate mathematically, and reason mathematically" (p. 123). The programs described here attempt to make that vision become reality in high-school classrooms. All are intended to be 3-year programs that meet university entrance requirements in mathematics upon successful (C or better grade) completion. Although the approaches differ, they require student involvement in applying mathematics to problem solving and real-world applications. Instructional activities are structured to promote mathematical discourse among students and between teacher and students. Skill practice is not as obvious as in traditional programs; rather, it is frequently utilized during the problem-solving process. Traditional algebra and geometry content is included in these programs, as well as a greater emphasis on statistics, probability, and discrete mathematics, particularly as supported with technology. As is always the case with mathematics curricula, these programs will be revised over time as they are used in more classrooms and as new research informs mathematics educators. After completing any of these 3-year programs, students are prepared to take either a pre-calculus course or an advanced statistics course.

Representative Programs

The November 1995 issue of *The Mathematics Teacher* is a focus issue whose theme is "Emerging Programs." We have selected four of the featured programs to examine in depth and have listed others at the end of this chapter. We encourage readers to refer to this journal issue for more information about secondary mathematics curricula that were new at the time of its publication.

A recent article (Martin, 2001) in *The Mathematics Teacher* describes a correlation study of the five NSF-funded high-school series with the NCTM PSSM document. The authors found that all series included a majority of the five PSSM content standards for Grades 9–12. When compared with the PSSM process standards, all series addressed at least 65% of those standards, with many aspects 85% or more. A lack of emphasis on formal proof was evident in all five series, while technology was generally an integral part of problem solving.

University of Chicago School Mathematics Project (UCSMP), Secondary Component A pioneer of new curricular programs was the University of Chicago School Mathematics Project (UCSMP), which began its work in 1983. Although this was before the NCTM *Curriculum and Evaluation Standards* document was written, the goal of UCSMP to develop mathematics programs appropriate for a broad middle group of students is consistent with the intent of the *Standards*.

The UCSMP secondary component begins with a course called *Transition Mathematics,* designed "for a student who has reached the seventh grade level in mathematics, regardless of age" (Hirschhorn, Thompson, Usiskin, & Senk, 1995). In other words, this course takes the place of a pre-algebra course. It provides not only pre-algebra content but also what might be called pre-geometry content. Although the next course, the first intended to meet college entrance requirements, is entitled *UCSMP Algebra* and is built around algebraic concepts, it also contains many geometry topics and some probability and statistics topics. The second high-school course, *UCSMP Geometry,* presents topics in a different order than most traditional textbooks, introducing coordinate and transformational geometries early in the course and developing proof-writing skills that include justification based on these forms of geometry, as well as those that are more Euclidean in nature. The UCSMP continues with courses entitled *Advanced Algebra; Functions, Statistics, and Trigonometry;* and *Pre-calculus and Discrete Mathematics*.

Real-world applications are included in all phases of the UCSMP curriculum. The curriculum assumes that classes have access to calculators (including graphing calculators) and computers with software that allow for various graphing and dynamic geometry, with lessons specifically calling for their use. The UCSMP program stresses students' independent reading of the text. Student assignments have four dimensions, as characterized by the acronym SPUR: skills, properties, uses, and representations.

College Preparatory Mathematics: Change From Within The College Preparatory Mathematics Project (CPM) received its initial funding in 1989 from California State Eisenhower funds. According to Kysh (1995), CPM has three major goals:

1. develop a rich integrated mathematics curriculum that will enable more students, especially those groups historically underrepresented in

mathematics, to succeed in a college-preparatory mathematics sequence;

2. base this curriculum on the best current wisdom of how people learn and the mathematics needed in an era of computers, and fit these topics into the context of current school programs with course titles Algebra 1, Geometry, and Algebra 2;

3. involve teachers fully in planning, developing, using, revising, and introducing to their colleagues the new materials and new teaching techniques.

After initial development of content goals (and other educational goals) and drafting of units and courses, each course in turn went through a period of feedback and revision. At the time of this writing, the initial three courses are fully developed and sold in paperback form at a much lower price than standard textbooks. The fourth year was developed and was beginning to be used at many CPM schools by 1997. CPM is distributed nationally, as well.

The Core-Plus Mathematics Project (CPMP)

Developed at Western Michigan University with NSF funding, the *Core-Plus Mathematics Project (CPMP),* published as *Contemporary Mathematics in Context,* is organized into four main strands: algebra/ function; geometry/trigonometry; statistics/probability; and discrete mathematics. These strands are interconnected by common local topics and unified by the fundamental themes of data, representation, shape, and change. The curriculum emphasizes mathematical modeling and features frequent use of graphing calculators as tools. The materials consist of a common core of mathematics experience/problem sets for students, along with more challenging applications and extensions for mathematically talented students—hence the title, Core-Plus. The curriculum is organized in multiweek units comprising several lessons, most of which are intended to take several days to complete.

This program shares an instructional design model with the *Connected Mathematics Project* (Grades 6–8), described earlier in this chapter, making the two programs a coherent 6-year package. The terms *Launch, Explore, Share and Summarize,* and *Apply* represent the four aspects of this teaching model. A problem is introduced in the Launch phase of the instructional design, which includes discussion questions to elicit student thinking about the problem. The next phase, Explore, has students in small groups investigating aspects of the problem through data collection, model construction, conjecture making, and verification. Third, students Share and Summarize their findings, justifying and critiquing each other's approaches and conclusions. Finally, in the fourth phase students Apply their

learning individually, becoming responsible for their own understanding and mastery of the core concepts and techniques included in the instructional sequence.

Additional tasks are provided as homework for each lesson, to be worked individually outside of class. These tasks include a variety of approaches: Modeling, Organizing, Reflecting, and Extending (MORE) the mathematics developed during class time. The Extending tasks are intended to be optional, allowing more mathematically inclined and motivated students to go "beyond the core" and pursue topics in greater depth. In terms of equity, this design offers open access to honors designation by making such extensions available to all members of a class. That is, any student can attempt those problems in the Extending section of each homework, and those meeting a previously agreed-upon level of attainment can earn honors credit for the class.

The Interactive Mathematics Program (IMP)

The Interactive Mathematics Program (IMP) curriculum was developed at San Francisco State University and the Lawrence Hall of Science (connected with the University of California at Berkeley), with major funding provided by the California Postsecondary Education Commission through Eisenhower funds. Additional components were funded by NSF. It is a problem-centered curriculum, with five major thematic units per year. Each unit integrates different mathematical content areas (algebra, geometry, trigonometry, and probability and statistics) around a central problem or theme. The delivery of instruction is student-centered, with group work the norm and the teacher commonly in a facilitator role. Students take responsibility for their learning and are allowed to use many approaches as they develop strategies and justification for solutions. Motivated by the central focus, students solve a variety of problems containing components needed to address the overarching problem of the unit. They develop the skills and concepts needed to solve the central problem during the course of the unit. Building confidence and persistence in students as they approach challenging mathematics is a central goal of this program.

All four of the programs described above have been evaluated by independent researchers as to the effectiveness of their curricula in meeting stated goals, the results of which are available from them upon request. The evaluation of the last two programs, CPMP and IMP, was funded by NSF. In general, evaluations show comparable or better results on standardized, norm-referenced tests by students in these programs compared with students at the same level in traditional programs. For example,

CPMP used the Iowa Test of Educational Development subtest, called the Ability to Do Quantitative Thinking, to collect data on students' ability to reason quantitatively. CPMP students scored significantly higher on this test than comparable students in more traditional programs. IMP student results on the SAT were compared to comparable non-IMP students. The results either showed no difference or showed higher scores of IMP students, even though IMP classes typically included a broader range of student abilities than comparison classes. In addition, there is evidence that students in these new programs do better than students in traditional programs in dealing with nonstandard problem situations. Finally, qualitative information collected from questionnaires and interviews with samples of students in these classes regarding their attitudes about mathematics and their ability to succeed in challenging courses indicate much improvement from the time students begin the new programs to when they complete them. Students in these *Standards*-based programs tend to continue to take more mathematics in high school than students in traditional mathematics programs. Thus, they graduate from high school better prepared for either the world of work or for continuing their education than are students who opt out of mathematics at the earliest possible opportunity.

One common area of agreement in the mathematics community is that all students should take mathematics every year they are in high school. Yet almost no states or districts require 4 years of mathematics coursework for high-school graduation. However, a graduation requirement of 2 or 3 years of college preparatory mathematics is becoming more common all over the United States. These increased requirements and expectations present new challenges to secondary mathematics teachers. School districts may address some of these challenges through implementation of *Standards*-based mathematics curricula.

One key factor in the implementation of all of these curricula is professional development. The NSF-developed programs generally require a week or more of professional development for each teacher for each year of implementation. The professional development enhances content knowledge and assists teachers in managing and directing classrooms that are more student-centered than they themselves have ever experienced. Forming collegial bonds with other teachers also helps to prevent reverting to old ways that feel more comfortable, despite their negative effects on student success. (Keep this in mind if you are hired to teach in a school that is using new curriculum.) Districts and schools sin-

cere about providing exemplary curriculum for all students will insist upon a strong professional development component. Take advantage of workshops, release time for curriculum-specific training, and other opportunities for you to work together with teacher colleagues in professional learning networks. More general information will be given about professional development in a later chapter. I (SM) attended 2 years of training for the IMP program with a colleague. Later, without training or collegial support, I began teaching a different, more traditional program, *Integrated Mathematics* (McDougal Littell). In spite of my previous training, I had to consciously avoid slipping back into a "telling" mode typical of my earlier teaching experience.

It is crucial to have the time to work with colleagues to do serious unit planning, discuss classroom management procedures, and review strategies to elicit the greatest success for your students. Many mathematics departments and district professional developers are working together to make such opportunities systemic, not just for new teachers, but also for experienced teachers. With ongoing collegial support and opportunities for continuing teacher professional growth, measurable progress in students' achievement is most likely to occur.

Set 4.2   Discussion Questions

 Questions with an asterisk appear in the Message Board section of the Companion Website at *http://www.prenhall.com/huetinck.* Go to Chapter 4 and click on the Message Board to find and respond to the question.

*1. Given the current failure rates in algebra and geometry, are we benefiting students by setting higher expectations that are more likely to be met through the use of *Standards*-based curricula, or are we harming students by setting them up for failure? What impediments or concerns do you see that need to be addressed if all students are to meet increased graduation requirements in mathematics?

2. Talk to at least one non-mathematics educator to get his perspective on the issue of increased graduation requirements, and report back to the class. Consider talking to a parent, business owner, school administrator, counselor, vocational educator, etc.

3. Examine some intervention programs used by schools in your vicinity for providing assistance to underachieving students. To what degree are they successful? How do they measure their success? To what is their success or lack of it attributed?

Sample High-School Instructional Sequences

Instructional Sequence 4.2 comes from Unit 2, "Patterns of Change," in Year 1 of the *Contemporary Mathematics in Context (Core-Plus Mathematics Project)* high-school curriculum. In this unit students collect and organize data; represent data and relations in numeric, graphic, symbolic, and verbal forms; and detect common patterns of change in variables. Keep in mind the possibility that students beginning this program in high school may have had a middle-school program such as those described above. What powerful mathematics these students will be able to do during high school!

FOR TEACHERS

Instructional Sequence 4.3 Modeling Bungee Jumping

Mathematical Content: Describing linear relationships with words, tables, and graphs; predicting (extrapolating) from a given graph; modeling linear growth with equations (PSSM Data Analysis and Probability Standard for Grades 9–12 and PSSM Algebra Standard for Grades 9–12)

Materials Needed: Rubber bands of like size, fishing weights, graph paper, meter sticks

Teacher Directions: Divide students into groups of 3 to 4 persons each. Demonstrate how the materials are to be used, and set norms for appropriate usage of the rubber bands. Student groups work together to collect and record the data and answer the questions on modeling bungee jumping. Have students continue to work through the MORE problems, some of which may be assigned as homework.

Source: Coxford, A. F. and Others (1997). Core-Plus/*Contemporary Mathematics in Context*. Chicago, IL: Everyday Learning Corp. Reprinted with permission.

FOR STUDENTS

Instructional Sequence 4.3
Modeling Bungee Jumping (page 1 of 3)

Directions: Read through the following information, and work in groups to solve.

Some amusement parks and other attractions around the world have bungee jumps for those daredevils who want the thrill of free fall from a high distance and the relief of being pulled back from what would surely be a fatal encounter with the ground below. Since people come in many sizes and weights, considerable planning and experimentation are needed before opening such jumps to the public. How can all of the people who try jumping be assured of both their safety and the thrill of coming close to the ground before being snapped up? Today we are going to model a bungee jump with materials available in the classroom. We are not going to try actual jumping!

Materials Needed: Rubber bands of like size, fishing weights, graph paper, meter sticks

1. In small groups, make a chain of rubber bands, and attach one weight at one end.

2. Use meter sticks to establish a way of measuring the amount of stretch with the initial weight. Make at least 5 trials with that weight, and find the average stretch length to fill in the table. Continue to gather data by adding more and more weights, each time taking 5 trials to obtain a corresponding stretch length.

Weight of Weights	Amount of Stretch

FOR STUDENTS

Instructional Sequence 4.3
Modeling Bungee Jumping (page 2 of 3)

3. Make a scatter plot of the data on graph paper. Refer to your scatter plot to answer the following questions:

   a. What does the pattern of points on your graph say about the pattern of change in the amount of stretch as the weight changes?

   b. Is it reasonable to connect the points on your graph and use the resulting graph to predict the amount of stretch for weights other than those you tested? Try it!

   c. How would you expect the patterns in your graph to be different from those of other groups? How would you expect them to be similar?

Modeling, Organizing, Reflecting, Extending

These are sample problems from the Core-Plus Mathematics Project, Course 1, Chapter 2, Section 1.

MODELING

Each of the following situations gives you some information about variables and relations among these variables. Then you are asked to make tables or graphs of the given information and to answer questions about the relationships. Keep an eye out for interesting patterns in the changes of related variables.

1. One key decision is the price to charge each jumper. The price will influence the total number of customers each day. Here are some data from a survey of park customers that were used to predict the number of bungee jumpers each day:

Price Charged	$20	$30	$40	$50	$60
Daily Customers	100	70	40	20	10

a. Describe the pattern relating price and the predicted number of customers.

b. Make a coordinate graph of the (price, customer) data, and explain how the pattern of that graph matches the pattern in the number data.

c. Predict the number of customers if the price is set at $25; at $45; at $100. Explain the reasoning that led to your predictions.

2. A radar gun was used by a test team taking a ride on a Ferris wheel. They aimed it at the ground during two nonstop trips around on the wheel, giving a graph relating height above the ground to time into the trip (see diagram of the Ferris wheel for data).

a. What is the highest the rider will be above the ground during the ride?

b. Sketch a graph that you believe would fit the pattern relating height above ground to time during the Ferris wheel ride, if the total time for the trip were 100 seconds. Write an explanation of the pattern in your graph.

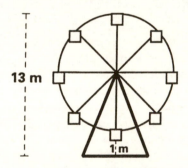

13 m

1 m

FOR STUDENTS

Instructional Sequence 4.3
Modeling Bungee Jumping (page 3 of 3)

ORGANIZING

3. Shown below is a pattern of "growing" squares made from toothpicks.

   a. Study the pattern and draw a sketch of the next likely shape in the pattern.

   b. Complete a table similar to the one below for the toothpick patterns.

   Toothpick Squares

   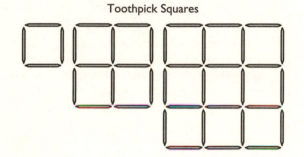

Number of Toothpicks per Side of Square	1	2	3	4	5	6
Area in square units	1	4				

   c. Sketch a graph of the relation shown in the (side length, area) data.

   d. Describe in words the relation between the area of a shape and the number of toothpicks in a side.

   e. Complete a table similar to the one below for different toothpick patterns.

Number of Toothpicks per Side of Square	1	2	3	4	5	6
Perimeter in units		8				

   f. Sketch a graph of the relation shown in the (side length, perimeter) data.

   g. Describe similarities and differences in the patterns of change in parts b and c.

REFLECTING

4. Do you think that all variables are related to each other? For each of the following pairs of variables, determine whether changes in one variable are related to changes in the other, and describe the pattern, if one exists.

   a. the height of an adult and the cost of a movie ticket;

   b. the amount of time spent on homework and the amount of money spent on lunch;

   c. the date on the calendar and the number of daylight hours;

   d. the TV channel setting and the TV volume setting;

   e. the pitch played by plucking a string and the tension on that string.

EXTENDING

The graph below shows data for hot dogs sold and profit in dollars at an amusement park. This graph is typical of a simple profit graph used in business. Find the coordinates of each labeled point on the graph, and explain what those co-ordinates tell about the hot dog business at the park.

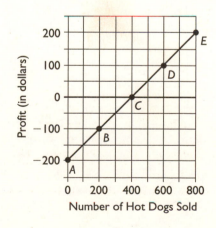

Source: Coxford, A. F. and Others (1997). Core-Plus/*Contemporary Mathematics in Context*. Chicago, IL: Everyday Learning Corp. Reprinted with permission.

Modeling in all kinds of mathematical situations is a keystone of CPMP. Of the seven units in Course 1, in addition to the introductory unit emphasizing basic forms of displays of data and Unit 2, "Patterns of Change," Unit 3 concentrates on linear models, and Unit 6 has students examine data related to growth and decay (exponential) patterns. Unit 3 in Course 2, "Patterns of Association," deals with correlation and how linear models, including the least-squares regression, relate to measures of correlation. Course 3 includes periodic models in Unit 3 and discrete models with recursive representations in Unit 7. Course 4 is now available for use in high schools.

Set 4.3   *Discussion Question*

1. The previous set of MORE (Model, Organize, Reflect, Extend) questions immediately follows the bungee jumping investigation in the curriculum, with only a brief definition of a variable and the explanation that a relationship between two variables may be described as a function if one value can be shown to depend on the other. Students were told that words, tables, and graphs can be used to show these relationships.

   Work through the sample MORE problems from the bungee jump section as you expect a student would. Then reflect on the previous knowledge and experience needed by students in order for them to complete the MORE exercises with reasonable success.

The set of lessons in Activity 4.4 is based on the "Pit and Pendulum" unit of Year 1 of the 4-year high-school curriculum *Interactive Mathematics Program*. An overview of the unit is provided so that you can understand how the mathematics is developed in a problem-centered unit.

The context for this 6-week unit is presented in excerpts from the Edgar Allan Poe story "The Pit and the Pendulum." The "big problem" of the unit is to determine whether the hero's escape is feasible. Students begin by gathering raw data on pendulums. The unit moves quickly to activities in which students participate in hands-on activities to develop the concept of the normal curve. The mathematical features of the normal curve and standard deviations are presented and discussed, and students are shown how to enter data and find standard deviations on calculators. Students return to the big problem more than halfway through the unit, where the activities shown in this text occur. In the final section, on curve fitting, students explore different

forms of graphs, particularly linear, quadratic, and square root functions, and develop equations to match these graphs. Then students return to the pendulum data and work in groups to develop an equation that fits their data. The culmination of this unit is a reenactment of the pendulum swing (without any dangerous blades) somewhere on the campus. Each group can then see how close its equation came to predicting the period of the 30-foot pendulum. Finally, they argue the reasonableness of Poe's story, based on their mathematical knowledge.

 For information about the On-line Pendulum lesson and software, go to **http://www.prenhall.com/huetinck** and click on Web Destinations for Chapter 4.

These lessons begin when students are asked to isolate variables and measure their effects on the period of a pendulum. Before beginning this activity it is essential to develop the mathematics of the normal curve, with the corresponding concept of what makes some values mathematically "ordinary" or "rare" when compared with previously established data. From this intuitive approach, students learn the characteristics of a normal distribution and the mathematical concept of standard deviation. Eventually, students find length to be the most significant variable in determining the period of a pendulum.

Complete Instructional Sequence 4.4 before moving into the next section.

ELEMENTS FOR SUCCESS IN TEACHING *STANDARDS*-BASED CURRICULA

Curriculum alone does not guarantee teaching success. In teaching *Standards*-based curricula, several other elements are important: curriculum-specific professional development, site-based joint planning time, a teaching role that emphasizes facilitation, flexibility to meet the needs of each group of students, and a willingness to reflect on students' work.

Professional Development

Not enough can be said for having curriculum-specific professional development in any *Standards*-based programs. Such training, whether designed by the developers, publishers, or local districts, should include the mathematical content contained in the particular text as well as the pedagogy needed

F O R   T E A C H E R S

Instructional Sequence 4.4 Predicting the Period of a Pendulum

Mathematical Content: Modeling nonlinear relationships with equations, predicting (extrapolating) from a model (PSSM Algebra Standards for Grades 9–12), using the normal distribution to identify relevant variables (PSSM Data Analysis and Probability Standard for Grades 9–12)

Materials Needed: Stopwatches (one per group of four students), circular washers, string, sticks for holding the top of the pendulum flat (see diagram), one large protractor per group, chart paper, markers, graphing calculators, and graphing calculator viewscreen

Directions: This instructional sequence may take several days for a class to complete. Homework will be related to the study of the normal curve. Students work in groups of four.

1. Have the class read an excerpt from Edgar Allen Poe's "The Pit and the Pendulum." Discuss whether the story is realistic. The mathematics done in this instructional sequence will help us look at that issue more objectively.

2. Distribute the following to each group: one stopwatch, several circular washers, around a yard of string, a large protractor, and a flat stick (or ruler) for holding the top of the pendulum on the table. Allow students time to read the directions and experiment with setting up a standard pendulum. As each group completes its setup, be sure the students understand how the data are to be collected. A full-class demonstration of a period of the pendulum is given. Have a large piece of chart paper organized in a table so that each group can record its five data points. As the groups complete this task, demonstrate entering the data on the graphing calculator viewscreen while students follow on their own graphing calculators. After the mean and standard deviation are calculated, draw a model normal distribution based on the gathered data and calculated statistics on the chalk- or whiteboard. This model should remain in the room until the next parts of the Instructional Sequence are complete. Discuss

with students the characteristics of a normal distribution, such as the bell shape and what it signifies; the location of the mean, median, and mode; how the amount of "spread" relates to the dispersion of the data, etc.

3. Tell each group which variable to work with, distributing the three possibilities (weight, length, amplitude) around the room. Repeat the trials as with the standard pendulum. Have each group record its results directly on the previously developed normal distribution for the period of a standard pendulum. Discuss which of the variables seems to have the most effect on the period of the pendulum. Length should be the obvious conclusion. Have students express what "significant" variation means to them.

4. Students will now try to collect and model data that will help them predict the period of a 30-foot pendulum. If students have not had the opportunity to explore various "families" of standard functions, they should do so before completing this activity. Using either graphing calculators or computer-based graphing tools, students should explore and record the shapes of the following nonlinear functions: quadratic, absolute value, cubic, exponential, and square root.

5. Give each group 2 yards of string. The groups are to collect data based on seven different string lengths, as indicated. Timing 12 periods is to relate the information to the Poe story. This time, each group works with its own data to determine a mathematical model as the groups are competing to best predict the amount of time needed to complete 12 swings (periods) of a 30-foot pendulum. Typical ways students arrive at a model are:
    - using the regression feature of graphing technology with different functions;
    - noting the shape is more like the square root function than any other and then experimenting to come up with a coefficient that makes the data nearly fit the model;
    - being very open and experimental with equations until one seems to work. This type of approach usually is in the form of a direct variation.

Source: *Interactive Mathematics Program,* Course 1, Key Curriculum Press, 1150 65th Street, Emeryville, CA 94608, 1-800-995-MATH. Reprinted with permission.

F O R   S T U D E N T S

Instructional Sequence 4.4
Predicting the Period of a Pendulum (page 1 of 2)

THE STANDARD PENDULUM

The pendulum that is illustrated below will be called the *standard pendulum* for the rest of the unit.

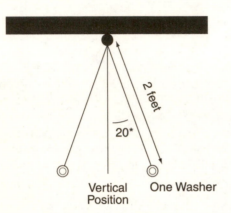

2 feet

20*

Vertical
Position

One Washer

Directions: As you study whether changing a pendulum affects its period, you will be looking at pendulums that differ in some respect from this standard pendulum.

You will compare the periods of these other pendulums to the period of the standard pendulum.

Here are the specifications for the standard pendulum:

Weight of bob	I washer
Length of string	2 feet
Amplitude	20°

Find the period of this standard pendulum, using the procedure agreed upon by your class, and record your result.

Then repeat the experiment, again recording the period. Continue gathering more data as time allows.

FOR STUDENTS

Instructional Sequence 4.4
Predicting the Period of a Pendulum (page 2 of 2)

GATHERING DATA ON THE STANDARD PENDULUM

Directions: This experiment is done in groups of 4. Group responsibilities:

1. Hold the pendulum. It is important to steady it on a flat surface.

2. Release the bob at the appropriate signal.

3. Hold the timing device, and tell the second person when to release the bob to start the time. Note the stopping time after 10 periods.

4. Record the results, and report out the five periods on the class chart.

Find the period of a standard pendulum by timing 10 periods and then dividing the result by 10. Repeat this process four times for a total of five trials per group. Record your results on the class chart. If time allows, there will then be a demonstration of using a calculator to enter the data and calculate the mean and standard deviation of the data. The normal curve representing the data will be drawn on the chalkboard.

DETERMINING THE RELEVANT VARIABLE

Each group will vary only one of the three conditions of the standard pendulum.

1. Does weight matter? These groups will only vary the number of washers. The length remains 2 feet and the amplitude stays at 30 degrees.

   a. Find the period of a pendulum with three washers. Do five trials.

   b. Find the period of a pendulum with five washers. Do five trials.

   c. Find the average period for each weight. Be prepared to record your results on the chalkboard.

2. Does length matter? These groups will only vary the length of the pendulum. Only one washer will be used as the bob, and the amplitude stays at 30 degrees.

   a. Find the period of a pendulum with a length of 3 feet. Do five trials.

   b. Find the period of a pendulum with a length of 1 feet. Do five trials.

   c. Find your average period for each length. Be prepared to record your results on the chalkboard.

3. Does amplitude matter? These groups will only vary the amplitude of the pendulum. Only one washer will be used as the bob and the length stays 2 feet.

   a. Find the period of a pendulum with an amplitude of 45 degrees. Do five trials.

   b. Find the period of a pendulum with an amplitude of 15 degrees. Do five trials.

   c. Find your average period for each amplitude. Be prepared to record your results on the chalkboard.

After recording the results on the normal curve, the class will discuss which variable(s) matter.

FINDING THE FUNCTION/CURVE FITTING

We will be attempting to predict the period of a 30-foot pendulum by finding a function whose graph seems to fit the data gathered on various shorter lengths. This time, we will measure the time for **12** periods. The following lengths are to be tested: 0.5 ft, 1 ft, 3 ft, 4 ft, 5 ft, 6 ft, 7 ft. Recall that we already have the data for a 2-ft pendulum. Each group will find the average time for five trials of the lengths assigned. Plot the 8 points on graph paper and as a scatter plot in your graphing calculator. Try to determine a likely function by trial and error using different regression models.

For those who really want to know, the physics formula will be shared at the end of this activity so you can see how close you came.

Source: *Interactive Mathematics Program*, Key Curriculum Press, 1150 65th Street, Emeryville, CA 94608, 1-800-995-MATH. Reprinted with permission.

to convey the content to students. Even when the topic is familiar, the presentation in a given book may be new and may elicit new understanding, even on the part of experienced teachers. In addition, attending professional development activities with colleagues lays the groundwork for the next element of success, working together at your site on curriculum implementation.

Site-Based Joint Planning Time

An atmosphere of collegiality is a plus in any professional situation, and particularly when implementing a new curriculum. When piloting a new program, two teachers teaching two sections each of a new course provide more information to the school than one teacher teaching four sections. If consistent improvement in student achievement can be shown, it is less likely to be attributed to a particular teacher's personality and style. In our experience, schools in which department members attend workshops and conferences together, meet together regularly to discuss curricular issues, and mutually agree upon appropriate assessments are most likely to show positive improvement in student outcomes, both academically and in attitudes about mathematics.

At some schools, all mathematics teachers teaching a certain course—say, Course 2—agree to have lunch together once a week and talk about implementation and assessment issues, perhaps agreeing on a common end-of-unit test for all of their classes. In other situations, teachers implementing a new program are given an extra planning period the first year of the program to put together all of the materials and strategies for delivering the program as intended. Even better—though rare and difficult to manage in a comprehensive high school because of scheduling conflicts—is a common planning period for two or more teachers teaching the same course. At the very least, having one other respected and trusted colleague with prior teaching experience with whom to share both successes and failures in a nonjudgmental setting is essential to your growth and feelings of efficacy.

Taking on a Facilitating Teaching Role

Teachers need to strive to involve students in the learning process as active participants, not passive receivers. Being a facilitator is not easy, however. It involves moving around a classroom and listening to the students discourse about mathematics, offering hints and suggestions only when asked by all members of a group. Facilitation involves patience when a group or class is "stuck" and willingness to allow some discomfort on the part of the students and for yourself as a teacher when an approach that seems obvious to you is not taken by your students. It means looking at false starts and wrong answers as opportunities to learn rather than mistakes to be avoided. It means picking up on a hesitant student's correct intuition about a problem and probing to bring out the insights that can benefit the entire class.

Although teaching this way is challenging, it is invigorating when you see students attempting a new approach to a problem on their own, persisting when the solution process does not come immediately, and requesting more opportunities to show their ability to handle difficult mathematical problems by applying the skills and concepts they have acquired.

Flexibility

No two classes of students are ever the same. An approach that works well with one group may be less successful with another, although we have found that good lessons generally achieve the desired objectives even when students react differently to them. You will need to look at expressions on your students' faces and other nonverbal ways they have of telling you whether they are "with you" in a given discussion or activity.

Many teachers have students keep learning journals to record their thinking about the mathematics they are doing, including what they understand and do not yet understand. The teacher reads these journals occasionally, perhaps once a week, and makes adjustments in instruction accordingly. Other teachers have students write a sentence or two at the end of each class period or at the beginning of the next period about what they understood and still need to learn. The teacher then reads these comments while checking in homework. Another effective strategy to use, particularly when students seem distracted and off task, is to assign different problems to small groups of students and have each group present its solutions on an overhead transparency to the entire class. These suggestions, and others, all have one goal—to involve students in doing quality mathematics.

Willingness to Reflect on Teaching Practices and Student Work

A recent practice in professional development is having teachers look together at anonymous student work on a single problem. Of necessity, the student work needs to go beyond basic computation and address applications or extensions of previously developed skills, concepts, and processes. A simple, yet useful structure for discussing student work involves three simple questions:

1. What do I know about the work I see?
2. What might I infer from the work I see?
3. What questions would I like to ask of the teacher and/or student about this work?

In our experience, such discussions lead to further independent reflection by teachers, resulting in new insights that inform their subsequent teaching practices.

Set 4.4   Discussion Question

 Questions with an asterisk appear in the Message Board section of the Companion Website at **http://www.prenhall.com/huetinck.** Go to Chapter 4 and click on the Message Board to find and respond to the question.

*1. Which of the preceding five elements for success in teaching do you anticipate being the most difficult to accomplish? Why?

USING PROBEWARE

Although many kinds of data can be collected apart from technological resources, the availability of various kinds of devices to collect, store, and depict data adds an exciting new dimension to student work in data analysis. Some probeware can be connected directly to computers so that the data collected are stored in the memory and displayed on the computer screen. Some probeware is associated with graphing calculators and can be used in the classroom. The results are shown on the graphing calculator view screen and/or on each student's calculator. Recent development in technology include "flash" technology, which allows graphing calculators to be connected to computers and then, via the Internet, to access additional programs that expand the capability of the calculator. For example, some graphing calculators designed for middle-school use do not include matrices. However, if the calculator is interactive with the computer, a program that gives the calculator that capability can be downloaded from the Internet to a student calculator.

Instructional Sequences 4.5, 4.6, and 4.7 use different kinds of probes to collect data. Common probes include those that measure temperature of liquids, light intensity, sound frequency, motion, pH, amount of pressure of a gas, and force. Even though specific probeware is mentioned in some of these classroom-tested lessons, other data collection and display devices can be readily substituted for the given technology.

One way we have seen teachers use probeware, where students have sufficient background, is to set up a series of different stations within the classroom and have students circulate in teams among the stations, gathering and analyzing the data. Students are responsible for reading and following direction sheets in order to collect and analyze the data both with technology and by algebraic means.

FOR TEACHERS

Instructional Sequence 4.5 Musical Sines (page 1 of 2)

Mathematical Content:
Applications of ratios, cyclical functions (PSSM Algebra Standard for Grades 9–12; Connections Standard)

Materials Needed:
Straws and tape; metric rulers; microphones/sound sensors, preferably one per group/station, connected to a computer or graphing calculator; built-in programs to collect and graph the data; rubber mallet; two tuning forks (ideally one octave apart)

Directions: This lesson has three main phases: Exploration, Concept Formation, and Summary/ Application. Extensions are suggested as a challenge to more advanced classes.

Background: Pitch, the difference between high and low tones, is the most obvious characteristic of sound. The difference in pitch is related to the frequency, in vibrations per second, of the object causing the sound. The greater the frequency, the higher the pitch. Changing the length of the air column in wind instruments produces notes of various pitches.

F O R   T E A C H E R S

Instructional Sequence 4.5 Musical Sines (page 2 of 2)

Exploration: Divide students into groups of four. Give each group four plastic straws and markers. Each student in the group uses a ruler and makes a mark on his straw as indicated.

Student A	9 cm	Student B	7 cm
Student C	5 cm	Student D	3 cm

Each student then bends his straw at the mark and tapes that end up against the straw. Then he holds the opposite end from the bent end to his lips and blows gently across the straw to make a whistling sound. Students will listen to each other's whistles and arrange the straws in order of pitch, from lowest to highest. Discuss findings as a class.

Extensions: Trigonometry students can model the sinusoidal functions by estimating amplitude, period, and displacement of the data. Harmonious tuning forks can be hit simultaneously, and the sums of the two functions modeled.

Concept Formation: Lead students in a discussion of the relationship between the length of a straw and the pitch of the sound that is made by blowing across the straw. Connect to string instruments and knowledge about them that students bring to the classroom. Demonstrate a graph of a sound wave to students via a tuning fork that can be struck and the sound recorded by appropriate probe ware connected to a display device. Ask questions such as:

1. What do you notice about the appearance of the sound wave graph?
2. If I hit a tuning fork with a lower sound, how do you think the graph would change? Then do so and compare the predictions with the actual graph.
3. How do you think the sound would vary if I had a turning fork with a higher sound?
4. Show students a transparency of the two sound waves given below. The top figure represents a C tuning fork with 262 Hertz (cycles per second) and the bottom one is the next higher octave of C at 524 Hz.

Summary and Application: Have students describe and sketch the graph they would expect to see for a pure note of 1056 Hz, using the same scale as the illustrated graphs.

Extensions: Have students produce sounds from various musical instruments and note the characteristics of the graphs. (Most musical instruments vibrate in a fundamental tone and overtones simultaneously. Thus, the sound is richer than that of tuning forks.)

Trigonometry students can model the sinusoidal functions by estimating amplitude, period, and displacement of the data. Harmonious tuning forks can be hit simultaneously and the sums of the two functions modeled.

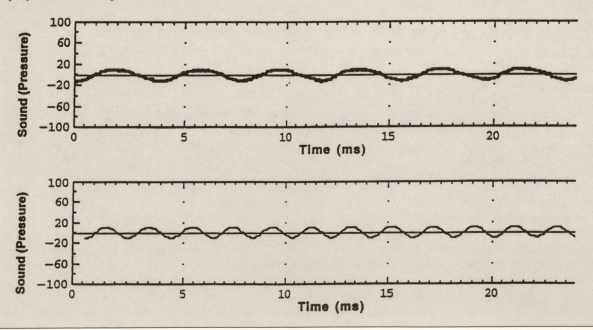

FOR TEACHERS

Instructional Sequence 4.6 Walk a Graph

Mathematical Content:

Modeling distance versus time graphs and velocity versus time graphs (PSSM Algebra Standard, especially analyzing change, for Grades 6–8 and 9–12)

Materials Needed:

Motion sensors, preferably one per group/station, connected to a computer or graphing calculator; built-in programs to collect and graph the data

Directions: The big idea of rate of change should be presented over time in a student's mathematical career, from simple additive and multiplicative patterns in elementary school to proportional reasoning in middle school to the concept of a derivative in calculus. Thus, middle-school students are best served by many different experiences, over time, with distance versus time graphs. We recommend a slow but connected progression for d versus t graphs to v versus t graphs so students can compare and contrast the meaning of the two types of curves. See the *Vertical Teams Tool Kit* (2000) for ideas on work-ing across grade levels with other teachers to prepare students for Advanced Placement Mathematics.

The directions are written as if each group of students has a motion sensor and graphing calculator or computer with which to work. This activity can also be modeled with one motion sensor connected to a display unit at the front of a classroom. It has been our experience that the motion detector does not work well at a distance less than 0.5 meter and can be complicated by extraneous objects near the walking path. Thus, the classroom needs to be organized so that each group has a clear path to use when gathering its data. It improves the data if the student who is walking holds a piece of poster board in front of himself to diminish the effect of clothes flapping.

Depending on students' previous experience with probeware, decide whether to have all of the equipment set for the students when they arrive in class and the computer/calculator program settings prepared. In any case, students need precise directions so that they can rerun the program and collect additional data as needed.

F O R   S T U D E N T S

Instructional Sequence 4.6
Walk a Graph (page 1 of 2)

Directions: Each part has three main phases: Exploration, Concept Formation, and Summary/Application. An Extension is suggested as a challenge.

Part 1 Distance Versus Time Graphs

EXPLORATION

Experiment with walking and looking at the *d* versus *t* graphs you generate. Practice getting smooth curves by repeating the data collection process several times while you modify your walking.

CONCEPT FORMATION

Working in groups, sketch and explain your predictions for the appearance of the graph obtained by each of the following methods. Verify or modify your answers by doing each method. Share conclusions with the entire class. Fine-tune the explanations, using correct mathematical vocabulary appropriate for your grade level.

1. Stand still a certain distance from the probe.
2. Walk backward away from the probe, and then stand still.
3. Walk backward away from the probe, and then walk toward the probe.

SUMMARY AND APPLICATION

Study the three graphs shown in the next column. Experiment and write a group summary of how they can produce similar graphs by walking certain ways. To assess your understanding of how to obtain each graph and the correct use of mathematical terminology and reasoning, chart your group's summaries. Compare the groups' similarities and differences, and refine your statements to be more complete and mathematically sound.

1.
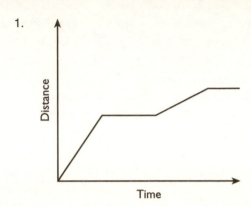

2.
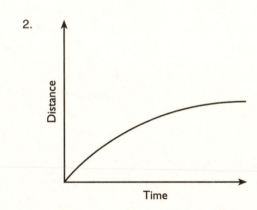

3.
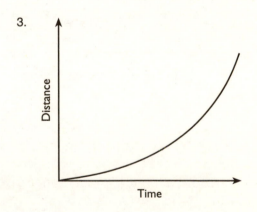

F O R   S T U D E N T S

Instructional Sequence 4.6
Walk a Graph (page 2 of 2)

EXTENSION

Try to walk a W or an M graph.

Part II: Change in Distance (Velocity) Versus Time Graphs
Note: The probeware program will need to be changed in order to do this type of graph.

EXPLORATION

Experiment with walking and looking at the v versus t graphs you generate and to get smooth curves.

CONCEPT FORMATION

Describe the speed (velocity) you used to make each of the previous three graphs. If the speed changed during the time the graph was made, label and explain what happened as a result of that change.

SUMMARY AND APPLICATION

Write your conclusions about the connection between distance walked and the speed of the person walking. Within each group, use a "read-around" process to clarify thinking.

EXTENSION

Explore how to make a constant (horizontal) v versus t curve. *Hint:* Think about a car's odometer, speedometer, and motion when the accelerator is pressed down.

F O R   T E A C H E R S

Instructional Sequence 4.7 Distance and Dimness (page 1 of 2)

Mathematical Content:
Nonlinear regressions (inverse square functions) (PSSM Algebra Standard Grades 9–12, especially the modeling component)

Materials Needed:
Light sensors, preferably one per group/station, connected to a computer or graphing calculator; built-in programs to collect and graph the data; mailing tube longer than 80 cm; masking tape; workable light socket with bulb available to each group gathering the data

FOR TEACHERS

Instructional Sequence 4.7 Distance and Dimness (page 2 of 2)

Directions: The lesson has three main phases: Exploration, Concept Formation, and Summary and Application. An Extension is suggested as a challenge.

Exploration

Ask students to explore or review the shapes of the equations for $y = x$, square root of x, x^2, $1/x$, and $1/x^2$. Ask them to predict which shape they think might most closely describe the graph of intensity of light plotted against the distance from the light.

Concept Formation

Slide the meter stick and probe toward the light to take data at 10 cm intervals. Take data at 70 cm, 60 cm, 50 cm, 40 cm, and 30 cm. Graph the data. Students with graphing calculators can transfer the data to their calculator to find the curve that best fits the data.

Summary and Application

1. Help students understand why the inverse relationship is to a squared factor rather than a linear one. Discuss how light spreads out as the surface of a sphere, with radius equal to the distance from the light bulb to the probe. The surface area of a sphere increases as the square of the radius. The light intensity is proportional to the inverse square as it spreads over a larger and larger area when the distance increases between the probe and the light bulb.

2. Have students write individual responses to the following questions: If I move so the brightness of the light measures one fourth the brightness of the light at an initial point, how far have I moved from the initial setting? If I move so the brightness of the light is nine times the brightness at an initial setting, how far have I moved?

Extension

Have students write their prediction as to how a dimmer or brighter light would affect the graph. If time and materials allow, test their conjecture with a bulb of a different wattage than the one used during the original experiment.

With the light bulb tightly inserted into the left end of the tube as pictured, students collect data on light intensity and distance, using probeware, as a precursor to finding a functional relationship that models the data.

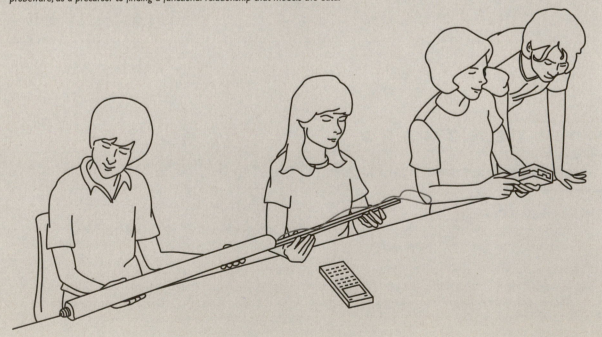

Summary

In this chapter you have seen examples of instructional sequences from *Standards*-based curricula for middle and high-school students. As you worked through the materials yourself you may have become more aware of the mathematical reasoning these materials elicit from students. Another feature of the exemplary curricula in secondary mathematics is the use of graphing technology. Thus, collecting and analyzing real data is an integral feature of 21st century mathematics. You were given several sample activities that use different data collection devices to develop mathematics concepts. We are sure you will continue to integrate the current technology that is available to you in all of your mathematics classrooms in order for students to see the relevance of mathematics to their world.

ASSIGNMENT

Locate materials for 1 year of one of the model curricula described in this chapter. This should include textbooks, modules, supplemental materials, assessments, and the like. Write a report describing the following:

1. the material resources provided with the program for the teacher;

2. additional resources needed to fully implement the program (technology, etc.);

3. the professional development available and/or required to implement the program;

4. any comments you would like to add, including comments from teachers using the program, if available.

ADDITIONAL ANNOTATED MODEL CURRICULA

Advanced algebra through data exploration: A graphing calculator approach. Murdock, J., Kamischke, E., & Kamischke, E. (1996). Berkeley, CA: Key Curriculum Press.

The authors—teachers at Interlochen Arts Academy in Michigan—developed this curriculum with the support of the National Science Foundation. Throughout the program, students integrate and link algebra with statistics, data analysis, functions, discrete mathematics, geometry, probability, and trigonometry. Conceptual understanding is promoted throughout, with contextual settings provided for meaningful problem solving.

Applications reform in secondary education (ARISE)/mathematics: Modeling our world.

COMAP (The Consortium for Mathematics and Its Applications) was awarded a grant by the National Science Foundation for the ARISE project in the fall of 1992. The project is designed to develop a comprehensive curriculum based on mathematical modeling for Grades 9 through 12. This curriculum, consisting of 4 years of high-school mathematics at the time of this printing, is applications driven and technology intensive. It is intended to meet the needs of all students. Practicing high-school teachers were heavily involved in the development of the curriculum, which demonstrates mathematical concepts in the contexts in which they are actually used. The mathematical core of a given problem situation, as presented on a brief video segment for each unit, provides the impetus to learn and apply the appropriate mathematical techniques and tools.

Integrated mathematics, Books 1, 2, 3.
Rubenstein, R. N., Craine, T. V., Butts, T. R. and Others (2000). *Integrated Mathematics Courses 1, 2, 3.* Evanston, IL: McDougal Littell.

Developed by a commercial publisher (McDougal Littell), this program combines typical exercises and student-based strategies in its approach to the core curriculum. Six mathematical strands are developed throughout the 3 years: algebra, geometry, statistics/ probability, logical reasoning, discrete math, and trigonometry. Active learning of students is encouraged through projects, explorations, activities, and discussion questions that are built into the student materials. Extensive support materials—practice sets, projects, alternative assessments, and support for non-English-speaking students—are provided for the teacher.

Systemic Initiative for Montana Mathematics and Science (SIMMS) /Integrated mathematics: A modeling approach using technology.

The SIMMS Integrated Mathematics curriculum takes full advantage of appropriate technology to the extent that the curriculum goals are impossible to achieve without it. Students must have access to function graphers, spreadsheets, a geometry utility, symbolic manipulators; electronic data collection devices, and word processors in order to carry out the research and analysis required in the modules.

Math Thematics; Six through Eight Mathematics (STEM). Funded by the NSF and developed at the University of Montana, these curriculum materials utilize technology and help students make connections with the sciences, language arts, and other fields that rely on mathematics, such as business. STEM materials are problem-centered, application-based, and provide opportunities for students to work together cooperatively on mathematics projects. New student assessment strategies incorporating technology were developed for use with the instructional materials.

INSTRUCTIONAL RESOURCES

Beckman, C. E., & Rozanski, K. (1999). Graphs in real time. *Mathematics Teaching in the Middle School, 5(2),* 92–99.

This article includes activity sheets to be used by students using motion detectors to develop the concept of slope.

Brueningsen, C., Bower, B., Antinone L., & Kerner, E. (2002 revision by Gastineau, J., & Cortez, W.) *Real world math with the CBL2 and LabPro.*® Texas Instruments.

This book contains a series of lessons using the Calculator Based Laboratory and related peripherals to develop various mathematical concepts.

Burrill, G. (1992). *Data analysis and statistics, addenda series,* Reston, VA: National Council of Teachers of Mathematics.

Teaching suggestions and student-ready worksheets are provided. Assessment of this type of work is discussed; samples of actual student work are given.

Burrill, G. (Ed.). (1994). *From home runs to housing costs; data resource for teaching statistics.* Palo Alto, CA: Dale Seymour Publications.

Drawing on materials collected from the Quantitative Literacy Project, this book contains data sets organized to be analyzed by specific statistical methods. Topics include line plots, measures of center, scatter plots, and simulation. Sample lessons and assessment ideas are also included. Oral and written discussion of the analysis and its relation to the data are emphasized.

Carlson, R. J., & Winter, M. J. (1998). *Transforming functions to fit data: Mathematical explorations using probes, electronic data-collection devices, and graphing calculators.* Berkeley, CA: Key Curriculum Press.

Two types of experiments are described in this supplemental book: Type 1, intended for students in pre-algebra and beginning algebra courses, and

therefore involving minimal function representation and transformations, and Type 2, for advanced algebra and pre-calculus students, where functions and their transformations play a major role. Data disks for both Windows and Macintosh formats are included and can be linked to graphing calculators with interface devices.

Fernandez, M. L. (1999). Making music with mathematics. *Mathematics Teacher, 92(2),* 90–95.

This article and series of worksheets specifically deals with sine waves generated by sound, as collected by probe ware. Samples of student work are included.

Hale, P. (2000). Kinematics and graphs: Students' difficulties and CBLs. *Mathematics Teacher, 93(5),* 414–417.

Johnson, E. C., & Young, D. A. (1998). *Data collection activities for the middle grades with the TI–73, CBL, and CBR.*® (1998) Texas Instruments.

This book is specifically geared to middle school students and the mathematics appropriate for that age group. Graphing calculators, motion detectors, and other data collection devices are integral to the activities.

Kohler, A. D. (2002). The dangers of mathematical modeling. *Mathematics Teacher, 95(2),* 140–145.

In this article, the author has his students investigate three different mathematical models to describe the growth of the U.S. population since 1790. Although they all fit the data equally well, they lead to very different predictions for the future. Issues are raised relative to assumptions made in selecting various models and the questions that need to be raised whenever models are selected to represent real-life situations.

Landwehr, J., & Watkins, A. E. (1986). *Exploring data.* White Plains, NY: Quantitative Literacy Series, Dale Seymour Publications. *Real world math with the CBL*™. Champaign, IL: Mathware.

The major goal of this supplemental book is to help students learn how to interpret data by using various kinds of plots and graphs. Many data sets are included, taken from a variety of real-world sources. Writing good descriptions of what plots reveal is emphasized. A teacher's edition, with answers and teaching suggestions, is sold separately. Although the lessons in this book are written for a particular technology, they can readily be adapted and used with other data collection devices.

REFERENCES

Advanced Placement Program® *Mathematics Vertical Teams Toolkit*. (1998) Austin, TX. The College Board.

Martin, T. S., Hunt, C. A., Lannin, J., Leonard, W. Jr., Marshall, G. L., and Wares, A. (2001). How reform secondary mathematics textbooks stack up against NCTM's *Principles and Standards. The Mathematics Teacher,* 94(7), 540–545, 589.

ADDITIONAL INSTRUCTIONAL SEQUENCES

Instructional Sequence 4.8   Straight or Curved
Instructional Sequence 4.9   Friction Car Motion
Instructional Sequence 4.10 Seismology and Data Analysis

When developing an appropriate regression model for nonlinear data, several approaches are possible. The following Instructional Sequences are examples of the most common approaches.

FOR TEACHERS

Instructional Sequence 4.8 Straight or Curved

Mathematical Content:
Using matrices and/or technology to identify and model quadratic relationships (PSSM Algebra Standard for Grades 9–12)

Materials Needed:
Textbook (Rubenstein et. al. (2002) *Integrated Mathematics, Book 3,* McDougal Littell); graphing calculators for at least every other student

Directions: Work through the three pages from the text as a student. Be prepared to discuss the strong points of the lesson and what you would do differently if you were presenting this content to students.

F O R   S T U D E N T S

Instructional Sequence 4.8
Straight or Curved (page 1 of 3)

Directions: Decide whether a quadratic model fits data. Use technology and matrices to find quadratic models.

Talk It Over

The table below shows the height loss in feet for a glider completing a circle at the given angle of bank.

Angle of Bank (degrees)	20	25	30	35	40	45	50
Height Loss in 360° Turn (feet)	108	91	81	74	71	70	71

1. Copy and complete the table at the left, using parts (a)–(e).

   a. Use a graphics calculator to find an equation of the least-squares line for the data. Let x represent the angle of bank and y represent the height loss in feet.

   b. Substitute the x-values from the data points to find the y-values of corresponding points on the least-squares line.

   c. Find the vertical deviation d between each data point and the least-squares line. Use the formula

   $$d = \text{actual } y\text{-value} - \text{model's } y\text{-value}.$$

   The deviation may be positive, negative, or zero.

   d. Find the square of each of the deviations, d^2.

   e. Find the sum of the squares of the deviations, $\Sigma\, d^2$. Statisticians use this value to measure how well a model fits a data set.

2. Look at the scatter plot shown. The data points at each end are above the least-squares line, and those in the middle are below the line. Do the points seem to lie on a curve rather than on a line? If so, what type of curve? Explain.

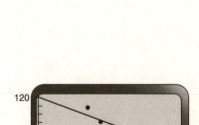

x	y-values		Deviation	
	Actual	**Model**	**d**	**d²**
20	108			
25	91			
30	81			
35	74			
40	71			
45	70			
50	71			

$\Sigma\, d^2 =$

Level Flight   Angle of Bank

Height Lost

FOR STUDENTS

Instructional Sequence 4.8
Straight or Curved (page 2 of 3)

The points in the scatter plot seem to lie closer to a parabola than to a line. In this case it is better to model the glider data by a **least-squares parabola,** which you can obtain by performing a quadratic regression using technology.

Sample
Find the least-squares parabola for the glider data, and compare it to the least-squares line.

SAMPLE RESPONSE

Step 1. Recall that the general equation for a parabola is $y = ax^2 + bx + c$.

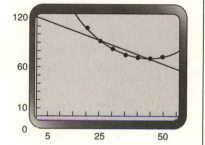

Use technology to perform a quadratic regression and find a, b, and c. A parabola that fits the data is $y = 0.068x^2 - 5.9x + 198$.

With technology, graph this quadratic model along with the scatter plot and the linear model.

Step 2. To decide whether a quadratic model or a linear model fits the data better, compare the sums of the squares of the vertical deviations from the data points to each model. Find which model has the smaller **sum of squares**.

x	Actual y-value	$y = 0.068x^2 - 5.9x + 198$	Deviation d	d^2
20	108	107.2	0.8	0.64
25	91	93.0	− 2.0	4.00
30	81	82.2	− 1.2	1.44
35	74	74.8	− 0.8	0.64
40	71	70.8	0.2	0.04
45	70	70.2	− 0.2	0.04
50	71	73.0	− 2.0	4.00

$$\Sigma d^2 = 10.8$$

The sum of the squares of the deviations from the data points to the quadratic model is 10.8. From *Talk It Over* question 1, you should have found that the sum of the squares of the deviations for the linear model is about 300.

The quadratic model has a smaller sum of squares, so the parabola is a better fit for the data set than the line.

The glider data in the sample was modeled using quadratic regression. You can also use a system of equations to fit a quadratic model to data. For this method, you need only three data points.

FOR STUDENTS

Instructional Sequence 4.8
Straight or Curved (page 3 of 3)

Exercises and Problems

1. How would you determine whether a linear model or a quadratic model fits a set of data better?

2. **a.** Use the least-squares quadratic equation from the Sample Response to predict the height loss for an angle of bank of 60°.

   b. The actual height loss is 80 feet. Explain why this value and the value in part (a) might be different.

   c. At about what angle of bank is there least height loss?

3. An advertisement for a sports car states that the car reaches its maximum power, measured in horsepower (hp), at a lower engine speed, measured in revolutions per minute (rpm), than other cars. Some estimated values on which this claim was made are shown here.

Engine Speed (rpm)	1,000	2,000	3,000	4,000	5,000	6,000
Engine Power (hp)	16	35	55	72	77	68

   a. Make a scatter plot of the data.

   b. Find a quadratic model for the data.

   c. At about what engine speed does the maximum engine power occur?

4. Look at the scatter plot that shows distance and roundtrip airfare. The data is shown below. For this problem, you can use a graphics calculator or statistical software.

World Travel	Mexico City	Cairo	London	Tokyo	Calcutta	Moscow	Rome
Air Distance From New York City (miles)	2,094	5,602	3,458	6,740	7,918	4,665	4,281
Roundtrip Airfare From New York City (dollars)	250	750	375	1,200	1,500	624	520

   a. Perform a linear regression and graph the least-squares line for the data.

   b. Find a quadratic model for the data points.

   c. Graph the parabola on the same scatter plot as the least-squares line.

   d. Which model seems to fit the data better, the *linear* model or the *quadratic* model? Explain.

FOR TEACHERS

Instructional Sequence 4.9 Friction Car Motion

Mathematical Content:
Use of graphed residuals to assist in selection of a nonlinear regression equation (PSSM Algebra
   Standard for Grades 9–12)

Materials Needed:
Activity sheets, data collection device with a motion detector and a toy friction car that is "revved" with
   a backward spin before releasing, display device to use with the graphing technology

Directions: Before beginning this activity, students should have experience using motion detectors and
their display devices. They should know how to store the collected data in various lists. Before students
attempt to collect the data, have them discuss what they think will happen to the forward motion of the
friction car from the time of release to the conclusion of the data collection. The initial challenge for the
students is to get a good set of data. You may either discuss ways of doing this before beginning the activity or not. In either case, you need to plan sufficient time for good data to be generated. The remaining directions for this activity are included in the worksheets.

FOR STUDENTS

Instructional Sequence 4.9
Friction Car Motion (page 1 of 2)

Directions:

1. Use the data collection device to get a smooth set of data of the motion of the friction car as it is
   released and moving away from the motion detector.

2. "Paste" the time data values in your first list; paste the motion data values in your second list.

3. Use your technology to make a scatter plot with time as the independent (control) variable. Remember to find an appropriate viewing window for the data. What was the viewing window?

4. Do a linear regression of the data.

   a. What is the linear regression equation, to the nearest hundredth?

   b. What is the r (correlation coefficient) value?

5. Paste the linear regression equation into the first function, then have your technology draw the
   graph along with the scatter plot.

6. Find the **residual values** (the distance each data point is from the regression line) by having your
   technology subtract the functional values of each data point from the actual data point. Put the
   residual values in a third list. For example, $L_3 = L_2 - Y_1(L_2)$ on the TI-83 will accomplish this.

7. Turn Y_1 and the first scatter plot off, and have your technology make a scatter plot of the residuals,
   (L_1, L_3). Remember to reset your viewing window to accommodate the data.

8. Look carefully at the pattern of residuals. Describe any patterns you see.

F O R   S T U D E N T S

Instructional Sequence 4.9
Friction Car Motion (page 2 of 2)

9. If the residuals from the linear regression do not fall both above and below the *x*-axis all along that line, a further examination of regression models is warranted.

10. Recall the shape of other parent functions you have studied. Select another that may more closely fit the friction car data.

11. Before continuing, turn off all previous plots and graphs, except for the scatter plot of the original data, which should be on.

12. Have your technology perform another regression.
   a. What is the regression equation, to the nearest hundredth?
   b. What is the *r* (correlation coefficient) value?

13. Paste the new regression equation into the second function, then have your technology draw the graph along with the first scatter plot. By observation only, tell whether you think this model better fits the data than the linear model and why.

14. Find the residual values (the distance each data point is from the regression line) by having your technology subtract the functional values of each data point from the actual data point. Put the values in a fourth list. For example, $L_4 = L_2 - Y_2 (L_2)$ on a TI-83 will accomplish this.

15. Turn Y_1 and the first scatter plot off, and have your technology make a scatter plot of the residuals, (L_1, L_4). Remember to reset your viewing window to accommodate the data. Describe the distribution of the residuals of this model. Give a mathematical argument as to whether this model better describes the data than the linear model.

16. If you are not convinced that you have the best model, try yet another regression, repeating the same process.

17. Write what you believe to be the best model connecting what the graph shows to what you know about the acceleration of any vehicle. Explain your answer.

Source: Adapted from a workshop given by Bob Drake and Sal Quesada of Roosevelt High School, Los Angeles.

A more advanced process for data analysis, sometimes called *linearizing,* is adapted from a talk given by Lew Romagnano at the Northeast Regional Conference of the NCTM in Philadelphia, Pennsylvania, in winter 1989. The process includes the following activities:

1. Graph the data, determine the independent variable, if possible, and put it on the horizontal axis.
2. Compare the pattern exhibited with a straight line. This is a critical step, sometimes referred to as "minimizing the residuals." The residuals refer to the horizontal distances from the actual plotted points to the line of best fit. The goal is to have these residuals be both small (near the plotted line) and randomly dispersed on either side of that line. For example, in the scatter plot below, the overall distribution of points above and below the linear model is about the same, but their distribution is not even, since the values above the line occur at both sides of the graph and those below occur in the middle. This is an indication that a nonlinear model is called for.

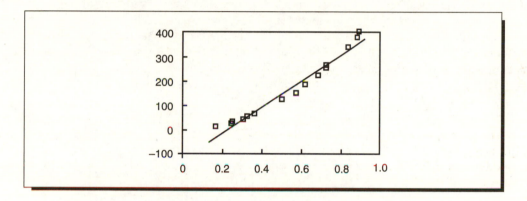

3. Re-express the y-values to "straighten out" the data points. In our example, since the data may be better represented by a quadratic function, we could re-express y as $\sqrt{y}$, thus "undoing" the quadratic relationship.
4. Find the linear model for the re-expressed data, using technology.
5. "Undo the re-expression" to find a model for the original data. In this case, we would square both sides of the linear model to get back to a function in y.

Instructional Sequence 4.10 uses a linearization approach with earthquake data.

FOR TEACHERS

Instructional Sequence 4.10 Seismology and Data Analysis (page 1 of 2)

Mathematical Content:

Linearizing exponential data by using semi-log plots (PSSM Algebra Standards for Grades 9–12)

Materials Needed:

Data set and directions for re-expressing the data, graphing calculators

Directions: The NCTM *Standards* emphasize data collection and analysis. To illustrate the usefulness of technology in the mathematics classrooms of California, we find excellent illustrations in seismology. The following activities are original investigations using factual data collected by Richter and Gutenberg at the California Institute of Technology in Pasadena. These activities feature applications of logarithms and linear regression analyses using graphing calculators.

Worldwide Mean Annual Frequency of Earthquakes

Magnitude (M)	Number of Quakes (N)	log (N)
> 8.0	1	0
7.0–7.9	18	___
6.0–6.9	108	___
5.0–5.9	800	___
4.0–4.9	6,200	___
3.0–3.9	49,000	___
2.0–2.9	300,000	___

Source: From data collected by Rediter and Guteinberg, 1918–1945.

To illustrate the power and convenience of using data transformation, have students study the data in the table above and then enter the data into two lists on a graphing calculator. Then graph the number of quakes as a function of the magnitude of the quake.

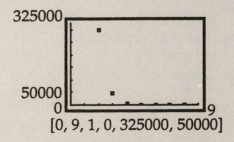

[0, 9, 1, 0, 325000, 50000]

Students will notice that the graph does not provide much information because the value 300,000 is so much larger than the other values that it dwarfs them. Ask students to discuss which type of function they think will best describe this relationship. Hopefully, they will come to the conclusion that the data appears to be exponential. Next have students redo this graph on the graphing calculator by completing the table and graphing the *logarithm* of the number of quakes as a function of the magnitude of the quake. (This can be done quite easily on the calculator by defining a new list in terms of the log of the list that contains the data for *number of quakes*.) The graph, which is commonly called a *semi-log plot,* should look like the one below.

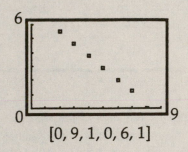

[0, 9, 1, 0, 6, 1]

Observe that a semi-log plot will be linear if the data set is exponential. However, the graph misrepresents data for the single magnitude 8.0 quake. There are quakes whose Richter number is greater than 8.0, but because log 1 = 0, the graph makes it appear as if this is impossible. Now ask the students to use a graphing calculator to find a line of best fit—either the least-squares line or the median-median line.

FOR TEACHERS

Instructional Sequence 4.10 Seismology and Data Analysis (page 2 of 2)

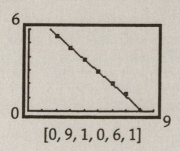

[0, 9, 1, 0, 6, 1]

The graph shows the least-squares regression line, $y \approx -0.895x + 7.354$. The correlation coefficient ($r = -0.9983$) is very close to -1, indicating a nearly perfect inverse relationship. For each increase of 1.0 on the Richter scale, there is a corresponding decrease of 1 in the log of the number of quakes.

No article on earthquakes is really complete without some discussion of Charles Richter and his coworkers at the California Institute of Technology, better known simply as "Caltech." They were well-rounded scientists, versed in mathematics, physics, and engineering, and built their own equipment. They traveled around hot southern California in Model A Fords to seismological sites that they had developed. They had to test their equipment and collect their data. They were patient mathematicians.

The reader may note that the data collection discussed in this article began in 1918 and ended in 1945 but was not published until 1954. With neither calculators nor computers, and using tables and interpolation, these scientists needed years of effort to finish writing a paper involving logarithms!

Source: Adapted, with permission, by Shirley B. Gray, California State University, Los Angeles, June 1997, *ComMuniCator,* published by the California Mathematics Council.

DATA-COLLECTING ACTIVITIES AND SOURCES

Sources of data for analysis generally come in two forms: data that are already collected and compiled—say, in a *world almanac*—or data that are collected through some classroom activity or experiment. Visual and graphic depictions of data abound in print media. Sources of graphs are newspapers (especially *USA Today*), magazines, and textbooks in other content fields. Two particularly engaging books on graphical display are by Tufte (1983).

Univariate Data Activities

Interesting data sets, such as those given in some of the annotated reference materials, are the keystone for this kind of activity. Typically, students are given a general set of instructions such as the following:

Use a current almanac to choose a data topic. Analyze the data to find range, mode, median, mean, and quartiles (as applicable). Identify outliers, if there are any. Make a visual representation of the data. Use the statistics and the visual depiction as the basis for summary statements about the data and/or to make predictions.

For information on Web-based sources of data, go to *http://www.prenhall.com/huetinck* and click on Web Destinations for Chapter 4.

Bivariate Data Activities

When students work with bivariate data, be aware that some pairs of data sets may not have any reasonable correlation, so no mathematical model is appropriate, although verbal descriptions may still show insights or suggest additional questions. For example, student height and GPAs would not seem to be correlated. Using the terminology of functions, neither variable makes sense as the dependent variable. Height does not depend on grades, nor do grades depend on height in a group of students of like age. Giving students examples of these kinds of data along with those that seem to have a functional relationship can contribute to their developing mathematical thinking and reasoning as related to statistical information.

Many data sets that are appropriately modeled by linear functions are direct variations. Technology-developed models of these kinds of data may, nevertheless, have an intercept, again leading to discussions as to the reasonableness of the model and the limits of technology. In the sets below, for example, the linear regression line of shoe length to size may not go through the origin. Depending on where the intercept occurs—above or below 0—a shoe of no length might appear to have a size, even a "negative" size. Such discrepancies between the mathematical model and the real world are typical in modeling situations and only reaffirm the need always to revisit the original situation and see whether the mathematical model makes sense. Some sources for linear data follow. The notion of slope as a ratio or rate is crucial when analyzing the related functions and their real-life meanings.

The following Lab Worksheet can be used by pairs of students in an algebra class to record the results of linear relations in data analysis experiments. With minor modifications, a similar form can be used for nonlinear experiments. This format can easily be adapted for use in data collection activities in almost any mathematics class.

LAB WORKSHEET–ALGEBRA EXPERIMENTS

Name(s): _____

Experiment: _____

Description of the experiment: _____

_____

_____

_____

Independent variable *x:* _____   Units: _____

Dependent variable *y:* _____   Units: _____

After gathering the data, draw a scatter diagram on graph paper. Find the equation of the line of best fit.

Labeled Drawing   Data Collection

Independent	Dependent

Answer the following questions in complete sentences:

1. What is the meaning of the *y*-intercept and slope?

2. What conditions would affect the line or cause another group's line to be different from yours?

3. Choose a value of *x* greater than any of your *x*-data, and use your equation to predict the value of *y*. Is it a reasonable answer? Why or why not?

4. Write a summary/conclusion.

Bonus: Write a problem that could be solved using this experiment.

Source: Adapted from a presentation by Louisiana Presidential Awardee Kay Fenton at the California Mathematics Council–South Converence, November 1997.

Another format for a lab report uses the following elements:

Introduction: Give the purpose of the experiment. What are you trying to find out by carrying it out?

Equipment and Setup: List the materials used, and draw a diagram of how the data were collected.

Procedure: Tell the steps taken to collect the data.

Analysis: Describe how statistics were calculated and how an equation was arrived at.

Conclusion: Tell how the results relate to the purpose. Give any limitations and suggestions for further exploration.

The following lists are not exhaustive but give some examples of bivariate data sources for linear and nonlinear relationships.

Linear Data

1. Ratios related to body parts are one potential source of linear data. Information collected from students creates interest and is readily available. Sensitivity to teenage issues is important here. Use seated height rather than standing height, for example, because upper torsos may have different proportions than overall height (a short boy may have a similar seated height as a tall girl, for example). Give students directions to measure two body parts of fellow class members, calculate their ratio, and make a scatter plot of the data. Some possible ratios include:

   • seated height to forearm length;
   • forearm length to foot length (with shoes on);
   • neck circumference to wrist circumference

   (In the book *Gulliver's Travels* by Jonathan Swift, the Lilliputians tried to construct clothing for Gulliver by the use of ratios. "Once around the thumb is twice around the wrist; once around the wrist is twice around the neck" comes from that political satire.)

2. A related ratio is shoe length to size, which can be used to predict the length of the latest basketball star's shoes (size 18?).

3. The notion of using measurable amounts to predict those that are not immediately measurable is a big idea in data analysis. A sports audience phenomena of the 1990s was the "wave." Started by any group in an arena or stadium, people would begin standing with their arms upraised, with people to their left following suit, and so on until the wave came full circle, back to where it began. A mathematical question based on this common happening is, "How many seconds does it take for the 'wave' to circle Dodger (or another) Stadium?" Students can collect data on how long it takes various numbers of them to do the wave and, with a little research about the approximate circumference of the given stadium, use a linear model to estimate a reasonable answer to the question. This could be varied by asking how long it would take for the entire school's student body to line up and do the wave.

4. The pi ratio can be estimated by measuring the circumference of various circular objects and their diameters. Tape measures or string are needed for this activity. Kitchen objects can be brought to the classroom for this activity—plates, saucers, pans, lids, etc. Other objects include rolls of tape, some bracelets, lamp shades, etc. After taking the two measurements for each object, students plot the diameter on the horizontal axis and the circumference on the vertical axis. The slope of the line that fits these points should approximate pi.

5. The ratio of volume (V) to mass (M) gives the density, thus a connection to science. The volume and mass of different sizes of wooden blocks can be determined by ruler and scale, respectively. Another connection to science is to measure spring lengths when stretched by different masses. Also, the "coefficient of restitution (or elasticity)" of a bouncing ball is found by comparing drop height to the height of the ball's first bounce.

Nonlinear Data

1. Ball bouncing also can produce nonlinear data if the consecutive heights of the same ball are plotted against the number of bounces. Technology can be used to collect and plot these data. Calculator-Based-Laboratory® (Texas Instruments) and Data Analyzer® (Casio) are two tools for collecting such data, along with motion sensors and display devices. Exponential decay curves are thus developed in real time.

2. Another way of modeling exponential change (growth and/or decay) is to use a large number of dice to represent a given population, with certain values of the dice representing the rate of growth or decay. For example, start with 50 dice representing an animal population that has a death rate of 16%. After a random throwing of all 50 dice, remove all of one number—say, the 6s—representing animals that died. Record the number of animals left. Throw the remaining dice again, following the same directions. Use the results to predict when that species of animal would be extinct, given the same conditions. Vary the activity by starting with 10 dice and adding 1 more each time a 1 is thrown, representing a birth rate of 16%. As a variation, use random-number tables to generate the birth and growth at different rates. The function to best model growth or decay based upon a common factor is the exponential function.

3. Technology, in the form of probeware, can be used to measure the drop in temperature of a cup of coffee over time as another example of exponential decay. The probeware comes in the form of a heat sensor that can be connected to a computer or a graphing calculator so that when it is placed in the cup, the data are graphed in real time, showing the shape of curve depicting the temperature decrease.

4. To extend measurement associated with circles, whole lentils or dried peas could be placed compactly inside lids one layer deep and counted, to give an area measure in beans. This result could then be compared with the circumference measure found by placing the same size of beans end-to-end around the lid. (Note that this is not the same as the typical area formula for a circle, based on its radius.)

5. The sine wave can be modeled with Slinky® toys and a motion detector. The detector is positioned face up, and the spring is above it. When a steady up-and-down motion is maintained over a period of time, the resulting graph is periodic. By estimating period and amplitude on the graph as well as any vertical or horizontal displacement, the sinusoidal function modeling the motion can be developed. The class level of such a modeling activity is probably pre-calculus.

6. Almanac data that may be useful include latitude of cities versus mean high temperatures in a given month, sports records over time (including separate statistics for women when available), populations of various countries over time, etc.

CHAPTER

5

Geometry and Algebra Redefined?

W
hy do geometry and algebra need to be redefined? They are historically established in the mathematics curriculum in the United States. During the 20th century, with few modifications, the underlying conception of algebra and geometry as they appeared in high-school textbooks has varied only in minor ways. As stated in the 1988 NCTM Yearbook, *The Ideas of Algebra, K–12* (p. 2), "the content of school mathematics in 1988 still bears a striking resemblance to the school mathematics of 1928, of 1948, or of 1968." Algebra is a content strand and/or a course dealing primarily with generalized arithmetic and procedures for solving various types of equations. In a somewhat dualistic way, geometry is both a study of a formal logical

system and a study of the characteristics of shapes, with theorems generally rooted in Euclid's system.

Yet, as in any field of endeavor, forces both inside and outside education contribute to changes in the discipline. Just as Newtonian physics has its place alongside the physics of relativity and as holistic medical practices are found to be a useful adjunct of science-based medicine, new developments in mathematics, educational psychology, and the use of technology can combine with traditional school mathematics to bring an understanding and appreciation of mathematics to more students. Mathematics is invented, not discovered, so new mathematics topics are continually surfacing. Some of the recent developments in mathematics have occurred because of the capabilities of computers and computer graphics. Fractal geometry is a notable example of a field of inquiry that is indelibly linked to multiple recursions made possible by the speed of modern data processors and the enhanced color graphics displayed on monitors.

The geometry and algebra dealt with in this chapter reflect the changes in those areas made possible and necessary not only by graphing computer technology but also by the practical demands of the future workforce for our youth. Students interested in pursuing technical careers need a basic understanding of algebra in order to be able to comprehend and use the equipment that will be available to them. Graphics design and the visual arts now make extensive use of computers, to name but two of the vocational areas that require modern skills alongside traditional hands-on experience. Therefore, all students, whether intending to attend college or not, should have sufficient understanding of algebra and geometry upon graduation from high school to be able to apply their concepts in the world they face in the future.

The NCTM *Principles and Standards for School Mathematics* (PSSM) include the conceptual underpinnings of algebra and geometry at the elementary level. Many resources have become available to help teachers of all grades implement the new vision of algebra and geometry for all students. The NCTM *Navigation* series is particularly useful. These booklets are organized by NCTM grade bands and Standards. Thus, there are four algebra booklets, one for each grade band (K–2, 3–5, 6–8, and 9–12) and a similar set for geometry. Each booklet includes a CD with blackline masters, selected articles, and applets of mathematics practices. They present current research-based ideas on the focus content area and include student activities that exemplify these approaches.

ABOUT THE ACTIVITIES FOR THIS CHAPTER

The activities in this chapter illustrate another standard that should be evident in work teachers have students do: multiple representations. For example, when your students use sketches, organized numerical information, and written logical explanations to solve a geometry problem, they demonstrate a deeper understanding of the mathematics than when they rely on a single representation. The geometry activities and illustrations show some ways this can be done. Likewise, the algebra activities stress multiple representations. Some activities, particularly Restaurant Rectangles, connect algebra and geometry.

As middle-school students work with integers on a number line and all four quadrants of the coordinate plane, they make a natural connection with geometry. However, measurement-based geometry is also important at the middle school, including the relationships between area, perimeter, and volume. Actual measurement of length and angle is a necessity in middle school. New versions of hands-on measurement tools help students overcome their misconceptions, especially regarding angle measure.

The role of technology in contemporary algebra and geometry cannot be ignored. Students can move easily from equations to graphs to tabular forms of functions. Dynamic computer graphic tools such as Nu Calc (the built-in application on Apple computers) and the Geometers' Sketchpad (available on multiple platforms) make it possible for students to participate in guided explorations based on visual depictions of algebraic functions or geometric shapes. However, generalizations based on visual models must be substantiated by deductive logic, a key element of all mathematics.

Set 5.1   Discussion Questions

1. What structural commonalties are there between algebra and geometry?
2. What mathematical topics rely on both algebraic and geometric understanding?

THE NATURE OF CONTEMPORARY GEOMETRY

The 1987 NCTM Yearbook, *Learning and Teaching Geometry, K–12,* presents many different articles about the place of geometry in the school mathematics curriculum. One of these, "Resolving the Continuing Dilemmas in School Geometry," summarizes the issues and makes some suggestions that recur in various forms in other articles (Usiskin, 1987, p. 30):

- Specify an elementary-school geometry curriculum by grade level.
- Do not keep students from studying geometry merely because they are poor at arithmetic or algebra.
- Require a significant amount of competence in geometry from all students.
- Require that all prospective teachers of mathematics, elementary or secondary, study geometry at the college level. (Author note: Two courses were required for mathematics teaching majors at my university—advanced Euclidean geometry and a non-Euclidean geometry course.)

Dynamic geometry software creates images and data that can be displayed to a large group via projection devices.

- Clarify the semantics used in discussion of geometry; avoid using such words as *approach* or *informal* as if they were well defined.
- Refine the level, quality, and quantity of discourse in discussion of the geometry curriculum.
- Analyze, from a curricular perspective, the various ways of conceptualizing geometry. (Usiskin feels that overdue emphasis has been paid to geometry as a logical system, to the detriment of other aspects of geometry, both practical and mathematical.)

The PSSM Geometry Standard has four components:

1. analyzing characteristics and properties of two- and three-dimensional geometric shapes and developing mathematical arguments about geometric relationships;
2. specifying locations and describing spatial relationships using coordinate geometry and other representational systems;
3. applying transformations and using symmetry to analyze mathematical situations;
4. using visualization, spatial reasoning, and geometric modeling to solve problems.

In this chapter we will present some of these other aspects of geometry that appear in *Standards*-based curricula.

For information about lessons and activities on modern middle school geometry and algebra, go to ***http://www.prenhall.com/ huetinck*** and click on Web Destinations for Chapter 5.

Three-Dimensional Geometry

Two geometry-related essays included in *On the Shoulders of Giants* (Steen, 1990) provide an overview of some overarching topics in the field of mathematics. One essay, "Dimension," talks about

how our being three-dimensional beings living in a three-dimensional world results in very young students having a natural sense of solid shapes. The author of this essay, Banchoff, laments the decline of solid geometry topics in the mathematics curriculum because he feels they are not only practical but also more understandable for young people. As a response to the need for earlier introduction of three-dimensional topics early in high-school curriculum, *Core-Plus (Contemporary Mathematics in Context),* introduces geometry in Course 1 by dealing with space-shapes first in Chapter 5, "Patterns in Space and Visualization."

Even though a quality mathematics education at the elementary level will include concept development through such three-dimensional shapes as cubes and pattern blocks, secondary students also need hands-on experiences with three-dimensional shapes. Not only does this address different learning styles by having students actually make and analyze structures, but students also develop appreciation for fields such as architecture and carpentry that rely on two-dimensional representations of three-dimensional objects. Topics such as isometric drawing, which were limited to the drafting curriculum in the past, now appear in most contemporary mathematics books.

The other geometry essay in *On the Shoulders of Giants,* "Shape" (Senechal, 1990) includes this statement: "Just as Shakespeare is not sufficient for literature and Copernicus is not sufficient for astronomy, so Euclid is not sufficient for geometry." After suggesting many shape-related mathematical explorations, Senechal summarizes why shape should be given adequate attention in the curriculum. One is the inherently interdisciplinary nature of the study of shape, particularly as combined with scale. Biology and art are but two content areas with obvious connections to the geometry of scale. For example, could the giant creatures of the movies, such as King Kong, really exist, based on what we know about structure? Also, the natural connection between hands-on activities and the study of shape beg for lessons involving students in building and exploring models. Furthermore, the study of shape is motivating and enjoyable to many students, as contrasted to the study of abstract postulates and theorems prevalent in all too many geometry classrooms. Finally, technology is making possible the study of shapes in ways that are new and different from ever before. New geometric discoveries are yet to be made!

Activities 5.1 and 5.2 require three-dimensional visualization to find relationships between geometric figures. These two activities can be presented as individual or group activities.

F O R   T E A C H E R S

Activity 5.1 Gumdrops and Toothpick Shapes

Mathematical Content:
Solid geometry, Euler's theorem (PSSM
    Geometry Standard for Grades 6–8)

Materials Needed:
Small gumdrops (30 or so per group),
    toothpicks (5 or so per group)

Directions: Divide students into groups of four. Give ground rules for the use of the gumdrops and toothpicks. Work with the class as they build the first polyhedron and complete the table, making sure the vertices, faces, and edges are correctly identified. It may be helpful to have a solid tetrahedron in the classroom so students who have difficulty seeing the faces can have a tangible example demonstrated. Note that when students build the square pyramid, there are two shapes for the faces—a square for the base and isosceles triangles for the lateral faces.

Monitor the groups as they work through the parts of the activity, making sure they answer the questions that require verbal answers.

When the groups are mostly finished, have members of various groups state the conjecture they wrote from 3(c). Record the conjectures on transparencies, chart paper, chalkboard, or whiteboard. Ask questions like the following to elicit student discourse:

■ What similarities do you see among the
    conjectures? What differences?
■ Are there any questions you would ask a
    group about their conjecture?
■ To what extent did building more shapes
    support your conjecture?

As the class continues to discuss the activity, ask:

■ What do we mean by a theorem? How are
    theorems helpful to us?

F O R   T E A C H E R S

Activity 5.2 Cubes in 2-D and 3-D (see For Students, p. 166)

Mathematical Content:
Using two-dimensional representations of three-
    dimensional objects to visualize and solve
    problems involving surface area and volume
    (PSSM Geometry Standard for Grades 6–8)

Materials Needed:
Isometric dot paper; at least 12 congruent cubes
    for each student, interlocking, if possible

Directions: Many students have trouble visualizing the isometric representation of cubes. They may need your help to see how to look at the

drawing. Holding a cube with the same orientation as the one in the drawing is helpful to these students. Likewise, students may need to build the shape represented in the second drawing in order to understand why 4 cubes are necessary under the given constraints.

Extensions: If the constraint that the figure must be freestanding were eliminated, several different solutions could exist for many isometric drawings. Students could explore the least cubes needed for such a shape, as well as the most.

Activity 5.1
Gumdrops and Toothpick Shapes

Directions: In groups, you will be building some **polyhedra**—three-dimensional shapes whose faces are polygons. Do not break the toothpicks to make the shapes. Push the points of the toothpicks into the gumdrops to form **vertices.** The toothpicks form the **edges** of the shapes.

1. The polyhedron with the fewest faces is a tetrahedron. Use four gumdrops and six toothpicks to make a tetrahedron. The faces of this tetrahedron should all be congruent equilateral triangles. Copy and complete this table for your tetrahedron.

Shape Name	Kind of Face(s)	Number of Faces (F)	Number of Vertices (V)	Number of Edges (E)
tetrahedron	equilateral triangle			

   a. Make a sketch of your tetrahedron.

   b. How many edges meet at each vertex of the tetrahedron?

   c. What happens if you remove just one toothpick from the shape?

2. Build a cube with toothpicks and gumdrops, and use it to complete the next row of the chart.

   a. Make a sketch of your cube.

   b. How many edges meet at each vertex of the cube?

   c. How is the cube different from the tetrahedron? In what ways are they alike?

   d. What common objects or structures are cubes?

3. Build a square pyramid—a shape with a square base and triangles coming to a point at the top. Complete the chart.

   a. Make a sketch of your pyramid.

   b. Describe a pattern you see in the chart.

   c. Make a conjecture about one thing you think will always be true for polyhedra.

4. Build four more different polyhedra, and complete the table for them.

5. Is there any consistent pattern relating faces, vertices, and edges? State the pattern as a formula.

6. Look up Euler's theorem in a geometry book, and compare it with your findings in Problem 5.

F O R   S T U D E N T S

Activity 5.2
Cubes in 2-D and 3-D

Directions: Isometric dot paper has dots placed so that isosceles triangles can be drawn easily. A three-dimensional representation of a cube can also be drawn on isometric dot paper. One way of doing this is shown. All drawings in this exploration will be based upon this example. In the drawing you see a cube as viewed from one edge. If this is hard for you to visualize, hold a cube in your hand and look at it from the edge until you see how the sides can be matched with lines on the drawing. Some edges of a cube are invisible in the following drawing.

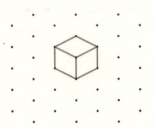

When cubes are drawn on isometric paper so that they appear to be stacked together, we assume that the shape can stand on its own when made with blocks. This means that, even when some cubes cannot be seen, if they are necessary for the shape to stand, we assume that they are part of the structure. For example, the structure below must be made of four cubes, even though only three can be seen in the drawing. Can you explain why?

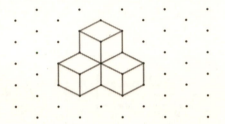

The volume of a shape formed by cubes is determined by counting the number of cubes, if they all are the same size. The surface area of a cube is found by counting the number of faces on all surfaces of the shape, even the bottom. If the top and bottom faces are left out, the number of cubes on the other faces is the lateral area.

1. Find the volume and surface area of the isometric shapes drawn below. Use cubes to help you, as needed.

2. Make a structure consisting of up to 12 cubes, and draw the shape on isometric paper. Then trade your drawing with a classmate, and see if each of you can construct the other person's 3-D structure, based on the other's drawing.

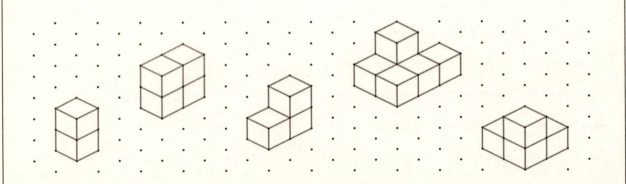

Geometry—More Than Euclid

Traditionally, a geometry course at the high-school level has served to contribute to students' understanding of the nature of shapes as well as the logical structure required to verify a hypothesis deductively. Unfortunately, research indicates that the standard textbook approach usually results in many college-bound students developing discomfort with and even dislike for geometry because of their inability to grasp the nature of deductive proof presented in two-column form (Senk, 1985). Other forms of deductive proof, including paragraph (Euclid's method) and flow proofs, are presented in many current textbooks.

The NCTM *Curriculum Standards* promote a broad set of geometry topics to be made accessible to all high-school students within the 3-year college preparatory core program, as well as topics to be explored at the middle-school level. In addition, it suggests presenting the notion of formal proof in Euclidean geometry from synthetic, analytic, and transformational perspectives. Furthermore, the concept of proof as justification of assertions through analytic reasoning should be developed informally over time, beginning long before high school. Thus, verbal and written responses to probing mathematical questions are important elements of K–8 mathematics, leading to a deeper understanding of and appreciation for the nature of mathematical proof by students at the high-school level.

The November 1998 issue of *The Mathematics Teacher* is a focus issue on the concept of proof. Referring back to an article on proof that appeared in a 1938 NCTM yearbook, the editorial panel of that journal suggested that we need to examine continually the role and appropriateness of proof at various stages of students' mathematical development. For example, how is the critical thinking that is necessary for understanding whether a proof is valid affected by stressing memorization of facts and procedures during the earlier grades? We found our ability to reason at the university level very much a function of the independent reading we did outside the standard curriculum that was offered during our high-school days. Certainly, the connection between language development and cognitive development is well researched. It would seem, then, that students' verbalization of mathematical reasoning and understanding is an important aspect of learning about mathematical proof. *Standards*-based curricular materials at all grade levels stress the use of mathematical language and the development of "mathematical literacy."

Three Perspectives of Formal Proof

Synthetic geometry goes back to Euclid and the Greeks. The structure of a formal logical system is illustrated by proving geometric relationships based upon the use of a rational sequence of definitions, postulates, and theorems. Even though the NCTM *Curriculum and Evaluation Standards* recommends decreasing the amount of attention given to the formal structure of Euclidean geometry, students at the middle-school level and even earlier can experience the challenge and satisfaction of dealing with probing questions that ask them to justify conclusions, explain how they know a given pattern always works, or find a counterexample to show that a pattern does not always work and is therefore disproved. Bringing in an emphasis on the NCTM Communication and Reasoning Standards through geometry topics promotes the mathematical thinking that we value in students.

Another perspective of formal proof, analytic geometry, was first used in the ninth century, but the concept as it is presently construed is rooted in the work of later mathematicians, notably Fermat (1596–1650) and Descartes (1601–1665). Fermat developed the fundamental theorem of analytical geometry, which is that, given a fundamental problem, one can find an equation to solve it. The combination of analytical geometry, the algebra of functions, and modern graphing technology has drastically altered the way function analysis can now be taught, even at the middle-school level.

A third perspective of formal proof, transformational geometry, is largely a product of the 20th century, with initiation by Felix Klein (1849–1925) in the late 19th century. Transformational techniques can be demonstrated both by some of the graphics technology and by a MIRA® or by a plane mirror. For example, students can discover rotations and translations as compositions of reflections by doing the appropriate constructions.

Even though a transformational geometry course is rarely required of prospective teachers of secondary mathematics, graphing technology makes it possible for their students to be introduced to several topics within this content area. Basic functions such as $y = x$ or $y = x^2$ are frequently introduced as "parent" functions in contemporary textbooks. Various changes in the parent graph are directly related to modifications of the symbolic representation of the function. Thus, analytic geometry, algebra, and transformational geometry are naturally integrated.

The important point is that the integration of algebra and geometry in exemplary examples of reformed curriculum is part of a long continuum of development within mathematics. The new component is graphing technology, such that, in keying in the equations, viewing the resulting graphs, and noting changes in the graphs resulting from changes made to the equations, students' understanding is enhanced. Even students who will not be attending college can be motivated by the prevalence of computer graphics in the modern world and the importance of mathematics-related technological understanding for many fields of work. Likewise, for students intending mathematics-intensive careers that require university study, an early start on the geometry of functions and the modeling capabilities made possible by a deeper understanding of the nature of these functions can only be beneficial.

All three approaches—synthetic, analytic, and transformational—have benefits and limitations. Consider a simple example of applying the SSS Triangle Congruence to problems presented synthetically, analytically, and transformationally.

I. Synthetic

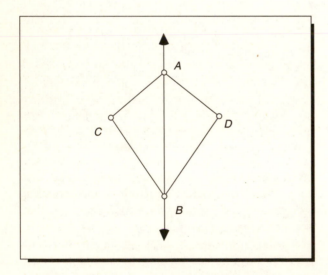

Given: $\triangle ABC$ and $\triangle ABD$ such that
$AC \cong AD$; $BC \cong BD$

Prove: $\triangle ABC \cong \triangle ABD$

Statements	Reasons
1. $AC \cong AD$, $BC \cong BD$	1. Given
2. $AB \cong AB$	2. Identity
3. $\triangle ABC \cong \triangle ABD$	3. SSS

QED

II. Analytic

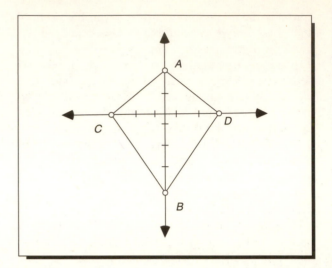

Procedure:
Use the distance formula to show corresponding sides have equal length;

$$AD: \sqrt{(0-3)^2 + (2-0)^2} = \sqrt{13}$$
$$AC: \sqrt{[0-(-3)]^2 + (2-0)^2} = \sqrt{13}$$
$$BD: \sqrt{(0-3)^2 + (-4-0)^2} = 5$$
$$BC: \sqrt{(0-(-3))^2 + (-4-0)^2} = 5$$

Then, since AB is a common side, use SSS to conclude that the two triangles are congruent.

III. Transformational

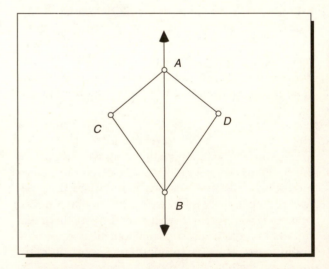

D is the image of C in AB. A is its own image, as is B. $AC \cong AD$, and $BC \cong BD$, since reflections preserve distance. $AB \cong AB$ (identity). By SSS, the two triangles are congruent.

Figure 5.1
Three Ways to Present Geometric Concepts

Synthetic	Analytic	Transformational
m(length AB) = $|B - A|$ Parallel lines are two lines on the plane whose distance from each other is constant.	$D = \sqrt{(x_1 - x_2)^2 + (y_1 - y_2)^2}$ Parallel lines on the coordinate plane have the same slope.	
Congruent planar figures have corresponding sides and angles equal.	Congruent figures in the coordinate plane have corresponding sides of the same measure and the absolute value of corresponding slopes equal.	Congruence is a one-to-one correspondence between two geometric figures that preserves distance and angle measure (Okolica & Macrina, 1992).
Perpendicular lines are two lines on the same plane that form right angles.	Perpendicular lines on the same plane have slopes whose product is -1.	Two lines are perpendicular if one is the reflection line of the other line in itself.
The midpoint of a line segment is equidistant from the endpoints of the segment.	The midpoint, M, of a line segment is found by $M = \dfrac{x_1 + x_2}{2}, \dfrac{y_1 + y_2}{2}$	One way of determining a midpoint of a line segment is that it lies on the line of reflection of one endpoint of the segment in the other.

Set 5.2 Discussion Questions

Questions with an asterisk appear in the Message Board section of the Companion Website at *http://www.prenhall.com/huetinck.* Go to Chapter 5 and click on the Message Board to find and respond to the question.

*1. Which proof do you find most convincing? most "elegant"? Why?

2. Which form of proof would you introduce first to young people? Why?

3. Discuss the advantages and disadvantages of each approach. Under what mathematical circumstances would the synthetic approach be most appropriate? the analytic approach? the transformational approach?

The table in Figure 5.1 compares the presentation of some geometric concepts as they are commonly presented synthetically, analytically, and transformationally.

Set 5.3 Discussion Question

Questions with an asterisk appear in the Message Board section of the Companion Website at *http://www.prenhall.com/huetinck.* Go to Chapter 5 and click on the Message Board to find and respond to the question.

*1. What are some other geometric concepts/theorems that can be expressed synthetically, analytically, and/or transformationally?

Inductive and Deductive Reasoning

Because of their nature, explorations lend themselves to inductive reasoning. Based upon observation and collected data, generalizations are made. It may be difficult for students to understand that a generalization is always open to revision, even if they see no counterexamples of it, unless the generalization is verified (proved) deductively. In contrast, a deductive conclusion always is true, because it is based on accepted statements and a logical structure. Herein lies a distinction between the scientific process—which includes mathematical discovery—and the logical structure of mathematical deduction. For example, when students notice that the midsegment of a triangle always appears to be parallel to the third side of the triangle in numerous examples using a dynamic geometry grapher, most will quickly conjecture that the parallel relationship between a midsegment and the third side of a triangle always will be true. Raising the possibility that this can never be conclusively verified by experimental means creates the need for a deductive analysis of the situation.

At a simpler level, some arithmetic relationships can be "proved" by visual means. Two that come to mind are the sum of the first n counting numbers and the sum of the first m odd numbers. See the following "proofs."

$1 + 2 + 3 + 4 + 5 + \ldots =$

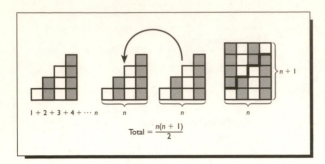

$1 + 3 + 5 + 7 + \ldots =$

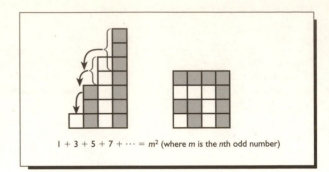

Only as students become more comfortable with an understanding of mathematical justification should more sophisticated techniques be introduced, such as mathematical induction.

Activities 5.3 and 5.4 promote mathematical reasoning in geometric situations for students at a wide range of levels. The follow-up questions and exten-

sions are essential if students are to go beyond simply completing the activity to thinking about and verbalizing what they have learned and finding additional mathematical extensions. In doing these activities, students can access significant geometric concepts at an intuitive level in preparation for formalized proofs.

F O R   T E A C H E R S

Activity 5.3 Growing Patterns

Mathematical Content:
Relationship between area and perimeter of
    similar figures (PSSM Geometry Standards for
    Grades 6–8 and 9–12)

Materials Needed:
Bucket of pattern blocks for each group of
    4 students

Directions: Using an overhead projector and transparent pattern block pieces, work through the first three problems with the entire class. Make sure students understand that the area of a given figure can be based on the assumption that a single unit of that shape represents one unit, regardless of the shape. If the green triangle is the basic unit of area, for example, the next larger similar shape is composed of four triangles, so the area is quadrupled. However, the perimeter, 6, is twice that of the original triangle.

At this point, have groups proceed on their own, giving directions such as these:

"Continue to answer the questions in this activity, using pattern blocks as needed, and sketching diagrams of your findings. Write the perimeter and

area of each figure, and compare how they grow as larger figures are made."

As students complete this activity, have one group present results for the orange squares, one for the beige rhombi, one for the blue rhombi, and one for the trapezoids. As it turns out, this activity cannot be done with the red hexagons.

Make sure the conjecture is stated and clarified.

Extensions:
- Have students make starting figures of more than one type of shape and repeat the activity, if possible. The key to this is determining the unit of area.
- Have students explain why the hexagon cannot be repeated as the other tiles can.
- Have students use graph paper and make other shapes, such as rectangles, moving to doubling and tripling their perimeters.
- As a high-school extension, students could make dilations of simple figures and verify the relationship between the scale factor and the area, first by measurement and then by generalized proof. Connections to coordinate geometry are important here.

Activity 5.3
Growing Patterns

Directions: In your group, duplicate one of the pattern block shapes, only larger, using only those shapes that are like the original shape. Start by using green triangles to build larger triangles with the same shape as the original green triangle. Answer the following questions in your group, and write your group responses on one sheet of paper.

1. What is the smallest number of triangles needed to make the next larger triangle? Make a sketch of the new triangle.

2. If the area of the green triangle = 1 triangular unit and its perimeter = 3 length units, what is the area of the new triangle? The perimeter of the new triangle? Count to verify.

3. How do the area and perimeter of the new triangle compare with the area and perimeter of the original triangle?

4. What is the next largest similar triangle formed by small green triangles? Make a sketch of this triangle.

5. What are its area and perimeter?

6. What patterns of areas and perimeters do you see?

7. Predict the number of triangles needed to form the next largest similar triangle. Is the pattern the same?

8. Select a different pattern block piece and repeat the process.

9. How does the pattern with this pattern block compare to the pattern with the triangle?

10. State a conjecture about how perimeter and areas grow when building similar geometric shapes.

FOR TEACHERS

Activity 5.4 Patty Paper Triangles

Mathematical Content:
Geometric constructions and related vocabulary (PSSM Geometry Standard for Grades 6–8)

Materials Needed:
Boxes of patty papers (the thin sheets used to separate hamburger patties before cooking, available in restaurant supply stores), straightedges

Directions: Provide each student with several pieces of patty paper and a straightedge. Demonstrate the first four steps with the students, checking for accuracy. For Steps 2–4, it is important to assign different students to draw different types of angles and triangles so that the class can see that the constructions work in all cases.

The groups continue to follow the steps in the exercise. Some students will have trouble working with the patty paper at first, so be sure they have several extra pieces of paper and work together as needed.

Questions to Ask: Use these questions, and others, to debrief the class about their results:

1. What appeared to happen when the three perpendicular bisectors were constructed? the three angle bisectors? the three altitudes? the three medians?
2. Did the lines coincide in all types of triangles? (Be sure to bring in an obtuse triangle if no group used one for its constructions.)
3. For the equilateral triangle, what is true of the four different constructions, and why? How does that affect the number of points of concurrence?
4. For the isosceles triangle, what is true of the four different constructions, and why? How does that affect the number of points of concurrence?
5. What is true of the number of points of concurrence of a scalene triangle?

For high-school extensions, these questions should lead to further assignments to use deductive reasoning to prove the relationships discussed during the debrief of this activity.

See Activity Notes to the Teacher for Selected Problems at the end of this book for alternative lessons for these concepts, one with a MIRA® and one using dynamic geometry software.

A postulate of Euclidean geometry is as follows: given a line and a point not on the line, only one line can be drawn in the same plane parallel to the given line. Non-Euclidean geometry came about as the result of assuming the parallel postulate of Euclidean geometry to be false. To the astonishment of many mathematicians, a consistent axiomatic system could be developed either with the assumption that no lines could be drawn parallel to the given line (now called *elliptic* or *spherical geometry*) or with the assumption that all lines in a given system are parallel and so do not intersect (now called *hyperbolic geometry*). The Russian mathematician Nikolai Lobachevski, one of the discoverers of hyperbolic geometry, gave his first lecture of non-Euclidean geometry at the University of Kazan in 1826 and later wrote many treatises on the subject. Other pioneers in the development of these geometries were Hungarian mathematician János Bolyai (1802–1860) and German mathematician Bernhard Riemann (1826–1866).

Non-Euclidean geometry is introduced in some of the newer curriculum programs, but not as a body of knowledge to be studied in depth. Instead, it is used as a tool for examining axiomatic systems. Spherical geometry, in particular, provides an excellent illustration of an axiomatic system in which the sum of the angles of a triangle is not 180° and two points do not determine a unique line, when a line is defined to be a great circle of the sphere. Since these mathematical conclusions can be visualized with a model of the globe, all high-school students can understand the concepts underlying these alternative systems and see that they also have practical relevance in the world. Math Connections, Course 3, is one example of a *Standards*-based curriculum that includes non-Euclidean geometry. Another way to introduce spherical geometry to secondary students is through the use of the Lénart Sphere and related activities (Lénart, 1996).

Geometric probability is another modern topic that combines the characteristics of geometric shapes

Activity 5.4
Patty Paper Triangles—A Practice Lesson (page 1 of 2)

Directions: You will need two to three patty papers for practice before beginning the exercise.

STEP 1

a. Draw a line segment with noticeable endpoints (marked with dots).

b. Fold the paper so that one endpoint is on top of the other.

c. Crease the paper.

d. What does this fold do to the segment?

STEP 2

a. Draw an angle with a vertex and two rays.

b. Fold the paper on the vertex so that one endpoint is on top of the other.

c. Crease the paper.

d. What does this fold do to the angle?

STEP 3

a. Draw a triangle.

b. Fold the paper so the base is folded over on itself, then slide the paper until the fold goes through the opposite vertex.

c. Crease the paper.

d. What does this fold give you?

STEP 4

a. Draw a triangle.

b. Fold the paper so that two vertices are on top of each other and gently crease just on the side between the two vertices. This is the midpoint.

c. Make a crease from the midpoint to the opposite vertex.

d. What does this fold give you?

Exercise: Working in groups of four, the designated member of each group draws a large triangle on one piece of patty paper and then traces the same triangle on the other three pieces. At least one of the groups should draw an equilateral triangle and another an isosceles triangle. Members of each group should then do the following, with one group member assigned to each task:

F O R   S T U D E N T S

Activity 5.4
Patty Paper Triangles—A Discovery Lesson (page 2 of 2)

STEP 1. PERPENDICULAR BISECTORS OF EACH SIDE

As in Step 1 of the previous practice lesson, crease the perpendicular bisector of each side of your triangle. Make a noticeable dot where the perpendicular bisectors intersect.

STEP 2. ANGLE BISECTORS

As in Step 2 of the practice lesson, crease the angle bisector of each side of your triangle. Make a noticeable dot where the angle bisectors intersect.

STEP 3. ALTITUDE OF EACH SIDE

As in Step 3 of the practice lesson, crease the altitude of each side of your triangle. Make a noticeable dot where the altitudes intersect.

STEP 4. MEDIANS

As in Step 4 of the practice lesson, crease the median of each side. Make a noticeable dot where the medians intersect.

Questions:

1. Write a conjecture about the crease lines formed in each step.

Stack the four triangles carefully, one on top of the other, and staple them together. Label the type of triangle your group used. Hold your group's triangle "sandwich" up to a window and look at it closely. Next, look at the triangle "sandwiches" made by each of the other groups.

2. Write a conjecture about the positions of the intersections of the creases in the equilateral triangle.

Explain why this is reasonable.

3. Write a conjecture about the positions of the intersections of the creases in the isosceles triangle.

Explain why this is reasonable.

4. Write a conjecture about the positions of the intersections of the creases in the other triangles.

Explain why this is reasonable.

with mathematical chance. This topic is introduced as early as in elementary grades through the study of fair and unfair games, using spinners. Exploration of geometric probability continues in the middle grades with area models for consecutive independent events and develops further in the high-school core curriculum, lending itself to many interesting and challenging problems that can be used as extensions for the most able mathematics students.

Noncomputer Tools for Geometric Measurement

Contemporary findings on learning theory based on cognitive psychology suggest the value of a variety of approaches and multiple tools for helping stu-dents develop their own understanding of geomet-ric concepts. Not only are traditional construction tools helpful in developing students' sense of geometry relationships, but new construction de-vices, manipulatives, and dynamic geometry com-puter programs also are readily available for classroom use. Indeed, today's teacher of geometry has many different avenues by which to develop lessons for students of all ages and abilities.

Traditionally, two basic tools for geometric con-structions have been the compass and the straight-edge. Particularly when it comes to compasses, many versions now are available (see Figure 5.2). For example, for situations in which safety is a con-cern, a compass without a metal point is available. For the teacher, a Circle Master® compass offers flex-ibility because it may be used with overhead pens as

Figure 5.2

Noncomputer Tools for Geometry Measurement

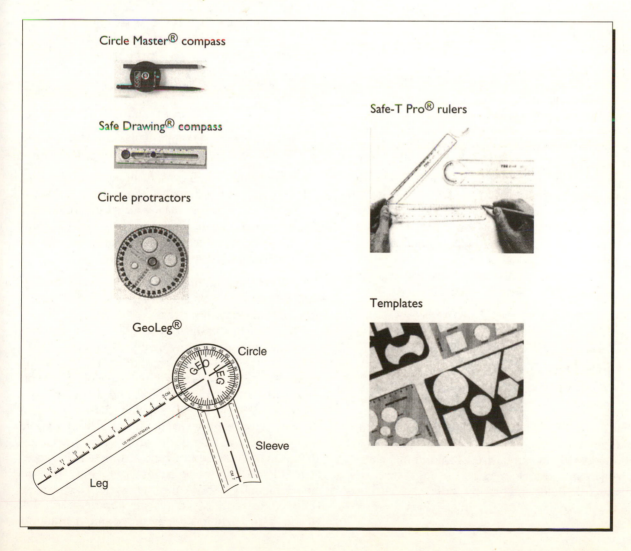

F O R   T E A C H E R S

Activity 5.5 Angle Sum of Triangles

Mathematical Content:
The sum of the angles of any triangle is 180°, $\angle 1 + \angle 2 + \angle 3 = 180°$
(PSSM Geometry Standard for Grades 6–8)

Materials:
A worksheet, pair of scissors and 3 GeoLegs for each pair of students

Directions: Have students work in pairs. They should have previous experience measuring angles with the GeoLegs. Demonstrate how to build a triangle with 3 GeoLegs on the overhead projector, having students following along. Then have them work through the worksheet as you circulate around the class monitoring their progress.

Extension: Have a student come to the overhead and demonstrate how the angles of a triangle can fit together to form a straight angle.

---

well as pencils. Likewise, when considering measuring tools, many types of instruments are currently available. For some students, a circular protractor may be less confusing than the standard semicircular one. The Barry protractor is very effective for younger students to relate directly the angle on a figure to its measurement, because the angle between the "jaws" is given by the placement of the pointer. In addition to standard and metric rulers, yardsticks, and meter sticks, flexible tapes may also be useful for measurements of curved distances. Some devices available, such as the Safe-T Pro® rulers, can even be used to measure dihedral angles of three-dimensional shapes. Templates may also be practical for assisting teachers and students in making more accurate drawings. Another tool is GeoLegs.® Activity 5.5 shows one of the many ways GeoLegs® can be used to support Geometry Standards.

 For more information on lessons and activities for Modern high school algebra and geometry, go to *http://www. prenhall.com/huetinck* and click on Web Destinations for Chapter 5.

THE NATURE OF CONTEMPORARY ALGEBRA

What is algebra? The word has different meanings for different people. Some say algebra is generalized arithmetic. Others emphasize its algorithmic nature. University algebraists stress its use in abstract systems such as fields and groups. Most associate algebra, at the very basic level, with variables expressed by symbols.

Four fundamental components of algebraic thinking are described in PSSM and the *Navigation* series:

1. understanding patterns, relations, and functions;
2. representing and analyzing mathematical situations and structures using algebraic symbols;
3. using mathematical models to represent and understand quantitative relationships;
4. analyzing change in various contexts.

Of course, these components take different forms at different grade levels and develop in sophistication over a student's school years.

"Algebra has its historical roots in the study of general methods for solving equations. The [PSSM] Algebra Standard emphasizes relationships among quantities, including functions, ways of representing mathematics relationships, and the analysis of change" (PSSM, p. 37). Within these two sentences, we see how the nature of school algebra has changed, mostly during the past two decades. If the mathematical concept of function is ascendant in secondary classrooms, preparing students in elementary school through systematic experiences with patterns plays an important role. If technology can help students move among numeric,

FOR STUDENTS

Activity 5.5
Angle Sum of Triangles

Mathematical Content: The sum of the angles of any triangle is 180°
 (PSSM Geometry Standard for Grades 6–8)

Materials:
A worksheet, pair of scissors and 3 GeoLegs for each pair of students

Directions: Work in pairs. You should have previous experience measuring angles with the GeoLegs. Demonstrate how to build a triangle with 3 GeoLegs on the overhead projector, having students following along. Then work through the worksheet as you circulate around the class monitoring their progress.

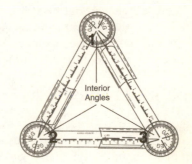

1. Measure and record the angles of the following triangles. (Round measures to nearest 5°.)

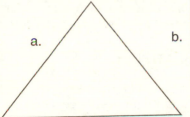 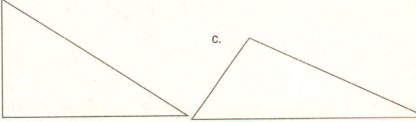

   Write a number sentence for each of the above triangles, showing the sum of the angles.

   a. _____   **b.** _____   **c.** _____

2. Using three GeoLegs, build a triangle with lengths of 18 cm, 10.5 cm, and 13 cm.

   Draw its shape.

   Look at and record its angle measures.

   What is the sum of the angles? _____

3. Hold the other two sides and decrease the length of the 18 cm side to 14.5 cm so that the lengths are 14.5 cm, 10.5 cm and 13 cm.

   Draw its shape and record its angle measures.

   What is the sum of the angles? _____

4. Two angle measures of a triangle are given. Build the triangles to find the third angle measure. Then verify the measure using this number sentence: $180° - (\angle 1 + \angle 2) = \angle 3$

   a. 45°, 70°, _____

   b. 95°, 50°, _____

5. Explain the angle sum of triangles.

Extension: *Why does the sum of the three angles equal 180°?* Did you know that the three angles of a triangle will fit together on a straight angle? Use a triangle from Example 1. Cut out each of the angles and fit them on this straight angle.

Source: Geoleg Program, P.O. Box 14754, Monroe, LA 71201, geolegs@aol.com.

symbolic, tabular, and graphic representation of data, we should develop lessons that encourage students to use these various forms and to engage in discourse that goes beyond what the technology shows to make logical connections. Teachers need to be prepared to assist students as they analyze data in order to develop appropriate mathematics models for the patterns of change the students discern.

Here we give a brief historical background in order to view the present from the perspective of past developments. We then examine some of the issues inherent in the goal of "algebra for all."

Historic Development of Algebra

Algebra began as a set of tools for solving practical problems. The tools were verbal recipes (algorithms) for the Babylonians, geometric representations for the Greeks, recipes again for the Arabs and medieval Europeans, and finally, letters and symbols for the people of the Renaissance. The name *algebra* is from the Latin translation of the Arabic title of al-Khwarizmi's book on algebra, which he wrote about A.D. 825.

Negative numbers had been around for centuries (generally thought of as debts) before Gerolamo Cardano (1501–1576) organized their use and rules. The need for square roots of negative numbers arose with the introduction of Cardano's formula for the root of cubic equations. However, the use of the terms *real* and *imaginary* as they are used in the modern sense first appeared in the work of René Descartes (1596–1650). The topic of algebra was later expanded to the study of the nature of roots of equations. Francois Viete (1540–1603) introduced the systemic use of letters for constants, which was carried further by Descartes in algebraic representation of geometrical quantities. Descartes made algebra into an organized body of knowledge in his book *Geometrie* (1636). Thus, algebra became a tool for representing numbers and numerical relationships by symbols, letters, and coordinate graphs.

Certainly this definition of algebra still underlies the content of most secondary-level algebra texts. The development of the real-number system, its subsets (natural numbers, whole numbers, integers, and rational and irrational numbers), and its properties provides the basis for the structure of algebra. Imaginary numbers are introduced later, after real numbers, usually along with solutions of quadratic equations representing parabolas. Except for a few topics such as matrices, the algebra primarily taught today in Grades 6–12 has the same content as that subject prior to 1824.

The year 1824 is significant because it marked a radical departure: algebra that cannot be reduced to geometry. In that year, Neil Henrik Abel (1802–1829) proved that it is impossible to solve the general equation above the fourth degree. In other words, except for special cases, the equation

$$ax^5 + bx^4 + cx^3 + dx^2 + ex + f = 0$$

cannot be solved by a finite number of arithmetic steps. In contrast, the quadratic equation provides a means to find the roots of the general equation, $ax^2 + bx + c = 0$ using addition, subtraction, multiplication, division, and taking a square root. These calculations can be represented geometrically and their solutions performed with straightedge and compass. After 1824, algebras were invented that cannot be reduced to geometry. For example, matrix theory is a part of modern algebra beyond the ability of the Euclidean tools. Algebra broadened in this century into a set of operations on a set of mathematical objects.

Today's School Algebra

Today's school algebra can be considered to be one of three types. First, it can be one of generative activities such as solving equations with an unknown and finding patterns and numerical relationships. Second, it can be transformational, such as in finding equivalent expressions. Third, it can be global in problem solving, modeling, proving theorems, and predicting new relationships. Through proficient development of skill in using the self-consistent system of definitions of mathematical entities and their properties, mathematicians can travel to new territories (Kieran, 1996). Unfortunately, K–12 students of mathematics all too infrequently get beyond the mechanics of algebra to appreciate the elegance and power of the subject for modeling and problem solving.

Researchers are working with classroom teachers to study mathematical activities that require students to generalize quantitative relationships other than with symbols. What kinds of classroom activities lead to algorithmic thinking that may be expressed verbally, in tables, or in graphs rather than with variables? What methods of equation solving are useful and understandable to students in addition to standard algebraic transformations? How are such nontraditional forms of mathematical thinking acknowledged and valued by teachers accustomed to standard approaches? Mathematics educators across the United States and in many other locations around the world are dealing with these questions. They are gathering evidence, based on student work, of the thinking processes entailed in this expanded notion of algebra, frequently called "algebraic thinking." This kind of work is neither to be considered in place of letter-symbolic algebra nor at a different level. Rather, it is another way of looking at how students do and understand mathematics.

At the middle-school level, the main algebra emphasis is linear relationships, building on proportional reasoning. Students work with discrete examples, building tables, plotting points, and generalizing in words and symbols. When first working with tables to arrive at generalizations, students often notice the recursive pattern and find it more difficult to arrive at an explicit formula. For example, when looking for patterns in the table below, where the increase in x is by 1, many students would notice the increase by 3 in the y column and would find the value for y that corresponds to $x = 10$ by successive counting on by 3 until the 10th term is reached. PSSM acknowledges that tendency of students and validates it. However, students need to see how the recursive pattern can help them write an explicit equation for the same relationship. In this example, the common increase of 3 indicates a pattern of linear growth. An equation that expresses y in terms of x must have 3 multiplied by x, with an adjustment made by adding a number that "works," i.e., where the equation, when evaluated for a given x-value, yields the related y-value.

x	y
1	4
2	7
3	10
4	13
...	
10	
x	

Activity 5.6, Square Patterns and Algebra, has students use various representations of a linear pattern to develop the concepts of slope and intercept. In covering this topic, a cautionary note is in order: When we teach slope as the measure of steepness of a line, we may inadvertently foster a misconception. For one thing, we can compare the steepness of two different lines only when their scales are the same. Furthermore, a greater concern is that the notion of slope as a ratio—an important idea in higher mathematics, as well as in many applications of mathematics—may inadvertently be downplayed. Slope as a measure of speed (the distance an object moves in a given amount of time) requires a different way of thinking than steepness. In this case, students have to measure both distance and time to find the rate of speed. After conducting a study on students' understanding of slope as "ratio as measure," Lobato & Thanheiser (2002) concluded that instructional activities that help students cope with the complexity of this concept should be encouraged, as it is more general and applicable than the notion of slope as steepness.

The question "What is algebra?" cannot be answered simply. Depending on the viewpoint, algebra may be primarily a tool to solve practical problems, a study of functions, a system with its own rules and logic, or more than all of these. The study conference of NCTM in 1992, Algebra for the Twenty-First Century, did not define algebra, but did develop some common principles. Two of these areas of agreement are emphasized in this text. The first is that algebra is not a discrete subject. In fact, the layer-cake approach of many high-school textbooks stemming from the division of algebra and geometry into separate courses has a rather short history. The integration of these two fields in exemplary reformed curricula is nothing new. A second commonality is that technology can greatly assist students in accessing an updated view of algebra.

Technology for Problem Solving

With the advent of technology, secondary-level students can and should enlarge their view of algebra, because they now have methods of representing relationships that may *not* require letter or symbolic form. "Technology" is used here in the broadest sense to include computers, probeware, graphing calculators, scientific calculators, four-function calculators, and even manipulatives. For example, spreadsheets are a visual technological tool for moving from the specific problem to a general approach. We may deal with families of functions connected to graphical or tabular approaches. A real situation may first be explored graphically with calculators or visually with manipulatives, then studied in symbolic format.

F O R   T E A C H E R S

Activity 5.6 Square Patterns and Algebra

Mathematical Content:
Developing slope and intercept through concrete models (PSSM Algebra Standard for Grades 6–8)

Materials:
Small square tiles for each pair of students, worksheet for each student

Directions: Set the stage by asking students about their understanding of slope by asking questions such as these:

- Where have you heard the word, slope, used? What does it mean?
- Why do we need to know slope? (Steepness of hills when building roads, roofs of buildings, predicting future outcomes, etc.)

Explain that students will be looking at some patterns made with squares. Have them take out their tiles and copy the patterns as you make them on the overhead.
   Point out that the first stage has three squares.

Then demonstrate the second stage.

- How many square tiles did it take to make this stage?
- What do you think the third stage will look like?
- Students in pairs create the third-stage pattern. Partners check for understanding. Have one or more students come to the overhead and make the third stage. If different patterns emerge, affirm them and say that you will choose one for the first example.

Distribute the work sheets. Students notice that the first three patterns are recorded for them.

1. Students create additional patterns.
2. Students begin to complete table, filling in the column for Total Tiles. Continue to complete the table and generalize to a formula.
3. Students move to the graph and plot the discrete points.
4. Students discuss where the slope is on the tile pattern, graph, and table.
5. Students note the number of tiles in the pattern right before the first stage and relate that to the concept of intercept.

Extension: Give students additional "starters" for linear patterns that they can build with squares and represent by table, graph, and equation.

Closure: Students respond to this writing prompt:

   Write what you have learned in this lesson. Include how slope and intercept are shown in this activity.

FOR STUDENTS

Activity 5.6
Square Patterns and Algebra

In this activity you will see how the algebra concepts of slope and intercept can be represented in several ways.

Student Directions:

1. Use the space below to record the first five steps of the pattern.

2. Complete the table.

3. Graph the number pairs from the table on the coordinate graph below.

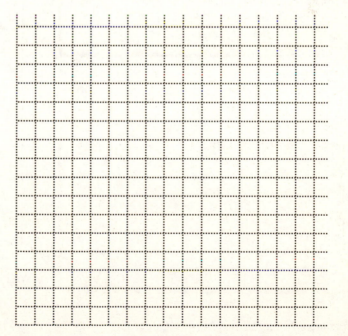

Step	Total Tiles
1	
2	
3	
4	
5	
20	
n	

Step 1

Step 2

Step 3

Step 4

Step 5

4. Discuss with a partner how the slope and intercept are represented in the concrete models, on the table, and on the graph.

The following example illustrates the multiple ways that a problem may be solved:

> You have finally been offered a paying job as a rock band drummer. Two different groups want you to play with them, but their contract offers are drastically different. Group 1 will pay a flat fee of $1,000 per concert. Group 2 will pay only $100 per concert but will double this amount for each additional concert day played. Which is the better deal? Why?

Method 1: Table

	Days			
	1	2	3	4
Group 1 Total	1,000	2,000	3,000	4,000
Group 2 Total	100	100 + 200 = 300	300 + 400 = 700	700 + 800 = 1,500

Method 2: Spreadsheet

A spreadsheet for six concerts:

Concert	Group 1 Daily	Group 1 Total	Group 2 Daily	Group 2 Total
Day 1	1,000	1,000	100	100
Day 2	1,000	2,000	200	300
Day 3	1,000	3,000	400	700
Day 4	1,000	4,000	800	1,500
Day 5	1,000	5,000	1,000	3,100
Day 6	1,000	6,000	3,200	6,400

Method 3: Graphing Calculator
A comparison of the graphs $y_1 = 100x$ and $y_2 = 100(2^x - 1)$:

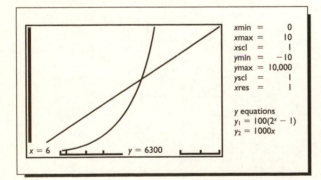

Technology-Related Insights into Quadratics   As students move into quadratic equations, graphing technology can play a role in helping them see the relationship between linear functions and quadratic

functions. Two examples of the unique way this can be done follow.

1. Using a graphing calculator, students graph simple linear functions, such as $y_1 = x + 3$ and $y_2 = x + 2$. By tracing, students note the x-intercepts of -3 and -2, respectively, and y-intercepts of 3 and 2, respectively. Next, by graphing $y_3 = (x + 3)(x + 2)$, students can see the product of those two lines graphed as a parabola that has the same x-intercepts and whose y-intercept is the product of the y-intercepts of the two lines, or 6. This visual relationship can be explored further, analyzed, and proved deductively for all cases.

2. With the second method, as shown in Winicki-Landman (2001), students use graphing technology to explore patterns of solutions of quadratic equations whose coefficients themselves have specific patterns, such as consecutive integers.

These and other kinds of explorations made possible by technology allow for students to interact with algebraic ideas in ways never before possible. As another exploration, have students try looking at patterns of factorable trinomials. For instance, if the first two terms are $x^2 + 5x$, what constants could the third term be in order for the trinomial to be factorable over the set of integers?

Set 5.4 Discussion Questions

Questions with an asterisk appear in the Message Board section of the Companion Website at *http://www.prenhall.com/huetinck*. Go to Chapter 5 and click on the Message Board to find and respond to the question.

*1. Write your own definition(s) of algebra, with examples to illustrate.
2. Give several examples of how your description of algebra would be reflected in classroom activities appropriate for middle school, Course 1, and advanced high-school algebra.
3. How will the two forces affecting the teaching of algebra, or Course 1 in an integrated program as described in this chapter, affect your own classroom?

What Is Algebra for All?

In the 1988 NCTM Yearbook, *The Ideas of Algebra, K–12*, Peggy House identifies two forces that are influencing the teaching of algebra. They are the growth and availability of computer technology for the secondary classroom and social demands on schools to be accountable to provide a better-educated workforce. Not only do students planning to enter traditionally technology-intensive careers such as engineering need to experience the problem-solving and modeling capabilities made possible by technology, but also students preparing for vocational careers after high school need a good understanding of algebra and the capabilities of technology. In an article in the *Los Angeles Times,* "The Science of Auto Body Repair" (1996), the owner of a technologically advanced auto body shop stated, "We're finding that we can't accept the people who were forced to go to the automotive side in high school because they couldn't conform to the scholastic side. They need the algebra and the math to run the machines."

The college-preparatory algebra course is a known gatekeeper to more advanced academic work or greater vocational opportunities, but unfortunately, a failure rate of 40% to 50% is typical. This leads to one obvious conclusion: teachers should introduce and build upon algebra concepts in the earlier grades. Also, the algebra course must change. The NCTM declared, "First year algebra in its present form is not the algebra for everyone. In fact, it is not the algebra for most high-school graduates today" (NCTM, 1994). The new curricula that we describe in the text are designed to present algebra topics in ways that give more students access to their understanding and use. A common character-istic of these materials is the inclusion of problems that can be approached in a variety of ways from a variety of levels. Activity 5.7 is an example.

As in geometry, current *Standards*-based textbooks present some topics at an earlier stage than was possible in traditional programs. Matrices, a topic dealt with more extensively in Chapter 6, are presented as early as middle school and are incorporated in significant ways in all of the 3-year high-school programs. Linear programming is developed in a Course 2 unit in the IMP curriculum and extended to a unit in Course 3, in which using a 9 × 9 matrix to solve a system of equations in nine variables is possible through the capabilities of technology. Composition of functions is introduced in Course 1 of MATH Connections through an example of a Rube Goldberg machine. Exponential growth and decay are introduced at the middle-school level and developed as early as Course 1, as in the ARISE (Mathematics: Modeling Our World) curriculum.

As experienced teachers, we have found our own understanding of mathematics to be enhanced and challenged when teaching these new materials to diverse student populations. We have revisited algebra and geometry ourselves to better anticipate what our students will need for the future. One can only wonder what the mathematics curriculum will look like 30 years from now, when most readers of this book will be nearing the end of their teaching careers.

FOR TEACHERS

Activity 5.7 Restaurant Rectangles

Mathematical Content:
Relationships between perimeter and area
    (PSSM Geometry Standards for Grades 6–8
    and 9–12)

Materials Needed:
Graph paper and square tiles for students;
    overhead transparency graph paper and tiles
    for demonstration and reporting; graphing
    technology and display device for Problem 5.

Directions: This activity may take several days of class time to complete. It may be broken down into different cases and worked on separately.

- Problem 1 is a typical constant perimeter problem. The graph is a discrete curve whose points lie on a downward-facing parabola. The smallest area occurs when the tables are in a line.
- Problem 2 holds one dimension constant. The graph of the other dimension versus the area is linear.
- Problem 3 is an exponential pattern involving doubling.
- Problem 4 has a common area that students need to find first. This graph is a curve and is explored in greater depth in the final problem.
- Problem 5 uses algebraic and technological tools to further analyze the graph in Problem 4. It is in the form of a rectangular hyperbola.

FOR STUDENTS

Activity 5.7
Restaurant Rectangles (page 1 of 2)

Directions: A restaurant owner wants to renovate her restaurant to provide meeting rooms for groups. She has to see what size and shape rooms will be needed for different sizes of groups. She will also need to order a reasonable number of tables and chairs for her needs.

Model the following problems on graph paper or with square tiles. Let one square on the paper represent a square table that seats exactly four people, and think of putting square tables together to make tables for more people. The perimeter represents the number of people that can be seated around the table, and the area represents the number of square tables needed to make the seating arrangement. A different orientation of an arrangement is considered separately, as the setup of the space would be different if the longer dimension were vertical rather than horizontal.

Keep in mind that many table arrangements in restaurants are "hollow rectangles" when no tables are needed in the middle. An example of such an arrangement is illustrated here. This arrangement of eight tables seats 12 people around the outside. However, the amount of floor space needed would be the same as if there were nine tables. Consider the unit of perimeter measure to be the side of a single square table and the unit of area measure to be the surface of one square table. (*Note*: A typical square table used in restaurants measures 3 feet on each side, so this arrangement would take up 81 square feet of room space, not considering space for chairs and movement.)

Help the restaurant owner with her planning by completing the items below.

1. A luncheon group has 12 members who wish to sit around one rectangle. Draw five different rectangles that can seat 12 people. Record the length, width, perimeter, and area of each arrangement.

   a. What are the variables in this case?

   b. What is the constant in this case?

   c. Graph the length versus the area of each arrangement of the 12 members.

   d. Describe the graph.

   e. Explain the relationship between the graphed variables.

   f. The restaurant owner must order 12 chairs for this group. What is the smallest number of square tables she would have to order to seat this group? Explain.

2. The debate society must always have four persons along one side of a rectangular arrangement. Also, since each debate has two participants, there must be an even number of people in attendance. The group will vary from 10 to 32 members. Draw several table arrangements that will meet these requirements. Record the length of the changing side, the area of each rectangle, and the perimeter of each rectangle. Look for a pattern to help you find values for the larger groups without drawing each diagram.

   a. What are the variables in this case?

   b. What is the constant in this case?

   c. Graph the length of changing side of the rectangle versus its area.

   d. Describe the graph.

   e. Explain the relationship between the graphed variables.

   f. The restaurant owner must order 32 chairs for this group. What is the smallest number of square tables she would have to order to seat this group? Explain.

FOR STUDENTS

Activity 5.7
Restaurant Rectangles (page 2 of 2)

3. The mathematical society has eight members. It meets monthly. When it meets, it sits at a one-by-three table arrangement. The members want to invite new people to join the club according to a mathematical design. For next month, they want to invite enough people to sit at a table arrangement that is twice the length and twice the width of their usual arrangement. How many people would they invite? Record the lengths of each dimension of the table arrangement, its perimeter, and its floor area. Continue the doubling pattern for two more months.

   a. What are the variables in this case?

   b. Is there a constant in this case? If so, what is it?

   c. Graph the length versus the area of each arrangement.

   d. Describe the graph.

   e. Explain the relationship between the graphed variables.

   f. How is this graph different from the graph of length versus area in Problem 1?

   g. How many square tables would the owner need to buy to seat 32 mathematical society members using this pattern?

   h. If she could buy only rectangular tables that seat three people on two sides and one person on each end, how many tables would the restaurant owner have to buy to seat all 32 members? Show a diagram of this seating arrangement.

4. The eccentrics club demands that the area of its rectangular table arrangement always be the same. The number of club members attending meetings ranges from 44 to 242. The restaurant owner orders tables that seat 10 people each on two sides and one person on each end for this group.

   a. How is this case different from the other cases?

   b. What is the constant in this case?

   c. Find a solution that uses the same number of tables in two different rectangular arrangements to seat 44 and 242 members of the club. Discuss the practicality of this solution.

   d. Find other arrangements of the number of tables used in Part c, and give their perimeter in terms of the maximum number of people that could be seated.

   e. Make a table that shows the length, width, area, and perimeter of the arrangements in Parts c and d.

   f. Make a graph of the length of the arrangement versus the area of the tables.

   g. How is this graph different from graphs in the previous problem?

5. The restaurant owner, who is a member of both the mathematical society and the eccentrics club, wonders about the patterns in Problem 4. She is limited to the constant area from that problem, but can use other sizes of tables to make additional rectangular arrangements.

   a. Using graphing technology, enter the points of the graph in Problem 4 so they appear as a scatter plot.

   b. Given the constant area of 120, write an equation that expresses the area in terms of the length and width. Solve for length.

   c. Substitute this expression in the equation for perimeter.

   d. Graph this curve as a function on the technology, and compare the curve with the scatter plot.

   e. What does this graph tell the restaurant owner about her design?

Summary

This chapter presented contemporary aspects of two strands of mathematics that have long histories. The geometry in today's *Standards*-based textbooks builds upon the tradition that began with Euclid more than 2000 years ago. However, those materials also include more current development in mathematics and technology that should be a part of your classroom. Similarly, since the formalization of algebra in the 9th century, equation solving has continued to play a major role. In today's classrooms, however, technology allows students deeper insight about the concept of functions as they can move easily from tables, to graphs, to equations and see how changing a feature of one of these representations affects the others. The activities in this chapter made use of different teaching materials in order to make these topics accessible at different grade levels and at different degrees of mathematical sophistication.

ASSIGNMENT

1. Figure 5.3 shows a copy of the table of contents from a 1963 Algebra 2 textbook. Locate a *Standards*-based Course 3 textbook, and compare the content of the two courses. Comment on the similarities and differences and possible reasons for the changes.

INSTRUCTIONAL RESOURCES

Blais, D. M. (1988). Constructivism—a theoretical revolution for algebra. *Mathematics Teacher, 81(8),* 624–631.
   This article describes how the paradigm of constructivist learning theory can influence the algebra curriculum.

Burke, M., Erickson, D., Lott, J. W., & Obert, M. (2001). *Navigating through algebra in grades 9–12.* Reston, VA: National Council of Teachers of Mathematics.
   This document addresses algebra as a process, expands the notions of variable, functions, algebraic equivalence, and change. Student activity sheets are included both as black line masters and on the accompanying CD-ROM.

Day, R., Kelley, P., Krussel, L., Lott, J. W., Hirstein, J. (2001). *Navigating through geometry in grades 9–12.* Reston, VA: National Council of Teachers of Mathematics.
   The geometry of transformations and coordinates are presented here, especially as connected to matrices. Some activities require the use of technology that produces geometric images. Student activity sheets are included both as black line masters and on the accompanying CD-ROM.

Friel, S., Rachlin, S., & Doyle, D. (2001). *Navigating through algebra in grades 6–8.* Reston, VA: National Council of Teachers of Mathematics.
   Topics include the use of mathematical models and different representations of algebraic concepts. Activities have students work with the 4 representation of functions and their interactions. Student activity sheets are included both as black line masters and on the accompanying CD-ROM.

Greenes, C. and Findell, C. (2001). *Groundworks.* Mountain View, CA. Creative Publications.
   Six big ideas of algebra (representation, proportional reasoning, balance, variable, function, and inductive reasoning) are developed for Grades 1–7 in this series of teacher resource booklets with reproducible student pages or consumable workbooks.

Hunt, W. J. (1995, December). Spreadsheets—a tool for the mathematics classroom. *Mathematics Teacher, 88(9),* 774–777.
   The author describes how his students model recursive processes through the use of a computer spreadsheet. Three such algorithms are illustrated: synthetic substitution, synthetic division, and Newton's method for approximating roots.

Lobato, J., & Thanheiser, E. (2002). Developing understanding of ratio-as-measure as a foundation for slope. In B. L. Litwiller & G. Bright (Eds.), *Making Sense of Fractions, Ratios, and Proportions,* NCTM 2002 Yearbook. Reston, VA: National Council of Teachers of Mathematics.
   This is a chapter from the referenced NCTM Yearbook. The yearbook comes with a collection of reproducible student activities related to the mathematical content of the articles.

Figure 5.3
Sample Table of Contents

CONTENTS

PART ONE

vii

viii · ALGEBRA, BOOK TWO

CONTENTS · ix

x · ALGEBRA, BOOK TWO

Source: Welchons, A. M., Krickenberger, W. R., and Pearson, H. R. (1963). *Algebra, Book Two, Modern Edition.* Boston: Ginn and Company. Reprinted with permission.

Marquis, J. (1989). What can we do about the high D and F rate in first-year algebra? *Mathematics Teacher, 82(6),* 421–425.

> This article gives suggestions about changes in the algebra class that are within a teacher's control. They include ideas on classroom structure, use of homework, after-class help, and assessment.

Mathematics Teacher, 91(8).

> This is a focus issue on the concept of proof.

Metz, J. (1994). Seeing the b in $y = ax^2 + by + c$. *Mathematics Teacher, 87(1),* 23–24.

> The relationship of the standard form of the quadratic equation and the coefficient of the linear term is discussed and illustrated. The article includes explanatory figures that can be enlarged and displayed on an overhead projector.

Nissen, P. (2000). A geometry solution from multiple perspectives. *Mathematics Teacher, 92(4),* 324–327.

> In this article, a geometry problem is solved using synthetic, coordinate, vector, and transformational approaches.

Okolica, S., & Macrina, G. (1992). Integrating transformational geometry into traditional high school geometry. *Mathematics Teacher, 85(9),* 716–719.

> Two classroom teachers describe how they move transformational geometry ahead of deductive geometry in their curriculum and continue to return to transformational principles throughout the course. They have found that doing this makes geometry more concrete for students, thereby increasing their comprehension.

Pugalee, D. K., Frykholm, J., Johnson, A., Slovin, H., Malloy, C., & Preston, R. (2002). *Navigating through geometry in grades 6–8.* Reston, VA: National Council of Teachers of Mathematics.

> The emphasis in this resource is on visualization, analysis, and informal deduction. Student activity sheets are included both as black line masters and on the accompanying CD-ROM.

Senk, S. L. (1985). How well do students write geometry proofs? *Mathematics Teacher, 78(6),* 448–456.

> The article reports the results of a study of geometry students done at the end of a school year. Only about 30% of the students in a full-year geometry course that taught proof reached 75% mastery of proof writing. The author includes implications and recommendations for mathematics curriculum changes in response to these findings.

Smith, L. (1993). Multiple solutions involving geoboard problems. *Mathematics Teacher, 86(1),* 25–29.

Smith, S. (1996). *Agnesi to Zeno: Over 100 vignettes from the history of math.* Berkeley, CA: Key Curriculum Press.

> Many fascinating stories of the history of mathematics, including several relating to algebra and geometry, make this a useful teacher resource.

Star, J. R., Herbel-Eisenmann, B. A., & Smith, J. P. III. (2000). Algebraic concepts: What's really new in new curricula? *Mathematics Teaching in the Middle School, 5(7),* 446–451.

> Using the exemplary middle school curriculum, the Connected Mathematics Project, as a reference, the authors identify and illustrate major differences between the algebra in its 8th grade materials and a typical algebra I textbook.

Usnick, V., Lamphere, P. M., & Bright, G. W. (1992). A generalized area formula. *Mathematics Teacher, 85(9),* 752–754.

Winicki-Landman, G. (2001). Searching families as a source of surprise. *Mathematics Teacher, 94(6),* 468–478.

> The series of worksheets included with this article has students connect different representations of linear and quadratic functions, formulate conjectures and generalizations about families of functions, and explore algebraic reasoning and proof.

ADDITIONAL ACTIVITIES

Activity 5.8   Kaleidoscopes
Activity 5.9   See It Geometrically, Confirm It Algebraically
Activity 5.10   The Oldest Living Proof
Activity 5.11   Probing Pentominoes

The first three activities are designed to integrate algebra, geometry, and technology on different conceptual levels. The activities are printed in a format to be used directly with secondary-level students. Initial instructions and descriptions follow. The fourth activity is a geometry investigation involving polyominoes.

F O R   T E A C H E R S

Activity 5.8   Kaleidoscopes

Mathematical Content:
Symmetry, angle measure, conjectures (PSSM Geometry Standards for Grades 6–8)

Materials Needed:
Two small rectangular mirrors hinged together; small object, preferably asymmetrical, to view in the mirrors; protractor for each pair of students.

Directions: For suggestions, see Activity Notes for the Teacher. Students will work in pairs and vary the angle between the mirrors and note the number of images they can see and the orientation of those images in order to discern patterns.

F O R   T E A C H E R S

Activity 5.9   See It Geometrically, Confirm It Algebraically (see For Students, p. 191)

Mathematical Content:
Family of parabolas, transformations (PSSM Algebra Standards for Grades 9–12)

Materials Needed:
Directions and a graphing calculator for each student (preferred, although students may also work in pairs); graphing calculator display device for the teacher; graph paper and straightedges for students

Directions: This is a guided discovery lesson. Students will gradually increase the complexity with which they are able to view quadratic equations in the form $y = a(x - h)^2 - k$ and visualize their shape and key characteristics before actually graphing them. It is assumed in this activity that students have had experience with graphing calculators, including the graphing of functions.

F O R   T E A C H E R S

Activity 5.10   The Oldest Living Proof (see For Students, pp. 192–193)

Mathematical Content:
Area relationships in circles, deductive and inductive reasoning
(PSSM Geometry Standard for Grades 9–12)

Materials Needed:
Geometer's Sketchpad® software and computer display device or a graphing calculator with dynamic geometry capabilities

Directions: This lesson can be presented in a lecture format by the teacher, with a student helper making the drawing while the teacher gives directions, or by a class in a computer lab. Previous knowledge with such technology is assumed. Specific instructions for making the figure are included in the Activity Notes for the Teacher.

F O R   S T U D E N T S

Activity 5.8
Kaleidoscopes

Directions:

1. Look into the mirror. Where is the image of your object? Stand the two mirrors with the hinge positioned as shown in the figure. Look in the mirrors at many different angles.

2. What happens to the number of images as the angle is increased?

3. When you hold up your right hand in front of a mirror, what hand does the image reflect?

4. When do you see a nonreversed image?

5. What is your conjecture about the relationship between the number of images and the angle between the mirrors?

6. What pattern do you observe with the reversed and nonreversed images?

Extension: The diagram shows the locations, as seen from above, of the Marshal and a man known as Fast Gun. Assume that both the mirror and the window in the saloon reflect images.

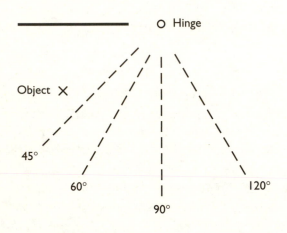

Move the mirrors to the angles shown in the figure. Complete the table:

Angle Between the Mirrors	Number of Images	Types of Image(s)
120 degrees		
90 degrees		
60 degrees		
45 degrees		

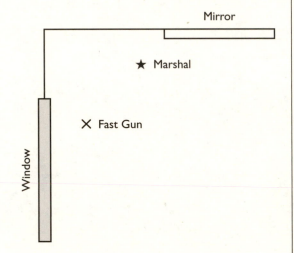

7. Draw all possible reflected images of Fast Gun and the Marshal.

8. What image(s) of Fast Gun could the Marshal actually see?

9. Add a deputy to the picture. Put her in a location where she can see reflected images of both the Marshal and Fast Gun.

FOR STUDENTS

Activity 5.9
See It Geometrically, Confirm It Algebraically

Directions:
Sketch each function on graph paper, and write the function equation under each sketch.

1. Graph the following functions on the graphing calculator. Then sketch the curves on graph paper using the same scale for each.

$$y_1 = x^2 \qquad y_2 = \left(\frac{1}{2}\right) x^2$$

$$y_3 = 3x^2 \qquad y_4 = \left(\frac{1}{4}\right) x^2$$

   a. In the equation $y = ax^2$, how does the value of the coefficient (a) change the curve?

   b. Write out three more equations with different a values that are both positive and negative. Sketch the curves you expect to see, and then use your calculator to check.

2. Graph the following functions on the graphing calculator. Then sketch the curves on graph paper.

   $y_1 = x^2 + 1 \qquad y_2 = x^2 - 4$
   $y_3 = x^2 + 3 \qquad y_4 = x^2 + 5$

   a. In the equation $y = ax^2 + c$, how does the value of c change the curve?

   b. Write out three more equations with different values of c that are both positive and negative. Sketch the curves you expect to see, and then use your calculator to check.

3. Graph the following functions on the graphing calculator. Then sketch the curves on graph paper.

   $y_1 = (x + 1)^2 + 1$
   $y_2 = (x + 2)^2 - 4$
   $y_3 = (x - 3)^2 + 3$

   Compare these curves with the first three in Problem 2. How does adding or subtracting a number to or from x change the graph?

4. Use the trace to find the vertex for each function of Problem 3, and record it on the sketch. How do the coordinates relate to the constants in the function?

5. Write the equation for the line of symmetry under each sketch for Problem 3.

6. We can think of transforming the parent equation $y = x^2$ to a family of different curves by changing the constants in the general form of the equation $f(x) = a(x - h)^2 + k$.

   a. Which constant in the general equation determines the shape? How?

   b. Which constant in the general equation reflects the curve about the x-axis? How?

   c. Which constant in the general equation shifts the curve horizontally? How?

   d. Which constant in the general equation shifts the curve up and down? How?

7. Sketch the expected curves for the following equations, and check your predictions on the graphing calculator. Remove the parentheses to write the equations in quadratic form. Graph the quadratic form to check your work in removing the parentheses.

$$y_1 = (x - 1)^2 + 1 \qquad y_2 = \left(\frac{1}{2}\right)(x + 2)^2 - 4$$

$$y_3 = 2(x - 3)^2 + 3 \qquad y_4 = 2(x - 5)^2 + 5$$

8. Why are the equations in Problem 7 said to be in the vertex form?

FOR STUDENTS

Activity 5.10
The Oldest Living Proof (page 1 of 2)

Hippocrates of Chios (about 450 B.C.) was the first person to construct a square equal in area to the area between the arcs of two different circles. This is the oldest surviving formal geometric proof. To make the appropriate sketch on the Geometer's Sketchpad, follow these steps:

1. To draw the circle and a diameter, draw a circle in the middle of the screen. Select the circle, and under <u>Construct</u> highlight <u>Point on Object</u>. To make a diameter, select line from the menu on the left. Select the center and the point on the circle (not the radius point from drawing the circle) and <u>Construct</u> a <u>Line</u>. Then select the circle and the line. Under <u>Construct</u> highlight <u>Point of Intersection</u>. Move the line so it is horizontal. To move the line, use the select arrow to "grab" the point on the circle; when the select arrow is horizontal, you can rotate the line about the center of the circle.

2. To construct a second diameter, again select the circle, and under <u>Construct</u> highlight <u>Point on Object</u>. Select the center and the new point on the circle and <u>Construct</u> a <u>Line</u>. Then select the circle and the line. Under <u>Construct</u> highlight <u>Point of Intersection</u>. Move the line so it is vertical.

3. To construct a square within the circle and label all the points on the figure, select <u>Segment</u> in the menu on the left panel. Select the four points on the circle. Use <u>Construct</u>, then <u>Segment</u> to draw the square. Select all the points, and under <u>Display</u> highlight <u>Show Labels</u>. Now your figure should look like the

one shown here. Although labeling of the intersection points may vary, A is the circle center and B is the radius. Moving either of these will change the size of the circle.

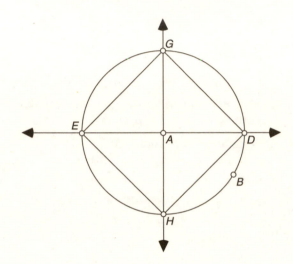

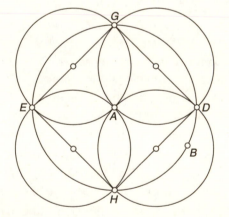

FOR STUDENTS

Activity 5.10
The Oldest Living Proof (page 2 of 2)

4. To draw four smaller circles—each with its center on the midpoint of each side of the square with the same diameter as the side of the square and hide lines—select each of the four segments. Use <u>Construct</u>, highlight <u>Point at Midpoint</u> to find the midpoint of each side of the square, which will be the center of each small circle. Select the midpoint and one neighboring corner (in that order); use <u>Construct</u> to draw <u>Circle by Center + Point</u>. Repeat this until there are four circles as shown in the figure. Select both lines; under <u>Display</u> highlight <u>Hide Lines</u>.

5. To highlight the interiors of the square and the circles, under <u>Display</u>, open <u>Shade</u> and click on 75%. Select the four corners of the square, then under <u>Construct</u> highlight <u>Polygon Interior</u>. Change the fill pattern to 50%. Select the large circle and under <u>Construct</u> highlight <u>Circle Interior</u>. Follow the same procedure to fill one of the smaller circles with 25% shading as shown.

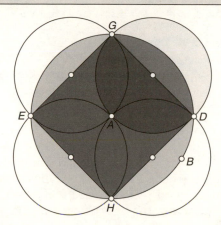

You have it easier than Hippocrates, since you are beginning with the figure he had to develop. Now prove that the area of the square does equal the four areas outside the large circle and inside the four small circles. This area that is the lightest filled area outside the largest circle and inside a small circle is called a **lune** (it does have a crescent moon shape). *Hint:* It may be easier to show that one-fourth the area of the square equals the area of one lune, rather than work with the complete figure.

F O R   T E A C H E R S

Activity 5.11 Probing Pentominoes

Mathematical Content:
Congruence, making 3-D shapes from 2-D nets, similarity (PSSM Geometry Standards for Grades 6–8)

Materials Needed:
Inch-square graph paper, scissors, tape

Directions: Students will identify the 12 pentominoes and explore various geometric features of these shapes.

F O R   S T U D E N T S

Activity 5.11
Probing Pentominoes

Directions: We are going to examine a certain type of polyomino. These polyominoes are made from connected congruent squares. You are probably familiar with the polyomino that is composed of two squares. It looks like this

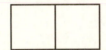

1. What is a common name for this figure?

Polyominoes can be joined only by entire sides, not at corners or at part of a side. Polyominoes made of three squares are sometimes called triominoes. Here are two triominoes.

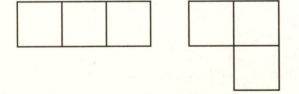

2. Are any other triominoes possible? Why or why not? If they are congruent, they are not considered different.

We are going to skip tetrominoes, those shapes made out of four congruent squares, and look instead at shapes made of five congruent squares. These shapes are called pentominoes.

Individually, use inch-square graph paper and trace the border of as many different pentominoes as you can. Then share your favorite pentomino with the class.

How can we name these pentominoes so we can talk about them together later?

EXTENSIONS

3. Explain how you can tell that no more pentominoes are possible.

4. Use scissors to cut out the pentominoes.

    a. Which can be folded into open-ended boxes?

    b. Which can be used to tessellate the plane?

5. If all of the 12 pentominoes were placed, without overlapping, inside an 8-inch by 8-inch checkerboard, how many spaces would be left uncovered? Can this actually be done?

6. What are the dimensions, in inches, of rectangles into which it might be possible to place all of the pentominoes without any empty squares? Draw these rectangles to scale and try it.

7. Use four pentominoes to make a larger pentomino that is similar to one of the original pentominoes. Find the perimeter and area of the new pentomino.

PART II

Teaching and Learning in the Classroom

Part II deals with the preparation for and delivery of instruction in a *Standards*-based classroom. Chapter 6 looks at both long- and short-range lesson planning, giving samples of lessons using explicit instruction, problem solving, and discovery as the pedagogical approach. Chapter 7 looks at discipline issues through the lens of promoting effective classroom communication—mathematical discourse as well as other means of written and oral strategies that promote student self-responsibility for learning. Two chapters, Chapters 8 and 10, address assessment. Chapter 8 concerns homework and grades. Chapter 10 looks at performance assessments and their uses, as well as the role of mandated external assessment. The assessment chapters are separated by Chapter 9, which deals with equity from the broadest perspective, including students qualifying for special education and gifted programs, although equity issues are addressed throughout the book.

CHAPTER

6

Planning Instruction

Planning is essential to success in teaching. If an actor falters in playing his part, the audience does not understand his message or purpose. Confused or uncertain about what they're seeing and hearing, the audience could lose interest. Likewise, a teacher must be clear about the presentation he is making in the classroom on any given day. In fact, the teacher has a more difficult task than the actor because the teacher interacts with "the audience" and must adjust the script as necessary to keep students involved.

Respect from the students is essential to a healthy learning environment. This respect will be seriously eroded, however, if students perceive a lack of planning by the teacher. Having a teacher who is unprepared gives students an excuse to come to class unprepared and perhaps even to pay less attention during class. Further, planning is one element of discipline. Thoughtful and well-planned, yet flexible, lessons suited to student abilities will prevent many minor discipline problems from developing. A teacher who plans carefully shows that he cares about student advancement and is a professional. In fact, detailed formal planning can compensate for a beginning teacher's lack of experience.

Planning proceeds from the general to the specific. Begin by asking numerous questions and, if possible, observe experienced teachers teaching in their classrooms to gain a broad overview of your teaching situation. Develop a perspective of the total course, become familiar with the individual units, and then make daily lesson plans for a unit or a week at a time. Illustrative examples based in innovative programs of study demonstrate planning tasks in this chapter. The chapter also includes strategies for developing effective lessons.

ABOUT THE SAMPLE LESSONS FOR THIS CHAPTER

Curriculum and Evaluation Standards for School Mathematics (NCTM, 1989) calls for increased attention to matrices, the mathematics topic for this chapter. There are many interesting applications of matrices, and the increasing sophistication of calculators and computer programs allows students to easily manipulate large and complicated matrices to access some of these complex problems. Thus, matrices provide numerous opportunities to address real-world situations. In addition, matrices can function as connectors within a curriculum, since they are a powerful mathematical tool in a broad array of contexts. Data display, solution of sets of linear equations, geometric transformations, representations of complex numbers and vectors, and use in trigonometry identities are topics employing matrices that extend throughout the secondary school mathematics program.

Activities in this chapter illustrate various ways to approach the teaching and learning of matrices using directed instruction, problem solving, and/or discovery-inquiry. The first two instructional sequences contrast the *Standards*-based traditional format curriculum from the University of Chicago School Mathematics Project (UCSMP) and the project-based Interactive Mathematics Program (IMP). The UCSMP is commonly taught by direct instruction, while the IMP teaching methodology relies heavily on cooperative groups and presentations by representatives from the groups, with conclusions monitored by the teacher. The lesson plan for UCSMP details both the teacher activities and the student activities. In contrast, the lesson plan for the IMP instructional sequence details only the student activities with hints to the teacher to ask questions to facilitate the class discussion to bring out salient points. It is appropriate to consider the type of lesson plan that best fits the material taught. Each of the lessons occurs in the third year of the program. The overall plan of teaching matrices in each of these 4-year textbook series is discussed in detail in the following sections: Semester Plan, Example Lesson Plan for University of Chicago

School Mathematics Project and Example Lesson Plan for Interactive Mathematics Project.

Take breaks from reading the text to work the matrix problems as a student would, and then shift to the perspective of a teacher, noting the differing levels of complexity and differing organizations of teaching matrices within the instructional sequences presented. This analysis will enable you to better understand the underlying structure of unique approaches. Sample Lesson 6.2, Organizing Matrices, is from a text for middle-school students, which begins with viewing matrices as a way to organize data similar to charts with which the students are familiar. Sample Lesson 6.3 is in the second chapter of the first year of a textbook series with matrix addition and subtraction immediately applied to solving secret codes, certainly a topic of high interest to beginning math students. Activity 6.4, Manufacturing Toys, is an excellent paper-and-pencil activity to assist discovery of the method of multiplying matrices within a contextual setting. This type of activity must be done before students begin using calculators to multiply numerical matrices so they understand the process and apply it intelligently with calculators. Without this sort of activity using labeled quantities in matrices with real-world meaning, students will multiply matrices to get non-sensical answers. Sample Lessons 6.4, Spinning Flags, and 6.6 explore transformations through matrices. Sample Lesson 6.4 is placed in the second year of a 4-year text series. In contrast, the UCSMP waits to introduce transformation with matrices until the third year, after students have studied transformations in detail in the previous geometry course. The last sample lesson, 6.8, uses matrix transformations in the higher-level mathematics of trigonometry.

The matrix sections taken directly from exemplary texts featured in Chapter 4 are included in this chapter. They have been selected so you can compare and contrast the variety of ways matrix mathematics can be ordered within an instructional sequence that may extend to as many as four texts in a series. These series use the spiral curriculum approach, where material is introduced at one level and then revisited at a higher level in later lessons. Knowledge of the general plan of your text and others in the overall series for your students is essential to planning instruction that is effective to facilitate student learning.

Note that the Directions section in each Activity is not aimed at the students, as in past chapters, but rather is aimed at the pre-service teacher or in-service teacher. These directions are designed to help you determine how you would plan to teach these lessons.

BROAD CONTEXTUAL OVERVIEW

Imagine that you are a recently hired teacher meeting with the department chairperson. You are offered some choices of classes to teach. Having made your decision, you then proceed to plan for your assigned classes, using a curriculum chosen previously by the department. It is this scenario that we shall address in this chapter.

As you gain experience you will participate with other members of the department in selecting curriculum. In time, you will become familiar with the NCTM *Standards*, as well as the curriculum documents at the state, district, and site levels. In addition to these documents, the department's curricular decisions will also be influenced by the expectations and characteristics of the community and the students served. For periodic curriculum selection, a committee will research statistics, obtaining data on the number of students who proceed to higher education and their test scores in order to identify the program that will best serve the students of that district. (The issues involved in curricular decisions are examined in detail in Chapter 12 in a discussion of professional growth.) However, it is never too soon for you, the beginning teacher, to become familiar with sources of information pertinent to your teaching situation. The more you learn about your teaching context, the more effective you will be in the classroom. Even if the courses and curriculum are preselected, you still have a multitude of professional decisions to make concerning planning and instruction that will lead to mathematical success for your students.

Before you start actual planning for instruction, however, you must understand the expectations of your colleagues, the abilities of your students, and the availability of resources. Each of these elements will influence both your long-range planning and your day-to-day organization. You should begin by collecting information about your instructional context.

Expectations

Of primary importance are the curricular expectations of your colleagues. Be sure to discuss these with your department chairperson or, ideally, an experienced mathematics teacher who is assigned to be your mentor. First, ask for any documentation concerning the courses you will be teaching. Departments have course descriptions ranging from brief statements to outlines of considerable detail. A course description will indicate the topics considered by the department to be of greatest importance for a specific course. Obtain all of the teacher's materials available for each of your courses. In some cases these materials may be no more than a teachers' edition text with teaching suggestions and problem answers added to the student version and/or a solution book. In contrast, some of the new curricula have a plethora of supplementary materials, including sets of overhead transparencies, software, books of additional problems, books of assessment items, and manuals offering project suggestions or enrichment activities. After reviewing these materials, discuss with a colleague each of the courses you are going to teach. It's preferable to work with a colleague who has taught the courses before.

For each of the courses you are to teach, ask the following questions:

- *What units should be taught by the end of the first semester?* Although this seems like an obvious question, we have taught in schools in which teachers new to the department did not teach the same topics that were taught in other sections of the same course. Because some students switched teachers due to necessary schedule changes at the beginning of the second semester, the students' lack of knowledge of some mathematical areas led to great difficulties. Likewise, ask what topics you are expected to have taught by the end of school year.

- *What topics are of primary importance for students who will be continuing to the higher-level mathematics course next semester?* Always remember that you are part of a community of teachers who work together to prepare students throughout a coordinated curriculum. Your colleagues will laud innovative additions to the stated curriculum, such as student-directed projects, if they know you are also adhering to effective instruction of materials identified as significant for mathematical progress in the department's program.

- *What is the department policy and/or expectation on grading?* The proportion of students receiving high versus low grades will be different for different courses. If possible, obtain a few tests and grading rubrics from teachers who have previously taught the same courses you are assigned in order to understand the prevailing school culture concerning grading. Inquire if there is a policy on quantity of recorded grades. Some schools require a weekly posting in the record book of at least one grade, whether from a quiz, unit exam, or participation activity. Is offering extra-credit work an option for the individual teacher, or is it assigned according to department policy? Is there a department final exam for all students in a given course? What percentage of a student's course grade is to be based on quizzes, tests, homework, problem of the week, project, and/or participation? This will vary from course to course. For example, effort made on homework will probably have a greater effect on the grade in a non-college-intended course than in a calculus course in which it may be considered only in cases in which a student's score is on the borderline between grades. Is the participation grade part of a citizenship grade or a work habit grade, or is it included in the academic course grade? How often are grade reports sent home? Can grades be entered directly into a computer, or must the official record be handwritten? Finally, obtain a copy of the grade report(s).

- *What are the school and department expectations on homework?* Especially for high-school students, a community may expect students to spend a certain amount of time on mathematics homework every evening, including or excluding weekends. Alternatively, a middle school may have a homework schedule in which mathematics and science teachers assign homework three specified nights a week, alternating with nights on which teachers of language arts and social studies make homework assignments. Of course, meaningful homework is a necessity; homework must never be assigned just for the sake of assigning it.
- *Are there other district, school, or department policies to consider while planning?* For example, does the mathematics department require math journals in each class? Does the school or district require portfolios upon graduation? If so, what mathematics elements, and how many examples of each, should be included in the portfolio from the courses under your responsibility? Do many students change courses once the year has begun? It will affect planning for the beginning of the school year if placement of students into classes can continue for more than the first few days.

Sometimes newcomers to teaching may feel that the answers to these questions and the decisions already made by the textbook authors leave them little room for individuality. This is not the case, however. The characteristics of the students in a particular class and other variables found in a given specific educational setting stimulate unique classroom procedures that will be effective for you. As a beginning teacher, ask for advice often, but never employ another teacher's methods exactly without careful thought. First, consider whether his teaching practice is one that is comfortable for you. Second, consider the parameters in your classroom compared with those in the classroom of the teacher advising you. Why will the recommended method work in your classroom? Can the suggested method be altered somehow to appropriately fit your situation? Do not expect to "get it right" the first time; none of us has done so consistently.

Community and Student Characteristics

Inquire about the characteristics of the community. Ask administrators about their impressions in working with parents. The obvious questions concern the socioeconomic level and the diversity of members of the community. You probably already made observations when applying for the position and driving through the area served by the school, but check to see whether your assumptions match those of your colleagues. How active is the PTA? In what ways do the parents support the educational community? How strong is their support? If the school district has more than one secondary-level school, how does your school compare with others in the district? Does the school serve only its surrounding community, or do students travel from other more distant areas with different demographics?

Find out some general information about the students in your classes before classes begin. Talk to experienced teachers in your department and the counselors at your site. However, if some comments are negative about a specific student, hold your judgment until you get to know him. Realize that students behave differently for different teachers and that you *must* draw your own conclusions about individuals. General student characteristics will vary depending upon the maturity and academic readiness of the students. Thus, when asking for information, be specific about the courses that you will be teaching. You can inquire about the expected level of expertise and general motivation level, realizing that this is only introductory information that you will refine as you begin teaching. Are there communities of students who have special needs? These may be students with disabilities and/or language deficiencies, or those who are gifted. Will communities of students with special needs be more likely to be enrolled in some classes than in others? How are you expected to work with and/or modify a program for students with special needs?

Have realistic expectations that emphasize the positive aspects of student abilities. As stated in the NCTM *Professional Teaching Standards,* "Teacher expectations have significant impact on what happens to children in school. Teacher expectations are founded on knowledge and beliefs about who their students are and what they can do. Teachers' understanding of the impact of students' age, abilities (both mental and physical), interests, and experience on their learning of mathematics are all important ingredients in building perceptions of students as individuals" (NCTM, 1991, p. 145). Remember, the planning process begins where the students are, and the curriculum is designed to build on their existing foundation to increase their understanding of mathematics.

Resources

Your classroom and its characteristics manifest the resources available to students. Please refer to the end of Chapter 2 for information on the impact on instructional planning of room shape, furniture and its arrangement, storage facilities, chalk- or whiteboard space, bulletin board space, and the use of an overhead projector.

Ask the following questions about additional resources:

When manipulatives are available, teachers can incorporate them in lessons that foster student understanding of mathematical concepts.

- How soon after the beginning of school will students be given their textbooks? In addition to textbooks, what additional written instructional materials are available for students? How are the quantity and condition of textbooks monitored?
- What computer facilities are available? Will you always have one computer in your room for demonstration purposes, or can one be checked out easily for use when needed? Do you have access to a computer lab? If so, what is the procedure for gaining access? What software is available? Is technical assistance available? If so, what are the characteristics of that assistance? How does the availability of computer hardware and software affect the content of your courses? What experience have students had in using computers within the school setting? Do many students have computers at home?
- What calculators are familiar to the students? Can students be expected to have their own? If some students cannot afford their own calculators, are classroom loaners available? Some schools have funds to help students purchase calculators, and others may offer graphing calculators to be "checked out" for the school year. Does your school have either of these arrangements? What can you do to facilitate calculator usage for your students? Are overhead projectors and view screens for calculators available?
- What manipulatives are available for your use? Are there demonstration sets for the overhead projectors and/or classroom sets for the students? What experience do students have in using manipulatives? How do the existing manipulatives fit into the content of your courses?
- What resources are available to assist you in working with students with special needs? Are there provisions for tutoring or extra assistance for students at risk in mathematics? Are there arrangements for enrichment through mathematics or computer clubs, contests, or science/mathematics fairs? Is there money for field trips?
- What clerical or school help can you expect? Does your school have student aides? If so, sign up immediately to receive this assistance. We have found that students can be very helpful in performing certain clerical duties, even if they cannot function as teaching aides. Do you have a photocopying budget? What machines are available? Can you request that an aide make photocopies of materials, or does a copy center facility exist for this purpose? If so, how much lead time is required?
- Is there a professional section of the library for the teachers? If so, what books, journals, and other materials are available? Peruse these materials while you plan.
- New teachers should not be reluctant to ask for money to assist them in teaching their classes or for professional development. As a participating mathematics department member, you should be aware of available financing sources. For example, how can you request funds for curricular materials? Inquire how resource books, calculators, computer software, and manipulatives are funded, because each may be funded from a different source. Is it common for members of your department to receive support for professional development? When considering your long-range plans, find out whether you should allot days to attend conferences or workshops. Many departments are especially supportive of new teachers willing to make the effort to enhance their teaching skills through conference attendance.

In gathering background information about the specifics of the courses you will teach, ideas about expectations of your colleagues, general information about your students, and characteristics of available resources, you are developing a broad overview of your teaching year. We strongly suggest, however, that you *do not* sit down and write months of daily lesson plans before school starts. To do so would probably result in a great deal of wasted time on plans that will require drastic revisions. Planning specific lessons requires knowledge of your students. Instead, move next to long-range planning, and then write daily lessons for only a week or a unit at a time. Throughout the year you will adjust the curriculum to best fit the needs of your students and to teach effectively within the educational culture.

Set 6.1 Discussion Questions

 Questions with an asterisk appear in the Message Board section of the Companion Website at *http://www.prenhall.com/huetinck*. Go to Chapter 6 and click on the Message Board to find and respond to the question.

*1. As a beginning teacher, what additional broad overview questions would you like to have answered for planning purposes?

2. Discuss specifics concerning different planning aspects for various courses and for students with differing abilities, backgrounds, and maturity levels.

Figure 6.1
Letter to Parents

Quartz Hill High School

September 8, 2003

Dear Parent/Guardian:

It is a pleasure to have your son/daughter in my math class. My goals this year are that your student develops a thorough grasp of the subject matter, broadens his/her skill to read mathematics for understanding, develops the ability to communicate mathematical concepts in written and oral form, and gains a sense of responsibility. He/she will have the opportunity to work independently and with others.

To achieve these goals and maintain a positive and effective learning environment, students must follow all school rules and regulations as well as my class rules. Please take a moment to review the Information Sheet given to your student in class today.

Should you have any questions or concerns, please send me a note or call me at Quartz Hill High School,   extension   . I value your ideas and welcome your suggestions.

Sincerely,

Christine LeBeau

- Detach Here -

Please complete and return this form to me by Monday.
Your signature indicates that you read the above letter and reviewed the Information Sheet.

Please Print
Student Name: _____ Course: _____ Period: _____

Parent/Guardian Signature: _____

Long-Range Planning

To begin to articulate the structure of a course for yourself, draft a letter to parents, a student information form, and a course information page. Following are examples of each of these. The letter to parents (Figure 6.1) sets the tone of pleasure in teaching, communicates expectations of students, and conveys a willingness to assist all students.

The student information form (Figure 6.2) is a means of collecting background information about each student and indicating interest in each as an individual. In developing the student information form, be sensitive to students. Because home phone and address are available to you in student records, it is permissible to ask for this information to have in your file. However, it may be construed as an invasion of privacy to ask for the student's work phone if he is employed part-time. Also notice that the sample form requests the name of a parent or guardian, not mother or father, which is a more comfortable request for students in many home settings.

Figure 6.2
Student Information Form

WHO ARE YOU?

☐ Freshman
☐ Sophomore
☐ Junior
☐ Senio
Math, Period ____

Last Name ______________ **First Name** ____________

Parent/Guardian's Name ______________________

____

Address ______________________________

City __________________ **Zip** ____________

Home phone ______________ **Birthday** ____________

. . . USEFUL INFORMATION . . .

Last Year's
Math Class __________ **Math Teacher** ____________

Grade Earned: 1st semester _____ **2nd semester** _____

School Attended ______________________

This Year's
School Activities ______________________

____

Career Interests ______________________

Valuable Facts about you, **e. g., reasons for special seating needs**

____

____

____

The Course Information Sheet (Figure 6.3) uses brief descriptions to convey the goals of the course, major elements of the course, and simple rules. Some schools require dissemination of grading procedures by the teachers, while others have a school or department policy that is sent to parents. After proceeding further in planning, revisit Figures 6.1 through 6.3 to revise them as necessary.

We suggest that you ask for student information on the first day of class and deal with course information and parent letters on subsequent days. Have an interesting activity with which to involve all students on the first day. Students will be more attentive to the course introduction if they do not receive too much at once. It is better to discuss rules briefly over several days than to dwell on them at length, which frequently causes students to "turn off."

Semester Plan

The next step in planning is to make a general semester plan. A semester plan includes the daily topics, test days, planned use of manipulatives, computer/calculators, or projects without the specifics of daily objectives, classwork problems, or homework assignments. Before beginning, get a copy of the school calendar to note vacation days and early-release days. Obtain either a large calendar with a different month on each page or a list of school days. To put all plans for different courses in the same place, use a teacher's plan book, which has calendarlike sectioned pages with rows for dates and columns for different courses. Look over the number of topics to emphasize, the planning recommendations from the publisher, and the number of days of instruction to form some general idea of how to space the units. There probably will not be enough days for all the elements desired. It will be necessary to make choices about topic and degree of emphasis based on school site expectations, students' abilities, and professional judgments about teaching mathematics.

The portion of a semester plan shown in Figure 6.4 is written for *Integrated Mathematics, Course 3,* developed in accordance with the NCTM *Standards* by the publisher, McDougal Littell. A case of materials accompanies each level of this course of study, including softbound books (*Warm-up Transparencies, Overhead Visuals, Teacher's Resources for Transfer Students, Assessment and Keys, Using TI-81 and TI-82 Calculators, Mac Emulation Software, Using Plotter Plus*) and disk (Multi-Language Glossary, Study Guide and Answer Key, Spanish Edition, Project Book, Practice Bank, Problem Bank, Activity Bank, and Project Book), in addition to hardbound

Figure 6.3
Course Information Sheet

GEOMETRY
INFORMATION SHEET

INSTRUCTOR: Christine LeBeau   QHHS PHONE:

CONTENT:

This course will develop logical thinking and visualization skills. It includes the study of geometric plane and solid figures, proofs, coordinate geometry, and transformations.

MATERIALS REQUIRED:

You must bring a pencil, standard lined, loose-leaf paper, your math text, and your homework to class everyday. Colored pencils, a ruler, a compass, a protractor, and graph paper will also be needed. A scientific calculator is not essential. However, it can be helpful when solving certain problems.

Only items necessary for this class may be on your desktop. I will confiscate any items distracting you from your study of geometry.

ASSIGNMENTS AND PROJECTS:

Assignments will be checked for completion on a daily basis. Late assignments will receive no credit. *Doing homework daily is critical to success in this course.*

Group and individual projects will be assigned throughout the year. Specifics will be provided when the project is assigned.

TESTS AND QUIZZES:

Expect a test worth 50 to 100 points after each chapter and a quiz worth 10–35 points at least once a week or after every two sections. Quizzes are generally unannounced. Cumulative semester finals will be worth 100–250 points each.

NOTE: A single absence on the day prior to a test or quiz will *not* excuse you from taking the test or quiz on the scheduled day.

ATTENDANCE:

Regular attendance and consistent study are two factors that contribute greatly to success in school. Attendance is expected. However, if you must miss a class, you are required to make up all missed work. **After-school work will be assigned for unexcused absences or tardies.**

MAKE-UP WORK:

Make-up work is available for *excused absences only*. There is no make-up for unexcused absences or for suspensions. To receive credit, late assignments *must have* the following information in the heading:

Name, Class, Period, and the appropriate *Assignment Number*.

You have one day for each day of absence to make up missed work. See me after class on the day you return in order to schedule a date to make up any missed tests or quizzes. *Failure to make up work in the required time will result in a zero for the work missed*

GRADING:

ACADEMIC ~ Grade is based on a cumulative point total determined by homework, classwork, projects, quizzes, and tests.

The grading scale is:

90 to 100%   A
80 to 89%   B
70 to 79%   C
60 to 69%   D
below 60%   F

WORK HABITS ~ Grade is based entirely on effort and is determined by the amount of assigned work completed and turned in.

CITIZENSHIP ~ Grade begins Satisfactory and will be lowered if SOS steps, After School Work, or Referrals are received. Outstanding will be awarded for above average cooperation

CLASS RULES:

1. BE PUNCTUAL ~ Be in your assigned seat ready to work when the bell rings.

2. BE COURTEOUS ~ Be kind to classmates in speech and actions. Show respect for others. Keep your behavior under control.

3. BE RESPONSIBLE ~ Follow directions and complete assignments carefully. Do your best work every day!

4. BE NEAT ~ Come to class appropriately groomed and dressed. Keep your desk and books free of marks. Clean up any mess on or around your desk. Take pride in yourself and in your classroom.

5. KEEP FOOD AND DRINK OUT OF CLASS ~ Absolutely no chewing gum, eating food, or drinking is allowed in class. **After-school work will be assigned for disregarding this policy.**

---

copies of the teacher's text and the student text. This wealth of materials allows the teachers to customize the course and requires choices because there is purposely more material than one instructor can use. Although at first the array of materials may overwhelm, begin with the teacher's text and utilize supplementary materials when needed. *Integrated Mathematics* has a format similar to traditional texts yet offers computer programs, calculator problems, manipulatives, ideas for applications lessons, activities for group work, and a unit project, as well as ex-

ercise sets. Further, the authors provide each unit with the following: overview, list of objectives, reference to *Standards* strands, list of support materials for each section, and a section planning guide with suggestions for daily planning.

The use of matrices builds through the 4 years of *Integrated Mathematics*. Matrices are introduced in *Integrated Mathematics Course 1,* Unit 3: Representing Data, by correlating spreadsheets to matrices as a method to display data. In *Course 2,* Unit 3: Linear Systems and Matrices introduces using

Figure 6.4

Long-Range Lesson Plan for First Unit of *Integrated Mathematics, Course 3* (McDougall Littell)

Sept. 5 (Th)	First day of school
	Introduce self to the class
	Students fill out the Student Information Forms
	Discuss course of study, rules, requirements
	Mathematics activity (course introduction)
Sept. 6 (F)	Go over mathematics activity
	Pass out Course Information Sheet
	Quickly review the layout of the text and main concepts in Unit 1
	Read "Plan a Park," the Unit 1 project, and discuss
	Discuss course of study, rules, requirements
Sept. 9 (M)	Sec 1.1 Algorithms with graphing calculator; scissors for triangle exercise
Sept. 10 (Tu)	Sec. 1.2 Using systematic lists; toothpick exploration
Sept. 11 (W)	Sec. 1.2 (Cont'd); Assign student work groups and allow time for organization on Unit 1 project
Sept. 12 (Th)	Sec. 1.3 Using statistics (trends); graphing calculator for box/whisker plots
Sept. 13 (F)	Short quiz; students work in groups on unit project
Sept. 16 (M)	Sec. 1.4 Using graphs and equations (right decisions); graphing calculator
Sept. 17 (Tu)	Sec 1.5 Systems of equations (matrices); graphing calculator with 2 variables
Sept. 18 (W)	Sec. 1.5 (Cont'd); matrices with 3 variables; graphing calculator
Sept. 19 (Th)	Sec. 1.6 Using diagrams (connections of maps, graphs, and matrices)
Sept. 20 (F)	Sec. 1.6 (Cont'd); coloring network diagrams; colored pencils
Sept. 23 (M)	Sec. 1.7 Maximizing and minimizing; graphing calculator
Sept. 24 (Tu)	Sec. 1.7 (Cont'd); group activity with center of mass of cups on strings through cardboard
Sept. 25 (W)	Sec. 1.8 Linear programming; graphing calculator
Sept. 26 (Th)	Sec. 1.8 (Cont'd); students prepare presentations for Unit 1 project
Sept. 27 (F)	Quiz; students present results of Unit 1 project
Sept. 30 (M)	Review for test
Oct. 1 (Tu)	Exam

technology and inverse matrices to solve systems of equations with two variables. In *Course 3,* Unit 1: Modeling Problem Situations reviews solving systems with two variables, leads into solving systems with three variables, and continues into graph theory. The text recommends a plan of 17 days for Unit 1, including 2 days for the unit project, 1 day for the unit review, and 1 day for the unit test. As the first unit of the year, it probably would be wise to allow 1 to 2 days extra to get the course started. (The example of the beginning of a long-range plan in Figure 6.4 assumes the students have books by the second day of class, which may not always be the case.)

Look over the units you will teach, and ask yourself the following questions:

- Does a series of lessons have an interesting variety?

- What material can be emphasized and added to certain units to make them particularly appealing to students? What material can be de-emphasized?
- What material can be enhanced with appropriate technology?
- Where might manipulatives assist students in understanding the important concepts?
- Will you assign homework daily? over weekends? for the day after a unit exam?
- How often will you give quizzes, and how much instructional time will they take?
- If you assign projects, will students be expected to complete them outside of class, or is it necessary for the students to use class time to work together?
- Will you assign a problem of the week? If so, will you take a few minutes of class time each day to encourage student progress on the problem, or will you give individual assistance?

Before writing a long-range plan, pencil in the approximate numbers of days required for each unit, including the exam day. Consult the teacher notes included with most curricula. Generally, a table at the beginning of the teacher's edition of a text indicates the number of days to be spent on a unit, with recommendations for deletions and extensions depending on class needs. Consider the following suggestions:

- Check for assembly days or standardized test days that will affect the time period of the unit. Generally, these days are announced only a few weeks before the change in schedule, so they will not be indicated on the school calendar for the year.
- If you want to conduct instruction on two concepts in the same day, the opportunity to do so is more likely to occur at the beginning of a unit. Generally, the first section is introductory and not too difficult. However, if you frequently introduce two concepts in the same day, the students will get confused when new material is introduced too quickly.
- Complete a unit before an extended vacation; otherwise, you may spend considerable time reteaching concepts forgotten over the holiday. If a vacation *must* fall in the middle of a unit, split the material into two parts for assessment.
- Always plan a review on the day before a unit exam to ensure that all students fully recognize the nature and scope of the material to be mastered. This also gives students one more opportunity to ask any questions they have about the unit material. Part of this review day may entail selected problems similar to those that will be on the exam so students can test aspects of their understanding. A review day will necessitate completing all topics to be on the exam 2 days before the test, which has the advantage of giving students a little more time to consolidate their knowledge.
- Avoid exams on Mondays—students just seem to do more poorly on a Monday. Also, avoid exams the day before a vacation because the attendance may be lower than average. Complete the semester plan by filling in topics on a day-to-day basis, and then reflect on it. Indicate when manipulatives, calculators, computers, and other teaching aids will be used. Carefully look over this sketch of the course. Does it look like an interesting course?

Consider ways the unit might be expanded or cut. *Integrated Mathematics* has many ideas for expansion, but beginning teachers frequently plan too much because they expect the students to comprehend more quickly than they do. If students have not had experience with graphing calculators or cooperative groups, this schedule will need to be sim-

plified. Is it best to cut the unit project, a section of lesser importance, or the group activities? Deleting experience with graphing calculators may make the course more difficult later on. On the other hand, developing expertise with the calculator now may take longer than it would if done later in the course. To answer the question of what to cut, think of the information gained during the development of the broad overview.

The long-range plan assists in setting goals for instruction, but it is *not* set in concrete. As the year progresses, changes to it will be necessary. The plan is a working document; make short notes to indicate where the timing had to be changed and why. For example, certain schoolwide standardized testing days may be annual events, so it will be helpful in future years to have this reduction in instructional time in mind at the beginning of the school year. Other events, such as a special assembly to encourage a winning football team, may occur occasionally. Note which concepts took more time or less time for your students than you had allotted. Be sure to consult the plan in following years. We have kept plans for the previous 5 years and consulted the lot when beginning a new year. With increased teaching experience, planning in subsequent years will go much more quickly and need less adjustment during the semester.

Unit Planning

Begin a unit plan with a concept map if the teacher's materials do not include one. The purpose of the concept map is to display in one-page pictorial form the main concepts in the unit and their interconnections. This technique for organizing information began in the area of reading and study skills to help students translate reading into thinking (Hanf, 1971). We have used it for planning our instruction and also have required students to make these maps to help them better organize information within a unit. First, write the main concept of the unit in the middle of a blank page and draw a circle or oval around it. A picture depicting the main idea may be included to assist memory. Then put major concepts in bubbles, shapes, or on lines around the central topic. Indicate the lesser ideas under each main concept. Lines drawn between the shapes and descriptors indicate connections.

The concept map in Figure 6.5 is drawn for a unit in Course 2 of the Core-Plus curriculum. This program, subtitled *Contemporary Mathematics in Context, a Unified Approach,* is heavily based in data analysis and applications. Matrices, briefly introduced in Course 1 as a method of displaying information, are reintroduced in the first unit of the

Figure 6.5
A Concept Map

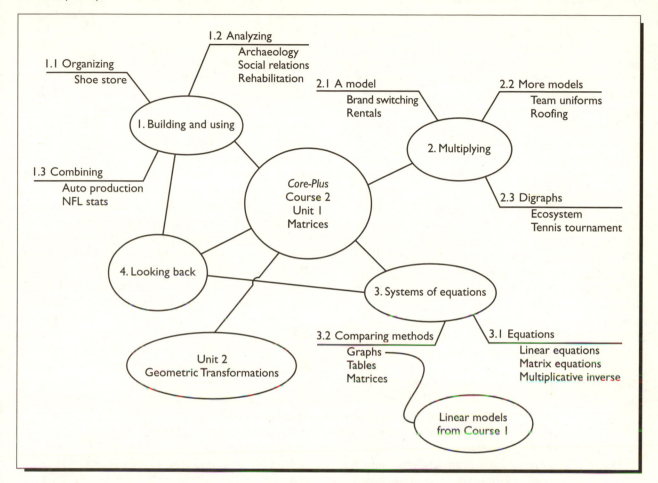

second year. The next unit of Course 2 expands the use of matrices to geometric transformations. Matrices and graph theory are employed to solve increasingly complex applications in subsequent years. Since the main concepts are embodied in detailed application problems, this concept map lists the specific applications in addition to the main concepts. Note that the *Core-Plus* implementation of matrices is quite different from the previous example curriculum from *Integrated Mathematics,* which primarily used matrices in solving equations in Course 3, with less emphasis on graph theory.

Consult the long-range plan and the unit plan suggested by the curriculum authors to make a brief outline of major concepts allotted on a daily basis. With experience, you will gain a feel for changing the units and activities presented in the text to others that seem of greater interest to your students and more attuned to your educational situation. The most important question to ask is, "Will these lessons actively involve students in learning mathematics?"

Balance: Pace, Sequence, Depth, Breadth, Skills, and Processes

Pacing is of primary importance in planning and instruction. Time available for instruction provides a constraint on learning. Teachers progress from one student activity to another based on their judgment of whether enough learners have gained the desired depth of understanding of the material, and also based on their view of the material left to be studied in the time remaining in the school year.

The definitions of enough learners and sufficient understanding of the material are not at all obvious. According to researchers, teachers generally move to new material when learners between the 10th and 25th percentile reach expected performance (Posner, 1987). These numbers vary according to the level and the perceived importance of the course. Teachers may expect almost all learners to excel in basic concepts but will advance more quickly from one topic to the next in upper-level high-school courses due to pressure to introduce a given number of chapters. Perceptions of the level of sufficient understanding depend on the standard of achievement used by the teacher. The achievement yardstick is based on either the relative performance of the other individuals in the class or on an absolute set of criteria, such as a set of specific standards or objectives. Information from students of previous years may also be considered in deciding the level of sufficient understanding.

Sequencing is of great importance in planning and executing instruction. To fully describe teaching, sequencing must be seen as the combination of classroom activities and mathematics topics in an instructional sequence. Another way to label these components is teaching methods and content of instruction. A wide variety of teaching methods gives rise to divergent approaches of sequencing; let us consider only two. The memorization method practiced by the Hebrews, the Spartans, and the Native Americans is reflected in the equivalent modern instructional organization of explicit instruction followed by guided practice followed by application/assessment. The Socratic method offers a sharp contrast wherein the teacher first asks questions to reveal students' lack of understanding or active misunderstandings. Then he asks questions to guide students to inquire and discover relationships for themselves (Posner, 1987). The mode of content presentation and sequencing of instruction both reflect and influence teaching methods.

Pacing and sequencing are the underpinnings of the contemporary concerns about content breadth and depth in the mathematics classroom. Content coverage indicates the potential of learning. It is essential to be ever aware that teacher coverage does not equate with student coverage. Furthermore, student coverage need not signify sufficient understanding by a large number of individuals in a class. Researchers indicate that what teachers cover does strongly influence what is learned, but they caution that content coverage facilitates learning only to a degree, "but may then depress it if too much is crowded into too short a time" (Barr, 1987). They also report that the textbook, rather than student ability, appears to have the greatest influence on what is covered in the mathematics classroom. This relates to the statement in the TIMMS Report that the U.S. mathematics curriculum is an inch deep and a mile wide.

Since the TIMSS report of secondary-level results released in 1998, there has been considerable debate of breadth versus depth. In addition to analyzing mathematics test scores of most countries, the report compared the curriculum of the United States and Japan. The Japanese students scored sig-

nificantly higher on the mathematics exam than the U.S. students at the eighth-grade level. Analysis of the textbooks and teacher practices of the two countries revealed that students in the United States spend many more years going over the same topic—8 years on average, compared with 3 years—and cover many more topics each year than do the Japanese. Instruction was examined through videotapes of 50 to 100 Japanese and U.S. eighth-grade classrooms. TIMSS summarizes U.S. instruction as emphasizing "familiarity with many topics rather than concentrated attention on a few," which leads to preoccupation with quantity rather than quality.

Entangled with the debate of breadth versus depth is the debate of skills versus processes. Some mathematicians have proposed that the goals of middle- and high-school mathematics should be to answer two questions: "What is mathematics? and Where and how is mathematics used?" (Devlin, 1997). Devlin recommended we reduce skills teaching and concentrate on the big picture to ameliorate math phobia and reduce ignorance about the true state of mathematics. Of course, this leads to other questions: What skills are essential? What topics best display the big ideas in mathematics?

Balance is required in all these matters. It is unfortunate that the debates around mathematics reform are couched in terms of opposites. The exemplary teacher sometimes teaches for mastery and sometimes for a broad view. The exemplary teacher sometimes emphasizes mastery of skills and sometimes concentrates on development of problem-solving strategies. The exemplary teacher sometimes teaches by explicit instruction and sometimes by inquiry-discovery. The choice of content detail, the balance between skill and processes, and the selection of mode of delivery should be guided by the aim of the instruction, by the nature of the material presented, and by student interest. For example, if the study of matrices will be treated in detail in a subsequent year, a brief introduction to matrices as a way of representing data is sufficient to familiarize students with the terminology and basic concept. It is sensible to use an explicit instructional approach to matrices as one way of organizing data, as students cannot discover something with which they are not familiar. On the other hand, overuse of teaching strictly by algorithm through explicit instruction easily leads to rote procedures that deaden the students' learning excitement. Incorporating an ample tool kit of methods and motivating problems from coherently developed materials into thoughtful and well-organized lessons sets the stage for success in instruction.

Alternative Schedules: Block, Teaming, Thematic, and Coring

When planning, we tend to assume an organization of daily classes of approximately one hour each for two semesters of approximately 18 weeks of instruction apiece. In current practice this traditional organization is becoming less common. A number of urban school districts have moved to year-round schedules to accommodate large student populations in areas where building new schools is impractical. Under most of these plans, two of the three different groups of students and teachers are present at the school site at any given time. Intersession classes may replace summer classes. The design is four-month-long semesters divided by two months of vacation. Although time of the school vacation(s) will vary, the classes fulfill the required number of contact hours (sometimes by extending the length of each period) as set by the state's department of education.

Many schools are moving to alternative types of scheduling in the effort to boost student achievement. Block scheduling formats vary widely. Examples are meeting 90 minutes per day for 10 weeks, meeting every other day for 90 minutes for a regular school year, or meeting four days a week for five hours, including one two-hour class per week. A number of middle schools have embraced the teams' approach with four teachers of mathematics, science, language arts, and social studies assuming responsibility for the same 120 students. These teachers can then decide how to allocate the instructional time and may plan thematic units across all the subject areas. Because it is sometimes difficult to schedule teams of four teachers, however, other schools pair the science and mathematics teachers. Two teachers have 60 students for two hours a day. The blocks of time enable teachers to implement cross-discipline connections and plan activities that may not fit into a one-hour time limit. Some high schools have organized the ninth grade into "families"—a form of teaming—to help the students transition from relatively small middle schools to larger high schools. A team of four teachers may or may not have block scheduling with the students. They do coordinate closely with each other, with counselors, and with parents to ensure student success. Coring has one teacher teaching both mathematics and science in a two-period block to the same group of students. This is commonly done at the sixth-grade level.

Following are some of our observations on these alternative schedules:

- Teachers we have interviewed and classroom research we have reviewed indicate agreement that a greater variety of teaching strategies is needed in the longer time blocks. After block scheduling has been in place for several years, mathematics teachers are nearly evenly split on whether the schedule is helpful to student achievement. Also, mathematics teachers seem no more in favor of or disappointed by block scheduling than teachers in other disciplines (Groves, 1997).

- Students' retention is perceived to be about the same from one scheduling format to another except under the system in which students finish a course in one quarter of a school year and may not take the next mathematics course for several quarters. Scheduling will need to be changed for the Advanced Placement classes so students finish the AP course in a timely manner just before the AP exam in May.

- Mathematics teachers perceive difficulty in completing instruction on the same number of topics as in a traditional schedule, but feel that their students have a greater depth of understanding. The research on mathematics achievement of students under block scheduling is inconclusive. Probably the different studies report contrasting results because the instructional practices and time devoted to staff development varies widely in addition to the myriad ways in which block scheduling is implemented (Kramer, 1996).

- To ensure success for the middle-school organization of cohorts of students assigned to a team of four teachers, the teachers should have a common planning period. Themes selected for continuity can be interwoven into the curriculum of each subject for the given grade level. For example, if the team decides on emphasis on Egypt as a theme, some history of mathematics can be included. However, the mathematics of the entire curriculum cannot be made subservient to the theme.

- When teachers of mathematics and science team up to teach students, connections and applications of mathematics to the real-world become natural and easy to effect. The only danger is that the mathematics will become a "servant" of data analysis. The field of mathematics is a significant achievement of thought and must not be considered only a tool for other disciplines.

- Teachers find some other benefits to alternative schedules. For example, they feel that the longer periods of instruction enable them to get to know the students better and allow more time to assist students of low achievement during class. Under many of the block scheduling plans, fewer courses taught per week means fewer preparations for the teachers and less paperwork, such as recording attendance.

- For specifics on how to implement alternative schedules, consult the literature on each different organization. Indeed, the possibilities are too vast to be described in detail in this text.

Set 6.2   *Discussion Questions*

 Questions with an asterisk appear in the Message Board section of the Companion Website at *http://www.prenhall.com/huetinck.* Go to Chapter 6 and click on the Message Board to find and respond to the question.

1. What questions would you ask students to answer on a "Who Are You?" sheet?
*2. How would you modify the Course Information Sheet shown in Figure 6.3?
3. Discuss how you might modify the concept map given for *Core-Plus* Course 2, Unit 1, to allow for the special needs of underachieving students; for students in a high-achieving class.
4. Articulate your position of how to attain balance in content breadth, depth, skill, and processes.

DAILY LESSON PLANNING

Although experienced teachers may not need to write daily lesson plans for each class, this is definitely a requirement for effective teaching by first-year teachers. To earn students' respect, a teacher needs to be well organized. The act of teaching requires simultaneous attention to student behavior and content material. Hence, it is necessary to make as many decisions as possible before class begins in order to avoid unnecessary distractions due to poor or inadequate planning. Vary from a plan as the situation demands, but realize that a plan, even if changed, acts as an anchor to maintain quality instruction.

If a lesson plan is to serve its purpose well, it needs to have the following elements or characteristics:

- *Objective, goal, or topic.* Many mathematics texts provide daily objectives. The main concept of the lesson may also be worded as a goal. Constructivist teachers may prefer to name a topic, since objectives have been closely associated with behavioral tasks in the past and implied a certain coverage, whether or not students were learning. The main point is to define the desired outcome of a lesson or sequence to serve as a guide in elic-

iting and assessing mathematical thinking. Consult a general methods text for detailed information about developing lesson plan objectives.

- *Student activities.* It is meaningless to use a lesson plan simply to list the teacher's actions. After all, teacher activity may or may not translate into student involvement and understanding. Thus, a teacher should either indicate students' activities as well as corresponding teacher activities or simply identify student activities to be elicited by the appropriate teaching situations. The examples of lesson plans in the next two sections illustrate each of these approaches.
- *A beginning, middle, and end.* Class may begin with a warm-up, the checking of homework, a discussion of the problem of the week, or an activity begun the day before. The central focus of the day's lesson will include further development of previous material or introduction of new mathematics concepts. The main lesson may be taught using large group, cooperative groups, or alternate large group and small group instruction, facilitated by the teacher with technology, manipulatives, or projects for active student involvement, as appropriate. Active instruction may continue nearly to the end of the period, allowing students a few minutes to get ready to move to the next class, or, students may be given the last 10 to 15 minutes of the class period to begin homework. Teachers working with block scheduling will need to alternate among a variety of activities in order to hold students' interest in the learning process over a class period of one and one-half to two hours. Classes of students with short attention spans will need frequent changes among activities to maintain involvement. A whole period or series of periods may be devoted to computer work, projects, or group work, but even these sessions should have a structured beginning, middle, and end to keep students on task. Assessment may be part or most of a day's lesson.
- *Approximate time allotted for each activity.* Consider including times in the daily lesson plan in order to pace yourself. Beginning teachers sometimes spend so much time going over homework or a warm-up activity that students do not get adequate instruction to be successful on new material. Realize, however, that estimates of time needed for activities will need to be revised often until you get to know your students and the material well.
- *Descriptors of activities.* Include enough description of the warm-up, INTO, or student activity so the exercise can be identified by an observer. The warm-up provides a short activity that generally is

a review to occupy the students at the beginning of the period while the teacher tends to clerical duties. It marks the beginning of instruction. The INTO, also called Set (as in "get ready, get set, go") or motivational activity, introduces the new material for the day, signals a change from initial activities such as homework discussion to the main lesson, and provides either a mathematical or a real-world context for the work to follow.

- *Brevity.* Try to limit the daily plan to one page, and definitely never go over two pages. A longer plan is difficult to follow without spending valuable class time flipping between pages. A one-page plan conveys the important elements of the lesson in an accessible format. Class notes required for any activity or set of problems are organized separately. Keep sequential lesson plans in a loose-leaf notebook for reference later.

- *Space at the end of the daily lesson plan for reflections.* At the close of the day, write both positive and negative thoughts about the lesson and their impact on future lessons. These notes will be extremely helpful when you teach the course the next time.

Note the form of the lesson plan sample for Sample Lesson 6.1. The most important segments are those in the classroom titled INTO, THROUGH, and BEYOND. The INTO (sometimes called a SET) is designed to signal a change from the beginning exercises to the new material that will be discussed this day or for the main activity of the lesson. This short interlude also gets the students ready—set to explore further—and serves to elicit student participation in the lesson to come. The THROUGH encompasses the main ideas for the class which are either an extension of previous work or a beginning of completely new concepts. The BEYOND provides the student with the opportunity to more fully comprehend the main lesson through additional activities that strengthen learning. Note that the teacher also has additional obligations before and after teaching the mathematics during the class period.

Example Lesson Plan for University of Chicago School Mathematics Project

Sample Lesson Plan 6.1 includes a one-page lesson plan based on three pages from Chapter 5 of *Advanced Algebra,* published by the University of Chicago School of Mathematics Project. The teacher's textbook is larger than the student text, with notes to the teacher in the margins. Including

annotations in the margins of a teacher's text is a common practice. Matrices are not introduced during Course 1 and Course 2 (algebra and geometry) in this textbook series. Chapter 4 of the third year (advanced algebra integrated) is devoted entirely to matrices. At that point the students study matrices to revisit and extend many of the procedures they have accomplished before without matrices. Chapter 4 explores matrices for the transformations executed previously in geometry, in addition to sections on storing data and multiplication and addition of matrices. (Note that multiplication is introduced before addition.) Chapter 5: Systems then introduces addition/subtraction, substitution, and using matrices to solve systems of equations. For brevity, the last example of this section is omitted, as are the problems labeled Covering the Reading, Applying the Mathematics, Review, and Exploration.

For the INTO exercise, masking tape is placed in a grid on the floor to represent large square graph paper with an x- and y-axis. Each of four students is assigned a value for the x-variable, such as -3, -1, 1, and 3, and asked to assume his correct position standing on the x-axis of the grid. Then each of the four students moves to the position on the y-axis that represents addition of $+3$ to his assigned number. Thus they stand to represent points on the given line $y = x + 3$. Three other students then stand on the x-axis to represent their assigned values of -2, 0, and 2. They then assume the negative of their value and move to the position on the y-axis that is the negative of their number to illustrate the line $y = -x$. The activity works best if the two lines intersect where x and y have integer values. The grid on the floor can be used again and again to integrate kinesthetic and visual learning with the abstractions of graphed curves. (The activity just described works best if students have had prior experience with "body" graphing of different lines and curves in previous sections.)

Example Lesson Plan for Interactive Mathematics Project

The Interactive Mathematics Project (IMP) is organized into four to seven units of study for each of the four years of the course in a format contrasting with that of the University of Chicago School Mathematics Project. The IMP teacher's notes are extensive in helping the teacher lead students to understanding. Class work is conducted with cooperative groups that are selected about every 3 weeks by randomly using a deck of cards. Students choose a card on entering the classroom. The four students with the same numbered card sit together; different suits are

FOR STUDENTS

Sample Lesson 6.1
Using Matrices to Solve Systems (page 1 of 2)

Mathematical Content: Using matrices to solve systems of two equations (PSSM Algebra Standard for Grades 9–12)

Materials Needed: Grid marked with chalk or masking tape on the floor

Directions: Note that the lesson plan for this lesson from the UCSMP begins with a kinesthetic exercise where students stand on points designated on a grid made with masking tape on the floor. Three students stand to represent one line, and another three students stand on the points marking an intersecting line. The rest of the class can determine the equation of the line, given the coordinates of each student, and then approximate the intersection coordinates of the two lines. Observe that the student activities are varied—*not* just observing, taking notes, and answering questions. The indicated activities get the students involved from the beginning and maintain their attention throughout the lesson.

Notice that $\begin{bmatrix} 1 & 3 \\ 2 & -1 \end{bmatrix} \begin{bmatrix} x \\ y \end{bmatrix} = \begin{bmatrix} x + 3y \\ 2x - y \end{bmatrix}$.

This means that it is possible to represent the system $\begin{cases} x + 3y = 22 \\ 2x - y = 2 \end{cases}$ as a matrix equation:

$$\begin{bmatrix} 1 & 3 \\ 2 & -1 \end{bmatrix} \begin{bmatrix} x \\ y \end{bmatrix} = \begin{bmatrix} 22 \\ 2 \end{bmatrix}$$

This is the **matrix form of the system**. The matrix $\begin{bmatrix} 1 & 3 \\ 2 & -1 \end{bmatrix}$ represents the coefficients of the variables, so it is called the **coefficient matrix**.

The matrix $\begin{bmatrix} 22 \\ 2 \end{bmatrix}$ contains the constants on the right sides of the equations. It is called the **constant matrix** for this system.

A system in matrix form can be solved using matrix multiplication. Just as the Multiplication Property of Equality allows both sides of an equation to be multiplied by any number, both sides of a matrix equation can be multiplied by any matrix. To solve, we multiply by the inverse of the coefficient matrix. By the theorem in Lesson 5-5, the inverse of $\begin{bmatrix} 1 & 3 \\ 2 & -1 \end{bmatrix}$ is found to be $\begin{bmatrix} \frac{1}{7} & \frac{3}{7} \\ \frac{2}{7} & -\frac{1}{7} \end{bmatrix}$.

Multiply both sides of the matrix equation by this inverse of the coefficient matrix. Because matrix multiplication is not commutative, the inverse matrix must be at the left on *each* side of the equation.

$$\begin{bmatrix} \frac{1}{7} & \frac{3}{7} \\ \frac{2}{7} & -\frac{1}{7} \end{bmatrix} \begin{bmatrix} 1 & 3 \\ 2 & -1 \end{bmatrix} \begin{bmatrix} x \\ y \end{bmatrix} = \begin{bmatrix} \frac{1}{7} & \frac{3}{7} \\ \frac{2}{7} & -\frac{1}{7} \end{bmatrix} \begin{bmatrix} 22 \\ 2 \end{bmatrix}$$

After the matrices are multiplied, the equation becomes

$$\begin{bmatrix} 1 & 0 \\ 0 & 1 \end{bmatrix} \begin{bmatrix} x \\ y \end{bmatrix} = \begin{bmatrix} 4 \\ 6 \end{bmatrix}.$$

The presence of the identity matrix verifies that the inverse matrix was calculated correctly. Thus

$$\begin{bmatrix} x \\ y \end{bmatrix} = \begin{bmatrix} 4 \\ 6 \end{bmatrix},$$

or $x = 4$ and $y = 6$. You are asked to check this solution in Question 3 at the end of this lesson.

In general, to solve the system $\begin{cases} ax + by = e \\ cx + dy = f \end{cases}$ by using matrices, rewrite the system as a matrix equation

$$\begin{bmatrix} a & b \\ c & d \end{bmatrix} \begin{bmatrix} x \\ y \end{bmatrix} = \begin{bmatrix} e \\ f \end{bmatrix},$$

which is of the form

$$M \begin{bmatrix} x \\ y \end{bmatrix} = K.$$

FOR STUDENTS

Sample Lesson 6.1
Using Matrices to Solve Systems (page 2 of 2)

Then multiply both sides of the equation by M^{-1}.

$$M^{-1}M \begin{bmatrix} x \\ y \end{bmatrix} = M^{-1}K$$

$$\begin{bmatrix} 1 & 0 \\ 0 & 1 \end{bmatrix} \begin{bmatrix} x \\ y \end{bmatrix} = M^{-1}K$$

$$\begin{bmatrix} x \\ y \end{bmatrix} = M^{-1}K$$

The last equation shows that the solution of a system is the product of the inverse of the coefficient matrix and the constant matrix.

Example 1

Use matrices to solve $\begin{cases} 9x = 3 + y \\ 2x - 3y = 5 \end{cases}$.

SOLUTION

Rewrite the first equation so that it can be put in matrix form.

$$\begin{cases} 9x - y = 3 \\ 2x - 3y = 5 \end{cases}$$

This is equivalent to the matrix equation

$$\begin{bmatrix} 9 & -1 \\ 2 & -3 \end{bmatrix} \begin{bmatrix} x \\ y \end{bmatrix} = \begin{bmatrix} 3 \\ 5 \end{bmatrix}.$$

The inverse of the coefficient matrix is

$$\begin{bmatrix} \frac{3}{25} & \frac{-1}{25} \\ \frac{2}{25} & \frac{-9}{25} \end{bmatrix}, \text{ or } \begin{bmatrix} .12 & -.04 \\ .08 & -.36 \end{bmatrix}$$

Multiply both sides of the matrix equation by the inverse matrix; the inverse matrix is always placed on the *left*.

$$\begin{bmatrix} .12 & -.04 \\ .08 & -.36 \end{bmatrix} \begin{bmatrix} 9 & -1 \\ 2 & -3 \end{bmatrix} \begin{bmatrix} x \\ y \end{bmatrix} = \begin{bmatrix} .12 & -.04 \\ .08 & -.36 \end{bmatrix} \begin{bmatrix} 3 \\ 5 \end{bmatrix}$$

$$\begin{bmatrix} 1 & 0 \\ 0 & 1 \end{bmatrix} \begin{bmatrix} x \\ y \end{bmatrix} = \begin{bmatrix} .16 \\ -1.56 \end{bmatrix}$$

So the solution is $x = .16$ and $y = -1.56$.

CHECK

Does $9 \cdot 16 = 3 + -1.56$? Yes, both sides equal 1.44. Does $2 \cdot 16 - 3 \cdot -1.56 = 5$? Yes.

Matrices provide an easy way to tell when linear systems have exactly one solution. The system

$$\begin{cases} ax + by = e \\ cx + dy = f \end{cases}$$

has exactly one solution only if the inverse of $\begin{bmatrix} a & b \\ c & d \end{bmatrix}$ exists.

This inverse exists if and only if its determinant, $ad - bc$, is not 0. This leads to the following theorem.

MATRIX-SOLUTION THEOREM:

A 2×2 system has exactly one solution if and only if the determinant of the coefficient matrix is *not* 0.

When the determinant of the coefficient matrix is 0, there is no unique solution. To determine whether the system has infinitely many solutions or none at all, you should find a solution to one of the equations and test it in the other one. Consider the system

$$\begin{cases} 6x - 9y = 10 \\ 62x - 93y = 310. \end{cases}$$

The determinant is $ad - bc = 6 \cdot (-93) - (-9) \cdot (62) = 0$, so there is no unique solution. The point $(\frac{5}{3}, 0)$ satisfies the first equation, but not the second. Thus the system has no solution; it is inconsistent.

Computer programs can find inverses of large matrices (often with dozens or hundreds of variables) to solve linear systems. Without such programs, you will solve a system of three equations with three variables using 3×3 matrices. The identity matrix for 3×3 matrices is

$$I = \begin{bmatrix} 1 & 0 & 0 \\ 0 & 1 & 0 \\ 0 & 0 & 1 \end{bmatrix}.$$

The calculation of the inverse of a 3×3 matrix is complicated, so we give it.

Source: Senk, S. L., and Others (1990). The University of Chicago School Mathematics Project, *Advanced Algebra*. Glenview, IL: Scott, Foresman and Company. Reprinted by permission.

F O R   T E A C H E R S

Sample Lesson Plan 6.1 Using Matrices to Solve Systems

Subject: Adv. Alg. Section 5-6 Using Matrices to Solve Problems

Date: November 10, 2002

Objective: Use inverse matrices to solve systems of eq. with 2 and 3 variables.

Instructional Materials: Text, "graph paper on floor," graphing calculator

TEACHER'S ACTIVITIES	STUDENTS' ACTIVITIES
Warm-up: 1, 3, 4, & 9 from Sec. 5-5	Exchange and correct from overhead
Discussion on Previous Homework:	Ask questions, present problems, and discuss
INTO: 4 students stand on grid for 1 line 3 stand on another line that intersects the first line	Review what a solution of eqs. means

THROUGH: Lesson

1. Show matrix form of a system	Take notes; ask questions
2. Review working ex. 1 in Sec. 5-3. What is being manipulated?	Provide steps using addition and subtraction Note that operations are on coefficients
3. Work same problem by matrices Work the ex. on p. 275	Take notes and ask questions
4. Ask these questions: Why should we use matrices? What must be the form of the eq.? Does the order of multiplication matter?	Answer questions and discuss
5. Present ex. 1 and 2	Discuss and take notes
6. Assign 1–9 on p. 279 to discuss Call on students	Pair-share discussions Pairs present answers

BEYOND

7. In your own words, why is an inverse matrix used to solve systems?	Write in journal

Begin Homework:

After working problems requiring solving systems of equations, sketch lines and check with TI by any method.

Homework: 12–15, 17–19 on pp. 280–281.

Lesson Reflections:

ordered with respect to the classroom walls. For example, all the 5s work together, and in all groups the hearts sit in the northwest position, clubs in the northeast position, etc. Frequent use of graphing calculators and manipulatives is incorporated into the units. Mathematics topics are listed in teacher materials for each day. A progressive discussion of a problem of the week (POW) is generally the first order of business. If the homework will be discussed immediately, the teacher stamps each student's work upon entering the room. Then students may add to their homework during discussion, and the stamp indicates the amount of work accomplished by the students at home.

Matrices are deployed in Course 3 to solve systems of linear equations and in Course 4 for geometric transformations and to develop trigonometry identities. Course 1 and Course 2 incorporate linear equations and linear programming. The latter topic is expanded with matrices in Course 3. The Course 1 "Overland Trail" unit looks at Western migration in the mid-1800s in terms of the many linear relationships involving modeling: what to take, expenses, rates of consumption and of travel, and time to reach the end of the trail. The Course 2 "Cookies" unit focuses on a classic linear programming problem to maximize the profits of a cookie store. The Course 3 "Meadows or Malls?" unit concerns a decision to be made about land use requiring linear programming and solution of a problem with 9 variables by matrices.

Sample Lesson Plan 6.2 and Sample Lesson 6.2 are the lessons for Day 19 and lesson plan for the subsequent discussion on Day 20 of the IMP 33-day unit, "Meadows or Malls?" with slight editing for brevity. The common form of a lesson plan illustrated in the previous section did not seem appropriate to us when teaching IMP. We found the following format more useful when planning for a project-based curriculum. The students' activities are listed using the four pages of notes contained in the teacher's materials for Day 20 to facilitate the discussion. The teacher guides the discussion to lead students to the understanding necessary to answer the questions.

Set 6.3 *Discussion Questions*

 Questions with an asterisk appear in the Message Board section of the Companion Website at ***http://www.prenhall.com/huetinck.*** Go to Chapter 6 and click on the Message Board to find and respond to the question.

*1. Compare and contrast the two lesson plan examples. These are only suggestions that should be altered when appropriate. What other helpful elements could be included?

2. Because writing daily lesson plans for all courses taught is a demanding task, especially the first time through a text, what measures will ensure ease of preparation?

F O R   S T U D E N T S

Sample Lesson 6.2
Inventing an Algebra: Meadows or Malls? (page 1 of 3)

A **matrix** is a rectangular array of numbers like:

$$\begin{bmatrix} 1 & -8 & 3 & -1 & -1 \\ 5 & 3 & 4 & -1 & -6 \end{bmatrix} \; or \; \begin{bmatrix} 1 & 1 & 1 \\ 2 & 1 & -1 \\ 3 & 2 & 1 \end{bmatrix}$$

or

$$[6 \quad 17 \quad 1/8 \quad -368]$$

The first matrix above has 2 rows and 5 columns. We describe the size (or shape) of this matrix by calling it a "2 × 5" matrix. (The expression "2 × 5" here is read "2 by 5.") When we call something an *m* by *n* matrix, the first number always tells how many rows there are, and the second number tells how many columns. (A row goes horizontally; a column goes vertically.)

The second matrix has 3 rows and 3 columns, so it is a 3 × 3 matrix. The third matrix has 1 row and 4 columns, so it is a 1 × 4 matrix. The individual numbers in a matrix are called **entries**. The plural of matrix is **matrices**. A matrix with the same number of rows as columns (such as a 3 × 3 matrix) is

F O R   S T U D E N T S

Sample Lesson 6.2
Inventing an Algebra: Meadows or Malls? (page 2 of 3)

called a square matrix. A matrix with one row often is called a **row vector**, and a matrix with one column often is called a **column vector**.

There is an *algebra* of matrices—that is, rules for adding and multiplying them. This worksheet will help you discover what those rules are. We would like you to discover the rules yourself, since we want you to feel that the rules are reasonable.

Here are some problems to work on:

1. A matrix could be used to keep track of students' points in a class. Each row could stand for a different student: Clarabell, Freddy, Sally, and Frashy. The first column might be for homework points, the second for oral reports, and the third for POWs.

   So, for the first grading period, we might have:

	Homework	Oral Reports	POWs (Problems of the Week)
Clarabell	18	54	30
Freddy	35	23	52
Sally	46	15	60
Frashy	60	60	60

   A matrix representation of this information might look like this:

   $$\begin{bmatrix} 18 & 54 & 30 \\ 35 & 23 & 52 \\ 46 & 15 & 60 \\ 60 & 60 & 60 \end{bmatrix}$$

   Here are the students' points in each category for the second grading period:

	Homework	Oral Reports	POWs
Clarabell	10	60	0
Freddy	52	35	58
Sally	42	20	48
Frashy	60	60	60

   a. Write their second grading period scores in a matrix.

   b. Figure out each student's total points in each assignment category for the two grading periods combined. Write those totals in matrix form.

   c. Congratulations! If you completed part b, you have added two matrices. Based on what you've done, write an equation showing two matrices being added to give the matrix you developed in 1b.

2. The Woos' bakery shop is open 6 days a week. Last week, their chocolate chip cookie sales were as follows: 30 dozen on Monday, 25 dozen on Tuesday, 27 dozen on Wednesday, 23 dozen on Thursday, 38 dozen on Friday, and 52 dozen on Saturday.

   For plain cookies, the sales on Monday were 30 dozen; on Tuesday, 28 dozen; on Wednesday, 40 dozen; on Thursday, 38 dozen; on Friday, 48 dozen; and on Saturday, 70 dozen.

   a. Use a matrix to represent the Woos' sales. Let each row be a different kind of cookie and each column a different day of the week.

   b. Make up sales numbers for the Woos for a second week. Show your sales in a matrix similar to that in problem 2a.

   c. Add their sales for the two weeks and show the totals in a matrix.

   d. Write the matrix addition equation that corresponds to your work.

3. Which of the matrix sums below do you think make sense? Explain why you think the others don't make sense:

   a. $\begin{bmatrix} 1 & 5 & 0 & -6 \\ 2 & -2 & 4 & 1 \\ 0 & 1 & -3 & 1 \end{bmatrix} + \begin{bmatrix} 8 & -4 & 0 & 3 \\ 3 & 2 & 4 & 5 \\ 1 & -3 & 3 & 6 \end{bmatrix}$

   b. $\begin{bmatrix} 1 & 5 & 0 & -6 \\ 2 & -2 & 4 & 1 \end{bmatrix} + \begin{bmatrix} 8 & -4 & 0 \\ 3 & 3 & 2 \\ 4 & 3 & 1 \end{bmatrix}$

   c. $\begin{bmatrix} -3 & 7 & 9 \end{bmatrix} + \begin{bmatrix} 7 & -3 & 5 \end{bmatrix}$

FOR STUDENTS

Sample Lesson 6.2
Inventing an Algebra: Meadows or Malls? (page 3 of 3)

d. $\begin{bmatrix} 5 & -4 & 2 & 1 \end{bmatrix} + \begin{bmatrix} 4 \\ -2 \\ 7 \\ 1 \end{bmatrix}$

4. What do you think has to be true of two matrices for it to make sense to add them?

5. Describe a rule for adding any matrices that fit your condition from Question 4.

Homework 19 and 20: Busing

There are two high schools in River City: East High on the east side of the river, and West High on the west side. (People in River City aren't very creative with their names.) In the past, the students who lived on the east side of the river went to East High, and those living on the west side went to West High. Some students needed to be bused to their schools.

Two things have led to a need to change the way students are assigned to schools: West High School has become overcrowded, while East has extra room. The town leaders decided community spirit would be enhanced if students from each side could know students from the other side of town.

Here are some facts about the situation:

- There are 300 high school students living on the east side and 250 living on the west side.
- East High can handle up to 350 students, and West High can handle up to 225 students.
- The average cost for busing per day will be:

  $1.20 for each east side student going to East High

  $2.00 for each east side student going to West High

  $3.00 for each west side student going to East High

  $1.50 for each west side student going to West High

Find out how many students to send to each school so that the busing costs are minimized.

Source: *Interactive Mathematics Program, Course 3,* Key Curriculum Press, 1150 65th Street, Emeryville, CA 94608, 1-800-995-MATH. Reprinted with permission.

FOR TEACHERS

Sample Lesson Plan 6.2 Inventing an Algebra: Unit Meadows or Malls? (page 1 of 2)

Mathematical Content:
Setting up equations for linear programming
  (PSSM Algebra Standards for Grades 9–12)

Directions: On Day 19 students discussed the page "Inventing an Algebra" and began "Homework 19 Busing." The homework assignment described in the teacher materials is to "set up the problem and decide what combination of equations they need to check. Tomorrow night (Day 20) they will solve those combinations and write up their overall solution." To gain an appreciation of the mind set of students on Day 20, work through the following problems.

Note that the lesson plan for this unit details *only* what the students are doing. If the students do not bring out the important answers to the questions posed, the teacher; may interject the questions into the discussion, however, the discussion remains student led.

F O R   T E A C H E R S

Sample Lesson Plan 6.2 Inventing an Algebra: Unit Meadows or Malls? (page 2 of 2)

Subject: IMP Course 3 Day 20

Date: May 10, '03

Mathematical Topics: Representation of a linear programming problem using eqs. and inequalities matrix algebra

Instructional Materials: No new materials

Beginning: Students get stamp on homework when entering class, students take notes and/or present on progress on POW

INTO   students share work on first part of homework with group, students discuss constraints and be sure 9 are listed

$$
\begin{array}{lll}
\text{I}   & E_e + W_e = 300 \\
\text{II}   & E_w + W_w = 250 \\
\text{III} & E_e + E_w \leq 350 \\
\text{IV}   & W_e + W_w \leq 225 \\
\text{V}   & E_w \geq E_e \\
\text{VI}   & E_e \geq O \\
\text{VII} & W_e \geq O \\
\text{VIII} & E_w \geq O \\
\text{IX}   & W_w \geq O \\
\end{array}
$$

THROUGH - Lesson

■ Discussion on Homework 19

Know must examine eqs in sets of four, but what must all four sets of linear equation/inequalities include? [equations I and II]

How many total combinations of equations are there to consider? [7C2 = 21 always including I and II]

Which of these combinations can be ruled out? [example - eqs. corresponding to VI and VII cannot both hold]

■ Discussion on Inventing an Algebra

Heart students (students who drew the card with hearts) from groups give results

Question 1 main points:

   Note the terminology of row, column, size and shape

   Note how the sum can be found directly from the matrices without looking at the data

   Explain what a few of the sums represent.

Question 2 main points:

   Why not set up with rows as day and columns as kind of cookie? [choice is arbitrary but consistency is necessary]

Question 3 main points:

   How do we know where to add zeros? [definitions are due to convention but must add matrices of same shape]

Questions 4 and 5 (reiterate main points in 1, 2 and 3)

   Any further questions or problems?

BEYOND

Begin homework 20, and complete the Busing problem at home.

Lesson Reflections:

STRATEGIES FOR EFFECTIVE INSTRUCTION

Each of these models is tied to certain learning outcomes. Explicit instruction is appropriate for teaching skills and procedures. Problem solving develops flexible thinking and allows for various problem approaches. Students learn to expand their repertoire of problem solving strategies by working together and seeing presentations of each other's work. Guided inquiry is an inductive approach that is appropriate in data collection and pattern recognition situations. In this approach, students are called to analyze the patterns they see, develop conjectures from these observations, and verify their conclusions deductively when possible. Sometimes in inquiry situations, a conjecture must be rejected and a more accurate conjecture posed for verification.

How to Study for Mathematics

Allow time in your planning and instruction to help students learn how to study mathematics. During the first week of instruction, discuss a summary of how to study for the course. It is most helpful if you write out several pages for the students to read and refer to as needed. An excellent resource for this discussion is *How to Study Mathematics* (NCTM, 1977). This 31-page (half size) softbound book is written to the student and serves as an excellent reminder of what teachers expect from, but do not always convey to, their students.

The following list is just a beginning; add to it as you gain teaching experience. As the year progresses, discuss with students your expectations. Ask your students to do the following with frequent reminders of how to study for mathematics.

- *Beginning a new unit.* Look over the table of contents to check the main ideas of the unit and see how these concepts relate to what you have or have not studied before. Skim the unit to look for new or familiar terminology.
- *Classwork.* Always come to class with supplies. Keep a record of assignments as completed, or mark off an assignment sheet provided by the teacher. Note briefly any difficult sections.
- *Homework.* Though the homework may seem easy at the beginning of the chapter, later sections build on the beginning, so don't ignore the easier material at the start of a unit. Look ahead on your schedule. If you will be busy on a given evening, try to get a start on that homework ahead of schedule.
- *Review.* Stop every several sections and think how the mathematics in this section relates to previous ones. Look ahead to get an idea of where the course is going next.
- *Study for an assessment.* Whether the assessment is a project or a written exam, do not fall behind in preparing for it. It is impossible to do well in mathematics by cramming. To practice for an exam, select a few homework problems from each section of the unit and work them *without* referring to the solutions. Check solutions only after finishing the problems.
- *Taking an exam.* Look quickly over the complete test to see the types and number of problems. Estimate how long you can spend on each, and try not to get stuck on any one problem. Be sure to show your work so the teacher can follow it. Ask yourself if the answer is reasonable. Spend all allotted time working on the test even if you have ample time to rework every problem, because you might catch a careless mistake at the last minute.
- *Get help as needed.* Know what help is available and use it. Do not wait until the night before the test, when it's too late.
- *Organization.* Keep materials orderly in a loose-leaf notebook. If papers are in a pile on the bottom of your locker or on the floor of your room, it will be especially difficult to be prepared for class.

In addition to making these suggestions, take time to go through some of these exercises with students to demonstrate the procedures recommended. Give students a few minutes the first day of a new unit to look over the materials and spend time discussing what is coming. List meaningful problems for students to rework when studying for an exam. Provide specific instructions concerning what should be included in an assignment. Although these practices seem obvious to teachers, students need instruction in *how* to learn as well as in *what* to learn. If students truly learn how to learn, their education becomes a self-directed lifelong process.

Explicit Instruction

As a mathematics student, you probably remember explicit instruction as the most common practice. With explicit instruction, the teacher is the main source of information. Different names have been used to express the same mode of instruction: mastery teaching, the Hunter model, and clinical teaching (Hunter, 1994, 1987). As a graduate student, I

(LH) was fortunate to have Madeline Hunter as a professor. She was an excellent instructor who practiced the methods she promoted. She did not intend her formulation to become a set procedure as required by some schools/districts for all lessons in all disciplines. Explicit instruction is not to be confused with lecture, but more actively involves the student. It "contains a highly organized set of interactions under the control of the teacher and focuses more on student learning than on teacher performance" (Armstrong & Savage, 1998). The Hunter model has seven components:

1. anticipatory set to develop readiness for learning;
2. teaching to an objective;
3. presentation of new material;
4. modeling the intended learning;
5. checking for understanding through teacher questioning;
6. guided practice with feedback by the teacher or other students;
7. independent practice either in class or as homework.

Some elements of the Hunter model may fit the reformed curriculum, but this mode of instruction is not consistent with the teacher in the role of facilitator in creating a mathematics community, the role that underlies the NCTM *Standards*.

In a balanced program, there will be occasions to use wisely explicit instruction, even if it is not in the prescriptive form of the seven steps. A case in point is Sample Lesson 6.3, an activity in a middle-school text, *Gateways*, a publisher-developed text subtitled *Algebra and Geometry, an Integrated Approach*. Since students at this level have never encountered matrices, a lesson that presents information and then tests for understanding is an effective approach. Matrices are introduced at the end of Chapter 5, Data Analysis in the *Gateways* text. The previous sections of the chapter introduce a number of types of graphs, such as circle, bar, line, scattergrams and histograms. Next, averages, stem-and-leaf plots, and box-and-whisker plots are discussed prior to the section on using matrices to organize data. The following elements from the chapter are provided: the reading, the Think and Discuss segment, and a portion of the Problems and Application segment.

Problem Solving

Teacher telling at times will help students make sense of mathematics. But more significantly the reform is "about posing interesting and challenging problems that will create a situation where the use

of mathematics is empowering" (Lappan & Briars, 1995, p. 148). Contextualized learning is a significant aspect of reformed learning and instruction. It is not sufficient that students be able to solve word problems such as mixture problems, rate/distance problems, and boat/current problems. Students must be able to solve these problems and also recognize the similar underlying structures. Thus, students realize the problem-solving techniques can be applied to new problems, similar in design, but not studied in prior examples.

Learning problem-solving techniques is important because life is not simple and unchanging. If life were static, the student would need to learn only a few solution methods and thereafter rely on memory and habit. Instead, throughout their lives students will need the ability to "formulate and solve problems involving quantitative thinking" (Henderson & Pingry, 1995, p. 233). To become an efficient problem solver is a skill valuable in many aspects of living. A general conceptual framework for problem solving has three elements:

1. orientation to the problem, with the student becoming involved to the extent that he begins to own the problem and therefore desires to solve it;
2. producing relevant thought processes that the student selects from his experience and knowledge and that of others to bring to bear on a possible solution;
3. testing hypotheses by deducing implications or by making predictions and checking the results.

Problem solving is a complex process, and teachers can assist students by asking questions and by supplying additional information when necessary (Henderson & Pingry, 1995).

Inquiry-Discovery

Teaching by inquiry, discovery, guided discovery, and the Socratic method are frequently used interchangeably for the teaching pedagogy that emphasizes the teacher as guide. One of the first books advocating the discovery approach, *First Lessons: Intellectual Arithmetic Upon the Inductive Method of Instruction* by Warren Colburn, was published in 1821. The book built on the Socratic method by suggesting sequences of questions to allow the student to develop mathematical concepts. Bruner (1966) and Davis (1966) used the term *discovery* or *guided discovery* to indicate learning of a process rather than the attainment of specific knowledge. Davis illustrates presenting the student with a "crisis dilemma" with an example of operations of a 2×2

F O R   S T U D E N T S

Sample Lesson 6.3
Matrices: Organizing Data (page 1 of 2)

Mathematical Content: Matrix vocabulary, reading data from a matrix (PSSM Representational Standards for Grades 6–8 and 9–12)

Materials: Text, supplementary data from a newspaper (optional)

Directions: Read the material and then work through the problems as a student. What questions could you ask as the teacher to help students understand? For either an extension or introduction, ask students to bring in an example of a data chart from the newspaper, and discuss if and how the data could be organized into a matrix.

One of the most common ways of organizing data is in a **matrix**. This is a two-dimensional table in which the rows (the horizontal groups of entries) and the columns (the vertical groups of entries) are labeled to indicate the meaning of the data. The plural form of *matrix* is *matrices*.

The following matrix contains data about the U.S. recording industry in the years 1986–1989. The entries represent approximate numbers of records, CDs, and tape cassettes shipped to stores, in millions.

	Records	**CDs**	**Cassettes**
1986	125	53	345
1987	107	102	410
1988	72	150	450
1989	35	207	446

The entries in the first row, for example, indicate how many of each item were shipped in 1986. The entries in the first column represent the number of records shipped each year. What do you think the entry 150 (in the third row and the second column) represents?

DIMENSIONS OF A MATRIX

The size of a matrix is expressed by giving its **dimensions**—the number of rows by the number of columns. The matrix above, for instance, is a 4-by-3, or 4×3, matrix. (The number of rows is always given first.) The individual entries can be referred to by their row and column numbers—in the matrix above, the entry in row 2, column 3, is 410. Sometimes subscripts are used to identify entries: The entry in row 2, column 3, can be called $e_{2,3}$, and we can write $e_{2,3} = 410$.

EQUAL MATRICES

A capital letter is often used to name a matrix. Let's take a look at two matrices, matrix A and matrix B. Do you notice anything special about the entries in these two matrices?

$$A = \begin{bmatrix} 1 & \frac{1}{2} & \frac{1}{3} & \frac{1}{4} & \frac{1}{5} \\ \frac{1}{6} & \frac{1}{8} & \frac{1}{9} & \frac{1}{10} & \frac{1}{20} \\ \frac{2}{3} & \frac{3}{4} & \frac{2}{5} & \frac{3}{5} & \frac{4}{5} \\ \frac{3}{8} & \frac{5}{8} & \frac{7}{8} & \frac{3}{10} & \frac{3}{20} \end{bmatrix}$$

$$B = \begin{bmatrix} 1 & 0.5 & 0.\overline{3} & 0.25 & 0.2 \\ 0.1\overline{6} & 0.125 & 0.\overline{1} & 0.1 & 0.05 \\ 0.\overline{6} & 0.75 & 0.4 & 0.6 & 0.8 \\ 0.375 & 0.625 & 0.875 & 0.3 & 0.15 \end{bmatrix}$$

We observe that corresponding entries in matrix A and matrix B have equal values. For example, $a_{1,4}$ of matrix A and $b_{1,4}$ of matrix B are equal; $\frac{1}{4} = 0.25$. Matrices whose corresponding entries are equal are called **equal matrices**.

FOR STUDENTS

Sample Lesson 6.3
Matrices: Organizing Data (page 2 of 2)

THINK AND DISCUSS

1. What is a matrix?

2. Why is a matrix used?

3. What are the dimensions of the matrix

$$\begin{bmatrix} 3 & 6 & 8 \\ 4 & 5 & 1 \end{bmatrix}?$$

4. Is matrix A equal to matrix B? Explain your answer.

$$A = \begin{bmatrix} 2 & 3 \\ 4 & 5 \end{bmatrix} \qquad B = \begin{bmatrix} 3 & 2 \\ 5 & 4 \end{bmatrix}$$

5. Construct a matrix with entries $e_{1,1} = 12$, $e_{2,1} = 15$, $e_{1,2} = 18$, and $e_{2,2} = 20$.

6. Refer to the table showing 1990 National League records.

    a. Which team had the best record?

    b. What was the total number of games won by the teams in the Western Division?

c. Which team scored the fewest runs?

d. Which team scored the most runs?

e. How is the table similar to a matrix?

7. Construct a 4-by-4 matrix in which $e_{a,b} = a + b$.

PROBLEMS AND APPLICATIONS

8. Consider the matrix $\begin{bmatrix} 5 & 2 & 1 \\ 2 & 15 & 10 \\ 4 & 21 & 22 \end{bmatrix}$.

    a. What are the dimensions of the matrix?

    b. What is entry $e_{3,2}$?

    c. What is the sum of the elements in column 2?

    d. What is the sum of the elements in row 3?

9. Consider the matrix $\begin{bmatrix} 3 & -4 & 8 \\ -9 & 5 & -4 \end{bmatrix}$.

    a. In what locations are the entries negative?

    b. In what locations are the entries even?

NATIONAL LEAGUE RECORDS IN 1990: FINAL STANDINGS

Eastern Division	W	L	Runs Avg.	Runs vs.
Pittsburgh	95	67	4.5	3.8
New York	91	71	4.8	3.8
Montreal	85	77	4.1	3.7
Philadelphia	77	85	4.0	4.5
Chicago	77	85	4.3	4.8
St. Louis	70	92	3.7	4.3

Western Division	W	L	Runs Avg.	Runs vs.
Cincinnati	91	71	4.3	3.7
Los Angeles	86	76	4.5	4.2
San Francisco	85	77	4.4	4.4
Houston	75	87	3.5	4.0
San Diego	75	87	4.2	4.2
Atlanta	65	97	4.2	5.1

Source: World Almanac and Book of Facts.

matrix. The student is first asked to find the matrix that multiplies a matrix to give a matrix of all zeros. Then the student is asked to find the identity matrix. Most students do correctly identify the matrix $\begin{bmatrix} 0 & 0 \\ 0 & 0 \end{bmatrix}$ in the first case but determine that the matrix $\begin{bmatrix} 1 & 1 \\ 1 & 1 \end{bmatrix}$ found through analogous thinking does not satisfy the condition of an identity matrix. The student must try a different tactic, and that process of discovering is the desired end. In contrast, Glaser (1966) focuses attention on the concept or generalization that is discovered. For our discussion this distinction between content and process is not significant because practicing teachers hope to encourage concept development in parallel with sound thinking processes.

Inquiry-discovery lessons can be either inductive or deductive, and sometimes are even discussed under the headings of inductive teaching and deductive teaching. The inductive method is an inference moving from specific examples to a generalization. Since an as yet unexamined case may disprove the generalization, the inductive conclusion must be qualified by some phrase such as "probably" or "it seems reasonable." The main point is for the student to connect common elements in a set of examples and make an abstraction based on that observation. The deductive method relies on presentation of certain principles from which students are to draw implications. Thus, the students make logical deductions from prior knowledge. This discussion is drawn from Cooney and Davis (1975) and includes a number of examples of strategies for using guided discovery in teaching secondary-level mathematics.

Cooney and Davis also suggest a number of important considerations when using discovery methods. Some of these are are follows:

- *Have the generalizations clearly in mind*. We would add that the teacher also should be open to student-generated methods that you may not have initially expected. Sometimes students can show new and interesting ways of thinking when allowed to discover.

- *Consider relevant factors before proceeding*. As pointed out earlier, certain material is more effectively understood by inquiry-discovery and other material by explicit instruction or problem-solving emphasis. In our experience, students frequently enjoy the freedom to explore in the inquiry-discovery mode, but this is true only if the discovery path is not too difficult or involved.

- *Plan the sequence of exploration activities or questions carefully*. We find it is not always easy to leave spaces narrow enough for the students to bridge with interest but not so wide that they get lost in building on concepts to find a generalization. Beginning teachers may be advised to begin with prepared materials. Sample Lesson 6.6: Spinning Flags and Sample Lesson 6.5: Manufacturing Toys, which follow, are examples of exemplary prepared materials designed to lead students to understanding through inquiry.

- *Reinforce the discovery by application*. When you request students to exercise further their generalization, it is more likely that they will transfer knowledge and retain concepts in addition to providing you with feedback as to the level of student understanding.

The lines drawn between explicit instruction, problem solving, and inquiry-discovery methods are not as important as the realization that an exemplary teacher can use the method appropriate to the mathematics and to the class. Students enjoy variety, and some students prefer and perhaps learn more effectively by one method than another. Just as manipulatives, calculators/computers, and innovative curriculum are part of an outstanding mathematics educator's tool kit, so are different methods of presentation. Any method requires planning as an integral part of instruction.

Sample Lessons 6.4 and 6.5 ably illustrate structured discovery lessons that lead students to understand multiplication of matrices in the first and transformations by matrices in the second.

 For information about Web sites with ideas for lesson study go to **http://www.prenhall.com/huetinck** and click on Web Destinations for Chapter 6.

F O R   T E A C H E R S

Sample Lesson Plan 6.4 Secret Codes and the Power of Algebra

Mathematical Content:
Matrices as a method to devise codes difficult to crack (PSSM Connections Standards for Grades 6–8 and 9–12)

Materials:
Text

Directions: The second chapter of *Mathematics: Modeling Our World, Course 1* deals with ways to make and break codes. Before this section, students have discovered that assigning letters to consecutive numbers results in a code that is easily broken because the frequency of letters in our language is known. In this section, they learn that the addition of a matrix functioning as a key makes codes much more difficult to break unless the key is known. Write a lesson plan including the questions you would ask to help students' understanding.

F O R   S T U D E N T S

Sample Lesson 6.4
Secret Codes and the Power of Algebra (page 1 of 3)

In this activity, you reconsider methods and representations you have already learned, to see if they can be adapted to produce a new coding method that foils the code cracker.

Recall that matrices are useful shortcuts for coding and decoding, particularly if you use a calculator with matrix features.

For example, suppose you use a shift +5 cipher to code the message "The package is in a locker at the airport." Since the message has 33 characters, you might store it in a 3 × 11 matrix.

Then you convert the letters to position numbers and add another matrix containing all 5s.

If the first matrix is entered as matrix [A] and the second as matrix [B] on a graphing calculator, the coded values are found quickly. All that's left is to take the message out of the answer matrix and either leave it as numbers or convert it to letters.

Of course, the problem with the coded message is that a code breaker can use knowledge of letter frequencies and linear patterns to crack your code.

1. Can you find a way to alter the process so that the code breaker will find no clues? Look very carefully at the matrices below. The shortcut not only offers a way to make coding easier, but it also offers a way to beat the code breaker if you modify the shortcut slightly. Discuss ways to do so.

2. When you have found a way to modify the shortcut, discuss whether your new method is easy to encode and easy to decode.

3. Also discuss whether your method is easy to communicate between coder and decoder.

4. Discuss the overall merits of your procedure. Is it a good coding method?

$$\begin{bmatrix} T & H & E & P & A & C & K & A & G & E & I \\ S & I & N & A & L & O & C & K & E & R & A \\ T & T & H & E & A & I & R & P & O & R & T \end{bmatrix}$$

A message stored in a matrix

$$\begin{bmatrix} 20 & 8 & 5 & 16 & 1 & 3 & 11 & 1 & 7 & 5 & 9 \\ 19 & 9 & 14 & 1 & 12 & 15 & 3 & 11 & 5 & 18 & 1 \\ 20 & 20 & 8 & 5 & 19 & 1 & 8 & 16 & 15 & 18 & 20 \end{bmatrix} + \begin{bmatrix} 5 & 5 & 5 & 5 & 5 & 5 & 5 & 5 & 5 & 5 & 5 \\ 5 & 5 & 5 & 5 & 5 & 5 & 5 & 5 & 5 & 5 & 5 \\ 5 & 5 & 5 & 5 & 5 & 5 & 5 & 5 & 5 & 5 & 5 \end{bmatrix}$$

Matrix coding with a shift +5 cipher

FOR STUDENTS

Sample Lesson 6.4
Secret Codes and the Power of Algebra (page 2 of 3)

Keys to Coding

Although a matrix is relatively easy for the coder and decoder to communicate between them, it is possible to make the communication even easier. It can be as simple as sending a single keyword, which is used to code with a **keyword matrix**.

For example, suppose a coder wants to send the message "Meet me at school" using the keyword *key*. Since *key* has three letters, store the message in a matrix of three columns.

Notice that since the number of letters in the message is not divisible by 3, a blank space is left at the end. You can also add meaningless characters like *X*s at the end.

Convert the letters of the message to position numbers and add to it a matrix containing the position numbers of the word *key* in each row.

1. The message is sent as 24 10 30 31 18 30 12 25 28 14 13 40 26 17.

   a. Explain why the message is hard to crack.

   b. Explain how the person receiving the message would use the word *key* to decode the message.

2. Use a 6 × 5 matrix with keyword *codes* to encode the message "The password is Captain Codeworthy."

3. Encode the word *package* using a 3 × 3 matrix with *bow* as the keyword. Use a two-step coding process that multiplies the coded values by 3, then subtracts the keyword. (You might get negative numbers in the resulting matrix.)

4. Decode each message. You are given the matrix dimensions, the keyword, and the coding process. [B] is the keyword matrix.

   a. 5 × 6, keyword *Monday*, [A] + [B]

   A T L X D K H Q A I F S V C U M T L B C R E Z

   b. 6 × 3, keyword *SAT*, 2[A] + [B]

   51 37 30 51 3 56 29 13 50 55 41 36 29 41 30 57 41

   c. 6 × 4, keyword *sing*, 5[A] − 2[B]

   27 87 67 31 −23 27 67 51 −33 82 12 11 27 −13 72 31 −23 −13 32

$$\begin{bmatrix} M & E & E \\ T & M & E \\ A & T & S \\ C & H & O \\ O & L & \end{bmatrix}$$

A message stored in a three-column matrix

$$\begin{bmatrix} 13 & 5 & 5 \\ 20 & 13 & 5 \\ 1 & 20 & 3 \\ 3 & 8 & 15 \\ 15 & 12 & \end{bmatrix} + \begin{bmatrix} 11 & 5 & 25 \\ 11 & 5 & 25 \\ 11 & 5 & 25 \\ 11 & 5 & 25 \\ 11 & 5 & 25 \end{bmatrix}$$

Matrix coding with the keyword key

FOR STUDENTS

Sample Lesson 6.4
Secret Codes and the Power of Algebra (page 3 of 3)

5. The plaintext message "Cryptograms are fun" was coded as S M Y P F T W M A M E F H Z F U Z. Find [B], the keyword matrix, for the coding process [A] + [B].

6. Using a 4 × 6 matrix, encode the message "No more magic tricks." Choose your own keyword. Keep it a secret. Challenge another student to figure out your keyword.

7. The message is "If you forget the password, you're sunk."

   a. Complete a tally sheet for the frequency distribution of letters in the plaintext message.

   b. Encode the message using a keyword matrix *study* and the process [A] + [B].

   c. Create another frequency distribution, this time with the coded message. Tally the number of times each letter appears in the coded message.

   d. Based on your observations of both frequency distributions, does a keyword matrix defeat the frequency pattern for the most common letters?

8. Conduct an experiment to confirm or refute your conclusions in Problem 7.

   a. Select a paragraph from a book or magazine you are reading. Instead of tallying every letter, do a frequency tally based on every fourth letter. Code the entire paragraph, using a keyword matrix that you choose. Do a frequency tally for the coded message based on every fourth letter.

   b. Repeat the experiment. Use the same paragraph, same keyword, and the same coded message. This time complete your tally based on every fourth letter, starting with the second letter in the paragraph instead of the first letter.

   c. Discuss the likely frequency distribution you would obtain by tallying every fifth letter from a paragraph encoded as in Problem 7.

   d. Write your discoveries from the frequency investigations. Conclude whether or not a keyword matrix is an effective way to thwart the frequency distribution of letters in the English language.

F O R   T E A C H E R S

Sample Lesson Plan 6.5 Manufacturing Toys

Mathematical Content: Multiplication of matrices (PSSM Connections Standard for Grades 9–12)

Materials Needed: Worksheets

Directions: In this activity students "discover" how to multiply matrices. The most difficult aspect of teaching matrices once students master the algorithm is to ascertain that they manipulate matrices in ways that make sense. This example is carefully constructed to show students that the operations they perform are reasonable and produce useful information.

F O R   S T U D E N T S

Sample Lesson 6.5
Manufacturing Toys (page 1 of 3)

The Cuddly Toy Company manufactures three types of stuffed animals: pandas, kangaroos, and rabbits. The production of each toy requires cutting materials, sewing, and finishing. This matrix shows the number of hours of each type of labor required for each type of toy.

	Panda	Kangaroo	Rabbit
Cutting	0.5	0.8	0.4
Sewing	0.8	1.0	0.5
Finishing	0.6	0.4	0.5

1. a. How many hours of cutting are required for a rabbit?

b. How many minutes of sewing are required for a panda?

c. What is the total number of hours of labor needed to produce two pandas?

The company has received orders for the months of October and November. This matrix shows the number of each type of toy to be produced each month.

	October	November
Panda	1,000	1,100
Kangaroo	600	850
Rabbit	800	725

2. a. How many kangaroos are to be produced in November?

b. What is the total number of rabbits to be produced in October and November?

c. How many toys must be produced in October?

3. The company needs to know how many hours of cutting labor will be needed in October.

a. How many hours are required to cut pandas in October?

b. How many hours are required to cut kangaroos in October?

c. How many hours are required to cut rabbits in October?

d. What is the total number of cutting hours needed in October?

4. Find the number of sewing hours needed in October for each type of toy and the total number of hours of sewing needed for the month.

a. Pandas

b. Kangaroos

c. Rabbits

d. Total

F O R   S T U D E N T S

Sample Lesson 6.5
Manufacturing Toys (page 2 of 3)

5. The process that you used to complete Problems 3 and 4 can be interpreted as a matrix operation. To find the number of finish hours, write the finish row of the first matrix next to the October column of the second.

$$[0.6 \ 0.4 \ 0.5] \begin{bmatrix} 1,000 \\ 600 \\ 800 \end{bmatrix}$$

Next, multiply the first number in the first matrix by the first number in the second, then multiply the second numbers, then the third numbers. Finally, add the products.

$$(0.6) \ (1000) + (0.4)(600) + (0.5)(800) = \underline{\hspace{1.5cm}}$$

6. Write the total number of cutting, sewing, and finishing hours found in Problems 3, 4, and 5 in this matrix.

$$\begin{matrix} & October \\ \begin{matrix} Cutting \\ Sewing \\ Finishing \end{matrix} & \begin{bmatrix} \underline{\hspace{1cm}} \\ \underline{\hspace{1cm}} \\ \underline{\hspace{1cm}} \end{bmatrix} \end{matrix}$$

7. We need to calculate the total hours for both October and November. The labor matrix and the order matrix are written below. Fill in the October totals from Problem 6, and calculate and fill in the November totals.

	Panda	Kangaroo	Rabbit
Cutting	0.5	0.8	0.4
Sewing	0.8	1.0	0.5
Finishing	0.6	0.4	0.5

	October	November
Panda	1,000	1,100
Kangaroo	600	850
Rabbit	800	725

$$\begin{matrix} & October \quad November \\ \begin{matrix} Cutting \\ Sewing \\ Finishing \end{matrix} & \begin{bmatrix} \underline{\hspace{1cm}} & \underline{\hspace{1cm}} \\ \underline{\hspace{1cm}} & \underline{\hspace{1cm}} \\ \underline{\hspace{1cm}} & \underline{\hspace{1cm}} \end{bmatrix} \end{matrix}$$

The process you have just completed is known as **_matrix multiplication_**.

8. To describe a matrix, it is customary to name the rows first and the columns second. The matrix containing the labor hours for each type of toy is called a labor-by-animal matrix. It would be incorrect to call it an animal-by-labor matrix.

   a. What is the correct way to describe the matrix containing the monthly order totals?

   b. What is the correct way to describe the matrix you obtained for Problem 7?

9. The company has three plants: one in the East, one in the Midwest, and one in the West. This matrix shows the hourly wage paid each type of worker at each plant.

	Cutting	Sewing	Fishing
East	7.50	9.00	8.40
Midwest	7.00	8.00	7.60
West	8.40	10.50	10.00

F O R   S T U D E N T S

Sample Lesson 6.5
Manufacturing Toys (page 3 of 3)

We wish to find the cost of producing each type of toy at each plant. Below are the plant-by-labor and the labor-by-animal matrices. Use the rows of the first and the columns of the second to complete the multiplication of the two matrices. Round your calculations to the nearest cent.

	Cutting	Sewing	Fishing			Panda	Kangaroo	Rabbit
East	7.50	9.00	8.40		Cutting	0.5	0.8	0.4
Midwest	7.00	8.00	7.60		Sewing	0.8	1.0	0.5
West	8.40	10.50	10.00		Finishing	0.6	0.4	0.5

	Panda	Kangaroo	Rabbit
East	_____	_____	_____
Midwest	_____	_____	_____
West	_____	_____	_____

Source: Froelich, G. W. (1991). *Connecting Mathematics, Addenda Series*, Reston; VA: National Council of Teachers of Mathematics. Reprinted with permission.

F O R   T E A C H E R S

Sample Lesson Plan 6.6 Spinning Flags

Mathematics Content: Transformation of a flag figure (PSSM Algebra Standard for Grades 9–12)

Materials: Text

Directions: The concept map for Unit 1 of Contemporary Mathematics in Context, Course 2 was displayed earlier in this chapter. Unit 2 of the same year expands use of matrices into geometric transformations. The following pages are about half of an investigation in the section called Transformations, Matrices and Computer Animation. Work through the problems as a student. What questions could you ask as the teacher to help students' understanding?

F O R   S T U D E N T S

Sample Lesson 6.6
Spinning Flags (page 1 of 2)

In the Flag Drill animation, the flag moves above and below a horizontal line. Think about how the flag could be transformed from a straight-up position to a straight-down position, as shown in the figure below.

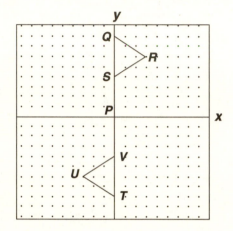

1. In your group, discuss at least two ways to transform the up-flag into the down-flag using one or more transformations.

   a. Did you, or could you, transform the up-flag into the down-flag by using a 180° rotation?

   - Which of the labeled points is the center of such a rotation?
   - Which point is the image of point *S*?
   - What is the pre-image of segment *UV*?

   b. What is the image of a point (x, y) under a 180° rotation about the origin? Assuming point *P* is located at the origin, verify your rule using points *P, Q, R,* and *S* as pre-images.

2. Using matrix multiplication and the general coordinate rule for a 180° rotation about the origin, you can find a matrix that represents the rotation. First, you will need to represent points as one-column matrices. So, (x, y) looks

   like $\begin{bmatrix} x \\ y \end{bmatrix}$, and its image under a 180° rotation,

   $(-x, -y)$, looks like $\begin{bmatrix} -x \\ -y \end{bmatrix}$.

a. Recall that matrices may be multiplied when the number of columns in the first matrix equals the number of rows in the second. Now, consider the following matrix multiplication. Determine the entries of the 2 × 2 matrix.

$$\begin{bmatrix} \rule{1cm}{0.4pt} & \rule{1cm}{0.4pt} \\ \rule{1cm}{0.4pt} & \rule{1cm}{0.4pt} \end{bmatrix} \begin{bmatrix} x \\ y \end{bmatrix} = \begin{bmatrix} -x \\ -y \end{bmatrix}$$

b. Compare your answer for Part a with that of other groups. Resolve any differences.

c. The matrix you agreed upon in Part b is a representation of a 180° rotation about the origin. When you multiply a point by the matrix, you get its image under the rotation. Check this by using the labeled points on the flag in Problem 1. Be sure to represent the points as one-column matrices and multiply with the point matrix on the right of the transformation matrix.

3. In a similar way, you can construct a matrix representation of a 90° counterclockwise rotation centered at the origin.

   a. Find the image of (2, 0) under a 90° counterclockwise rotation centered at the origin. Do the same for the points (2, 3) and (8, −5).

   b. What is the coordinate rule for a 90° counterclockwise rotation? Write your answer in the following form: $(x, y) \rightarrow (\rule{0.5cm}{0.4pt}, \rule{0.5cm}{0.4pt})$.

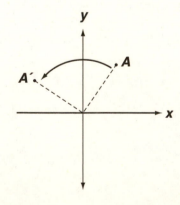

FOR STUDENTS

Sample Lesson 6.6
Spinning Flags (page 2 of 2)

c. Build a matrix representation for this 90° rotation by determining the entries of the 2 × 2 matrix below.

$$\begin{bmatrix} \underline{\quad} & \underline{\quad} \\ \underline{\quad} & \underline{\quad} \end{bmatrix} \begin{bmatrix} x \\ y \end{bmatrix} = \begin{bmatrix} -x \\ -y \end{bmatrix}$$

d. Now you have a matrix that models a 90° counterclockwise rotation about the origin. Multiply the matrix by the one-column matrices for the points (2, 3) and (8, −5). Check to see that you get the same answers as in Part a.

4. One advantage of a matrix representation of a transformation is that you can use it quickly to transform an entire polygon. Consider

$$\Delta ABC = \begin{bmatrix} 2 & 6 & 4 \\ 2 & 0 & -3 \end{bmatrix}$$

a. Sketch this triangle in a coordinate plane.

b. Multiply the matrix representation of ΔABC by the 90° transformation matrix. The result gives the image of ΔABC under a 90° counterclockwise rotation centered at the origin. When multiplying the two matrices, the matrix representation of ΔABC should be on the right of the rotation matrix.

c. Sketch the image triangle, $\Delta A'B'C'$.

d. When transforming a polygon using matrices, why should the matrix representation of the polygon be the factor on the right?

5. You have found matrices that represent 90° counterclockwise and 180° rotations about the origin. The matrix below represents another transformation.

$$A = \begin{bmatrix} 0.707 & -0.707 \\ 0.707 & 0.707 \end{bmatrix}$$

Source: Oxford, A. F. and Others (1997), Core-Plus *Contemporary Mathematics in Context:* Course 2, Part A, pp. 36–40, 102–109, 150–154: ISBN: 1–57039–483–0. Reprinted with permission by Glencoe/McGraw-Hill.

Summary

Planning is a significant underpinning of two of the six overarching themes of the *Principles and Standards for School Mathematics*. The first theme is a thorough understanding of the curriculum, including the standards germane to the course taught on the national, state, and local area. This must be backed by sensitive knowledge of where students are in their learning and how the teacher can build on that knowledge to achieve meaningful instruction. These themes are stated in PSSM as:

- *Curriculum.* A curriculum is more than a collection of activities; it must be coherent, focused on important mathematics, and well articulated across the grades.

- *Teaching.* Effective mathematics teaching requires understanding what students know and need to learn, then challenging and supporting them to learn it well.

The curriculum as we define it is much more than a set of materials; rather, it is what happens in the classroom. For students to develop mathematical power, the teacher must be well organized so that all the classroom time is spent on important mathematics. Coherence is necessary and is possible only if the teacher carefully considers the requirements of the course and uses a variety of teaching tools and methods to assist students along their way from naive thinkers to increasingly expert thinkers in mathematics. Foundational ideas must have a significant place in the curriculum, with a balance between the learning of skills and emphasis on problem solving.

The most brilliantly designed curriculum is of no value unless there is constant attention to the students' needs in learning mathematics. It is necessary to know the mathematics in depth, be able to use different pedagogical strategies, and be attuned to the students as learners. Exemplary teachers create a learning environment that is both challenging and supportive to learners at all ability levels. To do this, teachers are also lifelong learners through self-reflection and continuing improvement by interaction with colleagues on the site, at conferences, and during in-service opportunities.

ASSIGNMENTS

1. From one of the Additional Sample Lessons for this chapter, write a lesson plan for 1 day, including questions you will ask. Accompany your lesson plan with responses for this lesson that you might expect from the students.

2. Obtain a secondary-level text and write up a long-range plan for the first semester of the course. Assume your department chair has requested that you teach the important content of the first half of the chapters. Call a school district and get dates for school holidays and pupil-free days for a realistic calendar. Also ask about the time devoted to final exams. Be aware that high schools may devote 4 to 5 days to finals, while most middle schools do not set days aside for final examinations. Briefly indicate main topics for each day, including review days and exam days. Where appropriate to the material, indicate days on which manipulatives, computers, and calculators could be effectively employed.

3. Compare several different texts for the same course. If possible, contrast a traditional text with one of the reform-based programs highlighted in this chapter or in Chapter 4. What are advantages and disadvantages of the different approaches?

4. Interview a teacher who teaches on an alternative schedule. Ask how planning may be affected by organizations such as the following:

   - block scheduling;
   - team teaching across four disciplines or with mathematics and science.

INSTRUCTIONAL RESOURCES

Baroody, A. J., & Bartels, B. H. (2000). Using concept maps to link mathematical ideas. *Mathematics Teaching in the Middle School, 9(9)*, 604–609.

> The authors list 10 ways concept maps can assist meaningful learning. The thorough article also give teaching tips on getting started and illustrate some impressive concept maps, one of which was made by a student in Grades 4–5.

Barrett, G. B., & others. (1992). *Contemporary precalculus through applications*. North Carolina School of Science and Mathematics.

> Chapter 8, section 4, The Leontief Input-Output Model and the Inverse of a Matrix, shows the important use of matrices in the economics model of Wassily Leontief, who received the Nobel prize for this work. The concept of the inverse of a matrix is developed in this practical application.

Barrett, G. B., Bertkovich, K. G., Compton, H. L., Davis, S., Doyle, D., Goebel, J. A., Gould, L. D., Graves, J. L., Lutz, J. A., & Teapue, D. J. (1992). *Contemporary precalculus through applications: Function, data analysis and matrices*. North Carolina School of Science and Mathematics. Dedham, MA: Janson Publications.

> This text uses the Leontief Input-Output model as a vehicle for developing the necessity of inverse matrices. Wassily Leontief won the 1973 Nobel prize for economics for his use of matrices to analyze the American economy of 1958. He used 81 economic sectors grouped into 6 families. A simplified version of his model using 3 sectors enables the calculation of a demand matrix from the matrix multiplication of a technology matrix and a production matrix. This gives a method of finding the quantity of resources available for consumers given a certain level of production. Generally, society's demand can be estimated; however, analysts desire to calculate the quantity each sector of the economy should produce to meet society's expected demand. The argument leads to the method of finding an inverse, what matrices have inverses, and inverses that are difficult to calculate in a practical application that makes sense to students.

Froelich, G. W. (1991). *Connecting mathematics, addenda series*. Reston, VA: National Council of Teachers of Mathematics.

> Classroom-ready activities for making connections with functions, matrices, data analysis in reasoning and in problem solving are interspersed with thoughtful discussions of background information and teaching ideas.

Heid, M. K. (1995). *Algebra in a technological world, addenda series*. Reston, VA: National Council of Teachers of Mathematics.

> This book includes chapters on the future of algebra, changes in learning and their consequences, a functions approach, extending a functions approach, matrices, and symbolic reasoning from the viewpoint of reshaping instruction with technology.

Kramer, S. L. (1996). Block scheduling and high-school mathematics instruction. *Mathematics Teacher, 89(9)*, 758–768.

> This article from the column "Connecting Research to Teaching" is an excellent resource on block scheduling. A number of studies are reviewed, in addition to the responses to interviews conducted by the author.

Margenau, J., & Sentiowitz, M. (1977). *How to study mathematics*. Reston, VA: National Council of Teachers of Mathematics.

> This 33-page booklet is addressed to students, with hints on how to achieve success in mathematics. Many of the ideas are excellent for teachers to review to help their students develop good learning habits.

Productive use of time and space. *Educational Leadership, 53(3)*, 4–57.

> A large portion of this issue is devoted to nontraditional uses of time and space, including different types of block scheduling, connections to the world of work, year-round schools, multiyear teaching, and extended school hours.

Rubenstein, R. N., & others. (1992). *The university of chicago school mathematics project, functions, statistics and trigonometry*.

> Lesson 11-8, Matrices in Computer Graphics, is a novel and interesting lesson explaining and exploring how computer graphics software uses matrices to quickly transform pictures to simulate motion. The section is well written to interest students to explore this field further on their own.

Thompson, D. R., Senk, S. L., & Viktora, S. S. (1991). Matrices in the secondary school level. *Discrete Mathematics Across the Curriculum k–12*. Reston, VA: National Council of Teachers of Mathematics.

> This 1991 Yearbook contains a wealth of material for teaching discrete mathematics. Included are research references, an overview of the possibilities of including topics in discrete mathematics, and specific teaching ideas.

ADDITIONAL SAMPLE LESSONS

Sample Lesson 6.7   What Does *F(S) = KS* Do to the Area of the Unit Square *S?*
Algebra in a Technological World, Addenda Series (NCTM, 1995)

Sample Lesson 6.8   Matrices and Trigonometry *Discrete Mathematics Across the Curriculum, Yearbook* (NCTM, 1991)

Excellent resources for ideas and classroom-ready materials are the two NCTM books listed below. The examples were selected as rich and creative instructional methods of teaching matrices that may be infused into any secondary-level curriculum.

FOR TEACHERS

Sample Lesson Plan 6.7 What Does *F(S) = KS* Do to the Area of the Unit Square *S?*

Mathematical Content:
Geometric transformations with matrices (PSSM Geometry Standards for Grades 6–8 and 9–12)

Materials Needed:
Graph paper, graphing calculator

Directions: Students experiment with different matrices to transform the unit square. Students can do the operations with a calculator and then sketch their results on graph paper.

FOR TEACHERS

Sample Lesson Plan 6.8 Matrices and Trigonometry (see For Students, p. 237)

Mathematical Content: Trigonometry identities (PSSM Algebra Standard for Grades 9–12)

Materials Needed: Graphing calculator

Directions: By using the information provided, develop the equation for the identities of $\cos(\alpha+\beta)$ and $\sin(\alpha+\beta)$ in terms of the cos, cos, sin, and sin. This is novel approach seldom found in texts. Write a lesson plan, make up a set of classroom exercises, and develop a set of homework problems to change this yearbook information into an enrichment lesson.

F O R   S T U D E N T S

Sample Lesson 6.7
What Does $F(S) = KS$ Do to the Area of the Unit Square S? (page 1 of 2)

1. If $K = \begin{bmatrix} 1 & 2 \\ 3 & -2 \end{bmatrix}$, $KS = \begin{bmatrix} 1 & 2 \\ 3 & -2 \end{bmatrix} \begin{bmatrix} 0 & 1 & 1 & 0 \\ 0 & 0 & 1 & 1 \end{bmatrix} = \begin{bmatrix} 0 & 1 & 3 & 2 \\ 0 & 3 & 1 & -2 \end{bmatrix}$.

The effect of multiplying the unit square by K is shown in the diagrams below.

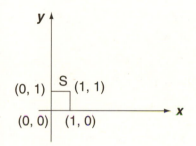

The unit square

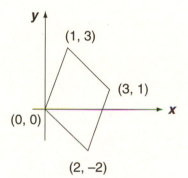

The unit square transformed by the function $F(S) = KS$

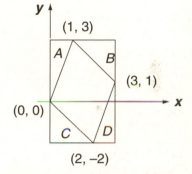

Area of S' = Area of rectangle − Areas of the four right triangles

Area of S' = Area of rectangle − Areas of the four right triangles

a. Find the area of the "enclosing" rectangle.

b. Find the area of each right triangle.

c. Find the area of quadrilateral S'.

d. How is the area of S' related to the value of the determinant of K? Test your conjecture on a few other transformation matrices.

e. Choose a different transformation matrix K, and find the area of the image of the unit square S under this transformation. How is the area of S' related to the value of the determinant of K?

FOR STUDENTS

Sample Lesson 6.7
What Does $F(S) = KS$ Do to the Area of the Unit Square S? (page 2 of 2)

2. What is the effect of any transformation matrix K on the area of R', where R is a rectangle different from the unit square?

3. What is the effect of any transformation matrix K on the area of P', where P is a nonrectangular parallelogram?

4. Make and test a conjecture about the effect on the area of the image of Q of $F(Q) = KQ$ when K is any 2×2 matrix and Q is any quadrilateral.

Source: Heid, M. K. (1995). *Algebra in a Technological World, Addenda Series*. Reston, VA: National Council of Teachers of Mathematics. Reprinted with permission.

F O R   S T U D E N T S

Sample Lesson 6.8
Matrices and Trigonometry

The use of matrices with transformations has a powerful payoff in trigonometry. In the previous section we discussed reflections about the *x*-axis, *y*-axis, or line $y = x$ and how composites of such reflections yield rotations of 90°, 180°, 270°, or 360° about the origin. A rotation about the origin by *any* magnitude can be represented by a 2 × 2 matrix.

A matrix for R_θ, a counterclockwise rotation of magnitude θ about (0, 0), can be determined by finding the image, under R_θ, of the points (1, 0) and (0, 1) on the unit circle. Recall that if the point $A = (1, 0)$ is rotated by magnitude θ about the origin, its image is the point $A' = (\cos\theta, \sin\theta)$. To find the image B' of $B = (0, 1)$ under R_θ, first observe that B is the image of A under a rotation of 90°. So B' will be the image of A' under a rotation of 90°. Applying a rotation of 90° to $A' = (\cos\theta, \sin\theta)$ yields $B' = (-\sin\theta, \cos\theta)$. Hence, the general rotation matrix for a counterclockwise rotation of magnitude θ about the origin is

$$R_\theta = \begin{bmatrix} \cos\theta & -\sin\theta \\ \sin\theta & \cos\theta \end{bmatrix}.$$

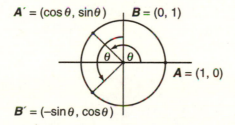

The matrix for R_θ can be very helpful in proving the identities for $\cos(\alpha + \beta)$ and $\sin(\alpha + \beta)$. A rotation of $\alpha + \beta$ can be considered as the composite of a rotation of β followed by a rotation of α. When a rotation of $\alpha + \beta$ is applied to the point (1, 0), the image is $(\cos(\alpha + \beta), \sin(\alpha + \beta))$. A rotation of first β and then α applied to the point (1, 0) gives

$$R_\alpha \circ R_\beta\,(1, 0) = R_\alpha(R_\beta(1, 0))$$
$$= R_\alpha(\cos\beta, \sin\beta).$$

So the matrix for the point $(\cos(\alpha + \beta), \sin(\alpha + \beta))$ is the product of the rotation matrix for α applied to the matrix for the point $(\cos\beta, \sin\beta)$. Answer:

Source: Thompson, D. R., Senk, S. L., and Viktora, S. S. (1991). Matrices in the secondary school level. *Discrete Mathematics Across the Curriculum k-12*, Reston, VA: National Council of Teachers of Mathematics. Reprinted with permission.

CHAPTER

7 Promoting Communication in the Classroom

In its *Principles and Standards for School Mathematics,* the National Council of Teachers of Mathematics (2000, p. 60) called communication "an essential part of mathematics and mathematics education" and selected communication as one of the main strands.

A rich conversation on mathematical concepts is essential to a *Standards*-based mathematics classroom. Using manipulatives, calculators, computers, and innovative curriculum all give the potential to enhance the discourse of the classroom. But according to the definitive literature on mathematics education, it is the classroom dialogue itself that speaks most of a teacher attaining best practice. Indeed, it is impossible to recognize a S*tandards*-based classroom without paying close attention to the oral and written interactions of the teacher and her students. Delivering exemplary instruction requires promoting communication in a community of mathematics learners.

The discourse must begin with attention to worthwhile tasks and will flower only in an atmosphere of trust and respect among all participants in the classroom. Both oral and written communication assist the learning process. The complex ways to integrate meaningful spoken or written dialogue in large-group, small-group, and individual settings require art in teaching; the lively dialogue in an interactive setting cannot be scripted.

According to the *Principles and Standards* (2000), four main attributes of communication teachers must enable their students to attain are:

1. "*Organize and consolidate their mathematics thinking through communication.*" When students grapple with methods of solving problems, they gain insights as they justify their thinking, question other students, and interact with thoughtful questions from their teacher. All too often, we expect students to convey solutions in organized mathematical symbols without placing equal importance on their ability to express in their own words what they are doing. As many of us have found, some students can mimic a mathematical process expressed in symbols without really understanding why the solution proceeds as it does. Through discussion, misconceptions can be identified and addressed. Reflection is intertwined with communication. When students can describe and defend their strategies, they refine, clarify, and consolidate their thinking.

2. "*Communicate their mathematical thinking coherently and clearly to peers, teachers and others.*" The essence of an accepted mathematical result is that it is recognized by the knowledgeable community of mathematicians. At all levels, students must develop their skills to listen, paraphrase, question, interpret, and offer their thinking to their own community of learners. This is possible only when the teacher has consciously tried to engender a cooperative learning atmosphere to support rich communication. An added benefit is that students are encouraged to take responsibility for their own learning.

3. "*Analyze and evaluate the mathematical thinking and strategies of others.*" Students must be able not only to clarify and express their own mathematical ideas, but also to evaluate, challenge, accept, and build on the thinking of others. This is the way our society advances its knowledge, and students must learn these processes. It is not easy to build on another's methods, which may be from a different perspective; however, this is precisely how experts advance their knowledge. Students need the opportunity to probe different approaches to problems to see the beauty and interconnections in mathematics. Through these efforts, students become critical thinkers.

4. "*Use the language of mathematics to express mathematical ideas precisely.*" We must not force premature use of mathematical language but help students develop connections between common words and their associated mathematical meaning until students mature in their understanding that terms generally have more precise meanings in mathematics than in everyday usage. Allow students to begin with their own language, and then refine it as you encourage them to communicate in formal mathematical language.

It is imperative to realize that communication can and should take multiple forms. Discussions, written full sentences, diagrams, drawings, spreadsheets, and graphs are all formats that can be effective and helpful. Classroom discussions, journaling, special projects, student-written problems, and quick-writes are just a few examples of techniques that encourage communication.

This chapter on communication concludes with specifics of discipline because effective classroom decorum proceeds directly from establishing a community of learners that is built on effective communication among all members of the classroom. The school culture, characteristics of the class, and personal attributes of the teacher all contribute to the climate of a classroom focusing on learning with a minimum of off-task behavior. The most valuable asset for the teacher in maintaining discipline is the presence of a productive community of learners.

ABOUT THE ACTIVITIES FOR THIS CHAPTER

The mathematical focus for this chapter is discrete mathematics. Discrete mathematics deals with separate rather than continuous mathematical entities. The existence of discrete mathematics as an identified topic of study began in the 1960s, and many reports of the 1980s and 1990s called for inclusion of the subject in all school mathematics programs. The digital electronic world of information, with its communication and increasing use of computers, emphasizes the need for discrete mathematics in the 21st century (Dossey, 1991). The NCTM 1991 Yearbook, *Discrete Mathematics Across the Curriculum K–12*, discusses the following reasons for including discrete mathematics in secondary schools:

1. Mathematics is alive.... Discrete mathematics is bursting with new developments and unsolved problems.

2. Problem solving and modeling are important .... Graphs and matrices in particular can be used to

model many interesting problems and can provide a new arena for teaching, learning, and appreciating mathematical modeling.

3. Discrete mathematics has many applications. . . . If we want to give a fair representation of mathematics and its applications, we should teach discrete mathematics along with the more traditional topics.

4. Discrete mathematics complements and enriches the traditional curriculum. . . . It simply broadens and enriches . . . and complements (Hart, 1991, pp. 74–75).

Activities in this chapter connect concepts related to matrices, the mathematical concept of the previous chapter, to digraphs, networks, conflict resolution, groups, and Markov chains. The use of calculators simplifies computations so students can explore the deep ideas in a variety of real-world problems. The selection from *Standards*-based curricula and exemplary references presents ways to teach these concepts that are only now becoming part of the regular secondary school curriculum. This mathematical context can be integrated into the curriculum and/or taught in a discrete mathematics course, which is becoming increasingly common as a mathematics elective.

The activities are loosely arranged in order of conceptual development from simpler to more complex uses of matrices and graphs. Activity 7.1 introduces graphs made up of vertices and edges and the generalizations that can be drawn about different configurations. Activities 7.2 and 7.3 move the student from matrices to graphs to directed graphs. Activities 7.4 and 7.5 introduce colors into graphs for conflict resolution. Activity 7.5 illustrates the use of matrix multiplication, which has two interesting applications in Activity 7.6. The final three activities in the chapter extend matrices to group theory, extended digraphs, and Markov chains. My favorites are Activity 7.7, "It's a SNAP" (suitable in any algebra class to introduce the basics of group theory without matrices) and Activity 7.8, "The Power of a Matrix" (illustrating fascinating applications of matrices and associated graphs. Markov chains provide fine material for the able student.

The mathematics for this chapter probably was not included in the traditional high-school courses you took. We purposely selected somewhat unfamiliar material to encourage you to look with fresh eyes at how best to develop the art of questioning with regard to topics not as common as algebra and geometry. Use the exercises to reflect on communication methods you can use as the instructor.

Note that the directions section in each Activity is not aimed at 6th- to 12th-graders as in past chapters. Rather, the directions address the preservice teacher or in-service teacher. These directions are designed to help you decide what questions you would ask to assist students learning in either whole-group, cooperative group, or individual instruction.

WORTHWHILE TASKS

The teacher is responsible for designing, shaping, and directing students' activities so the students grow intellectually in mathematics. In addition to using prepared materials, she may create or adapt tasks that capitalize on student questions and interests as an instructional sequence unfolds. Standard I of the *Professional Standards* states, "The teacher of mathematics should pose tasks that are based on

- sound and significant mathematics;
- knowledge of students' understanding, interest, and experience;
- knowledge of the range of ways that diverse students learn mathematics (NCTM, 1991, p. 25).

The document discusses three content considerations to identify worthwhile mathematics tasks whose richness leads naturally to mathematical discourse. First, activities should build on previous knowledge and lead to deepening conceptual understanding for future development. The task must be appropriate to the mathematical content. This principle seems obvious but is not always practiced. If the flow of the course requires a change of pace for a game, the content of the game must fit naturally into the curriculum. We do not condone playing games as a reward for good behavior, unless the activity enriches the students' progress in the course.

A second content consideration is that tasks should do more than provide an opportunity to find the right answer. It is far better to employ a mathematics activity that requires students to make decisions, speculations, or hypotheses than simply to assign problems emphasizing procedures to obtain *the* right answer. Worthwhile tasks may include problems with a range of correct answers, depending on students' reasonable assumptions. Thus, students not only do mathematics, they also gain an appreciation for "sense-making" answers.

The third content consideration discussed in the *Professional Standards* is that automaticity, or fluency, should be incorporated into a context of problem solving and reasoning. Teachers need to consider what areas of skill development and which memorized mathematics facts are necessary, as well as how to integrate such tasks into meaningful mathematics.

In summary, in judging the value of a task, mathematics teachers should be guided by the following statement:

> The tasks in which students engage must encourage them to reason about mathematical ideas, to make connections, and to formulate, grapple with, and solve problems. Students also need skills. Good tasks nest skill development in the context of problem solving. In practice, students' actual opportunities for learning depend on the kind of discourse that the teacher orchestrates (NCTM, 1991, p. 32).

Set 7.1   *Discussion Questions*

 Questions with an asterisk appear in the Message Board section of the Companion Website at *http://www.prenhall.com/huetinck.* Go to Chapter 7 and click on the Message Board to find and respond to the question.

*1. Give an example of a worthwhile instructional sequence from your experience as a mathematics student, and defend your choice.

2. Give an example of a learning activity that is not likely to be worthwhile, and explain why.

PROMOTING DISCOURSE

Discourse is essential to effective instruction. In asking a question, the teacher is, in effect, tossing the conversation to a student. Through discourse, the teacher provides information either directly or indirectly and continually assesses student progress. To teach effectively, she must listen to students, probe their thinking with thoughtful questions, ask questions to elicit responses to extend their knowledge, and adjust course activities as required to ensure students' progress in understanding. This is not easy! We have found that beginning teachers sometimes are afraid to toss the "conversational ball" because this puts the ball 'in the students' court' for a time. The inexperienced teacher then feels a loss of control. Ironically, the opposite is true. Students "turn off" to a lengthy period of teacher telling. They are likely to become disruptive when they are not involved and, at best, simply will not attend to the mathematical tasks at hand. Student engagement be-

gins with the belief that the mathematics under study is worthwhile and that nearly all students like to do activities within their abilities, even if occasionally the task may not interest them. A relationship of trust and caring between teacher and students ensures frequent passing of the "conversation ball" as guided by the teacher.

Establishing a Supportive Learning Environment for Discourse

An atmosphere of trust and mutual respect is essential for students to feel safe in entering into discourse. Be explicit in telling students that there is never a dumb question when anyone is seeking mathematical information. We all learn at different rates and sometimes do not hear information until we are ready to fit it into our schemas. Therefore, if a student asks a question that was answered only a few minutes before, she may simply have been unable to process the information when the answer was given previously. Thus, both the teacher and the class must honor requests to explain again or repeat the answer when necessary so that all class members can attain understanding. Many times the answer is more accessible if the wording of the answer, when given again, is altered. Of course, the teacher must model respect for student inquiries and requests for answers. Frequently remind students that it is better to be wrong than not to try and that no one may criticize efforts of another learner. Students must learn to question each others' assertions and offer different paths of thought while maintaining respect for all individuals.

Give students specific examples of poor questions. These are questions that distract from the mathematical discussion, such as, "On assembly day, when does this period end?" Other poor questions use *it* or *that one* instead of a descriptive term. Rather than second-guess a student's question about "it," ask the student to try to be more specific about what she wants to know. Of course, students' expressions of tentative hypotheses and alternative methods should be honored, even if the appropriate vocabulary is not yet in place.

If students are not accustomed to verbally participating in mathematics, some specific techniques can help in building their confidence when they are asked to respond before the whole class.

- Students pair-share before answering. It is less threatening for a student to present to the class after she has had the opportunity to verbalize ideas with a partner.
- Students use a small whiteboard or slate to display their answer to the teacher. This technique

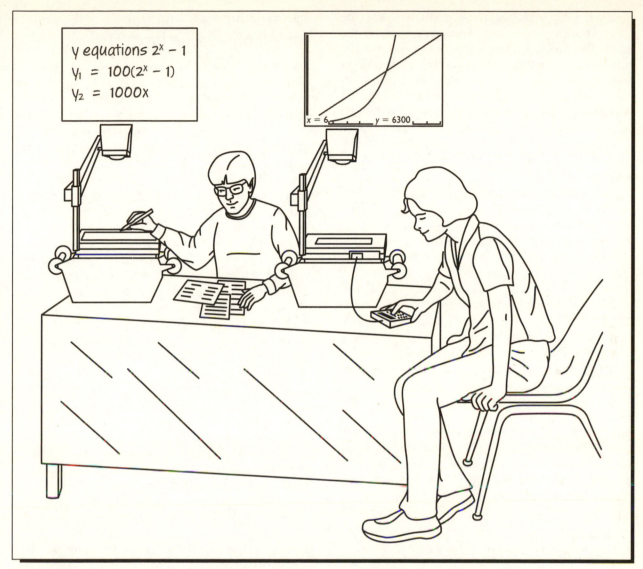

When two overhead projectors are set up in the classroom so that both images can be seen by all members of the class, the teacher can note the mathematics on one of them while a student uses a calculator attached to a projection device on the second projector.

is especially useful in middle school. The teacher can then call on students to explain what they have written.

■ When working with graphing calculators, let one student operate the calculator attached to the view screen so others can check their progress by matching their calculator screens to the projection image.

■ Groups of students write their conclusions on poster paper for display. The complete group stands at the front of the room to present, which alleviates the anxiety of being the single representative from the group asked to stand alone in front of the class.

■ Hand out overhead transparencies and pens for students to use in writing their solutions. The stu-

dents can present in pairs, with one writing out the solution and the other explaining it. Many students love to use the overhead projector after a little practice. If a solution is wrong, help the class make the correction, and express appreciation for the efforts of the presenter(s). Anyone can make a mistake, even the teacher!

Likewise, help students learn to work together in cooperative groups, small groups, or pairs. Cooperative groups were discussed in detail in Chapter 1. Peer tutoring is very effective if the tutors are instructed in how to ask questions to guide others to solutions instead of merely giving the peer the answer. The Pair Problem-Solving technique is a structured method. In this technique, two students work together. One is designated the listener, and the other is the problem solver. The problem solver explains aloud the steps taken to solve a problem. The listener actively participates by asking questions, requesting verification, and checking all conclusions. The problem solver is reinforced or debated at each step in the problem-solving process. The listener benefits from hearing the mental process and from testing for possible errors. This technique can be effective with students at all levels (Simmons, Perkins, & Colburn, 1986).

Give encouragement and light praise with statements such as "Good work" and "Alice has finished her classwork; has anyone else?" or show student work. Outstanding student papers displayed on bulletin boards provide the class with appropriate models of written work and praise the achieving students. Experience indicates that effusive praise for one individual is detrimental to the classroom climate. We think of this as the "birthday syndrome": If the birthday child is the only one to get presents, the party will easily get out of control as the other "guests" feel they also deserve attention. Thus, it is wise to give "party favors and prizes" to all, so everyone feels rewarded. Similarly, each of your students needs to hear appreciation of her efforts. Effusive praise of only a few students may send the detrimental message that the teacher is passing judgment on all ideas and is the sole source of mathematical authority. Research makes a strong case for limiting praise since it does not always empower students as thinkers and doers. The desirable message to send is that all students' thoughtful answers (even if incorrect) and problem-solving methods are valued (Schwartz 1996).

Set 7.2   *Discussion Questions*

Questions with an asterisk appear in the Message Board section of the Companion Website at *http://www.prenhall.com/huetinck.* Go to Chapter 7 and click on the Message Board to find and respond to the question.

*1. How will methods of establishing a supportive learning environment vary between students of different ability levels?

2. The establishment of a supportive learning environment is frequently influenced by the students' perception of the teacher. In your experience, how does this perception differ between middle-school and high-school students?

Questioning Techniques for Whole-Group Instruction

In whole-group instruction, the teacher generally aims questions at the ability level of the middle two thirds of the students. Some students will catch on more quickly than others; however, do *not* let these students answer all the questions. Even if they raise their hands repeatedly, ask them to let someone else respond. Keep track of who is replying by some simple method such as putting an X on a plastic overlay of the seating chart. All too often, teachers are misled into believing the class understands when, in fact, no more than four to five able students have answered all the questions. From time to time, ask a student to restate in her own words the solution of another student to double-check for comprehension.

There will also be some students who need considerably more instruction than the majority of the class. Plan time to assist these students either during or out of class. Make a list of students who have done poorly on the previous test. Check with these students, either individually during classwork time or during a tutoring session, to give them the additional help they require. Do this consistently during the unit—not only for several days before test time. If you wait too long, they may become overwhelmed.

Do not allow students to be lazy about participating. Good teachers don't *give* a good education to students; rather, they provide activities to motivate and encourage youngsters to become educated through success and failure. In the article "'Enabling' Undermines Responsibility in Students," author Landfried (1989) reminds us that enabling can have a negative connotation if the teacher coddles or rescues students instead of challenging them. The following passage illustrates the well-intended who teach the wrong lesson:

> The kids have Ms. Jones figured out. She can't stand silence and will answer virtually all of her own questions if they say nothing. Whenever students are actually asked to respond, a quick "I don't know" gets her off their backs. As a result, students say very little in class, their minds are elsewhere, and Ms. Jones essentially talks to herself most of the time (Landfried, 1989).

Wait Time   The best practice to adopt for questioning during whole-class instruction is threefold:

1. Ask the question.
2. Wait 3 to 5 seconds, counting silently, "One and two and three and four and five."
3. Call on a student by name to answer the question.

Waiting for 3 to 5 seconds can be a daunting situation to a beginning teacher. What can you do while you wait? An experienced colleague always has a bottle of water on her desk to drink from occasionally during a pause. With an expectant look on your face, you can maintain eye contact for a second with each of four or five students, or simply smile at a few students in turn as if you will call on one of them. It is imperative to call on a student *after* waiting the few seconds. Otherwise, if you call on a student and then ask her the question, the other students may cease to pay close attention because they know they will not be required to answer.

There are several different types of wait time. Studies of teachers indicate an average wait time of only 1 to 2 seconds after asking a question. Clearly, this is not sufficient time for in-depth consideration of any topic. If necessary, count to 5 slowly and silently to yourself to allow students time to think. Another type of wait time comes in the midst of a response. If the student halts after beginning to talk, wait again until the student regains her direction or requests assistance. If the student gets stuck, ask another student to help her out. Also, allow wait time for other students to join in the conversation. Wait time after a response gives other students the chance to challenge or complement the response. If there is no forthcoming additional dialogue from the class, then ask, "What do you think?" without indicating your opinion. This encourages students to look to each other for help instead of considering the teacher as the sole resource for mathematical information.

The art of questioning improves with experience. Richard Feynman, a Nobel prize winner and an excellent teacher, said the best teachers are those who can remember what it was like when they did not know the concepts. It is important to ponder how to break the ideas into manageable segments for a naive learner to grasp and connect to previously learned mathematics. Learning can be exciting, so do not spoil the fun by telling students exactly what to do and how

to do it. Sticking to a recipe limits creativity and dampens the exhilarating "Aha" that comes from figuring out a problem or making a connection. With practice, you will be able to match the question to the ability of the students to both lead and follow their thinking.

An important aspect in the art of questioning is to formulate questions that are neither too difficult nor too easy. If most of the class answers the question in less than 2 seconds, the question might be good for review but probably is not eliciting conceptualization along new avenues. If no student is ready after 5 seconds to volunteer a response or even talk when called upon, the gap is too great between the teacher's expectation and the students' level of knowledge. When this happens, first check that students *do* understand the problem as presented; perhaps the difficulty is something as simple as unfamiliar vocabulary. You can ask a student to state the question in her own words or to summarize the discussion as far as it has progressed. Continue the discussion with frequent stops to monitor understanding.

The TIMSS videos of instruction in the eighth grades in Japan and Germany illustrate whole-group interactions with students doing much of the instruction. In Japan, students are assigned a problem that can be worked four to five different ways. The teacher walks around the room while students work, noting the methods of different students. Then the students are asked to display and explain their various solutions. The teacher summarizes and gives further instruction and problems after the student presentations. The tapes of the German classroom are even more student directed, with the students leading and conducting debates on methods used.

Facilitating student participation in Activity 7.1 is heightened by periodic group discussion after each page of the activity. Since the material is likely new to students, this practice ensures that all are kept on track.

FOR TEACHERS

Activity 7.1 Graphs, Games, and Generalizations

Mathematical Content:
Edges and vertices of graphs and generalizations (PSSM Geometry Standard for Grades 6–8 and 9–12).

Materials:
Worksheets

Directions: Read the material and then work through the problems as a student. The first two pages are from *The Mathematics Teacher*, with an additional two teacher-written pages of extension. When teaching this lesson through whole-group discussion, what questions would you include in your lesson plan to facilitate student success in the assignment?

FOR STUDENTS

Activity 7.1
Graphs, Games, and Generalizations (page 1 of 4)

Figures of the sort below are called *graphs*. Each point indicated by a heavy dot is called a *vertex*, and each segment or arc connecting two vertices is called an *edge*. Each separated part of the plane formed by the graph is called a *region*. Note that graph (a) separates the plane into two regions, the region inside the graph and the region outside the graph.

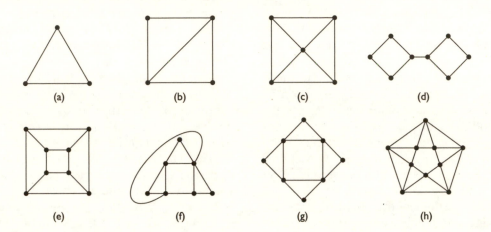

1. Complete the table below.

Graph	Edges (E)	Vertices (V)	Regions (R)	V + R
(a)	3	3	2	5
(b)				
(c)				
(d)				
(e)				
(f)				
(g)				
(h)				

2. Write down a formula relating the numbers *V, R,* and *E.*

3. Draw another graph of your own, and count *V, R,* and *E.* Does your formula also work for this graph?

4. How many regions would be formed by a graph with 5 vertices and 12 edges? Draw one such graph to verify your answer

FOR STUDENTS

Activity 7.1
Graphs, Games, and Generalizations (page 2 of 4)

A graph is said to be **traversable** if it can be traced in one sweep without lifting the pencil from the paper and without tracing the same edge more than once. Vertices may be passed through more than once.

5. Determine which of the graphs on the previous page are traversable. For those that are, mark the vertex where you start (S) and the vertex where you finish (F).

6. A vertex is said to be **even** if an even number of edges lead from it. A vertex is said to be **odd** if an odd number of edges lead from it. Complete the table below for the graphs on the previous page.

Graph	Number of Even Vertices	Number of Odd Vertices	Transversable?
(a)	3	0	Yes
(b)			
(c)			
(d)			
(e)			
(f)			
(g)			
(h)			

7. **a.** Can you traverse a graph if all the vertices are even?

   b. Can you traverse a graph if it has two odd vertices?

   c. Can you traverse a graph if it has more than two odd vertices?

   d. If a graph is traversable, does it matter at which vertex you start or at which vertex you finish?

F O R   S T U D E N T S

Activity 7.1
Graphs, Games, and Generalizations (page 3 of 4)

Extension: The mathematician Euler proposed the famous bridge problem in 1735. The city of Kalinigrad is located on the banks and on two islands of the Pregel River. The various parts of the city are connected by bridges, as shown in the figure below. Euler asked, "Is it possible to make a walking tour of the city that crosses each of the bridges exactly once?"

8. Answer this question by using the theorem you demonstrated on the previous page. This theorem can be stated, "It is possible to traverse a graph only if it has either 0 odd vertices or 2 odd vertices."

   a. Make a graph using the points marked *A, B, C,* and *D* as vertices that are connected by lines that go over the bridges. The lines connecting the vertices do not need to be straight lines as those of previous graphs.

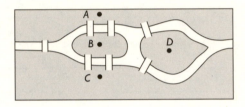

   b. What is your answer to Euler's question? (Show why.)

9. This is a similar problem where four different rooms are connected by doors.

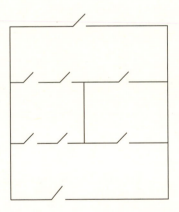

   a. Make a graph for this situation.

   b. Could a person go through every door only once? Show why.

FOR STUDENTS

Activity 7.1
Graphs, Games, and Generalizations (page 4 of 4)

10. Now that you know how to determine whether or not a graph is traversable, let's see if it is possible to determine whether or not you will come back to the same or different vertex after traversing a graph.

   a. Do you think you will come back to the same vertex where you started if the graph has 0 odd vertices? Give reasons for your answer.

   b. State your conclusion as a theorem.

   c. Will you come back to the same vertex after traversing a graph if there are 2 odd vertices? Give reasons for your answer.

   d. State your conclusion as a theorem.

   e. Explain why the theorem on the last page must be true in general.

11. Here is another city bridge problem. Is it possible to make a walking tour of this city and come back to the same place you started? Why?

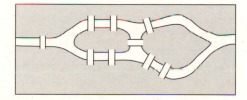

12. Make a room-and-door problem similar to this bridge problem.

Source: *Mathematics Teacher,* National Council of Teachers of Mathematics, Reston, VA, December 1988. Reprinted with permission.

Four Basic Principles   When questioning a whole class, it's helpful to keep in mind four basic principles. First, do not ask a question unless you want a thoughtful student response; to do otherwise is dishonest. Even though this may seem like a simple principle, many teachers do answer their own questions or ask "empty questions." We define an empty question as one that is extremely unlikely to be answered, such as "Right?" or "OK?" Only a very brave student will say, "No, it is not right," or, "No, it is not OK." If you answer your own questions, the students will learn to wait until you tell them the correct response and make no effort to figure it out for themselves. Students must expect to answer questions the teacher asks.

A second principle to keep in mind when questioning a whole class concerns embarrassing a student who will not know the answer. Some beginning teachers, in particular, are uneasy about this. Knowing your students will help to alleviate such worries. Try to match the question difficulty to the student's ability level in a subtle way; however, don't always ask the simplest question of the student least likely to know the answer. Even if that student is trying to learn, it may become obvious to the class and the student that you consider her to have low ability. In contrast, do not always call on the brightest student to answer all the most difficult questions; other students may excel more during discussion than they do on exams. Every few days, call on every student at least one time.

A third principle of whole-class questioning pertains to the student who says, "I don't know," repeatedly. Do not simply stop calling on her. Instead, go on to ask another student to assist and remark that you will come back later to the first student with another question. Then be sure to follow through. If the first student cannot answer a later question, repeat the question she missed first to get some mathematical response. Do this as many as three or four times during the period, always treating the reluctant student with respect. Consult with the student after class if this problem persists. Express that you care about her mathematical understanding, and continue to try to draw the student in to participate verbally.

The final principle of whole-class questioning is to develop thoughtful questions for your lesson plans. Conducting the class will be easier if you have planned ahead, instead of trying to make up clear and concise questions while teaching.

Do's and Don'ts   The book *Every Minute Counts, Making Your Math Class Work* is one of three small paperbacks written by David R. Johnson that incor-

porate many commonsense teaching ideas. Even experienced teachers read and reread these practical texts to remind themselves of ways to improve instruction. The following list of "try-to" questioning techniques is adapted in part from Johnson's text and in part from our experience:

- Try to follow up student responses with the question "Why?" This emphasizes the importance of knowing the procedure instead of being satisfied with only the answer. Also, it will help students who cannot answer the question to reason through the problem.

- Try to limit the number of questions that rely only on memory. A short answer to a simple question may elicit the correct vocabulary word or numerical answer, but does not indicate that the student can apply the concept or has mastery of the idea.

- Try to avoid repeating the student's answer, especially if you slightly reword it with upgraded vocabulary. To a certain extent, this devalues the student's ideas, because your rewording subtly indicates that the response should have been stated somewhat differently. If the student could not be heard by all the class, simply ask the student to repeat the response in a louder voice. This signals your appreciation of "student talk" as a valuable contribution to the class. An exception is when assisting a student who is struggling to verbalize an idea. You might say, "I think this is what you are saying . . . ," to help the student.

- Try to make it easy for students to ask a question at any time. When you are explaining a difficult concept, an interruption can be disconcerting, but if students are puzzled midway through an explanation, they will not progress with you through the discussion.

- Try to avoid asking questions that include the answer. This insults the students' intelligence and reinforces the view of the teacher as the sole provider of information, detracting from your efforts to maintain a community of mathematics learners.

- Try to avoid asking for oral group responses. The accuracy from this approach is questionable at best. The feedback is no more valuable than always calling on the same able students who volunteer.

- Try to leave an occasional question unanswered at the end of the period to extend learning beyond the classroom. Do carry through later to answer the question, or students will soon decide you do not really care whether they try to formulate an answer in these circumstances.

- Try to ask open-ended questions and avoid those that can be answered by yes or no.

Thoughtful open-ended questions can be a treasure trove for mathematical discussion, keeping students involved in learning. These questions are not easy to develop, however, so include some in your lesson plans, and keep good ones for use in later years (Johnson, 1982, pp. 9–13).

The following "try-not-to" suggestions from David Johnson are useful (though we found some of them to be "try-to" questions under certain circumstances).

- Try not to label the degree of difficulty of a question. Certainly, it is disconcerting for a student to be told a question is easy if she then is unable to answer it. However, if the question is difficult; it may be wise to tell the class. Tell them to think before responding, and allow a longer wait time to get a thoughtful reply.

- Try to avoid directing a question to a student for disciplinary reasons. In some cases this practice may be a gentle way to get a student on task. However, do not use the occasion to embarrass the student when she cannot answer. Sometimes you will be astonished to find a student who can quickly answer the question correctly and was on task when she did not appear to be.

- Try to avoid giveaway facial expressions to students' responses. As recommended by David Johnson, do not look disappointed when a wrong response is given and elated when a right one is offered. Sometimes a bit of acting is effective, however. Imagine that a teacher is reviewing with her class on the day before a test, and three or four students cannot answer a question on central concepts. The teacher may then rest her head on her desk for drama and say, "Now we really *have* to get to work to master these ideas—they are on tomorrow's test!" The drama will get attention but cannot be used too often.

- Seldom ask, "Do you want me to go over that again?" Johnson considers this question unlikely to get a response. However, we have asked this question occasionally and heard most of the class say yes. Students may need to go over difficult material again. But before starting from the top, ask a few questions to determine exactly where most of the students got lost. It is necessary to provide considerable wait time after this question to get an honest answer. If only a few students want to hear the concept explained again, do so for the small group while the rest of the class continues with classwork or homework.

- Seldom ask, "Do you have any questions?" In contrast to Johnson, we have used this question successfully with ample wait time. Students do re-

spond to this question, especially in higher-level mathematics courses of an abstract nature. We notice that beginning teachers use this question too often, however. When there is no response, the teachers assume everyone understands the material. Actually, a silent response can mean mastery or a complete lack of understanding. We have had a student respond, "I don't even know enough to ask a question." Dialogue between the students and teacher to find the specific difficulty must then follow, of course. Try to alter your approach and express the concepts from a different angle, checking frequently for understanding when revisiting the material.

Finally, teachers must listen carefully during a class discussion. Sometimes this requires patience in following a student's thinking, even when the students' thoughts do not appear to be headed toward conceptual development. We can be surprised by the direction a student takes. Learning from students adds immeasurably to the excitement of teaching. The following excerpt is a favorite of ours. It is published in a book of articles written by teachers and for teachers. The article, "Teaching Students to Think in Mathematics and to Make Conjectures," begins with an example that illustrates a teacher "interested in providing the setting wherein the students, through their own logical analysis and exploration, could arrive at the desired mathematical truths" (Borenson, 1986, p. 65).

Vignette 7.1   Teaching Students to Think in Mathematics and to Make Conjectures

The techniques suggested also will encourage novel insights and student creativity. Take the following incident, for instance. In an eighth-grade mathematics class, the teacher showed the class a parallelogram like the one shown here. The teacher asked the students if they thought any of the angles of a parallelogram are congruent. Renee raised her hand and said that angles *A* and *C* were congruent. "Tell us why you think so." "Those are alternate interior angles of parallel lines," the girl responded. At this point the teacher was in a state of disbelief. How could a student who had paid even the slightest attention to the class work come up with such a preposterous statement? The teacher began to wonder. The class had already done some work with alternate interior angles, such as the angles 1 and 2 in the second figure.

How could Renee make the kind of statement she did? The teacher, following the policy of encouraging students to defend their position, whatever it is, asked Renee to come up to the blackboard to show the class what she meant. . . . "I don't have to come up," Renee said. "Simply fold the parallelogram over so that *CD* lies on *AB*." The teacher hesitated for a second, trying to comprehend what it was that Renee was saying. At this point some astonishment began to show on the teacher's face with the realization that there was something to what Renee was saying. The students in the class started to smile gleefully at the teacher's astonishment and in the realization that Renee, a fellow student, had evidently hit upon something creative.

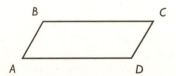

Sample parallelogram

Alternate interior angles

The teacher then drew a large parallelogram on a piece of paper in front of the class, cut it out, and rolled it over so *CD* coincided with *AB*. Then, lo and behold! angles *A* and *C* were alternate interior angels of parallel lines.

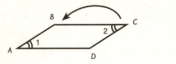

Rolling a parallelogram

This demonstration proved to the students and to the teacher that Renee was right! Her analysis was correct and logical, though at first it appeared as if she were way off base. Her novel argument demonstrated insight and skill at visualization—all of which would never have come to light if the teacher had not encouraged a student to defend the position she had taken, and if the teacher had not then attempted to understand that position.

Such moments do not occur every day. But they occur often enough in a teacher's career to be memorable, to add to the joy of teaching, and to add to the self-esteem of the students involved.

The interactions elicited during class discussions depend on the class's personality and the teacher's style. Some of these suggestions will work in some classrooms, and others will not. Some suggestions will be more effective for some classes than for others. The goal is to find modes of questioning that involve students in learning. Find what works, and measure success in students' movement toward becoming mathematically powerful.

Set 7.3 Discussion Questions

Questions with an asterisk appear in the Message Board section of the Companion Website at *http://www.prenhall.com/huetinck.* Go to Chapter 7 and click on the Message Board to find and respond to the question.

*1. The preceding discussion compares and contrasts our experiences in questioning techniques with those of David Johnson. Considering your experience as a student, observer, and teacher in training, compare and contrast your experience in questioning techniques with ours. Do you agree with our ideas? Why or why not?

2. Discuss how questioning techniques may vary depending on students' mathematical ability, maturity level, and learning preferences.

Questioning Techniques for Small or Cooperative Groups

Questioning techniques for students in small or cooperative groups vary somewhat from the methods used for whole-group instruction. Some questions will apply in both cases, but the setting is different. The teacher's main role in assisting small groups is to encourage the group to work collaboratively. Questioning should always reflect that perspective. Remind students to ask for help only when every person in the group agrees on the need for teacher assistance.

The teacher circulates throughout the room answering and asking questions, spending only a few minutes at a time with each group. In this dynamic setting the teacher cannot get caught too long with any one group, because other puzzled groups will put learning on hold until the teacher can help. The teacher must become adept at looking over the entire room while interacting with one group so that all students stay on task. The teacher is not only responsible for answering questions but also must ask questions of successive groups to ascertain whether each group is moving forward on the assignment.

Small-group interaction demands teacher flexibility. In contrast to whole-group instruction, each independent group of students may be working on a different problem when teacher and students begin to interact. After hearing a group's question, the teacher must first determine where the group is in the learning process. The next task is to be certain that all members of the group are at the same place in their understanding. Then the teacher asks questions to help students answer their question and checks that all the group members comprehend the answer. If the students are not able to answer their own question, the teacher can pose a related but simpler question and tell the group to think about it for a while before asking for help from her again. If there are different ways of working the problem, as there should be in group work, the teacher must be familiar with the differing potentially fruitful trains of thought to assist students to move along the path they have chosen. If the selected path will not lead to the desired learning, the teacher should ask questions or give counterexamples to lead the students to change their perspective.

The teacher should enlist interaction between groups. Best practice, especially for middle-school students, is to bring the class together from time to time to share progress. This may assist students who are not having success as readily as others. The teacher may also ask a student from a different group to provide some hints to a nearby group. The students must be instructed to ask leading questions when assisting instead of simply giving the answer, however. We have used the technique of asking a member of a less successful group to ask a question of a member of a group further along in conceptual development of the mathematics under study. The requesting group member should come to the teacher for further help only if the explanation sought from the student is not satisfactory. The explainer, in turn, may find that her group is not as certain as she first believed, when required to explain to a classmate. As teachers know, a topic is best learned when taught. In our experience, sometimes both groups come to the teacher for clarification, and therefore both advance their thinking.

Examples of Questions An excellent list of options for questions to evaluate and assist the progress of students is found in *Assessment Alternatives in Mathematics*, published by the California Mathematics Council and EQUALS (1989). This starter list is divided into different categories. A sampling of the published questions follows.

- *Problem comprehension.* What is this problem about? Would you please explain that in your own words? What assumptions do you have to make? Is there something that can be eliminated or is missing?
- *Approaches and strategies.* What have you tried? What did not work? How did you organize the information? Would it help to draw a diagram or make a sketch? How would you research that?
- *Relationships.* Is there a pattern? Let's see if we can break it down. What would the parts be? Can you write another problem related to this one?
- *Flexibility.* Have you tried making a guess? What else have you tried? Is there another way to (draw, explain, say . . .) that?
- *Communications.* Would you please reword that in simpler terms? How would you explain this process to a younger child? Which words were most important? Why?
- *Curiosity and hypothesis.* Can you predict what will happen? What do you think comes next? What else would you like to know?
- *Equality and equity.* Did you work together? In what way? How could you help another student without telling the answer?
- *Solutions.* Is that the only possible answer? Is the solution reasonable, considering the context? How did you know you were done?
- *Examining results.* What made you think this is what you should do? Is there a general rule? What questions does this raise for you? How would your method work with other problems?
- *Mathematical reasoning.* What were the mathematical ideas in this problem? What was one thing you learned (or 2 or more)? What are the variables in this problem? What stays constant?
- *Self-assessment.* What do you need to do next? What have you accomplished? Was your group participation appropriate and helpful?

Activity 7.2 is a set of classwork problems appropriate for group work. Consider how to use effective questioning techniques in this setting.

Questioning Techniques for Individual Assistance

Questioning techniques in a one-on-one situation differ in some fundamental ways from interacting with the whole class or with a small group. Only a few students, it is hoped, need to come in for help or receive assistance when most of the class is engaged in classwork. Thus, there is not the pressure to aim for the average ability of the class or the time constraint of spending only a minute or two with the student. If many students in a class need considerable individual assistance, change the curriculum or configuration of students to allow the students to succeed. The situation is untenable to both the students and the teacher if most of the students cannot accomplish the expected goals. In this discussion we will assume that only 10 to 15 percent of the students require individual help. We shall further assume a school organization wherein the teacher and students have at least some time to provide individual assistance during class, during a conference period, before or after school, or periodically during lunchtime (perhaps a duty shared by other teachers in the department).

With its many examples of effective questioning techniques, *How to Solve It* by George Polya (1988) belongs in every mathematics teacher's professional library. We shall use his methods to illuminate ways to help students individually, even though Polya's methods are effective in all situations of solving problems. Polya describes the task of the teacher:

> If the teacher helps too much, nothing is left to the student. The teacher should help, but not too much and not too little, so that the student shall have a *reasonable share of the work*. If the student is not able to do much, the teacher should leave him at least some illusion of independent work. In order to do so, the teacher should help the student discreetly, *unobtrusively*. The best is, however, to help the student naturally. The teacher should put himself in the student's place, he should see the student's case, he should try to understand what is going on in the student's mind and ask a question or indicate a step that *could have occurred to the student himself* (Polya, 1988, p. 1).

The ability to see the problem through the student's eyes is central to effective questioning techniques. In Vignette 7.1, presented earlier in this chapter, the teacher was able to view the problem through Renee's eyes. However, this is more difficult to facilitate in whole-group instruction than in the individualized setting. A useful metaphor for us is viewing a scene through a piece of colored glass. Each person sees the same scene through filters of a different hue. The empathetic teacher asks questions to see what the student sees through her colored window, which will not be identical to the view of the teacher. Students needing tutoring may have deficiencies in content background, novel ways of attaining knowledge, and/or diverse other special problems in addition to the immediate problem of learning the material under inspection. It is easier to respond to the needs of one student than many, but a one-on-one setting still provides challenges to the teacher.

Polya develops four main divisions and the corresponding four main types of questions: (1) understanding the problem, (2) devising a plan, (3) carrying out the plan, and (4) looking back. The following questions are examples of what to ask at each stage of problem solving:

- *Understanding the problem.* What is the unknown? What are the data? What is the condition?
- *Devising a plan.* Do you know a related problem? Here is a problem related to yours and solved before. Could you use it?
- *Carrying out the plan.* Can you see clearly that the step is correct? Can you prove that it is correct?
- *Looking back.* Can you check the result? Can you check the argument? Can you use the result, or the method, for some other problem? (Polya, 1988, pp. xvi–xvii).

There will be times when your efforts to assist students will fall short of your expectations. Remember, however, that learning proceeds at individualized rates. Meaningful interactions in mathematics cannot be hurried. Vignette 7.2 is an illustration.

FOR TEACHERS

Activity 7.2 From Graphs to Matrices

Mathematical Content:
Graphs, matrices, and digraphs (PSSM Geometry Standard for Grades 6–8 and 9–12)

Materials:
Worksheets

Directions: Work through this set, and make a list of questions you would expect students to ask if they worked in cooperative groups. What questions could you ask the groups to ensure that all students are contributing and processing the salient information?

F O R   S T U D E N T S

Activity 7.2
From Graphs to Matrices (page 1 of 4)

A sketched map (graph) of Mount Monadnock is given below. The heavy dots (vertices) represent rest stops, and the lines (edges) represent trails.

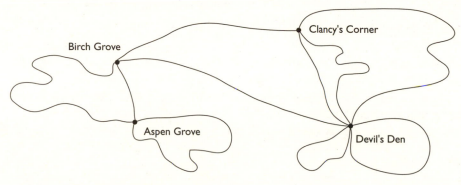

1. We can represent some characteristics of this map by using a table. In the table below, we write the number of trails from each rest stop to each other rest stop that do not pass through another stop. Note that two routes are possible from Aspen Grove to Aspen Grove (clockwise and counterclockwise). Complete the table below.

		TO			
		Aspen Grove	Birch Grove	Clancy's Corner	Devil's Den
FROM	Aspen Grove	2	2	0	0
	Birch Grove				
	Clancy's Corner				
	Devil's Den				

2. We can make writing the table easier by abbreviating the names of the rest stops. Or, if we agree that the rows (horizontal) and columns (vertical) represent the rest stops in alphabetical order, we can omit the names entirely and just write the numbers set off in brackets. Rewrite the table above, omitting the names.

$$\begin{bmatrix} 2 & 2 & 0 & 0 \\ - & - & - & - \\ - & - & - & - \\ - & - & - & - \end{bmatrix}$$

This ordered arrangement of numbers is called a *matrix*. Each number in the matrix is called an *element* of the matrix.

F O R   S T U D E N T S

Activity 7.2
From Graphs to Matrices (page 2 of 4)

3. Look at your matrix in Problem 2.

   a. Sum the elements in the third row. What does this number represent on the map? Sum the elements in the third column. What does this number represent on the map?

   b. Find the sum of all elements in each row. Find the total of these sums. How is this total related to the number of edges in the graph? Why?

   c. What type of integers appear along the major axis? (The major axis is the diagonal from the top left to the bottom right.) Why?

   d. Does the major axis form a line of symmetry for the matrix? What characteristic of the map is revealed by this symmetry?

4. Write the matrices corresponding to the graphs below.

   a.

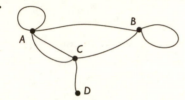

   b.

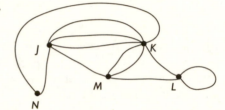

$$
\begin{array}{c}
\\
\text{From}
\end{array}
\begin{array}{c}
\\
A \\ B \\ C \\ D
\end{array}
\overset{\displaystyle \overset{\text{To}}{\begin{array}{cccc} A & B & C & D \end{array}}}{\left[\begin{array}{cccc}
\_ & \_ & \_ & \_ \\
\_ & \_ & \_ & \_ \\
\_ & \_ & \_ & \_ \\
\_ & \_ & \_ & \_
\end{array}\right]}
\qquad\qquad
\begin{array}{c}
\\
\text{From}
\end{array}
\begin{array}{c}
\\
J \\ K \\ L \\ M \\ N
\end{array}
\overset{\displaystyle \overset{\text{To}}{\begin{array}{ccccc} J & K & L & M & N \end{array}}}{\left[\begin{array}{ccccc}
\_ & \_ & \_ & \_ & \_ \\
\_ & \_ & \_ & \_ & \_ \\
\_ & \_ & \_ & \_ & \_ \\
\_ & \_ & \_ & \_ & \_ \\
\_ & \_ & \_ & \_ & \_
\end{array}\right]}
$$

   Do the properties you found in parts (b), (c), and (d) of Problem 3 hold true for these matrices?

5. Draw graphs corresponding to the matrices below.

   a.
$$
\begin{bmatrix}
0 & 1 & 0 & 1 \\
1 & 0 & 0 & 1 \\
0 & 0 & 0 & 1 \\
1 & 1 & 1 & 0
\end{bmatrix}
$$

   b.
$$
\begin{bmatrix}
2 & 1 & 3 & 1 & 1 \\
1 & 0 & 1 & 0 & 0 \\
3 & 1 & 0 & 1 & 0 \\
1 & 0 & 1 & 0 & 1 \\
1 & 0 & 0 & 1 & 0
\end{bmatrix}
$$

A •   •B

D •   •C

F •

E •   •G

I •   •H

F O R S T U D E N T S

Activity 7.2
From Graphs to Matrices (page 3 of 4)

6. To reduce traffic and slow soil erosion on Mount Monadnock, park rangers have decided to designate some ecologically sensitive trails as one-way trails, as shown below. For example, now just one way to travel from Aspen Grove to Aspen Grove is permissible—clockwise. Trails without direction arrows are two-way trails. Complete the matrix representation for the reconfigured Mount Monadnock trails.

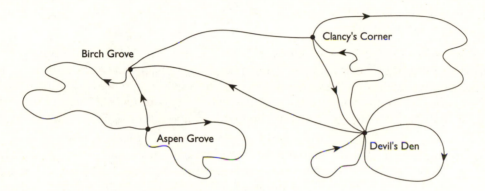

7. The graph in the last exercise is called a *directed graph* because some lines (edges) representing the trails can be traveled in only one direction. Look at the matrix in the last exercise.

a. Sum the elements in the third row. What does this number represent on the map? Sum the elements in the third column. What does this number represent on the map?

b. Find the sum of all elements in each row. Find the total of these sums. How is this total related to the number of edges in the graph? Why?

c. What type of integers appear along the major axis? Why?

d. Does the major axis form a line of symmetry for the matrix?

8. Write the matrices corresponding to the graphs below.

a.

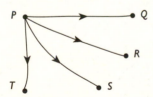

b.

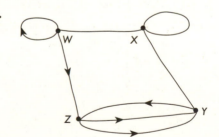

Activity 7.2
From Graphs to Matrices (page 4 of 4)

9. Draw directed graphs corresponding to the matrices below.

a.
$$\begin{bmatrix} 1 & 0 & 2 & 0 \\ 1 & 0 & 2 & 1 \\ 0 & 1 & 0 & 0 \\ 0 & 1 & 0 & 0 \end{bmatrix}$$

b.
$$\begin{bmatrix} 0 & 2 & 1 & 0 & 0 \\ 0 & 1 & 0 & 0 & 1 \\ 2 & 1 & 1 & 0 & 1 \\ 0 & 0 & 1 & 0 & 1 \\ 1 & 0 & 1 & 0 & 2 \end{bmatrix}$$

10. Sports teams often hold "kangaroo courts" in which players fine themselves and each other token amounts of money for mental mistakes. The Fighting Spartans girls basketball team held a kangaroo court after its first game. Alysha fined herself $2 for not going to the basket after she shot, and she fined Dawn $1 for missing a pick. Barb fined Alysha $1 and Cathy $3. Cathy fined herself $1, Alysha $1, Barb $2, and Edwina $2. Dawn fined Barb $1 and Cathy $2. Edwina fined Alysha $2 and Dawn $1.

a. Draw the directed graph and write the matrix representing who fined whom and for how much after the *first* game. Sum the elements in each row and each column. What do these sums represent? Who levied the most fines? Who was fined the most?

b. After the second game, Alysha fined Barb $3 and Edwina $1. Barb fined herself $2 and Cathy $1. Cathy fined Alysha $2 and Dawn $1. Dawn fined everyone on the team $2. Edwina fined Barb $1. Draw the directed graph and write the matrix representing who fined whom and for how much after the *second* game. Who levied the most fines? Who was fined the most?

c. Find the total fines levied by each player against each other player after the first two games of the season.

Source: *Mathematics Teacher,* National Council of Teachers of Mathematics, Reston, VA, February 1990. Reprinted with permission.

Vignette 7.2 Supporting Students' Methods for Sense Making

The task is to see how many lines it takes to connect each vertex of a polygon to the other vertices.

Teacher: How many lines have you drawn in the hexagon?
Student: Seven.
Teacher: Good. Is this point connected here? Eight. Let's go around. Now we know this guy is connected to everybody. How about this guy, is he connected to everyone? (lapse time)
Student: Yeah.
Teacher: So what are we saying? What did we say there was?
Student: There's 9, and then there is . . . there is 9 and 6 . . . , 15.
Teacher: Good. So now we created the figure. Let's see if we can find a pattern. Do you have your homework from the other night? (lapse time while student looks for the homework) Look at Set A. Look at Number 1. Does that look familiar to you? Look at what we have now. . . .
Stucent: OK.
Teacher: Does it look familiar to you?
Student: Yeah.
Teacher: Look at that; we made a connection. We are amazing people, aren't we? Does this make sense to you now?
Student: Yeah.
Teacher: Do you see how it's the same problem? (The teacher still is trying to help the student see she will get the same formula as two nights ago in the previous homework. The student wants to take the long way . . . still is stuck in the same mode.)

Student: Yeah. I see how it's the same problem as that, but could I have done it like this?
Teacher: OK.
Student: So I still can't do it this way, or . . . ? (Student is going to do it the long way. This student obviously needs more practice, and then maybe more connections can be made.)
Teacher: You still could do it this way (as on previous homework). You sure could. (Lapse time as teacher watches student make chart, compute differences, and start through the entire process to find the formula as done previously on the homework instead of building on an established pattern.)
Teacher: Good. When you're done with this one, start Number 3, and I'll come back over here, and we'll check and see if you are on the right track, OK?
Student: OK.

All questioning sequences to aid student understanding require listening and responding appropriately. The teacher in the vignette had hoped the student would recognize the homework connection and find a generalization. When the student was not able to do this, the teacher encouraged the student to work the problem in a longer but more comfortable, sense-making method for the student. The teacher listened with care and demonstrated the patience and wisdom to let the student work through the problems at her own pace. The teacher recognized the student's lack of transference, accepted it, and will follow up later to help the student make the generalization.

Imagine that your class began Activity 7.3 in class to be finished at home. If a student comes for tutoring after school, what additional examples could you pose to further that student's understanding?

FOR TEACHERS

Activity 7.3 Digraphs and Matrices

Mathematical Content:
Characteristics of matrices, digraphs, and data (PSSM Representation Standard for Grades 6–8 and 9–12)

Materials:
Worksheets

Teacher Directions: Although this material is not difficult, it is in a middle-school text, so the concepts would certainly be new to the students. How could you help a struggling student through tutoring one-on-one to internalize these definitions?

F O R   S T U D E N T S

Activity 7.3
Digraphs and Matrices (page 1 of 3)

Sample Problems

1. In this matrix of tennis matches of players *A, B, C, D,* and *E,* each entry represents the number of games the player listed in the row won against the player listed in the column.

Player *C* won 6 matches against player *B.*

$$\begin{array}{c} \\ A \\ B \\ C \\ D \\ E \end{array} \begin{array}{c} \begin{array}{ccccc} A & B & C & D & E \end{array} \\ \left[\begin{array}{ccccc} — & 4 & 6 & 7 & 3 \\ 6 & — & 4 & 2 & 1 \\ 4 & 6 & — & 5 & 9 \\ 3 & 8 & 5 & — & 6 \\ 7 & 9 & 1 & 4 & — \end{array} \right] \end{array}$$

a. Why are there five missing entries in the matrix?

b. How many times did each pair of players meet?

c. Who is the best player?

SOLUTION

a. A player cannot play against himself or herself.

b. For any pair of players, the total number of wins is 10. Therefore, each pair of players met 10 times.

c. Who is best is a matter of interpretation. Player *C* won the most games (24). However, player *A* beat player *C* 6 out of 10 times, and player *D* won half of the matches with *C.*

2. In this diagram, called a *digraph,* a route is defined as a road that travels through a city at most 1 time. Construct a matrix that shows the number of routes from the city listed in the row to the city listed in the column.

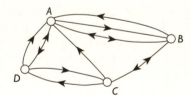

SOLUTION

$$\begin{array}{c} \\ A \\ B \\ C \\ D \end{array} \begin{array}{c} \begin{array}{cccc} A & B & C & D \end{array} \\ \left[\begin{array}{cccc} 0 & 3 & 3 & 3 \\ 5 & 0 & 3 & 4 \\ 5 & 7 & 0 & 4 \\ 5 & 7 & 5 & 0 \end{array} \right] \end{array}$$

FOR STUDENTS

Activity 7.3
Digraphs and Matrices (page 2 of 3)

Exercises

1. Complete the matrix by finding the perimeter and the area of a rectangle with each given length and width.

Length	Width	Perimeter	Area

$$\begin{bmatrix} 1 & 2 & & \\ 2 & 4 & & \\ 3 & 6 & & \\ 4 & 8 & & \\ 5 & 10 & & \\ 6 & 12 & & \end{bmatrix}$$

2. Create one 4-by-4 matrix in which

  a. the only entries are 1, 2, 3, and 4;

  b. every column contains 1, 2, 3, and 4;

  c. every row contains 1, 2, 3, and 4.

3. What values of w, x, y, z, and t will make these matrices equal?

$$\begin{bmatrix} 2 & x-2 & w \\ 3y & z+5 & 4-t \end{bmatrix} = \begin{bmatrix} 2 & 7 & 6 \\ 18 & 4 & 2 \end{bmatrix}$$

4. The labels of the rows and columns of the matrix below correspond to the vertices of the digraph. The matrix has an entry of 1 if there is an arrow leaving the row vertex and going to the column vertex. A 0 is placed trix.

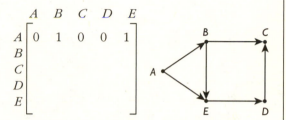

$$\begin{array}{c} \\ A \\ B \\ C \\ D \\ E \end{array} \begin{array}{ccccc} A & B & C & D & E \\ \end{array} \\ \begin{bmatrix} 0 & 1 & 0 & 0 & 1 \\ & & & & \\ & & & & \\ & & & & \\ & & & & \end{bmatrix}$$

5. Create a matrix in which $e_{a,\,b} = a \cdot b$.

6. In the windchill table, the rows represent wind speed, and the columns represent temperature.

  a. If the temperature is 0°F and the wind is blowing 35 miles per hour, what is the windchill?

  b. A windchill below −40°F is very dangerous. What combinations of wind speed and temperature are dangerous?

DETERMINING THE WINDCHILL FACTOR

Wind Speed	Actual Temperature (°F)																
	35°	30°	25°	20°	15°	10°	5°	0°	-5°	-10°	-15°	-20°	-25°	-30°	-35°	-40°	-45°
5 mph	33°	27°	21°	16°	12°	7°	0°	-5°	-10°	-15°	-21°	-26°	-31°	-36°	-42°	-47°	-52°
10 mph	22	16	10	3	-3	-9	-15	-22	-27	-34	-40	-46	-52	-58	-64	-71	-77
15 mph	16	9	2	-5	-11	-18	-25	-31	-38	-45	-51	-58	-65	-72	-78	-85	-92
20 mph	12	4	-3	-10	-17	-24	-31	-39	-46	-53	-60	-67	-74	-81	-88	-95	-102
25 mph	8	1	-7	-15	-22	-29	-36	-44	-51	-59	-66	-74	-81	-88	-96	-103	-110
30 mph	6	-2	-10	-18	-25	-33	-41	-49	-56	-64	-71	-79	-86	-93	-101	-109	-116
35 mph	4	-4	-12	-20	-27	-35	-43	-52	-58	-67	-74	-82	-89	-97	-105	-113	-120
40 mph	3	-5	-13	-21	-29	-37	-45	-53	-60	-69	-76	-84	-92	-100	-107	-115	-123
45 mph	2	-6	-14	-22	-30	-38	-46	-54	-62	-70	-78	-85	-93	-102	-109	-117	-125

FOR STUDENTS

Activity 7.3
Digraphs and Matrices (page 3 of 3)

7. Use the following matrix to determine who should be assigned jobs *A, B,* and *C* so that the jobs will be done in the minimum time. (The people cannot share jobs, and each must do one of the jobs.)

	Job A	Job B	Job C
Arti	6 hr.	5 hr.	4 hr.
Rita	5 hr.	4 hr.	2 hr.
Tria	6 hr.	3 hr.	5 hr.

8. The matrix represents a digraph. What is a possible graph for this matrix?

	A	B	C	D	E
A	0	1	1	1	1
B	0	0	1	0	0
C	0	0	0	0	0
D	0	0	0	0	1
E	0	0	1	1	0

9. Create a matrix showing the number of routes from point to point.

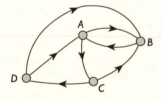

Source: From *Gateways to Algebra and Geometry: An Integrated Approach* by John Benson, Sara Dodge, Walter Dodge, Charles Hamberg, George Milauskas, and Richard Rukin. Copyright © 1994 by Houghton Mifflin Company. All rights reserved. Reprinted by permission of McDougal Littell, a division of Houghton Mifflin Company.

Listening

Listening is essential to communication. Dialogue is a conversation and not a take-turn discussion. All too frequently, however, a discussion is a take-turn situation with the speakers awaiting their opportunity to talk. The speakers listen to each other only for the opportunity of finding an opening to explain and defend their own views. A panel discussion is a prime example of this type of communication, and we have all been in situations with friends in which this kind of atmosphere prevailed. A common complaint in this setting is, "You aren't listening to what I am saying." In contrast, a conversation involves two or more individuals in exploring a topic of interest. The conversation has the aim of finding common ground, whether exploring new ideas or comparing differing viewpoints. A conversation invites participants to speak, listen, and react without a prescribed outcome.

"Is Anybody Listening?" is one of the articles on communication in the 1996 Yearbook, *Communication in Mathematics K–12 and Beyond* (Pirie, 1996, pp. 105–115). Pirie analyzed transcripts of teachers and students in the classroom to develop a four-part analysis of listening. Brief descriptions of her listening framework follow, embellished with examples from our experiences.

- Listening to the "What" involves the teacher attending to student use of mathematical words to become part of the language of the classroom. For example, a student described a step in solving equations as "take things off," which did relate to the physical example of changing weights on a scale but could not be translated to an equation with a negative number on the same side of the equation as the unknown. The words were the key to his difficulty, because he could not model negative weights in his conceptualization. Effective teacher listening to his precise words could help him understand what to do in a wider variety of problems.
- Listening to the "When" requires attention to the context as well as the words. This is particularly necessary when the teacher is using a word in a mathematical denotation and the student is referring to the word in everyday usage. I (LH) remember observing a teacher in training who was asked by a student which two of the three exterior angles to an angle in a triangle were necessary in the geometric construction of a given problem (extending two sides of a triangle at one vertex forms three angles outside the vertex). The teacher replied there are only two exterior an-

gles; the dismissal bell rang with the student shaking his head in bewilderment at the response. In the figure drawn there were three angles exterior to the angle in the triangle—the common usage of *external*—but there are only two exterior angles by geometric definition. The confusion arose from the difference in denotation between *exterior* in the mathematical context and the everyday use of the word. This difference in denotation is not uncommon. Also, sometimes an answer is true only in a specific context, and we can expand students' understanding by challenging their knowledge based on assumptions that they may have forgotten. For example, offer extra credit to geometry students who can draw a triangle with three 90-degree angles. When no one can figure it out, casually place a world globe in the room for several days until someone gets an idea—*on what surface to draw the triangle.* Students forget that they are studying plane geometry and too often state that *no* triangle has a sum of angles greater than 180 degrees. (In other words, context is significant.) Another example of listening to the "When" occurs in determining when it is mathematically correct to extrapolate or interpolate and when it is not.

- Listening to "How" a student verbalizes computations allows a glimpse into the students' misunderstandings. Sometimes this misunderstanding can even unwittingly be invited by the teacher's words. I (LH) remember once becoming very perplexed when grading a relatively easy test item that many students missed. They were to calculate the distance traveled from a velocity-time curve; instead, they were adding up all the area from the curve to the bottom of the piece of graph paper. I challenged the students the next day, "Did you believe that a larger piece of graph paper would result in a greater distance traveled for the same data?" They replied, "But you said 'the area under the curve.' " I should have been more careful to refer always to "the area between the curve and the x-axis—representing time." In another case a student teacher set up a word problem by telling the class to define $x + 10$ as the larger number and x as the smaller number because "you cannot subtract a larger number from a smaller number." Some students will remember those words in another context and become confused when subtracting positive and negative integers.
- Listening to "Everything" reminds us that students not only listen to our words but also our tone of voice and body language. Pauses, facial expressions, and quickness of responses give clues to students who do not focus on words alone. Two problems may arise that can be mitigated by

teacher sensitivity. The first is caused by the perceived imbalance of power between the teacher and the students. Students are reluctant to ask the teacher what her question means or to clarify what she is asking. The second type of difficulty is based on the assumption that both the teacher and the student are using identical words with identical precise definitions, when in fact each are using the mathematical term with a somewhat different meaning. The teacher must listen carefully so that neither of these situations is allowed to cut off communication.

The *1996 Yearbook, Communication in Mathematics,* is recommended for the breadth of topics discussed, such as multiple representations, word problems, writing, using literature, using technology, working with parents, supporting Limited English Proficiency students, and various forms of assessment. A wealth of examples of students' work, transcribed classroom interchanges, and vignettes elaborate the many ideas.

The intriguing view that listening can help us rethink what it means to teach mathematics is the subject of *Teaching Mathematics: Toward a Sound Alternative* (Davis, 1996). The double meaning of the word *sound* in the title refers to using the sense of sound to find a firm foundation for challenging common assumptions about teaching. Author Brent Davis advocates moving to the middle ground from "teaching as telling" to "teaching as listening" through reflections on his own teaching experiences and from a study of working with teachers. Definitions, examples, and discussions of three types of listening are woven into chapters discussing conceptual underpinnings, subject matter, formal education, cognition, and teaching.

Davis defines the following three types of listening:

1. *Evaluative listening.* Hearing is nearly synonymous with evaluative listening. The teacher asks questions from the lesson plan and deviates little from it. The teacher requests certain specific information and evaluates the students' responses as right or wrong. In this mode the responsibility of listening is mainly that of the learner.

2. *Interpretive listening.* In an exemplary classroom, the teacher is attempting to ascertain what the learners are thinking. The teacher and learner are constructing mathematics. Thus, the teacher must provide spaces for the learner to express mathematical ideas and methods in her own words. (These spaces are analogous to Polya's requirement that students do a *reasonable* amount of the work.) The listening involves both the teacher and learner as they converse about mathematics.

3. *Hermeneutic (the art of interpretation) listening.* "This manner of listening is more negotiatory, engaging, and messy," involving the hearing and heard in a project (Davis, 1996, p. 53). The split between the teacher and the students is blurred, with all focusing on a dynamic interaction.

The role of the teacher varies with each of these modes of listening. As an evaluative listener, the teacher maintains the central role of providing mathematical information in the traditional manner. As an interpretive listener, the teacher attempts to understand the view of the learner and orchestrates responses and activities toward a given outcome. As a hermeneutic listener, the teacher moves beyond orchestration to participate within a community of learners. The teacher moves from the position of asking, "How can I best tell this material?" to examining, "How can I know what the learner has learned?" In Vignette 7.3, Davis demonstrates hermeneutic listening from a study he conducted with a teacher (Davis, 1996, pp. 111–112).

Vignette 7.3   Hermeneutic Listening

Teacher: Number 1 [writing 1/6 + 3/12 + 2/24]: One sixth plus three twelfths plus two twenty-fourths. How much is that . . . Elaine?
Elaine: One half.
Teacher: Can you tell us how you got that?
Elaine: I can draw it.

Wendy (the teacher) held out the chalk, and Elaine came to the board to draw a picture of her arrangement of the pieces.

"It covers the same area as a half [piece], she explained. The sixth [piece] is as tall as a half [piece], and these three pieces [motioning across her diagram] are as wide as a half."

"So they're exactly the same size and shape as a half piece when you lay them out that way. Good. Did anybody get any other answers . . . Truong?"

"Six twelfths."

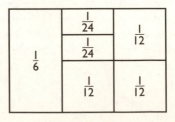

Elaine's Diagram

"Can you show us how you got that?"

"You can use that picture." Truong responded, pointing to Elaine's diagram. "You have three twelfths already; two twenty-fourths together is another twelfth, and the sixth can be cut into two twelfths. That's six twelfths altogether."

"OK. Good answer. Any other answers? . . . Van?"

"Four eighths."

"Four eighths? How can you get four eighths using these pieces?"

"Easy," Van announced, rising to go to the chalkboard. "Our fourth of a sixth plus one twenty-fourth plus a half of a twelfth is an eighth," drawing a dotted line across Elaine's diagram.

"You do that twice, so you can trade that for two eighths. Then, across the bottom, you have one fourth of a sixth and two halves of twelfths, twice, so that's two more eighths," adding more dotted lines and then simplifying the diagram by erasing the unwanted marks.

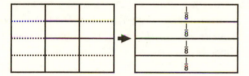

Van's Diagram

The lesson continued with an exploration of other possibilities, and students presented similar cases for other answers (which included 12/24, 2/4, and 1.5 thirds). More than half of the 45-minute time block was taken up in reviewing the homework "questions." The remainder of class time was spent in group work on another similar set of additive exercises that were developed by the students themselves. Wendy gave the additional instruction that groups were to find several different answers for each question and to explain why those answers were correct.

Davis advocates the framework of en activism—thinking founded upon seeking middle ways. En activist teaching focuses on what is happening in the classroom now, the possibilities for following actions, and the implications of those actions.

"In this conception, teaching can be neither about *telling* nor about *orchestrating*. Neither, however, are the acts of telling or orchestrating precluded in the en activist frame. I, the teacher, can still tell; I, the teacher, can still orchestrate. However, it is the learner, and not I, who determines whether I have told or orchestrated. The teacher must thus be attentive to the consequences of his or her interventions, attuned to the moment-to-moment activity of the classroom, and inquiring into the possibilities of the spaces that present themselves. He or she must be listening (Davis, 1996, p. 235).

Set 7.4   Discussion Question

1. Observe people talking to each other. Compare the body language of individuals engaged in conversation with that of individuals involved in a take-turn discussion, as defined in this section.

COMMUNICATION THROUGH WRITING

Writing provides a way to listen to students in order to become more fully informed of their cognitive (content) and affective (feeling) domains. Reading a student's written journal entry about how she works problems, how she defends answers, or where she gets stuck, a teacher can obtain a sense of the depth of that student's conceptual understanding. Writing affords access to the affective domain of how students feel about mathematics in general, their ability and success as mathematics students, and their perceptions of their development in the subject. Although most students find it easier to express themselves orally than in writing, many students will excel in written expression, especially if the format is precise enough to provide guidance but open enough to allow for differences of expression.

Writing can also help students to reflect upon their learning and reach "aha" experiences. Further, writing can assist students in clarifying their conceptual understanding. The first step to understanding the answer to questions is frequently a careful expression of the question. If students can write where they had difficulty in attaining a concept, this delineates the problem and enables the student to advance more easily to resolving a cognitive dissonance. The cognitive dissonance arises when students realize that the solution of the problem at hand is in conflict with their previous knowledge, beliefs, or methods. Writing helps students to shift their schemas to successfully incorporate previously gained knowledge with new information and to make connections in building an ever growing foundation of expertise in mathematics. Research indicates that writing gives students the opportunity to affirm and thereby strengthen their understanding of a concept even after they attain a solution (Ehrich, 1994).

Three Writing Approaches

Writing assignments can address the cognitive and affective domains through a combination of three writing approaches. These include providing answers to affective questions—that is, questions about students' feelings toward mathematics in general, as well as toward particular concepts and problems. A second approach is the think-talk-write approach, which couples writing with conversation. Finally, students can develop their ideas through regular writing in journals, with prompts directed toward their understanding of mathematics.

Affective Questions   Begin the practice of student writing on the first day of school. The student information sheet should contain at least several questions about students' expectations and students' feelings about mathematics. This information serves to inform you about the class before you get to know the students. We often asked, "Why are you taking this course?" If students answer, "Because I have to have it to go to college," or, "So I can take the next course," a conversation should ensue about mathematical reasons to take the class. This will provide the opportunity to preview the course content and to talk over reasons the mathematics of the course will be valuable. It is delightful to occasionally read, as we have, "Because I always wondered what algebra was about."

The student information sheet can request that students identify what they like most and least about mathematics and what they would like to change or retain in the mathematics classroom. In her book *Teachers Speak to Teachers*, Standera (1994) relates the answers given by one student and how this information informed her to help the student. Christi, a 3rd-year mathematics student, wrote the following answers: "The thing I like most about math is it's pretty easy, it comes easy to me. The thing I like least about math is all the equations I have to memorize. The thing I would change about math class is the people in it." Upon inquiry the teacher found that this student was considered to be good in math but not "good enough" to be placed in honors classes since she did not participate much during class. In conversation with Christi, the teacher decided that Christi resented not being in the honors program and therefore did not put forth her best effort. Although Christi was reluctant to discuss the last sentence of her response, she eagerly accepted the suggestion to transfer to an honors class, where she began to excel. Through information gained on the information sheet, you will also find students with low self-esteem in mathematics who can be encouraged to succeed (Standera, 1994).

Students should write responses to prompts selected to illuminate their understanding of significant mathematical principles. The students' writings will provide the teacher with valuable input for revising teaching strategies and identifying misconceptions. The Think–Pair–Share model discussed in Chapter 1 is a good method to encourage student journal writing after they have verbalized their thoughts to a peer.

Think-Talk-Write   Another way to approach writing is by the think-talk-write approach. Just as pair-share helps students verbalize for the whole class after sharing their thoughts with a partner, think-talk-write can assist students over the initial barrier of writing their thoughts by moving from talk to writing. Time for thinking, organizing ideas, and testing those ideas through conversation is built into this strategy. It is particularly effective when students are asked to explain, summarize, and reflect on big mathematical ideas. In the following example, seventh-grade students were studying measurement based on the *Mouse and Elephant* unit from the *Middle Grades Mathematics Project*, which explores the relationships between area and perimeter.

Vignette 7.4 Think-Talk-Write

Think

Teacher: For the next 30 seconds, think about the relationships between area and perimeter that you have observed over the past few weeks. No talking yet. I'll let you know when time is up. Ready? Go ahead and start thinking.

The students quietly reflect on the activities and discussions they have experienced.

Teacher: Now each person in your group is going to take a turn describing the relationship you have observed between area and perimeter. You have 60 seconds to talk while everyone else is listening. I'll let you know when it's time for the next person to talk.

The students begin talking. Initially, it is difficult for students to talk for 60 seconds—teachers might want to begin with periods of 30 seconds. The talk from one of the groups follows.

Talk

Jennifer: The relationship between the area of a shape and the perimeter of a shape is like the area of a shape is the inside and the perimeter is the outside.
Keisha: What I have observed is if you make one shape, you can find the area and perimeter of that same shape. You can add more tiles, the perimeter might

end up staying the same, and the area changes, or the area might stay the same, and perimeter might change. Like, for instance, we made the U shape in class. Many people changed the perimeter, but the area stayed the same, and many people changed the area, but the perimeter did not change.

George: The largest perimeter is a square. All the dimensions have to be equal. Mmmm . . . When you start with some numbers, once you get to the maximum number, they switch, and you get the same number at the end.

Fred: A relationship they have is when the perimeter of something stays the same but the area changes. One way is to make a chart with length, width, area. You have to multiply to get the area.

Write

Teacher: It's time to write. Describe the relationships you've observed between area and perimeter (Huinker & Laughlin, 1996).

The writing from this exercise showed that the students listened to each other. Understanding, misconceptions, and incomplete notions were all in evidence in the students' responses.

Journals Writing a journal entry requires students to go beyond "rote learning and challenges the students to use intellectual skills" (Nahrgang & Petersen, 1986). Journal writing can proceed along a number of different paths:

- The writing may be an integral part of the homework by requiring students to reflect upon their solutions for given problems. Or you may require students to write a few sentences about how they got stuck on any problem they do not fully understand. Thus, the homework and integrated remarks form a journal.
- The journal may be a separate notebook for writing in all subjects. If the school places an emphasis on writing, all teachers may require a certain number of journal entries for each subject and work together to improve students' ability to communicate through writing.
- The journal may comprise diarylike series of writing assignments to prompts provided by the teacher. Prompts might be on selected mathematical concepts—for example, "Explain the correlation between a network and an associated matrix." Prompts also can ask students to consider how the mathematics studied is related to real-world problems: "Give a setting outside the examples provided where a network can help analyze the situation." A third type of prompt requires students to reflect on their feelings and perceptions of their understanding, such as "What mathematics was the most difficult in this unit?" or "What mathematical information learned in this course are you most likely to remember and why?" or "How do you feel about your progress in this course?"

Whatever the form of the journal, it is important that you read and respond to the students' writing. Some teachers select a portion of the writing to read; others feel it is important to respond before asking the students to write again. Although this is an investment of time, it is well worth the added information you will gain about students' thinking and feelings. Research and experience indicate that writing is a unique mode of learning and an aid to learning (Nahrgang & Petersen, 1986). Your comments, which need not be lengthy, are personally addressed to the student, providing learning motivation. As you read and respond to the students' writing, you will be able to fine-tune more accurately your curriculum to meet the needs of the students.

It is recommended that assessment of journals be based on effort and completeness—*not* on content. Grades can lead students to try to interpret how you want them to respond. This defeats the two advantages of journal writing, individualized learning and discovery. But students do like to receive at least a few points for their efforts. A lack of effort should receive no credit. Brief comments such as "excellent," "thoughtful," "incomplete," or "explain further" accompanied by one point for acceptable remarks and two points for thoughtful remarks can be given. Correct the errors you find in the writing, bring them to the students' attention, and grade on the students' diligence in attending to the task (Nahrgang & Petersen, 1986).

After reviewing Activity 7.4, decide which of the three writing approaches discussed in this section would provide the most effective communication before the test. What is your rationale?

Learning Logs

A learning log is a spiral notebook used as a log to record class information such as agendas and assignments, learning activities done outside class, reflections on mathematics, and grades received in class. A log can be kept for one subject or maintained for a team of classes. The learning log has several purposes:

- for students to have one notebook in which to record their work, document the time spent outside class on homework, and reflect on their work;
- for students to use as a planning and time management tool;

- to open communication and create an ongoing dialogue between parents, students, and teachers through written comments;
- to encourage student responsibility for learning and achievement.

The teacher, student, and parent all have responsibilities. The teacher communicates with the student and parent whenever assignments are missing or a student's behavior is inappropriate by stamping ALERT in the log, accompanied by a brief explanatory note. The student writes in the log in class every day, records a daily record of time spent on each learning activity outside school, shares the log with her parent on a regular basis, and gives the log to the teacher for feedback when appropriate. The parent is to check the log often, respond to ALERT stamps, and encourage the student to view learning as a process.

The learning log is especially effective in middle school or the beginning years of high school to promote student success. The major benefit of the learning log is that it collects in one convenient place all the information the student needs to be successful. The focus is on the student's keeping a record of what she is studying and becoming responsible for her own learning. Parents can find out how their child is doing by reviewing the learning log at any time, so communication is ongoing. The log need not be graded.

Likewise, the teacher uses the log to respond to parent concerns and questions as well as to communicate with the student. Some examples of student entries follow:

- I need to redo HW #2 since I only had answers on my paper and did not show how I got the answers. I understand how I am to follow the problem-solving write-up, although I think I will need some practice with some of the strategies.
- I had trouble with problem #36 and #38 in HW #3. I talked with John from class and he was also having trouble. I did as much of the problems as

I could and showed what work I tried. We will have to ask for help tomorrow. (40 minutes) Showed Mom and Dad the Problem of the Week and we talked about it (5 minutes).

After reading entries such as these, the teacher can address efficiently the specific difficulties of individual students because the students have identified where they need help (Lewis, S., 1998).

Student-Written Problems

Inviting students to write problems, especially word problems, is a powerful learning tool. Students seldom stop to think about the necessary and unnecessary elements found in word problems. When students write word problems, they become aware of the structure of such problems, which is helpful for achieving solutions. We have used this technique in the following way:

1. After study and experience with a concept, ask students to write one to three problems involving the concept. The solutions should be entered on a separate page for later reference.
2. Collect the student-written problems, and distribute a portion of them to the class. The best situation is to select a reasonable number of the problems (look them over first for appropriate content) and type a sampling on a page. Do not change the problems as written. If time does not allow the reproduction of identical problems for use by all members of the class, simply mix the problems so each cooperative group has a different set of problems to solve.
3. The next day, the students work in groups to solve the problems.

Soon you will hear comments such as "This problem doesn't have enough information. We need to know . . . also," or "It is not clear what we are supposed to find," and even "There is no question to answer!" Ask the students to "fix" the unsolvable

FOR TEACHERS

Activity 7.4 Graphs, Colors, and Chromatic Numbers

Mathematical Content:
Graphs and colors to implicit conflict resolution (PSSM Representation Standard for Grades 6–8 and 9–12)

Materials:
Worksheets, colored pencils

Directions: After analyzing this activity, write out some journal prompts that would enable the students to communicate their understanding or misconceptions in writing.

FOR STUDENTS

Activity 7.4
Graphs, Colors, and Chromatic Numbers (page 1 of 3)

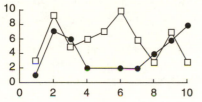

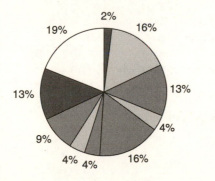

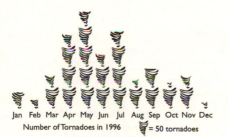

A graph is an important and powerful tool in displaying data and in solving problems. The examples in the left column show types of graphs that you have probably seen.

In discrete mathematics, two-dimensional graphs often use dots to represent vertices and line segments or arcs to represent edges. Let us begin with a simple example.

The diagram of Math Island shows attractions, denoted by the points $D, E, I, O,$ and P. The arcs or edges $IO, OD, ID,$ and IP represent roads joining the sites.

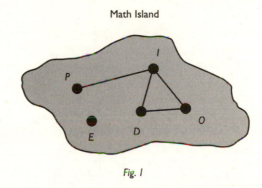

Math Island

Fig. 1

1. How many vertices (points) are pictured?

2. How many segments (edges) are pictured?

3. Can you drive from I to D by road? From P to E?

Simple graphs or pictures can help solve many problems.

Fractal Middle School has five clubs that meet 1 day per week during the after-school activity period. The principal wishes to spend the least amount of money to provide late buses after school and therefore wants the clubs to meet on the fewest days possible. Some students belong to more than one club and do not want to miss out on any of them.

Activity 7.4
Graphs, Colors, and Chromatic Numbers (page 2 of 3)

In the following graph, a segment connects two clubs if a student belongs to both.

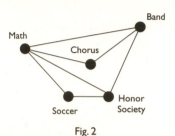

Fig. 2

Club participation

Students were asked to help the principal determine the lowest number of late-bus days.

One student decided to color the dots in the graph. If any were connected by two points, she made certain that the dots were a different color. After coloring the figure in several ways, she decided that the fewest colors she could use was three and that three buses would therefore be enough. That is, the math club would meet on one day, chorus and honor society on another day, and band and soccer on another.

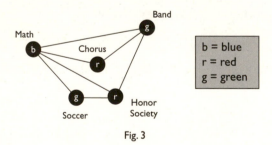

b = blue
r = red
g = green

Fig. 3

4. Do you think the principal could use just *two* buses?

The smallest number of colors required to color such a graph as the one above is called the *chromatic number* of the graph. The chromatic number for this graph is 3.

5. On a separate sheet of paper, color the Club Participation graph in a different way using

a. three colors;

b. four colors;

c. five colors.

6. Determine the chromatic number for each of the following graphs.

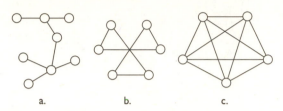

a.   b.   c.

A tropical fish hobbyist has six different types of fish: Alphas, Betas, Certas, Deltas, Epsas, and Fetas, which shall henceforth be designated by *A, B, C, D, E,* and *F,* respectively. Because of predator-prey relationships, water conditions, and size, some fish cannot be kept in the same tank. The following table shows which fish cannot be together.

Type	A	B	C	D	E	F
Cannot Be With	B, C	A, C, E	A, B, D, E	C, F	B, C, F	D, E

7. What is the smallest number of tanks needed to keep all the fish? To help answer the question, draw six points; one representing each type of fish and then draw a graph where each edge joins the vertices representing any two fish that are incompatible. Next, determine the chromatic number of your graph, and finally, obtain the answer to the original question.

More Coloring Problems

8. Determine the smallest number of colors needed for billiard balls in each of the following arrangements if no two balls of the same color can touch each other.

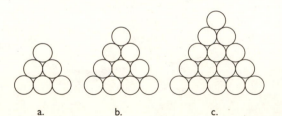

a.   b.   c.

FOR STUDENTS

Activity 7.4
Graphs, Colors, and Chromatic Numbers (page 3 of 3)

The road intersection shown needs traffic signals to handle the flow of traffic. Let us agree that two directions of traffic that cross will not be allowed to flow at the same time. We then need to set up and sequence traffic lights to ensure a safe traffic flow.

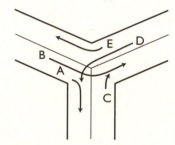

Traffic flow

9. Notice that traffic flows in five different directions, which will be represented by the vertices of a graph. We have drawn edges connecting vertices if the traffic directions they represent could intersect and indicate an accident. Next, color the graph, and determine the chromatic number. What does this number indicate?

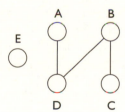

Graph of traffic flow

10. Draw a graph to correspond to the following traffic intersection. Determine the chromatic number of the graph, and describe traffic flow for the timing periods.

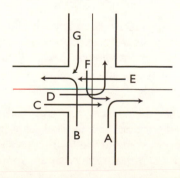

11. In a garden, certain plants should not be planted together in the same plot of land. Why not?

12. Baht A. Knee is planning a garden that will have Aspars, Beems, Carrows, Dubers, and Endove, henceforth denoted as *A, B, C, D* and *E*, respectively. In the conditions Baht planned to plant, he noted the following incompatibilities:

Type	A	B	C	D	E
Can't Plant With	B, C	A, C, E	A,	B, E	B, D

Use a graph and its chromatic number to determine the minimum number of garden plots necessary for Baht's garden.

Can you . . .

- construct a graph that has a chromatic number greater than or equal to 2?
- write an algorithm that will determine the chromatic number of a graph?
- produce a matrix for a graph that will show which vertices are different colors?
- write a definition for the edge chromatic number of a graph?
- write an algorithm to determine the edge chromatic number of a graph?

Did you know that . . .

- chromatic numbers can be used to solve scheduling problems?
- the famous "four-color-map problem" involves coloring regions in the plane?
- every planar graph has a chromatic number ≤ 4?
- the Welsh and Powell algorithm uses the degrees of vertices, the number of edges intersecting at a vertex, to color a graph?

Source: *NCTM Student Math Notes,* National Council of Teachers of Mathematics, Reston, VA, January 1998. Reprinted with permission.

problems. The students quickly grasp that problems must have certain characteristics to effectively bring out the salient ideas.

The next task is to conduct a conversation about the elements necessary in workable problems and those that are extraneous to the problem. Suggest that some problems be written with more information than required so students learn to select data appropriate to a solution, but warn students against wordiness. After relatively little experience, the students' problems will improve dramatically as students begin to recognize the structure of problems—something they might never have noticed before.

Students also enjoy the creativity in writing their own problems with interesting and imaginative contexts. Examples of student-written problems about maple syrup, football, sailing, and the circus are given in an article by Susan Larkin (1986) about the self-discovery of the advantages of student-written problems by a teacher. Another teacher testifies that students find fictitious stories to be as interesting as real problems and that writing problems helps them to learn to read problems more carefully (Fairbairn, 1993). He suggests providing the computation and asking students to provide the context.

Certain aspects of the learning situation will ensure that the exercise of students writing for students is productive and worthwhile:

- Approach the activity as an enjoyable change from textbook problems. Students will soon agree, even if at first they may not believe that writing problems can be their task.
- Remind students that comments must address the shortcomings or excellence of the written problems and not the individual who wrote them. At first students may not want to "sign" their problems for fear they will not be workable or clear to other students. Later, as students become more proficient at writing, they may want to get credit for their work. Since students love to see their names in print, consider "publishing" a classroom-tested collection of student-written problems.
- Begin with easy assignments, and advance to more difficult ones. The first attempts may just require students to change or improve textbook problems while they gain confidence in their writing ability.
- Recognize that students will need practice to write good problems. Tell students that writing problems is a difficult task but one at which they will improve with experience. Have students work together and peer-edit problems for clarity before turning their work over to you.

Continuing this practice over several years will give you a bank of interesting problems to draw from at other times in your curriculum.

Other Interesting Ways to Use the Written Word

The *1996 Yearbook. Communication in Mathematics K–12 and Beyond* (NCTM, 1996) includes a number of chapters on ways to incorporate the written word in teaching mathematics. The following list summarizes the main ideas of a few of the chapters and provides reference information for each:

- Children's trade books written for enjoyment are enhanced by adding explicit mathematical representations. Students can work in groups and use "think" balloons to add annotations. Physical arrangements designed from manipulatives can complement the books (Halpern, 1996).
- Mathematics teachers and reading teachers work together to help students learn how and why to read texts in order to construct mathematical meaning (Siegel, Borasi, Fonzi, Sanridge, & Smith, 1996).
- Literature offers quantitative relationships that provide a springboard for mathematical concepts. One unit in the *Interactive Mathematics Program* begins with Poe's story "The Pit and the Pendulum." Students analyze pendulums and develop statistics to determine whether the story is realistic in allowing the prisoner to escape the deadly pendulum. Tolstoy's story "How Much Land Does a Man Need?" describes land prices and areas and offers ample information to discuss estimation, rates, fraction, distance, currency, geometry, and trigonometry (Narode, 1996). The article in the *1996 Yearbook* gives suggestions about how to use this story in teaching mathematics.
- Students can exercise their creativity by writing rhymes, parodies, spin-offs from books or films, and songs that incorporate the mathematical concepts under study (House, 1996).

Set 7.5   *Discussion Questions*

Questions with an asterisk appear in the Message Board section of the Companion Website at **http://www.prenhall.com/huetinck**. Go to Chapter 7 and click on the Message Board to find and respond to the question.

*1. What experiences have you had in writing in mathematics? Were they helpful? Why or why not?

2. Review some of the instruction sequences presented in this text. What are some big ideas in the material for which writing could be an effective tool to help clarify students' understanding?

Go to Web Destinations for Chapter 7 at **http://www.prenhall.com/huetinck** to find links about Learning Logs.

Read through Activity 7.5 and decide which of the communication modes described in this section would be an exemplary lesson extension for that activity.

DISCIPLINE—FROM CONTROL TO COMMUNITY

Beginning teachers seldom experience difficulties in the classroom due to their knowledge of subject matter; rather, frustrations are most likely to arise from the demands of maintaining a learning environment relatively free from student disruptions. The foundation for good classroom discipline is laid through careful planning of worthwhile tasks using interesting methods. Further, good classroom discipline requires a teacher who respects students and strives to challenge them while providing ample opportunities for student success. However, it is naive to believe that innovative curriculum and empathy with students are sufficient to keep all students on task all the time. It is essential for teachers to think through possible responses to off-task behavior before a potentially disruptive situation happens in order to minimize the negative effects of some students on the learning process.

The primary element of successful classroom management is the teacher's firm understanding of the positive aspects of her role in discipline. In our experience, the beginning teachers who experience difficulty in maintaining discipline too often see it in negative terms. They are reluctant to correct students because they feel the students may resent the intervention or will not continue to like them. Consider first, however, that all of your students have the right to a productive lesson. Few students will misbehave often and intentionally, but those who do must not be allowed to interfere with the learning of the class. Sound discipline procedures help all students to practice self-control and take responsibility for their learning. It is a fact that the teacher cannot *make* a secondary-level student do anything, but the teacher can assist students in developing thoughtful regard for others and respect for the practices of democratic citizenship that are regularly expected in the classroom. Maintaining an environment that is advantageous to a community of mathematics learners is your responsibility as a teacher. Thus, encourage students to control their own behavior, but if some students misbehave frequently, take action to ensure that your classroom has a climate in which all can advance their understanding of mathematics.

We do not subscribe to the oft-quoted concept that the class must be disciplined before instruction can begin; we find effective classroom management is interwoven with instruction. If the majority of the class is involved in a worthwhile task, the off-task student can generally be brought into the activity by the attentive teacher who acts quickly and subtly to include the student without interrupting the flow of the class. Serious disruptions must be dealt with efficiently as well, so the learning of the class is not adversely affected. Your demeanor in the classroom will reflect how seriously you take your responsibility for student learning, your level of tolerance, your response to inappropriate behaviors, and how consistent you are. Establishing a climate conductive to learning is a continuing process that will become easier with practice as you remain consistently firm, fair, and friendly.

FOR TEACHERS

Activity 7.5 Conflict Resolution: Coloring Graphs

Mathematical Content:
Graph colors and conflict resolution (PSSM Representation Standard for Grades 6–8 and 9–12)

Materials:
Worksheets, colored pencils

Teacher Directions: After working these problems, design a problem like problem 6; but simpler with a shorter data chart. This could be an example to students to write their own problems of this type. What would be your instructions to the students for this assignment?

F O R   S T U D E N T S

Activity 7.5
Conflict Resolution: Coloring Graphs (page 1 of 3)

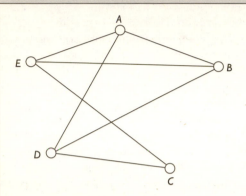

A conflict resolution graph.

1. In Lesson 1 you used graphs to represent a variety of real-world situations. Go back to Lesson 1 and identify the situations that involve conflict resolution.

2. The graph at left represents a conflict resolution situation.

   a. Make a table showing the conflicts among the vertices.

   b. When you use a graph to solve conflict resolution problems, it is helpful to mark the vertices in some way. Often a second label is added; the label might be times in one situation, zoo habitats in another. Mathematicians frequently use colors as an all-purpose method of labeling vertices and sometimes call conflict resolution problems vertex-coloring problems. To make the vertices easy to color, they use empty circles for the vertices and shade the circles with colors or write the first letter of a color inside the circle. Find a way to color the vertices of the conflict resolution graph by using as few colors as possible and with no two connected vertices colored the same.

3. **a.** Mathematicians call the number of edges that meet at a vertex its **degree**. Find the degree of each vertex in the conflict resolution graph in Problem 2.

   b. What does the degree of the vertex mean in the situation the graph represents?

4. To help determine the minimum number of colors that graphs need, mathematicians study groups of graphs that have something in common. For example, the graphs below are all empty graphs. An empty graph has no edges and represents situations with no conflicts.

   a. Explain why every empty graph needs only one color.

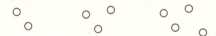

Empty graphs with 2, 3, and 4 vertices.

FOR STUDENTS

Activity 7.5
Conflict Resolution: Coloring Graphs (page 2 of 3)

b. Study the following three complete graphs. Find the minimum number of colors for each of these graphs. What can you say about the number of colors needed to color complete graphs? Explain.

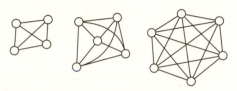

Complete graphs of 4, 5, and 6 vertices.

c. The following four graphs are cycles. Find the minimum number of colors for each of them. What can you say about the number of colors needed to color cycles?

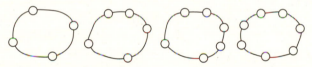

Cycles of 4, 5, 6, and 7 vertices

d. The following four graphs are trees. Find the minimum number of colors for each of them. What can you say about the number of colors needed to color trees?

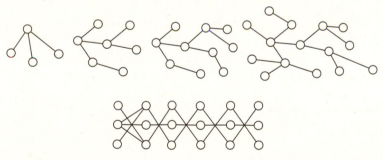

Five graphs that are trees

F O R   S T U D E N T S

Activity 7.5
Conflict Resolution: Coloring Graphs (page 3 of 3)

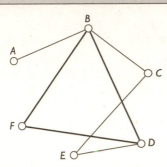

A graph with a subgraph that is a cycle of three vertices

Chemical	Incompatible With
a	b, d, f, h
b	a, j, k, l
c	i
d	a, l
e	g
f	a, l
g	e, i
h	a, j
i	c, g
j	b, h
k	b
l	b, d, f

5. Mathematicians find it helpful to know something about the number of colors that common graphs such as complete graphs, cycles, and trees require. That's because common graphs are often contained in large, unfamiliar graphs, and a large, unfamiliar graph needs at least as many colors as any of its parts. A graph that is part of another graph is called a **subgraph** of the graph that contains it. The vertices and edges of a subgraph are vertices and edges of the original graph. The subgraph shown here is a cycle of three vertices.

   a. Find another cycle that is a subgraph of this graph.

   b. Use your knowledge of subgraphs to analyze the graph in Problem 2. Does what you have learned about cycles prove that you used the minimum number of colors in your answer to part (b) of Problem 2?

6. The manager of a chemical storage facility keeps dangerous chemicals in sealed cabinets in case of leakage. However, some chemicals cannot be stored in the same cabinet with others because of the possibility of fire or explosion if the chemicals come in contact with each other. The table shows which chemicals are incompatible.

   a. Represent the chemical incompatibilities in a graph.

   b. Use your knowledge of subgraphs to determine a minimum number of colors for the graph.

   c. Try to color the graph with the minimum number of colors you found in part (b).

In summary, beginning teachers too often consider discipline to be the act of externally controlling students to do as the teacher asks. This concept of discipline is likely to lead to uncomfortable confrontational situations, however, rather than an environment of learning in which everyone is respected. We consider discipline to be encouraging student self-control and self-motivation so the entire class can be productive.

Kounin's Research

In the 1970s a significant body of research on discipline within the classroom was contributed by Kounin's analysis of the relationship between certain teaching behaviors and the resultant students' actions. Kounin moved from teacher interview to observations and then to videotapes to carefully analyze teacher-student interactions in 80 different classrooms. He sought teacher behaviors encouraging maximum student involvement while minimizing student misbehavior. The characteristics of teachers' overt attempts to stop misbehavior seemed to have little relationship to student behavior. Noting that deviant student behavior seldom occurred when students were engrossed in the lesson, he began to focus on management techniques of exemplary teachers to engage students (Kounin, 1970).

Kounin's principal concepts and teachings can be summarized as follows:

- The ripple effect is the effect of teacher words or actions to one student spreading to affect overall class demeanor. Although important in elementary school, the ripple effect was of little use with secondary-level students. Threats of punishment, clarity, firmness, and presence or absence of humor affected the targeted student but had little or no influence over other high-school students in the class. Older students were more likely to stay on task for teachers they held in high regard, so the interpersonal relationship between the teacher and the class was more important than remarks addressed to any one student.
- *Withitness* is a term describing the teacher's awareness of what is happening everywhere in the classroom at all times. This is a powerful trait in reducing student misbehavior, sometimes referred to as "having eyes in the back of one's head." The effective teacher continually looks over the classroom to see what is happening everywhere. It has been our experience that having good hearing provides an additional way to attain a reputation of withitness. It is important

for teachers to communicate their awareness. Making eye contact or simply saying a student's name aloud may be a sufficient response for keeping wayward students on task. At the same time, the teacher needs to be cognizant of the entire episode when admonishing students to get back to their lesson. To exhibit withitness, the teacher must correct the student who is the instigator and not other students misbehaving after the situation has evolved. If two situations of deviant behavior occur nearly simultaneously, the teacher must be able to quickly differentiate between the situations and react to the more serious disruption first. Timing is significant. Students expect teacher intervention at disruptions and might consider a teacher to be ineffective if she fails to respond quickly and appropriately. An immediate response helps to correct misbehavior before it escalates.

- Momentum and smoothness indicate the flowing movement of lessons from one activity to another, including introduction of an activity, involvement in the activity, closure, and transition to the next part of the lesson. Good classroom managers plan ahead so the momentum is not interrupted by logistical details. Teacher-initiated interruptions in the students' train of thought can escalate into student off-task misbehaviors. Kounin noted that slowdowns such as excessive time on directions, lengthy lectures on behavior, spending too much time on lesson detail, and breaking activities into too many parts caused delays leading to undesirable behaviors. He found that momentum and smoothness were the most significant behavior management techniques to maintain good classroom demeanor.
- Group alerting and accountability greatly assist focus in whole group instruction. The teacher alerts the group by first getting everyone's attention and then clearly and quickly advising the group of the requirements to accomplish the task at hand. Accountability lets students know that their performance will be assessed in some way, whether by grades or observation. In a group setting there are a number of ways to gauge individual understanding, such as requesting that students hold up small whiteboards marked with their answers, asking a question and then calling on a student at random, requiring students to manipulate objects, and asking students to record results on a flip chart or overhead transparency to share. Formats that require higher participation, instead of requiring only that students just sit and listen, also improve focus. The teacher should circulate within the room to check the

work of students who do not communicate to the class or teacher.

- Overlapping is the ability of the teacher to attend to multiple classroom events simultaneously. We might now name this essential teacher talent as multiple processing. Linear processing—attending to one happening at a time—simply is inadequate for effective classroom management. Monitoring student decorum, providing instruction, and considering reactions from the class to determine what comes next must all be considered at the same time. Unfortunately, it is too common for the teacher to be interrupted by a note from the office, a late student with a note to be signed, or some other clerical detail requiring her attention. Quickly dispatch these disruptions or deal with them near the end of the period. If, occasionally, a diversion must be handled immediately, give the class a task to do while you deal with the problem. Overlapping is an essential aspect of withitness.

- Satiation, valence, challenge arousal, and seatwork variety all refer to adjusting the pace and interest of activities to maintain student involvement. In the classroom, satiation (getting one's fill of the topic) brings boredom and frustration with too much repetition of a concept. Valence refers to the positive or negative reaction of students to an activity. To arouse student interest, teachers may offer challenges through extensions. Seatwork variety is a concept that explains itself. Students often work independently, and teacher talk is minimized through a teacher's good management.

Attention to all of these concepts when planning and delivering instruction improves a student's experience in the classroom. Finally, carefully consider the coherence of a lesson when planning. If it does not go as planned, make a note for future reference so the lesson will proceed more smoothly the next time you teach it.

Teachers can employ the management techniques pinpointed by Kounin to minimize student misbehavior. However, these techniques do not address disruptions arising from sources outside the classroom (Kounin, 1971). The essential elements to keep students involved provide a way to diagnose instructional problems and suggest means to remedy lessons that do not meet the teacher's expectations; however, a more comprehensive plan of discipline is necessary for a teacher to deal effectively with all types of misbehavior. Kounin's research gives insight into preventing off-task behavior, but it does not extend to methods of stopping deviant behavior when it does occur.

Vignette 7.5   One Teacher's Experience

One day in a high-school algebra class, a student was again distracting other students near him with disruptive behavior during a whole-class discussion. I had talked privately several times with this student but there had been no appreciable change in behavior. Politely but firmly I said, "Please take your things and report to the counselor's office. We will need to have a conference." The student surprised me by saying in a loud voice, "You can't make me." After a hesitation I replied, "You are right, I can't make you. Matter of fact, I don't even know what I can do because I've never had a student directly defy me before. (pause) However, I will find out what I can do. (pause) Perhaps you might wish you had gone to the counselor's office." This was entirely spontaneous for me, and I wondered if I had said the right thing. I was very careful to use a matter-of-fact voice with no hint of a threatening tone. I continued with the lesson to a class so quiet a pin drop could have been heard. After about 2 minutes, the offending student picked up his things and left the class. I briefly halted the discussion, looked at the clock, and wrote down the time. This was to signal the class that I would check the time stamp the student would receive upon entering the counselor's office.

The situation turned out better than I expected. The student, counselor, and I set out a behavior contract. I did not request or receive an apology. Our task was one of problem solving: how to eliminate the actions that had been disturbing the class. The student's attitude in the class was much improved for the remainder of the course.

Reflection: I learned several things from this experience. First, sometimes it is beneficial to tell students exactly what the penalty is for a given undesired behavior, and sometimes the student's imagination is so active that it is better not to be explicit. Second, it is best to be honest (I really didn't know what I could do and said so). The situation reinforced my resolve to always focus on my position of maintaining a positive learning environment for the class rather than be sidetracked by a disruptive student, even when it is difficult to remain cool.

I realize also that the experience had a successful outcome due to certain elements of the setting. First, I knew the class and that there was no clique of students ready to further aggravate the situation. The students knew that I always followed through with what I said I would do. I rarely sent a student out of class, so when I did so, it had a greater impact.

We all know that what works with one student or one class may not work with another. And what works for a teacher of one disposition may not work well for another. This experience of mine is only for consideration by other teachers, not for emulation. All teachers must develop interactions with students based on their own belief systems in a consistent framework.

Community in the Classroom

Visit the area in a university library devoted to discipline in education and you will quickly realize that this is a complex topic on which numerous volumes have been written. A variety of books summarize different theories of discipline, discuss practical examples, and provide lists of suggestions in order to maintain classroom decorum (Burden, 1995; Charles, 1996; Edwards, 1997; Emmer, Evertso, Clements, & Worshan, 1984; Good & Brody, 1997; Kohn, 1996; Levin & Nolan, 1996; Sotto, 1994). Each of these authors and researchers works from his or her basic beliefs about human nature in general and beliefs about young people in particular. Our combined experience of more than 35 years of teaching in secondary schools is that teachers are very fortunate that the vast majority of students enjoy growing and learning when they do not perceive insurmountable barriers to success. Unfortunately, some barriers may exist outside the school over which the teacher has no influence, and some students may have experienced extreme hardships for which school cannot compensate. As a result, a teacher cannot expect to lead all students to use fully their potential. Nonetheless, we have found that having a positive attitude that assumes students want to become productive adults is the best beginning for a personal discipline system.

When discussing community, terms such as *discipline* and even *management* may seem problematic. That is, *discipline* and *management* denote a teacher-dominated classroom, while *community* suggests teacher and students working together. The teacher exhibiting withitness strives for a student-friendly classroom with a climate in which no one interferes with the learning of another. The successful teacher allows the students as much freedom as possible but steps in quickly when any individual or group causes a degradation of the learning environment. Compliance or control are not important as long as students are advancing their knowledge. These ideas may be new to mathematics teachers in training whose college-preparatory mathematics classes in secondary school were traditionally taught. Classes using manipulatives, cooperative learning, calculators, or computers are frequently noisy and may not even appear disciplined to a casual observer. However, these active communities frequently have students more engrossed in learning than would be the case in a quiet, orderly community.

To ensure a healthy climate for learning but one in which students are not coerced in the name of discipline, we offer suggestions for bringing off-task students back to learning. The following list is an abbreviated sliding scale of actions in which the infractions progress from less serious to more serious.

1. If a student is being inattentive, talking out of turn, pestering another student, dropping paper on the floor, or carrying out some other relatively minor infraction, take the following action: Use strong eye contact with a shake of the head, say the student's name, or gain proximity to the student for a mild correction.

2. If a student is bringing and using items not appropriate to the class, such as magazines, radio and earphones, makeup, or pagers, take the following action: Either confiscate the item or tell the student that if it doesn't disappear from sight you must take it and turn it into the office. (Many schools have strict rules prohibiting certain electronic devices on school property.) Quietly collect magazines, makeup, soccer balls, and so on from the student, advising her to retrieve the confiscated item either at the end of class or at the end of the day. School policy determines the best action.

3. If a student persists in a pattern of disruptions such as getting up and walking around when inappropriate or touching another student in a way that annoys, take the following action: Begin by changing the students' seating arrangement. If that does not help the situation, ask the student to meet with you for a few minutes to discuss the behavior either after class, during lunch, or at another time that day. When you talk with the student, factually describe the offending action without negatively labeling the student. Ask the student for suggestions on how she might avoid the behavior. Be clear on what improvements must be made and assist the student in making them.

4. If a student has poor attendance, is excessively tardy, or makes frequent and thoughtless interruptions, take the following action: Notify her parent or guardian. Most schools have a well-delineated attendance and tardy policy that all beginning teachers should follow. It is essential to be prepared with dated records of the series of infractions, absences, or incidences of being tardy. If students are having these difficulties, it is likely their academic grade is suffering in addition to their citizenship and work habit ratings. Express to parents that you are concerned about their child's success in the course. Be prepared to discuss specifics concerning grades.

5. If a student is openly defiant and exhibits undisciplined behavior, take the following action: When you have determined that a pattern of disruption must be stopped and have had no

success with the aforementioned tactics, it is time for a parent conference with a counselor and/or an administrator. Serious problems such as evidence of substance abuse must be immediately reported to the administration. Schools have policies that must be strictly followed in such cases.

Networking Within the School

Always keep in mind that as a mathematics teacher, you are one member of an educational team. Seek assistance from your team members when necessary. You are sure to receive helpful hints for management and discipline from experienced teachers. Further, your department chairperson has the responsibility to assist you when possible. Be aware of the policies and procedures of your district and school. Most schools have an orientation session for new teachers before school starts. Included in this orientation are recommended and required methods of handling different classroom situations. Do not wait to ask for advice until a problem with a student or class is becoming quite difficult. Talk to counselors, and find out what course of action they recommend in given situations. Discuss discipline with your administrators to ascertain what types of problems they expect to handle and how and when they can assist you. Teachers who manage outside activities such as sports, school plays, clubs, and so on can be of great assistance if one of their stars is slipping in academics or citizenship.

Find answers for the following questions:

- Does your school have a quiet room to which you may send students who just need a time out of class? It's asking a lot to require energetic young people to sit 5 to 6 hours per day and pay attention.
- Can you ask a student to sit right outside the door if she is misbehaving? This is a simple alternative to sending the student to a special area; however, some administrators are uneasy about having students in the hallway. I (LH) had two seats just outside each classroom door for students who misbehaved. Occasionally a student would request that she be permitted to sit in the hall. One said, "I got in trouble with Teacher X second period and Teacher Y fourth period. This hasn't been a good day. I promise to work, but think I'd better sit by myself."
- Is there provision for detention? Who collects it? Many schools have detention detail collected by administration for certain infractions, but expect teachers to collect detention for other behaviors.

Do not assign detention if it lengthens your day unless you feel the effort is worth the result.
- What is the attendance policy? the tardy policy? Understand, follow, and document the steps the teacher should take before referring a student to the counselor or an administrator. If you do not agree with all aspects of the policies, wait for a few years of experience before you make changes.

A Personal Discipline System

Teachers in training who observe successful experienced teachers often remark on these teachers' "presence." Experienced teachers develop a personal system of discipline and classroom management based on their beliefs on how to be an exemplary teacher and their knowledge of themselves. They find efficient methods of communicating with students that fit their own personalities. They find ways to move students from activity to activity with minimum disruption in a manner that is consistent with their natural way of working with others. Successful teachers incorporate discipline into their classroom management. Seldom will a technique extolled by one teacher work in exactly the same way for another. Observe practicing teachers as much as possible, and note their methods that you expect to use comfortably and effectively in your classroom.

You will develop a personal system for discipline based on recommended best practice, educational theory, classroom research literature, suggestions from experienced teachers, your own experiences, and your expectations of students. The best action or reaction for the teacher to take depends on the situation, the established relationship with the student and class before the intervention, and the anticipated reaction of the student and class after the intervention. Sometimes one action will be best and sometimes another, so it is necessary to consider a variety of options. If one thing does not work to keep a student or students on task, try another. Reacting differently in different situations does not suggest drastic changes in your expectations of students. You will find some techniques more or less effective depending upon student maturity level, student ability level, and student background. As you build a personal system of discipline, these complexities will be incorporated.

Vignette 7.6 is one successful experienced teacher's reflection on his classroom management strategies and discipline policies. (Jack Bloom, Porter Middle School, Los Angeles Unified School District, wrote this piece specifically for this text.)

Vignette 7.6 One Teacher's Classroom Management Strategies and Discipline Principles

My first day of teaching began in the 7th week of school. The bell rang. Students rushed in from all entrances including the windows—knocking over desks and chairs if they happened to be in the way! Ten minutes passed before the students themselves decided to settle down to begin work. Students disrupted the class for whatever reason at any time, regardless of whether a lesson was in progress. Outbursts of laughter were a common occurrence. Students left their seats on a whim during class. This was truly an example of "majority rules."

This scene took place daily during the first few weeks of my introduction to the field of education. The students went through three different substitutes before I took over. The last teacher quit due to stress, claiming the students were deliberately programmed into his classes because he was hired as a long-term substitute. He confessed that everything he tried to do failed to alter their behavior in class. Something was definitely wrong with this picture.

Things didn't appear much brighter for me for a while. However, in small increments, I began to address different issues to sustain a learning environment. First, I continually reinforced the fact that I was going to stay as their teacher. Slowly the students began to realize that I was knowledgeable, fair, and made requests for behavior that benefited everyone.

Classroom Management Strategies

In order to create a positive learning atmosphere, I have found the following list of strategies useful when teaching students of varying ability levels and interests.

- Set clear, firm rules of expectations from the outset. As long as the parameters have been laid out and consequences listed, then the responsibility rests upon the students to follow the guidelines. You may even wish to enlist student input to establish guidelines in your classroom.
- Learn student names as quickly as possible. Thus you can identify the owner of the behavior, and ownership plays a key role in classroom control.
- Call home. This action sends a message both to the child and the parent regarding your concern toward proper classroom conduct.
- The ultimate goal is to establish a system you are comfortable with for the classroom and that works for your students. Every instructor is different, and what may work at one time for one classroom may not be as effective in another.

- The physical layout of your classroom is important for proper control. The arrangement of the desks and/or tables reflects a great deal about the style of instruction. Vary the mode of classroom instruction, and change the room arrangement according to the activity.
- It is important to obtain a comfort zone for both yourself and your students. After a period of time when you feel an acceptable level of classroom decorum, then encourage students to work in pairs or small groups.
- Try to adjust classroom instruction depending on the personality of the class. Present material in a multitude of ways with a variety of examples. (For example, using students' names in word problems stimulates interest.) Request that the students do problems on the board or overhead projector. Have students present a group lesson in front of their peers. (It encourages student participation in the instruction and allows for greater input, which offers the students more ownership of the lesson.) Assigning meaningful material pertinent to the topic of study enables the students to gain comprehension. Outside classroom projects allow students to be creative and develop critical thinking skills. Have the students make up problems highlighting the unit currently being studied.
- Make sure instructions are clear and concise.
- Provide a study guide to help the students organize and learn how to review for a chapter or unit test. Enrich your curriculum with skills not covered by the text.
- Try not only to be prepared—try to be overprepared. Empty time can bring chaos to a classroom.
- Plan activities and mode of instruction to avoid lag time. A warm-up at the beginning of class reinforces a prior lesson, allows the student an alternate strategy of study, and gives the teacher time for clerical duties. A 5-minute follow-up at the end of the period permits student feedback to ensure understanding, provides feedback to the teacher, and gives students a few minutes to neaten the area around their desks and get ready to go to the next class.

Tolerance for Struggling Students

Not all students learn at the same speed or level of comprehension. Projecting patience and tolerance rather than ignoring the slower students creates a positive learning climate. Be flexible by answering questions several times if necessary, give various examples, be patient with the slow learner, and look for signs of student understanding by "reading" facial expressions; all these actions are shown by a caring classroom teacher.

Feedback to all students is important, but especially to the struggling student. Return student work quickly so students can correct their mistakes before moving to new material. Provide frequent positive feedback for the class. "Good effort," "That was a creative approach," "It is great to see so many responses," and "I would like to return to that response in a moment" all are encouraging replies to student answers. The class will eventually pick up the positive messages from the teacher and mirror the respect given to even the slowest of students.

Discipline

Discipline probably is the topic most written about yet least understood. It deals with the interpersonal skills of the instructor and the diverse character traits of student dynamics. Students in a classroom are constantly testing the waters as soon as the opportunity allows.

Always prevent an open confrontation between yourself and a student. Students are very sensitive about being lectured in front of their peers, and many students will back the offending student regardless of the infraction simply because she is a fellow student. Offer an opportunity for the disruptive student to save face by suggesting an after-class discussion. This limits the possibility of a classroom confrontation, avoids any put-downs and student embarrassment, opens up a line of communication outside class, and allows reconciliation later.

Learn to prioritize disturbances. If students view the teacher as overreactive, they see what buttons they can push. Appear as calm as possible (regardless of internal stress) to reflect a stable image.

There are no guarantees, but a low-key approach lends itself to a more pleasant classroom environment. Demonstrating a willingness to negotiate without compromising the students' self-worth or your level of standards leads to long-term trust between you and your students.

Adaptability

Wouldn't it be great to have a room of gifted enthusiastic students, instant access to technical equipment for innovative instruction, a copy machine available at all times, a classroom set of textbooks and support materials you selected, and air conditioning/heating for proper climate control? The majority of us don't fall into such ideal situations as these. Rather, we find ourselves traveling to different locations across the campus to teach multiple courses in makeshift classrooms to students with special needs—without adequate instructional materials. This situation challenges the creativity of teachers to be as flexible as possible. Prepare to adapt to anything. One thing is certain: a sense of humor is essential for success.

Enlisting a support system and setting up a network for assistance eases the burden of feeling overwhelmed and alone. There are other teachers (mentors, neighbors, department teachers, core members, and colleagues with similar plights) to ask for guidance and help.

Learn to take personal pride and receive self-satisfaction in your efforts. Avoid falling into the negative "poor victim" role expressed by some teachers.

That has a tendency to spill over into the tone and conduct of the instructor and often is picked up by the class. Students need to feel that their class is special.

Summary

Specific techniques and appropriate behavior modification methods have been prescribed in many articles and publications. These are only guidelines. An effective program implements what works with the personality and style of the teacher. One instructor may emphasize a structured environment, while another may provide a less traditional framework. It is important to create a balanced approach to instruction through student participation and dialogue. Students receive messages from their teacher regarding classroom control; they are quick to learn what is allowed by different teachers in each class. They will adapt if consistency and fairness are maintained.

THE ART OF TEACHING

The vignettes in this chapter illustrate the art of teaching required in weaving together knowledge of students and deep understanding of mathematics to be able to initiate, guide, and respond to dynamic situations so that students' mathematics ability may grow. How to frame an instructional sequence? What part(s) to be large-group, small-group, or individual work? When to ask a question? Should answers be oral or written? When to be silent a few more seconds? What to ask next? Who to call on? When to recast a question or another's response? The teacher makes these decisions within a framework of pedagogy that assists but cannot be a prescriptive set of rules to follow.

Eisner has long advocated acknowledging the art and craft of teaching (Eisner, 1983). In researching the classroom actions of successful teachers, Flinders (1989) begins with Eisner's definition of art in the "broad sense to signify engaging, complex, and expressive human activity" (1989, p. 17). Flinders suggest we look for art in teaching in four modes:

1. *Communication.* Oral, written, and nonverbal clues such as eye contact, nods, smiles, leaning forward, or stepping to another space are coordinated to enhance communication.
2. *Perception.* Learning to see and hear students is essential, in addition to formulating a message. Intuitive receptivity demands flexibility and imagination to be able to move with the students to further mathematical understanding.
3. *Cooperation.* "The teachers I observed displayed various strategies for negotiating a co-

operative relationship with their students. Some of these strategies include: (1) using humor and self-disclosure to promote student solidarity; (2) allowing students to choose activities; (3) occasionally bending school and classroom rules in the students' interest; (4) providing opportunities for individual recognition; and (5) creating pockets of time that allow teachers to interact one-to-one with students" (1989, p. 18).

4. *Appreciation.* "The final art of teaching is appreciation" (1989, p. 19). This is something that teachers do. When teachers describe the intrinsic worth of their endeavors in a difficult job well done, this satisfaction is central to the daily work of the classroom.

There is no set of rules on how to be an outstanding teacher; it is not that simple. We are glad it is not. The lack of prescription demands that teaching be creative. The love we have for teaching comes from the excitement of the creative interaction with young people as they move from one place in their intellectual biography to the next. This excitement may not be there daily but it is evident often enough to give you the satisfaction that you have touched lives. Eisner (1983, p. 12) expresses this beautifully:

> The aesthetic in teaching is the experience secured from being able to put your own signature on your own work—to look at it and say it was good. It comes from the contagion of excited students discovering the power of a new idea, the satisfaction of a new skill, or the dilemma of an intellectual paradox that once discovered creates. It means being swept up in the task of making something beautiful—and teachers do make their own spaces and places. They provide, perhaps more than they realize, much of the score their students will experience

Set 7.6 Discussion Questions

 Questions with an asterisk appear in the Message Board section of the Companion Website at **http://www.prenhall.com/huetinck.** Go to Chapter 7 and click on the Message Board to find and respond to the question.

1. Discuss how Kounin's research is reflected in outstanding lesson plans.
2. Enumerate the positive elements of maintaining suitable classroom decorum.
*3. Compare and contrast your understanding of the science of teaching and the art of teaching.

Summary

Communication is at the heart of teaching and learning. Students become better mathematical thinkers as they can communicate coherent mathematical processes through oral or written explanations. By the time students are in high school, they should be good critics and self-critics who are able to use mathematical language accurately. As stated in the NCTM *Principles and Standards for School Mathematics* (2000), students must be able to exchange mathematical ideas effectively "to be prepared for the future."

This chapter suggests many ways of promoting discourse in a community of learners while conducting whole-group discussions, cooperative group work, or individual instruction. All these interactions require careful listening, as well as a variety of methods of encouraging written exchanges. The chapter also details ways to ensure control of the classroom as all move toward achieving this community of learners, since discipline is essential for an exemplary learning environment. The text discusses research and offers vignettes to assist you in developing a coherent personal discipline system. Finally, teaching is more an art than a prescription. We can suggest many methods and best ways of handling certain situations, but you will best know the personality of your students and your strengths and weaknesses. Therefore, you must put these ideas together into a coherent exemplary practice centered in your belief systems.

Communication is used not only to advance student thinking but also for assessment. In a *Mathematics Teacher* article, classroom teacher Kathleen Chapman describes her insights into her students' thinking through their journals. Some students judged able on the strength of their exams really did not have a clear idea of a major theme of the course. In contrast, "journals revealed abilities and mathematical awareness that had been masked by poor grades." She found, "A task ungraded is unheeded" (1996, p. 588–589). With experience, Chapman learned to set standards for journal writing and began using writing as one mode of assessment. Thus, this chapter is a good precursor to the next chapter, which is devoted to assessment.

ASSIGNMENTS

1. Using one of the four Additional Activities that follow, write a lesson plan that includes the question you would use to elicit discussion.

2. Based on your studies of educational psychology, knowledge of yourself, and expectations for your students, write a personal discipline plan that you expect to use when you begin teaching.

3. Develop a case study on one secondary-level student you can observe in a mathematics classroom. For several days observe the student's interactions with other students in the class and with the teacher. Interview the student about her goals and interests in school. Ask the teacher about her impression of this student. Reflect on what you have learned about the student and how this knowledge can inform teaching.

INSTRUCTIONAL RESOURCES

Berkman, R. M. (1994, February). Teacher as "kimp," *Arithmetic Teacher*, 326–328, Reston, VA: National Council of Teachers of Mathematics.

The teacher dons a baseball cap, which turns him into a "kimp," who asks very stupid questions assuming every possible misunderstanding to lead students into communicating precise mathematical thinking. It sounds like a delightful activity.

Chapman, K. P. (1996). Journals: Pathways to thinking in second year algebra. *Mathematics Teacher, 89(7)*, 588–589.

Davis, B. (1996). *Teaching mathematics: Toward a sound alternative*. New York: Garland Publishing.

This book draws on recent developments in a variety of academic fields such as cognitive theory, ecology, and critical discourse to propose how teaching can be reformed to better suit today's social and academic climates. The book's conceptual framework is a matrix with sections on the cultural, institutional, and interpersonal ramifications within each of the five chapters: conceptual underpinnings, subject matter, formal education, cognition, and teaching with illustrative teacher vignettes.

Elliott, P. C. & Kenney, M. J. (Eds.). (1996). *Communication in mathematics K–12 and beyond, 1996 Yearbook*. Reston, VA: National Council of Teachers of Mathematics.

The 28 chapters in this yearbook are grouped into four sections: challenges, value of discourse, writing, and discussing/assessing. Many examples are included of classroom conversations incorporating a variety of classroom-ready teaching ideas.

Johnson, D. (1982). *Every minute counts: Making your math class work*. Palo Alto, CA: Dale Seymour Publications.

This small volume is packed with commonsense ideas for teaching mathematics.

Kenney, M. J., & Hirsch, C. R. (Eds.). (1991). *Discrete mathematics across the curriculum. 1991 Yearbook.* Reston, VA: National Council of Teachers of Mathematics.

Specific ideas for teaching discrete mathematics are discussed for K–8, middle school, and high school, with theory and classroom-ready teaching ideas. Chapters on matrices, graph theory, counting methods, recursion, iteration, induction, algorithms, and project ideas provide an excellent resource for teachers at all levels.

Manouchehri, A., and Enderson, M. C. (1999). Promoting mathematical discourse: Learning from classroom examples. *Mathematics Teaching in the Middle School, 4(4)*, 216–222.

Classroom examples, a vignette, and a discussion of the vignette provide excellent information for enhancing classroom discourse.

Mathematics Teaching in the Middle School, 5(8), 478–546.

This issue explores different aspects of encouraging classroom communication with nine articles: "Never Say Anything a Kid Can Say!" "Word Origins: Building Communication Connections," "Understanding Student Responses to Open-Ended Tasks," "The Role of Definition," "Let's Talk About the Weather: Lessons Learned in Facilitating Mathematical Discourse," "Daily Journals Connect Mathematics to Real Life," "Fostering

Mathematical Thinking Through Multiple Solutions," "Using Counterintuitive Problems to Promote Student Discussion," and "Data Analysis Through Discourse."

McDuffle, A. R. (2000). Flying through graphs: An introduction to graph theory. *Mathematics Teacher, 94(8)*, 680–688.

> Four classroom-ready pages to teach graph theory are provided, along with a discussion of prerequisite knowledge required and a teachers' guide. These lessons would be excellent for a teacher just beginning to teach graph theory.

Pereira-Mendoza, L. (1993). What is a quadrilateral? *Mathematics Teacher, 86(9)*, 774–776, Reston, VA: National Council of Teachers of Mathematics.

> The teacher asks, "What is a quadrilateral?" and then draws a figure that fits the definition but is not a quadrilateral. For example, the answer, "a four-sided figure" results in a figure with sides of wavy lines. Through similar activities and imagined telephone descriptions, students learn to communicate concise mathematical definitions.

Thompson, D. R., and Rubenstein, R. N. (2000). Learning mathematics vocabulary: Potential pitfalls and instructional strategies. *Mathematics Teacher, 92(7)*, 568–573.

> A comprehensive list of vocabulary issues and examples is paired with the category of potential pitfalls in teachers using mathematical language that challenges students. The authors do a fine job of reminding us that many mathematically precise terms are seen as such by students. Various strategies can be employed to promote vocabulary development.

Van Zost, L. R. and Enyart, A. (1998) Discourse, of course: Encouraging genuine mathematical conversations. *Mathematics Teaching in the Middle School, 4(3)*, 150–157.

> The authors rightly assert, "Genuine mathematical conversations are rare in most classrooms." The story of the authors' journey to elicit discourse is interesting and instructive.

ADDITIONAL ACTIVITIES

Activity 7.6 Applying Matrices to Networks
Activity 7.7 It's a SNAP
Activity 7.8 The Power of a Matrix
Activity 7.9 Markov Chains

FOR TEACHERS

Activity 7.6 Applying Matrices to Networks

Mathematical Content:
Networks and the power of matrices (PSSM Geometry Standard for Grades 6–8 and 9–12)

Materials:
Problem and calculator

Teacher Directions: Which of the modes of communication discussed in this chapter would you use to facilitate understanding of this activity? Defend your choice.

FOR STUDENTS

Activity 7.6
Applying Matrices to Networks

The points *A, B, C,* and *D* in the diagram represent four rescue teams in a mountainous region, but because of differences in the radios and locations, not every team can communicate directly with every other team. The arrows indicate the possible directions of radio transmissions. For instance, rescue team *D* can communicate directly with rescue team *C,* but not with *A.* Team *D* can communicate with *A* if it uses *C* as a relay.

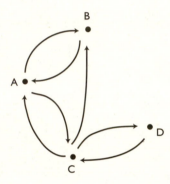

This is an example of a small network. Many networks (such as those involved with telephone communications) are extremely complex, and it is not easy to get the information we want at a glance. We can keep track of this information using an *adjacency* matrix *M,* shown to the right. In the matrix,

1 = direct communication
0 = no direct communication

$$\begin{array}{c} \text{To team} \\ \begin{array}{cccc} A & B & C & D \end{array} \end{array}$$

$$\text{From team} \quad \begin{array}{c} A \\ B \\ C \\ D \end{array} \begin{bmatrix} 0 & 1 & 1 & 0 \\ 1 & 0 & 0 & 0 \\ 1 & 1 & 0 & 1 \\ 0 & 0 & 1 & 0 \end{bmatrix} = M$$

What would the two-step communication matrix look like? We would want a 1 from *A* to *D,* because there is a two-step path $A \rightarrow C \rightarrow D$, which we could get by multiplying the 1 from the path from *A* to *C* by the 1 from the path from *C* to *D*. To this we would add the path through B, obtained as a product in a similar fashion. This "sum of products" sounds a great deal like matrix multiplication, and in fact, that's just what we need to get the two-step communication matrix!

1. Find M^2, the two-step indirect communication matrix.

2. What are the two 2-step paths from *A* to *A*?

3. How many paths from *D* to *B* are shown by the matrix? What points do you go through on these paths?

4. If M^2 gives the number of 2-step paths and *M* gives the number of 1-step paths, matrix $T = M + M^2$ gives the number of paths that take either one or two steps. Find *T.*

5. What does the 3, 2 matrix entry of *T* tell you?

6. One line of communication is still impossible, even with a single relay. Which one?

7. Find the matrix that will give the number of communication paths that take no more than 3 steps.

8. Can all rescue teams communicate with each other if 3 steps are allowed?

9. In the original diagram, *C* can send to *B* but *B* can't send to *C.* What could account for this?

FOR TEACHERS

Activity 7.7 It's a SNAP

Mathematical Content:
Operations and nonnumerical groups (PSSM Algebra Standard for Grades 6–8 and 9–12)

Materials:
Pegboard, rubber bands, activity sheets

Teacher Directions: To help students focus on operations and nonnumerical groups, begin the discussion with the translations of an equilateral triangle. We define the reorientation of the triangle with vertices *A, B,* and *C* as the operation and the triangle vertices as the nonnumerical set, called configurations. Emphasize that the reorientation always begins with the initial configuration. Ask the student how many different orientations are possible (6). For more detail in teaching this lesson, consult *The Mathematics Teacher*, April 1996, pp. 342–346.

FOR STUDENTS

Activity 7.7
It's a SNAP (page 1 of 3)

It's a SNAP is an activity that is played with a board of 9 pegs arranged in a 3-by-3 square array.

Using the three rubber bands and the top two rows of pegs, how many patterns can you make using the following rules?

- Every rubber band connects 1 peg in the top row with 1 peg in the middle row.
- Each peg is included once.

1. Sketch and label the patterns with letters of the alphabet. (There should be six different patterns.)

2. By stretching the rubber bands around the middle pegs, set up one pattern between the top two rows and another pattern (possibly the same) between the bottom two rows. Keep a given rubber band in the same plane; do not twist the rubber bands over each other as they pass around the middle pegs. Do the "SNAP" operation by removing the middle pegs to see the resulting pattern.

Example

3. By this procedure, fill in the following table:

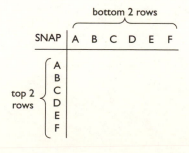

SNAP	A	B	C	D	E	F
A						
B						
C						
D						
E						
F						

F O R   S T U D E N T S

Activity 7.7
It's a SNAP (page 2 of 3)

Definition of a Mathematical Group

Following are the characteristics of a group:

- A group of elements is closed (that is, using the defined operation on any 2 elements yields an element in the group).
- The operation is associative.
- An identity element exists for the set and is the same element for the entire set.
- Each element in the group has a unique inverse.

Now let's see if the elements defined in the table you constructed define a mathematical group:

- Closure is satisfied since all SNAP operations give an element in the group.
- SNAP operations are associative, as can be seen in this example:

$(A$ SNAP $B)$ SNAP $C = E$ SNAP $C = B$
A SNAP $(B$ SNAP $C) = A$ SNAP $E = B$

- The identity is D, as shown in the table.
- With the SNAP operation, each of $A, B, C,$ and D is its own inverse. E is the inverse of F, and F is the inverse of E, so each element has a unique inverse.

Therefore, a group is defined by "It's A SNAP."

4. Is the SNAP operation commutative?

5. What can you conclude about groups and the commutative property?

FOR STUDENTS

Activity 7.7
It's a SNAP (page 3 of 3)

Additional Problems

1. The symmetries for the illustrated geometric figure are:

R_1 = rotation of 72 degrees
R_2 = rotation of 144 degrees
R_3 = rotation of 216 degrees
R_4 = rotation of 288 degrees
I = rotation of 360 degrees

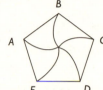

Due to the shape of the curves in the pentagon, the figure cannot be reflected about an axis.

a. Fill in the following table:

	I	R_1	R_2	R_3	R_4
I					
R_1					
R_2					
R_3					
R_4					

b. Are the conditions of a group met?

2. Does the following table define a group?

	I	A	B	C	D
I	I	A	B	C	D
A	A	C	D	B	I
B	B	I	C	D	A
C	C	D	A	I	B
D	D	B	I	A	C

3. Determine the possible symmetry operation for the following figures, and write out the corresponding tables. Do the tables form groups?

Source: *Mathematics Teacher*, National Council of Teachers of Mathematics, Reston, VA, April 1996. Reprinted with permission.

F O R   T E A C H E R S

Activity 7.8 The Power of a Matrix

Mathematical Content:
Directed graphs and matrix powers (PSSM Algebra Standard for Grades 9–12)

Materials:
Problems, graphing calculator

Teacher Directions: To understand this fascinating set of problems, you will have to work them completely. Quite possibly it would take over one class period to complete these problems. What teaching techniques and modes of communication would you use in teaching this material? Be specific in your description, including questions to ask, answers expected, and communication modes.

F O R   S T U D E N T S

Activity 7.8
The Power of a Matrix (page 1 of 5)

An ecosystem is the system formed by a community of organisms and their interaction with their environments. The diagram below shows the predator-prey relationships of some organisms in a willow forest ecosystem.

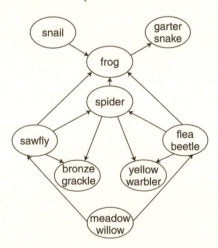

Willow Forest Ecosystem

Such a diagram is called a **food web**. An arrow goes from one species to another if one is food for the other. So, for example, the arrow from spider to yellow warbler means that spiders are food for yellow warblers.

Pollution can cause all or part of the food web to become contaminated. In this investigation you will explore how contamination of some species spreads through the rest of the food web.

1. First, think about the predator-prey relationships.

   a. Does the arrow from sawfly to spider mean that sawflies eat spiders or that sawflies are food for spiders?

   b. Spiders are food for which species? For which species are frogs food?

   c. The arrows are a very important part of this diagram. What are some ways to remember the meaning of the arrows?

2. Now think about the effects of pollution on the ecosystem.

   a. Suppose that all the frogs are contaminated by a toxic chemical that washes into the stream in which they live. Based on the predator-prey relationships shown in the food web, which other species in the ecosystem will be contaminated?

   b. If the sawflies are contaminated by a pesticide, which other species will subsequently be contaminated? Explain.

F O R   S T U D E N T S

Activity 7.8
The Power of a Matrix (page 2 of 5)

c. How far will the contamination spread if it starts with the yellow warblers?

d. Explain how the answers to parts (a)–(c) can be found by considering paths through the food web diagram.

The food web can be viewed as a ***directed graph***, or ***digraph***, where the vertices are the species and the edges are the arrows. You saw in part (d) of Problem 2, how finding paths through the digraph helps answer questions about the spread of contamination. Using matrices can help find paths.

3. The first step to finding paths is to construct the ***adjacency matrix*** for the food web digraph. The adjacency matrix is constructed by listing the vertices down the side and across the top of a matrix. Then write a 1 or a 0 for each entry of the matrix depending on whether or not the vertices are ***adjacent***; that is, whether or not there is a single arrow (directed edge) *from* the vertex along the side *to* the vertex along the top.

a. Construct the adjacency matrix for the food web digraph. Your teacher may have one started for you to complete.

b. Compare your matrix with the matrix constructed by other groups. Discuss and resolve any differences in your matrices so that everyone agrees upon the same matrix.

4. The adjacency matrix tells you if there is an edge from one vertex to another. An edge from one vertex to another is like a path of length 1. Now think about paths of length 2. A **path of length 2** from one vertex to another means that you can get from one vertex to the other by moving along two directed edges.

a. Examine the partially-completed matrix provided by your teacher, which shows the number of paths of length 2 in the food web digraph.
- Explain why the spider/garter-snake entry is a 1.
- Explain why the meadow-willow/garter-snake entry is a 0.
- Explain why the meadow-willow/frog entry is a 2.

b. Complete the matrix.

c. Compare your matrix with those constructed by other groups. Discuss and resolve any differences, so that everyone has the same matrix.

d. Enter the original adjacency matrix (which shows paths of length 1) into your calculator or computer software. Check that you have entered all the numbers correctly. With your group, make and test conjectures about ways to obtain the paths-of-length-2 matrix from the paths-of-length-1 matrix. If you don't find a way that works, check with another group.

5. a. Propose a method for using matrix multiplication to find the matrix that shows paths of length 3 in the food web digraph.

b. Carry out your proposal. Check several entries in your proposed length-3 matrix by examining the digraph to see if the entries really correspond to paths of length 3.

c. If matrix A is the adjacency matrix from the food web digraph, what does A^3 tell you about paths in the food web digraph?

Activity 7.8
The Power of a Matrix (page 3 of 5)

	Beetle	Frog	Grackle	Sawfly	Snail	Snake	Spider	Warbler	Willow
1-way Beetle									
Frog									
Grackle									
Sawfly									
Snail									
Snake									
Spider									
Warbler									
Willow									
2-way Beetle									
Frog									
Grackle									
Sawfly									
Snail									
Snake									
Spider									
Warbler									
Willow									
3-way Beetle									
Frog									
Grackle									
Sawfly									
Snail									
Snake									
Spider									
Warbler									
Willow									

Activity 7.8
The Power of a Matrix (page 4 of 5)

6. Suppose that the meadow willows are contaminated by polluted groundwater. They in turn contaminate other species that feed directly or indirectly on them. However, at each step of the food chain, the concentration of contamination decreases. Suppose that species more than two steps from the meadow willow in the food web are no longer endangered by the contamination.

  a. Which species are safe?

  b. How can the matrices A and A^2 be used to answer this question? Explain your reasoning.

You have seen that powers of an adjacency matrix give you information about paths of certain lengths in the associated vertex-edge graph. This connection between graphs and matrices is useful for solving a variety of problems. For example, it is often very difficult to accurately and systematically rank players or teams in a tournament. A vertex-edge graph can give you a good picture of the status of the tournament. The corresponding adjacency matrix can help determine the ranking of the players or teams. Consider the following situation.

The second round of a city tennis tournament involved six girls, each of whom was to play every other girl. However, the tournament was rained out after each girl had played only four matches. The results of play were the following:

- Emily beat Keadra.
- Anne beat Julia.
- Keadra beat Anne and Julia.
- Julia beat Emily and Maria.
- Maria beat Emily, Catherine, and Anne.
- Catherine beat Emily, Keadra, and Anne.

The problem is to rank the girls at this stage of the tournament, with no ties.

F O R   S T U D E N T S

Activity 7.8
The Power of a Matrix (page 5 of 5)

7. The first step in solving this problem is to find useful mathematical representations of the situation.

   a. Represent the results of the tournament at this stage with a matrix of 0s and 1s. A 1 should show that the player represented by the row beat the player represented by the column. For convenience, list the girls alphabetically.

   b. Think of the matrix as an adjacency matrix for a digraph, and draw the digraph.

   c. Compare your matrix and digraph with those of other groups. Does everyone's matrix and digraph show that Catherine beat Keadra? That Keadra beat Julia? Make sure that your matrix and digraph contain the same information about the results of the tournament as those of your classmates.

   d. Is it possible for two matrices or two digraphs to look different, yet both accurately represent the results of the tournament? Why or why not?

8. You now have two mathematical models of the tournament, namely, a graph and a matrix. Based on an examination of these models:

   a. If you had to rank one girl in first place right now, who would you choose? (Do not rank beyond first place.)

   ■ Give an argument based on the digraph that supports your answer.

   ■ Give an argument based on the matrix that supports your answer.

   b. Find two girls where neither one seems to be ranked clearly above the other.

9. To obtain further information about the performance of the players, sum each row of the adjacency matrix.

   a. What information does Keadra's row sum give you?

   b. Explain how you could use row sums to rank one girl over another.

   c. Based on the row sums, which girls appear tied?

   d. Give an argument for ranking Keadra above Julia.

   e. Give an argument for ranking Julia above Keadra.

10. To help resolve some of the unclear rankings, compute the square of the adjacency matrix.

   a. What do entries in the squared adjacency matrix tell you about the tennis tournament?

   b. What information does Keadra's row sum in the squared adjacency matrix give you?

   c. Investigate using row sums of the squared adjacency matrix to help rank the girls.

   ■ Have any ties or unclear rankings been resolved?

   ■ Do any ties remain?

F O R   T E A C H E R S

Activity 7.9 Markov Chains

Mathematical Content:
Powers of matrices and Markov chains (PSSM Algebra Standard for Grades 9–12)

Materials:
Problems, calculator

Directions: Matrices, graphs, probability, and systems of equations are connected in this activity investigating applications such as weather forecasting through Markov chains. This excellent culminating activity from The University of Chicago Mathematics Project, *Pre-calculus and Discrete Mathematics*, leads students through solving interesting real-world problems with matrices. This activity would have to be taught as part of a comprehensive unit on matrices. It illustrates only possible extensions of matrices and digraphs for a high-school curriculum.

F O R   S T U D E N T S

Activity 7.9
Markov Chains (page 1 of 6)

In this lesson, graphs and powers of matrices are combined with probability, limits, and systems of equations in a display of the interconnectedness of mathematics. The ideas of this lesson have wide applicability. We begin with an example involving weather.

Suppose that weather forecasters in a particular town have come up with data, represented in the following graph, concerning the probabilities of occurrence of mostly sunny days (*S*), rainy days (*R*), and mostly cloudy days (*C*).

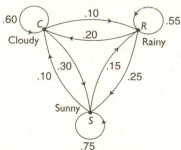

Interpret this directed graph as follows. The loop about point *C*, labeled .60, means that 60% of the time a cloudy day is followed by another cloudy day. The .10 by edge (*C, R*) means that 10% of cloudy days are followed by a rainy day. The .30 by edge (*C, S*) means that 30% of cloudy days are followed by a sunny day.

Now suppose today is cloudy. What is the weather likely to be two days from now?

F O R   S T U D E N T S

Activity 7.9
Markov Chains (page 2 of 6)

To answer this question, represent the graph by a matrix T, where the rows and columns of T are labeled C, S, and R. The entries of T are probabilities that one type of weather on one day is followed by a particular type of weather the next day. For instance, $t_{23} = .15$ because t_{23} is in row S and column R, and 15% of sunny days are followed by a rainy day.

$$
\begin{array}{c}
\begin{array}{ccc} C & S & R \end{array} \\
\begin{array}{c} C \\ S \\ R \end{array}
\begin{bmatrix}
.60 & .30 & .10 \\
.10 & .75 & .15 \\
.20 & .25 & .55
\end{bmatrix} = T
\end{array}
$$

Notice that each element is nonnegative (since each is a probability), and that the entries in each row add to I. A matrix with these properties is called a **stochastic matrix**. The matrix is indicated with the letter T to indicate that it contains the **transition probabilities** from one time period to the next.

In Lesson 11-5, you saw that the square of the adjacency matrix for a graph represents the number of walks of length 2 from one vertex to another. Here the square of T has a similar interpretation: the elements are the probabilities connecting weather 2 days apart.

$$
T^2 = T \cdot T =
\begin{bmatrix}
.60 & .30 & .10 \\
.10 & .75 & .15 \\
.20 & .25 & .55
\end{bmatrix}
\cdot
\begin{bmatrix}
.60 & .30 & .10 \\
.10 & .75 & .15 \\
.20 & .25 & .55
\end{bmatrix}
=
\begin{bmatrix}
.41 & .43 & .16 \\
.165 & .63 & .205 \\
.255 & .385 & .36
\end{bmatrix}
$$

Notice that the entries in each row still add up to I, so T^2 is also a stochastic matrix. Reading across the first row of T^2 shows that if today is cloudy, there is a 41% chance that it will be cloudy 2 days from now, a 43% chance that it will be sunny, and a 16% chance of rain.

T^2 can be multiplied by itself to yield T^4, which indicates the probabilities of various types of weather occurring 4 days later. Similarly, $T^4 \cdot T^4 = T^8$, and $T^8 \cdot T^2 = T^{10}$. In general, each entry of T^k indicates the probability that one type of weather will be followed by a particular type k days later.

$$
T^4 \approx
\begin{bmatrix}
.27985 & .50880 & .21135 \\
.22388 & .54678 & .22935 \\
.25988 & .49080 & .24933
\end{bmatrix}
$$

$$
T^8 \approx
\begin{bmatrix}
.24715 & .52432 & .22853 \\
.24466 & .52544 & .22990 \\
.24740 & .52295 & .22965
\end{bmatrix}
$$

$$
T^{10} \approx
\begin{bmatrix}
.24612 & .52458 & .22930 \\
.24563 & .52474 & .22962 \\
.24628 & .52426 & .22946
\end{bmatrix}
\approx
\begin{bmatrix}
.25 & .52 & .23 \\
.25 & .52 & .23 \\
.25 & .52 & .23
\end{bmatrix}
$$

FOR STUDENTS

Activity 7.9
Markov Chains (page 3 of 6)

The three rows of T^{10} are almost identical. This means that no matter what the weather is today, there is approximately a 25% chance of a cloudy day 10 days from now, a 52% chance of a sunny day, and a 23% chance of rain.

Weather is dependent on many factors. The key assumption in the model used here is that the probability of a certain type of weather tomorrow is only dependent on the weather today. When a situation can exist in only a finite number of states (above there are 3 states: C, S, and R) and the probability of proceeding from one state to the next depends only on the first state, then the situation is said to be an example of a Markov chain.

Markov chains are named after the Russian mathematician who first studied them, Andrei Andreevich Markov (1856–1922). Markov worked in a variety of areas of mathematics, with his greatest contributions being in the area of probability theory. He developed the concept of Markov chain from the theory of probability and applied it to a study of the distributions of vowels and consonants in Russian literature. His work is frequently considered to be the first research in *mathematical linguistics*, the mathematical study of language structure.

Recall that for the stochastic matrix T on the previous page, T^2 is also stochastic. In general, the kth power of any stochastic matrix is stochastic. This can be seen for the 2nd power of a 2×2 stochastic matrix as follows.

Because the entries in each row add to 1, the matrix has the form

$\begin{bmatrix} x & 1-x \\ y & 1-y \end{bmatrix}$ where $0 \le x \le 1$ and $0 \le y \le 1$. Its square is

$$\begin{bmatrix} x & 1-x \\ y & 1-y \end{bmatrix} \cdot \begin{bmatrix} x & 1-x \\ y & 1-y \end{bmatrix} = \begin{bmatrix} x^2 + y - xy & 1 - x^2 - y + xy \\ xy + y - y^2 & 1 + y^2 - y - xy \end{bmatrix},$$

which is also stochastic.

Furthermore, if a stochastic matrix T has no 0 entries, the rows of T^k will be nearly identical for large k. This indicates that over the long term, the proportions of the occurrences of the different states stabilize. You saw this for T^{10}.

Theorem (Convergence of Powers)

Let T be an $n \times n$ stochastic matrix with no 0 entries.
Then $\lim_{k \to \infty} T^k$ is a stochastic matrix with n identical rows.

Stable populations occur in populations of plants and animals, as the following example illustrates.

F O R   S T U D E N T S

Activity 7.9
Markov Chains (page 4 of 6)

Example: Consider a variety of rose that can have either a pale hue or a brilliant hue. It is known that seeds from a pale blossom yield plants of which 60% have pale flowers and 40% have brilliant flowers. Seeds from a brilliant flower yield plants of which 30% are pale and 70% are brilliant. After several generations of plants, what will be the proportion of pale and brilliant flowering plants?

SOLUTION

The transition matrix for this situation is

$$\begin{array}{c} \\ \\ Flower \end{array} \begin{array}{cc} & Offspring \\ & \begin{array}{cc} Pale & Brilliant \end{array} \\ \begin{array}{c} Pale \\ Brilliant \end{array} & \begin{bmatrix} .6 & .4 \\ .3 & .7 \end{bmatrix} \end{array} = T.$$

Let a and b be the proportion of plants with pale and brilliant flowers, respectively, when the population stabilizes. Then, the proportion of the flowers of the next generation that are pale will be $.6a + .3b$ because .6 of those produced by the pale flowers are pale, and .3 of those produced by the brilliant ones are pale. But since the population has stabilized, the fraction of the next generation that is pale must still be a. This results in the equation

$$.6a + .3b = a.$$

Similarly, the fraction of flowers in the next generation that is brilliant is $.4a + .7b$. Again, since the population has stabilized, the fraction that is brilliant must be b.

$$.4a + .7b = b.$$

To solve the system of two equations, add $-a$ to both sides of the first equation, and $-b$ to both sides of the second:

$$\begin{cases} -.4a + .3b = 0 \\ .4a - .3b = 0 \end{cases}$$

This system has an infinite number of solutions. But if a and b are the proportions of pale and brilliant flowers, then it is also true that $a + b = 1$. Thus the following system must be satisfied.

$$\begin{cases} .4a - .3b = 0 \\ a + b = 1 \end{cases}$$

This has solution $(a, b) = (\frac{3}{7}, \frac{4}{7}) \approx (.43, .57)$. So when the population stabilizes, about 43% of the plants will have pale flowers and 57% will have brilliant flowers.

CHECK

This matches the result obtained by calculating powers of T.

$$T^{10} \approx \begin{bmatrix} .42857 & .57143 \\ .42857 & .57143 \end{bmatrix} \approx \begin{bmatrix} \frac{3}{7} & \frac{4}{7} \\ \frac{3}{7} & \frac{4}{7} \end{bmatrix}$$

After Markov published his theory, his techniques were adopted by scientists in a wide range of fields. Albert Einstein used these ideas to study the Brownian motion of molecules. Physicists have employed them in the theory of radioactive transformation, nuclear fission detectors, and the theory of tracks in nuclear emulsions. Astronomers have used Markov theory to study fluctuations in the brightness of the Milky Way and in the spatial distribution of galaxies. Biologists have used Markov chains to describe population growth, evolution, molecular genetics, pharmacology, tumor growth, and epidemics. Sociologists have modeled voting behavior, geographical mobility, growth and decline of towns, sizes of businesses, changes in personal attitudes, and deliberations of trial juries with Markov chains.

FOR STUDENTS

Activity 7.9
Markov Chains (page 5 of 6)

Questions

COVERING THE READING

In Problems 1–4, consider the weather example.

1. a. If it is sunny today, what is the probability of rain tomorrow? **15%**

   b. If it is sunny today, what is the probability of sun tomorrow? **75%**

2. a. If it is rainy today, what is the probability of rain two days from now? **36%**

   b. If it is sunny today, what is the probability of rain four days from now? **≈22.9%**

3. Is T^{10} a stochastic matrix? **Yes**

4. a. In the matrix T^{10}, what does the number .24612 represent?

   b. What is the significance of the fact that the rows of T^{10} are nearly identical? **a) See margin. b) No matter what the weather is today, the probabilities for the weather in 10 days are about the same.**

In Problems 5–7, consider the rose example.

5. If a rose is brilliant, what is the probability that its offspring are brilliant? **0.7**

6. If a rose is pale, what is the probability that its offspring are pale? **0.6**

7. Using $T^{10} = \begin{bmatrix} \frac{3}{7} & \frac{4}{7} \\ \frac{3}{7} & \frac{4}{7} \end{bmatrix}$, calculate T^{20} and explain your result.

APPLYING THE MATHEMATICS

8. At each four-month interval, two TV stations in a small town go through "ratings week." They try to offer special programs that will draw viewers from the other station. During each period, MBC (Markov Broadcasting Company) wins over 20% of SBS (Stochastic Broadcasting System) viewers but loses 10% of its viewers to SBS.

   a. Draw a graph (like that shown at the beginning of this lesson) to represent the movement of viewers between stations. **See margin.**

   b. Write down the transition matrix. **See margin.**

   c. Using the method of the rose example, find the long-term distribution of viewers watching each station. **MBC: 67%; SBS: 33%.**

FOR STUDENTS

Activity 7.9
Markov Chains (page 6 of 6)

9. The British scientist Sir Francis Galton studied inheritance by looking at distributions of the heights of parents and children. In 1886 he published data from a large sample of parents and their adult children showing the relation between their heights. The following matrix is based on his data. Since he had to use volunteers in his study, he could not be sure that his sample accurately reflected the English population.

$$\begin{array}{c} & & \text{Child} \\ & \text{Tall} \quad \text{Med.} \quad \text{Short} \\ \text{Parent} \begin{array}{c} \text{Tall} \\ \text{Med.} \\ \text{Short} \end{array} & \begin{bmatrix} .53 & .32 & .15 \\ .30 & .34 & .32 \\ .15 & .36 & .53 \end{bmatrix} = T \end{array}$$

According to this matrix

$$T^2 \approx \begin{bmatrix} .399 & .326 & .274 \\ .315 & .327 & .358 \\ .255 & .326 & .419 \end{bmatrix} \text{ and } T^{10} \approx \begin{bmatrix} .321 & .327 & .352 \\ .321 & .327 & .352 \\ .321 & .327 & .352 \end{bmatrix}.$$

a. What proportion of the children of tall parents were short? **15%**

b. Use T^2 to tell what proportion of grandchildren of tall people were short. **27.4%**

c. Use T^{10} to predict the approximate proportion of tall, medium, and short people in the population in the long run. **32.1% tall, 32.7% medium, 35.2% short**

10. Prove for 2×2 matrices: If A is stochastic and B is stochastic, the product AB must be stochastic. **See margin**.

11. Consider the matrix T at the right.

    a. Is T stochastic? **Yes**

    $$\begin{bmatrix} .5 & .5 \\ .4 & .6 \end{bmatrix}$$

    b. Calculate T^2, T^4, T^8, and T^{16}.

    c. Find two numbers a and b such that $vT = v$ where $v = [a \; b]$ and $a + b = 1]$

    d. What do a and b represent? **b–d) See margin.**

Review

12. Find the total number of walks of length 4 which end at v_1 in the directed graph at the right. *(Lesson 11-5)* **24**

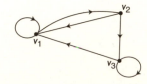

13. In the graph pictured below, determine the number of paths from A to G that contain no circuits. *(Lesson 11-4)* **10**

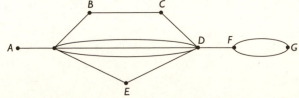

Source: Peressini, A. L., and Others (1992). The University of Chicago Mathematics Project, *Precalculus and Discrete Mathematics*. Glenview, IL: Scott, Foresman and Company. Reprinted by permission.

This chapter emphasizes using formative and summative assessment to provide information on individual student performance. Formative assessments occur on a day-to-day basis, both in direct and indirect ways. Students' oral responses, mathematical discourse overheard when moving around the classroom during group work, and evidence obtained from written classwork and homework are some of the sources teachers use for formative assessment. The main purpose of formative assessment is to provide the student (and perhaps parents/guardians) with the means to make improvements and corrections in mathematical understanding before a major test is given at the end of a unit of instruction. In contrast, summative assessment attempts to summarize the knowledge a student has gained at the conclusion of a unit of instruction.

This chapter deals with two of the four purposes for mathematics assessments identified in the NCTM *Assessment Standards for School Mathematics* (1995). One is the monitoring of student progress, and the other is evaluating students' achievement. In Chapter 10 we will look at using assessments to inform and improve instruction, as well as for program evaluation.

How does a teacher obtain and use information about student understanding of mathematics during the course of instruction and before a more formal end-of-unit assessment is given? The first part of this chapter presents suggestions for eliciting such information. If grades are to be given, as is the norm at most American secondary schools, then they should be a measure of attainment of identified content objectives. The construction of teacher-made tests that are fair and reasonable is addressed in this chapter, as well as issues dealing with grades and student evaluation.

ABOUT THE INVESTIGATIONS FOR THIS CHAPTER

The mathematics content of this chapter is patterns, the discernment of which some mathematicians claim is the link between different mathematical domains. Keith Devlin, Dean of Science of St. Mary's College of California, and the author of the book *Mathematics, the Science of Patterns* (1994), presented the following points to illustrate his view of mathematics during a commencement address to the 1997 mathematics graduates of the University of California at Berkeley:

- Arithmetic and number theory study the patterns of number and counting.
- Geometry studies the patterns of shape.
- Calculus allows us to handle patterns of motion.
- Logic studies patterns of reasoning.
- Probability theory deals with patterns of chance.
- Topology studies patterns of closedness and position.

"Mathematicians of all kinds now see their work as the study of patterns—real or imagined, visual or mental, arising from the natural world or from within the human mind" (Devlin, 1994). The mathematics focus in this chapter is on number patterns in varying contexts.

In *Standards*-based classrooms, the recognition of patterns in mathematics is key to student understanding of and appreciation for mathematics, in its rich and varied aspects. New curricular tools regularly provide pattern-based activities, lessons, and investigations for students. We characterize the activities in this chapter as investigations, since they share a process in which students observe and/or generate data, then look for, describe, and justify generalizations. Many of the investigations found in this chapter use recursive patterns. The PSSM Mathematical Reasoning and Proof Standard is referenced here because of the inductive and deductive

reasoning required when generalizing and verifying patterns. Investigations also tend to be rich in mathematical content, drawing on a variety of skills and concepts. Because they are more complex both mathematically and instructionally than typical exercises or hands-on activities, students generally need more than a single class period to complete them.

The regular use of investigations in the classroom allows you, the teacher, better to assess student conceptual understanding of the key topics in the unit. Through the use of a checklist or other ways of noting student involvement in the discussion of a particular problem, you can identify areas of student confusion or lack of comprehension. This enables you to address those areas, either individually or with the entire class, before the summative assessment.

FORMATIVE ASSESSMENT: MONITORING STUDENT PROGRESS

Before we look at specific suggestions for monitoring student progress, we need to note some essential differences in assessment of students in *Standards*-based programs in contrast with past practices. Throughout the school year, students in *Standards*-based programs should be aware of the mathematical goals and the performance levels that are expected. Clearly stated content goals should go beyond computational proficiency and include ability to demonstrate understanding and use of the language and symbols of each mathematical domain studied. In many of the traditional textbooks, lesson objectives are couched in behavioral terms and tend to emphasize procedural knowledge. Of primary importance in *Standards*-based curricula is the student's ability to apply mathematical tools to routine and nonroutine problems, not only in pencil-and-paper testing situations but in carrying out mathematical investigations.

Two-way communication between teacher and student, whether oral or written, is necessary to formative evaluation. In most traditional programs, this communication was limited to checking homework and answering individual questions during seatwork time. From our experience, most of those questions, not surprisingly, were about procedures used to arrive at the correct answers to exercises. This procedural emphasis in school mathematics in the United States was verified in the TIMSS report through data obtained on student questionnaires and by analysis of typical American lessons by university mathematicians. In contrast, *Standards*-based curricula stress in-depth reasoning about the overall structure of mathematics, help students make connections among mathematical topics, and have students practice the processes mathematicians use to approach and solve nonroutine problems. Appreciation of the role of mathematics in society and as a discipline also is promoted in *Standards*-based programs.

The Role of Homework

Determining whether and how to use homework in formative assessment can be tricky. In his synthesis of homework research, Cooper (1989) reviewed 100 research reports and 100 conceptual articles. In general, he found many gaps in the research. For example, he found no study comparing a feedback strategy for homework with a no-feedback strategy. However, some generalizations from his study are useful. For example, for middle-school students, more homework than 2 hours a night resulted in no improvement in achievement. On the other hand, there was a direct correlation between time spent on homework and grades obtained for high-school students, with the only upper limit being the time available in a day. The correlation between homework and grades at the high-school level needs to be reiterated clearly to students at the onset of each year.

Conflicting demands on students' time and energy are very real in our culture. Another relevant statistic from the TIMSS report is that American students tend to work more hours at jobs during high school than do their counterparts in most high-performing countries. Up to 10 hours per week actually had a positive correlation with grades, but when work ate up more than 10 hours, grades tended to show a downturn. One might speculate that students who worked a few hours found it necessary to manage their time better so that they could continue to maintain high-quality schoolwork, whereas students working more hours simply could not find adequate time to devote to homework, even when they were motivated. In any case, the value of spending individual time outside class not only in working exercises in a cursory fashion but also in reflecting on more thought-provoking problems and approaches needs to be reinforced frequently.

Cooper suggests some guidelines for homework policy, based on his findings. First and foremost, homework should never be given as punishment. Second, and pertinent to this chapter, the purpose of homework should be to diagnose individual learning problems. Third, in general, all students in the same class will be responsible for the same assignment.

Cooper goes on to assert that homework assignments should not be used to teach complex skills. Rather, they should be a combination of practice and review of material already covered and simple introduction to material about to be covered. A combination of skill review and applications of learned skills in different situations is recommended. He suggests a mixture of both mandatory and voluntary homework, with the caveat that voluntary homework should be intrinsically interesting. As quoted in *Newsweek* (Begley, 1998), Gary Griffin of Teachers College states, "Homework should be an opportunity to engage in creative, exploratory activity." More examples of alternative forms of assessment, some of them to be completed outside of class, will be considered in Chapter 10. Examples of voluntary homework assignments are extension problems included in many of the exemplary curricula described in Chapter 4. There is a qualitative difference between these problems and those expected to be successfully completed by all students. However, since all students have the right to work on their own to achieve greater proficiency and depth of understanding of a topic through such extensions, anyone may attempt them.

Management of Homework

We will suggest some management techniques that we have used for recording homework as well as the use of homework for diagnosing individual student difficulties. Many American teachers typically begin a class period by going over homework. While in some ways this is an efficient use of teacher and student time, it can lead to certain situations that impede student learning. For example, we have seen classes in which half or more of the period is devoted to discussing the previous night's homework. This practice, if it happens regularly, may result in less individual student perseverance on difficult problems, knowing that the teacher always does them in class the next day. Practically speaking, using so much of the period to go over homework also takes away from the time to present the lesson and check for understanding before the students leave with the next homework assignment. The following day students arrive truly needing more help. There is the potential of continuing in a cycle that is ultimately detrimental to the purpose of homework—to function as independent work that can be successfully completed by most of the students who were present during the lesson or instructional sequence.

Some teachers use a rubber stamp to mark students' papers at the beginning of the period to indicate that they completed the homework assignment, at least on quick examination. This strategy is nonjudgmental in that the quality of the homework is not assessed, yet it provides a measure of accountability that is lacking sometimes if students copy most of their homework problems while the class is going over homework. A teacher may stamp both the top of the homework paper and below the last completed problem. Then, in the space below the second stamp, students can copy problems they did not understand as they are discussed in class. In the same vein, some teachers have students do their homework in pencil and write any corrections in ink.

The practice of students exchanging and correcting papers still is effectively maintained in some classrooms. Of course, this is possible only in checking and correcting short answers. Some teachers have students go over their homework in small groups, helping one another with problems not completed at home. On occasion, we have collected the previous night's homework immediately after class begins, without going over any problems, and then spot-checked a few crucial exercises or problems in the homework to assess the level of understanding of individual students. This is most effective, although more time-consuming, when combined with brief comments written on the papers of students having difficulty. Collected homework containing comments must be returned promptly, however, in order for the feedback to be useful to students.

As a time management strategy, some teachers collect homework once a week in a packet and return it in the same way. This works best when students are given answers to selected problems daily and are motivated to work each day on homework, not waiting until the night before the homework is due to complete the entire packet. Without feedback, however, any homework checking and marking may become a practice in assessing quantity, not quality, and the use of homework as a means of obtaining information about individual student performance in order to provide intervention prior to a formal assessment is not met.

In short, there is no one best way to use homework as a formative assessment tool for individual students, but taking some time to go over homework papers is necessary.

Many math teachers now have their own Web sites. This makes it possible for their students with on-line access to confirm homework assignments. Additional teacher-designed activities can be put on their Web site, and links to specific topics may be made available through that medium. Chapter 11 provides more specific suggestions regarding the use of the Internet to help students and parents access various mathematics resources. Publishers also maintain Web sites specific to their textbooks. Frequently these Web sites offer homework assistance to students.

Set 8.1   *Discussion Questions*

Questions with an asterisk appear in the Message Board section of the Companion Website at *http://www.prenhall.com/huetinck.* Go to Chapter 8 and click on the Message Board to find and respond to the question.

*1. When have you been assigned homework that helped you attain a deeper understanding of the material you were studying? Be specific. What made the assignment meaningful and challenging?

2. Select a textbook that is commonly used in your area. Go online to the publisher's Web site, and examine the electronic resources the publisher provides teachers, students, and families. Report your findings to the class.

Gathering and Interpreting Evidence

What other classroom practices help a teacher identify individual barriers toward attaining the mathematics learning goals of the class? The *Standards* and other reform documents emphasize the development of self-reliant students who take responsibility for their own learning. Student self-assessment and self-evaluation can be encouraged as a means to this goal.

Sometimes self-assessment is part of a learning log or journal kept by the student. Logs and journals as components of teacher-student communication are covered in much more detail in Chapter 7. For the purposes of this chapter, we will note that some teachers have a practice of using the last 5 minutes of a class for students to write a journal entry describing what they understood from the lesson and what they needed help with. The teacher collects the journals periodically, reads the entries, and responds with comments to the students. Sometimes, student feedback is written at the conclusion of the homework, to be read by the teacher each day when checking the homework. In either case, these entries are confidential, to be read only by the teacher and not to be discussed in class, except in general terms. Investigation 8.1 has students use the recursive features of calculators to reveal patterns. Note the directions to the students to describe the process they used. If you use this activity in the classroom, we suggest having students demonstrate their process by using the display device.

Stallings and Tascione (1996) provide a framework that Tascione and her students developed collaboratively to use to guide self-assessment. It includes the following parameters:

1. proper procedure;
2. evidence of work;
3. neatness and legibility;
4. correct answer;
5. effort and/or understanding.

The first four items were ones the students in the class originally identified. They reflect the students' conceptions of mathematics upon entering the class and are quite consistent with TIMSS students' responses showing their perception of mathematics as essentially procedural. The fifth item deals with conceptual understanding. This item was suggested by the teacher and agreed upon by students after a class discussion as a primary element of assessment. To have evidence for the five items, after a major assignment or a test, students write about the extent to which they did or did not meet high standards in the five areas. Not surprisingly, Tascione's students had the most difficulty responding to the fifth item, sometimes confusing procedural correctness with conceptual understanding or believing they had made a trivial mistake when, instead, the mistake indicated to the teacher a deeper lack of clarity about the mathematical underpinnings of the problem that was missed.

The opportunity for students to express themselves and defend their reasoning provides additional information beyond the test itself that the teacher can use when assigning grades. Students' grades might be raised if they were able to show their deeper understanding of the material through written explanations. This format allows the teacher to see how a student perceives the extent to which his performance meets the class goals. Further, access to students' self-assessments gives the teacher insight about a student's mathematical strengths and weaknesses that are not evident through other means.

Some teachers use individual and/or group quizzes as tools for formative assessment. Such quizzes cover only one or two major concepts from a unit of study and can inform both teacher and students as to the degree of understanding of those concepts. Figure 8.1 provides examples from a quiz that was given during an Algebra I unit on simple functions. This assessment was used to determine whether students mastered the concepts related to distance/speed/time graphs through activities using CBLs (calculator-based laboratories) and motion sensors, similar to Activity 4.5 in Chapter 4. Work through the quiz, putting yourself in the place of a student in

a *Standards*-based classroom where technology was used effectively to support the mathematics.

Many informal ways of assessing individual understanding occur in *Standards*-based classrooms. When students are working in groups, simple checklists can be used to obtain evidence of individual students' dispositions toward mathematics. Figure 8.2 shows a sample checklist from the NCTM *Curriculum and Evaluation Standards* (1989, p. 235).

A favorite problem that relies on visualization and numerical patterns associated with geometric shapes is the Painted Cubes problem. We have seen many variations of this basic problem. The particular version in Investigation 8.2 comes from *Wonderful Ideas* (Janes, 1994–95).

Set 8.2   *Discussion Question*

1. Suppose you are using the Painted Cubes investigation as group work in a class. Make a list of actions you would observe in order to determine whether students are working effectively together toward a correct solution to the problem.

Many teachers offer individual help to their students outside of class time, such as before school, during lunch, or after school. Students who work with the teacher on such a basis provide an excellent opportunity for two-way feedback. This means more than simply showing a student how to approach a given problem or master a procedure. It means first asking the student what he already understands, where he feels unsure of himself mathematically, and what he thinks the teacher might do to help him meet the learning goals of the class. Again, the goal is for the student to develop independent learning, including knowing where and how to ask for assistance.

As stated in the NCTM *Assessment Standards for School Mathematics* (1995), effective monitoring of student progress requires clarity about several criteria:

- the mathematics to be learned;
- the kinds of evidence necessary to describe students' progress in learning that mathematics;
- the variety of equitable assessment methods and tools available to collect evidence of students' learning;
- the criteria for interpreting that evidence and making valid inferences about what students are learning;
- how those interpretations are to be communicated to students in ways that support the achievement of instructional goals (p. 44).

Figure 8.1
Sample Quiz: CBL Motion Graphs

Part I. Answer the following questions in the space provided. Use the graphs to help.

1. What do you do to create a horizontal line on a time-distance graph?

____

____

2. How do you create a straight line that slopes up?

____

____

3. How do you move so the graph goes up steeply at first, and then continues up gradually?

____

____

4. Which object is moving faster? ___________
What does the intersection of the two lines mean?

____

____

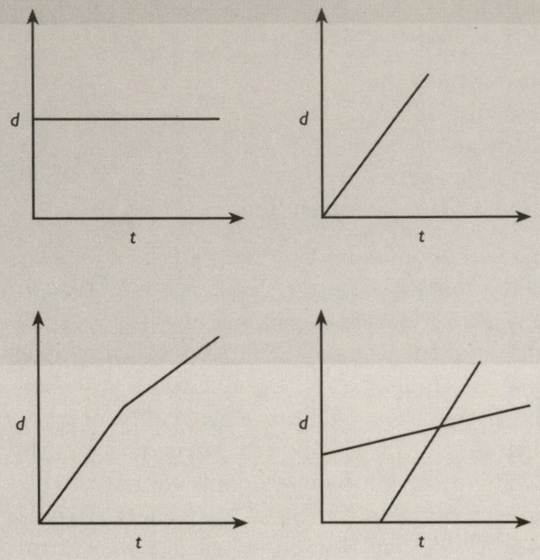

Part II. Sketch a graph of the scenario described. Label the axes with the appropriate name and scale (Distance, Time, Speed, etc.).

5. You are walking down the street from home at a steady pace, stop for a few minutes to look at the new houses that are being built, and then turn around and walk right back home.

6. John is riding his bicycle up a hill, then rides at a steady pace for a few minutes, speeds down the hill, and comes to a sudden stop.

7. You are rocking back and forth in a rocker in front of the TV set.

8. Your mother is driving you to school. On the way she stops once at a red light. When she comes to the school zone, she slows down. When she gets to the school driveway, she stops and lets you out. She drives away at a safe speed.

Source: Adapted from materials developed by Robin Rubenstein, Presidential Awardee from Nevada.

Figure 8.2
Mathematical Disposition Checklist

Grades 5–8

In the middle grades, students' mathematical dispositions become more apparent in their daily work. A checklist of actions that demonstrate mathematical disposition can be used to help record students' progress. Such a checklist can be completed by a teacher while focusing on five students during a class period. Over six weeks, each student's mathematical disposition can be evaluated at least once. A sample checklist is given below.

Mathematical Disposition Checklist

Name					
	Student 1	**Student 2**	**Student 3**	**Student 4**	**Student 5**
Date: **Action Observed**					
Confidence: Initiates questions.	✓		✓	✓	
Is sure answers will be found.		✓	✓	✓	
Helps others with problems.	✓			✓	
Other/note:				*Challenged the solution of another student*	
Flexibility: Solves problems in more than one way.	✓	✓			
Changes opinion when given a convincing argument.			✓	✓	
Other/note:		*created new problem by changing cond.*			

Source: National Council of Teachers of Mathematics, (1989). *Curriculum and Evaluation Standards for School Mathematics,* Reston, VA: The Council. Reprinted with permission.

Set 8.3   Discussion Question

 Questions with an asterisk appear in the Message Board section of the Companion Website at *http://www.prenhall.com/huetinck.* Go to Chapter 8 and click on the Message Board to find and respond to the question.

*1. Recall a class you attended in which you were aware of the teacher's efforts to obtain formative assessment information about you as an individual. Describe the techniques used by the teacher and the extent to which you believe the teacher was able to help you improve your understanding and achievement of the content through these means.

F O R   T E A C H E R S

Investigation 8.1 Iteration All Over Again

Mathematical Content:
Recursion, exponential growth, irrational numbers
(PSSM Algebra Standard for Grades 9–12)

Materials Needed:
Activity sheets, graphing calculators

Directions: Work through this investigation as a student would. Then, develop a short prompt to assess the main concept of the lesson. Assume that students may use calculators with recursive features during the quiz.

F O R   S T U D E N T S

Investigation 8.1
Iteration All Over Again (page 1 of 2)

Explore the recursive nature of your calculator by pressing the indicated keys. Describe the resulting patterns.

5 (enter) + 3 (enter) (enter) (enter) (enter)

3 (enter) × 5 (enter) (enter) (enter) (enter)

See if the same procedure works for other operations, including powers and roots.

Since calculators vary, you need to know the extent to which your calculator can perform these repeated procedures. They will save you time when used correctly.

Iteration is the word used to describe the process of applying a mathematical procedure over and over again, using the previous answer to generate the next answer. When working with functions, you begin with $f(x)$, and the next iteration is $f(f(x))$, then $f(f(f(x)))$, and so on. The following exercises are intended to be worked using calculators with iterative features.

1. Each year, on your birthday, your grandfather deposits $100 into a savings account that pays 10% per year, simple interest. If he began when you were born, how much money would be in your account when you turned 18? Describe the process you used to determine your answer, and show the yearly amounts.

2. One of the fastest-growing urban areas in the country is Las Vegas, Nevada. In 1980 its population was 164,670, and in 1990 its population was 258,670 (source: *World Almanac*), an annual growth rate of about 4.6%. Use iteration on your calculator to estimate the population of Las Vegas in 2000 if the same growth rate continued. Describe the process you used to determine your answer, and show the yearly amounts.

3. A historical way of approximating square roots can be easily replicated with the repeating functions of a calculator. It involves successive averaging. For example, say we are trying to find the square root of 40. We select any number between 1 and 40 to begin the process—say, 5. We then have the calculator find the average of that number and the quotient of 40 divided by that number. It looks something like this on the calculator:

5 (enter)

.5(ans + 40/ans)

F O R   S T U D E N T S

Investigation 8.1
Iteration All Over Again (page 2 of 2)

When you try it on your calculator, the values should quickly appear to approach the "black hole" of 6.3245. . . . This is an excellent approximation of $\sqrt{40}$, as you can check by using the square root key. Try this procedure on another positive integer, and show the results of the first 10 iterations.

4. Try this iterative procedure:

1 (enter)

1/(1 + ans) (enter)

Continue to press (enter), counting the steps until the first five digits are exactly repeated. This pattern converges around a value often called the Golden Ratio, a mathematical characteristic of what is said to be the most artistically pleasing rectangle. See the diagram below showing the geometric characteristics of such a rectangle. A possible research project is exploring the use of the Golden Rectangle for thousands of years by architects, sculptors, and painters.

The mathematical characteristics of the Golden Ratio can be shown by developing a set of geometric figures based on a square with side length of 1 unit inscribed in a semicircle. All values are approximate, rounded to the nearest thousandth. The 1×0.618 rectangle and the 1.618 rectangle are both Golden Rectangles; that is, their corresponding sides form a "reciprocal ratio" $\frac{1}{0.618} = \frac{1.618}{1}$.

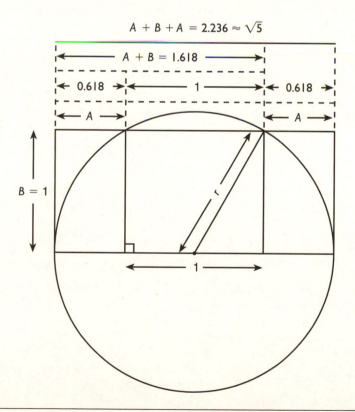

Source: Adapted with permission from a presentation at a math seminar on June 11, 1994, by Tom Walters, Wilson High School, Los Angeles.

SUMMATIVE ASSESSMENT: EVALUATING AND GRADING STUDENT ACHIEVEMENT

This section emphasizes the development and use of teacher-produced tests in *Standards*-based classrooms. Some examples of items from teacher-made tests are given, along with opportunities for you to develop specific types of test items. At the conclusion of this chapter, you will be asked to create a test on a *Standards*-based unit of study. Later, in Chapter 10, alternative assessment techniques will be explored, including performance assessment. In Chapter 10 we also will discuss the ubiquitous reality of standardized tests and how to deal with them in the classroom, since their primary uses are for external comparisons and program evaluation.

Promoting Balance Through Tests

College Preparatory Mathematics: Change From Within Assessment Handbook, Math 1 (1997) discusses the issue of reconsidering assessment. In courses in which the content focus has moved from facts and procedures to deeper understanding and application of mathematical tools, and where in-struction has changed from the teaching-by-telling mode to a more student-centered mode, assessment also must change. The writers state some possible unfortunate consequences if teachers continue to use only traditional testing in a *Standards*-based course (p. 8):

- Teachers will never know whether students have succeeded in developing problem-solving skills or conceptual understanding.
- Students will be left feeling that, regardless of what we say, the only important mathematics is the manipulation of facts and symbols.
- Advocates of *Standards*-based mathematics programs will not be able to convince others of the value of using a different approach when their students score only slightly higher than their peers on traditional assessment instruments and there is no other evidence of deeper learning.

With those cautions in mind, here are some suggestions to consider when preparing a summative test, based upon our experience.

Test Design and Construction

The purpose of a unit exam is threefold: a learning experience for students, a means of assessment for the teacher to use, and a self-evaluation experience

FOR TEACHERS

Investigation 8.2 Painted Cubes

Mathematical Content:
Surface area, geometric patterns (PSSM Geometry Standard for Grades 6–8)

Materials Needed:
Student activity sheet, at least 27 linking cubes per group, sticky dots, clear transparency film, water-based transparency markers

Teacher Directions: Divide students into groups of 3–4. Each group has a set of the materials listed. Before using sticky dots, make sure they can easily be removed from the linking cubes. Alternatives might be water-based markers or small squares of sticky paper.

Have a 3 × 3 × 3 cube built before the class meets, and hold it up as students work under your guidance to answer the questions. Show students how the sticky dots in different colors can be attached to unit faces of the cube in order to get an accurate count. Remind them to include all faces of the cube in their count, including those on the bottom.

Students enter the responses for the 3 × 3 × 3 cube in the table. They continue to build additional cubes, as needed, to complete the table. Have them write out their discussion of patterns on transparencies and on a group reporting form.

Groups report on a single pattern they found. When all groups have presented their summaries, make sure the key generalizations are clear to all students. As an individual assessment, have students individually find the values for a 6 × 6 × 6 cube.

FOR STUDENTS

Investigation 8.2
Painted Cubes

face

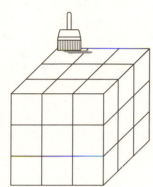

- This is a **unit cube**. It will be used in this Puzzler to build bigger cubes.
- The **face** of a cube is the square side. Every cube has six faces.
  Imagine building this $3 \times 3 \times 3$ cube with 27 unit cubes and then painting the entire outside surface of the cube.

1. After you have painted the cube. . .

  a. How many of the 27 unit cubes have only one face painted?

  b. How many of the 27 unit cubes have exactly two faces painted?

  c. Exactly three faces painted?

  d. Zero faces painted?

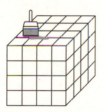

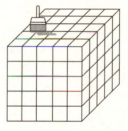

2 x 2 x 2 cube   4 x 4 x 4 cube   5 x 5 x 5 cube

2. Imagine painting the three cubes shown above. Fill in the chart below.

3. For each cube, give the following information:

  a. the number of unit cubes in each larger cube;

  b. the number of unit cubes that have. . .

  - only one face painted;
  - exactly two faces painted;
  - exactly three faces painted;
  - zero faces painted.

4. What patterns can you discover in the chart?

Size	Number of Unit Cubes	Number of Unit Cubes with Paint on Exactly . . .			
		0 Faces	1 Face	2 Faces	3 Faces
$2 \times 2 \times 2$					
$3 \times 3 \times 3$					
$4 \times 4 \times 4$					
$5 \times 5 \times 5$					

Source: Janes, Nancy Segal (Ed.). *Wonderful Ideas*, PO Box 64691, Burlington, VT (nancy@wonderful.com).

for students. The exam should not be feared; rather, it should be seen as an opportunity for students to show what they know and can do.

Keep in mind that published exams included with a textbook will not necessarily reflect your emphases and expectations. A test prepared by you will better match your preestablished curricular goals. The task is simplified by technology now available that allows teachers to create quality tests combining items written by the curriculum developers with teacher-generated items. Some curricular programs provide computer disks of test items that can be modified, while others provide item banks of problems from which to choose in designing a test. In the final analysis, you and your students will be best served by your custom-designed exams tailored for the particular learning experiences of your classroom.

Writing the Test   We suggest waiting to finalize the test until shortly before the test is scheduled, that is, 3 to 4 days prior—not the night before! The exception to this rule of thumb is when using a departmentalized test. Even then, however, you will need to review the test yourself a few days before it is scheduled to determine whether you have given appropriate attention to the emphasized content. As you begin writing your own tests, be aware of any available technology for this purpose, especially software that has mathematics test preparation capabilities such as built-in equation writers. If you do not own such software yourself, your school may have a site license that allows you to use the software on your own computer for professional purposes. In addition to software for producing mathematical symbols and equations, consider using links to graphing calculators to download viewscreens to be electronically pasted onto the test for student reference. A mathematical interpretation of the calculator display allows the creation of items that assess more than the ability to push certain buttons on the calculator. Rather, the student can demonstrate mathematical understanding by interpreting what he sees on the display.

Although writing a test that requires students to show what they know about a given unit of study may seem to be rather straightforward, beginning teachers often are surprised by the results of what they considered a reasonable exam. The first tests that we wrote at the beginning of our careers gave us disappointing results. Observing students during the tests and subsequently grading the tests led us to conclude that our tests were too long and too difficult. Since then, we have often seen new teachers misjudge appropriate length and difficulty of

teacher-developed tests. One way to more accurately gauge your tests is to consider the time an average student needs to complete the test. A general rule that we have used is to take the test "cold" ourselves, completing all the items in the way we expect students to do, and then multiply the time we took by 3. Students become very discouraged when unable to complete tests, particularly when they know the material.

Also related to the actual time needed for students to take the test is the number of pages the test contains. Having many pages of items, even though the number of items is not excessive, tends to discourage students and adds to the complications of test grading. Try to conserve space—wide margins are not needed, and the font used should be a simple one that is readable when relatively small. Allow space to show work, but request that students attach their own paper rather than leaving large areas of work space on the test copy.

To save grading time, provide answer blanks for problems with short answers. Otherwise, students may not clearly indicate their own answers, especially if they are rushing to finish a test. This strategy is especially helpful for multipart problems. If students see a space in which to respond to each of the parts, they are less likely to skip a part.

Further, because a test should fairly assess a student's mathematics knowledge, directions should be clear and concise. It is fair and even desirable to include some problems requiring approaches slightly different from those used in class to demonstrate understanding and not just parroting of demonstrated methods. Also, it is fair to have some problems include extraneous details so that students have to choose the pertinent information to solve them.

Including diagrams, drawings, tables, and graphs can enhance a test, but they should be clear and accurate. Computer drawing tools and clip art for mathematics can be a boon to the teacher, but hand-drawn graphics are quite acceptable when carefully done. Non-mathematical visuals add interest and relevance to problems, and there are many opportunities in geometry, for example, to include such items on a test. An innovative example is shown in Figure 8.3.

Test Content   To provide a range of difficulty appropriate for a majority of class members, include a variety of types of items on the test. A few "enhanced" multiple-choice items, for which students are required to show their work, help students develop test-taking skills that should serve them on standardized assessments. Hart (1994) describes

Figure 8.3

Example of a Non-Mathematical Diagram

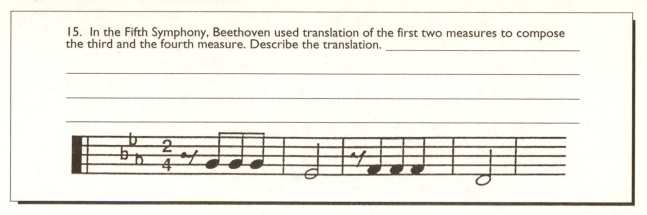

15. In the Fifth Symphony, Beethoven used translation of the first two measures to compose the third and the fourth measure. Describe the translation. _____

_____

_____

_____

an enhanced multiple-choice question as a multiple-choice item that has been improved to make it more than a passive-recall item. Several examples of enhanced multiple-choice items for eighth grade appeared in *A Sampler of Mathematics Assessment*, provided to all California public schools in 1991 by the California Department of Education. An example of an enhanced multiple-choice item follows:

When a number is divided by 7, the remainder is 4. What is the remainder when twice that number is divided by 7?

a. 1 b. 2 c. 3 d. 4

Overall, a test should require students to demonstrate basic recall of important information, use correct mathematical terminology and/or symbols, and apply mathematical tools in contextual situations. The variety of items on the test also should allow for different levels of achievement. Students who have been in class, participated in lessons, and done their homework should be able to get a passing grade. Students whose knowledge exceeds the basic standards of the class should be able to demonstrate their competence by solving more difficult problems, extensions of applications problems, or extra-credit items. One type of item that allows students with deeper content knowledge to show the extent of their knowledge is known as *open-ended*. The example in the next column is an open-ended problem adapted from the same source as the enhanced multiple-choice item.

Imagine that you are at a meeting of the math club, which just concluded selling ice-cream bars to raise funds. Here is a summary of the last sale:

Flavor	Number of Bars Ordered	Number of Bars Sold
Chocolate	375	283
Vanilla	125	119
Strawberry	250	203
Orange	100	74
Lemon	100	56
Cherry	50	50

You are in charge of presenting a plan for the next ice-cream order, based on this information. The leftover bars still are available. The flavors given above are the only choices, but the club does not have to order every flavor. Prepare a presentation to the club in which you justify your plan mathematically. Your plan should include your recommendations and why you think they are best economically for the club. You may use tables and diagrams as well as words in your presentation.

Test Administration and Follow-Through

When conducting a review for a test, help the students focus on those aspects of the unit that are most clearly related to the mathematical objectives for the unit. A review day can be deadly unless students are given some way to use their time productively. One strategy that we have found helpful is to create or select a series of review problems (many texts have a series of review pages) that address the important procedures and concepts of the chapter. Have students work those problems on the chalkboard or on a dry-erase board for classmates to copy and then discuss. The copied problems then become the core material to study for the test. This strategy was most successful when many problems were put on the board at once, by many different students. The goal was maximum involvement by the greatest number of students in the review process. Various game-type activities such as the frequently used formats of bingo and Jeopardy are sometimes used as part of a review.

Begin the test with encouragement to the students. During the test, allow only questions dealing with the test directions themselves. If students have questions about specific items, have them raise their hands quietly and come to your desk so as not to disturb other students. Let students know when half of the period is passed and when 5 minutes remain in the test period. Some teachers plan to devote the last 5 minutes of the test period to reflective time for students to write how they think they performed on the test and why. If you choose to do this, let students know ahead of time, and structure the test and test period to make this practice feasible.

You should decide ahead of time whether students will be allowed to take their exams out of the classroom when their tests are returned. Once an exam leaves the classroom, its security is compromised, yet there is value in having students rework missed items. With the technology for test creation that is available today, it is much easier than in the past to create different, yet equivalent, versions of a unit test and to modify a test each year as instruction varies. We have found considerable value in having students correct mistakes made on exams and give explanations of the sources of their errors, be they computational or conceptual. In some instances, teachers provide a separate form for test correction. This form has two columns: one for the actual work, showing the corrections, and the other an explanation of the original error and an indication of what is now understood about the problem solution that was not clear before. Students should have all tests returned to them in a timely manner and have the opportunity to review their performance.

Set 8.4   *Discussion Question*

Questions with an asterisk appear in the Message Board section of the Companion Website at **http://www.prenhall.com/huetinck.** Go to Chapter 8 and click on the Message Board to find and respond to the question.

*1. If you were going to be assessed for your knowledge of mathematics, which form(s) of assessment from those given below would you choose? Why?

- multiple-choice tests;
- performance assessments (showing knowledge of and ability to use mathematics);
- essays;
- open-ended problems;
- projects;
- other (explain).

Sample Test Items

This part of the chapter gives examples of a variety of test items written by prospective and new teachers for the given content.

The first area of content that we will address is Algebra 1. The first item in Figure 8.4 deals with order of operations. Notice that the item, as written, goes beyond the actual calculation to have students explain their understanding of how the rules apply to this particular exercise. The second part of that item has students apply their understanding in a different context: they know the answer and have to work within the given constraints to make the entire problem correct. The next two items are in an "extended true/false" format with the vocabulary of coordinates and functions as the topic. The directions require students to rewrite the response that makes any false statement true. The final Algebra I item presented in Figure 8.4 uses a fairly typical matching format in which students identify algebraic representations of patterns given in tabular form. Again, the nature of the item requires students to perform some additional calculations and to use reasoning skills, not simply to recall facts. Note that matching tests should *not* have lists of equal length. Varying the list length diminishes elimination and guessing. Also, students may be told that an answer can be used more than once.

The first unit of the *Interactive Mathematics Program* (IMP), Course 1, is entitled "Patterns." In this unit, students learn to discern and describe patterns presented in many different types of situations, both contextual and purely mathematical. A favorite investigation for many of us who have taught this unit is Consecutive Sums (see Investigation 8.3). When given this problem to begin as classwork in groups, many students experienced both discomfort at the expectation that they were going to come up with the patterns on their own and excitement about being able to start working on the problem immediately. In other words, this is a very accessible

Figure 8.4
Sample Teacher-Made Items for Algebra I

4. Consider the following expression: $4 \times 8 - 3(3 + 2)^2 + 8 / 2 \times 2$
   a. Danny evaluated this expression and came up with −41. Do you agree or disagree with his answer? Explain why you agree or disagree.
   b. Where could you put a set of parentheses to arrive at the solution of −41?

True or False: Read each statement very carefully. If you think that a statement is true, circle True. If you think that the statement is false, circle False and write the answer that makes the statement true.

11. The graph of (1, −4) is in Quadrant II.   True / False

12. The inverse of the relation {(4, 0), (9, 2), (−1, −5)} is {(−4, 0), (−9, −2), (1, 5)}. True / False

Match each relation in Column A to the correct equation in Column B.

	A							B
16.								a. $y = 2x - 1$

16.

x	−6	−3	0	3	6	9
y	−2	−1	0	1	2	3

17.

x	−3	−2	−1	0	1	2	3
y	−5	−3	−1	1	3	5	7

18.

x	−6	−3	0	3	6	9
y	−2	−1	0	1	2	3

19.

x	1	−1	0	2	−2	3
y	1	5	3	−1	7	−3

B

a. $y = 2x - 1$
b. $y = 4x + 5$
c. $y = -2x + 3$
d. $y = -4x + 5$
e. $y = 3x$
f. $y = 2x + 1$
g. $y = 1/3x$
h. $y = x + 4$
i. $y = -2x + 1$
j. $y = 2x - 3$

problem that uses simple arithmetic but stresses sophisticated reasoning processes. Contrast that with consecutive integer problems that occur in most traditional Algebra I textbooks.

The three teacher-written test items in Figure 8.5 are related to geometry at the college-preparatory level. The first is a short-answer item that asks students to apply the concept of perimeter to a novel situation, thereby eliciting some reasoning on their part. The second is also a short-answer problem. It requires students to integrate their knowledge of coordinate geometry with knowledge of characteristics of a parallelogram. Note that there is more than one correct solution approach (through showing opposite sides parallel or through showing that opposite sides have the same length). The third item is a more standard proof. However, students can use different proof formats.

Figure 8.5
Sample Teacher-Made Test Items for Geometry

1. A square has sides each measuring 6 cm in length. Describe a rectangle, a triangle, and a regular hexagon that have the same perimeter as the square given. (5 points each)
   a. rectangle

   b. triangle

   c. regular hexagon

2. Martin and Lisa Jefferson wanted the design of their new patio to be made up of colored brick laid out in the shape of parallelograms. They made a pattern for the design on graph paper, as shown below. Is the figure a parallelogram? Justify your answer. (5 pts.)

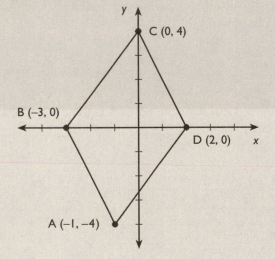

3. In isosceles trapezoid *ABCD*, $\overline{QA}$ bisects ∠*BAD* and $\overline{PD}$ bisects ∠*CDA*. If ∠*BAD* ≅ ∠*CDA* and ∠*B* ≅ ∠*C*, prove each of the following by either 2-column, paragraph, or sentence approach:
   a. Δ*ARD* is isosceles.
   b. Δ*PCD* = Δ*QBA*
   c. Δ*PQR* is isosceles.

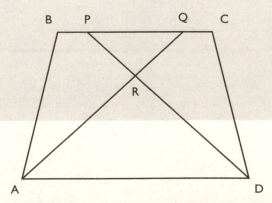

FOR TEACHERS

Investigation 8.3 Consecutive Sums

Mathematical Content:
Patterns in numbers, justification (PSSM Problem
Solving Standards for Grades 6–8 and 9–12)

Materials Needed:
Statement of the problem for each student, 2–3
sheets of large easel paper, several water-
based colored markers for each group

Directions: As a learner, work on this problem
with colleagues. Then develop an assessment
item to be answered individually by students
who have completed this task.

As a teacher, divide students into groups to
work on this investigation. Clarify the directions,
making sure students understand the vocabulary
in the problem, especially the word *consecutive*.
Make sure students are aware that all possible
sums are to be found for each number.

Note that the group is to assign itself homework and come prepared to complete the initial
task the following day. In our experience in doing
this activity with students, many of them have difficulty describing the patterns in words. Rather
than cut the activity short, it is better to continue
into a third day, including a writing activity as
homework the second day. Continue to ask probing questions to elicit student precision in their
descriptions and to have students justify the patterns.

FOR STUDENTS

Investigation 8.3
Consecutive Sums

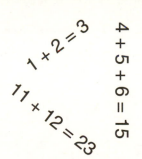

This problem is about **consecutive sums**; that is, sums where the numbers being added differ by 1. Examples of consecutive sums are:

$$2 + 3 + 4, 8 + 9 + 10 + 11, \text{ and } 23 + 24$$

since the numbers 2, 3, and 4 are consecutive; the numbers 8, 9, 10, and 11 are
consecutive; and the numbers 23 and 24 are consecutive.

The sum $3 + 4 + 6$ is not a consecutive sum, because the numbers are not
consecutive. A consecutive sum must have *at least* two terms being added.

Problem: For each number from 1 to 35, find *all* the ways to write it as a consecutive sum.

Explore. Look for patterns. Are there numbers that are easy? Are there any that are impossible?

Note: This is a group activity. Figure out ways that the members of your group can work together.
Near the close of the period, you will be asked to summarize what you have done so far and to assign
yourselves homework.

In two days your group should produce a display of some sort on a large sheet of paper that shows
your results and includes summary statements of *all* the patterns you discovered.

For tonight, your group must assign homework to each member for the group to use tomorrow.

Source: Fendel, Dan, et al. (1997). Patterns Unit, *Interactive Mathematics Program Book 1,* Key Curriculum Press, 1150 65th Street,
Emeryville, CA 94608, 1-800-995-MATH. Reprinted with permission.

Recursive patterns need a clear notation. One of the best-known recursive patterns, partly because of its many manifestations in natural phenomena, is the one named for Fibonacci, who in 1202 wrote a book entitled *Liber abaci*. Investigation 8.4 begins with his famous rabbit problem.

Finally, the two sets of teacher-produced items in Figure 8.6 concern the content area of statistics. The first set uses a true/false format to assess students' understanding of the vocabulary of statistics and probability. As before, this format is extended by having students show how to change false statements into true ones.

Figure 8.6
Sample Teacher-Written Statistics Test Items

True or False (3 points each)
(If a statement is false, indicate how to change the statement into a true statement.)

1. _____ A set of data cannot have more than one mode.
2. _____ An outlier can affect the mean.
3. _____ A compound event consists of one or more simple events.
4. _____ The interquartile range contains 25% of the data.
5. _____ If an experiment is repeated many times and the probability for each event is the same, then the events are equally likely.

Use the graph for Problems 6 and 7.
The following graph represents test scores for a 100-point math test:

Stem	Leaf
4	4 4 5 5 5 9
5	1 2 2 3 4 4 4 6 7 9
6	0 1 1 2 3 3 5 6 8
7	2 7 9 9
8	0 0 2 5
9	0 8

6. Use the information in the stem-and-leaf graph to explain the following statements:
   a. More students scored in the 60s than in the 70s and 80s.
   b. The mode of the scores if 45.
7. Given that your teacher gives grades 90–99 = A, 80–89 = B, 70–79 = C, 60–69 = D, 59 and below = F, use the information to convince your teacher that the test was either too easy or too hard.

FOR TEACHERS

Investigation 8.4 Fibonacci Fauna and Flora

Mathematical Content:
Recursive patterns, Fibonacci numbers, mathematical history (PSSM Connections Standard for Grades 6–8 and 9–12)

Materials Needed:
Activity sheet, quarter-inch graph paper

Directions: Have students work in pairs on this activity. High-school students will need to understand the recursive notation as it related to this sequence. Middle-school students may be more informal, using verbal description of the recursive patterns.

This investigation provides a good opportunity for students to use technology to investigate the real-life applications and history of the Fibonacci sequence. If you choose to extend this investigation beyond what is given on these pages, many resources exist.

 For one of the most comprehensive Web sites on Fibonacci numbers, go to *http://www.prenhall.com/huetinck* and click on Web Destinations for Chapter 8.

FOR STUDENTS

Investigation 8.4
Fibonacci Fauna and Flora

A famous mathematician from the past, Leonardo de Pisa, commonly known as Fibonacci, posed a problem about population growth in rabbits in 1202. Fibonacci made three assumptions about rabbits for his study:

1. It takes a newborn rabbit 2 months to be able to have babies.

2. A male/female pair of rabbits can produce a mixed pair (one male, one female) each month after they mature.

3. Siblings can mate, and no rabbits die during the 1st year.

Fibonacci's well-known question is, "How many pairs of rabbits will there be at the end of each month (until the end of the first year)?"

1. The diagram below shows the pattern to the end of the fourth month. See if you can complete the pattern for the first year.

The pattern you may have noticed is that, after the first month, the next month's total is the sum of the previous 2 months' total. This pattern is called the **Fibonacci sequence**. Here are the first several terms in the sequence:

1 1 2 3 5 8 13 21 34 55 89 144 . . .

The Fibonacci sequence is an example of a **recursive** sequence, that is, a sequence whose terms are given in relation to previous terms. For the nth term, $F_{(n)}$ in the Fibonacci sequence, we could say mathematically that $F_{(n)} = F_{(n-1)} + F_{(n-2)}$

2. Try another example of recursion. Suppose there is a newborn pair of mice, one male and one female. They can have babies in 9 weeks and every 3 weeks thereafter. Suppose they have eight babies each time, four male and four female, and the babies continue the pattern, with none dying. How many mice will there be at the end of each 3-week period, up until the eighth period (24 weeks)?

(*Note*: Problems 3 and 4 require some research.)

3. You may use live plants in your community to answer this question, or you may use accurate pictures of plants in books. List at least 10 plants whose parts are related to the Fibonacci sequence. Make a sketch to illustrate.

Example: An apple has a cross-section that is a five-pointed star; 5 is a Fibonacci number.

4. Find a plant that has a spiral arrangement (pine cones, sunflowers, pineapples, daisies, etc.). Count the pieces that make up the spiral, and compare your results with the Fibonacci sequence.

5. Use a sheet of graph paper to draw a Fibonacci spiral. Start with a unit square. Draw another unit square next to it, forming a rectangle. Draw a two-unit square connected to the original two unit squares to form another rectangle. Continue by drawing a 3-unit square connected to the others to form a larger rectangle. If this pattern continues, you can make a spiral by connecting the appropriate opposite vertices of the squares, in order.

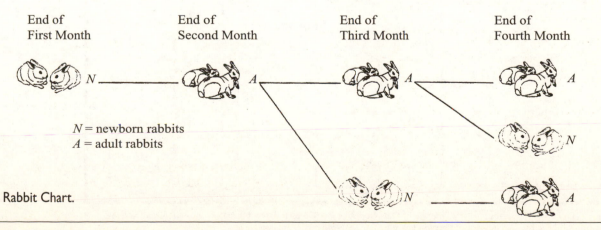

| End of First Month | End of Second Month | End of Third Month | End of Fourth Month |

N = newborn rabbits
A = adult rabbits

Rabbit Chart.

Source: NCTM Student Math Notes, National Council of Teachers of Mathematics, Reston, VA, January 1996. Reprinted with permission.

In the second set of items, students interpret a stem-and-leaf plot representing a particular given situation with which all students are familiar. The first two questions require short explanations as answers. The last has students use the mathematics as a basis for presenting a convincing argument.

The next investigation concerns Pascal's triangle, a well-known number pattern. Although the exercises included in the investigation concentrate on various number patterns revealed in Pascal's triangle, another important application is to the topic of binomial probability. A partially blank Pascal's triangle is provided in Figure 8.7.

Grade Determination

In *Standards*-based classrooms, the expectation is that student grades more clearly reflect the various ways students have of showing their understanding of and ability to apply the mathematical content of a given course of study. Yet teachers frequently disregard much of the evidence and continue to rely on scores received on traditionally formatted tests as the major determinant of grades. The following study shows how even well-intentioned teachers who agree with the philosophy of the *Standards* err on the side of tradition when it comes to their own tests.

Senk, Beckmann, & Thompson (1997) conducted a study of assessment and grading practices in 19 mathematics classes in five high schools in three states. They looked at high-school mathematics teachers' assessment practices in much more detail and over a longer period than any previous study. They examined the relationship between assessment and grading as well as teachers' perspec-

Figure 8.7
Pascal's Triangle

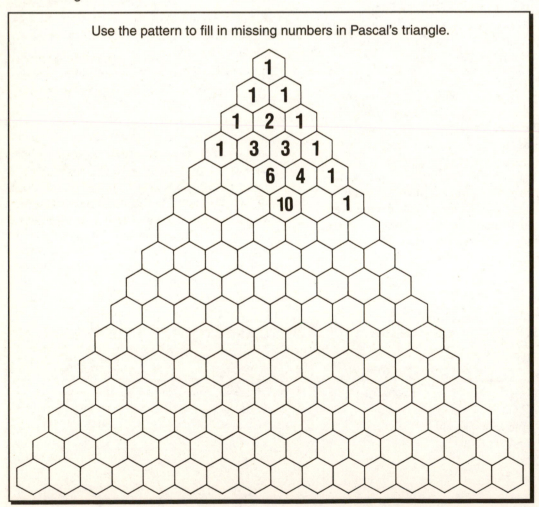

Use the pattern to fill in missing numbers in Pascal's triangle.

Source: From *Visual Patterns in Pascal's Triangle* by Dale Seymour. © 1986 by Pearson Education, Inc., publishing as Dale Seymour Publications, an imprint of Pearson Learning Group. Used by permission.

tives on their practices. The mathematics courses involved in this study comprised topics only in the core high-school curriculum of the *NCTM Curriculum and Evaluation Standards* (1989) for Grades 9–12. Thus, basic math, pre-algebra, and calculus classes were not included in the study. The teachers in the study were better prepared in mathematics than the national average and participated in professional development activities to a greater extent than their peers. University of Chicago School Mathematics Project (UCSMP) materials (see Chapter 4 in this text for additional information) were used in 12 of the 19 classrooms. Calculators were allowed in all classrooms and were required by 11 teachers. A general finding on classroom tests was that they still consisted mainly of low-level (simple recall, etc.) questions, very few problems set in realistic contexts, and very few items that took advantage of students' use of technology. These teachers also used other assessments (quizzes, homework, written reports, etc.) in their classrooms. About 77% of a student's grade was based on tests and quizzes, on average. Homework accounted for another 15% of grades. Other forms of assessment made up the remainder. In general, although several teachers in the study commented that they learned much more about their students' understanding through written and oral explanations, the amount of time needed to prepare and process these newer forms of assessment was a real issue. The reality is that grades appear to be here to stay and easily scored tests are less of a burden to the teacher. As we consider grading in this part of the chapter, the challenge of teaching and assessing deeper levels of understanding remains, as well as communicating the meaning of grades to students and parents.

Two articles in the October 1994 issue of *Educational Leadership* raise questions as to the rationales and uses of grades. In the first (Kohn, 1994), Kohn identifies three possible rationales for grading: sorting students, motivating students, and giving students feedback. He then provides arguments and studies to refute all three of these rationales. The detrimental effect on learning as a result of sorting students is well documented (more attention will be given to this topic in Chapter 9, on equity). For now, Kohn is among those educators who believe that using grades as a sorting mechanism sends a message in direct opposition to Kohn's proposition that students would learn more in schools if the atmosphere became more encouraging and less judgmental. The studies he cites present little evidence to support the rationale for grades as motivating, at least in a positive way. Finally, grades, as such, provide very little useful feedback. Formative assessments are better able to provide this. A typical grade, whether expressed as a number or letter, is an amalgamation of data and, as such, cannot give the student specific suggestions for improvement. As an alternative to assessment tied to grades, Kohn proposes a "support" model of assessment with five principles:

1. Assessment of any kind should not be overdone.
2. The best evidence we have of whether we are succeeding as educators comes from observing children's behaviors.
3. We must transform schools into safe, caring communities.
4. Any responsible conversation about assessment must attend to the quality of the curriculum.
5. Students must be invited to participate in determining the criteria by which their work will be judged and then to play a role in weighing their work against those criteria.

FOR TEACHERS

Investigation 8.5 Pascal Patterns

Mathematical Content:
Recursive number patterns, combinations, Pascal's triangle (PSSM Reasoning and Proof Standard for Grades 6–8)

Materials:
Activity sheets

Directions: Work through this investigation as a student, then write one assessment item asking for student reasoning based on the patterns in Pascal's triangle.

When using these activities with students, make sure they understand the structure of Pascal's triangle and, in particular, can complete the next row, given a current row.

F O R   S T U D E N T S

Investigation 8.5
Pascal Patterns (page 1 of 2)

Sum Patterns

1. a. Find the sum of the elements in the first few rows of Pascal's triangle. Fill in the table below:

Row	0	1	2	3	4	5	6
Row Sum	1	2					

b. What is the pattern of the sums?

c. How can you relate the row number to the sum of that row?

d. How can you express the sum of the elements in the 20th row?

the 100th row?   the nth row?

2. a. Where is the element that will give the sum of the first 4 elements of the first diagonal $(1 + 2 + 3 + 4)$ the first 5 elements of the first diagonal?

b. Where is the element that will give the sum of the first 4 elements of the second diagonal $(1 + 3 + 6 + 10)$?

c. What is the pattern that will give the sum of any number of elements in any diagonal?

3. a. Find the sum of *all* the elements in Pascal's triangle down to and including the first 6 rows. Fill in the table below:

Row	0	1	2	3	4	5
Triangular Sum	1	3				

b. If you see a pattern, then you can fill in the following table without adding all the elements.

Row	6	7	8	9	10
Triangular Sum					

c. What is the rule?

FOR STUDENTS

Investigation 8.5
Pascal Patterns (page 2 of 2)

Additional Exploration Questions

1. Look at a completed Pascal's triangle with at least 10 rows. Describe a consistent way to use the triangle to find consecutive Fibonacci numbers.

2. The six numbers that surround a given number in the interior of Pascal's triangle are called a ring. Investigate the products of the six numbers in a ring. What conclusion can you make? Justify why this conclusion will always be true for any rings in Pascal's triangle.

3. Find patterns for figurate numbers in Pascal's triangle: triangular numbers, square numbers, pentagonal numbers, hexagonal numbers, etc. Remember:

   Triangular numbers are 1, 3, 6, 10, 15, 21, . . .
   Square numbers are 1, 4, 9, 16, 25, 36, . . .

4. Show how the rows in Pascal's triangle describe the number of subsets of each size in a given finite set of items. For example, if the given finite set contains five elements {a, b, c, d, e}, there are subsets containing zero, one, two, three, four, and five elements.

5. Describe how the coefficients in the binomial expansion $(x + y)^n$ can be found in Pascal's triangle.

In the second article, Guskey (1994) points out several fallacies about grades, based upon a review of the literature on the subject. Grades are not essential for instruction. In fact, they can hinder instruction by placing the teacher in two mutually incompatible roles—advocate and judge. Assigning a single letter or number grade requires abstracting a great deal of information about a student into a single symbol. That symbol conveys very little meaning to students and parents and is somewhat arbitrary, as subjectivity always is a part of grading. An example of the impossibility of being totally objective that has occurred in our classrooms is when two students have exactly the same number of points (or percentages) near the end of the year but have progressed at different rates. One has improved remarkably over the past several weeks to get to that point, and the other's grade has been dropping, with recent work substandard. Should those two students receive the same grade? Guskey cites research that shows, counterintuitive to some beliefs, that holistic scoring procedures tend to have greater reliability than analytic procedures. In other words, grading systems based on rubrics clearly identifying components of excellence are likely to have more consistent results among students than systems that are primarily based on a combination of test and quiz scores. From other research studies, he notes the reward value of good grades but negates any punishment value of bad grades. Finally, he agrees with Kohn in insisting that grades should never be based on the normal curve but instead in reference to a common set of learning criteria.

Set 8.5   Discussion Questions

Questions with an asterisk appear in the Message Board section of the Companion Website at **http://www.prenhall.com/huetinck.** Go to Chapter 8 and click on the Message Board to find and respond to the question.

1. Discuss the pros and cons of grading on a curve. (In most situations we have seen, this practice ranks students by some numerical score then approximates a normal distribution by arbitrarily choosing cutoff points that result in a few A's, a few more B's, a large number of C's, fewer D's, and a very few failing grades.)

*2. Describe an experience you have had in which a grading system was used that you feel fairly represented the knowledge gained in the class.

Despite all of the cautionary findings, more than likely you will be expected to give summative grades to your students on a regular basis. In the age of electronics, numerical grade calculation is much easier than it was previously. Many schools have site licenses for a particular piece of grading software, or you can use a spreadsheet to make up your own system. These programs allow teachers to keep up-to-date records and to easily modify them when changes are needed (say, when students revise unsatisfactory responses to an open-ended problem in order to meet the minimum standards required, or if the lowest test score is dropped at the end of the semester and the student's grade is calculated based on the remaining test scores). The programs also allow for differential weights to be given to different types of projects or assignments.

New-teacher in-services in most school districts frequently include the district's grading guidelines and system, and many mathematics departments have standard percentage equivalents for grades. Find out about these practices as soon as you can in order to better prepare your own system to be as consistent with those practices as seems feasible. In one district we know, students receive three marks for each subject: the letter grade (A–F), work habits grade (E, S, U for excellent, satisfactory, unsatisfactory), and a cooperation grade (E, S, U). The letter grade is the only one that affects grade point averages and college entrance requirements, as it is based upon demonstrated content knowledge. Work habits and cooperation grades can affect participation in school events and eligibility for awards. The three types of reporting also help the teacher communicate to school counselors and parents possible causes of poor content achievement.

Most schools require some form of midterm reporting to provide notification to students, parents, and counselors of progress toward the class goals. Standard forms on which to handwrite personal comments and suggestions usually are available for teachers to send home to parents and have signed and returned to show evidence of ample warning of problems with student achievement (and discipline, addressed in Chapter 9). Some districts require comments for every unsatisfactory grade that is given, providing students and parents with indications for the means of grade improvement. Those comments may be on a menu in a database to be used for computerized grade reporting. Whatever the form, accountability is a reality, both for teachers and their students.

A useful tool to allow students to participate in the grading process is an assignment sheet. We have used a simple format, sometimes provided to the students on a handout but most often put on the overhead projector for students to copy and keep on their own paper. Many teachers use the following categories: Date; Assignment; Possible Points; Points Earned. By maintaining an up-to-date assignment sheet, students know immediately where they stand in terms of points and missing work. Absent students also have a quick way to find out what they missed when absent: copy a friend's assignment sheet. If grades are based on simple percentages— i.e., the ratio of total possible points to total actual points—a student can quickly calculate his grade at any time. This is efficient and allows students an opportunity to compare their records with the teacher's if any discrepancies appear.

However, when moving to a *Standards*-based program involving different types of assessment, this system is not as effective. For example, if performance tasks are scored on a 4-point rubric, which is common, how does that (or should it) translate into a grade? The standard percentages no longer make sense in performance assessments based on rubrics. For example, if a rubric score of 3 out of 4 represents good performance, that certainly cannot be easily translated into 80%, rather than 85% or even 79%. We will deal with these issues in greater detail in Chapter 10, but be aware at this point that the total assessment picture in *Standards*-based classrooms becomes both more complicated and, it is hoped, more authentic than simple numeric calculations. The patterns in Activity 8.6 are numerical versions of palindromes—words or phrases that read the same read forward or backward. Although there is a recreational aspect to palindromes (the numerical version is sometimes called numberdromes), they have a mathematical basis. Consider the criteria you would use to assign a grade to this set of problems, or the type of item you would use to evaluate student understanding of the mathematics of palindromes.

 Go to **http://www.prenhall.com/huetinck** and click on Web Destinations for Chapter 8 to find more information about palindromes.

Cheating

What about cheating? There are techniques to combat cheating, but the best overall strategy is to be attentive and to get to know your students and their work. That means taking some time to talk to them about their understanding of mathematics, to listen to them as they discuss mathematics with their classmates, and to read and correct enough of their written work to know their strengths, needs, and personal styles. Let them know that you want them to convey their understanding to you, and explain explicitly how they can do that. For example, give credit when a student makes an oral presentation of a problem solution to the class. Problem presentations are hard to copy, especially if the solution is open to further questions from the class. Valuing student thinking sets a classroom tone that the focus of mathematics is understanding and application. Nevertheless, there always seem to be a few students whose main goal is a good grade, based on quickly arriving at answers rather than the satisfaction of knowing and understanding the content. This is less true when using *Standards*-based curriculum, as students are drawn into the lessons, often despite themselves, and the level of participation and discourse, takes away some of the impetus for cheating.

Be willing to take a stand against cheating when the situation is in your control. It is unlikely that you will ever know for sure who did their own homework, for example. The best you can do is to manage copying when it appears in your class. Our cheating policy on tests was strict; student(s) caught copying received a 0 on the test. However, because we always dropped the lowest test score of the semester, they had an opportunity to make amends for the one mistake by not repeating it. A different technique was never to give a test score less than 50 except for cheating, which continued to have a penalty of a 0. Thus, students were not as tempted to cheat when they felt completely lost during a test because averaging in a 0 on a test is much more detrimental than averaging in a 50.

Having at least two versions of each test so that students sitting close to each other have different tests is a practical necessity, especially when students sit next to one another at tables. Sometimes, if two papers on a written assignment seem exactly alike, ask the two students involved to tell you how they want their *one* score distributed—cut exactly in half, or more of the score given to one person? If you are consistent and offer reasonable ways for students to redeem themselves and not repeat the behavior, it usually stops. If it does not, counselors and parents need to be involved in a conference with you.

F O R   T E A C H E R S

Investigation 8.6 Palindromic Numbers/Numberdromes

Mathematical Content:
Number theory, algebra (PSSM Algebra and Reasoning and Proof Standards for Grades 9–12)

Materials Needed:
Activity sheets, scientific calculators

Directions: This investigation requires knowledge of at least one year of algebra. As you work through the exercises, make a list of the mathematical skills students will use to complete the investigation. Middle-school students can complete page 2, and a follow-up assignment to "reverse and add" is accessible to all students. The challenge for students who have had algebra is to set up accurate equations to represent the given patterns. Simplifying them leads to a derivation type of proof.

F O R   S T U D E N T S

Investigation 8.6
Palindromic Numbers/Numberdromes (page 1 of 2)

Directions:

1. Work through the "Palindromes" worksheet on the next page.

2. Select two other non-palindromic two-digit numbers, and apply the reverse-and-add process until you obtain at least one other numberdrome. Show your work. *Comment*: It is an unproved conjecture that all numbers can be turned into numberdromes by this process.

3. Describe the palindromic characteristics of the true mathematical sentences below. Verify by calculation if you choose.

$$12 \times 42 = 24 \times 21 = 504$$
$$13 \times 93 = 39 \times 31 = 1{,}209$$
$$24 \times 84 = 48 \times 42 = 2{,}016$$

What must the mathematical characteristics of the digits be in order for these kinds of equations to be true? Verify your response. (*Hint*: You may need algebra.)

4. Describe the palindromic characteristics of the true mathematical sentences below. Verify by calculation if you choose.

$$12 \times 63 = 36 \times 21 = 756$$
$$13 \times 62 = 26 \times 31 = 806$$
$$24 \times 63 = 36 \times 42 = 1{,}512$$

What must be the mathematical characteristics of the digits in order for these kinds of equations to be true? Verify your response. (*Hint*: You may need algebra.)

Extensions

5. Some additional numberdrome patterns are given below. (*Hint*: Part (b) involves mathematical relationship using ratios.

   a. $201 \times 204 = 402 \times 102$
      $103 \times 602 = 206 \times 301$

   b. $132 \times 462 = 264 \times 231$
      $123 \times 642 = 246 \times 321$
      $233 \times 664 = 466 \times 332$

   c. $13^2 \times 62^2 = 26^2 \times 31^2$

   What must be the mathematical characteristics of the digits in order for these kinds of equations to be true? Verify your response. (*Hint*: You may need algebra.)

6. Can you find any four-digit numerals that have palindromic products similar to the number above? If so, describe what you did to find the numerals.

FOR STUDENTS

Investigation 8.6
Palindromic Numbers/Numberdromes (page 2 of 2)

Palindromes

Abadaba wrote:

    BOB   ANNA   EVE   RADAR   SPACECAPS

1. Does each word read the same when the letters are taken in reverse order?

Words such as these are called word palindromes.
Abadaba found sentence palindromes:

NIAGARA,   O ROAR AGAIN
A MAN,   A PLAN,   A CANAL: PANAMA

2. Do the sentences read the same when the letters are taken in reverse order?

Of all palindromes, Abadaba liked number palindromes the best:

1 3 3 1	6 1 7 1 6	4 0 8 8 0 4
2 5 4 5 2	8 8 8 8 8	1 2 3 4 3 2 1

3. Do the numbers remain the same when the digits are taken in reverse order?

4. Make up four 4-digit number palindromes.

    a. _____   **b.** _____   **c.** _____   **d.** _____

5. Make up four 5-digit number palindromes.

    a. _____   **b.** _____   **c.** _____   **d.** _____

Abadaba wrote:
```
   1 2
 + 2 1
   3 3
```
He reversed the digits in 1 2 and added.
The result is a number palindrome after one reversal.

Abadaba wrote:
```
     3 7
   + 7 3
   1 1 0
 + 0 1 1
   1 2 1
```
He reversed the digits in 3 7 and added.
The result is *not* a number palindrome.
He reversed the digits in 1 1 0 and added.
The result is a number palindrome after two reversals.

Source: Adapted from a presentation by John F. Moelter at the Los Angeles City Teachers' Mathematics Association Conference on March 14, 1998.

Summary

This chapter introduced various methods for assessing individual performance, mainly through observation and testing. Research on homework was shared. Teacher-created samples of various types of test items were presented. The difficult issue of grades was discussed. In a *Standards*-based classroom, student goals must include understanding the mathematics underlying their work. One way to push to this deeper level is to have students regularly work on challenging investigations rather than only complete computation-based exercises.

ASSIGNMENT

1. Design a unit test to be taken individually. Identify the *Standards*-based unit of instruction (text, chapter, other instructional material) upon which the test is based. Use the suggestions discussed previously in this chapter to construct a test of appropriate length and level of difficulty, with a variety of types of items. Submit a final version of the test completely formatted, with all diagrams included. Also submit an answer key.

INSTRUCTIONAL RESOURCES

Becker, J. P., & Shimada, S. (1997). *The open-ended approach: A new proposal for teaching mathematics.* Reston, VA. National Council of Teachers of Mathematics.

Translations of open-ended problems from Japanese schools are included in this book, along with methods of evaluating higher-order thinking.

Bush, W. S., & Leinwant, S. (2000). *Mathematics assessment: A practical handbook for Grades 6–8.* Reston, VA: National Council of Teachers of Mathematics.

Twenty samples of assessment tasks developed by teachers are presented in this resource. Suggestions for selecting and developing assessments make this a valuable tool for mathematics educators.

Compton, H. C., Foster, A. B., Greer, A. S., Mosier, J. A., Romagnano, L., & Rubino, C. (1999). *Mathematics assessment: A practical handbook for Grades 9–12.* Reston, VA: National Council of Teachers of Mathematics.

Ideas for creating, locating, and modifying assessment tasks are given here as well as ways to grade, report, and use assessment data.

Long, V. M., Clark, G., & Corcoran, C. (2000). Anatomy of an assessment. *Mathematics Teacher, 93(4),* 346–348.

The authors give an example of a rich mathematical task along with criteria for assessing the student work on the task. Student samples are shown.

NCTM *Student Math Notes.* Reston, VA: National Council of Teachers of Mathematics.

Published as an online supplement to the NCTM *News Bulletin*, these are secondary-level student pages that classroom teachers may use without permission. We have found them to be a good source of extensions in many topic areas. For example, the January 1996 *Student Math Notes* topic is "Those Fascinating Fibonaccis!"

Seymour, D. (1986). *Visual patterns in Pascal's triangle.* Dale Seymour Publications, White Plains, NY.

This 138-page book, which still is available, contains student worksheets, solutions, and many pages showing and describing additional number patterns associated with Pascal's triangle.

ADDITIONAL INVESTIGATIONS

Investigation 8.7   Mathematical "Black Holes"
Investigation 8.8   Trains
Investigation 8.9   Rod Staircases
Investigation 8.10 Guatemalan Weaving Patterns

The additional investigations have students look at numerical patterns generated in different ways and draw conclusions about them. The first, 8.7, examines procedures for generating sequences of numbers that eventually seem to "settle down" to a consistent looping pattern or single value, regardless of the starting value. Investigation 8.8 uses Cuisenaire rods to build "trains" of different lengths. By organizing the resulting patterns, students can identify values related to Pascal's triangle. Cuisenaire rods are also used in Investigation 8.9 to build patterns of "staircases." Not only does each staircase result in a pattern that can be represented algebraically, but all of those algebraic patterns can also be related by a broader generalization. The final investigation, 8.10, examines numerical patterns actually used by Guatemalan natives who weave fabrics; students generalize and justify possible outcomes generated in this way.

FOR TEACHERS

Investigation 8.7 Mathematical "Black Holes"

Mathematical Content:
Recursive patterns that converge or repeat (PSSM Reasoning and Proof Standard for Grades 9–12)

Materials Needed:
Activity sheets, scientific calculators

Directions: First work through these problems as a student. Have examples of each of the patterns ready as your class works through them.

Students may work in pairs and use calculators to verify the patterns that emerge. Be sure students address Problem 2(b), where the algebra connection is used to show why the "black hole" results from following the directions.

F O R   S T U D E N T S

Investigation 8.7
Mathematical "Black Holes"

Directions: Follow the procedures below to discover some mathematical patterns that may surprise you.

A black hole in space is a place where the gravity is so intense that nothing that comes near it, even light, can escape from being drawn into it. The following explorations have been characterized as mathematical black holes by some.

1. **a.** Follow the procedure and see where it leads:

   ■ Pick any positive integer.

   ■ If it is odd, multiply it by 3 and then add 1 to get the next number.

   ■ If it is even, divide it by 2 to get the next number.

   ■ Starting with the number you selected, record the sequence produced.

   Continue to follow the procedure until a pattern occurs.

   b. Pick another positive integer and apply the same rules to get another sequence.

   c. Share your results with someone else in the class.

   d. Write conjectures about the results of applying the procedure to any number.

   e. Can you find numbers that have fewer numbers in the sequence before the pattern begins? Give an example.

   f. Can you find numbers for which the sequence is long before repeating? Give an example.

   g. Why might this process be called a mathematical "black hole"?

2. Choose any number. Add 12 to it. Multiply the result by 2. Subtract 4. Divide by 4. Finally, subtract half the number you started with. What number results?

   a. Follow this procedure with several different starting numbers and see whether it leads to a mathematical black hole. Show your work.

   b. Show mathematically what is happening when this procedure is used. (*Hint*: Algebra can help you here.)

   c. Create a procedure that will always result in the black hole 6, regardless of the beginning number.

3. **a.** Try this procedure to get a numerical "whirlpool."

   ■ Select two one-digit positive integers.

   ■ Create a third number by multiplying the first number by −1 and adding the result to the second number.

   ■ Create a fourth number by multiplying the second number by −1 and adding the result to the third number.

   b. Continue the procedure until you notice a pattern. Describe the pattern. Do you think "whirlpool" is an appropriate name for this type of pattern? Why or why not?

   You will need a scientific calculator for Problem 4.

4. Chose a positive integer. Find its square root. Find the square root of the answer, using repeat functions of your calculator, if possible.

   a. Continue to find the square roots of each subsequent answer until you are "drawn in" to a number. What is the number?

   b. Compare your results with those of others in your class. What conjecture can you make about this process?

FOR TEACHERS

Investigation 8.8 Trains

Mathematical Content:
Patterns, combinations, Pascal's triangle (PSSM Reasoning and Proof Standard for Grades 6–8)

Materials Needed:
Activity sheets, Cuisenaire rods for each pair of students

Directions: Have students build trains of lengths 1 through 6, using Cuisenaire rods in as many combinations as possible. Note that Problem 9 can be solved with Pascal's triangle. If students already have worked with that structure, they may recognize the pattern.

FOR STUDENTS

Investigation 8.8
Trains (page 1 of 2)

Part 1

1. How many trains can you make whose total length is 3?

$$\boxed{1} \;+\; \boxed{2} \;=\; 3$$

The order of the cars counts! So we can also have:

$$\boxed{2} \;+\; \boxed{1} \;=\; 3$$

Can you find the other two trains of length 3?

2. How many cars do these trains have?

a. $\boxed{1} \;+\; \boxed{2} \;+\; \boxed{2}$

b. $\boxed{1} \;+\; \boxed{1} \;+\; \boxed{2} \;+\; \boxed{2}$

c. $\boxed{1} \;+\; \boxed{3}$

d. $\boxed{1} \;+\; \boxed{1} \;+\; \boxed{2} \;+\; \boxed{1} \;+\; \boxed{1} \;+\; \boxed{3}$

F O R   S T U D E N T S

Investigation 8.8
Trains (page 2 of 2)

3. a. How many trains can you build whose length is 1?

   b. How many trains can you build whose length is 2?

   c. How many trains can you build whose length is 4?

   d. How many trains can you build whose length is 5?

   e. How many trains can you build whose length is 6?

4. How many cars are in each of the trains you just built? Place your answer next to the trains you just built.

5. Name at least two ways to categorize the trains.

6. Organize your data into a chart or table.

7. Fill in the following table:

Length of Train	Number of Different Trains with the Given Number of Cars					
	1 Car	2 Cars	3 Cars	4 Cars	5 Cars	6 Cars
Length 1						
Length 2						
Length 3						
Length 4						
Length 5						
Length 6						

8. Describe the patterns you found. (3–5 sentences)

9. Find a shortcut to determine how many trains of length 10 have 5 cars.

Source: Adapted from a Structured Exploration used in the Leadership in Urban Mathematics Reform (LUMR) project funded by the National Science Foundation to the Educational Development Corporation of Newton, MA.

FOR TEACHERS

Investigation 8.9 Rod Staircases

Mathematical Content:
Linear patterns, surface area and volume (PSSM Algebra and Connection Standards for Grades 9–12)

Materials Needed:
Activity sheets, linking cubes for each group (preferable to Cuisenaire rods, although they may be used as shown in the activity)

Directions: Students work four to a group. We prefer linking cubes because the parts of the staircase can be built to stay together. This helps students count to find the surface area. Build and discuss the three-step staircase with the entire class to make sure students understand what they are required to do. Assign different groups different sizes of staircases to make and analyze. As groups complete their individual tables, have them complete a class chart, either on the chalkboard or on chart paper. Have students notice the patterns in the formulas for *n*, and see if they can verbalize a generalization of the pattern for all cases.

Comment: Sometimes students come up with different forms of the formula. So long as they are equivalent and make sense, all forms should be accepted.

Extension: See if anyone can come up with a "mega-formula" that will work for all cases.

FOR STUDENTS

Investigation 8.9
Rod Staircases (page 1 of 3)

Directions: In this Activity, you will build "staircases," and use certain geometric features to develop patterns that can be described algebraically.

Objective: Students will experience how to collect data, record them, and use them to make a prediction on the results for the general case.

Materials: Whether working individually or in groups, students will have sets of Cuisenaire rods or linking cubes with which to work.

Exploration: The goal is to make staircases of a varying number of steps, each staircase the same color (each rod having the same length). Each step of the staircase is to be offset 1 unit. The area of the face of the smallest cube is 1 square unit, and its volume is 1 cubic unit. This cube is the standard by which all measurements are to be determined.

FOR STUDENTS

Investigation 8.9
Rod Staircases (page 2 of 3)

In a three-step staircase, each step is 3 units long. It should look like the following.

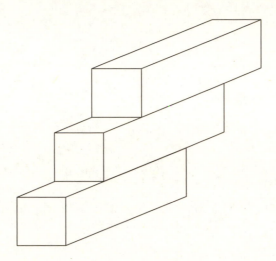

Work together to complete entries on the following chart for a 3-unit staircase.

3 UNITS		
No. in Staircase	**Volume**	**Surface Area**
1		
2		
3		
4		
5		
6		
…		
n		

F O R   S T U D E N T S

Investigation 8.9
Rod Staircases (page 3 of 3)

Build a Staircase

Working in groups or individually, complete the remaining charts for stairs having steps of lengths 4, 5, and 6.

3 UNITS		
No. in Staircase	Volume	Surface Area
1		
2		
3		
4		
5		
6		
…		
n		

4 UNITS		
No. in Staircase	Volume	Surface Area
1		
2		
3		
4		
5		
6		
…		
n		

5 UNITS		
No. in Staircase	Volume	Surface Area
1		
2		
3		
4		
5		
6		
…		
n		

6 UNITS		
No. in Staircase	Volume	Surface Area
1		
2		
3		
4		
5		
6		
…		
n		

Source: Adapted from *Algebra for Everyone* Discussion Guide for videotape of the same name. (1991) NCTM, Reston VA.

FOR TEACHERS

Investigation 8.10: Guatemalan Weaving Patterns

Mathematical Content:
Number patterns, ethnomathematics (PSSM Reasoning and Proof Standard for Grades 6–8)

Materials Needed:
Activity sheets

Directions: Have students work in small groups. Work through a few examples of how the patterns are constructed with the students. Then, each group is to continue to explore patterns of various lengths, trying to see if they can come up with numbers that follow the system and result in the "ultimate values" from 1 to 9. Depending on the amount of time taken, discussion into the reasons behind the results could be extensive or could be left as extensions for extra credit.

If there are any school or community resources that can provide examples of this native craft, it could be very enriching and validating, especially if there are students from Central America in your classroom.

FOR STUDENTS

Investigation 8.10
Guatamalan Weaving Patterns (page 1 of 2)

Some Guatamalan weaving uses a cross-stitch pattern. The indigenous people who create the weaving have developed number patterns related to their weavings. These patterns result in "ultimate values" that have sacred meaning. See some examples below.

One Cross

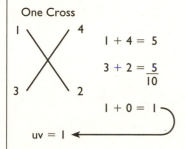

$$1 + 4 = 5$$
$$3 + 2 = \underline{5}$$
$$10$$
$$1 + 0 = 1$$
$$uv = 1$$

Two Crosses

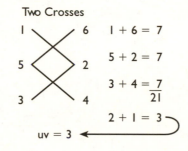

$$1 + 6 = 7$$
$$5 + 2 = 7$$
$$3 + 4 = \underline{7}$$
$$21$$
$$2 + 1 = 3$$
$$uv = 3$$

Two Crosses

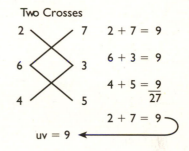

$$2 + 7 = 9$$
$$6 + 3 = 9$$
$$4 + 5 = \underline{9}$$
$$27$$
$$2 + 7 = 9$$
$$uv = 9$$

Explanation: The number pattern always begins in the upper left-hand corner and then follows the broken line segment to the bottom; jumping across, it follows the other broken line segment back up to the top. Once all the numbering is complete, adding across should produce the same sum for each row. Then find the sum of these numbers and add the digits of that result until arriving at a single digit. That is the "ultimate value."

The table below is set up to see if you can find at least one example of each ultimate value for each cross-stitch pattern. Once that is done, make conjectures about the results, and report out your findings.

Pattern　　　　　　　　　　　　　　　Ultimate Value

Pattern	1	2	3	4	5	6	7	8	9
✗ (1,4,3,2)									
✗✗		1,6/5,2/3,4							2,7/6,3/4,5
✗✗✗									
✗✗✗✗									
✗✗✗✗✗									

FOR STUDENTS

Investigation 8.10
Guatamalan Weaving Patterns (page 2 of 2)

Pattern Worksheet

One Cross

Sums

$\_\_ + \_\_ = \_\_$
$\_\_ + \_\_ = \_\_$

Total ☐
Ultimate Value = ___

Sums

Total ☐
Ultimate Value = ___

Sums

Total ☐
Ultimate Value = ___

Two Crosses

Sums

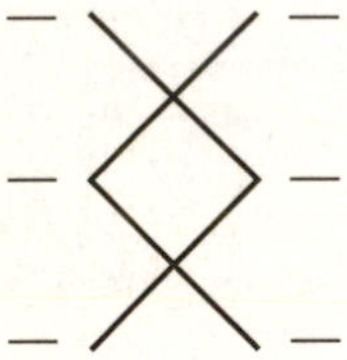

$\_\_ + \_\_ = \_\_$
$\_\_ + \_\_ = \_\_$
$\_\_ + \_\_ = \_\_$

Total ☐
Ultimate Value = ___

Sums

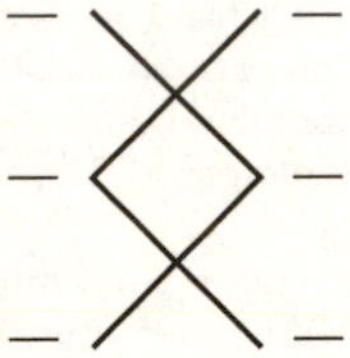

Total
Ultimate Value = ___

Sums

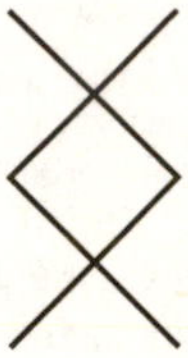

Total
Ultimate Value = ___

Three Crosses

Sums

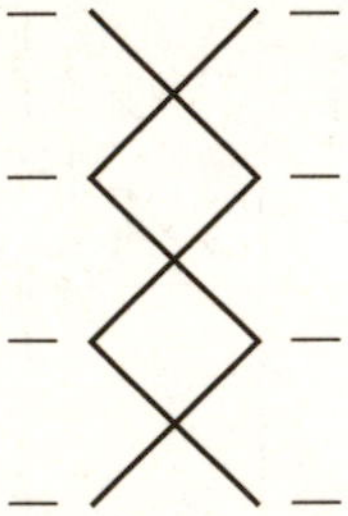

$\_\_ + \_\_ = \_\_$
$\_\_ + \_\_ = \_\_$
$\_\_ + \_\_ = \_\_$
$\_\_ + \_\_ = \_\_$

Total ☐
Ultimate Value = ___

Sums

Total
Ultimate Value = ___

Sums

Total
Ultimate Value = ___

Continue more practice in the same manner on other paper.

CHAPTER 9

Student Equity

The methods and curriculum for *Standards*-based mathematics education are founded on the belief that mathematics must be a conduit for all students—not a filter resulting in underrepresentation of certain groups in fields dependent upon higher mathematical skills. Shirley Malcolm discusses how mathematics can become the great equalizer:

Mathematics is the critical filter for all kinds of things in life: jobs, understanding news and advertising, recognizing information that will protect us from being duped. Unfortunately, people seem really attached to the old nature/nurture controversy. The notion of a math gene still seems to be floating around and we can't seem to get rid of it. No one talks about a reading gene, even though reading is similar in terms of the skills that it represents. Yet we want some way of distinguishing our kids in terms of mathematics ability. I think it's very unhelpful.

Maybe what we have is the "Lake Wobegon" effect—Garrison Keillor's notion of the town where all the children are above average. Maybe this emphasis on a math gene has been one way of affirming our children's specialness (and through them, our own?). Maybe mathematics carries some special "cachet" because of its perceived difficulty.

I think we should return to an idea espoused by David Hawkins in a 1990 *Daedalus* article: that mathematics and science can in fact be the great equalizers within education. Science and mathematics empower everyone who learns them, regardless of background. Success in these fields depends primarily on diligence and imagination—characteristics that can be found in abundance in all children. We must learn to see in these programs the magnificent opportunity to reduce rather than widen differences through excellent instruction that can have life-changing consequences (Malcom, 1997, 30–35).[1]

The fundamental issue for educators is how to provide equal opportunities for all students and simultaneously attend to individual student differences. This is a problem of balance that will be with you throughout your entire teaching career. There are no pat solutions. We know that one size does not fit all. When and how do we separate groups of students to better attend to their unique needs? When and how do we include all students in a classroom that echoes our democratic principles? Sensitivity to student differences, caring that all students succeed, and understanding how different students learn mathematics are the basic attributes that will assist in finding this balance.

ABOUT THE ACTIVITIES FOR THIS CHAPTER

The mathematical emphasis in this chapter is nonstandard problems, by which we mean problems that do not lend themselves easily to solution by familiar algorithms. All of the problems can be approached in a variety of ways from informed assumptions, number sense, algebra, geometric concepts, or first solving a simpler problem and extending the method to the problem posed. Students could begin with drawings, manipulatives, calculators, or mathematical symbolism. Persons with strong mathematical backgrounds may struggle with some of these problems since wide experience with textbook problems may not assist. In fact, the use of algebraic equations is the most laborious way to solve some of the problems. If this is true for you, perhaps these nonstandard problems will provide the opportunity for you to reflect sympathetically about the difficulties experienced by secondary level students who regularly approach mathematics without the benefit of experience of the expert.

---

[1] Excerpts reprinted with permission from Malcom, S. (1997) Making mathematics the great equalizer. In L. A. Steen (Ed.), *When Numbers Count: Quantitative Literacy for Tomorrow's America.* Copyright © 1997 by College Entrance Examination Board. All rights reserved.

The selected problems all "have legs." By this we mean each can be extended to more complex problems leading to rich mathematical connections, and none is just a unique puzzle to be solved. An example of a problem "without legs" is, "What is the number formed when each of the digits is placed in alphabetical order according to the first letter in the name?" This may be fun to figure out but does not lead to enriched mathematical thinking.

The problems are ones that can be accessed by a variety of paths, ranging in difficulty from pre-algebra to calculus. Thus, the problems are equalizers in that students of a wide range of ability and mathematical background can still solve the problems. Nonstandard problems require mathematical thinking and creativity, so the students excelling in their solutions may not always be those receiving the highest grades in a mathematics course. This may be something for teachers of secondary level mathematics to consider in determining appropriate teaching methods and assessment practices.

 For more information about content specific problems, go to *http://www.prenhall.com/ huetinck* and click on Web Destinations for Chapter 9.

TRACKING

When mathematics teachers first hear the word *tracking,* their response frequently is, "We don't track. They do that in English with Basic English, English, and Honors English at each grade level." Of course, mathematics in most secondary-level schools *has* been tracked, but we call the levels by different names, such as General Mathematics, Algebra Concepts, and Algebra for the three different tracks of low, average, and high mathematical ability. Tracking is meant to describe broad divisions within a program, separating students into groups of basic, average, and college-bound levels of ability for all academic subjects.

In the past, students were separated during middle school and continued on the same track during high school. This type of rigid segregation of abilities has become much less common in recent years, however. Previously, students might remain on the basic track for as many as three years, primarily practicing computations, with little exposure to problem solving. In contrast, many schools today give all students the opportunity to at least become familiar with algebraic and geometric concepts, even if the symbolic formalism is not foremost in all courses. Also, most schools provide avenues for a student to move between different tracks, since her maturity level and interests may change during the secondary-level years.

Ability grouping refers to the clustering of students based on their measured or perceived performance, either within a class or within a department. However, in current usage terms such as *ability grouping* and *tracking* have become less precise. The following discussion details the reasons for modifying tracking in program design and gives examples of how detracking can be implemented.

The Study of Schooling

Over 27,000 individuals contributed to the data for *The Study of Schooling,* which formed the basis of John Goodlad's book, *A Place Called School.* A selection of 38 schools in 13 communities from seven sections of the country provided maximum diversity and representativeness "in characteristics of the student population, family incomes, and other ways" (Goodlad, 1984, p. 18). A continuum of 12 years of schooling was examined in each community, since the selected elementary schools fed their students to the secondary schools included in the study. More than 20 trained data collectors spent almost a month in each community, collecting a large array of information through surveys, questionnaires, interviews, visits, and existing data sources from educators and community groups. Over 1,000 classrooms were studied. Ten themes were defined to "help us see that schooling has a common set of characteristics and that school-to-school differences result from the sum total of how these characteristics manifest themselves in each school . . . school functions . . . school's relevance in the lives of its students . . . how teachers teach . . . the circumstances surrounding teaching . . . the distribution of resources for learning . . . equity . . . implicit curriculum . . . satisfaction . . . the need for data" (p. 29–31).[2] Issues of equity were raised when access to knowledge was examined within entire school populations.

Based on a subset of the data from *The Study of Schooling,* one of John Goodlad's graduate students, Jeannie Oakes, wrote a persuasive book, *Keeping*

Track: How Schools Structure Inequality. In the preface to Oakes's book, John Goodlad states:

> There were clear differences between upper and lower tracks in regard to the content and quality of instruction, teacher-student and student-student relationships, the expectations of teachers for their students, the affective climate of classrooms, and other elements of the educational enterprise. . . . Not only do individual schools differ widely in the quality of education they provide, but also it appears, quality varies substantially from track level to track level within individual schools.

Oakes examined differences in the day-to-day classroom lives of 13,719 teenagers in 25 junior and senior high schools. Based on information from administrators, counselors, and teachers, the classes were categorized into high, average, and low tracks. Classes of English and mathematics were selected for analysis, since nearly all the schools tracked in these disciplines.

In mathematics there was considerable difference between high tracks and low tracks with regard to access to knowledge considered high status for its societal value and access to higher education. The students in high tracks experienced activities that "demanded critical thinking, problem solving, drawing conclusions, making generalizations, or evaluating or synthesizing knowledge" (Oakes, 1985, p. 76), while the low-track classes emphasized arithmetic facts and computational skills. Time on task varied between high and low mathematics tracks, with a greater percentage of classtime spent in instruction, more time spent on homework, and less time spent on off-task behavior by students in the high tracks, which would advantage them by providing a greater opportunity to learn. Among other things, students were asked their perception of the quality of instruction by responding to a series of questions describing teacher enthusiasm, verbal clarity, task orientation, and use of praise and criticism. The high-track classes were more frequently characterized by the teacher behaviors considered to promote learning:

> Educational equality can be interpreted to mean that students are provided with the resources necessary to ensure that they are all likely to acquire a specified set of learnings. This might be translated in schools to mean that resources are allocated and instruction designed so that those entering schools least likely to do well are given the best schools have to offer. Certainly, we found no evidence of this kind of equality operating in schools. Indeed, we found the opposite to be the case. Those least likely to do well were given the least in the three areas of school experience we studied. Those most likely to do well were given the most (Oakes 1985, p. 135).

---

[2] Goodlad, J. I. (1984), *A place called school: Prospects for the future* (New York: McGraw-Hill Book Company). Reproduced with permission of the McGraw-Hill Companies.

Modifications of Tracking

In our opinion, the tracking practices studied in the 1970s in *The Study of Schooling* have been somewhat mitigated, but we still have a long way to go. I (LH) am haunted by the insight of one of my students over 25 years ago in an individualized instruction class with a curriculum of mainly computational practice and skill development. He said, "The problem is that when we get in the low classes, we can't learn enough to get out of them." This seemed a tragic situation. This young man realized his mathematical shortcomings were being compounded by being in basic mathematics, but he did not have the wherewithal to break out of the track. Since then, social scientists and educational psychologists have found through research what many practitioners have discovered through experience: intelligence is not a single factor; learning ability can be modified; students who cannot always retain the multiplication tables still can participate successfully in problem-solving activities; students preparing for college, as well as those preparing for work, must be critical thinkers who can make hypotheses, evaluate information, draw conclusions, and make generalizations.

Many high schools have moved from three tracks to two, based as much on student interest as on demonstrated ability. This is a step in the right direction because *The Study of Schooling* did find much less difference between high and average tracks than between average and low tracks. Nonetheless, rigid broad program tracks must be replaced by flexible ability groupings that enable students to change programs when they are willing to study during school breaks or put a concentrated effort into challenging classes. Also, there should be multiple paths to a college-intended course. For example, some students may need pre-algebra for a year before entering a first-year course in integrated algebra and geometry, while other students will not. Teachers and counselors must keep in mind that students mature at different rates; therefore, there will be age differences among students in the same mathematics course.

Adam Gamoran advocates decrease of either tracking or ability grouping but recognizes that in some cases high-track students perform better in homogeneous groupings than do similar students in heterogeneous classes. He suggests certain aspects of ability groupings in secondary schools can improve instruction for the low groups:

- Teachers hold high expectations and encourage students in their endeavors.
- Teachers and students have opportunities for verbal interaction.

- The lower tracks are not assigned to weak or inexperienced teachers; rather, teachers are rotated through different ability groupings.

Under these conditions, the lower-level classes may help students to catch up—or at least not to fall further behind (Gamoran, 1992). We would add that schools should provide tutoring and resources such as manipulatives, calculators, and computers equitably to all levels of classes. Many schools assist the low-ability students by allowing relatively low student/teacher ratios in these classes, since the students may have greater need of individualized teacher contact than in higher-level classes.

Strategies for Detracking

There is a continuing debate on beginning tracking in the middle school. Sociology professor Elizabeth Useem found that some schools track students out of advanced mathematics at an early age. Tracking favors high-ability students, and in the United States only about 17% of eighth-grade students are in the track leading to calculus. Since calculus is a gatekeeper course for more than half of college majors, and students exposed to calculus concepts in high school are more likely to pass calculus at the university level, she advocates policies to encourage greater numbers of students to receive a more challenging curriculum than the 6% who now persist to calculus in high school.

Research into policies of 26 school districts around Boston illuminated sharp contrasts between districts with similar communities. Community B encouraged 40% of seventh-graders to start in the advanced track, while Community A restricted 18% of their seventh-graders to take a comparative curriculum. The department chairman in Community B likened being sorted on math as similar to participation in sports. If a student is cut from soccer, it is very difficult for that student to try out for that sport again. The same is true in mathematics; if the student is sorted out early, it is next to impossible for later success in higher mathematics. He said, "Calculus is not for everyone, but many more people should take it." Another district espoused the philosophy of separating the best students in the fourth grade, which effectively filtered many students from advanced mathematics.

In her article "You're Good but Not Good Enough," Useem recommends curricular changes and a conscious effort of all school personnel to increase the number of students who tackle the tougher mathematics courses. The College Board now publishes a document of nearly 300 pages to assist educators across Grades 6 through 12 to form a Vertical Team to work together "to increase the number and diversity of students who pursue and

Vignette 9.1 Japanese Algebra Example: One Student's Solution

1	2	3	. . .	14	15	Number of Days
170	160	150	. . .	40	30	Amount in Older Brother's Wallet
105	100	95	. . .	40	35	Amount in Younger Brother's Wallet

succeed in advanced mathematics at the precollege level as a worthwhile and achievable goal" (Useem, 1997, p. 1). The guide is broad in its focus, ranging from how to get all stakeholders involved to examples of specific supporting activities in the classroom.

Japanese Heterogeneous Classes Perhaps we can learn how to further detrack by examples from the Japanese, whose students all experience the same national mathematical curriculum until after the ninth grade. At the end of the ninth grade, they take exams that separate students into tracks with differing career paths. Their early curriculum is founded upon problems that can be solved in multiple ways.

At an early presentation of the analysis of classrooms in Japan, Germany, and the United States for the TIMSS (Third International Mathematics and Science Study), a video of an eighth-grade Japanese algebra lesson was shown (NCSM Research Session, San Diego, 1996). At the beginning of the period, the students are given the following problem:

> Two brothers went to the temple every day to pray and gave an offering for their mother who was ill. One brother had a wallet with a total of 18 coins, with the value of 10 yen apiece. The younger brother had a wallet with a total of 22 coins, of value 5 yen apiece. They agreed to each put one coin per day in the donation box until their wallets were empty. One day the boys noticed that the younger brother had more money in his wallet than did his older brother. On what day did this occur?

A manipulative on the board represented two large sets of pockets, circular cutouts stood for the 5-yen and 10-yen coins, and a rectangle denoted the donation box. The teacher carefully explained the problem, even demonstrating moving coins from the pockets into the donation box for the first day. The teacher then gave the students about 15 minutes to solve the problem while he circulated throughout the room, answering questions and taking notes on the methods used by the students.

At the end of this time, the teacher asked a student to come to the board and share his method. The first student used the manipulative and removed pieces from each set of pockets (wallets) until he showed the day that the total amount in the wallet with 5-yen pieces was greater. A second student came to the board to display his method, which consisted of the table shown in Vignette 9.1.

The third student wrote an equation on the board $(180 - 110 = 70)$ to represent the difference between the total amount of money in the two wallets in the beginning and then reasoned that the difference in the donation was 5 yen per day. He said since 70 divided by 5 is 14, this is the day when the wallets would have the same amount. Therefore, he said, on the 15th day one wallet would hold more than the other. A fourth student set x equal to the number of days and set up two equations: $y = 180 - 10x$ and $y = 100 - 5x$, where y is the amount of money after x days. She set the two equations equal to find the 14th day and then added 1 to get the answer of the 15th day. The last student presenter discussed inequalities and explained that the conditions were met not only on the 15th day but also for the remaining days that each boy would have some money. He set up the same equation as the previous student, replacing the equal sign between the two equations with the appropriate inequality sign.

These five solutions were on the board simultaneously. The teacher discussed the various methods and expanded upon the last solution, demonstrating the use of inequalities. The teacher assigned a similar homework problem and asked students to use inequalities to solve it.

This problem is outstanding because it provides a measure of success to a spectrum of sophisticated approaches, as is required in a nontracked classroom. While the students were working, the teacher made notes on the methods used and called students to present their solutions in increasing order of sophistication. We assume that not all students received the same grade for the right answer but assessment was based on process and not only on the right answer. Another important note is that nearly the entire class period was taken with only *one* problem, discussed in considerable detail. Furthermore, only one similar problem was given for homework. This pace is a good strategy for heterogeneous classes.

The oft-heard comment after seeing this type of classroom is, "We have too much to cover to spend so long on one problem, however, rich it is." But the TIMSS report found that U.S. math classes go over the same concepts for eight years, whereas the Japanese expect their students to have mastery after 3 years. Since we teach so many more concepts in a year, we have to review again and again. So there are two ways to look at the time spent. Of course, there are many significant differences between the Japanese and U.S. cultures. Nonetheless, we can learn ideas from the Japanese for dealing with students of varying learning styles and mathematical competence in a single classroom.

Try the two problems in Activities 9.1 and 9.2. The Mini-Camel problem in Activity 9.1 is presented during the first year of the Interactive Mathematics Program as a problem of the week. Previously the students had been given a Cory Camel problem, where Cory has 1,000 bananas to take to market 1,000 miles away. The students have so much difficulty with that problem that they work this problem before returning to the Cory problem. This process teaches the valuable lesson of developing a problem with smaller numbers to find a process that can work for a problem with larger numbers. Try working the triangular area problem in Activity 9.2 in four roles: (1) as a middle-school student with access to graph paper but without knowledge of the formula for the area of a triangle; (2) as a middle-school student who uses the for-

mula for the area of a triangle; (3) as a second-year algebra student with access to graphing calculators; and (4) as a calculus student.

Detracking in the United States   Methods to approach detracking in 10 secondary schools were documented by a group of researchers based at the University of California, Los Angeles. Educators in the examined schools, disenchanted with the divisions among students created by tracking, worked to restructure their schools to increase overall student achievement by detracking to improve equity and excellence. The schools varied widely in location (Northeast, Northwest, Midwest, South, and Southwest) and size (from 500 to 3,000 students). The schools all had socially and economically diverse student populations. Most of the schools began by eliminating low-level tracks. Detracking proceeded differently in the schools according to different subject areas. Here we will highlight the methods used to detrack the mathematics programs.

Some schools established heterogeneous benchmark classes—for example, requiring all students to take 1 year of algebra. Other schools required all students to begin the ninth grade on a college preparation set of courses. For the most part the schools either opened access to honors programs or provided honors activities within heterogeneous classes, such as through challenge projects. One

F O R   T E A C H E R S

Activity 9.1 Mini-Camel

Mathematical Content:
Patterns, algebra, (PSSM Reasoning and Proof
   Standard for Grades 6–8 and 9–12)

Materials:
Problem, objects to manipulate (optional)

Directions: Here are some questions that might help you to develop a strategy to solve this problem.

1. What would happen if Mini-Camel made just one trip? Do you think this is the best solution to the problem?

2. What would happen if Mini-Camel went part of the way with a load, then went back to pick up more bananas and repeated that process? Try some possible distances to see how she could end up with no bananas left behind and the most left to carry to the next stopping point.

3. Continue this process, trying to maximize the number or remaining bananas after each leg of the journey, and not leaving any bananas behind.

FOR STUDENTS

Activity 9.1
Mini-Camel

Directions: What is your first reaction to the problem? (Most will say it cannot be done.) Since it cannot be done in one run, consider the situation where the camel can take the bananas a certain distance to a drop stop, return, take more, etc. Remember that the camel must eat one banana each mile, whether going to or from the market. Find an answer by trial and error, or try to maximize the camel's loads when she begins from each drop spot along the way. In other words, how far should the camel take each load to a drop spot so she continues to the next drop spot with a full load?

Like Corey Camel, Mini-Camel also owns a banana grove. But Mini-Camel's harvest consists of only 45 bananas, and Mini-Camel can carry at most 15 bananas at a time.

The marketplace where Mini-Camel's harvest can be sold is only 15 miles away. Like Corey, however, Mini-Camel eats one banana during each and every mile she walks.

1. How many bananas can Mini-Camel get to market?

2. Explain how Mini-Camel achieves this result.

3. Discuss how the Mini-Camel problem is related to POW 13: Corey Camel, and explain how the mini-POW could help you solve the POW.

Note: Your POW write-up asks you to refer to your work on this assignment, so you'll need to keep a copy of your notes from this mini-POW.

Source: Fendel, Dan, et al. (1997). *Interactive Mathematics Program*. Key Curriculum Press, 1150 65th Street, Emeryville, CA 94608, 1-800-995-MATH. Reprinted with permission.

FOR TEACHERS

Activity 9.2 Finding the Area of a Triangular Region

Mathematical Content:
Area; algebra, advanced algebra, or calculus,
(PSSM Reasoning and Proof Standard for
Grades 6–8 and 9–12)

Materials:
Problem, graph paper

FOR STUDENTS

Activity 9.2
Finding the Area of a Triangular Region

Directions: Be certain to mark and construct the figure as shown and check it with the teacher. Talk with your group about possible approaches to solving the problem.

On a piece of centimeter graph paper, draw a rectangle *ABCD* and a triangle *EFG* formed by folding the rectangle so that point *A* touches side *CD* at point *F*. How far from *D* should point *E* be located to maximize the area of triangle *DEF*? (You might want to simplify the problem by giving a value to the *ABCD* rectangle, such as 12 cm by 8 cm.)

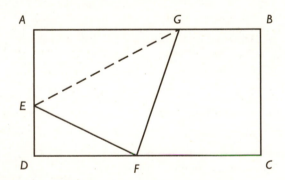

school encouraged minority students to take advanced placement classes through a "Jaime Escalante" campaign, wherein students needing extra academic assistance were given opportunities to take resource classes in place of an elective, repeat courses during off-session, or attend after-school tutoring sessions. In addition, mathematics homework sessions and summer challenge programs boosted enrollments of underrepresented minority groups in higher mathematics courses. For low-achieving students, certain schools adopted reform mathematics curricula integrating strands of algebra, geometry, statistics, probability, and logic. At one school the teachers piloted an integrated mathematics and engineering program that emphasizes the mathematics in vocational skills. These educators are continuing to work to reform their schools, in spite of some community pressure due to ingrained beliefs that the traditional organization of a school should be maintained (Oakes, 1996).

Set 9.1   *Discussion Questions*

 Questions with an asterisk appear in the Message Board section of the Companion Website at *http://www.prenhall.com/huetinck.* Go to Chapter 9 and click on the Message Board to find and respond to the question.

1. What are the disadvantages of a tracked program?
*2. A number of strategies for detracking are discussed. Consider the broad spectrum of the educational community within a district. What elements must be in place for detracking to succeed?
3. Talk to friends who did not continue in higher-level mathematics. Ask them to describe their experiences with the mathematics program in which they were enrolled as secondary-level students.

MATHEMATICS REFORM AND MULTICULTURAL/ MULTIETHNIC STUDENTS

What research basis is there for claiming the teaching strategies promoted in the Standards lead to higher mathematical achievement for economically disadvantaged students? One project had middle school students engage in cognitively challenging tasks similar to those you see in this book while the teachers use questioning techniques and other strategies to elicit mathematical discourse from the students. This project, based at the University of Pittsburgh, is referred to as QUASAR.

The QUASAR Project

"QUASAR is an educational reform project aimed at fostering and studying the development and implementation of enhanced mathematics instructional programs for students attending middle school in economically disadvantaged communities" (Silver, Smith, & Nelson, 1995, p. 9). The purpose of the project, begun in 1989, was to prepare middle-school students for high-school college preparatory courses or technical career training by decreasing the number of tracks and increasing access to challenging mathematics, with assists of special support services. Cooperative groups have been used to foster communities of learners who communicate and collaborate in mathematical thinking. Problems selected often have multiple entry and exit points, more than one right answer, and use a wide range of intellectual skills. The following vignette summarizes a class session dealing with the topic of surface area and volume.

Vignette 9.2   *A QUASAR Inquiry*

Each group was given a set of 24 cubes, and students were asked to construct a rectangular solid, or box, using all 24 cubes; to draw a sketch of the solid that they constructed; to find the area, surface area, and dimensions of the box they constructed; and to record their results. After a brief presentation and discussion of the task, Mr. Henderson set the groups to work as he circulated around the room, checking on the process of each group. Once a group completed a cycle for one solid, it was encouraged to continue the process with a different solid. When the groups had made enough progress, members of each group presented their group's results, which were compiled in the table shown here.

Dimensions	Surface Area	Volume
1 × 1 × 24	98	24
1 × 2 × 12	76	24
1 × 3 × 8	70	24
1 × 4 × 6	68	24
2 × 2 × 6	56	24
2 × 3 × 4	52	24

Students were then asked to make a generalization about the solids and the compiled data in the table. A student noted that longer boxes had greater surface areas than shorter, more compact boxes, and the class agreed with this analysis. Mr. Henderson asked the class to explore how the surface area would be affected if a "compact" rectangular solid were cut in half and the two halves were placed end-to-end to make it longer, or if one of the "long" solids were cut and reassembled to be more compact. After exploration in small groups, followed by whole-class discussion, the class concluded that (a) the surface area increases as the height decreases and the length and width increase, and (b) the surface area decreases as the length, width, and height become numerically closer. Mr. Henderson then asked students to speculate about the smallest surface area possible for a 24-cube rectangular solid, if they were allowed to "cut up" the cubes. After some discussion, the group came to the conclusion that a cube would have the smallest possible surface area. The lesson concluded with students writing in journals about the relationship between volume and surface area.

This task illustrates several features of the kind of mathematics instruction teachers are striving for in QUASAR classrooms. It was exploratory in nature. It involved the integration of basic skills (multiplication and/or addition in calculating volume and surface area) with higher-level processes (making and testing conjecture, making judgments, and forming generalizations based on patterns in data). The task also accommodated multiple modalities of information processing and answer production, since it involved spatial, visual, written, and oral communication.... The task was accessible to all students in the class, yet it offered sufficient challenge for the most able student in the class. The organization of students into cooperative groups allowed students with different abilities and interests to bring their knowledge and talents to bear on the completion of the task (Silver et al., 1995, pp. 33–34).

The parallels between the efforts of the QUASAR educators and the NCTM *Standards* are many. In addition to using explorations with multiple methods, the QUASAR teachers created a comfortable atmosphere for questioning, making hypotheses, testing conclusions, and attaining understanding.

The QUASAR educators have the challenge of working with linguistically diverse learners, as well as students whose life experiences may be quite different from those of the teachers. Some of the teachers are bilingual, and this helps to build communities of learners that discuss mathematical ideas in more than one language. Discourse may move freely back and forth from English to Spanish, and students have access to materials in both languages.

Sometimes the teachers have been surprised by a mathematical answer that reflects the life of the community rather than the desired calculation. For example, students were asked to calculate whether it was best for a student to buy a weekly pass or to pay a daily fare to ride the bus to school. The costs given indicated a better value for 5 days of round-trip fare than for a weekly pass. Still, most of the students believed the weekly pass was the best plan. When discussing this problem with the students, the teachers discovered that the students realistically imagined their families using the pass in the evenings and on the weekends. Thus, they reasoned the weekly pass was the better deal.

Stories, games, dramatic play, poems, storytelling, and music were some of the innovative methods used to create interest in mathematical problems. At one school of predominantly African-American students, the African game Wari became the context for lessons on reasoning strategies:

QUASAR teachers are ordinary people engaged in extraordinary efforts to develop enhanced instructional programs for their students under very difficult circumstances. They are typical of middle school mathematics teachers all over the country in that the majority have elementary certification with limited formal training and background in mathematics, with many completing only a mathematics methods course in college. There is also predictable diversity among project teachers—many are novice teachers with no more than 5 years of experience, whereas others have more than 20 years of experience; most are eager to participate in efforts to change mathematics instruction, but others see little need for change; many share background experiences and racial or ethnic identities similar to those of their students, and a few do not. Although typical in the ways just noted, most teachers in project schools are exceptional among middle school mathematics teachers in their commitment to improving the life chances of their students and in their willingness to exert extra effort to accomplish that goal. In their efforts, teachers are supported by their resource partners, who provide guidance and a sustained reflective presence; by their principals, who try to buffer the project from outside influences that would destroy it before it could become fully established; and by each other, drawing strength from the solidarity that develops as they work together to build new forms of instructional practice that work well for their students (Silver et al., 1995, p. 14).[3]

[3] Silver, E. A., Smith, M. S., & Nelson, B. S. (1995). The QUASAR project: Equity concerns meet mathematics education reform in the middle school. In W. G. Secada, E. Fennema, & L. B. Adajian (Eds.), *New Directions for Equity in Mathematics Education*. Cambridge, MA: Cambridge University Press in collaboration with the National Council of Teachers of Mathematics. Reprinted with the permission of Cambridge University Press.

Making Mathematics Meaningful

We know we must make mathematics meaningful for underrepresented students in technical professions, but how do we do it? In an ethnographic study of eight teachers successful with African-American students, G. Ladson-Billings identified the following common characteristics of these classrooms:

> Students treated as competent are likely to demonstrate competence, . . . Providing instructional scaffolding for students allows them to move from what they know to what they do not know, . . . The major focus of the classroom must be instructional . . . Real education is about extending students' thinking and ability beyond what they already know, . . . and effective pedagogical practice involves in-depth knowledge of students as well as of subject matter (Ladson-Billings, 1995, pp. 137–140).

The following vignette of Ms. Rossi, an Italian American, encapsulates these characteristics. Before class she explained that she would set the context for her students by beginning with information about the origins of algebra. Algebra first appeared in the writing of an Egyptian, Ahmes, about 1700 B.C. Therefore, this was part of the students' heritage.

Vignette 9.3   Notes from an Observer

The entire time I observed her class that morning, Ms. Rossi and her students were involved in mathematics. Although they were engaged in problem solving using algebraic functions, no worksheets were handed out and no problem sets were assigned. The students, as well as Ms. Rossi, posed problems.

From a pedagogical standpoint I saw Ms. Rossi make a point of getting every student involved in the mathematics lesson. She continually assured students that they were capable of mastering the problems. They cheered each other on and celebrated when they were able to explain how they arrived at their solutions. . . .

Ms. Rossi moved around the classroom as students posed questions and suggested solutions. She often asked, "How do you know?" to push the students' thinking. When students asked questions, Ms. Rossi was quick to say, "Who knows? Who can help him out here?" By recycling the questions (and, consequently, the knowledge), Ms. Rossi helped her students understand that they were knowledgeable and capable of answering questions posed by themselves and others. However, Ms. Rossi did not shrink from her own responsibility as teacher. From time to time, she worked individually with students who seemed puzzled or con-

fused about the discussion. By asking a series of probing questions, Ms. Rossi was able to help students organize their thinking about a problem and develop their own problem-solving strategies (Ladson-Billings, 1995, pp. 134–135).[4]

A number of schools with low-income and minority students are proving that their students can succeed in higher-level mathematics. The two examples in Figure 9.1 are taken from *Setting Our Sights: The Measure of Equity in School Change* (Johnson, 1996).

Practicalities

From the examples discussed, it is clear that ethnicity, linguistics, culture, and socioeconomic levels combine to affect the practice of teaching in today's schools. Many students have a cultural background and speak a language quite different from their teacher's. At present, one in five students in the United States is not a native English speaker. Although it might be best to have bilingual teachers who can teach mathematical concepts both in English and the native tongue (Khisty, 1995), this is seldom possible. Difficulties arise even when teachers acquire a second language through college courses, since probably they will not become familiar with mathematical concepts as expressed in the academically learned language. Many classrooms have students with a mix of different first languages, so it is not possible to arrange bilingual education—one native language and English—for the class. You must develop methods, using the available resources, to provide all your students with mathematical knowledge.

Some suggestions for teaching a diverse community of mathematical learners follow:

- Assume that all students in your classes can succeed.
- Do not expect or accept that students who are recent immigrants can take mathematics without linguistic assistance, based on the premise that mathematical symbols are nearly the same in all countries. This is the worst possible travesty, trapping students in computational practice instead of helping them to develop critical thinking

---

[4] Ladson-Billings, G. (1995). Making mathematics meaningful in multicultural contexts. In W. G. Secada, E. Fennema, & L. B. Adajian (Eds.), *New Directions for Equity in Mathematics Education.* Cambridge, MA: Cambridge University Press in collaboration with the National Council of Teachers of Mathematics. Reprinted with the permission of Cambridge University Press.

Figure 9.1
Evidence of Success in Teaching Low-Income and Minority Students

The graphs in this figure show the result of a five year attempt to increase the number of students enrolled in college preparatory mathematics in an urban high school. They show the increase over time as students not only completed algebra but continued to take additional academic mathematics courses in subsequent years. What the graph is not able to show is the dedication and hard work on the part of teachers and administrators at that school toward access to higher education for their students. Although this is data from a single school, many urban schools across North America are achieving similar results, aided by exemplary curricula and research-based pedagogy.

Opportunity High School 5-Year Course Trend   The data in the bar graph describe changes over 5 years in an urban high-school mathematics department that purposely began offering algebra to all of its predominantly low-income African-American student body. This was prompted by a district thrust and several different improvement initiatives. A group inside Opportunity High School that felt a very high level of dissatisfaction with current outcomes took on the challenge of change, led by a committed principal. As the data show, this school changed the status quo. They then took the initiative beyond algebra to increase the levels of enrollment in other college-preparatory courses. Over a 5-year period, the school's mathematics department dramatically increased the number of college-preparatory mathematics courses from 47% to 83%. These data challenge naysayers who don't believe that these kinds of changes are possible with the described student population. In addition, this underscores that *fundamental changes often occur over a period of time, rather than instantaneously.*

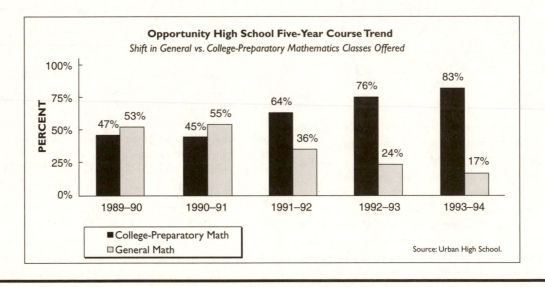

skills. As a teacher, refuse to use lists of vocabulary that only translate mathematical operations; these lists will do nothing to help students understand mathematics. Rather, insist that the students have the same language support systems in mathematics as they receive in other disciplines.

■ Remember that arriving immigrant students over 6 years of age generally take 6 to 7 years to approach grade-level proficiency in English (Cummins, 1991). That youngsters can converse in English does not mean they are proficient enough to understand and communicate deep mathematical concepts. Be cautious in forming an opinion of the language ability of your students.

■ Do not assume that all Hispanic immigrants speak a common Spanish language. Some Hispanics may immigrate from Brazil, where the major language is Portuguese; others come from different countries in South America or from different regions within these countries and speak a

Figure 9.1
(continued)

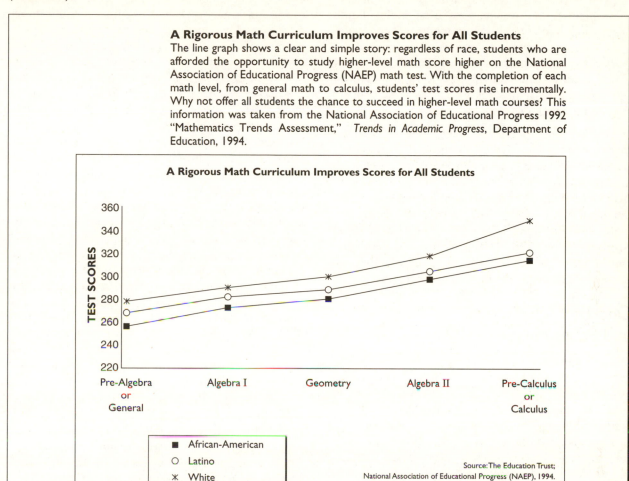

A Rigorous Math Curriculum Improves Scores for All Students
The line graph shows a clear and simple story: regardless of race, students who are afforded the opportunity to study higher-level math score higher on the National Association of Educational Progress (NAEP) math test. With the completion of each math level, from general math to calculus, students' test scores rise incrementally. Why not offer all students the chance to succeed in higher-level math courses? This information was taken from the National Association of Educational Progress 1992 "Mathematics Trends Assessment," *Trends in Academic Progress*, Department of Education, 1994.

Source: Johnson, R. S. (1996). *Setting Our Sights: Measuring Equity in School Change.* Los Angeles: The Achievement Council. Reprinted with permission.

dialect that may not be easy for even a bilinguist to understand. We know Mexican immigrant mathematics teachers in our graduate program who say that sometimes they cannot communicate with as many as half of the Hispanic students in a class. This is due not only to regional dialectics, but also to differing versions of the Mayan language. It seems to be more widely known that not all Asians speak the same language, even if from the same country.

■ When possible, pair more fluent English speakers with those less fluent, but check to see that they can communicate and get along well together. It is appropriate to change groups periodically so students learn to work with different students. Also, mix students occasionally in cross-cultural groupings.

■ Check that all students are progressing in their communication of mathematics as well as their use of English. Try to help students develop conceptual understanding, even if their use of English is limited. Waiting until their English is fluent to begin word problems in mathematics will unnecessarily hold them back academically.

■ Be sensitive to the types of assignments that the students most enjoy. For example, if they like to do projects or cooperative learning, be creative in adapting the main curriculum so it is project based or has cooperative activities.

■ Do not avoid types of assignments that students may find difficult, such as writing out their solutions in complete sentences. Provide scaffolding and assistance so they can begin to experience success. If computers are accessible, perhaps writing on the computer will be more exciting to them than pencil-and-paper assignments.

- Even if you have traditional texts, you can use problems and investigations from multicultural resource books to "hook" students into the main concepts presented in your texts.
- Techniques such as using body language, everyday objects as manipulatives, and pictorial representations assist all students, and especially those with language deficiencies.

One way to address diversity issues in mathematics is to select activities and tasks that are mathematically rich and have multiple solution strategies at different levels of mathematical sophistication. Activities 9.3 and 9.4 are excellent for evaluating students' problem-solving abilities because neither activity can be solved by a textbook algorithm. Algebra can be used for Activity 9.3, and geometry can be used for Activity 9.4. Alternatively, students can approach both activities by finding patterns.

Dealing With Cultural and Economic Diversity

Do not assume that all students have attended school the years previous to the grade you teach. Students may have come from countries where it was too expensive or too dangerous to attend school regularly. A student new to schooling will need explicit instructions concerning the bell schedule, where to sit, and perhaps even in deportment. We recall students enrolled at the beginning of middle, school who had not attended school before.

Try to build a curriculum that is relevant to the experiences of your students outside the classroom. In his provocative article "Race, Retrenchment, and the Reform of School Mathematics," William Tate offers the following example of an empowering mathematics project for a class of African-American students. The class identified 25 problems that were negatively affecting their community. One of these problems was the large number of liquor stores within a 1,000-foot radius of the school. The students studied the economics of the situation to propose mathematically based incentives to induce the liquor store owners to relocate farther from the school. Thus, "mathematics is more than just numbers short of context (i.e., in-school knowledge). Instead, mathematics is embedded within the culture of their daily struggles" (Tate, 1994, p. 482). This example illustrates Tate's main point that a mathematics pedagogy should be built on the students' experiences and prepare them to participate in a democratic society.

Furthermore, for the student who does not know some of her elementary arithmetic facts, investigate the previous educational experience of the student, rather than assuming low ability. Whatever the cause of the deficit, the student needs access to tutoring. Information about the student's educational background will increase the effectiveness of the tutoring. Likewise, give specific instructions about how to organize notes, homework, and so on, but do not be rigid if these instructions are not always followed. Perhaps school is the only place in this student's life that is organized, and these are skills that take time to learn.

In addition, be sensitive to the school culture. Sometimes, even in relatively affluent schools, certain groups of students do not wish to be seen carrying books. If you run into this, try to get a classroom set of texts so the student has one at home and can use another at school. Or, if photocopying facilities are available, make copies of homework problems so that the pages can be folded into a pocket for concealment.

Of course, it is never appropriate to make a negative remark about any student's clothes or cleanliness. You have no idea of the living conditions of the student. You may show concern during an individual conversation, however. In fact, this is how I (LH) learned that one of my students was living in his car and washing up at the city park. His mother thought he was staying with his father, and his father believed him to be with his mother. In addition, some students may be homeless children who, though living with a parent, are making do in sad circumstances. In these cases, youngsters are doing well to stay in school, and appearance is low on their list of priorities.

If a student does not do her homework, it may be because doing it is really quite difficult due to her home environment. Under certain circumstances, assigning detention with tutoring available may be a sound educational practice. I (SM) have had students thank me for assigning detention when they came in after school to get caught up on homework. It showed I cared enough to be there to help them, and they expressed appreciation for the little extra push. The following suggestions are other ways a teacher can be receptive and responsive to students' needs:

- Begin a file of interesting mathematics problems from different cultures. It is *not* enough to note cultural diversity simply by celebrating certain special days.
- Be aware of the religious customs of your students to be certain you do not make assignments that might interfere with their religious practices. For example, do not set the due date of an important assignment to conflict with a significant religious holiday.

FOR TEACHERS

Activity 9.3 Crossing the River

Mathematical Content:
Patterns, algebra, (PSSM Reasoning and Proof
    Standard for Grades 6–8 and 9–12)

Materials:
Problem, overhead projector

Directions: Place the student page on an overhead projector. Ask students to solve the problem
individually or to work in groups and solve it together. Require that students describe how they
solved the problem.

Extension: Determine the number of trips for x
adults and 2 children. Does the pattern change if
x is odd? How does the pattern change if the
number of children is odd?

FOR STUDENTS

Activity 9.3
Crossing the River

Directions: All the individuals can row, including the children. Who should be in the first boat?
Develop a pattern.

Eight adults and two children have a boat and need to cross a river. The boat can hold EITHER one adult OR up to two children. Everyone can row the boat. What is the smallest number of river crossings necessary for the adults and children to cross the river?

Source: Adapted from materials developed by Educational Development Corporation for the Leadership in Urban Mathematics Reform
Project funded by the National Science Foundation.

FOR TEACHERS

Activity 9.4 Cutting the Cake

Mathematical Content:
Patterns, geometry, area of a triangle, (PSSM Reasoning and Proof Standard for Grades 6–8 and 9–12)

Materials:
Problem, overhead projector, graph paper

Directions: Pass out graph paper. Post the "Cutting the Cake" problem on the overhead projector in front of the whole class, and ask students to solve the problem. Students can work individually or in groups. Require students to describe how they solved the problem.

FOR STUDENTS

Activity 9.4
Cutting the Cake

Directions: The fact that the amount of icing must be the same for each child rules out cutting horizontally along a side. Consider the simpler problem of cutting a round cake. Write down the steps, assuming you do not have a protractor but can measure the distance around the cake. The problem is much easier to visualize if you use graph paper. What size square might simplify the problem? Why did you pick these dimensions? Cut the square cake, using your dimensions for cutting the square cake. What can you say about the triangles formed on top of the cake?

Six friends come to Mary's birthday party. She has a square cake that is iced on the top and on all four sides. How can she cut the entire cake so that each of the seven youngsters has the same amount of cake and the same amount of icing?

- Remember that punctuality, competition, eye contact, questioning ideas, and individual work have values in certain cultures that may vary considerably from those of the typical American middle class.

- Keep significant goals in perspective. It is important for a student to be engaged in mathematics; it is not important that her name be written in the upper left-hand corner of the paper instead of the upper right-hand corner (or to be sometimes left off).

- Get to know the community where you teach and where your students live.

- Assume that all students in your classes can succeed, but do not despair if occasionally you cannot reach someone.

Vignette 9.4 One Teacher's Answer

How do you embrace diversity? What would be the evidence that you have done just that? As an educator and specifically a high school mathematics teacher, these are important questions. Let me begin with my classroom. My instructional techniques and curriculum choices are guided by the following guidelines:

1. All students will be given the opportunity to learn, and high-level learning will take place.
2. There is never time to waste.
3. I will move all students forward, no matter the level at which they begin.
4. Good teaching takes into account student differences and similarities, whether they are language, cultural, and/or economic. These differences are a challenge for all of us, but they are not barriers.
5. As a woman and a Mexican American, I am a role model; my learning is continuous.
6. Math is important.
7. All students can learn.

How do these "rules to teach by" affect my classroom? Students know very quickly that there is learning to be done every day. It is not good enough that most are doing their work, but my mission is for all to be engaged in the learning experience. If language is an issue, then bilingual materials, sheltering techniques, student language partners, etc., are utilized to ease the transition as the students become more English proficient. I share with them my life struggles and triumphs. I share with them the goals and aspirations I have for my children and how they are no different than the ones I hold for them. Math is a tool that they will use throughout their life, and the study of it is rewarding and often times fun. Every student in my class is given the opportunity to achieve, and many do, but I know more can do better. If more time is needed to learn, then my classroom is open during lunch and sometimes after school. My actions and attitude convey to my students that they all can learn, they all can achieve, and I will be there to motivate, encourage, and support them in this effort.

What does this have to do with diversity? After all, items 4 and 5 are the only ones that address diversity directly. Good teaching practices are appropriate for all students. The language, economic, cultural, etc. background of the students are what make the class unique, and they need to be recognized and addressed, but they do not change the rest of my goals.

As department chairperson, I remind members of the goals our department strives to maintain:

1. All students will be given the opportunity to learn, and high-level learning will take place.
2. There is never time to waste.
3. All students will move forward, no matter the level at which they begin.
4. Good teaching takes into account student differences and similarities, whether they are language, cultural, and/or economic. These differences are a challenge for all of us, but they are not barriers.
5. Math is important.
6. All students can learn.
7. Our learning is continuous.
8. Communication within the department is important.

Why is it that my goals and those of the department are so much alike? We communicate; we communicate a lot. We communicate with our feeder school and share our goals and vision. We hire new teachers who share our vision. We want all students to achieve, and at a high level. We are respected by other departments, and we take pride in that. One of our missions is for our AP Calculus and AP Statistics classes to reflect the diversity of the school. We have moved forward in that direction. We want all students to continue to take math the full 4 years of high school. We continue to make strides in this area. When you embrace diversity within your classroom and department, you strive for all students to achieve. If there is a student need, be it economic, cultural, language, etc., you address it as a department and act on it. Almost all department members participate in our after-school tutorial program, and many open their classrooms during their lunch hour. We look for and receive outside funding.

There will always be circumstances beyond our control. In a perfect world all students would come into the classroom on equal footing. This is not possible, but good teaching and challenging curriculum are. These are the things that will help equalize the playing field.

Yvonne Mojica
Verdugo Hills High School,
Los Angeles Unified School District

Set 9.2 *Discussion Questions*

 Questions with an asterisk appear in the Message Board section of the Companion Website at *http://www.prenhall.com/huetinck.* Go to Chapter 9 and click on the Message Board to find and respond to the question.

*1. We all have some prejudices even beyond those of color, ethnicity, or cultural background that may affect our classroom demeanor as a teacher. Honestly evaluate any prejudices you might have. Consider how you can ensure that these attitudes do not adversely affect students in your charge.

2. What type of information might you gather to better assist you in providing equal opportunities for mathematical success for students in a diverse class?

*3. With which of the bulleted practicalities on pages 370 and 375 do you most strongly agree? With which do you disagree? Explain your reasoning in either case.

GENDER DIFFERENCES

The results from research on gender differences in motivation and in achievement have changed in the past 20 years. In the early 1980s researchers began to find decreasing gender differences in achievement in mathematics and science, where previously females consistently had performed more poorly than males. A summary of some of the more than 600 programs funded by the National Science Foundation and the American Association for the Advancement of Science from 1966 to 1982 produced real gains in helping women to excel in science and mathematics. Strong academic emphasis, multiple strategies, and systems approaches were common elements in the more effective programs. In particular, achievement in mathematics was nearly equal for males and females until the fifth grade, when females began falling behind. The gender differences became more pronounced in high school (Huetinck, 1990). An analysis of large numbers of students taking the state-mandated California Assessment Program exam, combined with observation research, prompted a hypothesis that girls did better than boys in elementary school as long as there were algorithms to follow in problem solving. When females reached higher-level

courses, they were less able to try novel solutions, perhaps because they had internalized the rules so well that their creativity suffered (Marshall, 1984). Gender differences in mathematics achievement are declining, but they still are significant at the advanced mathematics course levels (American Association of University Women, 1992).

Two Classroom Research Studies

In spite of the decreasing gender gap on mathematics achievement tests, today's educators still must be sensitive to gender differences in the classroom that have been observed by seasoned teachers. Following are two brief summaries of classroom research performed by collaborative groups of teachers in their secondary-level classrooms. One group investigated gender differences in calculator use, and another group studied differences in patterns of interactions in boy/girl pairs.

In the first study the teacher-researchers collected data consisting of student attitude surveys, students' open-ended written responses, classroom observations, and interviews with students. Both genders found calculators to be useful and fun, but males self-reported that they are more likely to play and explore with calculators than was reflected in the females' self-reported preferences. When comparing students in the 6th and 12th grades, there was a tendency for greater numbers of older males to agree that "Guys know more about calculators." However, females at both grade levels did not agree with this statement. The older males were more confident when using calculators than the male sixth-graders, while the girls did not gain in confidence when comparing the two grade levels. Classroom observations documented considerably greater use of the calculators by males. When interviewed, the females said they wanted to work out the problem doing all the steps instead of using the calculator. The most telling event was when one TI-92 was brought into the sixth-grade classroom, and 73% of the males signed up to try out the calculator, while none of the girls did so. Since attitudes and behaviors toward calculators seem to change from middle school to high school, it is imperative that middle-school teachers give all students extensive experience on scientific and graphing calculators. These teachers recommend that each student needs access to her own calculator and that females need to be encouraged to use the calculators for explorations. The researchers concluded, "It appears that as the students grow older, and the calculators become more sophisticated in their applications beyond basic operations, the greater the gap between males and females in their interest and usage" (Perfect, 1997, p. 71).

In the second study, teacher-researchers analyzed videos of high-ability girl/boy pairs solving the Painted Cubes problem (Investigation 8.2). The students were given manipulatives and calculators to solve this nonstandard problem. The females were somewhat more verbal than the males, as evidenced by giving longer and more frequent explanations. They more frequently took the lead by asking questions and giving suggestions about how to proceed. The data indicated that the females, even though high achieving, were much more insecure than the males in making mathematical decisions. They frequently demonstrated the need for reassurance and validation when working. The researchers recommend giving encouragement to all students, with the understanding that the reassurance appears to be of greater importance to the females (Widdel, 1996).

The differences noted in these two studies indicate possible reasons fewer females than males persist in taking higher-level mathematics. Certainly, sophisticated use of calculators and confidence to attack original problems are necessary for success in advanced courses. These classroom research results seem to mesh with other recent research on differences in problem-solving approaches by males and females. Gender differences in approaches to solving problems by high-ability mathematics students were analyzed for SAT mathematics problems identified as either conventional or unconventional. Females tended to follow a classroom-learned, algorithmic approach, while males were more likely to use unconventional methods. Furthermore, high scores correlated well with confidence and persistence toward mathematics, while use of conventional strategies correlated with attitudes of dislike and belief in the irrelevance of mathematics (Gallagher, & DeLisi, 1994). This fits with the teacher-researcher observations that females are much less secure when solving a demanding, uncommon problem, such as the Painted Cubes problem.

In our experience, higher-level mathematics courses do require less use of algorithms and a greater independence in constructing knowledge than in courses typically found in middle school or the first 2 years of high school. If females are especially insecure with problems that do not fit an algorithmic approach, they may be less likely to enroll in higher-level mathematics, even when they have high mathematical ability. Thus, the innovative problems found in many of the reformed curriculum may be of special benefit to females to allow them practice and success using unconventional solutions.

The checklist in Figure 9.2 was developed as part of a gender-equity intervention program. It is easy to see how all students will benefit when a teacher can implement these objectives (Koontz, 1997, pp. 193–194).

Set 9.3 Discussion Question

1. What are some specific tactics that you as a teacher can use to encourage gender equity?

SPECIAL EDUCATION

Students With Mild Learning Disabilities

Identifying and assisting youngsters whose low ability in mathematics is based on learning disabilities is complex. In 1975 federal law, the Education for All Handicapped Children Act (EHA), mandated that special-education students be placed in the least restrictive learning environment for success in learning. Learning-disabled students may be youngsters with mental retardation, serious emotional disturbances, autism, traumatic brain injury, attention deficit disorder, attention deficit hyperactivity disorders, or other specific learning disabilities. Identification of learning disabilities is difficult because many factors may contribute to low achievement. Standardized tests are not a good criteria for identifying learning disabilities. Low motivation, prior mathematics instruction, cultural bias of tests, immaturity, and other noncognitive factors may explain low test scores. Furthermore, probably there is no one cognitive factor for the learning disability.

With experience in interacting with students at a range of age levels, maturity, and mathematical ability, you will become sensitive to students who might have learning disabilities. Ask yourself these questions: Does the student have an attention deficit, such as difficulty in paying attention to steps of problem solving or modeling the teacher? Does the student have visual-spatial deficits, such as difficulty using a number line, keeping her place on a worksheet, or differentiating between certain numbers? Does the student have auditory-processing difficulties, such as participating in oral drills? Does the student have memory problems in retaining

Figure 9.2

Classroom Observation Checklist

In creating a gender-fair program, the teacher—

1. fosters a climate of openness by
   - calling students by name, and
   - moving around the classroom;
2. encourages student interaction and cooperation by having students
   - work in small groups using varied roles (reporter, recorder),
   - respond to other students,
   - explores others' points of view,
   - listen to explanations by many students, and
   - use manipulatives cooperatively;
3. demonstrates an attitude of acceptance by
   - accepting all valid student responses,
   - giving supportive comments to incorrect answers, and
   - probing further the "I don't know" responses;
4. encourages students to gather and organize information by
   - having students classify and categorize data,
   - having reference materials readily available, and
   - having students record data in journals;
5. provides visual cues to develop cognitive strategies by using appropriate charts, pictures, mathematics manipulatives, and models;
6. makes connections to past concepts and applications;
7. elicits the verbalization of students' reasoning by
   - posing "if … then" and "what if …" questions,
   - posing questions at different levels of Bloom's taxonomy, and
   - calling on both sexes equitably at each question level;
8. promotes silent reflection by
   - giving appropriate wait time,
   - withholding a "correct" response, and
   - requesting more responses even after a "correct" response is given;
9. encourages equity by
   - referring to women and minority scientists and mathematicians,
   - reflecting on her or his own teaching to ensure equitable instruction;
   - encouraging females to perform traditional male tasks (load computers, move desks),
   - using gender-fair language (scientist, . . . she; doctor, . . . she), and
   - holding high expectations for females and minorities.

Source: Koontz, T. (1997). Know thyself, the evolution of an intervention gender-equity program. In J. Trentacosta & M. J. Kenney (Eds.), *Multicultural and Gender Equity in the Mathematics Classroom: The Gift of Diversity*, 1997 Yearbook. Reston, VA: National Council of Teachers of Mathematics. Reprinted with permission.

mathematics information or perform poorly on review material? (Miller & Mercer, 1997).

Public Law 105-17—Individuals With Disabilities Education Act (IDEA) Amendments of 1997—has brought about many changes to the 1975 legislation. As before, each student has a vital document called the Individualized Education Program (IEP) prepared by educators, parents, and when appropriate, the student. This document spells out the services the student will receive. The main change

in the law with regard to the general education teacher is that she is now a member of the IEP team who shall, "to the extent appropriate, participate in the development of the IEP of the child" [Section 614(d)(3)]. The IEP includes determining positive appropriate behavior interventions when necessary, assigning certain supplementary learning aids and services, and possibly modifying programs for the youngster. Other changes significant to the general education teacher include emphasis upon participation of youths with disabilities in general education classrooms, in the general curriculum, with aids and services as needed, and in State and district assessment programs (*News Digest,* National Information Center for Children and Youth with Disabilities, 1997).

The main effort is not to identify the students, but rather to try strategies to assist in learning whether a student is identified as requiring special education. Try to implement interventions before referring a student to a special-education program. Keep a variety of student work, and see if you recognize patterns of success and special difficulties. Analyze what the student knows and does not know. Ask the student how she feels about mathematics and whether she is confident in doing a particular activity. Then, if the student is moved to a special-education program, the preliminary information on the student's learning patterns will be of great value to the special-education teacher.

Carnine (1997) has found the following strategies to be effective for students with learning disabilities:

- Teach clusters of information around a central idea. For example, instead of expecting students to use different formulas for volume of different geometric objects, concentrate on the one relationship of base times the height. Treat the pyramid and the sphere as special cases for which there is not a single height.
- Teach conspicuous strategies. For example, assist students in developing a set of steps for working a problem (rather than providing the procedure). As students continue to use the explicit steps, they will eventually master a strategy.
- Use time efficiently. Do not try to do too much too quickly; proceed at a comfortable pace for the students.
- Focus on big ideas instead of emphasizing details.
- Ease into complex strategies. For example, begin with a simplified data chart of a few entries, or use a protractor with the angle scale in only one direction, so students do not get overwhelmed by new material.
- Use a strand organization with a variety of related concepts over several days, so students receive the review as needed but do not get bored with practice of one problem type for a long time in 1 day.
- Use manipulatives in a time-efficient manner.
- Clearly communicate strategies explicitly with scaffolding into self-directed learning accompanied by consistent feedback.
- Provide practice and review to facilitate retention.

From our experience, we would add that situations that could possibly distract students should be kept to a minimum. For example, have materials necessary for the day's lesson on students' desks when they arrive in class to avoid the distractions inherent in passing out items after the class has begun. Also, check frequently for understanding of vocabulary words you might expect the students to know. It is too easy to blame low ability on mathematical deficiencies when students, even native English speakers, really are having difficulties in verbal or written comprehension.

Thoughtful use of manipulatives can be especially helpful for instruction of the learning disabled. "Structured situations involving manipulatives help these students, organize their thinking so that they begin to see relationships or follow the flow of a computational procedure" (Thornton & Wilmot, 1986, p. 38). These researchers recommend using manipulatives to talk through a problem, write up a model, record the entire solution, and discriminate between new and previous learning. However, you cannot assume that students with mild learning disabilities will react in the same way to manipulatives as you might. It is important to be explicit in the use of manipulatives and to help students focus on the significant characteristics of the manipulative that aid in understanding. For example, Baroody (1993) recommends using number sticks of trains of number cubes instead of Cuisenaire rods. Because youngsters must relate the color and length of the rod to a code to find its representative length, it is easier simply to count the cubes in the number train when using number sticks.

Most importantly, we have found that students with learning disabilities or general low mathematics ability need the teacher's considerable encouragement and frequent reminders of their progress. Try to administer quizzes and return them quickly. Have students keep a record of their daily work, even if it is only a check on their homework or classwork. Weekly, lead students in calculating the status of their accumulative grade. A low-ability student is apt to remember that she got a B on one quiz but forgets the zeros on several assignments, and is genuinely surprised when the total grade is not a B. If it pleases the students, and it generally does, stamp their papers for effort shown. While the class does desk work, try to talk a few minutes each week to each student about her progress in the course: The lack of retention of these students does not pertain only to mathematical facts. They seldom remember their difficulties or even their successes.

If you become impatient with a low-ability student, try to recall an activity in which you were involved that was difficult for you. Perhaps you were always the last to be chosen for a sports team, sang in a group even though it was hard to find the notes, or hated to write because it was difficult to be creative. Then realize that these youngsters have spent many hours daily for years of their lives in schooling in a similar situation in which it is difficult for them to do well. They recognize that others their age can perform the task more easily. When you put yourself in their shoes, patience returns.

High Achievers and Mentally Gifted and Talented Students

Students who are high achievers or mentally gifted and talented generally are characterized by above average ability, high levels of task commitment, and creativeness. Because these students tend to be curious and natural learners, educators sometimes feel it is less necessary to provide for their needs than for students of low ability. Based on our experience, we completely reject this attitude. High-ability students need programs designed to assist them to reach their full potential. Furthermore, the most capable students are many of our leaders of the future, so society is wise to teach them how to use their talents.

HR 4127, the Gifted and Talented Students Education Act of 1998, set forth categorical block grants to support programs and services for gifted and talented students. Some provisions of this act include the following:

- Funding is based on state student population, with a minimum of $1 million per state.
- Decisions on how to best serve these students are left to state and local districts.
- Evaluation is required of program effectiveness.
- Federal funds must supplement and not supplant state and local funds allocated for gifted education.
- No more than 10% of the money received by the state can be used for state education agency and administration.

The law allows states to distribute money to public schools for programs and services in four areas: professional development for general education teachers, school counselors, and administrators; implementation of innovative programs and services for high-ability students; use of emerging technology, including distance learning; and technical assistance to states and local school districts.

One way to address the needs of gifted and talented students is to provide them with qualitatively different and more challenging materials or extensions to problems. Many of the activities in this book include extensions for this purpose. Activities 9.5

and 9.6 are number sense challenges for middle-school students and high-school students, respectively. The answer to the question in Activity 9.6 is not difficult, but explaining why takes thought.

 For more interesting problems of the same type as Activity 9.5, visit *http://www. prenhall.com/huetinck,* and click on Web Destinations for Chapter 9.

There are a number of forms of curriculum arrangement for the most able students:

- "Curriculum compacting is a flexible, research-supported instructional technique that enables high-ability students to skip work they already know and substitute more challenging content" (Reis & Renzuilli, 1992, p. 51). Students take a pretest to demonstrate a high level of understanding of the next unit of concepts. The teacher then prescribes enrichment materials providing academic challenges as a replacement for practice on topics the student already understands. Depending on the students' interests and needs, the work may be individualized or group work.
- Grade telescoping programs are designed to enable high-ability students to progress through middle school and high school in fewer years than the regular program.
- Early admission to college may take different forms. This is especially effective if grade telescoping is combined with a special college program that provides support systems to students who begin taking college courses early. Some junior colleges admit high-school students to certain classes before they graduate from high school. Some 4-year colleges have special programs of full enrollment of students several years younger than the average college freshman. These colleges provide support systems including assigning these students to certain college advisors, establishing networks among the students, and even providing a central place where the students can meet and socialize with peers of the same age group.
- Acceleration commonly is used in mathematics by beginning students early in middle school with algebra and geometry concepts, enabling them to begin high-school classes 1 to 2 years ahead of the average student. A review of studies finds that bright students are not harmed socially or psychologically by being accelerated in their program (Rogers & Kimpston, 1992). The only problem we have seen with the approach is that this program

F O R   T E A C H E R S

Activity 9.5 Guess My Number If You Can

Mathematical Content:
Patterns, number theory, (PSSM Reasoning and
  Proof Standard for Grades 6–8 and 9–12)

Materials:
Problem

Directions: Provide individual students with Activity 9.5, and ask them to try solving the problem. Have students first work the problem as individuals. If students continue to struggle, assign pairs to solve it together and provide explanations orally and or in writing.

F O R   S T U D E N T S

Activity 9.5
Guess My Number If You Can

Directions: If this problem seems quite complicated, simplify it. Find a number that fulfills these conditions without a remainder. Once you have this number, how can you find the number from the given problem? Think of the processes you used to find the number and write an explanation that another student could use if they were stumped.

I'm thinking of a number. Put away your calculators, they won't help you this week. Here are the only clues I'm going to give you:

My number when divided by 2 has a remainder of 1.
My number when divided by 3 has a remainder of 2.
My number when divided by 4 has a remainder of 3.
My number when divided by 5 has a remainder of 4.
My number when divided by 6 has a remainder of 5.
My number when divided by 7 has a remainder of 6.
My number when divided by 8 has a remainder of 7.
My number when divided by 9 has a remainder of 8.

Well, maybe one more clue: My number is the smallest integer for which the above clues hold true.

After you find my number, I want you to tell me *how* you can find my number. I will not accept guess and check or trial and error as the reason this week.

I want you to practice using words like:

divide NOT goes into

multiply NOT timesed

factor

product

quotient

divisor

dividend

Good luck! This one may be harder for you to explain than to solve.

Go to Web Destinations for Chapter 9 at
http://www.prenhall.com/huetinck for a
link to more extensions on number sense
problems under content specific sites.

F O R   T E A C H E R S

Activity 9.6 The Locker Problem

Mathematical Content:
Patterns, number sense, (PSSM Reasoning and Proof Standard for Grades 6–8 and 9–12)

Materials:
Problem, graph paper, overhead projector

Teacher Directions: Display the following problem on an overhead projector. Ask students to use the graph paper to make their "locker" charts.

Extension: The real beauty of this problem is to explain the "why" of the result by considering odd and even numbers of factors. Have students consider the numbers of odd or even factors as they write mathematical explanations for the outcome.

F O R   S T U D E N T S

Activity 9.6
The Locker Problem

Directions: This activity is not simple. Make a chart of each pass by the lockers, tabulating whether they are open or closed.

There are 500 students and 500 lockers, numbered 1 through 500. Suppose the first student opens each locker. Then the second student closes every second locker. The third student changes the state of every third locker. The fourth student changes the state of every fourth locker. This process continues until the 500th student changes the state of the 500th locker. Which lockers are open?

supplants all other creative ways to challenge the high achievers. We hope it is used in conjunction with additional avenues to promote the intellectual growth of high-ability students.

- Concurrent enrollment involves attending classes both in junior high and senior high schools on the same day. Students may be in academic higher-level classes at the high school (frequently, mathematics and English) and take other classes at the middle school or junior high school. The greatest problem is the logistics of arranging transportation and coordination of classes with time for travel.

- Mentoring of a student by a practicing mathematician or college mathematics professor may be appropriate for the exceptional student beyond the usual high-school curriculum. This is especially effective if the student is pursuing a topic of interest and can demonstrate progress in a science and mathematics fair. Certainly, mentored high-school mathematicians have done very well in the nationwide Westinghouse Talent Search.

- Advanced placement classes allow students to take college courses in high school. The students receive college credit or advanced standing in higher education according to their level of proficiency demonstrated on exams administered by the College Board. Many mathematics students take courses and exams in Calculus AB, Calculus BC, Computer Programming, and Statistics. Materials including suggested texts, course outlines, and problems from old exams can be obtained from the College Board.

- Special programs for high achievers and gifted and talented students may be one of three general types. First, students with an interest in science and mathematics attend a school with a special curriculum that offers a rich array of electives. Many of these programs have enrollments of 300 to 500 students within a large secondary-level school. We know of successful secondary-level programs of this type that collaborate closely with a nearby public institution, as, for example, the city zoo, the county hospital, and a state university. Second, special programs within a school may be available based on identification of either gifted or highly gifted status according to state and district standards. We know of one highly gifted program in which students begin taking Calculus and Biology Advanced Placement courses (and exams) in the ninth grade. Third, programs for gifted and talented students may be available on a pull-out basis, in which students from different schools regularly meet at a central site.

- Some districts and states have publicly funded academies, frequently on a boarding school basis, for the exceptionally gifted. Competition frequently is keen for openings in these schools, but you should encourage interested students to apply even if it means you will miss having them in your class.

- Summer-school options may include special classes held at the school site or outside programs designed for high-achieving students. You should become aware of the many nationwide programs as well as the financial support available, so you can inform able students of these opportunities. Our students who have been fortunate enough to be accepted into these programs frequently have had marvelous life-changing experiences.

- Out-of-school activities that appeal especially to the mathematically capable may be arranged by the school, such as visits to industries, universities, or museums, with talks and demonstrations centering on practical and research applications of mathematics. To make these field trips meaningful, the teacher must ensure a valuable learning experience by preparing both the students and speakers at the visited institution. For example, the teacher should confer with the speaker about the topic to ensure it will be within the interest and intellectual grasp of the students. The students can be prepared by reading and discussing material about the upcoming activity.

Many of these options overlap and support each other. For example, we know a college professor who teaches a summer class in number theory for high-school students. These students then present their impressive work at the state science fair.

Set 9.4 *Discussion Questions*

 Questions with an asterisk appear in the Message Board section of the Companion Website at *http://www.prenhall.com/huetinck.* Go to Chapter 9 and click on the Message Board to find and respond to the question.

1. How can you recognize students with mild learning disabilities?
*2. What mathematical support will you employ to assist students with mild learning disabilities?
3. What are desirable program characteristics for high-achieving students?

Summary

One of the six basic principles of the *Principles and Standards for School Mathematics* (2000) (p. 12) is the equity principle, which states, "Excellence in mathematics education requires equity—high expectations and strong support for all students." Furthermore, equity is at the core of the vision of this document to improve mathematics education for all students. There are three main elements to the equity principle:

- "Equity requires high expectations and worthwhile opportunities for all."
- "Equity requires accommodating differences to help everyone learn mathematics."
- "Equity requires resources and support for all classrooms and all students" (2000, pp. 12–14).

This chapter selected only four topics under the broad term of equity: tracking, multicultural/ multiethnic education, gender differences, and special education. We expect that you will receive greater depth and breadth of discussion and learning during your professional career on these are other related issues, because each of these topics could be the subject of a complete course. The material presented in this text, of necessity, is simply an introduction to a particularly significant set of topics that will be ever more important as we travel further in the 21st century while our nation becomes more and more diverse. We must increasingly use *Standards*-based curricula, technology, and reasonable and appropriate support. We must even confront our own beliefs to provide access and opportunities for all students to succeed in mathematics.

ASSIGNMENTS

1. Select an important concept in the core curriculum—information that all students should be able to access. Design a series of lessons for a class with students with mild learning disabilities. Design lessons around the same concept for a high-achieving class. What differences did you incorporate in the two sets of lessons?

2. In the future when computers are readily available for all students upon command, envision how detracking might be enhanced. Describe the various elements of the role the teacher will be able to fill in this classroom.

3. Make a tape of yourself teaching a lesson. (Do check with the administration first to be certain it is permissible.) Focus on your ability to engage all students in the lesson. Do you call on some students more than others? What types of students are those? After analyzing the first tape, make another and see if you are able to increase the level of involvement of the students. (If you don't, do not get discouraged. Realize that a number of factors may intercede to change substantially the learning situation even with the same class. We all just keep working on this most important aspect of teaching.).

4. Find a school in your area that has challenged or is making a concerted effort to challenge all students. Interview the mathematics department chairperson to find out what methods she was able to successfully employ.

5. Interview a secondary-level counselor to become familiar with the different programs available at a given school in your area.

INSTRUCTIONAL RESOURCES

Baroody, A. J. (1993). Introducing number and arithmetic concepts with number sticks. *Teaching Exceptional Children, 60(2)*, 7–11.
This excellent article details how youngsters with learning difficulties may more easily grasp number concepts using segmented number sticks rather than Cuisenaire rods, whose length must be deduced by comparison to a color or code. The article reminds us that naive learners may have difficulties with manipulatives that those experienced in mathematics may not see.

Brandt, R. S. (Ed.). (1992). *Educational leadership, 50(2)*.

The entire October journal is devoted to detracking for equity and providing equitably for student differences.

Callahan, W. (1994). Teaching middle-school students with diverse cultural backgrounds. *Mathematics Teacher, 87(2),* 122–126.

This article has good suggestions about working effectively with Hispanic and Haitian students, based on the author's experience in teaching middle school in Florida.

Cooney, T. J., & Hirsch, C. R. (Eds.). (1990). *Teaching and learning mathematics in the 1990s, 1990 Yearbook*. Reston, VA: National Council of Teachers of Mathematics.

The book is divided into seven parts: (1) new perspective on teaching and learning; (2) effective models and methods for teaching and learning; (3) the role of assessment in teaching and learning; (4) cultural factors in teaching and learning; (5) contextual factors in teaching and learning; (6) implications of technology for teaching and learning; and (7) professionalism and its implications for teaching and learning. Many of the articles have vignettes and teaching examples of particular interest to new teachers.

Dick, T., & Kubiak, E. (1998). Issues and aids for teaching mathematics to the blind. *Mathematics Teacher, 90(5),* 344–349. Reston, VA: National Council of Teachers of Mathematics.

The article provides recommendations for teachers of blind students, in addition to a list of resources and suppliers.

Edwards, C. A. (Ed.). (1999). *Changing the faces of mathematics: Perspectives on Asian Americans and Pacific Islanders*. Reston. VA: National Council of Teachers of Mathematics.

This is one of a series of books addressing ways to increase access to quality mathematics for diverse learners.

Feigenbaum, R. (2000). Algebra for students with learning disabilities. *Mathematics Teacher, 93(4),* 270–274.

The teaching and learn strategies used in LD classes are described in detail. The author also discusses how these students fared in later courses taken outside the special algebra classes.

Fennema, E., & Leder, G. C. (Eds.). (1990). *Mathematics and gender*. New York: Teachers College, Columbia University.

In 1985 Fennema and Peterson proposed the Autonomous Learning Behavior model as a way to study gender differences. The researchers contributing to this volume impart considerable information about possible sources of gender difference in mathematics and implications of the Autonomous Learning Behavior model.

Hankes, J. E., and Fast, G. R. (Eds.). (2002). *Changing the faces of mathematics: Perspectives on indigenous people of North America*. Reston, VA: National Council of Teachers of Mathematics.

This is one of a series of books addressing ways to increase access to quality mathematics for diverse learners.

House, P. A. (Ed.). (1987). *Providing opportunities for the mathematically gifted*. Reston, VA: National Council of Teachers of Mathematics.

This small book touches on the many aspects of gifted education. It includes a comprehensive list of resources and references for the teacher who wants more information on the subject.

Hynd, G. W. (Editor-in-charge). (1997). *Journal of learning disabilities*.

The issues of January–February and March–April feature a two-part series on mathematics education. This is a rich source for teachers of mathematics and teachers in special education to combine their expertise in meeting the needs of students with learning disabilities.

Jacobs, J. E., Rossi Becker, J., and Gilmer, G. F. (Eds.). (2001). *Changing the faces of mathematics: Perspectives on gender*. Reston, VA: National Council of Teachers of Mathematics.

This is one of a series of books addressing ways to increase access to quality mathematics for diverse learners.

Jamski, W. D. (Ed.). (1990). *Mathematical challenges for the middle grades from the arithmetic teacher*. Reston, VA: National Council of Teachers of Mathematics.

The book includes 125 uncommon problems for students at all levels.

Jitenda, A., & Xin, Y. P. (1997). Mathematics work—problem solving instruction for students with mild disabilities and students at risk for math failure: A research synthesis. *Journal of Special Education, 30(4),* 412–437.

The review summarizes 14 intervention studies and classroom implications for solving word problems.

National Information Center for Children and Youth with Disabilities. (1997, August). The IDEA amendments of 1997, *News Digest, 26,* 1–39.

A comprehensive overview is provided with a point-by-point examination of the major changes of IDEA 97 contrasted with the previous IDEA. Included are sections of a simplified overview, next steps, references and resources, selected organizations, general provisions, assistance for education of all children with disabilities, and information concerning infants and toddlers.

Rafferty, Y. (1997). Meeting the educational needs of homeless children. *Educational Leadership, 56(4),* 48–53.

The article paints the sad picture of the plight of the homeless child. Suggestions are given to educators to "address the needs of homeless children, to promote their academic success, and to make the classroom a haven in a heartless world."

Scherer, M. M. (Ed.). (1997/1998). *Educational leadership: Reaching for equity.*

The entire December/January journal is devoted to issues and practical solutions within the broad spectrum of equity.

Sobel, M. A. (1988). *Reading for enrichment in secondary school mathematics.* Reston, VA: National Council of Teachers of Mathematics.

These interesting topics and nonroutine problems can be good starting places for projects for high achievers.

Stern, F. (2000). Choosing problems with entry points for all students. *Mathematics Teaching in the Middle Grades, 6(1),* 8–11.

This article is right in the spirit of the activities in Chapter 9, with ideas for more problems that can be accessible to all students, including using manipulatives, data charts, calculators, and patterns.

Strutchens, M., Johnson, M. L., and Tate, W. F. (Eds.). (2000). *Changing the faces of mathematics: Perspectives on African Americans.* Reston, VA: National Council of Teachers of Mathematics.

This is one of a series of books addressing ways to increase access to quality mathematics for diverse learners.

Thornton, D. A., & Wilmot, B. (1986, February). Special learners. *Arithmetic Teacher,* 38–40. Reston, VA: National Council of Teachers of Mathematics.

This article gives practical suggestions for using manipulatives with learning handicapped and with gifted students.

Thornton, C. A., & Biey, N. S. (Eds.). (1994). *Windows of opportunity: Mathematics for students with special needs.* Reston, VA: National Council of Teachers of Mathematics.

This comprehensive book is divided into four parts: (1) current issues; (2) classroom episodes; (3) promising practices; and (4) the challenge and the promise. There are suggestions for vignettes and examples of exemplary practice for middle-school teachers.

Trentacosta, J., & Kenney, M. J. (Eds.). (1997). *Multicultural and gender equity in the mathematics classroom: The gift of diversity, 1997 Yearbook.* Reston, VA: National Council of Teachers of Mathematics.

Through 28 different articles, the book thoughtfully probes five general areas of equity: (1) issues and perspectives; (2) classroom cultures; (3) curriculum, instruction, and assessment; (4) professional development; and (5) future directions. Examples are included of successful practice with diverse populations, as well as homogeneous minority groups such as American Indians.

Volpe, B. J. (1999). A girl's Math Olympiad team. *Mathematics Teaching in the Middle School, 4(5),* 290–293.

Excellent ideas are given for coaching a girls' Olympiad team at this very important age to best interest girls in the study of mathematics.

Wiest, L. R. (2001). Selected resources for encouraging females in mathematics. *Mathematics Teacher, 94(1),* 14–18.

Four pages of detailed information and Web sites are listed for increasing knowledge and improving instruction for females in mathematics. These include biographical resources and self-help resources for girls.

ADDITIONAL ACTIVITIES

Activity 9.7   Diophantus
Activity 9.8   The Checkerboard Problem
Activity 9.9   The Popcorn Problem
Activity 9.10   12 Bags of Gold
Activity 9.11   The Boat Problem

FOR TEACHERS

Activity 9.7 Diophantus

Mathematical Content:
Patterns, algebra, (PSSM Reasoning and Proof Standard for Grades 6–8 and 9–12)

Materials:
Problem

Directions: Work this problem yourself, using several approaches that you predict your students might use.

FOR STUDENTS

Activity 9.7
Diophantus

Directions: This problem is easier to work *without* algebra. Guess what kind of number you would expect. How small? How large? What type of number? Trial and guess will give the right answer, which you can verify with algebraic methods.

Diophantus was a famous Greek mathematician who lived in Alexandria, Egypt, in the third century A.D. After he died, someone described his life in this puzzle:

He was a boy for 1/6 of his life.
After 1/12 more, he acquired a beard.
After another 1/7, he married.
In the 5th year after his marriage, his son was born.
The son lived half as many years as his father.
Diophantus died 4 years after his son.

How old was Diophantus when he died?

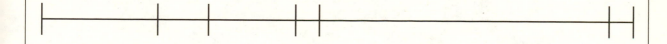

F O R   T E A C H E R S

Activity 9.8 The Checkerboard Problem

Mathematical Content: Patterns, number sense, (PSSM Reasoning and Proof Standard for Grades 6–8 and 9–12)

Materials: Problem, graph paper, colored pencils, colored transparency paper

Directions: Try working this problem from both a whole-part and a part-whole perspective in order to anticipate possible student approaches.

Extension: What would be the pattern if the board were a rectangle? For example, what if the board were 9 × 7 instead of 8 × 8?

F O R   S T U D E N T S

Activity 9.8
The Checkerboard Problem

Directions: You see before you a typical checkerboard consisting of 64 black and white squares. Keeping in mind that a square is a right-angled figure with four equal sides, *how many different squares (of all sizes) do you calculate to be shown above?* (*Note:* squares that partially overlap are still considered different.)

FOR TEACHERS

Activity 9.9 The Popcorn Problem

Mathematical Content: Patterns, algebra, geometry, (PSSM Reasoning and Proof Standard for Grades 6–8 and 9–12)

Materials: For algebra: worksheets, ruler, paper, tape; for advanced algebra and calculus: worksheets, graphing calculator

*To see ways this problem can be approached by students at different mathematical levels, see the Teaching Notes for this activity beginning on page 513.

FOR STUDENTS

Activity 9.9
The Popcorn Problem

Directions: Use the detailed instructions appropriate to your course. Be sure to answer all the questions in order.

Introduction: Real-world problem situations are very useful to show the value and utility of mathematical thinking. When combined with a technology rich solution method, they also add an exciting dimension to the mathematics teaching and learning processes. The popcorn problem situation outlined in this article can be used with middle-school or pre-algebra students and then revisited every year while the student progresses through the study of algebra and culminating with the study of calculus. And each year the level of mathematical intensity can be increased. At every level many important mathematical connections can be investigated and explored by the student. This is a problem situation to cherish!

The Problem: Equal squares of side length x are removed from an 8.5-inch-by-11-inch piece of cardboard, as shown in the figure at left. A box with no top is formed by folding along the dashed lines. How much popcorn will this box hold; that is, what is the volume of the box? Is there a box of *maximum* volume? Show your reasoning.

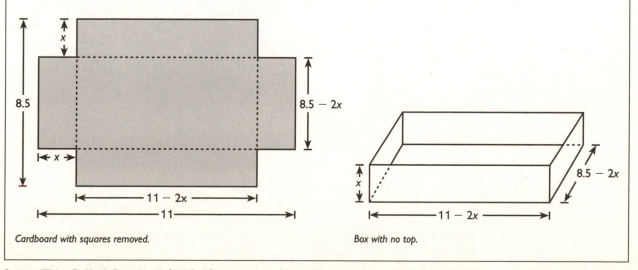

Cardboard with squares removed.   Box with no top.

Source: Waits, B. K., & Demana, F. (1992). *The popcorn problem: The power of visualization and the TI-81.* Columbus, OH: Ohio State University. Reprinted with permission.

F O R   T E A C H E R S

Activity 9.10   12 Bags of Gold

Mathematical Content: Logic, (PSSM Reasoning Proof Standard for Grades 6–8 and 9–12)

Materials: Problem, manipulatives

Directions: Read this problem and be sure you understand what it asks you to do. A suggested strategy is to work through a similar problem that is less complicated and use that information to help you solve this problem. If you have not done the 8 Bags of Gold problem (Activity 1.9), ask your teacher how it differs from this problem and begin with it.

F O R   S T U D E N T S

Activity 9.10
12 Bags of Gold (page 1 of 2)

Directions: A much easier problem to start is as follows: If only one bag of 8 is less in weight, what is the minimum number of times the balance must be used to find the light bag? The problem with 12 bags of gold with one *either* heavier or lighter is a much more complicated problem, with many scenarios to consider. Don't stop before examining all possibilities. This problem of the week will definitely take some time to understand. Complete all the steps in the write-up. Use 12 pieces of the manipulatives, and label them 1 through 12 to keep track of the bags of gold.

Here we are back with our economical king. Thanks to your class's work on the Eight Bags of Gold POW (Activity 1.9), he found the thief in a very economical manner. Now, since he has been so economical, he has even more gold.

The 8 bags got too heavy to carry, so he had to switch to 12 bags. Of course, each of his 12 bags holds exactly the same amount of gold as each of the others, and they all weigh the same. Well, . . . maybe not.

Rumor has it that one of his 12 trusted caretakers is not so trustworthy. Someone, it is rumored, is making counterfeit gold. So the king sent his assistants to find the counterfeiter. They did find her, but she wouldn't tell them who had the counterfeit gold she had made, no matter how persuasive they were.

F O R   S T U D E N T S

Activity 9.10
12 Bags of Gold (page 2 of 2)

All the assistants learned from her was that one of the 12 bags had counterfeit gold and that this bag's weight was different from the others. They could not find out from her whether the different bag was heavier or lighter.

So the king needed to know two things.

- Which bag weighed a different amount from the rest?
- Was that bag heavier or lighter?

And, of course, he wanted the answer found economically. He still had only the old balance scale. He wanted the solution in two weighings, as in the other problem, but his court mathematician said it would take three weighings. No one else could see how it could be done in so few weighings. Can you figure it out?

Find a way to determine which bag is counterfeit and whether it weighs more or less than the others. Try to do so using the balance scale as few times as possible. Keep in mind that what you do after the first weighing may depend on what happens in that weighing. For example, if the scale balances on the first weighing, you might choose bags for the second weighing different from the bags you would choose if the scale does not balance on the first weighing.

Note: The problem can be solved with only three weighings, without any tricks, but it is very hard to cover every case.

Write-up

1. *Problem statement.*
2. *Process.* Based on your notes, describe what you did in attempting to solve this problem.
   a. How did you get started?
   b. What approaches did you try?
   c. Where did you get stuck?
   d. What drawings did you use?
3. *Solution.* Since this problem is much more difficult than Eight Bags of Gold, you shouldn't be too disappointed if you don't get a solution using just three weighings. Your task is to give the best solution that you found. Explain fully which cases your solution works for and which cases it doesn't work for.
4. *Evaluation.*

Source: Fendel, Dan, et al. (1997). *Interactive Mathematics Program.* Key Curriculum Press, 1150 65th Street, Emeryville, CA 94608, 1-800-995-MATH. Reprinted with permission.

FOR TEACHERS

Activity 9.11 The Boat Problem

Mathematical Content:
Geometry, (PSSM Geometry Standard for Grades 9–12)

Materials:
Problem, computer (optional)

Directions: Depending upon your course and availability of technology, this problem can be solved with the use of dynamic geometry software, spreadsheets, programming on a graphing calculator, or calculus methods. Make sure students draw the figure and understand the dynamics of the problem before proceeding.

FOR STUDENTS

Activity 9.11
The Boat Problem

Directions: Draw a diagram of the problem situation, labeling the known features of this problem and identifying the unknown distance by a variable. Use the tools provided by your teacher to continue the solution process.

Suppose a boat is located 30 miles from shore and must get a passenger to a hospital that is located 60 miles down shore from the boat's current position. The boat travels at 20 mph, and the ambulance that meets the boat travels at 50 mph. Where should the ambulance meet the boat to minimize the amount of time needed to reach the hospital?

Source: *Lessons in Mathematics for the Classroom and for Inservice Sessions with Alternative Assessment Procedures.* (1994). University of Northern Iowa: Cedar Falls, IA. Reprinted with permission.

CHAPTER 10

Focus on Performance Assessment

In Chapter 10 we will look at using assessments for informing and improving instruction and for program evaluation. Because of their very nature, performance tasks give the teacher and students feedback as to the current level of achievement and suggest ways for teacher and students to improve future outcomes. In this chapter we will also look at various forms of assessment provided by external sources to monitor and evaluate the instructional program. In addition to state and locally mandated reports of academic progress, the No Child Left Behind Act, passed by the federal government in 2001, requires schools and states receiving federal education funds to have strong systems of accountability based upon student performance. Mathematics is one of the content areas included in the accountability system. Continual progress is the stated goal, especially for students in low-performing schools. Hence, mathematics educators need to call upon our professional, intellectual, and personal resources to help our students and those of our colleagues meet this challenge.

The NCTM contrasts two perspectives on assessment, summarized in Figure 10.1, which is based on a visual packet provided to help teachers understand new directions and rationales in assessment.

Figure 10.1
Old and New Perspectives of Assessment

19th-Century Perspective	21st-Century Perspective
■ Use of *norm-referenced standardized tests, *chapter tests associated with texts, criterion-referenced mastey tests,* and/or state-administered profile tests	■ Use of multiple sources of evidence
■ Fragmented, essential view of mathematical knowledge*	■ Mathematics as a socially constructed body of knowledge and learning as an active, exploratory process involving students' reinvention of key mathematical concepts
■ Dispensary approach to teaching, in which teachers impart a body of information to passive learners	■ Facilitative role for teachers
■ A collection of summary scores should be normally distributed*	■ A student's level of performance should be compared with specific performance standards, not other students' performance
■ Externally imposed assessments are more valuable than teacher assessment	■ Teachers are the primary assessors of student performance and value student participation in an open, equitable process

*__Norm-referenced tests__ are developed by commercial testing companies, based on a reference sample representing a profile of students nationwide. The tests use multiple-choice items to distinguish between high- and low-performing students and arrive at results in which there is a normal distribution of correct responses for each grade level and subject. Their purpose is to obtain a measure for comparing students across schools and school districts, as measured by percentiles, with the reference group used to establish the norm.

__Standardized tests__ take place under standardized conditions. The directions are scripted so that all students taking the test hear the same thing before they begin and generally have the same amount of time to complete the test. Exceptions such as extra time may be made for special-education students whose Individualized Education Plans (IEPs) specify additional conditions for taking such a test.

__Criterion-referenced mastery tests__ require all students taking them to meet a certain achievement level in order to establish their attainment of a particular goal. An example is a state-required graduation test in mathematics, requiring that students meet a set level of proficiency in order to receive a high-school diploma.

__The fragmented, essential view__ of mathematical knowledge stresses facts and procedures to learn. Assessments stress correct answers and the use of algorithms and procedures previously demonstrated and practiced in class.

__The normal curve__ is used as the model for assessing achievement for large-scale tests for which results are presented in summary form. Tests are constructed so that some scores will be in the lowest quartile. This assumption about performance often continues to the classroom level, so that some students are expected to excel, many to do average work, and some to fall behind.

The summary in Figure 10.1 includes brief explanations of key terms.

The use of 21st-century types of performance assessments—both those organized as part of reformed curricula and those mandated by districts and/or states—is increasing nationwide. As the word *performance* indicates, students must do more than select from a set of multiple-choice answers on this type of assessment. Rather, they are expected to show their reasoning, justify their approaches to the given problem situation, and sometimes arrive at a product that meets given criteria. The tools that the student has used during regular class time continue to be available while the student is completing the performance assessment.

Ideally, the performance assessment is part of the curriculum—not separated from it, as is a traditional test. When incorporated into the regular instructional program, performance tasks can help both teachers and students gain useful information for improving achievement. With specific performance standards in the classroom, no longer are students compared with each other; rather, they all are challenged to meet at least the minimum level of proficiency on the given task. In such a classroom, the normal curve is no longer a model of expected student achievement. Through a combination of performance activities included within the ongoing instructional program (sometimes called "embedded" assessment), students are given ways beyond typical end-of-unit tests to show achievement of course and grade-level performance standards in content as established by the school and district.

In the first part of this chapter, we look at the way performance tasks are built into exemplary curricula. We then examine the issues of developing consistent rubrics for assessment of performance tasks. Student involvement in the development and use of rubrics is an important component of instructional design in classrooms in which performance assessment is an integral part of the class. It is hoped that your district and state will include performance assessment as a component of their total assessment system, based on the knowledge that performance assessment can be both less intrusive on the implementation of *Standards*-based curricula and more informative to the classroom teacher.

Since standardized test results too frequently are used as the basis of public statements related to educational evaluations, the classroom teacher needs to take mandated testing seriously. Norm-referenced tests, SATs, and other tests whose school and district results are made available to the public often are referred to as "high stakes" tests. Of course, the SAT also is high stakes for individual students, since their scores may directly affect university admissions.

Keep in mind, however, that there is a limit to what standardized tests can tell the individual teacher about classroom practices. In many situations, the results of such testing become available after the school year is over. Even when looking at the previous year's results for individual students, the teacher is able to see only what types of problems students did well on and what types they did poorly on. That is, the reasons for poor performance can only be inferred. Perhaps the topic was not addressed prior to the test. Perhaps the student was ill during the time the material was covered in class. For reasons such as these, standardized testing should intrude as little as possible on implementation of the selected curricular program. Ideally, the state or district assessments are well matched to *Standards*-based curricula. However, there may be instances in which instructional choices are made solely with the "test" in mind. These situations are discussed in the middle portion of this chapter. Near the end of this chapter, we discuss the use of such performance assessment results to inform instruction.

ABOUT THE ACTIVITIES FOR THIS CHAPTER

The mathematical emphasis in this chapter is applications. The ability to apply mathematical knowledge and processes in new and novel situations is a goal for all students of mathematics. Realistic, rather than contrived, applications can now be incorporated into the classroom, thanks, at least in part, to technology.

The National Board for Professional Certification defines an applications assignment as one that engages students in "the application of important mathematical principles to disciplines and/or contexts outside mathematics *or* the application of important principles in one domain of mathematics to another domain." The messy numbers of real data are no longer a stumbling block to conceptual understanding. The visual aspects of graphing calculators and computers help students view geometric representations of information that was tedious to plot and analyze before the availability of these electronic tools for the classroom. Applications problems are well suited to performance assessment, as frequently they are multistep and can be approached in various ways through the use of different mathematical tools.

Activities 10.1–10.7 provide examples of performance assessment. Many of them include a rubric for assessing student work. The additional activities, 10.8–10.13, are released items from various state and other externally designed assessments.

PERFORMANCE TASKS AND RUBRIC ASSESSMENT

"A performance assessment in mathematics involves presenting students with a mathematical task, project, or investigation, then observing, interviewing, and looking at their products to assess what they actually know and can do" (Stenmark, 1991, p. 13). This kind of assessment is essential as you strive to determine how well students can apply their mathematical knowledge. Performance assessment is, by its nature, criterion referenced. Learning goals and levels for the class and for a given activity are clearly stated so that all students know what is expected. The students understand that they will be given many opportunities to demonstrate their knowledge, both in the form of teacher-written tests and through other activities in which students show their ability to describe, connect, and apply the mathematics they have learned.

Performance assessment, used in a formative sense during the course of a unit of instruction, reflects your goals in teaching a particular curriculum and therefore can be used to inform your ongoing planning of classroom activities. Performance levels are established and clearly communicated with the intent that every student can attain them. Clark (1997) describes this communication between teacher and students as "a reciprocal relationship between teacher and student that produces learning as the result of a two-way interaction" (p. 19). Generally, this communication includes expectations that students will use mathematical language and symbols correctly within the context of the task they are given, apply mathematical tools appropriate for the grade level in completing the tasks, and be able to demonstrate the use of mathematical reasoning at the expected level of sophistication of the course they are taking.

Performance assessments do not replace standardized tests. Rather, they provide direct information to the teacher, students, and families about the mathematics a student is able to understand and use. As an analogy, think of what you value when selecting a plumber. Many states require plumbers to pass a multiple-choice test on the "book knowledge" needed in that vocation. Would knowing a plumber's score on a multiple-choice test on the vocabulary and regulations of that occupation be sufficient when a broken pipe needs to be repaired? Most of us would agree that proven hands-on personal expertise and reliability characterize a competent plumber. We might be glad to know that the plumber is certified by a licensing agency and is knowledgeable concerning the regulatory aspects of the profession. Nonetheless, performance on the job is the ultimate standard: We want a plumber who has satisfactory results when repairing our pipes based on knowledge of the tools of the trade and the ability to solve the unique problem in our home. In the same way, the skills and knowledge tested on typical standardized multiple-choice assessments might provide a baseline of information to the teacher and student about comparisons based upon a normal distribution. It is through performance assessment, however, that specific information about students' ability to apply the mathematics they know can best be elicited and used to improve classroom instruction related to desired student outcomes.

Standards-based mathematics programs have strong applications components and varying degrees of real-world connections. Some programs, such as *Mathematics: Modeling Our World (ARISE)*, consist almost totally of applications problems incorporating skill development within the context of the given problems. Other programs separate into separate problem sets applications activities, exercises on computational skills, and lessons promoting the development of mathematical concepts. We will show examples from these curricula of different applications tasks, projects, and investigations, some with accompanying rubrics. Each of these types of assessments is described in the section of the chapter in which it is illustrated.

Step 1: Identify Outcomes

The first step in the design and/or selection of performance tasks is the identification of the desired achievement outcomes to be assessed by the task. Ideally, these tasks grow out of the selected curriculum. Such tasks have mathematical goals that cannot be measured by multiple-choice tests or other types of assessments in which only the answer is considered when scoring. In general, mathematics outcomes best measured by performance assessments include demonstrating understanding of mathematical concepts, using various problem-solving strategies to solve nonstandard mathematical problems, and connecting among topics within mathematics and between mathematics and other disciplines. Students in exemplary classrooms have many opportunities within the regular curriculum to demonstrate their achievement of the outcomes for the class through a combination of mathematical calculations, visual depictions (graphs, diagrams, pictures), and verbal explanations/ justifications.

We begin our examples of performance assessment with performance tasks, which are focused and concise activities that are to be completed individually, in class, and within a limited amount of time. Our examples come directly from specific curriculum, as well as from other published sources that are listed in the chapter references. Similar activities are used by some state assessment systems. See the Additional Activities at the end of this chapter for examples of such items.

Performance Tasks For the purpose of this chapter, we define performance tasks as items small enough in scope and required complexity to be completed in a class period or less. The purpose of tasks of this size is primarily to assess whether students understand and can use specific mathematics concepts or skills.

We recommend starting with performance tasks that already have been developed with rubrics included. With practice and some patience, you and your students will become better able to specify and identify the characteristics of the different levels of the rubric. At some point, after you have experience with rubric scoring, you may want to modify previously used tasks or develop your own tasks for class use.

When developing your own performance tasks, you need to keep in mind the mathematical objectives for the course you are teaching. In *Standards*-based programs, one mathematical objective is the development of students' mathematical reasoning.

Usually, for teachers and students to assess such reasoning, a task requires students to show a *series of logical steps* that they used to solve the given problem, along with some kind of *accompanying justification or rationale,* based on mathematical concepts previously developed. In a classroom setting, students could give the reasoning orally, but in this chapter we give only examples of tasks with written responses.

Stein et al. (2000) identify characteristics of tasks according to their cognitive demand. At a low level of demand, tasks have students rely on memorizing facts or procedures or do not require students to justify or explain their reasoning. By contrast, tasks with higher-level demands involve using multiple approaches and probing for deeper levels of understanding. These high-demand tasks may also require considerable effort on the part of students and involve some anxiety when a solution path is not obvious.

Exemplary curricula contain many activities asking students to apply mathematics in realistic situations. The first example, Activity 10.1, is from the unit "All About Alice," from the Interactive Mathematics Program (IMP), Course II. The content focus on exponents and logarithms uses Lewis Carroll's classic *Alice in Wonderland* as the setting for developing the concepts and rules for exponent use. Activity 10.1 is a classwork activity that occurs about 2 weeks into the unit, as well as the associated homework that follows the activity. Notice that students are given a real-life context for using exponents to estimate large and small numbers.

ply their knowledge of quadratic equations and parabolas. This task appears as Activity 10.2, "Path of a Rocket." Tools used during instruction, such as the graphing calculator, may be used during the assessment.

Note how Activity 10.2 includes the three criteria stated earlier. First, a clear mathematical objective is identified—applying what is known about a parabola to a given situation. Second, the requirement to show the work leading to the solution of the problem means that students are to write a series of steps that reflect their understanding of the procedures needed to meet the requirements of the problem. Finally, students are expected to justify what they did by discussing the results in the context of the given situation.

When performance tasks are part of a curriculum, a scoring rubric generally is provided. The 4-point rubric provided in the CPM program for the "Path of a Rocket" activity is shown in Figure 10.2. These points indicate the students' level of attainment on the particular task. Translating the rubric scores into grades is not automatic, as the purpose of the assessment is less to determine a grade than it is to establish a student's quality of understanding of the concepts involved. For example, a score of 2 may indicate the need to review quadratic equations with some student, perhaps in a tutoring situation, so that the student can solve similar problems successfully in the future.

Set 10.1   *Discussion Question*

Questions with an asterisk appear in the Message Board section of the Companion Website at *http://www.prenhall.com/huetinck.* Go to Chapter 10 and click on the Message Board to find and respond to the question.

*1. How would you assess the students' understanding of the core concepts of these activities in order to determine what you needed to do next with the class?

The *Assessment Handbook* provided with the College Preparatory Mathematics (1994) curriculum includes a Course 3 task whose purpose it is to assess students' ability, after three years of CPM, to ap-

Figure 10.2
Rubric for "Path of a Rocket" Activity

Rubric Scores
4 Found an equation and determined the time that the rocket hit the ground. Time can be found either algebraically or using a graph. Small algebraic or arithmetic error is acceptable.
3 Found equation but did not find the time the rocket hit the ground. Made a small error in finding the equation of the parabola.
2 A reasonable graph is given and an attempt at the equation was made.
1 Only a graph is given, and no attempt at the equation is made.

Note: College Preparatory Mathematics Educational Program. 1233 Noonan Drive, Sacramento, CA 95822.

F O R   T E A C H E R S

Activity 10.1 Big Numbers

Mathematical Content:
Operations with exponents, scientific notation (PSSM Number and Operation Standard for Grades 6–8)

Materials Needed:
Activity sheets, scientific calculators

Directions: Work through the exercises as students would. Predict the parts that would give the students difficulty. Then think of future activities or assignments that would be appropriate for students who have difficulty, as well as activities or assignments to challenge or verify the understanding of successful students.

F O R   S T U D E N T S

Activity 10.1
Big Numbers (page 1 of 2)

Scientific notation is sometimes helpful in working with big numbers.

   In some of the problems in this activity, you are given information in scientific notation. You can use what you learned in *Homework 16: Warming Up to Scientific Notation* to simplify the computations.

FOR STUDENTS

Activity 10.1
Big Numbers (page 2 of 2)

You will probably want to write your answers in scientific notation. But you do not necessarily need to give exact answers for these problems. Use your judgment about the amount of precision that is appropriate in each case.

1. A computer can do a computation in $5 \cdot 10^{-7}$ seconds. How many computations can the computer do in 30 seconds?

2. A leaking faucet drips a drop per second. If there are 76,000 drops of water in a gallon, how many gallons would drip in a year?

3. Measurements show that Europe and Africa are separating from the Americas at a rate of about 1 inch per year. The continents are now about 4,000 miles apart. Assuming that the rate has remained constant, how many years has it been since the continents split apart and started drifting?

4. In 1990 the gross national debt of the United States was $3,233,313,000,000. The 1990 census showed 248,709,873 U.S. citizens. About how many dollars per citizen was the national debt in 1990?

5. One atom of carbon weighs approximately $1.99 \cdot 10^{-23}$ How many atoms are there in a kilogram of carbon?

6. The mass of the earth is $5.98 \cdot 10^{24}$ kg. The mass of the sun is $1.99 \cdot 10^{30}$ kg. Approximately how many earths would it take to have the same mass as the sun?

7. Light travels at a speed of approximately 186,000 miles per second. (That's *very* fast.) A **light-year** is the distance that light travels in a year. Approximately how many inches are there in a light-year?

8. For simplicity, suppose that a grain of sand is a cube that is 0.2 millimeter in each direction. About how many grains of sand packed tightly together would it take to make a beach that is 300 meters long, 25 meters wide, and 5 meters deep?

Source: *Interactive Mathematics Program Year 1,* published by Key Curriculum Press, 1150 65th Street, Emeryville, CA 94608, 1-800-995-MATH. Problems 1–4 were adapted from problems in *Algebra 1,* by Paul A. Foerster, Addison-Wesley Publishing Co., 1990, pp. 401–406. Data in Problem 4 taken from *Information Please 1996 Almanac,* 49th edition, Houghton-Mifflin. Reprinted with permission.

FOR TEACHERS

Activity 10.2 Path of a Rocket

Mathematical Content:
Quadratic functions and their graphs, applications (PSSM Algebra Standard for Grades 9–12)

Materials Needed:
Problem statement, graphing calculators

Directions: Work out the problem yourself. Show your work, and state your results clearly. Share your work with a partner, and discuss whether you think the rubric scores included in the CPM program are usable in a classroom. Be prepared to discuss your points with the class.

FOR STUDENTS

Activity 10.2
Path of a Rocket

Directions: Read this problem and work independently to produce a complete solution. You may use any tools that we have been using in class, including a graphing calculator.

A small rocket fired from the bottom of a hole 5 meters below ground level reaches a height of 3 meters above the ground on the way up after 4 seconds. The rocket also is 3 meters above the ground after 8 seconds.

Find the equation of the parabola that models the path of the rocket, and find the time when the rocket hits the ground.

A complete response includes

a. a clearly labeled graph;

b. the work leading to the equation;

c. your results clearly stated.

Source: Reprinted with permission by CPM Educational Program (College Preparatory Mathematics: Change From Within Algebra I). Sacramento, CA.

The Mathematics Diagnostic Testing Program (MDTP) of the University of California provides a set of "written response items" for teachers to use as performance tasks to improve their instruction toward the goal of strengthening students' ability to "think and communicate effectively about mathematics" (1996). A general 4-point scoring rubric is provided with the tasks, with rubrics for specific items written with more detail unique to the given tasks. Teachers also are provided with an "Essence Statement" for each task. This statement emphasizes the key mathematical features of the task and suggests extensions of the task. A sample item is given in Activity 10.3.

Step 2: Develop Rubrics

When creating your own performance assessments, the next step after writing the task is to develop holistic rubrics to use when scoring them. We suggest developing the rubrics before you give the task to your students, as the process of developing the rubrics may cause you to clarify the directions given to students as they are presented the rubric. For example, if students are to show their range of mathematical understanding by presenting more than one way of depicting or solving the problem, the directions to the task should clearly stipulate that.

As you develop and adapt performance tasks and rubrics relevant to your students and curriculum, you will want to consider that, according to knowledgeable sources on rubric assessment (Stenmark, 1991; Danielson, 1997), it is important to have an even number of points possible, usually 4 or 6. Even though it seems more logical to use a 5-point rubric that is easily translated into standard grades, it has been found that scorers are less discriminating with such a rubric. The natural tendency is to place many students in the middle scoring category (a 3 on a 5-point rubric) without examining the nuances of differences that indicate when more work is needed (1 or 2 on a 4-point rubric) versus communicating to students that they have shown satisfactory achievement of the learning goal (3 or 4 on a 4-point rubric). Even though teachers of many content areas, such as language arts, have successfully used a 6-point rubric, most mathematics teachers seem to prefer a 4-point rubric. To give you an idea of the extent of the details needed for a 6-point rubric, an example of such a holistic rubric is shown in Figure 10.3 along with the performance task for which it was written. This rubric was developed by the California Assessment Program to help teachers score solutions to the given mathematics problem. For our illustrative purposes in this chapter, however, we will use a 4-point rubric.

Should you choose to develop your own rubrics for a given task, keep in mind the following guidelines:

- Identify the key mathematical elements that determine whether a paper is acceptable or unacceptable. This is a similar process to a "binary sort" in computer lingo.
- Identify specific differences between a paper that is barely unacceptable and one that is clearly full of errors and/or misunderstandings. This will help you clarify the difference between a score of 1 and a score of 2.

 For a link to a generic mathematics rubric go to **http://www.prenhall.com/huetinck** and click on Web Destinations for Chapter 10.

FOR TEACHERS

Activity 10.3 Bear Flag Written Response Item

Mathematical Content:
Area, percents (PSSM Geometry and Number and Operation Standards for Grades 6–8)

Materials Needed:
Student worksheet, General Scoring Rubric

Directions:
1. Work out the Bear Flag Activity yourself.
2. Develop specific written rubrics for the categories 0–4, based on the General Scoring Rubric.
3. Compare your rubric with one or more classmates or colleagues, and refine them for clarity and specificity.
4. If possible, try the activity with a group of pre-algebra students, and use your rubric to score the papers with comments to the students.

F O R S T U D E N T S

Activity 10.3
Bear Flag Written-Response Item (page 1 of 2)

Student Name: _____ Class: _____ Score

Bear Flag Essence Statement

Algebra Readiness - Decimals

The task is to estimate the percent of a flag that is covered by a bear icon. This requires the solution of sub-problems for which work should be clearly shown. To fully accomplish the task, student work will be evaluated on the presentation of the solution as well as its accuracy.

- To begin the problem, student work in Part A will demonstrate a conceptual understanding of area by providing a reasonable strategy for estimating the area of the bear. This might include counting grid units (and fractional portions thereof) covered, adding the covered parts of columns or rows, or using inscribed or circumscribed rectangles. It is essential that a thorough explanation be given for the process that determines the estimate.
- To complete the task, student work in Part B will demonstrate that the area of the flag is 88, either by counting squares or by multiplying the number of rows by the number of columns. In addition, student work will show that the percent of the flag covered by the bear is obtained by dividing the bear area estimate (from Part A) by 88 and multiplying the result by 100.

Possible Extensions for Class Activity:
Discuss and compare different estimation methods; examples might include using areas of inscribed and circumscribed rectangles, counting squares covered by bear, and counting squares not touched by bear and subtracting from area of flag.

Discuss methods for improving estimates; examples might include further subdivision of grid and estimating portion of each square touched by bear.

Pictured below is the California Club's flag, which is white with a bear.

1. Estimate the area of the bear in square units. Explain how you arrived at your estimate.

2. Use your estimate to find the percent of the flag covered by the bear. Explain.

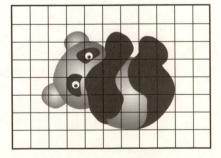

F O R   S T U D E N T S

Activity 10.3
Bear Flag Written-Response Item (page 2 of 2)

GENERAL SCORING RUBRIC FOR WRITTEN RESPONSE ITEMS		
Category	**Score**	**Description**
No Response	0	Either the work is not attempted (i.e., the paper is blank), or the work is incorrect, irrelevant, or off task. The response may minimally interpret or restate the problem but does not go beyond that.
Minimal	1	The response demonstrates only a minimal understanding of the problem posed, and a reasonable approach is not suggested. Although there may or may not be some correct mathematical work, the response is incomplete, contains major mathematical errors, or reveals serious flaws in reasoning. Requested examples may be absent or irrelevant.
Partial	2	The response contains evidence of a conceptual understanding of the problem in that a reasonable approach is indicated. However, on the whole, the response is not well developed. Although there may be serious mathematical errors or flaws in reasoning, the response does contain some correct mathematics. Requested examples provided may fail to illustrate the desired conclusions.
Satisfactory	3	The response demonstrates a clear understanding of the problem and provides an acceptable approach. The response also is generally well developed and presented but contains omissions or minor errors in mathematics. Requested examples provided may not completely illustrate the desired conclusions.
Excellent	4	The response demonstrates a complete understanding of the problem, is correct, and the methods of solution are appropriate and fully developed. The response is logically sound, clearly written, and does not contain any significant errors. Requested examples are well chosen and illustrate the desired conclusions.

EXPLANATORY NOTES

1. Rubrics for specific items should always be used with this general rubric and the following notes about specific rubrics.
2. The following excerpt from MDTP Guidelines for the Preparation of Written Response Mathematics Questions provides a context for this general rubric. The statement of the question should be explicit and clear. The extent to which students are to discuss their reasoning and results should be explicit. The extent to which students are to provide examples, counterexamples, or generalizations also should be clearly stated.
3. Although the categories in the General Scoring Rubric are meant to indicate different levels of understanding and accomplishment, teachers should expect that some student responses may be on the boundary between two categories and may be scored differently by different teachers.
4. Teachers may wish to designate some outstanding responses in the Excellent category as exemplars.

NOTES EXPLAINING HOW TO USE SPECIFIC ITEM RUBRICS

Scoring of written responses is to be based upon both the correctness of the mathematics and the clarity of the presentation. In scoring, do *not* "mind read" the presenter, instead, only grade the presentation. Grade each response on the actual mathematics written and on the quality of the presentation of that mathematics. Unexecuted recipes or prescriptions should receive minimal credit. The specific scoring rubric for an item outlines the mathematical development necessary for the given scores. In addition to the formal mathematics, it is essential that students show their work and clearly present their methodology. The evaluation of each response should be based in part upon its organization, completeness, and clarity. A score of 1 or 2 may in some cases be based simply upon the mathematics called for in the rubric. Scores of 3 and 4 require effective presentation as well as appropriate mathematics. The mathematics called for in specific rubrics is necessary, but not sufficient, for these scores.

Figure 10.3
Example of a 6-Point Rubric

Example 2—Survey of Smoking
The journalism class of Exeter High School surveyed 100 of the school's 2,000 students about their smoking habits. The results of the survey follow:

38	Never smoked
11	Current smoker who has smoked less than 1 year
24	Current smoker who has smoked more than 1 year
18	Quit smoking less than 1 year ago
9	Quit smoking more than 1 year ago
100	Total

Write a short article that could appear in a school newspaper about the results of the survey. Include five statements that show interpretations or conclusions you derive from the survey data.

SMOKING SURVEY TASK RUBRIC

Level	Description of Work, by Each Performance Level
6	The student states five conclusions or interpretations, several of which evidence insightful comparison or synthesis, predict trends, discuss sampling techniques, demonstrate thinking about other issues for research, or in some way offer provocative questions. The response reflects analysis of the data and reveals unusual insight and variety of dimensions. Observations or interpretations are presented effectively either in a list of statements or in the format of an article.
5	The student demonstrates various dimensions of thought in completing the task of giving five conclusions or interpretations of the data. For example, stating that 29 percent (11 plus 18) of those surveyed made a decision about smoking within the last year is a different dimension from reporting that 38 percent had never smoked, or even adding 18 to 9 to get the fact that 27 percent had quit smoking. The student understands that extrapolation from the sample to the total student population mandates addressing sample reliability issues. Conclusions and interpretations are expressed effectively in either a list of statements or an article.
4	The student gives five conclusions or interpretations that are correct in concept but may have minor errors. The student understands the major implications of the survey and recognizes the possibility of bias in the sample. The explanation is successful, but it may lack detail.
3	The student gives an incomplete or superficial list of conclusions or interpretations, one or more of which may have major errors. For example, the response extrapolates to the entire student body without qualification. The conclusions or interpretations may be derived from the same line of reasoning. For example, changing each of the five numbers to percents of those surveyed or of the student body would give five conclusions from the same dimension or line of thought. The results are, on a whole, given coherently.
2	The student attempts to interpret or draw conclusions from the data but makes major conceptual errors or omissions. The response may make no reference to either the sample set or an extrapolation to the whole student body. For example, the student may simply state that 38 percent had never smoked. The student attempts to communicate, but the statements are unclear or fragmented.
1	The student copies the data or attempts to restate information given in the problem. No conclusions or interpretations are attempted, and the response reflects no understanding of the mathematical concepts. Any communication attempted is muddled, irrelevant, or superfluous.

Source: Pandy, Tej. (1991). *A Sampler of Mathematics Assessment.* California Department of Education, Sacramento, CA. Reprinted by permission of the California Department of Education.

- Give specific criteria for distinguishing between a paper that is acceptable, but just so-so, and one that clearly shows good understanding of what is asked in the task, correctly applies appropriate mathematical tools to the task, and uses clear mathematical reasoning to explain the solution process. This will help you identify papers as having scores of 3 or 4.

As a classroom teacher, I (SM) would on rare occasions give more than 4 points for performance that clearly was superior in all mathematical aspects.

Step 3: Identify Anchor Papers

The third step in creating your own performance assessments is the identification of "anchor papers" exemplifying the various performance levels, as established by the rubrics. In an extensive testing system, such as statewide assessment, the large quantity of student papers virtually assures a good set of exemplars for each rubric level. At the classroom level, however, it may be difficult to identify clear exemplars. Indeed, there may even be none at the highest level if students have never experienced

performance tasks before doing them in your class. In those cases, the best strategy may be to begin with published materials that include exemplars gleaned from classroom field-testing. Examples of such published materials include those by Danielson (1997) and the Balanced Assessment Program (Shannon, 1998). Exemplar papers may also be provided during professional development specifically geared to the type of curricular programs we are highlighting in this book.

After an initial experience with performance tasks, you certainly will have student work that illustrates at least some of the aspects of one, two, three, and four papers. As time goes on, you will develop a good collection of student work to use as examples. It is wise to get both student and parent permission to use actual classroom work in this way, especially if student work is to be shared or used as examples during teacher in-services. Parental permission slips are provided with some of the exemplary programs. A sample of one of these is shown in Figure 10.4. Of course, the students' names must always be removed from their papers before using them as exemplars.

Figure 10.4
Sample Parental Permission Slip

(date)

Dear Students and Parents,

Research on teaching and learning tells us that both can improve when student work is used to inform instruction. The mathematics department is planning ongoing professional development that has teachers working together to review student work in mathematical problem solving. Our goal is to improve all of our students' ability to apply mathematics in many different situations, both real-life and purely theoretical. We will remove names from the papers we share among ourselves and maintain the anonymity of the students whose work we select and bring to our inservices.

Will you please sign the agreement below and have your student return this paper to the mathematics teacher tomorrow? If there are any questions, please do not hesitate to contact the school at (phone number). Thank you for your cooperation.

(mathematics teacher)_____

I give my permission for the work of (student's name) to be shared with others in a professional development setting. I understand that the student's name will be removed from the paper before it is shared.

(student signature)_____ (date)_____

(parent signature)_____ (date)_____

Some teachers make overhead transparencies of student responses to use as a basis for class follow-up discussions of the task. This is one way that performance assessment may affect instruction. These discussions should not only stress the task that has been completed but should also provide students with concrete suggestions as to how they can improve their performance in the future.

If a group of teachers using the same curriculum and set of learning objectives works together on performance assessment in order to assure uniformity of expectations and scoring, it is more likely that consistency will be achieved. Teachers report to us that such an experience is a very stimulating and rewarding form of professional development that fosters greater understanding of both the mathematics involved and the nature of students' learning. In this type of professional development, teachers also discuss their instructional practices, thereby learning new classroom strategies from one another.

Ongoing Projects   For the purposes of this book, ongoing projects will be assigned to be done over time, with the majority of the work to be completed outside of class. Of course, some class time may be spent checking progress or verifying interim steps along the way. Projects frequently require a product that illustrates the application of mathematical principles to a given situation or problem. In some cases, the product is limited to a written report. Frequently, however, a physical model or poster display also is created.

We define ongoing projects as work done over time toward the completion of an application of the mathematics being learned during a unit of study. Most of the work is done outside of class time, although progress checks can help alleviate the tendency to procrastinate. Projects are completed by individuals or by small groups. Assessment criteria, usually in rubric form, are given when the assignment is first made. Assessment of the final project is based on these rubrics. Notice the various forms of assessment criteria included with the projects described in this section. "Designing a Fountain" is an integral part of a textbook unit and the 4-point rubric is given in that textbook. The "Music Company Project" from a published set of middle school performance tasks includes a list of specific directions to the students. See Teacher Notes p. 520 for matrix form of rubric that is provided for assessing student work. The "Dream House" project is teacher-developed and includes a list of steps to be followed in order to complete the project. We can imagine considerable discussion between the

teacher and the students where the steps for this project are clarified and quality criteria for the final work are discussed.

Set 10.2   *Discussion Question*

Questions with an asterisk appear in the Message Board section of the Companion Website at *http://www.prenhall.com/huetinck*. Go to Chapter 10 and click on the Message Board to find and respond to the question.

*1. How would the scoring rubric for an eighth-grade class be different from that for a high-school third-year college prep math class?

Step 4: Score Student Work

The fourth step in the process of creating a performance assessment is scoring, with justification. This step takes time. The teacher delineates the key components of each rubric level with sufficient specificity to explain a given score.

Although the time involved is a drawback of performance assessment, we have found this drawback to be mitigated by the amount of useful information about individual students and a class that a teacher obtains when using performance assessment. In fact, using such assessment to inform current instruction to better ensure students' grasp of mathematical concepts is likely to decrease reteaching in future courses. We also have found that a combination of performance assessments and conventional tests leads to a more comprehensive assessment of student capabilities. Some recommend that performance tasks not be announced as a test, but rather be embedded in the everyday activities of the class as a learning experience. The benefit, they claim, lies in students' being able to rework unsatisfactory papers and, through doing so, learning to take more responsibility for meeting the standards for their class.

Step 5: Revise

Within the ongoing process of performance assessment, there may be a fifth step: revision. Student work that falls below the minimum standard is returned, with specific suggestions concerning the nature of the improvement needed to bring the work up to standard. In terms of a 4-point rubric system, students with ratings of 2 might have some evidence of work that, with some correction, would bring it to a 3. Students with ratings of 1 may have to start over again or try an entirely different solution strategy to bring their work up to a 3. In terms of grades, the intent would be for students to achieve at the C level after revision. Students with ratings of 3 and 4 most likely would become the B and A students, respectively. The class goal would be for all students to achieve a C or better. The revision step is not included, of course, when the performance assessment is part of a culminating activity for a unit or school year.

A second potential difficulty of which the individual teacher—especially one just beginning to use performance assessment—needs to be aware is the tendency to give the best papers or projects in the class the highest possible score, even if none of them truly meets that level of the rubric. This natural tendency can be alleviated by working with other teachers to develop tasks, set rubrics, and score student work. "Blind scoring," in which students' names are not visible and/or in which teachers score the papers of each other's classes, is a way of attempting to alleviate this concern. Ultimately, students can benefit by being held truly accountable to a high standard and by understanding that rubric scoring is not like grading on a curve. Instead, it provides a consistent standard that all can satisfactorily attain. A caution—do not hesitate to have most students revise their work before finalizing their score. There is a tendency to give.

Projects

Another example of a project contained within a curricular program is "Design a Fountain," found in *Integrated Mathematics 2* (Rubenstein et al., 2002). The content focus of Unit 4, which includes this project, is quadratic functions and graphs. The project is described at the beginning of the unit. In cooperative groups, students are to design a fountain that has at least two intersecting water arcs. Constraints are given on the height of the water, the angle at which the water comes out of each nozzle, and the speed at which the water leaves the nozzles. Students are to write equations that model arcs meeting the constraints and to make a poster that includes both a sketch of the fountain and mathematical graphs of the parabolas that model the path of the water. Throughout the unit, students are given the mathematical tools that they need to complete the project. A summary of the scaffolding provided for the students follows:

Lesson 1: Students are given a formula for the path of the water arc and to explore. Use a graphing calculator to explore how changing the velocity and/or angle of the arc affects the appearance of its graph.

Lesson 2: Students work together outside class and measure the distance from the nozzle of a hose to where the stream of water lands on the ground when the nozzle is held at a 45-degree angle.

Lesson 3: Students use the data gathered in Lesson 2 and the equation given them in Lesson 1 to find the maximum height of their water arc above the ground.

Lesson 4: Students are given a problem situation that specifies the desired height of a water arc and the desired distance from beginning to end of the arc. Students are asked to work backward with the formula to find the water velocity that would be required to make the arc work. They also are asked to discuss the reasonableness of their solution.

Lesson 5: Students research examples of fountains to consider different design elements that they might want to use.

Lesson 6: Students apply their knowledge of the discriminant, the main concept of the lesson, to their fountain project.

Lesson 7: Students apply the concept of the lesson, solving simultaneous quadratic equations, to find where two arcs in a fountain would intersect.

The final project is presented as a poster that includes labeled sketches and graphs of the parabolas involved, accompanied by the algebraic equations used to make the graphs.

We have seen many examples of students' fountain posters and have been impressed by their work. Teachers tell us that students who complete the fountain project have a much better understanding of how algebraic functions can model real-world phenomena than students they had previously who had no similar applications experience. The most exciting aspect of these projects to me (LH) was to see students become "shining stars" who previously had been B or C students in regular classwork. Creative approaches and the ability to persevere in solving complex problems are too infrequently highlighted in other mathematics activities. It was delightful to see students gain respect from their peers when they excelled in such projects.

A colleague recently related a dramatic instance of a student succeeding far beyond expectations. The 10th-grade Special Education students enjoyed the "Spatialization" unit from the Middle Grades Mathematics Project. One student with multiple learning disabilities worked diligently through the exercises, building blocks and drawing pictures in perspective. He became so interested in designing that he successfully tackled the project of designing a room addition for his father's office.

The following suggested 4-point rubric for the fountain project is adapted from the one provided in the curriculum for the teacher:

4 Students use the equation for the path of a parabolic water arc correctly in designing their water fountain. Their sketch of the fountain is accurate and clear, and includes the heights and widths of all water arcs. The graphs of the water arcs are drawn correctly, and the equations of the arcs, stream angles, and water speeds are free of error. The poster is attractively presented and shows a fountain design that is supported by the mathematics of this unit.

3 Students' posters lack some of the details regarding heights and widths of the water arcs, the equations of the arcs, the measures of the stream angles, or the water speeds. The sketch of the fountain is somewhat rough and could be improved. There may be some minor errors in applying the mathematics needed to design the fountain.

2 Students' posters are lacking in many essential details. The sketch of the fountain is careless and demonstrates superficial work. Students do not fully understand how to use the equation for the path of a parabolic water arc to design their fountain.

1 Students' posters show a sketch of a fountain, but most details are missing or are incorrect. The equations of the arcs are incorrect, as are other data associated with them. Students whose work received a rating at this level should be encouraged to speak with their teacher as soon as possible to review their work and to make a new start on the project.

A common type of application problem that appears as a project in most of the new curricula is the development and use of surveys. Danielson (1997) includes such a task, which appears here as Activity 10.4. She provides a 4-point rubric for middle-school students participating in this survey project. Many of the features of a rubric for projects are similar to those of rubrics for performance tasks. However, usually there are more parts to a project that is completed over time. Thus, the rubrics should be rigorous enough to require students to give extra effort beyond that given in class in order to complete all aspects of the project well.

A group of five teachers working on a master's of arts in education with a mathematics emphasis conducted a descriptive study investigating the attitudes of their students toward cooperative long-term proj-

A group of students work together to build a "dream house" to scale.

ects in mathematics. All of the projects were completed outside class after one period of introductory instruction. Activity 10.5, the "Dream House Project," is one of three projects used with students in Grades 7–12. Santamaria (1996) used three types of instruments to gather data on student responses:

1. attitudinal questions, to which students could respond by circling the one of four answer choices that most nearly described their feelings regarding the cooperative project;

2. open-ended questions about the same topic;

3. student interviews.

Upon analyzing the data, Santamaria concluded that females strongly preferred working in groups more than males did, that student achievement and preference for cooperative work on projects are inversely related, and that students with little or no experience in cooperative groups liked the project assignment better than students who had previous experience in cooperative groups. When all of the students were questioned about their beliefs concerning the importance of this type of long-term project, middle-school students, in general, felt more strongly positive than high-school students. However, a large majority of students at all grade levels involved felt that mathematics projects were valuable in helping them apply their mathematics knowledge outside the classroom.

The *Contemporary Mathematics in Context (Core-Plus)* curriculum, in contrast to projects that occur during the course of a school year, has a culminating "capstone" unit that ties together major content objectives of the year toward a given outcome. For example, at the end of the first year of Core-Plus, students are to plan a school fund-raising carnival. Students work both in groups and individually to complete the project. Several suggested

FOR TEACHERS

Activity 10.4 Music Company

Mathematical Content:
Designing and conducting surveys, collecting and
analyzing data, communicating results both
graphically and verbally (PSSM Data Analysis
and Probability Standard for Grades 6–8)

Materials Needed:
Student directions, scoring guide

Directions: Make a list of topics your students
would have become relatively proficient in before
you could give this as a culminating activity. Compare your list to the five categories on page 520 of
the Scoring Guide in the Teacher Notes.

FOR STUDENTS

Activity 10.4
Music Company

Mathematics Standards Assessed

- Number operations and concepts
- Functions and algebra
- Statistics and probability
- Problem solving and mathematical reasoning
- Mathematical skills and tools
- Mathematical communication

Directions: A music recording company is trying to decide which groups to record on its label. The
company has asked you to help by determining which groups are most popular with students today and
which will be the most popular for several years. The company has asked for your recommendations,
supported by clear reasons.

To complete this job, you might:

- Determine students' favorite musical groups and groups they think they will like in the next few years.
  This means that you must design a survey instrument of some kind.
- Conduct the survey of students.
- Analyze your data by organizing it into a table.
- Summarize your findings by making some type of graph or graphs.
- Calculate how many recordings could be sold to students in your entire school.
- Write a summary to the recording company, in which you recommend which artists it should record.

Source: Danielson, Charlotte (1997). *A Collection of Performance Tasks and Rubrics: Middle School Mathematics*. Larchmont, NY: Eye
on Education. Reprinted with permission.

FOR TEACHERS

Activity 10.5 Dream House Project

Mathematical Content:
Scale drawings/proportions, budget calculations
(PSSM Measurement and Connections
Standards for Grades 9–12)

Materials:
Activity sheets

Directions:
1. Develop a series of questions you would pose to your students before they started this project. These questions will lead to a "criteria chart" that will remain posted in the classroom during the period of time students are working on the project. This set of criteria is the basis for determining the grades or scores given to the completed project.
2. Establish your time line for checking the progress of each group. Include a general sequence of steps, and specify what evidence you will require from each group during the process. This might vary depending on the amount of direction needed by a given class.

FOR STUDENTS

Activity 10.5
Dream House Project (page 1 of 2)

Introduction: You and the other members of your group want to build a dream house. As a group, you have to present an architectural model and a written report of floor covering cost.

You will have opportunities to work with your group in class but must plan on meeting outside of class, as the in-class time will not be sufficient to complete the project. You will work more efficiently by assigning jobs to different members of the group. You can create an action plan that lists all jobs to be done, who will do them, and when the jobs are due. (This can be part of your written report.) It is very important for the group to work cooperatively and for all members to do their share. This is a learning experience for the future, when you will be required to work with people every day.

When researching floor covering cost for your financial part of your report, don't be afraid to go into different stores and ask questions. You can also get estimates over the phone, getting listings from the yellow pages. Be polite, identify yourself and your school, and say why you are calling. Have your questions prepared in advance. Most people will be happy to answer your questions.

Report due: _____

FOR STUDENTS

Activity 10.5
Dream House Project (page 2 of 2)

Materials:

scissors   graph paper

rulers   poster board

Specific Steps:

1. The size of your house has to be at most 40′ × 50′.

2. Rough draft done on notebook paper.

Minimum Requirements	Optional
a. Living room	Extra bedroom
b. Kitchen	Family room
c. Master bedroom	Extra bathrooms
d. Full bath	Fireplace
e. Hallways connecting all rooms	TV room
f. Closets in each bedroom	Workout room
g. Front and back doors	Jacuzzi, spa
h. Laundry room	Dining room
i. Floor covering	

3. **a.** All dimensions to scale. (I used 1/4″ per foot.)

   b. All walls are 8′ high.

   c. All doors are 7′ high and 3′ wide.

   d. All hallways are 3′ wide.

CREATION OF FLOOR PLAN

4. **a.** Do your rough draft in your notebook.

   b. After the rough draft has been approved by the teacher, lay out the perimeter of the house on 1/4″ graph paper.

CONSTRUCTION AND ASSEMBLY OF WALLS

5. Cut to scale poster board in long strips. Walls are to be placed directly on top of your floor plan lines and attached to the graph paper. (All doorways and windows should be cut out before attaching walls to floor plan.)

   Hints: Apply tape to base of walls, and secure floor. Then line up adjacent wall, and tape corner. Begin with exterior walls.

COST PLAN

6. Write a report of the floor-covering costs. You have a total budget of $4,000 to cover cost of materials (*Example:* tiles, hardwood, carpeting, linoleum or a combination), labor, and taxes. Investigate and shop around to find the best prices. Bring in at least two different companies' estimation of labor and materials cost to back up your choice of covering.

investigations using different aspects of the mathematics of the course are provided. They include the following ideas:

- *Planning*. Use a project digraph to identify and schedule tasks for the carnival.
- *Floor plans*. Given certain constraints, make a floor plan to scale on graph paper for booths needed for the carnival.
- *T-shirts*. Use the mathematics of this book, including NOW/NEXT tables, to show the cost of producing various quantities of shirts, as well as the sales price and an analysis of the selling price and quantity needed to produce a given profit.
- *Money making*. Analyze data from the previous 3 years (i.e., the number of tickets sold to parents) in order to best predict the pattern of sales for this year. In addition, analyze mathematically the investment of profits in an interest-bearing savings account.
- *Games 1*. Design a ring-toss game with a certain size of rings and 2-liter bottles of soda. Analyze the expected number of ringers when the bottles are placed at varying distances apart.
- *Games 2*. Analyze a basketball free-throw contest by designing and carrying out a simulation of the activity.

To finish the capstone, each group chooses three investigations to complete and share with the class. Each student then writes a report to the principal of the fictitious school where the carnival is to be held, explaining how mathematics was used to assure the success of the carnival.

We hope you recognize that the projects described here are integral to the curriculum, in contrast to the way projects sometimes have been used in mathematics classes. We have seen projects assigned as additional work, possibly for extra credit, but separate from the curriculum. While this use of projects may be valid, the projects cannot be tied directly to instructional decisions, as are the projects included in *Standards*-based curricula.

The Instructional Resources listed at the conclusion of this chapter identify some sources of tasks, investigations, and projects. As you select from these materials in your instructional planning, consider the mathematical objectives of the course for which they are to be used. Choose projects that support the curriculum and from which you and your students can gain useful information about their level of mathematical understanding.

Investigations

An investigation is a mathematical situation that is presented to students with the goal of exploring different aspects and arriving at summary conjectures. As such, an investigation is more inductive than a project. A project is based upon applying previously learned mathematics to a particular situation, so it is more deductive. When assessing student work on an investigation, a teacher looks for the logical processes of mathematics and the connections students are making with previously learned material. In many investigations, some outcomes are expected, but others may occur that the teacher had never considered. For example, when using a dynamic geometry graphing tool, students may discover new relationships, techniques, or theorems that are not part of a typical geometry class.

Investigations are embedded in the *Interactive Mathematics Program* (IMP) in the form of problems of the week (POWs). These problems are posed once a week and are due a week from the date of assignment. Students may discuss problem approaches briefly during each class period, but the bulk of the problem solving is to be done individually outside of class. The day the POWs are collected, one or two randomly chosen students are asked to present part or all of their solution. Over the year, all students should have an opportunity to present their work. Most of the POWs are investigative in nature, and all involve nonstandard problem solving. Many other contemporary curricular programs, at both the middle- and high-school levels, include investigations in lessons that may take more than one day to complete. In addition, some teachers using more traditional curricula "open up" their programs by including POWs they have developed or obtained from a variety of sources.

The following format is used consistently throughout the IMP curriculum for students' write-ups of POWs (Fendel, Resick, Fraser, & Alper, 1997, p. 11):

1. *Problem statement*. State the problem clearly in your own words. Your problem statement should be clear enough that someone unfamiliar with the problem could understand what it is that you are being asked to do.

As a teacher of this curriculum, 1 (SM) found students struggling with or not taking this part of the problem-solving process seriously. As a consequence, they tended to make incorrect assumptions that led to incorrect results.

Go to Web Destinations for Chapter 10 at **http://www.prenhall.com/huetinck** to find a link to a website with Problems of the Week (POWs) in middle school math, algebra, and geometry.

2. *Process.* Describe what you did in attempting to solve the problem, using your notes as a reminder. Include things that did not work out or that seemed like a waste of time. Do this part of the write-up even if you did not solve the problem.

At first, students tended to throw away all scratch-paper work and turn in only work that showed a successful approach to the POW. Over time, however, they began trying more approaches and including unfruitful attempts in the work they turned in, which was very informative to me as a teacher.

3. *Solution.* State your solution as clearly as you can. Explain how you know that your solution is correct and complete. If you obtained only a partial solution, give that. If you were able to generalize the problem, include your general results. Your explanation should be written in a way that will be convincing to someone else—even someone who initially disagrees with your answer.

Keeping in mind the possibility of revision, having students give as much of an answer as they were able was very useful to my subsequent instruction, whether the follow-through involved individual students or the entire class.

4. *Extensions.* Invent some extensions or variations to the problem. That is, write down some related problems. They can be easier, harder, or about the same level of difficulty as the original problem. (You don't have to solve these additional problems.)

The quality of the extensions varied greatly. Sometimes they were very ingenious; at other times, only cursory, rather shallow changes were made to the original problem. It was difficult for me, the teacher, to determine how much weight to give to this portion of the process in assessing the total POW. In retrospect, I think stressing the importance of a quality extension as a way for high achievers to show their capabilities would be an effective way of dealing with extensions.

5. *Evaluation.* Discuss your personal reaction to the problem. For example, you might respond to the questions below.
   - Did you consider it educationally worthwhile? What did you learn from it?
   - How would you change the problem to make it better?
   - Did you enjoy working on it?
   - Was it too hard or too easy?

The investigation in Activity 10.6, "Spirolaterals," was adapted from a problem of the week appearing in IMP, Year 1 (Fendel, Resick, Fraser, & Alper, 1997, p. 400). Additional sources not in the IMP material were used to provide a real-life context to the problem (see reference list). Spirolaterals (this spelling was used in the 1973 *Scientific American* article that was the basis for many of the ensuing activities) also occur in some of the exemplary middle-school curricula.

FOR TEACHERS

Activity 10.6 Spirolaterals

Mathematical Content:
Conducting trials, making conjectures, justifying generalizations (PSSM Reasoning and Proof Standard for Grades 6–8)

Materials Needed:
Activity sheets, 1/4-inch-square and isometric graph paper

Directions: Work through the investigation yourself, as a learner. Then write a 4-point rubric to be used in an eighth-grade class to assess student responses.

You may want to have students from two classes trade anonymous papers and work through the Eight-Step Development of Mathematics Performance Criteria (Figure 10.5). Spirolaterals can be done as a small-group activity.

FOR STUDENTS

Activity 10.6
Spirolaterals

AS THE WORM TURNS

"Certain prehistoric worms fed on sediment in the mud at the bottom of ponds. For efficiency, they would not retrace paths which had already been traveled, since little food was left there. Worms had innate 'rules' regarding how close to the eaten path to stay, how far to go before turning around, how sharp a turn to make, etc. These rules varied from species to species, and paleontologists can trace the development of species and determine the similarity of different species by comparing fossil records of worm tracks" (*Science,* 21 November, 1969).

Today we are going to do a mathematical investigation inspired by these prehistoric worms. We will start with certain assumptions:

- worms travel in straight lines until they turn,
- worms move forward in positive integral increments,
- worms can cross their own trails, but they stop if they get to their starting location and orientation.

Example
A worm travels paths of lengths 3, 5, 2. At the end of each path, the worm turns right 90°.

Use grid paper to see what happens. We will start the worm going forward in the "up" direction on the grid.

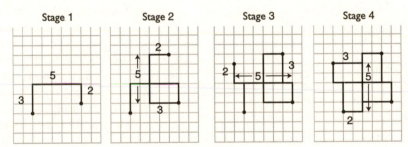

Stage 1   Stage 2   Stage 3   Stage 4

Result
After four repeats of this pattern, using the given assumptions, the worm returns to the starting point. This spirolateral pattern is closed.

Your task: explore other spirolaterals
try to find some patterns
explain why a pattern works the way it does
try other numbers in a sequence
try other sequence lengths
try other rules for turning

Describe and illustrate your findings. Use any mathematics you know to justify your conclusions and generalizations.

EXTENSIONS

- Write a program for your calculator or computer to do spirolaterals.
- What if the worms could change a rule if they came to a path that was already eaten?
- You suggest one.

Source: *Interactive Mathematics Program Year I,* published by Key Curriculum Press, 1150 65th Street, Emeryville, CA 94608, 1-800-995-MATH. Reprinted with permission.

PERFORMANCE CRITERIA

Mathematics classrooms in which performance criteria are clearly stated and students understand that they are expected to meet these criteria have the potential to become true learning communities, where students participate in establishing their own high standards. Clark (1997) provides an eight-step process for developing performance criteria in a classroom in which reciprocal obligations between teacher and student are practiced—that is, where there is an agreement that "it is the student's responsibility to demonstrate understanding and the teacher's responsibility to provide the opportunity and the means for that demonstration." The eight steps are presented in Figure 10.5. This information is provided here to hold before us

Figure 10.5
Eight-Step Development of Mathematics Performance Criteria

Step 1	Pose an open-ended task suitable for the unit, and let the students do the task.
Step 2	Distribute three samples of other students' attempts at the same task, and ask the class (in groups of four or in pairs) to identify the best and worst attempts and to find reasons for their decision.
Step 3	Share all the things that students feel distinguish a good solution from a bad one, add some of your own as necessary (with the endorsement of the class), and generate a list of criteria for good performance.
Step 4	Develop as a class a grading scheme by which the criteria can be translated into a grade or score for the task.
Step 5	Ask the students to apply the new criteria to their solution to the problem and to make evaluative comments on their own work.
Step 6	Ask the students to apply the grading scheme to their solution and generate a grade for their work.
Step 7	Have the students submit their solution with their evaluative comments and grade.
Step 8	"Second-grade" the work to check for shared understanding of the agreed criteria and consistency in their use.

Source: Clark, David (1997). *Constructive Assessment in Mathematics.* Key Curriculum Press, 1150 65th Street, Emeryville, CA 94608, 1-800-995-MATH. Reprinted with permission.

the ideal in a *Standards*-based classroom of having students take responsibility for their own learning. We extend this notion to include students participating in meaningful self-assessment.

Portfolios

"A portfolio is purposeful collection of student work that exhibits to the student (and/or others) the student's efforts, progress, or achievement in a given area" (*Constructivist Assessment in Mathematics,* California Mathematics Council, 1994, p. 55). Students have been developing portfolios for many years in the arts and in writing as evidence of their ability to perform competently within criteria established for those content areas. In recent years, teachers at all levels have experimented with student portfolios in mathematics. There still is a need for more classroom-based research on the use of portfolios for student assessment in mathematics (Bright, 1998; Asturias, 1994). Carefully developed and managed portfolios can be a useful tool for student self-assessment. Indeed, when used as one aspect of end-of-unit assessment, portfolios have informed instructional practices. In this chapter, that is the focus of their use. The function of portfolios as a means of communicating to parents the nature and extent of their children's performance and growth in mathematics is discussed in Chapter 11. Later in this unit, we will discuss how portfolios also can be a tool for external evaluation and program effectiveness reviews.

Many of the *Standards*-based programs incorporate portfolio assessment as a summative activity at the end of each unit and as a self-evaluation process at the end of the year. In other *Standards*-based classrooms, teachers have developed portfolio systems that not only provide current information about student progress but also can be carried to the next mathematics class to provide that teacher with more complete information about the student than typically is available through cumulative records.

The following types of entries are frequently included in mathematics portfolios:

- student-selected homework assignments showing growth over time in understanding key mathematical concepts/procedures;
- problem-solving activities (problems of the week, etc.);
- summary writing of the key areas of learning in the unit and areas the student feels a need to work on;
- assignments a student is proud of, and why;
- reflection on specific areas of learning gained through group activities;
- other items specific to the curriculum and/or class assignments.

Figure 10.6
Expected Contents of a Portfolio

"All About Alice" Portfolio

Now that "*All About Alice*" is completed, it is time to put together your portfolio for the unit. Compiling this portfolio has three parts:

- writing a cover letter in which you summarize the unit;
- choosing papers to include from your work in this unit;
- discussing your personal growth during the unit.

Cover Letter for "All About Alice"
Look back over "All About Alice" and describe the central theme of the unit and the main mathematical ideas. This description should give an overview of how the key ideas were developed in this unit.

As part of the compilation of your portfolio, you will select some activities that you think were important in developing the key ideas. Your cover letter should include an explanation of why you are selecting each particular item.

Selecting Papers From "All About Alice"
Your portfolio from "*All About Alice*" should contain

- *Homework 17: An Exponential Portfolio;*
- *"All Roads Lead to Rome";*
- a homework or class activity in which you used exponents to solve the problem;
- a homework or class activity that involved graphing;
- *Homework 8: Negative Reflections;*
- A Problem of the Week—Select one of the two POWs you completed during this unit (*"More From Lewis Carroll"* or "*A Logical Collection*").

Personal Growth
Your cover letter for "*All About Alice*" describes how the unit develops. As part of your portfolio, write about your personal development during this unit. You may want to address this question:

How do you think you have grown mathematically over your second year of IMP?

You should include here any other thoughts about your experiences with this unit that you want to share with a reader of your portfolio.

Source: *Interactive Mathematics Program Year 1* published by Key Curriculum Press, 1150 65th Street, Emeryville, CA 94608, 1-800-995-MATH. Reprinted with permission.

Sample Unit Portfolio At the end of each of the five yearly units, an IMP student adds to his portfolio, following given guidelines. At the end of each year, students are given time to review their portfolios and decide which papers they will retain to indicate to their next IMP teacher the extent of their mathematical competence and confidence. Homework 20 from the "All About Alice" unit informs students of the expected contents of the portfolio for that unit (see Figure 10.6). As homework, students build their portfolios, following those guidelines.

My students (SM) found it helpful to do a prewrite activity in class on the day a portfolio write-up was assigned. The activity included group development of a concept map of the mathematical content of the unit. The development of a concept map is a useful strategy for all students; in fact, even those of my students who were not native English speakers gained more confidence in their use of mathematical vocabulary through the prewrite strategy. English teachers at my school were very helpful in showing me how this kind of activity could be carried out in a mathematics class, and I would recommend that kind of professional collaboration. Cross-curricular projects involving language arts and mathematics are particularly viable, both at the middle-school and high-school levels, when students are using the type of exemplary curricula described in this book. Through a joint process, the mathematics teacher ensures that the mathematics is correctly described, and the English teacher can reinforce good standards of written academic communication.

Set 10.3   Discussion Questions

 Questions with an asterisk appear in the Message Board section of the Companion Website at **http://www.prenhall.com/huetinck.** Go to Chapter 10 and click on the Message Board to find and respond to the question.

1. What do you think you would learn about your students by reading a complete set of portfolio items for the "All About Alice" unit (see Figure 10.6)?
2. How might your instructional practices for the next unit be modified as a result of the portfolio reviews?
*3. What issues concern you regarding portfolio assessment as a tool to inform instruction?

As an example of mathematical applications and how they are related to authentic assessment, we will look at the seventh-grade module "Getting in Shape" from MathScape (1998). The theme of this unit is geometric design. The focus of the unit is the mathematics of triangles, polygons, and circles, as well as critical thinking aspects involved with tiling (tessellations). The final project of this module is for students, working individually, to create a geometric design that uses figures they have studied in the unit and to write a report that explains the mathematical relationships used in their design. Activity 10.7 presents Homework 4, used as embedded assessment within the MathScape program. Typically, an embedded assessment is a regular assignment that the teacher spends more time looking at and scores by a rubric.

A unique feature of the MathScape program is the student self-assessment it includes. Each unit is broken into "phases," each approximately a week long. At the end of each phase, both a skill quiz and a student self-assessment sheet are provided. A copy of the Phase 1 Self-Assessment given to students following Activity 10.7 is provided in Figure 10.7.

Set 10.4   Discussion Questions

1. Do you think a copy of a student's work on Homework 4 (Activity 10.7) might be appropriate to include in a portfolio? Why or why not?
2. What information might the teacher be able to glean about student understanding of mathematics from Homework 4 as contrasted to homework consisting only of skill practice?

Figure 10.7
Student Self-Assessment

Phase One
Student Assessment Criteria

Does my work show that I can ...

- classify angles and triangles correctly?
- take accurate angle measurements?
- create a tessellation that clearly shows a repeating pattern and has no gaps or overlaps between the triangles?
- describe triangles, giving details about the sum of angle measures, the lengths of sides, and lines of symmetry?
-
-

Source: *MathScape* (1999). Chicago, IL: Creative Publications. Reprinted with permission.

FOR TEACHERS

Activity 10.7 Tiling With Triangles

Mathematical Content:
Classifying and measuring triangles, tessellations (PSSM Geometry Standard for Grades 6–8)

Materials Needed:
Worksheet, student self-assessment rubric

Directions: Work through the assignment yourself. Then answer the Discussion Questions in Set 10.4.

FOR STUDENTS

Activity 10.7
Tiling With Triangles

Applying Skills: Tell whether each pattern below is a tessellation. If it is, sketch the figure or figures used to create the tessellation.

1.

2.

3.

4.

5. Sketch an example of a triangle that *cannot* be used to create a tessellation. If this is not possible, write "not possible."

6. Sketch a triangle on an index card, and cut it out. Use your triangle to draw a tessellation.

Extending Concepts: Use the tessellation to answer the following questions.

7. How many times does each angle of the triangle appear at any given tessellation vertex?

8. What is the sum of the angle measures of a triangle?

9. What is the sum of the angles at a tessellation vertex?

10. Use your answers to Problems 7–9 to explain why any triangle tessellates.

In the language of transformations, a slide is called a **translation,** a flip is a **reflection,** and a turn is a **rotation.** The tessellation below can be created by moving the triangle in position 1 sequentially to positions 2, 3, 4, 5, and 6.

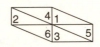

11. Identify which transformation (a translation, reflection, or rotation) would move the triangle from

   a. position 1 to 2;

   b. position 3 to 4;

   c. position 4 to 5;

Writing:

12. Suppose a fourth-grader asked you how to make a tessellating pattern with triangles. Write a step-by-step list of instructions for your young friend. Make your directions clear and simple to follow. Draw pictures to illustrate the steps.

Source: *MathScape* (1999). Chicago, IL: Creative Publications. Reprinted with permission.

District Performance Assessment Systems

Some districts include portfolio assessments as a component of their entire student assessment program. When practiced districtwide, a commonly agreed-upon format and set of criteria are established. An example of a portfolio system based on performance standards is the one developed as part of the New Standards assessment system. A summary of the content of the New Standards portfolio system for middle school is given in Figure 10.8, with comments.

A sample of the type of entry sheet that is provided with the New Standards portfolio system is shown in Figure 10.9. Students are to complete entry sheets for each item in their portfolios, justifying their selection and their mathematical understanding that the selection shows. If such an assessment were part of a district's assessment program, the district would be responsible for identifying and training scorers, scoring and validating student work, and communicating the results to students, parents, teachers, and the community.

Figure 10.8
The New Standards Portfolio System

Middle Grades Mathematics

Conceptual Understanding Exhibit
Prepare four entries for the Conceptual Understanding Exhibit, one in each of these areas of mathematics:
1. Number and Operation
2. Geometry and Measurement
3. Function and Algebra
4. Probability and Statistics

Problem Solving Exhibit
- There is one entry in the Problem Solving Exhibit. This entry is a collection of four problems.

Project Exhibit: Putting Mathematics to Work
Prepare one entry per year for the Project Exhibit. Typical entries are projects involving research and applications of mathematics over a period of 3 weeks or more.

Select one per year from the following kinds of project:
- Data Study
- Mathematical Modeling
- Design of a Physical Structure
- Management and Planning
- Pure Mathematics Investigation
- History of a Mathematical Idea

Skills and Communication Exhibit
Separate pieces of work are not required for the Skills and Communication Exhibit. Entries submitted for the first three exhibits might be ample. If not, a few additional pieces of work may be included here to fill important gaps.

There are two entry slips: one for skills and one for communication. On these entry slips you are asked to tell us where to look in your other exhibits for evidence of your mathematical skills and your ability to communicate mathematically.

Source: Reprinted with permission from New Standards™. The New Standards™ assessment system includes performance standards with performance descriptions, student work samples and commentaries, on-demand examinations and a portfolio system. For more information, contact the National Center on Education and the Economy, 202-783-3668 or http://www.ncee.org.

Figure 10.9
Sample Portfolio Entry Sheet

Name	Date
Conceptual Understanding Exhibit	**Entry Slip #2**
Geometry and Measurement	

Enter two or three pieces of evidence that show you understand the concepts listed below. Identify the concept or group of concepts for which you are providing evidence. Show that you can use the concepts to solve problems.

_____ use relationships between figures involving congruence, similarity, and projections, and describe them in transformations

_____ analyze geometric figures and use deductive methods in proofs

_____ work with measures of length, area, surface area, volume, and angle; and non-geometric measures of weight, monetary value, and time

_____ use and determine formulas for area, surface area, and volume of different figures

_____ study geometric patterns including sequences of growing shapes, and describe the patterns in terms of properties of the *n*th stage

_____ use quotient measures such as speed and density, and relate them to slope and "per unit" amounts

_____ understand the structure of standard measurement systems, including the relationship of the units, unit conversions, and the analysis of units used to measure quantities such as length, time, and speed

_____ solve problems involving map scales and other scale diagrams

For example, you might submit a problem that uses geometric and measurement ideas to analyze the dimensions and properties of shapes. A comparison of the ratio of surface area to volume of a pine tree and a cactus, for example, might be explored.

Title of Piece	Circumstances (Mark all that apply.)	Where is it?
	_____ Alone _____ Group _____ Homework _____ w/feedback _____ Other:	_____ Here (It's attached.) _____ Not Here. Look in Exhibit _____ Entry _____
	_____ Alone _____ Group _____ Homework _____ w/feedback _____ Other:	_____ Here (It's attached.) _____ Not Here. Look in Exhibit _____ Entry _____
	_____ Alone _____ Group _____ Homework _____ w/feedback _____ Other:	_____ Here (It's attached.) _____ Not Here. Look in Exhibit _____ Entry _____

Source: Reprinted with permission from New Standards™. The New Standards™ assessment system includes performance standards with performance descriptions, student work samples and commentories, on-demand examinations and a portfolio system. For more information, contact the National Center on Education and the Economy, 202-783-3668 or http://www.ncee.org.

THE ROLE OF EXTERNAL ASSESSMENTS

The NCTM Assessment Standards (1995) discuss the use of student assessment in program evaluation. A key ingredient, according to this document, is that any evaluation process, whether it be at the na-tional, state, or local level, *must include teachers*. In addition, several shifts in program evaluation practices may be necessary:

- moving away from relying on oversimplified evidence from a single test or test format (traditionally one standardized, norm-referenced test);
- presenting disaggregated data giving breakdowns of results in various groupings rather than as single scores representing a school;

- including and honoring teachers' professional judgments about students' performance along with other evidence. (NCTM, 1995, p. 67)

Standardized Tests

Standardized testing remains a fact of life in the United States. Many conclusions about students and schools are based upon standardized test results. The media publishes results as if schools could be compared through this means. So you will be better informed about the nature of standardized tests and what they can and cannot tell the public, we are providing some information put together by knowledgeable sources in this area.

One source is James Ridgeway of the National Institute for Science Education (NISE) at the University of Wisconsin at Madison (Ridgeway, 1998). He was involved in the Balanced Assessment project funded by the National Science Foundation (NSF). In the *NISE Brief* (January 1998), Ridgeway states, "Exclusive dependence on standardized tests of technique in mathematics and science poses a substantial threat to educational reform" (p. 7). He goes on to suggest that several dimensions need to be included in assessment of *Standards*-based programs. They include mathematical content, mathematical process, types of goals (pure mathematics, applications, etc.), and circumstances of performance (oral presentation versus written description, individual versus group work, etc.). Such dimensions, Ridgeway claims, are essential for guiding and monitoring the reform and for communicating to stakeholders the expectations for students in the *Standards*-based programs.

W. James Popham, University of California at Los Angeles, has written an essay about standardized testing intended to be read by parents (Popham, 1998). As one day you may be in the situation of interpreting test results and the information they can and cannot provide to parents, we present a brief summary of some of Popham's main points.

First, standardized tests compare an individual test-taker's performance to the performance of students in a "norm group," representative of the U.S. student population, who have previously taken the same test. Parents often misunderstand this type of performance measure. When test results are expressed as percentiles, it is important for parents to understand that a score at the 60th percentile does not mean their child answered 60% of the items correctly. Instead, it means their child scored as high as or higher than 60% of the students in the group used to norm the test.

A question to be considered is the validity of test results given to a student group whose demographic composition is considerably different from that of the group used to establish the norm. This may be particularly true in urban and other areas in which the ethnic composition and/or the socioeconomic profile of students may be very different from the national norm.

Popham argues that standardized tests should not be used to evaluate teachers or schools, for several reasons:

- There is likely to be a mismatch between the content the test measures and what teachers actually are teaching, especially since curriculum is a local choice.
- These tests are designed to give a spread of student results, so there is a very strong tendency to omit items that cover content most students are likely to know.
- Standardized tests are revised only every 5 to 10 years, so a school's test scores may be artificially boosted by familiarity with the test.

Finally, Popham notes that standardized test scores tend to correlate with high socioeconomic status. Poor performance therefore should not imply that educators in a low-performing school are not doing a good job (or that educators in a high-performing school are doing a good job). Popham concludes, "Judging educational effectiveness with test scores is like measuring mileage with a teaspoon. It just doesn't work" (p. 4).

Author and speaker Alfie Kohn is a well-known critic of the increased number of standardized tests imposed upon students and their uses as gatekeepers to promotion or graduation. At a conference of educators in June 2000, he stated, "The emergency consists of a top-down, heavy-handed, corporate-style, test-driven approach to school reform that is squeezing the intellectual life out of our schools" (International Education Summit, Wayne State University, Detroit, Michigan). Kohn voices a concern that many educators have: Teaching to the test may not really increase my students' knowledge, but it may make them feel education is irrelevant and meaningless to their lives.

The SAT Another high-stakes test in the United States is the Scholastic Achievement (formerly Aptitude) Test (SAT). The SAT plays a crucial role in determining access to higher education and profoundly influences the type of learning and assessments regarded by schools as important. Indeed, many textbook programs include assessment items that are structured to have a similar format to the SAT. Recently, the SAT changed part of its mathematics format to include "open response" items. These items are open in the sense that multiple-choice answers are not provided. Rather, the student works out the problem and then bubbles in the values that represent the correct answer to the problem.

Because of the impact of student SAT scores on college admissions, results on this battery of standardized, norm-referenced tests also are used, inappropriately, to judge schools. School test results are available on the Internet, and school averages are widely publicized. Again, many factors beyond the school's control contribute to SAT scores. As more students aspire to attend a university, more are also taking the SAT tests than ever before. Particularly in schools whose student body consists largely of students from low-income families and/or traditionally underrepresented groups, average test scores over time might actually drop as students who previously would never have been encouraged to consider continuing their academic education past high school now take the SAT. Further, many of these students have less access and means to participate in SAT preparation courses. Since these courses claim to increase SAT scores, students not taking them may be at a disadvantage. Weissglass (1998) is among those who question the assumptions of the SAT and its role in limiting educational opportunity for certain groups of students.

The validity of the SAT for college admissions has been called into question recently, most notably by the University of California system. Many eastern universities had discontinued its use for admissions purposes already. Behind these decisions was the awareness that SAT scores are not very strong predictors of later success at the university, especially for students from low-performing schools. Further, the claim that one could not prepare for the SAT was belied when students were able to increase their performance on the SAT through test preparation programs. Interestingly, the test's name, originally the Scholastic Aptitude Test, was changed to Scholastic Achievement Test, and now stands solely as three letters.

If the intended egalitarian purpose of the SAT—to identify students intellectually able to succeed in advanced educational, regardless of their background—has not been met, it is time for another look. Several changes in the SAT have been proposed. One is the addition of a written essay along with the single-answer format. Another is the increased reliance on the ACT, which purports to measure what students actually should know, based upon the high-school curriculum. The Educational Testing Service benefits financially whenever anyone takes either test. The criticism that big business benefits from all the school accountability measures is another issue, one that will not be discussed in this book.

Federal Requirements The recent reauthorization of the federal Elementary and Secondary Education Act is known as the No Child Left Behind Act. The impact of this legislation has begun with the 2002–2003 school year. A key element is the accountability for improvement in student achievement. All students, including minorities, low-income, disabled, and English learners, must become proficient in state academic standards for reading and math in Grades 3–8. If a school fails to make adequate yearly progress for 2 consecutive years, corrective actions must be taken. Penalties will be imposed if progress continues to wane. Eventually there will be a takeover of a "failing" school district by a receiver or trustee until adequate yearly progress is made.

You and your fellow teachers will be faced with the reality of administering standardized tests and seeing the results printed in local newspapers. Your students' futures may be affected by the tests they take. The public may judge your school as inferior if its test scores are low. The encouraging news is that it is possible, and even desirable, to continue to engage your students in tasks you consider educationally worthwhile because they have depth and to have increased standardized test scores. The two are not mutually exclusive. Schools that build test-taking skills into homeroom or class warm-ups are maintaining an appropriate balance. They are continuing to provide stimulating curricula for their students while also providing them with tools to succeed on standardized tests wherever they occur.

Local school control is a fundamental tenet of the education system in the United States, so there has never been an official national curriculum. However, the U.S. Department of Education has administered a voluntary set of tests at the 4th, 8th, and 12th grades for several decades, based on commonly agreed-upon content, including mathematics, at those grade levels. This National Assessment of Educational Progress (NAEP), often called the "Nation's Report Card," will become more important as the No Child Left Behind Act is implemented, with each state expected to participate. Results of the NAEP are not reported at the individual student level. Rather, a sampling of students at the tested grade levels are administered the test, and the results are compiled across the entire country, by various student subgroups and geographic regions.

Having each state participate is essential as a type of quality control, because content standards and levels of proficiency vary across states.

 For information about the Nation's Report Card, go to **http://www.prenhall.com/huetinck** and click on Web Destinations for Chapter 10.

Performance Assessment

If performance assessment is part of a district or state's total assessment program, as it is in some places, professional development usually is an integral component. Since such assessment frequently is done only at specific grade levels, the establishment of grade-level standards necessarily precedes the development of tasks. The move to such standards is common in most states and districts at this time. The national Goals 2000 project required that participating districts develop such standards in an open process, with input from many stakeholder groups. Some compensatory education programs, such as Title 10, require that students be assessed by multiple means, including, but not limited to, standardized tests. As you begin your teaching career, it's likely that you'll encounter grade-level standards linked to performance assessment.

States that have developed and used multiple types of assessment include Arizona, California, Connecticut, Kentucky, New Jersey, Oregon, and Vermont. Some Canadian provinces also use performance assessment as part of their provincial assessment system. The National Science Foundation funded the *Balanced Assessment* project's development of performance tasks, complete with classroom field testing, revision, rubric refinement, and student samples. Released items from state assessments, the *Balanced Assessment* project, and other sources were provided to members of the National Council of Supervisors of Mathematics. These tasks, samples of which appear in the Additional Activities at the end of this chapter, may be used by the classroom teacher in appropriate places within a given curriculum. They may provide the basis for professional development when a group of teachers administer the same task to their students and then meet afterward to discuss the results and implications for classroom instruction. Additionally, they may be used to give students experience with this type of assessment before they take a mandated performance assessment in a district or state.

Advanced Placement Tests

Another form of testing based on a national set of curriculum expectations is the Advanced Placement (AP) program. These tests, administered in May each year, give motivated, high-achieving students the opportunity to pass rigorous exams and thereby possibly earn college credits while still in high school.

Most high schools offering AP classes also give students an extra grade point simply for taking the classes. That is, a C grade in an AP class, usually worth 2 points toward a student's grade point average (GPA), instead earns 3 points, and so on. Some universities are concerned about grade inflation at the high-school level because of this practice, not only for AP classes, but also for designated honors classes. University admission officers on campuses where entrance is very competitive may actually find themselves denying admission to students with a 4.0, or straight-A, average because so many other students have greater than a 4.0 average. There is much discussion in many states on limiting the amount of extra points students may be allowed while in high school. The University of California, for example, currently limits the number of additional grade points that students may include in the GPA to 4. There also is a concern that students may avoid elective classes that might be of interest to them if those classes do not have the potential to add extra points to their GPA. Nevertheless, AP exams are sure to be a part of the high-school program in the foreseeable future.

The first mathematics exam of this type was the AP calculus exam. This test is now given at two levels, the AB level and the BC level. The AB course is structured to be equivalent to a one-semester beginning calculus course. The BC course is equivalent to a second calculus course. For several years, students have been allowed to use graphing calculators on one part of the test but not on the other part.

Students receive scores ranging from 1 to 5, with 5 being the highest. Although a 3 is considered "passing," different universities have different policies about accepting AP scores in lieu of students taking calculus at the university level. The AP exams are criterion-referenced, with a set of standards for each score, regardless of the number of students attaining that score. So, in a sense, the AP calculus exam is a performance assessment. Teachers from all over the country meet at one location and do the scoring. Although individual student results of all AP exams, on a 5-point scale, are provided to schools as well as to the students (usually during the summer after the tests were taken), teachers do not see individual student work from the exam unless they are selected to participate in the national scoring during the summer.

The number of students taking AP calculus at the high schools in the United States is growing, but the percentage of students each year taking the AP exam still is extremely small, especially when compared with percentages in other countries, according to the TIMSS 12th-grade study. And despite the well-known success of underrepresented students in specific schools, such as those in East Los Angeles' Garfield High School as illustrated in the film *Stand and Deliver,* the proportion of Latino and African-American students succeeding on this test nationally still is far smaller than their numbers in the general population.

On a national level, a new mathematics-related test was developed—the AP statistics exam—first administered in May 1997. Students who do well on the AP statistics exam may receive credit for a non-calculus-based introductory college-level statistics course. The open-response section of this test includes a rubric scoring component. Teachers who participate in the national scoring use a rubric system developed in collaboration with the American Statistical Association. Together, teachers and statisticians work to identify the characteristics of an exemplary response. As an aid to improving instruction and thereby achievement in AP statistics, the open-response questions from past exams are provided to teacher-scorers, along with several examples of student work, the scores given to the work, and the rationale for the scores, based on the scoring rubric. In many locations, teachers who participated in the scoring gave workshops at conferences and in their districts so that other teachers could benefit from the professional discourse

prompted, comparing the student work in the samples with the work of their own students.

In a similar manner, teachers of all levels who use performance assessment to inform and improve classroom instruction find it to be a valuable tool for ascertaining a clearer picture of how students are able to apply and use their mathematical content knowledge. Through ongoing performance assessment, teachers are better able to identify common misconceptions or lack of clarity about concepts and work with students to correct their thinking before the culminating activities leading to a grade. It is then more likely that the grade is a summary of a student's total mathematical ability than grades based predominantly on one type of assessment.

Summary

The first part of this chapter looked at assessment to inform instruction. Only when teachers can see evidence of what their students are thinking can they design effective instructional strategies. The activities in this chapter were selected to elicit thinking and verbal reasoning on the part of students.

The other main emphasis of this chapter was assessment used for program evaluation. The appropriateness of externally imposed standardized tests for this purpose was discussed from several points of view. Examples of test items from various assessments systems were shared. The implications of the federal No Child Left Behind Act will be played out over time, during which external assessments will be used to measure schools' effectiveness in educating their students.

ASSIGNMENTS

Select two of the Additional Activities from the end of the chapter, and do the following:

1. Describe the content contained in each selected task, and identify a class for which you think this task is appropriate.
2. Describe the mathematical experiences students would have before performing the tasks as individuals and the classroom conditions during the assessment.
3. Tell how the results of the assessments would be communicated to your students and any other follow-up activities you might provide.
4. Explain how your subsequent instruction would be affected by your students' outcomes.

INSTRUCTIONAL RESOURCES

Balanced assessment for the mathematics curriculum. Parsippany, NJ: Dale Seymour Publications.

A series of field-tested secondary tasks, with sample student responses, in six packages:

Middle grades assessment package 1 (1999)
Middle grades assessment package 2 (2000)
High school assessment package 1 (1999)
High school assessment package 2 (2000)
Advanced high school assessment package 1 (1999)
Advanced high school assessment package 2 (2000)

Danielson, C. (1997). *A collection of performance tasks and rubrics. Middle school mathematics.* Larchmont, NY: Eye on Education.

In addition to the 24 performance tasks, with a specific rubric matrix provided for each, the author gives rationales and processes for the development and use of performance assessment.

DeMeulemeester, Katie. (1995). *Math projects: Organization, implementation, and assessment.* Palo Alto, CA: Dale Seymour Publications.

This resource and its companion publication, *Encyclopedia of Math Projects and References,* also is available in a database software version. This excellent resource includes four parts: Part One contains specific examples for different presentation formats; Part Two includes an Organizational Checklist and discussion of project design features; Part Three provides many of the organizational tools, such as forms and handouts to be used in conjunction with projects; Part Four deals primarily with classroom management issues.

Murphy, R. (1999). Changing assessment practices in an algebra class, or "Will this be on the test?" *Mathematics Teacher, 92(3),* 247–249.

This article documents the author's experience with implementing assessments more nearly aligned to the NCTM *Standards* in her algebra classrooms. Sample items are given, some of which include writing and rubric assessment.

New Standards Performance Standards. (1997). Vol. 2—Middle School, Vol. 3—High School. Rochester, NY: National Center on Education and the Economy and the University of Pittsburgh.

This document provides performance descriptions in four areas: mathematics, English language arts, science, and applied learning. Samples of performance tasks are included, accompanied by student work illustrating the achievement of the standards and commentary justifying their selection.

Romagnano, L. (2001). The myth of objectivity in mathematics assessment. *Mathematics Teacher, 94(1),* 31–37.

In this article, the author addresses the topic of test reliability. Rather than accepting false dichotomies as "objective versus subjective," he urges mathematics teaches to consider ways to make their assessments more consistent and useful. Sample items from various sources are used in the discussion.

Rubenstein, R. N., Craine, T. V., Butts, T. R., Cantrell, K., Dritsas, L., et al. (2002). *Integrated Mathematics 1, 2, 3.* Evanston, IL: McDougal Littel/Houghton Mifflin.

In addition to projects included in student textbooks, the Teacher's Resource Kit—one of which is available for each year of the program—contains additional booklets on projects and alternative assessments.

Seymour, D. (1996, compiler). *Encyclopedia of math topics and references: A resource for projects and explorations.* Palo Alto, CA: Dale Seymour Publications.

This resource and its companion publication, *Math Projects,* also comes in a database software version. Over 250 topics are listed alphabetically with descriptions, level of difficulty (from middle-school to advanced high-school courses), and related resources in the form of books and magazines.

Stein, M. K., Smith, M. S., Henningsen, M. A., & Silver, E. A. (2000). *Implementing Standards-based mathematics instruction: A casebook for professional development.* New York: Teachers College Press.

The first part of this book, based on the Ford Foundation–funded QUASAR Project, takes teachers through a process for identifying middle-school performance tasks with high cognitive demand. The remainder is a series of cases developed during classroom implementation of the project and teachers' facilitated discussions of their work.

Stylianou, D. A., Kenney, P. A., Silver, E. A., & Alacaci, C. (2000). Gaining insight into students' thinking through assessment tasks. *Mathematics Teaching in the Middle School, 6(2),* 136–143.

ADDITIONAL ACTIVITIES

Activity 10.8   Miles of Words
Activity 10.9   Get a Clue
Activity 10.10 Planning a Bookcase
Activity 10.11 Effective Tax Rates
Activity 10.12 Insect Population
Activity 10.13 Wall Posters

These activities are additional samples of different types of performance tasks. Activity 10.8 asks students to use approximation techniques to assess the likelihood that a statement made could be true. Activity 10.9 has middle-school students organizing information and then drawing reasonable conclusions. Students are given written and pictoral information in Activity 10.10 and asked to find the least expensive way to obtain a bookcase. "Effective Tax Rates" (Activity 10.11) has students not only calculate such rates, but also generalize beyond the given situation. Exponential growth is the mathematics underlying Activity 10.12, placed in the context of an insect population. Finally, Activity 10.13 requires students to apply their knowledge of areas of rectangles to a real-life situation.

FOR TEACHERS

Activity 10.8 Miles of Words

Mathematical Content:
Estimation, rates, unit conversions (PSSM Problem Solving Standard for Grades 9–12)

Materials Needed:
Statement of the task, scientific calculators

Directions: As an assessment item, this task should take 15–20 minutes for students to complete. As embedded in a lesson, the extensions suggested in the Teacher Notes can be used to deepen student understanding to rate as a function of time.

FOR STUDENTS

Activity 10.8
Miles of Words

This problem gives you the chance to assess the reasonableness that 40,000 words were uttered in a 200-mile train journey.

The following excerpt appears on the first page of a fictitious novel:

> "Alan sat next to an elderly man during his train ride to Penn Station. The two men sat side by side for the entire 200-mile trip. Over that distance Alan uttered about 40,000 words to the stranger. When the train stopped at Penn Station, the two men departed, and they never saw each other again."

1. Find a reasonable figure for the rate, in words per minute, of normal spoken language. Show all of your calculations, and explain your reasoning.

2. Make an estimate of the average speed of a train in miles per hour.

3. Discuss in detail this statement: "Over that distance Alan uttered about 40,000 words . . . " Is this statement reasonable? Why or why not? Show all of your calculations, and explain your reasoning.

Source: This task comes from High School Assessment Package 1, developed by the project *Balanced Assessment for the Mathematics Curriculum*. Balanced Assessment packages, comprising additional tasks and instructional support, are published by Dale Seymour Publications. Further information can be obtained from the publisher or the project Web site: http://www.educ.msu.edu/MARS. Reprinted with permission.

FOR TEACHERS

Activity 10.9 Get a Clue

Mathematical Content:
Venn diagrams (PSSM Reasoning and Proof Standard for Grades 6–8)

Materials Needed:
Statement of the task, extra paper

Directions: The intended level of this task is sixth grade. It is expected that students will need around 30 minutes to complete it. Although the Venn diagram, to be correct, should be the same from student to student, the analysis of the information will vary. Thus, the rubric for this task should include clear mathematical support for the student's choices.

FOR STUDENTS

Activity 10.9
Get a Clue

Directions: Demonstrate your mathematical knowledge by giving a clear, concise solution to the problem. Your score will depend on how well you

- explain your reasoning;
- show your understanding of the mathematics in an organized manner;
- use charts, graphs, and diagrams in your explanation;
- show the solution in more than one way or relate it to other solutions;
- investigate beyond the requirements of the problem.

The Problem: Ms. Sommers, the owner of Maple Grove Campground, wants to update her facilities to provide more recreational opportunities for campers. She interviews 300 campers and lists the eight favorite recreational activities of men, women, and children, as shown in the table below.

Campers	Activities
Men	basketball, swimming, fishing, boating, bicycling, hiking, jogging, Frisbee golf
Women	hiking, tennis, jogging, swimming, aerobics, walking, bicycling, volleyball
Children	inline skating, basketball, volleyball, bicycling, Frisbee golf, skateboarding, swimming, miniature golf

Use a Venn diagram and sound reasoning to determine some new activities she could include at her campground. Explain your reasoning.

Source: Adapted from Foster, D., Gillian, S., Price, J., McClain, K., Martinez, B., & others (1995). *Interactive Mathematics: Activities and Investigations*. Westerville, OH: Glencoe, division of Macmillan/McGraw-Hill Publishing Co.

FOR TEACHERS

Activity 10.10 Planning a Bookcase

Mathematical Content:
Measurement applications, calculations of cost (PSSM Connections Standard for Grades 6–8)

Materials Needed:
Activity sheets

Directions: Even though this was an item for an individual to complete during a state assessment, it could be used as a homework assignment to be followed by a class discussion.

FOR STUDENTS

Activity 10.10
Planning a Bookcase (page 1 of 2)

At its last meeting, the French Club voted to obtain a bookcase for the club's growing collection of literature. You receive the following memo from Mr. Collins, the faculty sponsor of the club:

> To: President of the French Club
> Re: Bookcase for the club
> From: Mr. Collins
>
> Spradlees offers the lowest prices in the area, but Sally suggested we might save money by making the bookcase in the wood shop here at school. The club's cash reserves are low, so saving money is important. Mr. Howey said we can use the shop tools and supplies at no cost, if we pay for the wood. He will help with construction. The bookcase will go against the wall, between the desk and the file cabinet, in a space a little over 6 feet wide.
>
> Please analyze the situation and determine which is better: making or buying the bookcase. Can we save money by making it ourselves? I have enclosed an ad with lumber prices to help you estimate construction costs.
>
> We need to decide about the bookcase at today's meeting. Since you will not be there, please prepare a written report for the club to use as the basis for our decision. Be sure to include
>
> - a clear explanation of the possibilities you considered and how you estimated their costs;
> - a comparison of relative costs of different possibilities;
> - your recommendation for what we should do and why.
>
> Thanks.

Write a report responding to Mr. Collins's memo. Include drawings or other graphics, if needed, to effectively communicate your findings and your suggested course of action.

F O R   S T U D E N T S

Activity 10.10
Planning a Bookcase (page 2 of 2)

Goodwin's Lumberyard

Kiln-Dried Pine Shelving

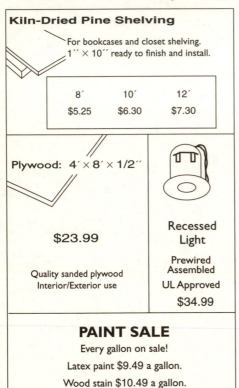

For bookcases and closet shelving.
1″ × 10″ ready to finish and install.

8′	10′	12′
$5.25	$6.30	$7.30

Plywood: 4′ × 8′ × 1/2″

$23.99

Quality sanded plywood
Interior/Exterior use

Recessed Light

Prewired
Assembled
UL Approved
$34.99

PAINT SALE
Every gallon on sale!
Latex paint $9.49 a gallon.
Wood stain $10.49 a gallon.

Back-to-School Sale!
Unfinished Pine Furniture

Bookcase 6′ × 4′ × 10″ $59.87

Bookcase 6′ × 2′ × 10″ $24.87

Typing Table $25.87
3′ × 24″ × 18″

File Cabinet
$49.87

Open 9 A.M. to 9 P.M.

Shop before 11 A.M. and get an extra 10% off!

SPRADLEES

Source: Released by the Connecticut State Department of Education.

FOR TEACHERS

Activity 10.11 Effective Tax Rates

Mathematical Content:
Percent applications (PSSM Number and Operations Standards for Grades 6–8)

Materials Needed:
Activity sheet

Directions: This is a released item from the high-school portion of the National Assessment of Educational Progress (NAEP) test, administered to a representative sample of students across the United States each year. How would your students fare on this item?

FOR STUDENTS

Activity 10.11
Effective Tax Rates

Directions: This problem requires you to show your work and explain your reasoning. You may use drawings, words, and numbers in your explanation. Your answer should be clear enough so that another person could read it and understand your thinking. It is important that you show all your work.

The Problem: One plan for a state income tax requires that persons with incomes of $10,000 or less pay no tax and persons with incomes greater than $10,000 pay a tax of 6% only on the part of their income that exceeds $10,000.

A person's effective tax rate is defined as the percent of total income that is paid in tax. Based on this definition, could any person's effective tax rate under this plan be 5%? Could it be 6%? Explain your answer. Include examples if necessary to justify your conclusions.

Source: Adapted from a 1992 National Assessment of Educational Progress item.

FOR TEACHERS

Activity 10.12 Insect Population

Mathematical Content:
Exponential growth (PSSM Algebra Standard for Grades 9–12)

Materials Needed:
Activity sheet

Directions: This task could be used to introduce exponential growth.

FOR STUDENTS

Activity 10.12
Insect Population

Over a 1-year period, an insect population is known to quadruple. The starting population is 15 insects.

1. Make a table or graph to show the growth of the population from 0 through 6 years.

2. How many insects would there be at the end of 10 years?

3. Write a mathematical statement that describes this growth.

4. Would your statement or formula correctly describe the insect population after 50 years? Justify your answer.

Source: Adapted from Kentucky Department of Education 1993–94 released tasks.

FOR TEACHERS

Activity 10.13 Wall Posters

Mathematical Content:
Area, scale (PSSM Reasoning and Proof Standard for Grades 6–8)

Materials Needed:
Activity sheet, graph paper

Directions: This would be a good problem to do in small groups.

FOR STUDENTS

Activity 10.13
Wall Posters

Directions: Explain your answer thoroughly. Show all of your work, computations, charts, graphs, etc. You may use a calculator.

The Problem: Steve has a wall in his room that measures 13 feet long and 8½ feet high and is totally bare. He wants to hang automobile posters that are 3 feet wide and 2 feet high. What is the greatest number of posters he can hang so that the posters do not overlap?

Source: Adapted from Kentucky Department of Education Middle School released tasks.

PART

Ongoing Development

Part III, the final and briefest part of the text, addresses a teacher's professional responsibilities beyond the classroom. Chapter 11 gives examples of ways to involve parents and the community in support of mathematics education. Chapter 12 talks about ongoing professional growth as both a benefit and a necessity to a successful career as a mathematics teacher.

CHAPTER

11

Communicating With Parents and Community

We believe it has always been a part of a teacher's responsibility to interact professionally with others beyond the classroom and school environments. Teachers are part of a professional community, and mathematics teachers should take advantage of opportunities to share professional experiences and growth with other educators and colleagues. In addition to professional outreach opportunities, teachers can involve themselves with various elements of the school community, local business entities, governmental officials, and educational resources such as libraries and museums. In this chapter we will look at ways teachers work with these important community constituents to provide relevant classroom activities.

The first contact you have with the families of your students may be sending letters to parents. Many schools require that teachers write a description of the

Figure 11.1
Sample Letter to Parent

Dear Family,

Our class will soon be studying the mathematics of rates, ratios, proportions, and percents in a unit called "Buyer Beware."

In this unit, students take on the role of consumer reporters for an imaginary magazine called "Buyer Beware." Students discover the mathematics of economics as they learn to make decisions involving matters of money. Students come to see mathematics as a useful tool because they are actively involved in mathematical activities that are related to everyday expenditures.

The first phase of the unit focuses on rates and unit prices. The class begins by comparing the unit prices of different-size packages of the same-brand product. They learn to interpret and create price graphs as a useful tool for comparing unit prices.

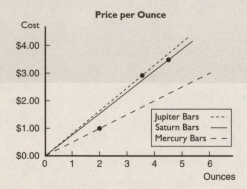

Then we will move on to ratio and proportion, learning to use equivalent ratios and cross products to solve proportions. The last phase of the unit covers percents. The work with percents will include estimation and calculation of percents as well as reading and interpreting circle graphs. The final activity of the unit involves planning a banquet within a budget.

An educated consumer knows how to make wise decisions when it comes to buying goods and services. An educated consumer uses critical thinking to evaluate advertisements, unit prices, sale prices, and discounts. An educated consumer knows how to plan and organize a budget. By the end of the unit, the students will have applied what they learn about the mathematics of rates, ratios, proportions, and percents to situations similar to those faced by consumers every day. In addition to these everyday applications, understanding of the concepts of ratio and proportion are also important for later work with algebra.

Sincerely,

Source: *MathScape,* (1999). Chicago, IL: Creative Publications. Reprinted with permission.

course being taught, general expectations for the class, grading standards, and other details such as procedures concerning the use of graphing calculators. An example of a teacher-written parent letter is shown in Chapter 6. The sample letter in Figure 11.1 informs parents about the content of the seventh-grade unit "Buyer Beware" from the *MathScape* curriculum.

Clear communication between parents/responsible adults and the school is essential. Whatever their background and experience, parents everywhere want their children to receive a good education.

As a new teacher, you have an early opportunity to establish a cooperative relationship with the parents of your students through an activity, sometimes called back-to-school night, usually held near the beginning of the school year. Also, some schools conduct open-house-type activities near the end of a school year, at which student achievement is highlighted. In addition, you may teach at a school that schedules parent conferences to coincide with the end of a grading period, when report cards are sent home. Further, when a particular student in your class is having difficulty with mathematics or classroom behavior, it is your obligation to inform the parent/guardian in writing and/or arrange for a face-to-face conference. This chapter presents suggestions and practical tips for preparing for parent presentations and conferences.

We recognize that the changing nature of the family in our society results in many different family configurations. You may be dealing with single-parent families; "blended" families; multigenerational immigrant families; students living with guardians, grandparents, or foster parents; and even an occasional "emancipated" young adult. Older brothers and sisters may play a major role in seeing that their younger siblings are progressing as expected in school. For the purpose of simplicity, however, we will use *parent(s)* generically to refer to the adult(s) assuming responsibility for your students.

One of the studies documenting the relationship of parent involvement to student achievement was published by Shaver and Walls in 1998. The study looks at Title I parent involvement at the elementary and middle-school levels. Findings indicate that increased student achievement in both reading and math, as measured by standardized test scores, correlate to parent involvement.

As you seek ways of encouraging more mathematics involvement for your students, you may want to consider mathematics clubs and contests. These may be locally based but often afford opportunities for students to organize and/or participate in activities involving other students and schools, even to national and international levels. Communicating with the community to gain support for projects and to highlight students achievement is important to the success of extracurricular activities. We discuss mathematics clubs and contests in this chapter, including some organized by groups committed to providing recognition for outstanding student participants.

Assignments and activities involving the broader local community as well as the students' parents can enhance student appreciation of and involvement in mathematics. This chapter incorporates some ideas for activities such as these. It will quickly be apparent that, as a teacher, you will need creativity should you decide to plan and implement ideas for the particular school community in which you teach.

Finally, we include some current information and strategies for incorporating the world of the Internet into your classroom. The information we share will be general because of the rapid changes that occur with this technology. Some of these applications could be combined with the activities of this chapter.

ABOUT THE ACTIVITIES FOR THIS CHAPTER

Activities in the body of this chapter deal primarily with number sense, estimation, and measurement. The PSSM Number and Operations Standard in-

cludes the ability to "compute fluently and make reasonable estimates" at all grade levels. Number sense at the middle-school level concerns predominantly the ability to understand and use various representations of rational numbers, fractions, decimals, percents, and integers. Additionally, both at the middle- and high-school levels, basic skills include understanding the representation of very large and very small numbers through scientific notation as expressed through pencil-and-paper calculations and by technology. Other mathematical abilities needed by secondary students before completing high school are recognizing the reasonableness of such amounts through comparison with known entities and knowing the number of significant digits appropriate to the nature of measurement. The interplay of technology and mathematics requires a deep understanding of these concepts, developed through the kinds of lessons presented in this chapter.

In Activity 11.1 students estimate earnings based on a graph. The next two activities elicit student understanding of number relationships in fractions and decimals. Orders of magnitude and estimation of large numbers are needed in Activity 11.4. Communicating the usefulness of math through Activity 11.5 is a bit of a diversion, but one where students are encouraged to express to others an appreciation of the beauty and applicability of mathematics to the world.

The remaining activities continue the connections to mathematics outside of the classroom. Sample math contest problems are shared in Activities 11.6 and 11.7. Estimation can be used as a way to involve community members in a math fair, as described in Activity 11.8. Activities 11.9 and 11.10 require different degrees of involvement of adults sharing with students how they use math in their world of work.

SCHEDULED SCHOOL-BASED EVENTS

Back-to-School Nights

The first time you see your students' parents is likely to be at a back-to-school night scheduled early in the semester. It is important that you present information to them in a professional yet friendly manner. During a typical back-to-school night, parents follow their student's schedule and move from class to class, each time hearing from the teacher about the course, homework expectations, materials used, and the like. If an innovative curriculum is being introduced, some mathematics departments go beyond the typical 10 minutes allotted in the traditional format. To educate the parents regarding the new curriculum, the math department might make a longer presentation to inform parents of the rationale for the selection of the program and to describe its mathematical content. Often, once parents have an opportunity to work through a few of the activities, they realize that their children are not being used as experimental subjects and can accept that the new program was chosen to address the weaknesses of the previous program.

If innovative technology is to be used in the classroom, a brief demonstration may be helpful to illustrate how its use will enhance and extend student learning. If Internet activities are to be a part of the class, find out which families have access. For those who do not have access at home, provide information about other access sites, such as the local library. The minilesson provided in Activity 11.1 is a good one for back-to-school night. If direct online time is not appropriate, technological aids such as Web Whacker can be used to save information gathered on the Internet for review later. With Web Whacker, all of the screens and pathways used for the lessons are displayed during the playback.

 Go to Web Destinations for Chapter 11 at **http://www.prenhall.com/huetinck** to find links to the Census Bureau Web site and many other graphs.

The depth of analysis expected in a lesson such as Activity 11.1 will vary according to the grade level and mathematical background of the students. For example, "Analyze as completely as possible" will be the only directions necessary for high-school students with previous experience in statistics. Middle-school students might be given more structured questions, such as those in the directions.

Addressing Issues Around Number Sense
Unfortunately, many adults have a limited view of mathematics as the study of numbers and basic operations. Therefore, if computational practice is not obvious in *Standards*-based curricula emphasizing problem solving, parents may become concerned that their children are not being prepared for college. This concern, expressed during parent interviews in the early 1990s, was noted by the National Center for Research in Mathematical Sciences Edu-

cation (NCRMSE) in a study of schools reforming their mathematics programs.

Of particular interest to us are findings that teachers in some of the schools involved in the study did not recognize the importance of informing and involving parents until after parents began complaining to school administrators and board members. This conflict could have been prevented. When educators incorporate communication with parents into the change process, they can elicit considerable support for new programs. Effective presentation of student data, pertinent research findings, and expectations of colleges and universities will enhance the quality of communications with parents. One group of teachers, for example, videotaped a presentation by a university admissions officer stating unequivocally that the new *Standards*-based programs in mathematics were given equal weight as traditional programs in the admissions process. This tape was then used during a parent meeting to dispel rumors that students with certain courses listed on their transcripts received preferential treatment during the admissions process.

Activities and ideas about the mathematical area of number sense appear in this chapter because they can connect parents' expectations with the goals of *Standards*-based mathematics programs. For example, the goal, of middle school, in the area of numbers, is for students to gain number sense for rational numbers in all their forms. The NCTM Middle School Addenda Series booklet *Developing Number Sense* (NCTM, 1996, p. 11) offers many teaching suggestions and worksheets to use with the middle-school age group:

> Evaluating number sense is best accomplished through class discussion, dialogues with individual and small groups of students, and examination of individual journal entries (rather than by pencil-and-paper tests).

The next two activities—Activity 11.2 on fractions and Activity 11.3 on decimals—are examples of assignments that foster the development of number sense at the middle-school level. Going over activities such as these at a back-to-school night will help parents understand that your expectations are not only for building computational skill, but also for a deeper recognition of how number operations work with rational numbers.

Continuing through the middle-school level and at the high-school level, number sense broadens to include orders of magnitude. By the time students complete a high-school mathematics curriculum, they should have a sense of "largeness" and "smallness" of quantities and should be able to use this sense to estimate reasonable answers to problems. Famous

F O R   T E A C H E R S

Activity 11.1 Census Data Line Graph

Mathematical Content:
Number sense, statistics (PSSM Data Analysis
  and Probability Standard for Grades 6–8)

Materials Needed:
Graph from Census Bureau Web site

Directions: Have middle-school students answer questions such as these about the graph:

1. Give an example of a job for which a
   person with each level of education might
   best qualify.

2. In the age group 25–29, which group
   earns the highest annual salary? About
   how much is this amount?
3. Which group has the greatest increase in
   earnings over the age groups? Give a
   possible reason for this increase.
4. Which groups' earnings became "flat" over
   their earning lifetime?
5. During which interval do the earnings of
   people with a doctoral degree appear to
   decrease the most? Can you think of a
   possible reason for this downward change?

F O R   S T U D E N T S

Activity 11.1
Census Data Line Graph

**Earnings Trajectories for Full-Time, Year-Round Workers by Educational Attainment Based
on 1997–1999 Work Experience**

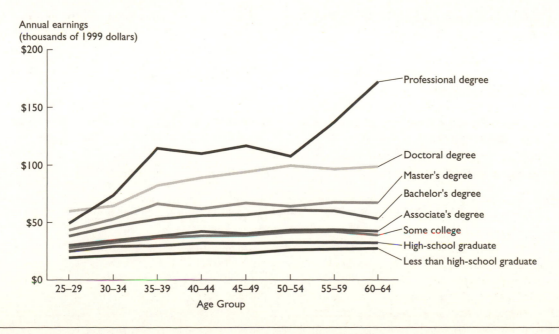

Source: U. S. Census Bureau, *Current Population Surveys*, March 1998, 1999, and 2000.

F O R   T E A C H E R S

Activity 11.2 Operations on Fractions

Mathematical Content:
Fractions, number sense (PSSM Number and
   Operations Standard for Grades 6–8)

Materials Needed:
Student worksheet

Directions: Display the number line, and ask students questions such as those listed and others that come to mind. Encourage students to justify their answers by explaining their reasoning.

See Activity Notes for the Teacher at the end of this book for suggestions on how this activity can be used for formative assessment.

To the Teacher: This activity is presented in the evaluation section of the *Curriculum and Evaluation Standards for School Mathematics* (NCTM 1989, p. 203). It is useful for clarifying students' understanding of the effects of certain operations on fractions.

F O R   S T U D E N T S

Activity 11.2
Operations on Fractions

1. If the fractions represented by the points *D* and *E* are multiplied, what point on the number line best represents the product?

2. If the fractions represented by the points *C* and *D* are multiplied, what point on the number line best represents the product?

3. If the fractions represented by the points *B* and *F* are multiplied, what point on the number line best represents the product?

4. Suppose 20 is multiplied by the number represented by *E* on the number line. Estimate the product.

5. Suppose 20 is divided by the number represented by *E* on the number line. Estimate the quotient.

FOR TEACHERS

Activity 11.3 Exploring Equivalent Expressions With Decimals

Mathematical Content:
Decimals, number sense (PSSM Number and
    Operation Standard for Grades 6–8)

Materials Needed:
Student worksheet

Directions: Ask students to compare various
expressions with the expression 12.8 × 48 and to
choose those that are equivalent. As the students
study each expression, encourage them to verbalize their thinking. As an extension, have students develop additional equivalent expressions.

See Activity Notes for the Teacher at the end
of this book for suggestions on how this activity
can be used for formative assessment.

FOR STUDENTS

Activity 11.3
Exploring Equivalent Expressions With Decimals

Which of these expressions have the same product as 12.8 × 48? Explain your thinking.

1. 128 × 4.8

2. 10.8 × 50

3. 128 × 4 × 0.8

4. 64 × 9.6

5. 2 × 32 × 9.6

6. 6.4 × 96

7. 25.6 × 24

8. 2 × 6.4 × 4 × 12

Source: Reys, B. J. (1996). *Developing Number Sense in the Middle Grades,* NCTM Addenda Series, Grades 5–8. Reston, VA: National
Council of Teachers of Mathematics. Reprinted with permission.

estimation problems, called "Fermi" problems because they are attributed to the physicist Enrico Fermi, offer opportunities to apply understanding. For example, a Fermi problem that often is quoted is, "How many piano tuners are there in Chicago? (Fermi worked at the University of Chicago for some time.) At first this seems like a nonsense question, or one that is utterly impossible to answer; however, a series of facts, combined with estimation, can produce an answer that is reasonable. Pertinent information might include the overall population of Chicago, an estimate of the number of pianos there, how often they would need the services of a piano tuner, how much work a piano tuner would need to make a living, etc. On a more local note, we know of a high-school physics teacher who, on the first day of class, asked his students to find a way to estimate the height of the local water tower. They could not use direct measure, nor could they call city hall. He reports that students came up with many ingenious ways to complete this assignment.

In this fascinating essay "On Number Numbness" (1985), Douglas Hofstadter laments what he calls the "appalling innumeracy of most people . . . when it comes to making sense of numbers that run their lives" (p. 116). He then gives several examples of Fermi-type problems, with the goal of getting an answer in the correct order of magnitude. Some of these problems are listed in Activity 11.4. It might be particularly appropriate to offer this special challenge to your class tied in with a study of scientific notation. To involve parents, give homework assignments that have students work with family members to write and solve Fermi-type problems related to numerical information with which they are familiar.

 Go to Web Destinations for Chapter 11 at **http://www.prenhall.com/huetinck** to find a Web site with Fermi-type questions designed for upper-elementary students.

Offering Assistance to Parents   Parents whose background in mathematics is weak still can help their children by providing a home environment in which homework is a priority and in which their children are encouraged to use educational resources available for them in the community, such as tutoring programs. Many parents may feel uncomfortable with the types of assignments students in exemplary programs may be expected to do at home, from problems of the week to proj-

ects and data collection activities. As a teacher, you should be aware of materials prepared especially for parents of mathematics students. On back-to-school night you might distribute to parents handouts similar to Figures 11.2 and 11.3, adapted from the California Mathematics Council (CMC) *ComMuniCator*. Note that some of the documents on the Resources list also are available in languages other than English.

Figure 11.2
Helping at Home

Parents often ask how they can help their children with mathematics at home. Good questions—and good listening—will help your children make sense of mathematics, build their confidence, and encourage mathematical thinking and communication. A good question opens up a problem and supports different ways of thinking about it. Here are some you might try. Notice that none of them can be answered with a simple yes or no.

Getting Started
What do you know now?
What do you need to find out?
How might you begin?

While Working
How can you organize your information?
Can you make a drawing to explain your thinking?
Are there other possibilities?
What would happen if…?
Can you describe the strategy you're using to solve this?
What do you need to do next?
Do you see any patterns?
Can you make a prediction?
What assumptions are you making?

Reflecting About the Solution
Is your solution reasonable?
How did you arrive at your answer?
Can you convince me your solution makes sense?
What did you try that didn't work?

Responding
Your response is as important as your initial questions. Try to avoid stopping as soon as you hear the "right" answer. Responses like these give your children a chance to clarify their thinking.

Why do you think that?
Tell me more.
Can you explain it in a different way?
Is there another possibility?

Activity 11.4 Numerical Horse Sense

Mathematical Content:
Orders of magnitude, number sense (PSSM Number and Operation Standard for Grades 6–8)

Materials Needed:
List of questions

F O R   S T U D E N T S

Activity 11.4
Numerical Horse Sense

Directions: Estimate the answers to these questions, writing a step-by-step rationale for each problem. Each of your answers should be expressed as a single non zero digit followed enough zeros to make a number that is a reasonable answer to the question.

1. How many basketballs would fit into your classroom?

2. How many licks would it take for everyone in your school to eat a double-scoop ice cream cone?

3. How old would you be a million minutes from today?

4. What is the total yearly income of all U.S. major league baseball players?

5. How many dogs are there in the United States?

6. How many fingernails get painted each week in Los Angeles?

7. How many cell phones are there in the world?

8. How many blades of grass are there on a football field?

9. How many glasses of water would it take to fill an Olympic-size swimming pool?

10. Create an estimation problem for your classmates to answer.

Figure 11.3

Mathematics Resources for Parents

Family Math—the Middle School Years, by Virginia Thompson and Karen Mayfield-Ingram Berkeley, CA: Lawrence Hall of Science, University of California.

Figure This! (www.figurethis.org) includes a collection of math challenges for middle-school students and their families, along with solutions and related information.

Math at Home: Helping Your Children Learn and Enjoy Mathematics/Matemáticas en la Casa: Ayudando a Sus Niños a Aprender y Disfrutar de las Matemáticas. These booklets are available from the Sonoma County (California) Office of Education, www.scoe.org.

Math Is Power (www.mathispower.org) provides problems for students and resources for parents from the National Science Foundation.

Mathematics for All—Plus is a series of 8 half-hour video programs for families of children in Grades 4–6; also available in Spanish. Go to http://www.learner.org for further information.

Principles and Standards for School Mathematics Outreach CD (Reston, VA: National Council of Teachers of Mathematics). This CD includes PowerPoint presentations, handouts, and videos for use in speaking to parents and the wider community about the messages of the *Principles and Standards for School Mathematics.*

Set 11.1   Discussion Question

 Questions with an asterisk appear in the Message Board section of the Companion Website at ***http://www.prenhall.com/huetinck.*** Go to Chapter 11 and click on the Message Board to find and respond to the question.

*1. Discuss with your colleagues effective ways to involve parents in helping their children learn mathematics.

Open Houses

Events that bring parents into the school to observe evidence of student achievement provide you, the teacher, with a unique opportunity to have your students communicate to their families their mathematical growth during the year. The suggestions that follow assume that the student is attending the open house with her adult family members. Countryman and Schroeder (1996) describe how one middle school successfully incorporated student-led parent-teacher conferences into both spring and fall open houses. In mathematics classes where students have developed portfolios during the year, this practice can be particularly effective. We have also heard high-school teachers comment on the effectiveness of having their students, using their portfolios, make presentations to family of the

mathematics they have learned during the year. Providing the portfolio for the parents to look at with their student helps to verify the mathematical connections and applications students can do beyond the basic skills, thus supporting the goals of the contemporary programs.

Also, math projects such as those discussed in Chapter 10 can be displayed during an open house. It is important that classroom displays of projects should be clearly identified as part of the curriculum, embodying the use of mathematical tools needed by students continuing to advance their mathematics education. We have seen a wide variety of math projects, including posters, physical models of surfaces of revolution, Hyperstudio projects, and animation projects done as high-school AP calculus class assignments. We would not limit the notion of projects to any grade or subject level.

A high-school teacher gave her mathematics students the assignment shown in Activity 11.5—create an ad to promote mathematics. The project, which spread to all members of the department and to many levels of classes, was scheduled in the spring so that it could be displayed during open house.

Typical report card formats provide a parent minimal information about the actual knowledge of her child. The report cards with which we are familiar have, at most, a letter grade (or numerical average) relative to the course content; some indication of student's work habits during class and on out-of-class assignments; some indication of cooperation with the teacher, other students, and school

FOR TEACHERS

Activity 11.5 Math Ad

Mathematical Content:
Mathematics appreciation, applications (PSSM Communication Standard for Grades 9–12)

Materials Needed:
Activity sheets

Teacher Directions: Have students respond to the following:

1. Describe a movie trailer, billboard, or TV commercial that recently got your attention.

2. What visual images do you remember from that ad? What words do you remember?

3. What visual images do you think most people have about mathematics? What words would they use to describe mathematics?

4. In your group, brainstorm some positive images and words related to mathematics.

Now let us look at a project that you will be doing.

FOR STUDENTS

Activity 11.5
Math Ad (page 1 of 2)

Advertise That Product: Math

As you well know, advertising is a powerful way to attract people's attention to get them to buy a product. Movies entice with trailers, previews, and billboards to attract the public to see their show. Billions of dollars are poured into advertising to get the attention of the public to buy any conceivable commodity.

As math students and math "consumers," we wish to share our love, knowledge, and genuine passion for math with the world. We want "those" out there to know what they are missing if they are not on the math bandwagon. Where else could you experience the thrill of a calculator solving a 5×5, 6×6, 10×10, 100×100 matrix in seconds except on your flashy new TI-83? The power . . . The glory . . . AaaHHHHHH it is too much to behold to keep it to ourselves. We must share. *We must advertise. We must let the world know how great math can be.*

WHAT TO DO

1. Find a group of executives from Period 3 or 5. No fewer than 2, no more than 5.

2. Plan your strategy. What campaign is going to grab the public's attention? What kind of poster, ad, presentation will be unforgettable? How will you be able to handle the crowds when they come banging on your door, asking for more of your product? Today the classroom . . . tomorrow the world!

3. It's a dog-eat-dog world out there, and we have to get our presentation in by (date_____).

4. A lot is riding on this project—a whole test grade. It had better be good. What would my boss (teacher) say; better yet, what would my parents say if I didn't turn out a great product? Better get cracking. Where is my staff? Hold the phones!

FOR STUDENTS

Activity 11.5
Math Ad (page 2 of 2)

**ADVERTISING MATHEMATICS
EVALUATION FORM**

Names: _____

_____

_____

_____

Creativity (10) _____
Good idea? Carried out well? Clever?

Originality (10) _____
Entertaining? (Grab your attention, interesting)

Overall Appeal (10) _____
How does it look? Is it presented well?

Does it really advertise math? (35) _____
Is it clear that what you are trying to say is math related?

Neatness (10) _____
Organized, planned out, reflects careful thought, layout, design, graphics

Intriguing (10) _____
Does it "sell" the product (math)?

Shows effort and is well timed (not rushed) (15) _____

Source: Adapted, with permission, from Beverly Gleason, Santa Monica High School, Santa Monica, CA.

rules; and a small space for either specific written comments or those selected from a computer menu. The sample school report card shown in Figure 11.4 (Clark, 1997, Chapter 10) expands upon that standard format to provide more detailed information to parents without being burdensome for the teacher to complete. A progress report of this type can be used to increase communication to the home. Comments about the student's strengths as well as deficiencies always are appropriate and enlightening.

Parent-Teacher Conferences

Because student discipline was discussed in Chapter 7, we will not dwell on parent conferences called to improve the behavior of a student. However, upon your request or that of a parent, a conference may be arranged to discuss a student's poor achievement. This assumes that you have first worked with the student and talked with her about your concerns relative to her academic performance. Students may tell you of personal situations that interfere with their time or

Figure 11.4
Sample School Report Card Format

Name: _____   Tutor group: _____

Subject: Mathematics 8   Semester 1

The Year Eight program aims to continue the development of student numeracy and awareness of space and shape and begins to consolidate algebraic skills and use them to model real situations. Knowledge of concepts associated with chance events and the analysis of data continues to be developed. Students build on their earlier project experiences by preparing an entry in the Mathematics Talent Quest. Problem solving is encouraged through work on Task Center activities, and work involving computers and calculators is integrated throughout the semester's units.

Work requirements		**Graded assessment**	
1. Skills and standard applications	☐	1. Graphs of experiments	☐
2. Problem solving and modeling	☐	2. Integers, Cartesian coordinates	☐
3. Project work	☐	3. Correlation	☐
S = Satisfactory completion		4. Pyramids, compass constructions	☐
N = Unsatisfactory completion		5. Ratio and rates	☐
Attitude and management		6. Bookwork	☐
1. Acceptable class behavior	☐	7. Project: Mathematics Talent Quest	☐
2. Ability to work independently	☐	8. Problem solving: Math Task Center	☐
3. Completion of set tasks	☐		
4. Ability to work cooperatively	☐		
5. Motivation	☐		
6. Participation in discussion	☐		
H = High M = Medium L = Low			

Descriptive comments: _____

_____

Teacher's signature: _____

Source: Clark, David (1997). *Constructive Assessment in Mathematics*, Key Curriculum Press, 1150 65th Street, Emeryville, CA 94608, 1-800 995-MATH. Reprinted with permission.

attention to schoolwork. If the situation warrants a referral to a school counselor for assistance, that should be the next step. Talk briefly with the counselor beforehand to prepare her for the student conference. At this time, you might give your perspective on a possible positive intervention to help the student refocus on the work in your class. The next step, if necessary, is a meeting with the student's parent.

A parent conference may be difficult to arrange, due to working parents' schedules and your own availability. Even so, we urge you to work with the counseling staff at your school to communicate with parents, to the degree that is reasonably possible, especially when a student who has been doing well shows a sudden negative change in her performance. In some cases, parents may not be aware of the pressures their child is facing in or beyond the classroom. Indeed, almost all of the parents with whom we have conferred were very grateful that we were concerned enough about their child as an individual to make the effort to discuss her potential problems with them before the difficulties escalated.

The approach that we have found most effective is to treat parents as partners with the school in preparing young people for a successful future. When that attitude is conveyed, the responsibility must also be shared, with parents doing their part whenever their child is beyond the jurisdiction of the school. Be aware, however, that parents of adolescent students face the challenge of trying to foster their child's growing self-reliance while requiring her to accept realistic boundaries that they have established.

Electronic Communication With Parents

If your school provides after-school or Saturday tutoring, be aware of the procedure involved in assigning students to the programs, and inform parents of this information as needed. (Some teachers allow a certain amount of makeup credit for students whose work and attendance at tutoring are verified.) Other after-school assistance may be available in your school community—in churches, youth centers, colleges, and the like. Again, this information can be provided both to students and parents as a resource.

Some schools have a phone-in system that provides parents information about homework assignments and automatically notifies them in the evening of their child's absence from school that day. Other schools have homework hot lines via telephone, Internet, or a districtwide instructional television program that students can watch to see, for example, mathematics problems being worked and discussed.

Many teachers have their own Web sites where students and parents can access information about homework and have online interactions with the teacher about assignments. Should you want to set up a Web site for class communication, we recommend you become informed of any school and district policies on this subject for your own edification and protection.

Most of the activities described in this section are scheduled at the school and involve parent participation. The focus has been specifically on activities that contribute directly to communication between you and the parents of your students regarding the mathematics achievement in your class. Be aware, however, that many other activities involving parents may also take place at your school that do not directly involve your classroom but may, nevertheless, affect your students' lives. Indirectly, your classroom may

be affected by parent-led projects benefiting your entire school. In schools in which there are active parent organizations, for example, funds may be raised for materials not covered within the school budget. You may be able to give input as to how such funds might be allocated. In some locations, funds for technology are obtained by parents and the community. You might be called upon to suggest a recipient for a scholarship raised for a deserving student.

Further, a range of social services may be available as well. In schools in which vision, health, and dental assistance is provided, you may be able to play a part in seeing that your students' health needs are met, with positive consequences for their achievement. Classes may be offered to teach parents English. Information on social and mental health services may be provided. The school may support connections between members of the community and local law enforcement agencies to prevent and combat crime. Also, political forums often are held at school sites.

Many of these support services may be carried out beyond your classroom without your needing to be involved. But as you get to know your school community, it is to your advantage to become familiar with supportive services available and the needs that exist. A close connection between the school and its stakeholders is beneficial to all concerned.

MATHEMATICS CONTESTS AND CLUBS

Mathematics contests may be local, regional, state, national, or international. As you continue in your professional life, you may find these kinds of activities to be very rewarding. They give you a unique opportunity to work with motivated students and learn at the same time. Some schools require teachers either to develop elective "modules" for students or to take responsibility for students' extracurricular activities in some way. For those of us who love mathematics, showing students some aspects of mathematics not dealt with in a typical classroom is very enjoyable. Coaching students preparing for a contest or including contest preparation as part of a club's agenda are two ways you may become involved in extracurricular activity.

Mathematics Contests

We used the Internet to search for information about national mathematics competitions. One such site is mathcounts.org. This site provides information about the annual MATHCOUNTS problem-solving competition for seventh- and eighth-grade students. The chapter (regional) competitions generally are held on a Saturday in February. From there, student teams go on to compete at the state level. Finally, state teams compete for the national championship.

Even though you may not be involved at this time in MATHCOUNTS, some preservice teachers are involved in after-school tutoring of students preparing for the first level of this competition. Sara McCoy (McCoy & Reinke, 1997), writes in the NCTM publication *Mathematics Teaching in the Middle School* of such an experience while she was a student at Oklahoma State University. During the fall semester she met with a team of junior-high stu-

dents once a week for an hour and a half to go over sample problems from the handbook provided by the organization.

A sample problem from the handbook is given in Activity 11.6. What McCoy learned from her initial experience with the problem sets was that students needed to develop their number sense rather than rush through the problems to get the right answers. She then modified her approach by selecting one problem at a time for students to work on in small groups, present to each other, and then discuss. Furthermore, she found it very productive to give these bright students problems whose solutions required physical models. She concluded the article by saying, "It [the MATHCOUNTS tutoring] is an experience that I need[ed] to become an effective teacher."

 Go to Web Destinations for Chapter 11 at **http://www.prenhall.com/huetinck** to find out more about MATHCOUNTS.

FOR TEACHERS

Activity 11.6 MATHCOUNTS Sample Item: Back to School

Mathematical Content: Ratio, permutations, fractions (PSSM Number and Operations and Reasoning and Proof Standards for Grades 6–8).

Materials Needed: Activity sheets

FOR STUDENTS

Activity 11.6
MATHCOUNTS Sample Item: Back to School

Directions: Solve the problems, showing your reasoning.

1. On the first day of school, Mrs. Addemup welcomed her students with the following math problem: There are 27 students registered for this class, and the ratio of girls to boys is 4:5. How many more boys than girls are registered in this class?

2. Once Mrs. Addemup finished taking attendance and going over the problem on the board, the principal called her over the intercom to tell her to take her class to the auditorium for the Beginning of Year Assembly. Each teacher was called individually to escort his/her class to the auditorium when it was the class's turn. The school has 4 sixth-grade classes, 3 seventh-grade classes, and 4 eight-grade classes. If the sixth-grade classes went first, then the seventh grade, then the eighth grade, in how many different orders could the 11 classes have been called to the auditorium?

Source: www.Mathcounts.org

Another competition is called the American Mathematics Competition, sponsored by the American Mathematics Competitions (AMC) organization. This competition is given annually at the individual school and then sent to the headquarters at the University of Nebraska–Lincoln to be scored. Calculators are allowed but not required on this exam. Recognition in the form of certificates and other prizes is awarded at the school and state levels. A 2002 released item is given in Activity 11.7.

 Go to Web Destinations for Chapter 11 at *http://www.prenhall.com/huetinck* to find out more about the American Mathematics Competition.

The International Mathematical Olympiad (IMO) is a mathematics competition for the best and brightest high-school students from countries around the world. It is held annually around mid-July, each year in a different country, and lasts for about 10 days. Each country is permitted to send a delegation of six students, a team leader, and a deputy team leader. During two days of testing, students are given a total of six problems to solve individually, with content consisting of topics from the high-school curriculum, excluding calculus. In 1998, a first occurred: the United States team had a female member. Furthermore, she received a silver medal for her outstanding performance in the competition.

The limited space in this chapter precludes our providing an extensive description of other large-

FOR TEACHERS

Activity 11.7 American Mathematics Competition Sample Item: Exponents

Mathematical Content:
Exponent rules, number sense (PSSM Algebra Standard for Grades 9–12)

Materials Needed:
Problem statement

Directions: This is an example of the type of problem a math club might look at together or that a group of students preparing for a mathematics competition would discuss.

FOR STUDENTS

Activity 11.7
American Mathematics Competition Sample Item: Exponents

Directions: Solve the following problem. You may use a calculator.

How many ordered triples of positive integers (x, y, z) satisfy $(x^y)^z = 64$?

Source: www.unl.edu/amc

scale competitions, so we will mention only one more for illustrative purposes. Each year a competition is sponsored by the Junior Engineering Technical Society (www.asee.org/jets). A unique challenge is presented to teams of students each year. In the 1997–98 school year, the challenge was to build a safe shopping cart that a toddler could not fall from or easily tip over. The winners were a team of young women from West Perry High School in Elliottsburg, Pennsylvania. Fittingly, they named their entry the "Queen of Carts."

In many parts of the country, mathematics competitions, field days, and mathematics/science fairs are organized by professional organizations (often NCTM affiliates), county offices of education, and local school districts. It has been our pleasure to be involved with such extracurricular activities. We have seen teachers, students, and supportive parents benefit when the activity is the culmination of a year-long effort to increase the problem-solving ability of all students in a classroom. The MESA (Mathematics, Engineering, Science Achievement) project also organizes local and regional competitions for students participating in that elective program at the middle and high schools.

In a somewhat different vein, the 1996 annual Westinghouse Talent Search was won by an 18-year-old student, Jacob Lurie, who developed the mathematical topic of surreal numbers (April 7, 1996, *New York Times* magazine). Every year the top 40 winners of this national competition with scholarships and prize money.

Mathematics Clubs

Mathematics clubs with which we are familiar generally have had one or more of the following purposes, beyond a broad goal of fostering interest in and enthusiasm for mathematics:

- become familiar with mathematics topics outside of the scope of the standard high-school mathematics curriculum—for example, topology;
- prepare members for participation in mathematics competitions;
- develop and sponsor mathematics contests for other schools in the area.

Clubs with a main focus on preparation for competitions generally function in a way similar to the MATHCOUNTS tutoring described earlier in this chapter. The faculty sponsor(s) act as coaches for the students as they work through and discuss challenging problems, with the intent of entering and doing well in competitions.

When a club decides to develop and sponsor mathematics contests for other (usually younger) students, certain aspects of leadership development are necessary. Students will have to write problems for the exam, publicize the competition, raise money to reproduce materials and perhaps offer refreshments to the participants, monitor the activities, develop a fair scoring and assessment procedure for determining winners (if that is the nature of the contest), provide entertainment while the scoring is being completed and checked, and provide prizes. We found sponsorship of such extracurricular activities to be very exciting.

To prepare for or sponsor competitions, the club will need many challenging math problems. NCTM publishes books on contest problems at the high-school level. Refer to the References at the end of this chapter for further information.

When I (SM) was a junior-high teacher, my students were given the opportunity to participate in a Math Field Day sponsored by a mathematics club from a nearby high school. Because this was in an urban area, 15 to 20 schools participated in any given year. Individual written exams were given for Grades 7 and 8; an algebra exam was given for Grade 9. Nowadays, the algebra exam might be at the eighth-grade level, however. Interestingly, the seventh- and eighth-grade tests were reputed to be harder, year by year, than the algebra test because more of the problems were of the nonstandard type requiring reasoning and creative thinking. Following the written exam, students participated in strategy game elimination tournaments. The games included three-dimensional tic-tac-toe and hex. There was a refreshment break as well. The awards ceremony was held in the school library, where a student magician was performing tricks while the final results were being tabulated and organized. My students gained a great deal of pride and satisfaction in their strong performance and enjoyed participating in the activity.

A number of my (LH) students entered the high-school science and mathematics fair with mathematics projects good enough to then proceed to the county and even, in some cases, to the state science fair. One student's study won a prize at the Science, Mathematics, and Technology State Fair. She explored the different methods that calculators and computers use to generate random numbers and analyzed which generated the most randomized list of a given length. Other projects examined hidden patterns in chaotic systems, the central limit theorem, the most economical volume for the honey cell, an algorithm for magic squares, and fractal geometry. We set up the high-school math-science fair in the large wrestling room, thanks to the class that usually met there giving up its space for the week. Teachers could bring their classes to the fair during the week it was set up, and many math and science teachers did so. One evening during the week was open house, when parents enjoyed seeing the students' exhibits. The students were very proud of their accomplishments; they were praised not only by their families but also by their peers. Even if they did not win a prize, the students who went to the county and state fairs greatly enjoyed the experience of talking to high achievers in math and science from other areas. Figure 11.5 is a sample of the type of rubric used to score math fair projects.

If you have the opportunity to coach or sponsor extracurricular mathematics activities, we encourage you to consider doing so. Many students have chosen mathematics-related careers because of such opportunities. I (SM) am one of them, thanks to Mr. Arvin Orahood, my ninth-grade algebra teacher, who coached me and other students and took us to a regional mathematics competition at which students from my small rural school did well in competition with much larger schools.

Figure 11.5

A Rubric for Scoring Math Fair Projects

JUDGES WORKSHEET – MATHEMATICS AND COMPUTERS

☐ NUMBER   DIVISION (CHECK ONE) ☐ JUNIOR   ☐ SENIOR   CATEGORY

MATHEMATICS AND COMPUTERS CREATIVITY (25 points total)   CIRCLE APPROPRIATE NO.

	MIN				MAX
1. The level of mathematics or computer usage for this project is not commonly taught at this grade level.	1	2	3	4	5
2. The project is original or represents a new point of view or modified point of view of a known topic.	1	2	3	4	5
3. The mathematical concepts or methods of computer programming are used ingeniously.	1	2	3	4	5
4. Interpretation of results shows student's creative involvement.	1	2	3	4	5
5. Student shows understanding of the mathematical or computer science context related to the project.	1	2	3	4	5

MATHEMATICS AND COMPUTERS CREATIVITY TOTAL ►

ANALYTICAL METHODS (30 points total)

1. The purpose is clearly and succinctly stated.	1	2	3	4	5
2. The background theory to support the project is explained.	1	2	3	4	5
3. All initial conditions are given.	1	2	3	4	5
4. The conclusions follow logically from the hypothesis or initial conditions.	1	2	3	4	5
5. The measure of development found in references and the amount of original work is well defined.	1	2	3	4	5
6. The project shows depth of study and effort.	1	2	3	4	5

ANALYTICAL METHODS TOTAL ►

PRESENTATION (20 points total)

1. The visuals are clear, clean, neat, and easily understood.	1	2	3	4	5
2. The written descriptions show correct grammar and spelling.	1	2	3	4	5
3. Mathematical symbols or computer program readouts are standard or carefully explained.	1	2	3	4	5
4. Computational or programming methods are completely shown or outlined in detail.	1	2	3	4	5

PRESENTATION TOTAL ►

BACKGROUND (25 points total)

1. The study is complete within the scope of the problem.	1	2	3	4	5
2. The appropriate literature has been searched.	1	2	3	4	5
3. All original calculations or computer programs are available.	1	2	3	4	5
4. Special mathematical, computational, or programming skills are evident.	1	2	3	4	5
5. A well-organized and neat notebook clearly demonstrates the student's involvement in all aspects of the project.	1	2	3	4	5

BACKGROUND TOTAL ►

TOTAL POINTS FOR PROJECT ►

ADD COMMENTS OR CLARIFYING STATEMENTS (USE REVERSE SIDE IF NECESSARY)

....

SIGNATURE OF JUDGE   DATE SIGNED

COMMUNITY-BASED MATHEMATICS ACTIVITIES

As part of their membership in the University of Missouri Mathematics Teachers Organization, a group of preservice teachers planned a mathematics fair to motivate students and involve parents in looking at mathematics in a new way (Reys & Wasman, 1998). The fair was organized as a series of booths, each developed and run by a team of two to three college students. A one-page handout describing each

activity was prepared for families to take home with them after the fair. One of the booths stressed estimation. Activity 11.8 includes samples of the types of questions that might be part of such an estimation booth exhibit. These questions come from several different sources.

Many schools and teachers sponsor and promote activities that either bring the community into the school to participate in a mathematics-related event, show students how people in their community use mathematics, or take mathematics activities out to the community. We will share a few examples of these activities.

FOR TEACHERS

Activity 11.8 Estimation Contest

Mathematical Content:
Number Sense, estimation (PSSM Number and Operations Standard for Grades 6–8)

Materials Needed:
List of questions similar to those given in this activity, collections of items to use in estimations competitions (numbers of beans in a jar, etc.), a system of collecting estimates

that identifies the estimator, answers prepared ahead of time

Directions: Make signs or charts that say:

Write your best estimate of this answer on the answer sheet provided, along with your name. If you win, you will need to describe your method when you claim your prize.

FOR STUDENTS

Activity 11.8
Estimation Contest

1. How many paper clips would be needed to reach end to end from the floor to the ceiling?

2. How many seconds are there in a year?

3. What is the population of this city, according to signs posted when entering?

4. If you had $1 million and gave away $50 an hour, how long would it take to give away the whole amount?

5. What is the average number of hairs on the human scalp?

6. How many Boy Scouts are there in Pakistan?

Barnes (1993) describes a teaching module used in a mathematics class for high-school juniors and seniors. This type of project might be beneficial to the college-preparatory student as well, but the amount of time devoted to guest speakers would have to be limited. The assignment was to interview someone in the community to find out how that person uses mathematics in the course of her job. Then the students were to ask the person to help them write a short worksheet (no more than five problems) illustrating the mathematics used in her particular line of work. Students could also ask the person to come and speak to their class on the same topic. Barnes's assessment of the project was that it was very successful. Students learned not only about mathematics but also that people in their community cared enough to arrange their schedules so they could come and speak to the class. Students became aware of career options and the training they would need in order to be qualified for certain careers.

In a much more limited way, I (SM) gave the assignment presented in Activity 11.9 on the first day of a high-school math class. My students also gained new insights about how mathematics is used in the workplace. The following day, working in groups of four, students debriefed their homework and completed a summary sheet to be turned in as part of their groupwork. With a more advanced mathematics class, the types of mathematics listed could include the topics covered in the class, or the assignment could be more open-ended, such as that described in the Barnes article.

Another example of involving the community was described by Tibbs and Jordan (1994). Students make a Career Poster summarizing the outcomes of an interview with someone who uses mathematics on the job. Activity 11.10 includes the assignment sheet for the career poster.

A program called Math Options, described by VanLeuvan, Smith, Dion, Simon, & Kaplan (1996), is specifically directed at increasing female participation in careers in mathematics and science. Seventh-grade girls were targeted for this activity, sponsored by Pennsylvania State University's Ogonz campus, located in the Philadelphia area. Five girls and their teachers from each school were invited to attend. Role model presenters from the community engaged the students in hands-on activities related to their particular fields and participated in career panels. The junior-high students had many opportunities to interact with professionals.

FOR TEACHERS

Activity 11.9 Math on the Job

Mathematical Content:
Career applications, data representation (PSSM Connections Standard for Grades 6–8 and 9–12)

Materials Needed:
Homework directions, reporting sheet, poster, and book, *"When Are We Ever Going to Use This?"* (optional and helpful)

If either the book or the poster is available, go over with students. The poster is a summary of the book. People in different jobs were given a list of mathematical topics and asked to identify the ones they used the most in their work. The poster reports the data in tabular form, with check marks indicating the topics chosen. The book goes into more details as to how the mathematics is used in various jobs. The set was originally published by Dale Seymour Publications, now a subsidiary of the Pearson Learning Group.

Directions: On the day of this assignment, read the homework directions with students, and discuss them so that everyone understands what to do.

On the following day, have groups of four tally their responses on the reporting sheet. Have them summarize and report their findings.

Extensions:
1. Have students make a graph to represent their findings.
2. Have students write a summary of their findings, including some rationale for the information they received.
3. Activity 11.10 could be an extension of this activity.

F O R   S T U D E N T S

Activity 11.9
Math on the Job

Data Collection
This is a data-collecting assignment. You are to ask five adults about the kinds of math they use on their jobs or at home. Complete this sheet, and bring it back tomorrow.

   To the adult who provides the information: First write the name of your occupation in one of the provided blanks. Then place a check mark in the column next to any math concepts you use on your job. Also check whether you use a calculator on your job. Thank you for helping the high-school math student collect these data.

Adult #1 Occupation: _____

Adult #2 Occupation: _____

Adult #3 Occupation: _____

Adult #4 Occupation: _____

Adult #5 Occupation: _____

Concept	Adult #1	Adult #2	Adult #3	Adult #4	Adult #5
Decimals	_____	_____	_____	_____	_____
Percents	_____	_____	_____	_____	_____
Estimation	_____	_____	_____	_____	_____
Fractions	_____	_____	_____	_____	_____
Proportion	_____	_____	_____	_____	_____
Statistical graphs	_____	_____	_____	_____	_____
Formulas	_____	_____	_____	_____	_____
Algebra	_____	_____	_____	_____	_____
Geometry	_____	_____	_____	_____	_____
Trigonometry	_____	_____	_____	_____	_____
_____	_____	_____	_____	_____	_____
Calculator	_____	_____	_____	_____	_____

Group Report

Number of Adults Giving Information: _____

Concept	Total Number of Checks
Decimals	_____
Percents	_____
Estimation	_____
Fractions	_____
Proportion	_____
Statistical graphs	_____
Formulas	_____
Algebra	_____
Geometry	_____
Trigonometry	_____
_____	_____
Calculators	_____

As a group, find a way to organize and report the information you received.

FOR TEACHERS

Activity 11.10 Career Poster

Mathematical Content:
Career applications (PSSM Communications and
Connections Standards for Grades 6–8 and
9–12)

Materials Needed:
Career Poster Directions for all students;
Overhead transparency version for teacher
use.

FOR STUDENTS

Activity 11.10
Career Poster

Student Directions:
Interview someone who uses mathematics in his
or her job. Ask the person to give you an example of a problem encountered in his or her work.
You do not have to understand the problem
yourself.

Make a poster. The title of the poster should
be the name of the career, such as "Engineer" or
"Carpenter." On the poster you should include
three things:

1. the mathematics problem given to you by the
person you interviewed;

2. a paragraph explaining in general what the
problem is about and how it is used;

3. a picture to illustrate the job. It can be a
photograph of the person you interviewed, or it can be a picture cut from a
magazine showing a person in that occupation.

On the back of the poster, you must put three
things:

1. your name and class;

2. the name of the person you interviewed and
the name of the place where she or he
works;

3. the daytime telephone number of the person you interviewed. The number will enable me to verify any of the information, if
necessary.

This assignment will be graded. The grade will
be based on these things:

1. *Accuracy and completeness.* You must follow
instructions for the interview and poster.

2. *Neatness.* Please print your title. Your paragraph should be typed or printed neatly in
ink.

3. *Timeliness.* The poster must be turned in
on or before the due date.

This assignment is due _____.

Source: Adapted from Peggy Tibbs and Janette Jordan, "Sharing Teaching Ideas," *Mathematics Teacher* (September 1994).

An amusement park ride becomes part of a mathematics activity when students use indirect measurement techniques to determine the approximate height of a Ferris wheel.

A similar format is followed at Expanding Your Horizons career awareness days held at many campuses around the country for girls in Grades 6–12 and their parents. This program began at Mills College in Oakland, California, in the late 1970s. Role model speakers and hands-on activities are components of these Saturday events held at universities and colleges. An additional component is parental involvement. Parents have special sessions, including sessions at which they can hear panel presentations by women in careers requiring strong mathematics and science backgrounds. The girls can ask the presenters and representatives of the host institution about admissions requirements, support services, scholarships, and the like.

Other successful activities we have seen include "Math in the Mall" and "Math Trails," popular in many parts of the country. In 1998 Ron Lancaster of Hamilton, Ontario, won an unprecedented second Hilroy Fellowship, a very prestigious award in Canada, in recognition of the Math Trails he designed in downtown Toronto for his seventh-grade students. These trails helped students connect their mathematics learning to the art, architecture, and science present in the city, as described in the July/August NCTM *News Bulletin*. Likewise, many theme parks sponsor mathematics and science activities for students. At Magic Mountain in Valencia,

California, for example, students measure distance, velocities, and accelerations of different rides. In San Diego, a Math Day is an annual event at the Sea World attraction. Certainly, mathematics is everywhere, and students' appreciation of the subject can be enhanced by experiences such as those described, carried out outside the classroom.

THE INTERNET: EXTENDING MATHEMATICS TO THE CYBERWORLD

At home, at work, and in public libraries, most Americans have access to the Internet. Given this, we do not include detailed information in this chapter about the mechanics of getting on the Internet or searching for a specific topic. Instead, we focus on applications for teaching mathematics. We envision the following possible uses of the Internet in classrooms:

- locate collections of data to use for statistical analysis;
- find graphs to be explained mathematically;
- share information about particular topics among educators and/or students (for example, some

teachers set up a Web site where their students shared findings about spirolaterals—see Chapter 10 for the lesson—with students in other schools);

- research a famous mathematician or mathematical theorem;
- create Web pages to share ideas on a particular type of mathematics or related project;
- import video clips to illustrate mathematical concepts;
- locate lessons plans correlated to PSSM;
- interact with other teachers regarding classroom issues;
- read articles on mathematics education research and issues.

 Go to Web Destinations for Chapter 11 at **http://www.prenhall.com/huetinck** to find out more about lesson plans correlated to PSSM *(Illuminations).*

Various organizations provide newsletters and conferences for teachers wanting to keep abreast of technology in the classroom. One of these is Computer-Using Educators (CUE). We have found CUE's articles helpful in raising issues regarding computer usage. Each newsletter has a section in which technology is reviewed, as well as a list of opportunities for grants to bring more computer technology into the classroom.

Summary

Any successful school is a mini community that serves all of the people associated with it—employees associated with the schools, as well as the parents and neighborhood within which the school is located. This chapter gave you ideas on

- communicating with parents about your classroom goals through letters, back-to-school night presentations, and open house activities;
- involving students, parents, and community members in mathematics-related activities outside of the school day—contests, math fairs, classroom speakers, and the like.

The estimation, measurement, and data collection and depiction activities in this chapter support both of these types of interactions.

ASSIGNMENTS

1. Use the library or the Internet to find information on mathematics contests for middle- and high-school students. Go beyond what is included in this chapter, and provide information about how students can become involved, what is required financially and in terms of time, and what, if any, limitations on student participation exist.

2. Identify the kinds of homework assistance available for students in a given school community. A school counselor may be a good source for this information. Emphasize assistance that is available and accessible to most students. You may include community sources, such as churches and social service centers, as well as those within the public education structure.

INSTRUCTIONAL RESOURCES

Giannetti, C. C., & Sagarese, M. M. (1998). Turning parents from critics to allies. *Educational Leadership 55(8),* 40–42.
   The authors provide specific suggestions for dealing with parents and engaging them in productive ways toward the success of their children.

Little, C. (1999). Counting grass. *Mathematics Teaching in the Middle School, 5*(1), 7–10.
   Relates a scenario of an estimation activity implemented in the schoolyard. Sampling techniques were used to estimate the number of blades of grass in the soccer field. A worksheet is included.

Schneider, Leo (compiler). (2002). The Contest Problem Book VI (MAA) 1989–1994. Reston, VA, NCTM.
   Contains 180 challenging problems and some techniques for solving.

ADDITIONAL ACTIVITIES

These activities present extensions of ideas on number sense and measurement.

If middle-school students are given the kinds of problems to work on and discuss as those given in Activity 11.2, and if number sense continues to be developed as students move through the core high-school curriculum, then problems such as these will seem natural. However, often this is not the case, and students entering college find this set of problems quite difficult, as was shared by university mathematics professor Millie Johnson of Western Washington University at a Viz-Math seminar in October 1998 at California State University, Northridge.

Measurement is a separate standard in PSSM. As defined in that document (p. 44), "measurement is the assignment of a numerical value to an attribute of an object, such as the length of a pencil." Students who attain this standard can:

- understand measurable attributes of objects and the units, systems, and processes of measurement;
- apply appropriate techniques, tools, and formulas to determine measurements.

We have frequently found high-school students with misconceptions about measurement. A basic concept regarding measurement is that it is always approximate, as the scales used are continuous and things being measured are discrete. Many times, estimation of a measurement is sufficient, depending on the context. For example, it is better to underestimate when determining the weight limit of an elevator, whereas one should overestimate the amount of paint needed to cover the walls of a room—within reason, of course. The degree of accuracy needed depends upon the situation as well. Tool and die makers must make machine parts with a great deal of precision, using the notion of tolerance. The amount of water needed to cook a certain amount of spaghetti, on the other hand, is generally not measured precisely.

Activities 11.11, 11.12, and 11.13 deal respectively with hands-on length measure, time measure, and using scaling and approximation to indicate large distances. Precision and degree of accuracy become more important as students use mathematics tools in various applications, especially in science. Sets of direct measures of natural phenomena and data collections describing large populations tend to have characteristic distributions that can be analyzed with statistical methods. A bell curve will be more meaningful to students who have collected data through experiments or measurements that exhibit this shape. The final activity of the chapter, 11.14, has students use maps of different scales to estimate places that are given distances from their school.

FOR TEACHERS

Activity 11.11 Advanced Number Sense

Mathematical Content:
Pre-calculus notation, number sense (PSSM Number and Operations Standards for Grades 9–12)

Materials Needed:
Worksheet

Directions: Have students work in pairs to complete the worksheet, giving a written rationale for each response. Different pairs report their response and rationale to the class.

FOR STUDENTS

Activity 11.11
Advanced Number Sense

1. For each of the following expressions, determine which of the lettered points on the number line shown above is closest to the given number.

   a. $n \times p$

   b. $k \times p$

   c. $l + p$

   d. $\sqrt{n}$

   e. $|k|$

   f. $\dfrac{1}{p}$

   g. $2l$

   h. $\dfrac{1}{q}$

2. Determine the truth value of each of the following expressions.

   a. $h < p$

   b. $h \times k < 0$

   c. $\dfrac{k}{l} > 1$

   d. $p + k \times l > 0$

   e. $|h| > m$

   f. $|1 + l| > l$

   g. $\sqrt{kl}$ is imaginary

Source: From Elich, J./Cannon, L.D., *Precalculus*. 2nd Ed. (1999) Harper Collins.

FOR TEACHERS

Activity 11.12 Length Measure

Mathematical Content:
Length measure, statistics (PSSM Measurement and Data Analysis Standards for Grades 6–8)

Materials Needed:
Activity sheet, metric tape measure

Directions: Have students, in pairs, measure the length of the classroom to the nearest centimeter. Collect the data and have students use the data to make a stem-and-leaf plot and a box-and-whisker plot to depict the results. Discuss the results, using the Possible Discussion Questions as a guide.

Extensions: Have students make comparative box-and-whisker plots of different classes' results, either on chart paper or with technology.

FOR STUDENTS

Activity 11.12
Length Measure

Possible Discussion Questions

1. What do the data show us?

2. Is it possible for the results to be different, even if everyone did her best to be accurate? Why or why not?

3. What could be done during the measurement process to have a smaller range of answers?

4. Is it appropriate to measure the length of the room in centimeters? Why or why not?

5. How far off does a measurement have to be to be considered wrong?

Source: Adapted from the 1989 NCTM *Curriculum and Evaluation Standards*.

FOR TEACHERS

Activity 11.13 Time Is Relative

Mathematical Content:
Time measurement, statistics (bell-shaped distributions) (PSSM Measurement and Data Analysis Standards for Grades 6–8)

Materials Needed:
Stopwatch for every pair of students, charts and sticky dots for recording information

Directions: In this experiment students explore the accuracy of timing 5 seconds with a human-operated stopwatch. The purpose is to develop a bell-shaped distribution and understand why that shape makes sense when actually measuring all kinds of data, even when supposedly measuring the "same" amount of time.

Provide the following instructions to the class:

You will take turns timing 5 seconds. One person watches the second hand on a clock or watch. The second person holds the stopwatch. The first person says "Start" at the beginning of 5 seconds and "Stop" at the end of 5 seconds. The second person tries to start and stop the stopwatch based only on the oral commands. After each attempt, record what is actually shown on the stopwatch, to the nearest tenth of a second. You can expect to be close to 5 seconds but not exactly at 5.0 seconds. Why? Repeat with the first person giving the commands for a total of 5 times, then trade and repeat the process 5 more times. Each pair then makes a line plot of the 10 data points on a single sheet of paper.

Post a large time line, going from 4.5 to 5.5 seconds with intervals of 0.1 marked, at the front of the classroom. One student from each pair will use sticky dots to record the pair's results as part of the large line plot. Follow with a discussion, using the possible Discussion Questions and others.

Overall, students should see why bell-shaped distributions make sense when things are being measured.

FOR STUDENTS

Activity 11.13
Time Is Relative

Directions: Nobody is a perfect timer. In this experiment you will explore how accurately people can time things. Students, in pairs, will take turns timing 5 seconds. One student from each pair comes to the front and uses "sticky dots" to record the pair's results on the large class chart. A discussion follows.

Possible Discussion Questions

1. What do the data show us?

2. Is it possible for the results to be different, even if everyone did her best to be accurate? Why or why not?

3. What could be done during the measurement process to have a smaller range of answers?

4. What are some situations when measuring to a tenth of a second or less very accurately would be important? How is this done?

5. How far off does a measurement of 5 seconds under the conditions in this classroom have to be to be considered wrong?

FOR TEACHERS

Activity 11.14 Thinking About Distances

Mathematical Content:
Linear distance, scale, magnitude (PSSM Number and Operations Standard for Grades 9–12)

Materials Needed:
Activity sheet, access to local maps and maps showing locations up to 500 miles from your school

Extensions: Use Internet resources (Project GLOBE) to find out more information about global data collection of information useful to earth scientists.

Source: This activity is based on a lesson from the *Mathematics: Modeling Our World* first-year curriculum (see Chapter 4), which has a unit on Landsat, a satellite system to monitor Earth's resources.

FOR STUDENTS

Activity 11.14
Thinking About Distances

Directions: The Landsat 5 satellite orbits Earth at an altitude of approximately 700 km (440 miles). An airplane typically flies about 9.7 km (6 miles) above Earth. Use maps to explore the significance of those distances in the following exercises.

1. Locate five places that are about 9.7 km away from your school. The place should not be a home, but some community feature that you could point to when driving past, such as a shopping mall, a cemetery, another school, a park, etc. Describe how you determined the distance for each place.

2. Locate five places that are about 700 km from school. Again, describe how you determined the distance. Do you think the distances you determined in this exercise are as precise as those in Problem 1? Why or why not?

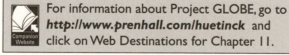

For information about Project GLOBE, go to **http://www.prenhall.com/huetinck** and click on Web Destinations for Chapter 11.

CHAPTER
12

Professional Growth

You are embarking on a profession that truly makes a difference. Over the course of your teaching career, you may provide meaningful educational opportunities to thousands of young people, whom you will guide in attaining skills essential to successful adulthood.

In an ideal first teaching assignment, as a beginning teacher you would have a mentor teacher designated to provide you with assistance as needed. This mentor teacher could offer general information about the expectations of the community and the mathematics department, give practical guidance in working within the school structure, and assist with suggestions on handling difficult situations, if such arise. In addition, the school site and/or district ideally will arrange workshops and professional activities to facilitate teacher development, although these are generally voluntary.

Indeed, this is an ideal, because in the United States there seldom is such support for beginning teachers. This lack complicates the task of colleges and universities that are preparing beginning teachers. The credential experience thus must include information and coaching about continuing professional growth, even for teachers who must be largely self-directed and might not consider professional growth activities to be a priority during the first year of teaching. As a matter of fact, the first year will be quite demanding. Nonetheless, you must make the effort to continue to grow if you wish to become an exemplary teacher. Objective evaluation and effective self-reflection are essential, especially in the first year of teaching. Therefore, in this chapter we discuss avenues of teaching enhancement that will become more important to you as you master basic elements of classroom management and begin to focus your teaching preparation on improving the quality of instruction in your courses.

ABOUT THE ACTIVITIES FOR THIS CHAPTER

The mathematics content in this chapter involves subjects that are beyond the core curriculum recommended for all students. The mathematics is embedded in instructional sequences written by exemplary mathematics classroom teachers. They have gone beyond preparing innovative lessons for their students to conducting workshops and presenting at conferences to share their successful teaching ideas with colleagues. The lessons frequently include scripting for teacher and student interaction, so do not need introductions written by the authors, as has been the practice in previous chapters. Also, because the answers frequently are included in the discussions, teacher notes for this chapter are not provided. All of these exemplary lessons are at the end of this chapter.

Some of the activities approach important mathematical concepts from an uncommon viewpoint with unique uses of technology. Other activities bring in areas of mathematics not often found in the secondary level curriculum. Work through these examples to release your own creativity to develop fascinating and effective learning experiences for your students. As you increase your teaching skills, you will come to find great pleasure in designing or writing original lessons.

NCTM PROFESSIONAL STANDARDS FOR TEACHING MATHEMATICS

In March 1991, the National Council of Teachers of Mathematics (NCTM) published *Professional Standards for Teaching Mathematics* to supplement the *Curriculum Standards,* a set of documents later joined by the *Assessment Standards.* Together these three publications define the direction for mathematics education envisioned by a consensus of mathematics educators, business and industry leaders, and parent organizations. The table of contents for the *Professional Standards* is divided into four main sections:

1. standards for teaching;
2. standards for evaluation of teaching;
3. standards for professional development;
4. standards for the support and development of teachers and teaching.

The first section describes the desirable attributes of an exemplary mathematics program (which were treated in detail in other chapters of this text): selecting worthwhile mathematical tasks, establishing classroom discourse to support high-level mathematical thinking, and characteristics of a learning environment conducive to learning. The fourth section of the *Professional Standards* discusses the responsibilities of policy makers, school systems, and higher education through credential programs and is not germane to the scope of this text. The second and third sections are extremely pertinent, however, as they detail issues of teacher evaluation and professional development—elements of importance to beginning teachers. These sections of the *Professional Standards* are the focus of the first part of this chapter. Later, the chapter describes the professional certification process as constituted in the *National Board Professional Teaching Standards.*

NCTM PRINCIPLES AND STANDARDS FOR SCHOOL MATHEMATICS

The *Principles and Standards for School Mathematics* (2000) document "builds on and consolidates messages from the previous *Standards* documents" (p. 6). The volume is divided into four main parts. The first part describes the six overarching themes, which are equity, curriculum, teaching, learning, assessment, and technology. Where appropriate, these themes have been described in previous sections of this text. The second part of the document describes the mathematical content and processes students should know. The content standards are Number and Operations. Algebra, Geometry, Measurement, and Data Analysis and Probability. The process standards are Problem Solving, Reasoning and Proof, Communication, Connections, and Representation. Four chapters delineate specifics of these standards for the four separate grade bands of pre-kindergarten through Grade 2, Grades 3–5, Grades 6–8, and Grades 9–12. The final portion of the document discusses the steps necessary to obtain the vision embodied in the *Principles and Standards.*

The activities in this text indicate the PSSM strand and grade level for the related standard. Of course, these placements are open to interpretation, as many of the activities not only address several strands simultaneously but also address both content and process standards. We hope that the suggested standards are just a beginning to further your understanding of their application.

The central portion of the document provides many examples of how the standards can be used. The content standards begin with a one-page summary of the expectations for the given grade level. Then examples of each of the expectations are displayed. The process standards also begin with a one-page summary of what instructional programs should enable students to accomplish. Then each section answers the questions "What should communication look like in these grades?" and "What should be the teacher's role in developing communication in these grades?"

The title of the last chapter of the PSSM is "Working Together to Achieve the Vision." Each of the six main principles is discussed in turn through the posing of thoughtful questions. The roles and responsibilities of all persons concerned with education—including students, teachers, administrators, policy makers, university faculty, families, and community members—must work together to make this vision of mathematics teaching and learning a reality. As a classroom teacher, you will be a significant partner in this effort.

For information about the NCTM Web site, go to *http://www.prenhall.com/huetinck* and click on Web Destinations for Chapter 12.

EVALUATION

Evaluation is an essential activity that enables teachers to move from professional status as novice to outstanding teacher. Effective evaluation is cyclical and is based on gathering data, reflecting on the data, and acting to improve instruction. The cycle continues as the teacher again gathers data and repeats the cycle. All good teachers, regardless of years of experience, continually reevaluate their teaching as they experiment informally or formally to better meet students' needs and to design instruction to increase their mathematical understanding. This evaluation can be based on data from a variety of sources: observation and self-reflection, students, school-site colleagues, and outside observers such as university educators or district personnel. The complete evaluation cycle may take only the few minutes required to present a concept and decide how to alter the learning experience to ensure greater understanding of more students. In contrast, the evaluation cycle may take a year or more when a new curriculum is begun or a course

is substantially changed to include experimental elements such as outside projects or alternative assessments.

The *Professional Standards for Teaching Mathematics* discusses four primary assumptions about evaluation:

1. *The goal of evaluating the teaching of mathematics is to improve teaching and enhance professional growth.* The teacher is the key to high-quality mathematics education for students.... Professional development extends and expands teachers' abilities to make good decisions by giving them access to a deeper understanding of mathematics, a greater repertoire of teaching strategies and the ability to match their repertoire to the needs of all students....

2. *All teachers can improve their teaching of mathematics.* Although experienced teachers might be more adept at self-analysis, beginning or struggling teachers can also reflect ... and arrive at some conclusions on how their teaching can be improved.

3. *What teachers learn from the evaluation process is related to how the evaluation is conducted.* .... When written evaluation reports for a teacher's personnel file are produced, a spirit of sensitivity, mutual respect, and concern for professional growth as the primary purpose of evaluation are especially important.

4. *Because teaching is complex, the evaluation of teaching is complex. Simplistic evaluation processes will not help teachers realize the vision of teaching mathematics described in these standards* (NCTM, 1991, pp. 72–73).

Evaluation by a Supervisor

During the first year of teaching, a positive evaluation as a nontenured teacher by a supervisor is of primary importance for retention. Tenured teachers generally are formally observed one to two times a year, but probationary teachers may be observed from four to eight times during a school year. It is hoped that the supervisor will be present for at least one entire class period and observe several different types of lessons before writing an evaluation for the semester or year. School policy may include a pre-conference at which the teacher discusses his goals for the year, goals for the unit, and plans for the lesson in preparation for the supervisor's visit. One supervisor might ask the teacher when he would prefer to be observed, while another will favor an impromptu visit. There should be a post-conference with the supervisor to discuss the classroom observations before the written report is finalized. The report should include a general description of the classroom and activities observed, commendations for good practices, recommendations for alternative practices, and joint suggestions for implementation. The common practice is that the teacher signs the final document and keeps a copy in his files. The original is placed in the teacher's permanent district personnel file.

Whether the evaluation is a paragraph of assessment accompanied by a checklist or a lengthy descriptive narration, a supervisor is looking for the following elements:

- student involvement in the classwork, as evidenced by the number of students working on the task at hand and whether the students maintain interest until the end of the period;
- the ability of the students to interact with each other and to be supportive of each others' efforts;
- effective organization of the learning activity, including evidence of lesson planning, careful supervision, and management of equipment;
- a friendly and respectful rapport between the teacher and students;
- selections of lessons difficult enough to challenge the students but within their capacity to achieve success;
- use of a range of classroom activities and instructional materials to help students master concepts;
- an attractive learning environment.

Attaining tenure, a process of several steps, generally requires at least 3 years of successful teaching experience on contract as a probationary teacher. Some localities that have a deficit of qualified mathematics teachers may hire college graduates as emergency credential teachers who teach full-time while proceeding in a program to attain a credential. Unfortunately, these beginning teachers too frequently are in a sink-or-swim situation, with no more than a few weeks in a summer how-to-teach class before being handed a full assignment. Also, since contracted emergency teachers are hired only after no credentialed teachers can be found, their schedules are the last to solidify and may consist of the classes most difficult to manage. Some districts may hire uncredentialed teachers as long-term substitutes, which is even less desirable for the beginning teacher, because the job can be terminated at any time (there is no contract, and generally, there are no benefits). The more desirable route for both the beginning teacher and his students is to complete a credential program and then be hired as a probationary teacher. Commonly, emergency hires have no legal rights for retention. A probationary teacher would be assessed by his supervisor according to district policy for recommendation to the school board for tenure after several years of successful performance.

The granting of tenure is a significant step for both the teacher and the school administration. Within the first several years of teaching, you should know whether you wish to remain at your school. If there is good cooperation between department members and support by the administration in curriculum and discipline matters, you probably have found a position that fits you. If this is not the case, then move to another school or district. Common practice is to grant only 6 to 10 years' advance on the salary schedule when moving into a new teaching position, so it may be very expensive in lost salary to change districts after about 6 years. The granting of tenure is important to the administration because this indicates its confidence in your continuing positive contributions to your educational community. A tenured teacher has certain legal and academic protections beyond those of a probationary teacher that require full documentation to effect removal.

In addition to classroom observations, the administration will consider other informal sources of information in determining whether to confer tenure. A teacher will gain a reputation by word of mouth among the students. Although a few students might be quite negative and others overly effusive about a teacher's ability, over time students' opinions are meaningful. Administrators gain a sense of your classroom management skills on an ongoing basis through informal comments by students. Further, participation in school activities, community or parent activities, and assistance in departmentwide tasks demonstrate the teacher's professional and personal qualities. Some evaluation checklists may include items concerning professional attitudes, such as the following: implements constructive suggestions; analyzes/evaluates own teaching consistently; meets commitments and deadlines; maintains good rapport with faculty and staff; and assumes/fulfills professional responsibilities. Extremely important attributes for a beginning teacher are the willingness to listen to experienced teachers and the ability to implement suggestions from supervisors. Your department chair and administration realize you may not be an exemplary teacher in just 3 years and will recommend tenure from evidence that you wish to continue to grow to excellence in the profession.

An evaluation practice currently gaining favor is to involve teachers as active participants through preparation of a portfolio demonstrating their teaching abilities. This portfolio can contain samples of student work from different classes, associated lesson plans, and student assessments. (Think ahead and ask some students if you can keep or copy their work so you do not need to construct the portfolio after returning work to the class.) Carefully select a few items that showcase your competence at working with students of differing ability levels and ages. Portfolio selections also should demonstrate a variety of successful modes of instruction. The portfolio then serves as a focus for analysis and discussion of your teaching capabilities, ensuring evaluation of the complexity of teaching as recommended by the *Professional Standards*. The following vignette demonstrates how this procedure can work.

Vignette 12.1 Teaching Portfolios Support Evaluation

Doug Reid teaches 1st-year algebra at Jefferson High School. He voices concern to his mathematics supervisor, Yolanda Hernandez, that his total evaluation last year was based on only two classroom observations. Yolanda is concerned about this also, but she explains that her responsibilities make it virtually impossible for her to visit each teacher more than two or three times a year. During the conversation, she indicates a willingness to base her evaluation on information provided by the teachers, if they can suggest a reasonable way of doing this.

After considerable deliberation, the teachers and Yolanda decide that the teachers will provide portfolios for her to consider and that she will base part of her evaluation on these portfolios. The teachers decide that the portfolios will contain sample lesson plans and student activity sheets they have used, various problems they have used for "warm-ups" or "attention-grabbers," special materials they have created for students, chapter quizzes and tests, notes on computer software and other materials, and a description of what they consider to be their best lessons.

Doug is skeptical about the idea. He thinks the creation of a portfolio will be a lot of extra work that won't really help him improve as a teacher. Yolanda emphasizes that the teachers should not prepare additional materials but rather should see the portfolio as a means of collecting information on teaching that has already occurred. That is, the portfolio should be seen as a means of *collecting* information rather than *creating* information. Doug thinks this is an important point; it eases his mind that he won't have to be doing "busy work" for the sake of evaluating his teaching.

As the portfolio develops, Doug comments, "I'm beginning to see the value of the portfolio. Although it takes a little time to select and compile lesson plans, activities, and chapter tests, it turns out to be two pronged—it is valuable for my own analysis as well as for the supervisor's. Yolanda can use this to assess my short- and long-range goals and provide feedback on my

quizzes and tests. Actually, it is less work than I had originally imagined."

Yolanda indicates that the portfolios are helpful in keeping her in touch with what the teachers are doing. Actually, she is surprised that they provide as much information as they do. She notes, for example, that Doug's algebra tests tend to overemphasize computational algorithms. She offers several alternative items that he can use in subsequent testing. She likes his warm-up activities and compliments him on the way he begins the algebra classes.

At a faculty meeting later that month, the principal compliments the department for its innovative approach to improving instruction. She is particularly pleased that the teachers and the supervisor have worked together in a professional way in developing procedures for evaluation (NCTM, 1991, pp. 86–87).

Reflective Teaching

Regardless of the mode of evaluation used in your school, it is far preferable to begin self-analysis of your teaching before being formally observed by a supervisor. Thus, you can demonstrate your interest in the main goal of evaluation, which is to improve instruction. Following are some ways to get started in collecting data that can become methods of initiating private self-reflection.

Review of Lesson Plans   Each day, spend just a few minutes making a brief note at the bottom of the day's lesson plans about what worked best and the pitfalls, if any, that you encountered. Sometimes, if you teach the same lesson to two different periods, you may change practices in the second teaching to improve the lesson or note that some elements worked better in one class than they did in the other. Personality, ability level, or time of day can sometimes make a difference. Note these observations for reference in later lessons and for reference if you teach the same course in subsequent years.

Student Feedback   Ask students from time to time to comment on different aspects of the course content. An easy way to begin is to request a quick-write on "What I understand so far in this unit" and "What I do not understand so far in this unit." This practice is especially easy to institute if students write in journals from time to time, but individual written student responses can be equally helpful. Thus, a teacher can appreciate the difficulty of certain concepts, as perceived by the students, that may not match his preconceptions about the complexity of the course content. The comments also may highlight a teacher's need to review given areas of mathematics that he finds somewhat difficult to present. Experienced teachers know that we understand a concept best after being able to teach it successfully.

Near the end of the first semester, ask students to list two things they would like changed in the course and two things they would like to remain the same. These are much broader categories than understanding about content. You probably will be amazed by the variety of responses. One excellent veteran teacher was asked by a number of students to change her outdated nail polish color! This was their only request for change, so she willingly complied. A teacher should consider all requests, act on some of them, and perhaps even discuss some with the class as a whole; however, he need not ascribe equal value to all suggestions.

Videotape of a Class

As you gain confidence in teaching, videotape a class. If you are self-conscious about alerting the students, you can set up the video camera on a back file cabinet in a shoe box with a hole cut to accommodate the camera lens. Be sure it is set up so most of the room is visible, including the area you will mainly occupy. (Some schools may require permission from all parents whose students are in the video, if the tape will be used in professional development where supervisors or university personnel will view it. Generally, permission is not necessary if you are the only one to view the tape for use in self-analysis. Ask an administrator about school policy.) Select one or two aspects of the video for focus.

If the video is taken from a stationary position in the room, the sound quality may be poor and the view of the room will be limited. Any analysis probably will concern overall characteristics of the class rather than sufficient details to use in analyzing whether students are learning.

Pick a few of the following questions to ask yourself:

- Do I have any distracting habits, such as saying "OK" many times?
- Do I recognize raised hands equally from students sitting in different parts of the room?
- Do I favor calling on students of a certain gender or certain students who are sure to know the answer, and do I spread the questions equally to students located in all areas of the classroom?
- Am I surprised by student activity made visible in the video that I do not notice while teaching?
- Do I allow sufficient wait time and patience for students to formulate and articulate their ideas?
- Do students talk to each other about mathematical concepts?

- Do I circulate to all parts of the classroom?
- During group work, do I ever get stuck assisting one group while other students waste time waiting for my attention?
- How much time during the period is lost instructional time?
- Do I have a friendly but commanding presence?

After making observations from the tape, formulate resolutions to make at most two changes. Do not be too hard on yourself—just try to change a few aspects of your teaching at a time. An excellent practice is to videotape yourself weeks later and see whether you have improved in the areas you targeted. Then consider one or two additional aspects of teaching to change at a later time in your next self-evaluation cycle.

Weekly Log

Keep a weekly written log. This may be especially important early in your teaching career, when things may not go as planned. Briefly record your successes and frustrations. State what you would like to accomplish in the coming week. Then periodically read earlier entries. You will learn much about yourself as a teacher and will undoubtedly be heartened to see growth over time in increasing successes.

Class Discussion

From time to time, take the last minutes of the class to talk to your students. Ask several what they learned that day or during the past week. Ask them what information is of the greatest importance to relay to students who were absent. Was the material difficult or easy? Are there other ways to answer this question? You might share what you have learned during the week.

Feedback From Colleagues

After you have done some preliminary reflecting and are becoming comfortable in your role as a teacher, ask a colleague to provide support and feedback on a lesson. Be quite specific about your goals for the lesson, and define the focus to be considered for recommendations. With the assistance of an experienced teacher, you can begin to analyze ways to design curriculum to maximize student involvement. The following vignette illustrates this approach.

Vignette 12.2   Collegial Support in Professional Growth

Art Heyen has been reading various articles in the *Mathematics Teacher* about the importance of emphasizing mathematical processes when teaching mathematics. He decides to make a concerted effort this year to incorporate these ideas into his teaching. At the beginning of the year, he meets with Diane Rowen, an experienced mathematics teacher, to discuss how his teaching could become more process oriented. Diane suggests that he start with a few selected topics to "get the feel of it" and then work from there. Diane offers suggestions for a lesson on graphing parabolas that Art could use later in the year....

In November, Art is ready to teach the lesson on graphing parabolas. He invites Diane to observe the lesson and make suggestions. He indicates that he has had moderate success with other lessons in which mathematical processes have been emphasized. He complains somewhat about it taking so long to find good materials but notices that the students seem more interested in mathematics this year than any of the previous two years that he has been teaching.

Art typically teaches the lesson on graphing parabolas by modeling several graphs and helping the students locate the vertex and several other points, which are then plotted. After several demonstrations, he assigns practice problems. This year he will teach the topic with a greater emphasis on conceptual development.

Art begins the lesson by passing out graphing calculators that have just recently been obtained. He asks the students to write down three statements or words they associate with the equation $y = ax^2 + bx + c$. Some of the phrases are *quadratic equation, parabola,* and *horseshoe-shaped.* One student mentions that if $x = 0$, then $y = c$. Art asks what this means, but the student is not sure. Diane thinks Art might have spent more time helping the student reason through his conclusion.

Art asks the students to use the graphing calculators to graph the cases when $a = 0.24$, -0.5, 1.4, and -8 and b and c both are 0, and then sketch and label the graphs on the same set of axes on the graph paper he has presented....

As the students work on questions, Art and Diane walk around the room and check the students' progress. Diane notices that one student has drawn a horizontal line for one of the sketches. She asks if it is possible for the graph of a quadratic function to be a horizontal line. The student seems puzzled. After rechecking his figures, the student finds that he had entered $y = 4^2$ on the calculator rather than $y = 4x^2$. A student who is listening claims that you could get a horizontal line. Diane asks her how this could happen. The student argues that it can happen when the a and b coefficients are 0 because then you have a constant function. Both Art and Diane are impressed with the student's reasoning, even though they recognize an error in her thinking.

Art asks the students to consider . . . $y = 3x^2 + 10$, $y = 3x^2 - 5$, $y = 3x^2 + 5$, $y = 3x^2 - 10$. . . .

On the basis of the graphs they have sketched, the students are then asked to consider the following questions: Without using the calculator, indicate whether the graph of each of the following equations will open upward or downward, whether the graph will

be relatively narrow or wide, and where the graph intersects the y – axis. Then sketch the graphs on a sheet of graph paper: $y = -(1/4)x^2 - 4$, $y = 5x^2 + 4$, $y = -x^2 + 7$, $y = (1/3)x^2 - 6$. . . .

After school, Art meets briefly with Diane to discuss the lesson. He mentions that he wanted to cover more material—particularly the relationship between the value of the discriminant and the number of intercepts. He realized that it would be easier to just tell the students what he wants them to know, but he was very pleased with their ability to communicate mathematics in their written statements and to use inductive reasoning to figure out what the sketches of the last set of graphs will look like.

Diane concurs. She was particularly pleased with Art's repeated efforts to encourage the students to write statements about what they had discovered. She suggests that next time he might begin the lesson by asking the students what the graph of the equation $y = 1.5x^2 - 3x + 4.2$ [that is, an equation that the students wouldn't normally encounter] would look like. After students' conjectures are recorded, the lesson could be developed, following which the equation could be revisited to determine its graph. The students could use their knowledge developed in the lesson to determine its graph.

Art likes the suggestion. He sees this fitting in with his intention of helping students to reason mathematically. Diane thanks Art for inviting her into his classroom. She compliments him on his efforts to improve his students' ability to use mathematical processes (NCTM, 1991, pp. 100–103).

With practice in reflection, you will begin to ask yourself questions that delve into students' efforts to become mathematically powerful, such as:

- Am I encouraging students to explain, justify, and hypothesize?
- What is my evidence for student understanding? Does this include all students?
- Are the students exploring alternative strategies for problem solving?
- Am I modeling the mathematical thinking that I hope my students will use?
- Do the students take time to try to figure out a problem whose solution is not immediately apparent?
- How do I encourage students to take initiative in answering their own questions?
- In addition to discussion, does my class use other means of communication such as reading and writing?
- Do my students feel comfortable in requesting manipulatives or calculators when these tools might aid their understanding?

Set 12.1   *Discussion Questions*

 Questions with an asterisk appear in the Message Board section of the Companion Website at *http://www.prenhall.com/huetinck.* Go to Chapter 12 and click on the Message Board to find and respond to the question.

*1. Consider yourself a practicing teacher whose evaluator has asked for an appointment for a room visit. What characteristics would you include in the lesson for that day?

 2. List several self-evaluation techniques you would be comfortable using for self-reflection as a beginning teacher. Expand on these techniques to delineate exactly how you would apply them in your classroom.

 3. How would you relate your practice to the NCTM Standards?

CONTINUING PROFESSIONAL DEVELOPMENT

Enhancement of teaching ability comes as a result of experience coupled with the desire and effort for continued professional development. To gauge your progress, consider differences between novice and expert teachers identified by research. Expert teachers have more complex conceptual systems than novice teachers, which enable them to better organize, interconnect, and access both content knowledge and pedagogical knowledge. Therefore, they are more efficient than novices in planning for instruction and in interacting with their students. Expert teachers plan more in their heads—actually thinking through possible scripts—and, because of previous experiences, need not modify their plans as often as novices. When they must think on their feet, expert teachers have greater stores of demonstrations, powerful explanations, and methodologies to utilize than do novice teachers. During instruction, expert teachers efficiently use instructional and management structures. They and their students are aware of certain practices that are carried out with little instruction. Thus, expert teachers dispatch classroom routines more easily than novice teachers with little monitoring, which allows better focus on conceptual development (Brown & Borko, 1992).

Professional Organizations

Active participation in professional organizations and subscriptions to journals written for mathematics teachers allow the networking with experienced teachers that is essential for professional growth. Membership in a professional organization often entitles you to a number of useful resources. The National Council of Teachers of Mathematics is the largest national organization for mathematics teachers in Grades K–16. Membership provides the following written materials, as well as an 800 telephone number and a Web site for additional information:

- *Teaching Children Mathematics (TCM)* is a monthly journal focusing on pre-K through elementary grade levels. Classroom teaching tips, reviews of books, technology updates, and investigations provide teaching ideas applicable not only for elementary school but also, frequently, in secondary schools.

- *Mathematics Teaching in the Middle Schools (MTMS)* is a monthly journal aimed at addressing the needs of middle-school children, with articles on technology assessment, real-world problems, reviews, materials for bulletin boards, and special sections for students.

- *Mathematics Teacher (MT)* emphasizes ways to present concepts for Grades 8–12 and for 2-year junior colleges. Classroom-ready materials, innovative teaching ideas for higher-level mathematics, calendar features, a sharing section for teachers, and technology tips are included.

- *NCTM News Bulletin* keeps mathematics educators informed about current issues and events in mathematics education. *Students' Math Notes* are enclosed five times a year, comprising four pages of classroom activities.

- *NCTM Educational Materials and Products Catalog* lists more than 200 publications and other teaching materials useful not only for teachers and students but also for parents and the community. Included are yearbooks, mathematics content addenda, collections of activities centered around a theme, and books on research in mathematics education.

- *Journal for Research in Mathematics Education (JRME)* details research in the teaching and learning of mathematics at all levels.

- *Mathematics Education Dialogues* is a publication that provides a forum for discussion of timely issues in mathematics education that cut across all educational levels.

During an in-service, mathematics and science teachers participate in a model lesson where they use probeware and graphing calculators to collect and analyze the acidity of a certain solution.

Participation in Projects, Conferences, and Workshops

On many a Friday after school, we have wondered why we signed up to participate in a Saturday conference/workshop. This was especially true when we had children at home and found Saturdays the best time for doing chores and running errands. But after the Saturday conferences adjourned, we knew why we continued to attend such events—to recharge the batteries. It is exciting to learn new ways to reach your students. Even sharing ideas over lunch with other mathematics teachers is invigorating. Teachers should make the effort to attend at least one conference/workshop per semester, even when they wonder if they have the time. Of course, it is best if your school allows release time, and it is especially valuable if at least several members of your department can attend the same conference and come back and share their experiences. Over time you will collect a variety of teaching ideas as you move from novice to expert teacher.

A number of conferences and workshops are available for mathematics teachers. The National Council of Teachers of Mathematics (NCTM) conducts one national and nine regional meetings each year. In addition, state mathematics teachers organizations hold regular conferences, as do some large school districts. Not only can a teacher participate in sessions as a learner, he will generally find the exhibit area the best place to learn of new materials for instruction. Workshops aimed at development of certain concepts, such as infusing technology into practice or becoming familiar with a particular curriculum, probably will be offered locally. Many mathematics teachers belong to the organization Computer-Using Educators, which also holds local and regional conferences. Also, conferences aimed specifically at middle-school teachers are being offered more frequently. Involvement in all of these experiences adds depth and variety to the teacher's tool kit of content and pedagogical knowledge.

A longer time commitment is required for participation in teacher enhancement projects such as those funded by the National Science Foundation, the Woodrow Wilson Foundation, NASA, and universities that sponsor professional growth opportunities for teachers. Most of these programs include a summer institute for which teachers receive an honorarium and perhaps college credit. The institutes promote introduction to new curriculum, increased understanding in certain fields of mathematics, innovative uses of technology, and most important, networking among teachers. In some nationwide projects teachers can meet colleagues from different states and learn much about education in other areas. Likewise, some programs are simple in structure, such as a local group of colleagues who meet over several years to increase their effectiveness in their classrooms.

Two Projects Supporting Reflective Practice

A description of two projects follows. The first is *Structured Exploration,* developed by the Education Development Center, Inc., under the auspices of the Leadership for Urban Mathematics Reform (LUMR). The second is *Mathematics Teaching Cases,* developed by the Far West Laboratory for Educational Research and Development (now called WestEd). We selected these two examples because they succinctly demonstrate steps for growth through reflective practice and because each of these programs can be utilized by a district, or even by a single school, for teachers at all levels of experience. Perhaps your school or district can elicit assistance from one of these professional development groups to institute one of these programs or a similar program to help you and your colleagues examine their practices.

Recent professional development strategies encourage teachers to examine and reflect upon their teaching and their students' learning. Time is provided, generally outside of the school day, for teachers to gather as colleagues, with a lead teacher trained as a facilitator. A group process encourages teachers to reflect on their own and others' classroom practices and ways to adapt their own classroom practices to improve student learning. We have observed several instances of this form of professional development and were particularly struck by the quality of the dialogue among the participating teachers. The mathematical content focus was maintained, and deep issues regarding student misconceptions and ways to overcome them by modifying instruction were discussed at length. Teachers felt the time was well spent, and they were energized to return to their classrooms with new approaches and a positive attitude about working with their students.

Structured Exploration   *Structured Exploration* begins with a meeting of mathematics teachers working together on a mathematics investigation intending to reveal students' algebraic thinking. These teachers complete the investigation on their own and share some solution approaches with one another. During the next week or two, the teachers give the investigation to at least one class and reflect on the student thinking revealed by reading their papers. The teachers bring a sample, including high, low, and middle papers, to the next meeting and participate in a facilitated discussion of what they can infer about student thinking from reviewing the collective group of papers. Hearing other teachers' inferences about student work is an important part of the process, as is discussion of the classroom situations under which the investigation was presented.

Of course, these three different reflections—on one's own thinking, on one's students' thinking, and on one's colleagues' thinking—do not take place in isolation or in a neat sequence. Rather, all three occur at each step in the reflecting process. Through continuing discussion over a period of time and over several problems, "teachers internalize mathematics as a way of thinking, rather than only as a compilation of discrete topics and procedures; they can begin to encourage similar thinking in their students" (Kelemanik, 1997, p. 1).

When working through the steps of the process, the teacher may ask the following questions:

Step 1: Doing Mathematics With Colleagues

- Reflecting on one's own thinking . . . How am I making sense of the mathematics? How did I come to look at and approach the mathematics in this investigation in the way that I did?
- Reflecting on colleagues' thinking . . . How were our approaches alike or different? What assumptions or intuitions led to each of our approaches? What are the mathematical connections between the different approaches?
- Reflecting on students' thinking . . . How might students' approaches be similar to or different from mine or my colleagues? What mathematical assumptions might students make in working on this investigation?

Step 2: Collecting and Analyzing Student Work

- Reflecting on students' thinking . . . Since I am working only from what I see on the student's paper, what inferences am I making about the student's thinking from his or her written work? What do I think I know about how the student thinks about the underlying mathematics? How can I find out whether my inferences are accurate?

- Reflecting on one's own thinking . . . How am I making sense of the mathematics in this piece of student work? How does the student's approach compare with my own? How did I come to look at and approach the mathematics in the ways that I did?

- Reflecting on colleagues' thinking . . . How were the inferences drawn from a piece of student work similar or different? What questions did my colleagues have and why? What are the mathematical connections between the different approaches?

In structured exploration, real data guide the conversation. Teachers work on a common investigation and bring in student work from that same investigation. This makes it easier to examine and compare the different approaches taken within the same investigation, and to reflect on the mathematics. In this way, the process emphasizes the role of teacher as learner and researcher. Teachers have the opportunity to focus on what they can learn from the investigation and the student work. These are insights that shape their role as instructors. In order to be effective instructors, capable of supporting rich mathematical thinking in students, teachers need to understand how such thinking develops across and within grades and what its various manifestations are. Investigating mathematics through a structured exploration process helps them do this" (Kelemanik, 1997, pp. 1–5).[1]

Mathematics Teaching Cases

Mathematics Teaching Cases focuses on fractions, decimals, ratios, and percents. The materials include 30 case studies for discussion that fall into the following categories: "Inside Student Thoughts," "Making Sense or Memorizing Rules?" "Teaching as Questioning," "Reflecting," "Manipulatives Aren't Magic," "What Next?" "Connections," and "This Wasn't My Plan." Each vignette is followed by several suggested readings. The textbook with the cases is accompanied by a separate *Facilitator's Discussion Guide.*

As in the *Structured Exploration,* having a trained facilitator is key to the effectiveness of this professional development strategy. In contrast to *Structured Exploration,* the *Mathematics Teaching Cases* model (see Figure 12.1) uses written descriptions of a real classroom situation in which a teacher was confronted with an instructional dilemma—students did not understand a fraction concept for which instruction had been provided. Using a facilitated format, teachers look at the facts of the case and then identify and discuss issues raised by the case. The insights gained about students' misconceptions

prove valuable to a teacher trying to decide what to do next in the classroom, especially at the middle-school level, where fraction/rational number understanding is key to further progress in mathematics.

The purpose of discussing cases is *not* to criticize the teachers, but to collaborate in reflection and critical examination on practice, and to generate different points of view on situations for which simple answers do not exist. The cases have been carefully crafted to provide thoughtful discourse for professional development. Following are some of the questions and issues raised by this case that are noted in the *Facilitator's Discussion Guide:*

- Language issues . . . Should the teacher have avoided using *take* and stated the problem another way? How might this have been done? Do students need to understand the language used in this way at some point?

- What is a whole? . . . The idea that the whole may be a part of something *or* a set of things must be developed if students are going to acquire a deep understanding of basic fraction ideas.

- Multiplying by a fraction . . . Amanda pointed out the relationship between multiplying by a fraction and dividing by a whole number. Why does this work?

- Beliefs about teaching . . . Should the teacher have given a little more guidance? How much guidance can a teacher give and still be teaching from a constructivist point of view?

- Conceal or reveal students' incorrect solutions? . . . The teacher in the take one-third case purposely called on several students to present their solutions without first checking to see whether the student had the correct solution. . . . What does it do to a student's self-esteem to display an incorrect solution? (Barnett, Goldstein, & Jackson, 1996, pp. 2–3)

Set 12.2   *Discussion Questions*

Questions with an asterisk appear in the Message Board section of the Companion Website at **http://www.prenhall.com/huetinck.** Go to Chapter 12 and click on the Message Board to find and respond to the question.

*1. Work through a nonstandard mathematics problem with a fellow mathematics educator. Together, discuss the three cycles of *Structured Exploration* by examining your thinking.

2. Determine and write up how you would teach the "Take One-Third" lesson in Figure 12.1.

---

[1] *Structured Exploration* © 1997 Education Development Center, Inc., Newton, MA. Reprinted with permission.

Figure 12.1
Sample Case Study From *Mathematics Teaching Cases*

Take One-Third

As my seventh- and eighth-graders entered our classroom and found their seats, their attention turned to the "starter problem" written on the overhead. I asked them to work on it silently in preparation for the day's lesson on multiplying fractions.

> *On your own, draw a picture where you take ⅓ of 1⅓.*
> *Hint: Start with a picture of 1 ⅓.*

I finished administrative tasks as the students worked, then walked around to look at their pictures. I decided to ask Linda and Bob to show their solutions on the board, so that I could illustrate the use of both continuous and discrete fractions. We turned first to Linda's picture.

"How did you start the problem, Linda?"

"I just drew 1 and ⅓," she said.

"So this circle represents a whole, and this piece is ⅓ of another equal-sized whole?"

"Yeah."

Several students commented that they had drawn very similar pictures. I asked Linda to explain how she solved the problem.

"I just took away ⅓ from 1 and ⅓," she answered, as she crossed out the ⅓.

"Listen to what you just said," I prompted.

"I just took away ⅓ from 1 and ⅓," Linda insisted.

"What operation did you say out loud?" I asked.

"Take away—subtraction."

When I directed her attention back to the problem on the overhead, she looked confused, saying: "Take ⅓ of 1⅓. I don't get it. This is weird."

Still hoping the class would be able to discover the proper procedure on its own, I switched to Bob, expecting that his solution would be both correct and easier for the class to understand.

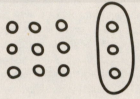

He explained how he started. "I thought of 9 spots being in the whole and then 3 more would be ⅓."

"So how did you find ⅓ of 1 1⁄3?"

"I just took ⅓," he replied, indicating three of the spots.

"You should take 4," Jim and a few other students cried out. I asked them to think about what it means to take ⅓, giving a hint by pointing to the denominator.

"Divide them into 3 equal groups," Amanda volunteered, "and you get 1 of those groups or ⅓."

Source: Barnett, C., Goldstein, D., & Jackson, B. (Eds.). (1994). *Mathematics Teaching Cases: Fractions, Decimals, Ratios and Percents. Hard to Teach and Hard to Learn.* Far West Laboratory for Educational Research and Development. Portsmouth, NH: Heinemann. Reprinted with permission.

Vignette 12.3 One Teacher's Experiences

In 1986 I first became aware of the field of operations research and its emerging topics that have made up the basis of courses in discrete mathematics. After hearing Henry Pollock of Bell Laboratories speak, I attended a series of workshops sponsored in our school district that were presented by professors of mathematics from a nearby university. Upon completing more work in the field of discrete mathematics, I started a pilot course at my high school in 1988 for students who had completed Math Analysis but were not inclined to take Advanced Placement Calculus. The course content often is appealing to students attracted to the humanities because of its practical applications to social choice, business and finance, marketing, optimization, and other decision-making fields.

The course was well received by the students, and I began giving presentations to other teachers on the topics of discrete mathematics at workshops and eventually at conferences, seminars, and institutes on both local and national levels. For example, I presented a 3-week course for mathematics teachers as part of a National Science Foundation grant for 3 years. I worked as the West Area Coordinator part-time and as the Teacher Coordinator for a local project. The NCTM was preparing the first national standards at that time and asked our network to read and amend the first draft. I was delighted to see the topics of discrete mathematics included at all grade levels, as well as a separate course in high school.

Over the next several years I worked with several mathematics advisors for our school district on having

Figure 12.1

Sample Case Study From *Mathematics Teaching Cases (continued)*

Then I attempted a real life example that would relate Bob's problem to the previous day's lesson. I asked them to imagine that Bob's items were Popsicles and to think about ⅓ of all of them. Bob could get one part, his brother another equal part, and his mom another third. His dad is on a diet. How many Popsicles would it be fair for Bob to eat? Jane and several students said 4, a few said 3. I called on Jane to explain.

"⅓ of 12 is 4. You just divide," she replied.

"So we weren't supposed to take away ⅓. These are division problems," Max realized. "why didn't you tell us?" The whole class was a little unhappy with my "deception."

All this took place in a general math class in a medium-sized suburban middle school with 850 students. There were twenty seventh-graders and six eighth-graders in the class. I had chosen fractions as one of my teacher-evaluation curricular areas for the year.

I had begun the unit by giving a pretest on basic fraction concepts and operations, including some word problems. Because the scores were on average very low, I decided to spend a couple of months working with these ideas so my students would show substantial growth on the post-test.

We spent the first few weeks developing meaning for fractions, placing a strong emphasis on being able to draw a picture of a fraction amount. Most pictures showed subdivisions in rectangles. with number lines being used occasionally. I offered examples of work with discrete fractions, such as ¹²⁄₂₄ meaning 12 of the 24 original pieces

of candy in a box, which in turn means the box is half full. By the time we reached the current lesson, the students also had some experience drawing representations of subtraction problems such as:

$$\frac{1}{2} - \frac{3}{8}$$

On the day before this lesson the students had worked on pictures that introduced the concept of fraction multiplication. They had sketched problems such as ⅓ of 27 pieces of gum and had figured ¼ of 16 candles. The word *multiplication* had not been formally used at this point.

So here we were trying to begin a lesson on multiplying fractions, and now Linda's work had revealed that she thought we were talking about subtraction. Then, from Bob's example the class had impulsively concluded that "you just divide." I wondered if it had been a mistake to follow my usual custom of having students experiment with a new concept on their own before the formal lesson. Was it practical—or possible—to capitalize on these misunderstandings and proceed with the lesson? Or should I have started over and approached the lesson by giving a little more guidance?

I now see that similarities in the language of multiplying and subtracting fractions call for a careful choice of words. But beyond that, my own understanding of fractions has been shaken by Max's statement. It seems that you do divide when multiplying fractions. But how am I going to make sense of that to my students?

the course offered on a districtwide basis. Most were unable or unwilling to make headway with their superiors. There was a string of reasons—changing personnel, political consideration, waiting for the entire mathematics curriculum to be revised, and so on. I did keep pushing by meeting with each new appointee and updating the materials and textbook lists as new ones became available. Finally, this year a course in discrete mathematics is in the official list of course offerings by my large urban school district. The topic of discrete mathematics has also been incorporated into all of the integrated mathematics materials in the last few years so that future courses in discrete mathematics will begin at a higher level and advance to greater depths than is now possible.

The empowerment that I gained as a result of working in professional development activities gave me the confidence to determine the curriculum for my own courses and the ability to work collaboratively with my colleagues. I discovered that it is possible for one teacher, after years of rather isolated classroom teaching, to make

changes not only in her own classes but on a much broader scale when there is support from a network.

Kathy Blackwood
Venice High School
Los Angeles Unified School District

THE NATIONAL BOARD FOR PROFESSIONAL TEACHING STANDARDS

A set of portfolio items can be submitted to the National Board for Professional Teaching Standards (NBPTS) for the candidate (the teacher) to obtain national certification—a high honor for any teacher. Educational Testing Service (ETS) oversees the development of assessment materials, operations and scoring under a grant from the U.S. Department of

Education and the National Science Foundation in collaboration with exemplary teachers.[2] Teachers wishing to become certified by the National Board prepare four portfolio entries and take a content exam at an examination center to demonstrate their expertise. The portfolios are assessed by practicing classroom teachers who have demonstrated excellence in instruction, have participated in professional growth activities, and are specially trained as NBPTS evaluators. The portfolio requirements are geared to subject area and to student age. Some states and some school districts give salary increases of up to 15% for board certification, provide mentors for the process, and pay for the exam.

The standards written by ETS allows certification candidates to select examples of their practice to illustrate what accomplished mathematics teachers should know and be able to implement in their classroom. (These NBPTS standards are consistent with but not identical to the NCTM *Standards*.)

While there is a separate statement of the scoring criteria for each of the portfolio entries, in general, the *Standards*—and therefore, the assessment—rest on a fundamental philosophical foundation expressed in the National Board's five core propositions:

- Teachers are committed to students and their learning.
- Teachers know the subjects they teach and how to teach those subjects to students.
- Teachers are responsible for managing and monitoring student learning.
- Teachers think systematically about their practice and learn from experience.
- Teachers are members of learning communities (*Mathematics Adolescence and Young Adulthood*, 2002–2003, p. 3).

A set of documents is available from NBPTS to guide teachers in preparing entries, including hints for videotaping and how to make good selections. The portfolio preparation is to take place during the teaching in one school year and is designed to sample practices already in place. Brief descriptions of the three types of portfolio entries follow:

1. *Samples of students' work entitled "Developing and Assessing Mathematical Thinking and Reasoning."* The written commentary must be not longer than 12 typed pages and includes two student responses to two activities from the chosen instructional sequence. These activities must "support each other in developing student understanding of an important mathematical idea

and give you information about each student's understanding" (2002–2003, p. 3). In four main sections, the applicant: (1) describes the instructional context of the class selected; (2) relates, the planning of the students' understanding to the pertinent concepts; (3) analyzes the students' responses for evidence of achievement of learning goals and conceptual understanding; and (4) reflects on the next steps for instruction and if and how to use the lesson again. The NBPTS documents include a number of questions to consider for each section, which assist the teacher in providing the information requested.

2. *Two entries based primarily on videotape clips:*
   - *Instructional Analysis: Whole Class Mathematical Discourse.* The teacher videotapes a whole class as he engages the class in exploring a concept, technique, and/or reasoning method of mathematics. The tape is 15 minutes long. The written commentary—a maximum of 12 teacher-written pages and 2 pages of instructional materials—includes instructional content, planning, analysis of evidence of students' mathematical communication and thinking evidence on the videotape, and reflections on the videotape and lesson. Each section includes questions for the applicant to consider when composing the portfolio entry.
   - *Instructional Analysis: Small Group Mathematical Collaborations.* The 15-minute video made for this entry features the teacher interacting with small groups of students engaged in exploration and discussion. The entry highlights how the teacher enables students to be at least partly responsible for their own learning and that of their group. The written commentary is similar in form to the Whole Class entry.

3. *Documented accomplishments: contributions to student learning.* This entry gives applicants the opportunity to communicate their professional work outside the classroom with parents, family, community, and colleagues. One section is entitled "Families and Communities," and the other is "Contributing to the Professional Community."

4. *Mathematics content exam.* The applicant takes an exam from the areas of algebra, geometry, statistics, discrete mathematics, and calculus.

Several restrictions apply on the time period of the instruction and the age of the students featured. The three first entries listed above must come from different units of study, different lessons, and different times during the same calendar school year in which the candidate applied. In addition, 51% of the students must be between the ages of 14 and 18 for

---

[2]Materials in this section are reprinted with permission of the National Board for Professional Teaching Standards, from *Adolescence and Young Adulthood/Mathematics Standards for National Board Certification*, November 1996. All rights reserved.

Adolescence and Young Adulthood certification. For the Middle School Mathematics: Early Adolescence certification, the majority of students must be between 11 and 15 years of age. The pieces of the Early Adolescent portfolio are quite similar to those of Adolescence and Young Adulthood portfolio.

 For information about NBPTS, go to **http://www.prenhall.com/huetinck** and click on Web Destinations for Chapter 12.

Set 12.3 *Discussion Questions*

 Questions with an asterisk appear in the Message Board section of the Companion Website at **http://www.prenhall.com/huetinck.** Go to Chapter 12 and click on the Message Board to find and respond to the question.

1. Design and discuss a lesson that would show the teacher's talents in whole-group discussion to be submitted to NBPTS.
2. Design and discuss a lesson that would show the teacher's talents in small-group discussion to be submitted to NBPTS.
*3. Point out the differences to consider when planning the whole-group video and the small-group video.

LIFELONG LEARNING

After you become comfortable in your teaching environment, you probably will want to extend your teaching abilities and content knowledge, as most teachers do. In addition to the avenues of involvement in professional organizations mentioned earlier, you may become interested in further formal schooling or becoming a teacher leader.

Master's Degree

Both for reasons of salary increase and for love of knowledge, consider beginning a graduate-level program about 3 to 5 years after you begin teaching. The program may be housed in a university's school of education or in a department of mathematics. Some master's degree programs are beginning to include the NBPTS entries as part of the required course work. With a cohort of fellow teachers and help from college professors, you can get practice making videos and writing up teaching experiences to apply later for national board certification.

Online Professional Development

With the increasing use of computers, more and more innovative ways are available for online professional development. We would like to recommend one of these that is currently free, funded by the U.S. Department of Education, The PBS Teacherline. The program has five key components: the Virtual Mathematics Academy, Facilitated Learning Modules, TeacherLine Certification Program, Community Center, and Resources. The first two provide particularly interesting assists to individual professional growth.

The Virtual Mathematics Academy, developed by NCTM and PBS Teacherline, helps teachers in the four grade bands to apply the six principles in the PSSM. You can investigate strategies through interactive activities, video resources, and key resources. Then reflect on what you have learned after designing and putting plans into action. Teachers can use multiple resources, including videos from NCTM Academy Institutes, NCTM publications, PBS Mathline, and lesson plans. The application proceeds through a self-paced four-step process: define, explore, plan, and implement. In addition, there are opportunities for interaction on discussion boards and chats with experts. The anticipated focus will be on teaching algebra and geometry.

The Facilitated Learning Modules explore pedagogical issues in mathematics and technology integration. This segment is designed to meet the standards of the International Society for Technology in Education (ISTE) and the NCTM. Through modules of videos, slides, and animation simulations, you can implement what you learn and merge theory with real-life scenarios. Renowned producers have made the modules in two categories focusing on mathematics and technology. Each module contains announcements, reading, assessment, assignments, video clips, activities, a recommended schedule, and a facilitator's guide. These modules are appropriate for either preservice or inservice teachers. Each module may be easily integrated into other professional development programs on any level.

Some school districts currently give professional development credits for salary promotion based on these materials, as do some university extension programs. This program is only one of several online professional development opportunities, which will surely be increasing in the next few years.

 Go to Web Destinations for Chapter 12 at **http://www.prenhall.com/huetinck** for links to teacher preparation.

Summary

Teachers love to learn as much as they love to teach. The common reason for continuing professional development is to improve facility in teaching by keeping abreast of new curriculum, pedagogy, and technology. Also, we may want to study new areas of mathematics or take higher-level mathematics courses than those required for a teaching credential. Teachers can enhance their programs by reflection through projects, conferences, further degrees, and special certification. The real reason we continue in lifelong learning is that it keeps alive the joy of teaching.

INSTRUCTIONAL RESOURCES

Aichele, D. B., & Coxford, A. F. (1994). *Professional development for teachers of mathematics*. Reston, VA: National Council of Teachers of Mathematics.

This 1994 NCTM Yearbook includes 29 articles grouped under the headings of professional development issues and perspectives, initial preparation of teachers of mathematics, and professional development for practicing teachers of mathematics.

Evaluating educators. (2001). *Educational Leadership, 58(5)*, 6–68.

This issue, of value to all educators, begins with a discussion with Lee Shulman about good teaching. Following this are discussions of merit pay, ideas of how to evaluate experienced teachers, and ways to help struggling teachers.

Hart, L. C., Schultz, K., Majee-ullah, D., and Nash, L. (1992, September). The role of reflection in teaching. *Arithmetic Teacher, 40(1)*, 40–42.

This is a very friendly article about how to become a reflective practitioner.

Johnson, R. W. (1993, October). Where can teacher research lead? One teacher's daydream. *Educational Leadership*.

This article introduces the wide subject of classroom research in reflective teaching—a subject beyond the scope of this text.

Keeping teaching fresh. (2000). *Educational Leadership, 57(8)*, 8–75.

This issue contains 19 articles devoted to keeping teaching alive for teachers, administrators, professional developers, university professors, and even substitute teachers.

Lubienski, S. T. (1999). Problem centered mathematics teaching. *Mathematics Teaching in the Middle School, 5(4)*, 250–256.

The subtitle, "Three teachers search for understanding of problem-centered instruction," is an appropriate description of the journey of three teachers who collaborate to improve learning for their students.

Nielsen, L. J., & de Villiers, M. (1997). *Is democracy fair? The mathematics of voting and apportionment.* Berkeley, CA: Key Curriculum Press.

This book has 18 activities exploring the real-world applications of mathematics in differing methods such as making election decisions and in methods of apportionment. Calculator explorations and research questions are considered in each activity.

Panasuk, R. M., and Sullivan, M. M. (1999). Powerful connections: An opportunity for professional growth. *Mathematics Teaching in the Middle Schools, 5(1)*, 46–52.

The article describes a long-term professional development project involving all the teachers of an urban middle school in collaboration with a university. A significant element of the success of this project is that the teachers themselves selected the methods to investigate more effective teaching practices.

Stein, M. K., & Smith, M. S. (1998). Mathematical tasks as a framework for reflection: From research to practice. *Mathematics Teaching in the Middle School, 3(4)*, 268–275.

The use of reflective practices incorporated in the Quantitative Understanding Amplifying Student Achievement and Reasoning (QUASAR) Project is explained as a vehicle to make teachers aware of how they teach and how their students perform.

EXEMPLARY LESSONS

F O R   T E A C H E R S

Exemplary Lesson 12.1 Voting (page 1 of 2)

I have found students (and teachers) to be surprised at the many ways there are to conduct an election other than the plurality method. At the start of a unit on voting, small groups should brainstorm on various ways to select a class favorite "anything."

They will usually come up with plurality, run-offs (There are different types of run-offs.), and some kind of a point system (as in sports seedings) with a little prodding. After studying various methods, the following activity is helpful in having students realize where they can use math in their lives. I've had students develop this idea for their semester projects also.

An application of voting methods to personal decision making.

Liz is a senior in high school trying to make a decision on which college to attend next fall. After many applications, she has been accepted by several and has narrowed her choices down to four schools for final consideration. The criteria that she considers important are cost, location, prestige, and size. First she ranks each school according to these categories.

| Rank | Criteria (Weight) | | | |
	Cost (3)	Location (2)	Prestige (2)	Size (1)
First	UCLA	UCLA	Harvard	Harvard
Second	USC	USC	Stanford	Stanford
Third	Stanford	Stanford	UCLA	USC
Fourth	Harvard	Harvard	USC	UCLA

Liz considers the cost to be the most important factor, so she weights it by 3. Location and prestige are equally important (weight 2), and size is least important (weight 1).

1. Which school is the Condorcet winner? Explain why there is not always a winner by this method. How can you amend the method to find a winner?

2. Use the Borda method to determine the winner. You can give 4 points for every first-place vote, 3 for every second place, etc.

3. Suppose Liz decides between the first two schools that accepted her application, USC and Stanford. The next acceptance is from Harvard, which she puts up against the winner from the first two schools. Finally, she decides between that winner and UCLA. Would the "agenda effect" make any difference if the acceptances came in a different order? Why?

4. Make up a problem similar to this one where you need to make a decision in your own life.

FOR TEACHERS

Exemplary Lesson 12.1 Voting (page 2 of 2)

Answers

1. <u>UCLA (7)</u> vs USC (1); <u>UCLA (5)</u> vs Stanford (3); <u>UCLA (5)</u> vs Harvard (3). UCLA is the winner in all two-way votes, but there is not always one that can win over all others. Then you could use Duncan Black's method of counting the number of wins each has in two-way votes.

2. UCLA: $3(4) + 2(4) + 2(2) + 1(1) = 25$
   USC: $3(3) + 2(3) + 2(1) + 1(2) = 19$
   Stanford: $3(2) + 2(2) + 2(3) + 1(3) = 19$
   Harvard: $3(1) + 2(1) + 2(4) + 1(4) = 17$

3. <u>USC (5)</u> vs Stanford (3); <u>USC (5)</u> vs Harvard (3); USC (1) vs <u>UCLA (7).</u> It would not matter which order the offers came in because UCLA can win over all 3.

4. Answers will vary. Some examples might be about which elective to take next semester, with whom to go to the prom, where to go on vacation, what job to take, etc.

Source: Kathy Blackwood. Used with permission.

F O R   T E A C H E R S

Exemplary Lesson 12.2 Iteration and Home-Screen Programming (page 1 of 3)

Iteration, the act of repeating a process over and over, has taken on a new ease and importance because of the TI-82/83 answer key. Applied to a series of well-formed commands linked by colons, iteration can be used by students and teachers to create simple exploratory "programs" without ever leaving the home screen. These programs have many virtues, including their ease of creation and modification and the simplicity with which they can be interrupted and resumed after examining a stat plot of partial results.

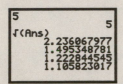

Figure 1

1. When we pick a number and enter it using the **enter** key, we sometimes refer to that number as a *seed,* and the calculator considers it to be its last answer. It is interesting and frequently instructive to seed the calculator with any number and then iterate it under an operation using the **ans** key. For example, if we enter 5 and then try the square root of **ans,** we see a sequence of numbers converging on 1 as we repeatedly hit the **enter** key. Figure 1 illustrates this idea. Let's expand on this technique.

Figure 2

2. Simple interest is routinely explored in many basic math classes using the $i = p \cdot r \cdot t$ formula in a straightforward fashion, but the problem becomes much more interesting when we let the interest compound (that is, when we let the interest accumulate along with the principal). In the interest of simplicity, let's take $100 compounded at 8% yearly. If we start with 100 **enter,** then 1.08**ans** is our recursive formula, and **enter, enter, enter** produces the account balances when interest is paid. The most difficult thing about this process is counting the number of years, and here is a way of solving that problem. The calculator understands the terms of the sequence (0, 100) to be **ans(1)** and **ans(2),** so our recursive statement is built to modify both, and we can let the calculator do the counting for us, as shown in Figure 2.

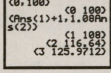

Figure 3

3. The final skill we need to start writing programs is simply an understanding of linking commands with colons. Figure 3 is an example. When we press the **enter** key, 1 is stored into both *A* and *B*. Then a three-step process that temporarily stores the sum and then moves everything down is repeated, forming the Fibonacci sequence. This is what I call a "home-screen program." The next step will be to add commands allowing us to save the data to the lists for examination with "zoom stats" as we work.

FOR TEACHERS

Exemplary Lesson 12.2 Iteration and Home-Screen Programming (page 2 of 3)

4. Let's return to the simple-interest example above and fancy up the commands as shown in Figure 4. The top line sets a counter, N, to 0, fixes an initial amount of money in A, and sets the interest rate at 8% before clearing out lists 1 and 2 to store the partial results. After that is done, the next command line starts the counter, stores it as list 1, calculates the new balance, and stores that to list 2. Some partial results are shown in the center of Figure 4. We can, at any time, pause to view a stat plot of the balances to date. We might even want the class to model the results with an equation in $y =$ to reinforce the exponential idea.

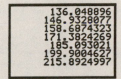 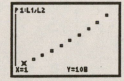

Figure 4

It is easy to quit back to the home screen and pick up the iteration where we left off. Those interested might want to include a "round, 2" command in the iterated statement to return a nicely formatted result.

Here is the best part. At any time, using the "2nd enter" process, we can retrieve the initial commands, edit any part, and repeat the experiment. For example, in the left-hand screen above, $(1 + I)A + 100$ **store** A will let us see the long-term effect of an extra annual deposit of $100.

5. Infinite series is another fruitful area for investigation using home-screen programming. A simple example is the alternating harmonic series for ln 2.

The terms are $1 - \frac{1}{2} + \frac{1}{3} - \frac{1}{4} + \cdots$. It is slow to converge but easy to compute. Figure 5 illustrates the program. These command lines start to look very familiar after a while, but there are two or three new ideas here. We need to produce alternating signs, hence the power of -1. We need to accumulate a series total, so setting T to 0 and adding each new fraction to it will accomplish that, and the last command, showing T as a fraction, is not necessary but adds a new dimension to the activity. Note that the fraction notation breaks down at some point. The last screen is a zoom stat of the data. We still have some way to go to .69315, but we can pause at any time, look at the graph, and go back to collect more information. Students might also want to graph $y = \ln 2$ on the screen for comparison. As long as the correct stat plot is turned on, moving back and forth is easy.

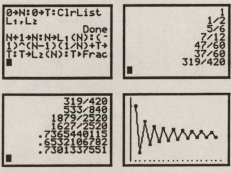

Figure 5

FOR TEACHERS

Exemplary Lesson 12.2 Iteration and Home-Screen Programming (page 3 of 3)

6. A more interesting series is the one for e^x, $1 + x + \dfrac{x^2}{2!} + \dfrac{x^3}{3!} + \cdots$. The simplest case would be just to find e, so let's work on that first. Figure 6 shows the sequence of commands to be iterated. Note that the first line is identical to the previous exercise and that the second line is even easier, so why don't you try the problem yourself before reading the code in detail?

Did you peek? Students should be encouraged to test the results with paper and pencil to at least convince themselves that the iteration is working. Note how much faster this series converges to e. The 10th term is already to 2.7182815. Would you agree that visualizing the convergence adds to students' understanding?

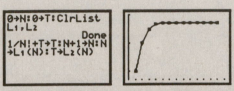

Figure 6

7. The final example involves a nice application of Euler's method to a simple velocity/height problem. It was suggested to me by an outstanding teacher and good friend, Allen Martin from Loyola High School in Los Angeles. In the problem a ball is thrown up with an initial velocity of 60 ft./sec. Without invoking equations of motion, what can we conclude about the velocity and height over time? Let's assume a constant velocity for a small increment of time—in this case, .1 sec. Calculate the resulting changes in v and h, and store the results (See Figure 7). The second screen is a partial picture, and the third compares the result, shown as a dotted curve with the equation of motion. Play with the chosen time interval, D, to refine the calculation. Working on a problem like this requires a careful discussion of the modeling assumptions involved, and I would certainly want the students to hand calculate the first few data points.

So where do we go from here? I have demonstrated a selection of applications of the home-screen technique, but it is in no way exhaustive. Newton's method for roots and the logistic population model are topics easily explored using these techniques. I am almost continuously running into new situations where this type of investigation can be rewarding. You are encouraged to apply the idea if you feel that it would be productive.

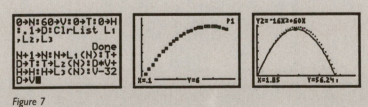

Figure 7

Source: Tom Walters, twalters@lausd.k12.ca.us. Used with permission.

FOR STUDENTS

Exemplary Lesson 12.3
The Unit Circle (page 1 of 2)

This activity about the unit circle would be done in the demonstration mode since students do not have access to a class set of T1-92s.

The figure—including circle, point A, point P, segment OP, measure of angle, and coordinates of P—would be prepared before class.

During class we would move point P and see how the measure of the angle and the corrdinates of point P change. P would then be animated and the data for one complete cycle of P on the circle would be collected.

We would investigate the data—developing that the *x*-coordinate is the cosine of the angle and the *y*-coordinate is the sine of the angle.

The graphs of the angle vs *x*-coordinate and angle vs *y*-coordinate would be created.

Directions: Follow the numbered directions.

1. Clear **sysdata.** There are two ways to do this. On home screen, type **Delvar sysdata** and press **ENTER.** Machine responses "done." The second way is to go to **2nd VAR-LINK** and manage it from that screen.

2. Open a new Geometry figure. Call it unitcirc. **APPS 8 Geometry 3 New**

3. Press **F8 9:** or ♦**F** to get the format screen. You need to turn on the coordinate axes.

4. Place the number 1 on the screen: **F7 6:Numerical Edit.**

5. Transfer this number to the *x*-axis: **F4 9:Measurement Transfer.** Point to the number and press **ENTER.** Point to the *x*-axis and press **ENTER.** A point should appear on the *x*-axis at the 1-unit scale mark. Call it point *A*.

6. Draw a circle with center at the origin and a radius of 1: **F3 1.** Point to the origin (be sure you get the message "this center point") **ENTER.** Then point to the point *A* you created on the *x*-axis (wait for message "this radius point") **ENTER.**

7. Find the equation of the circle: **F6 5: Equation & Coordinates.** You need to point to the circle **ENTER.** You may want to drag the equation to another location.

8. Locate a point on the circle **F2 2: Point on Object.** Call it point *P*.

9. Draw a segment from this point to the center of the circle: **F2 5:Segment.**

10. Mark the angle: **F7 7: Mark Angle.** Mark the angle starting with the point on the *x*-axis, next to the origin, and the point on the angle. The order is very important. Measure the angle: **F6 3:Angle.** Point to the mark. **ENTER.**

11. Find the coordinates of the point on the circle: **F6 5: Equation & Coordinates.**

12. Now collect some data: **F6 7:Collect Data 2: Define Entry.** Point to angle measure **ENTER;** point to *x*-coordinate **ENTER;** point to *y*-coordinate **ENTER.**

13. To store the data, **F6 7: Collect Data 1:Store Data ENTER.**

14. Animate the point that is on the circle and on the terminal side of the angle. Animate it in a counterclockwise direction, and make sure it goes around the circle at least once: **F7 3: Animation.** When the message "this point" appears, press down the hand, and use the right portion of the cursor pad to pull out the spring to the right.

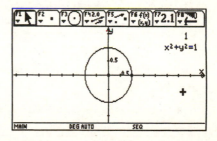

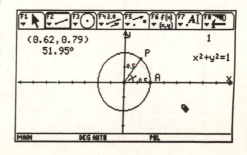

F O R   S T U D E N T S

Exemplary Lesson 12.3
The Unit Circle (page 2 of 2)

15. Now go to the Data Matrix Editor, **APPS 6 2: Open.** Find "Sysdata" **ENTER.** Remember the angle measure is in c_1, x-coordinate in c_2, and y-coordinate in c_3.

16. Do a plot **Setup F2 F1.** We want *a scatter, c1, c2.* To see the plot, **♦E Window, F2 ZOOM 9: Zoom Data.** What is the equation of this curve?

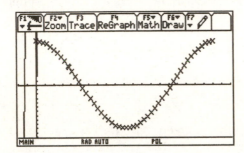 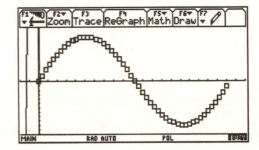

17. Also plot c_1 and c_3. What is the equation of this curve?

18. Go back to your data: **APPS 6 2: Open.** Find "Sysdata" **ENTER.** In c_4, type in $c_2^2 + c_3^2$. What happens?

DATA	∠	x coor	y coor		
	c1	c2	c3	c4	c5
1	66.251	.40274	.91532		
2	72.	.30902	.95106		
3	79.2	.18738	.98229		
4	86.4	.06279	.99803		
5	93.6	⁻.0628	.99803		
6	100.8	⁻.1874	.98229		
7	108.	⁻.309	.95106		

$c4=(c2)^2+(c3)^2$

19. In c_5, type in $\cos(c_1)$. In c_6, type in $\sin(c_1)$. What are your observations? Be sure you are in ***degree mode***.

DATA	x coor	y coor		cos(c...	sin(c...
	c2	c3	c4	c5	c6
1	.40274	.91532	1.	.40274	
2	.30902	.95106	1.	.30902	
3	.18738	.98229	1.	.18738	
4	.06279	.99803	1.	.06279	
5	⁻.0628	.99803	1.	⁻.0628	
6	⁻.1874	.98229	1.	⁻.1874	
7	⁻.309	.95106	1.	⁻.309	

$c6=\sin(c1)$

Source: Kathy Layton. Used with permission.

FOR TEACHERS

Exemplary Lesson 12.4 Dr. Pepper on the Ramp (page 1 of 4)

INTRODUCTION

The new Advanced Placement Calculus syllabi emphasize the idea that derivatives are functions whose values are rates of change. Below is an example of how simple technological devices can be used to bring this idea to the forefront as students encounter the concept of a derivative for the first time. The lessons described have been successfully used in a number of school settings. This paper presents an example of how the use of technology can enliven and enhance the introduction of a core mathematical idea.

OUTLINE OF A TECHNIQUE FOR INTRODUCING THE CALCULUS OF QUADRATIC FUNCTIONS THROUGH DATA ANALYSIS

This lesson comes from the W. M. Keck Curriculum Project course called *The Mathematical Analysis of Change*. It is in teaching the MAC course that the lessons and assignments summarized below have been taught at several schools over the course of the past five years. The cover includes graphs of the position function and associated velocity function. In creating descriptions of these functions students are led to a correct conjecture about the relationship between a quadratic function and its derivative.

Attached to the end of this short summary is a data set collected by use of a motion sensor placed at the top of a ramp about 10 feet long. A piece of tape had been placed across the ramp so that its upper edge was 6 feet from the front of the motion sensor. The sensor was activated as a can of Dr. Pepper was released to roll down the ramp.

The lessons and assignments summarized have also been experienced by teachers in workshops given on the MAC course. My experience is that they constitute a very effective technology-based introduction to a central idea—there are patterns in changing rates of change whose description can be discovered and related to the descriptions of patterns in other data sets arising from the same event. The students come to see this as one of the goals of calculus.

SUMMARY OF KEY STEPS IN THE DISCOVERY OF THE DIFFERENTIAL CALCULUS OF QUADRATIC FUNCTIONS:

Step #1: FINDING A PATTERN IN THE (TIME, POSITION) DATA POINTS:

The students take part in a monitoring of the movement of the can of Dr. Pepper down the ramp. The coordinates of the data points attached to this summary were obtained in the same way, and they are transferred to a pair of lists in the students' calculators. The students then speculate on the type of function whose graph might at least come very close to passing through the data points.

Because of previous experience with motion data the students suggest trying a quadratic model. In teaching the course we guide the students to selecting a representative sample of three data points. Then they use the coordinates of these data points to write a system of three linear equations whose solution they expect will be the coefficients of a quadratic model function for all the data points expressed in a standard form. Even though students choose different triples and the coordinates of their solutions differ depending on this choice, the quadratic graphs generated using these various solutions visually seem to fit the data points very well.

F O R   T E A C H E R S

Exemplary Lesson 12.4 Dr. Pepper on the Ramp (page 2 of 4)

For the purposes of the lessons to follow, it has been our choice to base the quadratic on samples of three data points rather than make use of our calculator's Quadratic Regression command, though doing so is a reasonable option.

Step #2: SEEKING A SPEED NUMBER FOR THE CAN AT ONE POINT ON ITS DESCENT DOWN THE RAMP.

The students are asked how fast the can was moving as it crossed the upper edge of the tape. Recall that the upper edge of the tape is six feet from the front of the motion sensor. At first students discuss dividing six by the time it took to reach a position closest to six feet. This would be the time for data point (1.375, 6.0534). However, this suggestion eventually gets replaced when they recall that in order for the motion sensor to function properly, the can had been started from a position about 1.5 feet in front of the sensor.

Students come to suggest computing an average speed based on the two data points (1.350, 5.9273) and (1.375, 6.0534). They think this is the best number to use as the speed as the can crossed the front edge of the tape which can be computed from the available data points.

Step #3: SEEKING A PATTERN IN A COLLECTION OF AVERAGE SPEEDS COMPUTED FROM THE DATA POINTS:

We discuss how to use the average speeds computed from the Dr. Pepper on the ramp data as the coordinate of a new set of data points. After considering some options, it is decided to pair these average speeds with the center of the time intervals. In assignments students then use consecutive data points in triples to compute a few of these data points. The average velocity is computed from the first and third data points, and the result is paired with the time measure from the middle data point.

To facilitate the collection of these (time, average velocity) data points from the (time, position) data, the following simple program is used.

```
PROGRAM: VELDATA
:ClrList L1, L2
:ClrHome
:Output (4,1"NUM
BER OF VELOCITIE
S TO BE COMPUTED
")
:Prompt N
:Output (4,1, "TIME BETWEEN
SENSOR READINGS")
:Prompt I
: For(C, 1, N, 1)
: Output(4,1, "MIDDLE TIME")
: Prompt T
: Output(4,1, "EARLIER POSITION")
: Prompt E
: Output(4,2, "LATER POSITION")
: Prompt L
: T→L1(C)
: (L-E)/(2*1)→L2 (C)
: End
```

FOR TEACHERS

Exemplary Lesson 12.4 Dr. Pepper on the Ramp (page 3 of 4)

During a lesson the students use their calculators to generate 8 to 10 (time, average speed) data points using triples of their own choosing. They are then asked whether they think there might be a pattern in this data. Because of their previous experience, they suggest looking at a scatter plot. It is always a pleasure to note the surprise some openly express when they see that these data points appear to be at least nearly collinear. When we use our calculators' Linear Regression commands on our data sets, the results usually show a correlation coefficient impressively close to 1. In doing this I have seem correlations greater than 0.999.

Once in a while a students will comment on the fact that the y-intercept of their linear model for the (time, average speed) data points is fairly close to the linear coefficient of their quadratic model for the (time, position) data points. Some have also noticed that the slope of the model line for the (time, average speed) data points is about twice the quadratic coefficient of their quadratic model. These comments are noted as "interesting."

Step #4: Seeking a Pattern in a Collection of Average Speeds Computed From in a New Way:

In assignments the students are led to recall how well the various quadratic functions we found fit the original (time, position) data points. It is then suggested that we might try computing average speeds indirectly from the quadratic models rather than directly from the data points. This is a very crucial change.

The following simple program is then to use a new collection of (time, average speed) data points. Before it is run, the students need to enter as Y1 a description of their choice of a quadratic model for the (time, position) data points. **This should be done in a way that uses the greatest number of digits possible in the coefficients.** If QuadReg is used, the regression equation can be transferred to the Y1 position.

```
PROGRAM: VELMDL
: ClrList L1, L2
: ClrHome
: Output (4,1, "NUM
BER OF VELOCITIE
S TO BE COMPUTED
")
: Prompt N
: Output (4,1, "TIM
E BETWEEN SENSOR
READINGS")
: Prompt I
: For(C.1,N,1)
: Output(4,1, "MIDDLE TIME")
: Prompt T
: ClrHome
: T→L1(C)
: )Y1(T+I)-Y1(T−I
))/(2*1)→L2(C)
: End
```

FOR TEACHERS

Exemplary Lesson 12.4 Dr. Pepper on the Ramp (page 4 of 4)

The students find that the (time, average speed) data points generated with this program are always so close to perfectly collinear that their calculators invariably give a correlation coefficient of 1. This happens regardless of their choices for the middle times they enter as they run the program. This also happens regardless of the particular quadratic expression they have entered as Y1 in the function list before running PROGRAM VELDATA.

THE REALLY NEAT DISCOVERY FOR THE STUDENTS IS THAT THE Y-INTERCEPT OF THEIR LINEAR MODEL FOR THE (TIME, AVERAGE SPEED) DATA POINTS IS ALWAYS EXACTLY THE SAME AS THE LINEAR COEFFICIENT OF THEIR QUADRATIC MODEL AND THE SLOPE OF THEIR LINEAR MODEL IS ALWAYS EXACTLY TWICE THE LEAD COEFFICIENT OF THEIR QUADRATIC MODEL.

This discovery prompts an algebraic analysis of the symmetric different quotient expression used to compute average velocities using positions computed from any quadratic model. But more significantly, it gives the students the opportunity to share in the excitement in finding simple patterns in the mathematical analysis of real events, which has been such a powerful motivation in the history of mathematics.

Dr. Pepper on the Ramp Data Set

Time (in seconds)	Position (in feet)	Time	Position
0	1.5268	0.85	3.5578
0.025	1.5449	0.875	3.6587
0.050	1.5629	0.900	3.7631
0.075	1.5881	0.925	3.8639
0.100	1.6133	0.950	3.9720
0.125	1.6285	0.975	4.0800
0.150	1.6709	1.000	4.1880
0.175	1.7069	1.025	4.3033
0.200	1.7465	1.050	4.4149
0.225	1.7825	1.075	4.5301
0.250	1.8257	1.100	4.6490
0.275	1.8653	1.125	4.7678
0.300	1.9122	1.150	4.8902
0.325	1.9626	1.175	5.0091
0.350	2.0130	1.200	5.1315
0.375	2.0706	1.225	5.2611
0.400	2.1318	1.250	5.3908
0.425	2.1930	1.275	5.5276
0.450	2.2579	1.300	5.6573
0.475	2.3191	1.325	5.7869
0.500	2.3875	1.350	5.9273
0.525	2.4667	1.375	6.0534
0.550	2.5315	1.400	6.1902
0.575	2.6108	1.425	6.3307
0.600	2.6792	1.450	6.4587
0.625	2.7484	1.475	6.6151
0.650	2.8448	1.500	6.7473
0.675	2.9421	1.525	6.8888
0.700	3.0033	1.550	7.0329
0.725	3.0861	1.575	7.1805
0.750	3.1797	1.600	7.3282
0.775	3.2698	1.625	7.4722
0.800	3.3598	1.650	7.6198
0.825	3.4570		

Source: Richard Sisley, Polytechnic School, Pasadena, CA. A description of a series of lessons which have been used to introduce the calculus of quadratic functions from the W.M. Keck Curriculum Project, Course III, The Mathematics of Change.

FOR STUDENTS

Exemplary Lesson 12.5
Kepler's Law (page 1 of 4)

Amazingly, using hundreds of years of observations and some trigonometry, astronomers by the time of Copernicus had rather accurately surveyed the solar system (at least out to Saturn, the farthest planet visible with the naked eye). The proportions of the solar system in terms of astronomical units (the distance from Earth to the Sun) were worked out, although the proper scale was not known.

Copernicus had data very similar to this table:

Planet	Distance (in AU)	Period (in Earth years)
Mercury	0.387	0.241
Venus	0.723	0.615
Earth	1.00	1.00
Mars	1.52	1.88
Jupiter	5.20	11.9
Saturn	9.53	29.5

1. Enter this data into List1 and List2 on your TI-82/83. Make a Stat Plot of the data, and sketch your results here:

2. What's wrong with this display? How could this be corrected?

3. Make List1 = log List1 and List2 = log List2. Plot the data again, and sketch your results here:

4. Find the best line through the data, sketch it through your data points, and write its equation (rounding a and b to the nearest hundredth).

5. What is r? _____ What kind of correlation is this? _____

FOR STUDENTS

Exemplary Lesson 12.5
Kepler's Law (page 2 of 4)

We have the equation:	$y = 1.5x$
Which actually represents:	$\log P = 1.5(\log D)$
Use the laws of logarithms:	$\log P = \log (D^{1.5})$
Drop the logs:	$P = D^{1.5}$
	$P = D^{(3/2)}$
Square both sides:	$P^2 = (D^{(3/2)})^2$
Simplify exponents:	$P^2 = D^3$

This is Kepler's law of periods, which states that a planet's period squared is equal to the cube of its distance from the sun. Kepler discovered this by simply playing with the numbers in Copernicus's table. While Kepler believed that Earth isn't at the center of the universe, Earth is at the center of his calculations (D is measured in AU's, the distance of Earth from the Sun, and P is measured in Earth years). That's why Earth was right at the origin of your graph.

Later discoveries of planetary bodies—Uranus, Neptune, various asteroids, and Pluto—all conformed nicely to Kepler's law of periods, falling neatly on the line you drew. (You may confirm this for extra credit.) But soon other orbiting systems were to be discovered. When telescopes were invented, systems of satellites were discovered around Jupiter and Saturn. Let's look at this newer data:

Jupiter	D (in km)	P (in days)	Saturn	D (in km)	P (in days)
Io	422,000	1d 18h 28m	Rhea	526,000	4d 12h 29m
Europa	671,000	3d 13h 14m	Titan	1,230,000	16d
Ganymede	1,070,000	7d 3h 42m	Iapetus	3,580,000	79d 7h 12m
Callisto	1,880,000	16d 16h 32m			

FOR STUDENTS

Exemplary Lesson 12.5
Kepler's Law (page 3 of 4)

When these two new satellite systems were discovered, everyone was very excited to see if Kepler's law of periods also described the motion of these moons that weren't orbiting the Sun but were orbiting the giant planets. Will these moons fall right in line with the planets when we plot their periods and distances from their primary bodies?

To find out, put these sets of data in List3, List4, List5, and List6. (You'll have to convert days/hours/minutes to decimal days.) To compare the Jovian and Saturnian systems with the solar system, we have to convert the units of the original two lists (remember we changed List1 and List2 into logarithms of themselves). Convert the two lists back to their original values. (Do you remember what function is the inverse of the log function?) Then convert List1's units from astronomical units to kilometers, and List2's units from Earth years to days.

$$\text{astronomical units} \times \frac{150{,}000{,}000 \text{ kilometers}}{1 \text{ astronomical unit}} = \text{kilometers}$$

$$\text{years} \times \frac{365 \text{ days}}{1 \text{ year}} = \text{days}$$

6. Check with a classmate to see if all six of your lists agree. Now to graph all the data, let's use the same trick we used before: change all your lists into common logarithms of themselves. Then turn on all three Stat Plots. Stat Plot 1 will be List1 vs. List2, Stat Plot 2 will be List3 vs. List4, and Stat Plot 3 will be List5 vs. List6. Use Zoom Stat to see the answer to our question. Sketch your results here:

7. Describe what you see. What's the same and what's different when you compare our new systems with the solar system?

FOR STUDENTS

Exemplary Lesson 12.5
Kepler's Law (page 4 of 4)

8. Do linear regressions on all three lines, and write their equations here. (The first one is done for you.)

    a. solar system: $y = 1.5\,x - 9.71$ _____

    b. Jovian system: _____

    c. Saturnian system: _____

9. Now transform these logarithmic equations into the curves they represent. (The first one is done for you.)

$$\log P = (3/2)\log D - 9.71$$

$$\log P = \log (D^{(3/2)}) - 9.71$$

$$\log P = \log (D^{(3/2)}) - \log (5.13 \times 10^9)$$

$$\log P = \log [D^{(3/2)}/(5.13 \times 10^9)]$$

$$P = D^{(3/2)}/(5.13 \times 10^9)$$

We see that for each system, we have a different relationship of this form

$P = k\,D^{(3/2)}$.

That is, for each system, the period of an orbiting body is *proportional* (by some factor, k) to the "three-halves power" (the cube of the square root) of its distance away from its "primary body."

Kepler's law turns out to be just a special case of a more general theory of gravitation. The man to formulate this general theory of gravitation was none other than Sir Isaac Newton. Essentially, Newton figured out what the constant of proportionality, k, was composed of. Let's compare the special case to the general case:

Kepler: $P = kD^{(3/2)}$

Newton: $P = \dfrac{2\pi}{\text{sqrt}(GM)}\,D^{(3/2)}$,

where "sqrt" means square root, G is the universal constant of gravitation, and M is the mass of the primary body.

Source: Scott Malloy, Brea Olinda High School, Brea, CA.

Activity Notes to the Teacher for Selected Problems

CHAPTER 1

Activity 1.2: Basketball and Volleyball Players

A Venn diagram can be drawn with two intersecting circles, one representing basketball players and one representing volleyball players. Eight persons are basketball players, 10 are only volleyball players, and 5 play both sports (in the intersection).

Activity 1.3: All, Some, or None

The following are possible responses. They are not intended to be the only correct responses or to exhaust the possible correct responses.

a. All the shapes are similar.
   Some of the shapes have sides larger than a centimeter.
   None of the shapes contains an obtuse angle.
b. All of the shapes are quadrilaterals.
   Some of the shapes have the horizontal dimension as the longer one.
   None of the shapes contains an obtuse angle.
c. All of the shapes are polygons.
   Some of the shapes contain a right angle.
   None of the shapes is congruent.
d. All of the shapes are concave.
   Some of the shapes have five sides.
   No two of the shapes are convex.
e. All of the shapes are conic sections.
   Some of the shapes have a vertical major axis.
   None of the shapes contains an angle.
f. All of the shapes appear to have line symmetry.
   Some of the shapes contain a line segment.
   None of the shapes is an open figure.
g. All of the shapes are complex figures.
   Some of the shapes are composed of line segments.
   None of the shapes is a simple closed curve.

h. All of the shapes are angles.
   Some of the shapes are acute angles.
   None of the shapes is a straight angle.

Activity 1.5: Build a Rectangle

A possible solution is 5 by 15 rectangle. It can be divided into three 5 by 5 squares. Its perimeter is 40.

Activity 1.7: Condo Neighbors

A complete chart would look like this.

	Anita	Becky	Jonquil
Chemist		X	
Radio Announcer	X		
Doctor			X

Since the radio announcer feeds Jonquil's cat when the owner is gone, Jonquil cannot have that occupation. The chemist taps on Anita's wall. Since Becky lives in the middle condo, she is the only one who can tap on Anita's wall and must be the chemist. Anita is therefore the radio announcer, and Jonquil is the doctor.

Activity 1.8: No Homework

Contrary to what might be students' first reaction, all necessary data are given.

Candace McNeil does not do math homework on Thursday.
Ernie Blatt does not do homework on Tuesday for his English class.
Francisco Fong does not do homework on Friday for his French class.
Lila Gamboa does not do homework on Monday for her science class.
Lamont Hicks does not do homework on Wednesday for his social studies class.

Activity 1.9: Eight Bags of Gold

Number the bags 1 through 8. First balance bags 1, 2, 3 against 4, 5, 6. There are only two different possible outcomes of this weighing:

1. If the bags balance, then either bag 7 or bag 8 is light. Balance bag 7 and bag 8 to see which is lighter.
2. If the bags do not balance, set the heavier three bags aside. Then place one of each of the bags from the lighter side on either side of the scale. If these balance, the third bag is the lightest. If these do not balance, choose the bag on the lighter side.

CHAPTER 2

Game Show Activities 2.1–2.3

This is a counterintuitive problem. Therefore, to be certain your students understand, it is best to work the problem at least two different ways.

The easiest way for students to grasp this problem is through geometric probability. By using the spinner illustrated in Activity 2.1, students soon realize that to win without switching, the needle must land on the prize which has 1/3 the area of the spinner dial. To win when switching, the first spin must land on 2/3 of the dial which is not a prize. Thus, switching is the better strategy to win.

2.1 Game Show: A Discovery Simulation With a Spinner (Endogenous)

After all the groups have recorded their 40 trials on the overhead, total the figures to get a large data set. The number of wins when "switching" compared with "not switching" should be near the ratio of 2:1.

2.2 Game Show: Drawing Tree Diagrams (Exogenous)

The tree diagram solution by Shaughnessy and Dick (1991) is shown in Figure A.

2.3 Game Show: Calculate Probability (Didactic/Scaffolding)

Most students who first encounter the Game Show Problem assume that the probability does not change when the host opens the door, so it does not

Figure A
Tree Diagram Solution for Activity 2.2

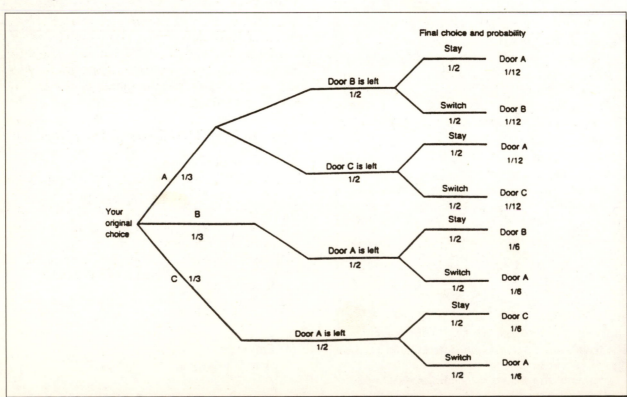

Source: Shaughnessy, J. M., & Dick, T. (1991). Monty's Dilemma: Should You Stick or Switch? *Mathematics Teacher, 91*, 252–256.

make any difference whether the contestant switches. Because the host always opens a door with the goat, the probabilities do change. The questions about the cards are designed to lead students to the concept that removing some losers changes the probability of winning.

If you stick to your first choice, you have a 1/3 probability of winning because there is only one door with a car and you must pick it or lose. If you must switch, you can pick either goat initially because the host will open the door to the goat not selected. Thus you have a 2/3 probability of winning.

Activity 2.5: Odd or Even?

Possible outcomes are $8 + 0$, $8 + 4$, $8 + 1$, $4 + 0$, $4 + 4$, $4 + 1$, $3 + 0$, $3 + 4$, and $3 + 1$. Five of these sums are even, and four of the sums are odd. Therefore Patricia has an advantage.

Activity 2.6: A Fair Deal for the Carrier?

The simplest way to work this problem is to calculate the average expected for each week and compare it to getting paid $5 per week.

If students want to compare all the different possibilities, they will probably need to make tables to see how the expected values are played out. The students should recognize at some point that it is best to consider the totals for 60 weeks, because this is the lowest common denominator for the fractions of probability. Since the paper carrier should earn $300 in 60 weeks without betting, none of the options are better than getting paid $5 per week. The column on the left lists the probabilities for each of the six cases, and the total amount of money expected in 60 weeks is listed in the third column.

		Amount Expected in 60 Weeks	Amount per Week
1. P ($2) = ½	P ($6) = ½	$240	$4.00
2. P ($6) = ⅔	P ($2) = ⅓	$280	$4.67
3. P ($9) = ½	P ($1) = ½	$300	$5.00
4. P ($15) = ¼	P ($1) = ¾	$270	$4.50
5. P ($20) = ⅙	P ($2) = ⅚	$300	$5.00
6. P ($20) = ⅕	P ($1) = ⅘	$288	$4.12

Another method is to calculate the weekly average for each possibility, which is shown in the last column.

Activity 2.7: A Fair Dart Game?

This is a simple way to introduce geometric probability. Since the dark areas are 19/36 of the total area, the game is biased toward the player. The quadrants in opposing corners have the same count so only the two top quadrants need to be analyzed.

Activity 2.8: Probable Triangles

Part I Students should find that the sum of the lengths of any two sides must be greater than the length of the third side.

Part II Divide the students into 12 groups, and have two groups each explore one column and record their results on the transparency or board at the front of the room. The two groups working on the same column will verify their answers. There are six cubed permutations, or 216 different arrangements.

Part III There are 111 permutations that result in triangles: 6 are equilateral, 63 are isosceles, and 42 are scalene. The probability of obtaining an equilateral triangle is 6/216, of obtaining an isosceles triangle is 63/216, of obtaining a scalene triangle is 42/216, and that of not getting a triangle is 105/216.

Extension

The number of combinations for all different lengths is $6 \times 5 \times 4 = 20$ (or use the equation for combinations of six numbers taken three at a time). The number of combinations for two similar lengths is $6 \times 5 \times 2$ divided by 2 (for the repeats of the same number) = 30. There are six combinations of equal lengths. The sums of these values yield a total of 56 combinations.

Activity 2.9: The Triangle Problem

1. Table values will vary.
2. The sum of the lengths of two sides must be greater than the length of the third side.
3. The inequalities are $AX + XB > CD$, $AX + CD > XB$, and $XB + CD > AX$, using the figure given in the problem.
4. Substituting $AX = d$, $XB = (L - d)$, and $CD = L/2$ gives the following set of inequalities:

$$d + (L - d) > L/2$$
$$d + L/2 > (L - d)$$
$$(L - d) + L/2 > d$$

Simplify:

$$L > L/2$$
$$d > L/4$$
$$d < 3L/4$$

5. The first statement was a given, so it yields no new information. The second and third inequalities show that X must fall between $L/4$ and $3L/4$ for the three segments to produce a triangle. Since this length is 1/2 of the sample space, the probability of the three segments forming a triangle is 1/2. According to the analysis, breaking the dowel at a random point is equivalent to randomly choosing a point on a line segment.

Activity 2.10: Mix and Match

Game I is not fair because there is 2/6 probability to mix and 4/6 probability to match. Game II is fair for each probability is 1/2. An interesting way to view this is shown below:

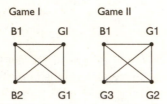

Where BI refers to the first blue object, GI to the first green, etc.

The connecting lines between the letters show 4 ways to connect a B and a G (match), but only 2 ways to connect either a B and another B or two G's (mix). Thus the probabilities are 4/6 and 2/6. Similar reasoning leads to probabilities of 3/6 and 3/6 for Game II.

CHAPTER 3

Activity 3.1: Pattern Block Addition of Fractions With Unlike Denominators

Students should draw figures similar to those below:

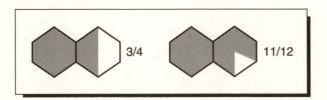

Their procedure described in pictures or words might be: To get the common denominator, trade each fraction of blocks for the smaller same-color blocks that cover. Then add the fractions.

Activity 3.3: Add and Subtract Positive and Negative Integers

Students seldom have difficulty with addition; however, subtraction—especially subtraction of a number with a greater absolute value from one of smaller absolute value—is more difficult. Several students will get the idea that adding zeros to the Work Space in the form of equal pairs of dark and light beans will enable them to subtract as, for example, in Problem 6: $+5 - (-9)$. The storage area labeled "Extra Pieces," separate from the Work Space, keeps all the objects in view and seems to help students take this step in understanding. Picture representations of students' answers should resemble those shown in Figure B.

We have found this method of introduction to be superior to memory tricks or discussion of absolute value for enhancing the understanding of students at every level.

Figure B
Picture Representations of Solution to Activity 3.3

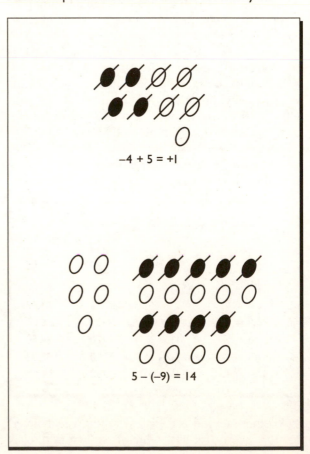

Activity 3.4: Completing the Square With Algebra Tiles

Problems 2 and 3 are shown below.

2.

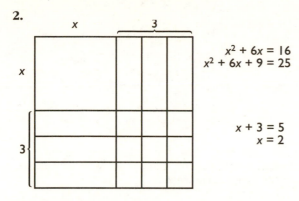

$$x^2 + 6x = 16$$
$$x^2 + 6x + 9 = 25$$

$$x + 3 = 5$$
$$x = 2$$

3.

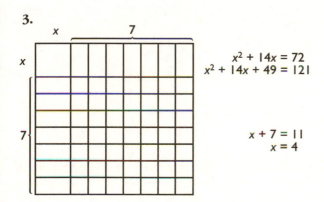

$$x^2 + 14x = 72$$
$$x^2 + 14x + 49 = 121$$

$$x + 7 = 11$$
$$x = 4$$

4. a. Quadratic equations have two solutions. (Students at lower levels may not know this.)

b. There can be only one answer by this method, since there cannot be a negative area.

5. Figure is as shown:

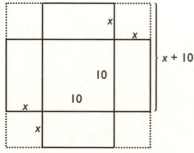

From the figure:
$$x^2 + 10x = 39$$
$$4 \cdot x(x + 10) + 10^2 = (2x + 10)^2$$
Substituting 39 for $x^2 + 10x$:
$$4 \cdot 39 + 10^2 = (2x + 10)^2$$
$$256 = (2x + 10)^2$$
$$16 = 2x + 10$$
$$x = 3$$

Activity 3.5: More About Area, Perimeter, and Right Triangles

Triangle	Area of Leg 1 Square	Area of Leg 2 Square	Area of Hypotenuse Square	Area of Triangle
A	1 sq. unit	1 sq. unit	2 sq. units	½ sq. unit
B	4 sq. units	4 sq. units	8 sq. units	2 sq. units
C	9 sq. units	9 sq. units	18 sq. units	4½ sq. units

Activity 3.8: The Terminators

Fractions whose decimal equivalents terminate have only powers of 2s and/or 5s as denominators. Look for any relationships between the powers and the number of digits in the decimal form.

When denominators are prime numbers other than 2 and 5, the number of digits in the repitand can be no more than 1 less than the number itself. For example, all decimal equivalents of fractions with 7 as a denominator have 6 repeating digits. Furthermore, the digits in the first half of the repitand are 9s, complements of those in the first half. For example, the repitand for ⅐ is 142857, 1 + 8 = 9, 4 + 5 = 9, and 2 + 7 = 9. You may find other interesting relationships.

Activities 3.11–3.12: Exploring Exponential Functions With Paper Folding and the Ozone Layer*

The answers to these problems illustrate an important property of the nature of exponential relationships. A constant change in the independent variable will create a constant *percentage* change in the dependent variable, as shown on the right side of Figure C. This contrasts with what happens for linear functions (left side of Figure C).

Paper Folding

1. See table below.

Number of Folds (n)	0	1	2	3	4	5	6
Number of Sections (S)	1	2	4	8	16	32	64

2. a 1,024 sections
3. a 13 folds
4. 9.19; 3.2 is not a whole number

*Graphic Algebra, Explorations With a Graping Calculator, Key Curriculum Press, 1150 65th Street, Emeryville, CA 94608, 1-800-995-MATH. Reprinted with permission.

Figure C
Linear and Exponential Relationships

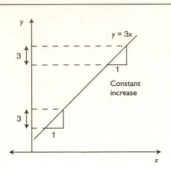 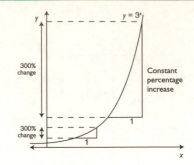

For **linear** functions, a constant change in x produces a constant change in y.

For **exponential** functions, a constant change in x produces a constant percentage change in y.

Ozone Layer

1. 50×0.99^2; 50×0.99^3; 50×0.99^6
2. 49 km
3. a. in the year 2064
    b. in the year 2133
    c. in the year 2202
    d. reduces to half previous value every 69 years
4. 618 years from 1995, or 2613

Number of Years Since 1995 (t)	0	10	20	30
Thickness of Ozone Layer in km (W(t))	50	45.2	40.9	37.0

5. See table above.
6. a. −9.56%; 9.56%
    b. −9.56%; 9.56%
    c. −9.56%; 9.56%
    d. Every 10 years the ozone layer reduces by 9.56%.
7. After each year, it loses 1% of a smaller thickness than the original 50 km. So after 10 years, it loses less than 10% of its original thickness.

Activity 3.13: The Pythagorean Theorem With Geometer's Sketchpad

The scripts for this activity using Geometer's Sketchpad follow.

Right Triangle
Given:
1. Point [A]
2. Point [B]

Steps:
1. Let [j] = Segment between Point [B] and Point [A].
2. Let [k] = Perpendicular to Segment [j] through Point [A].
3. Let [C] = Random Point on Line [k].
4. Let [m] = Segment between Point [B] and Point [C].
5. Let [n] = Segment between Point [A] and Point [C].

Boxon Right Triangle
Given:
1. Point [A]
2. Point [C]
3. Object [j]

Steps:
1. Let [B] = Image of Point [A] rotated 90 degrees about center Point [C].
2. Let [k] = Image of Object [j] rotated 90 degrees about center Point [C].
3. Let [D] = Image of Point [C] rotated 90 degrees about center Point [B].
4. Let [m] = Image of Object [k] rotated 90 degrees about center Point [B].
5. Let [n] = Segment between Point [A] and Point [D].

Hexon Right Triangle
Given:
1. Point [A]
2. Point [C]
3. Object [j]

Steps:

1. Let [B] = Image of Point [A] rotated 120 degrees about center Point [C].
2. Let [k] = Image of Object [j] rotated 120 degrees about center Point [C].
3. Let [n] = Image of Object [k] rotated 120 degrees about center Point [B].
4. Let [E] = Image of Point [C] rotated 120 degrees about center Point [B].
5. Let [p] = Image of Object [n] rotated 120 degrees about center Point [E].
6. Let [F] = Image of Point [B] rotated 120 degrees about center Point [E].
7. Let [q] = Image of Object [p] rotated 120 degrees about center Point [F].
8. Let [G] = Image of Point [E] rotated 120 degrees about center Point [F].
9. Let [r] = Segment between Point [A] and Point [G].

CHAPTER 4

Instructional Sequence 4.1: Egg Dimensions

6. **a.** The equation of the least-squares regression line for warbler eggs is $y = 0.688x + 1.147$, to the nearest thousandth.
   b. The regression line value of 12.6 mm is 0.1 mm larger than the actual value.
   c. This line seems to be a good predictor of eggs in this category.
7. **a.** The equation of the median fit line is $y = 0.733x + 0.321$.
   b. The median fit line is slightly lower than the least-squares regression line.
8. **a.** The slope is the coefficient of x.
   b. Round the slope to 0.7 or 7/10. Select any point on the line. Move right of it 10 units and up 7. The new point should be on or very close to the regression line.
   c. If the length of the egg increases by 10 mm, its width increases by 7 mm.
9. **a.** The y-intercept, the other value in the equation, is where the graph of the line intersects the vertical axis.
   b. There is no meaning for the y-intercept in this situation.

Instructional Sequence 4.2: Breaking Bridges

Problem 1: Answers will vary somewhat.

3. For 6 layers, the breaking weight would be approximately 50 pennies; for 7 layers, approximately 58 pennies.
4. For 2.5 layers, the breaking weight would be approximately 21 pennies; for 3.5 layers, approximately 28 pennies.

Instructional Sequence 4.3: Modeling Bungee Jumping

Modeling

1. **a.** As the price increases, the number of daily customers decreases.
   b. The points on the graph are high at the left when the price is the least and go down to a low on the right when the price is the most.
   c. At $25, there are 80 customers; at $45, 30 customers; at $100, no customers. These values came from connecting the dots in the scatter plot and then reading the coordinates of the given points.
2. **a.** 13 m

Organizing

3. **b.**

Number of Toothpicks per Side of Square	1	2	3	4	5	6
Area in square units	1	4	9	16	25	36

d. As the number of toothpicks per side increases, the area increases rapidly, since the sides are squared to get that value.

e.

Number of Toothpicks per Side of Square	1	2	3	4	5	6
Perimeter in units	4	8	12	16	20	24

g. Both patterns show an increase as the number of toothpicks on a side increases. The area pattern increases more with each additional side, while the perimeter pattern increases at a steady rate.

Reflecting Students may justify different responses from those given.

4. a. not related
   b. not related
   c. related—This is a cyclic pattern that will have different times for most and least daylight hours, depending on location on the globe.
   d. not related
   e. related—The more tension on the string, the higher the pitch.

Extending

Sample responses follow:

A (0, −200) shows that $200 was spent on supplies before any hot dogs were sold.

B (200, −100) shows that the hot dog stand is still $100 in the red when 200 hot dogs have been sold. We might also assume that each hot dog is sold for $0.50.

C (400, 0) is the breakeven point where the sales and the costs are equal.

D (600, 100) and E (800, 200) give two examples of making a profit: $100 when 600 hot dogs are sold and $200 when 800 hot dogs are sold.

Instructional Sequence 4.4: Predicting the Period of a Pendulum

Gathering Data The following chart may be useful for student groups to use as they gather data.

Trial (10 periods)	1	2	3	4	5	6	7	8	9	10	Mean
1											
2											
3											
4											
5											

A class chart may take the following form:

Group/Means	1	2	3	4	5
1					
2					
3					
4					
5					
6					
7					
8					
.					
.					
.					

The pendulum data are then transferred to a group histogram. With eight groups, each group having found five means, the histogram will have 40 data points. The points, when graphed, should have a bell-shaped distribution. This gives students a visual, intuitive depiction of the normal distribution. *Save this group histogram for use the following day.* If more than one class is doing this activity, the group histograms may be combined to have an even better picture of likely periods of the standard pendulum.

Either at the end of this period or the beginning of the next period, students should learn to enter the class data into their calculator and use the calculator to find the mean and standard deviation. Locating the standard deviations on the histogram is helpful, as students can see that most, if not all, of the data lie within the 95% probability range.

Determining the Relevant Variable

As described, each group will now modify the standard pendulum by varying one of the three variables (length, weight of bob, angle of release). Note that each group changes its variable twice and performs five trials each time to obtain a mean period. As on the previous day, it is suggested that students time 10 periods and then divide by 10 for each trial.

Students then compare their new outcomes with those of the previous day. They put their results on the group histogram (maybe with different colors for different variables) and see whether their results are "ordinary" or "unusual," based on the normal distribution data. They should see that length is the only variable that regularly affects the period in a significant way.

Finding the Function/Curve Fitting

In the IMP curriculum, several previous assignments had students look at various "parent functions" (x^2, $\sqrt{x}$, $|x|$, $\sin x$, etc.) and sketch them on class charts, which still hang in the room.

All groups will vary the length and gather data, as indicated, with five trials per length. Then each group will plot its eight points on graph paper and compare the shape of its discrete graph with the graphs students have previously explored. They should see the resemblance to the $y = \sqrt{x}$ graph charted earlier. However, when making a scatter plot on the calculator and comparing it to the basic square root function, they see that their points do not lie on that curved line. From there, the groups experiment with coefficients, either inside or outside of the radical, until they find a function whose graph seems to be a good approximation of their data. It is likely that each group will come up with a different variation of the function. They evaluate their function for $x = 30$ (or trace it) to predict the period of the pendulum in Poe's story.

The culminating activity has students setting up a 30-foot pendulum at their school and using stopwatches to time its period. SM's school had a three-story building with open stairwells so that a 30-foot pendulum could be made and used. The group with the closest prediction, based on its function, then received a prize.

The formula for the period, P (in seconds), of a pendulum is $P = 2\pi \sqrt{L/g}$, where L is the length of the pendulum and g is gravity.

Instructional Sequences 4.5–4.7

Each of these activities is in an inquiry mode, so the answers should be discussed and critiqued as they occur.

Instructional Sequence 4.8: Straight or Curved

Possible answers for Talk It Over follow.

1. **a.** Answers may vary slightly due to rounding. One result is $y = -1.16x + 121.6$
   b.–d. See completed table at the top of the next column.
2. The data points seem to be in the shape of a parabola. See the Additional Sample provided in the Teacher's Edition as a guided practice activity to use with the class.

x	y-values Actual	Model	Deviation d	d2
20	108	98.4	9.6	92.16
25	91	92.6	−1.6	2.56
30	81	86.8	−5.8	33.64
35	74	81	−7	49
40	71	75.2	−4.2	17.64
45	70	69.4	0.6	0.36
50	71	63.6	7.4	54.76

Instructional Sequence 4.9: Friction Car Motion

The teacher will be in a facilitative role during this exploration. A quadratic regression is the best model for the acceleration of the friction car. Some students may conclude a different regression equation is a better fit. This is an opportunity for mathematical discourse in the classroom about the graph and what it tells the informed observer about the nature of the motion of the moving vehicle.

Instructional Sequence 4.10: Seismology and Data Analysis

Rather than giving the page to the students, give them only the data in Table 1 and then guide them through the rest of the process developed in this instructional sequence.

An extension activity for nonlinear regression is to use the data given in Wallace's (1993) article and follow his reasoning to produce appropriate models for the records for men and women in the 800-meter run. These models can be used as the basis for a discussion of the following question: Will the women's record be faster than the men's, i.e., will women's record time ever be less than men's for the 800-meter run?

CHAPTER 5

Activity 5.1: Gumdrops and Toothpick Shapes

Representative answers follow.

1. 4 faces, 4 vertices, 6 edges
   b. 3 edges
   c. The shape collapses.

2. 6 faces, 8 vertices, 12 edges
  b. 4 edges
  c. The faces are squares.
  d. building blocks
3. 5 faces, 5 vertices, 8 edges
  b. The number of faces plus the number of vertices is 2 less than the number of edges.
  c. This pattern will always be true for polyhedra.
4. Responses may vary.
5. Yes: $F + V - 2 = E$
6. One form of Euler's Theorem is:

$F + V = E + 2$ (the number of faces + the number of vertices = the number of edges + 2)

Activity 5.2: Cubes in 2-D and 3-D

1. Let V = volume and S = surface area.

$V = 2$	$S = 10$
$V = 4$	$S = 16$
$V = 3$	$S = 14$
$V = 6$	$S = 24$
$V = 4$ or 5	$S = 18$ or 22

Activity 5.3: Growing Patterns

Representative answers follow.

1. 4
2. Area is 4 space units. Perimeter is 6 length units.
3. The new area is 4 times the old area. The new perimeter is 2 times the old perimeter.
5. Area = 9 units. Perimeter = 9 units.
6. The area increases by a larger amount with each larger triangle. The perimeter grows by 3 units with each larger triangle.
7. 16 triangles. Area = 16. Perimeter = 12. Yes, it is the same pattern.
8. Patterns will vary.
9. Answers will vary.
10. In general, areas grow by larger and larger amounts each time, and perimeters grow by the same amount each time. Hexagons cannot be duplicated as larger hexagons, but the quadrilaterals in the set of pattern blocks all follow a similar growth pattern.

Activity 5.4: Patty Paper Triangles

Representative answers follow.

1. The crease lines formed in each part appear to intersect in one point.
2. The intersections of the creases in the equilateral triangle appear to coincide. This is reasonable because the median, angle bisector, and altitude of right triangles are the same line.

3. The intersections appear to lie on a line. Isosceles triangles are symmetric.
4. The intersections of the four types of coinciding lines associated with triangles will lie on a line. Two alternative forms of the triangle discovery lesson follow (pages 489 through 492).

Activity 5.6: Square Patterns and Algebra

Step 4

Step 5

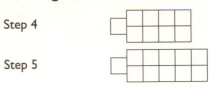

Step	Total Tiles
1	3
2	5
3	7
4	9
5	11
:	
20	41
.	
n	2n + 1

4.

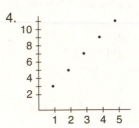

Activity 5.7: Restaurant Rectangles

1. Five discrete arrangements are represented in this table.

l	w	P	A
5	1	12	5
4	2	12	8
3	3	12	9
2	4	12	8
1	5	12	5

The plotted points lie on the graph of the function $A = l(6 - l)$, a parabola.

(continued on p. 493)

Activity 5.4
Alternative I MIRA Triangles—A Discovery Lesson

Directions: You will need two to three blank papers for practice before beginning the exercise. Always use the MIRA with the bevel edge down and toward you.

Construction 1:

a. Draw a line segment with noticeable endpoints (marked with dots).

b. Hold the MIRA roughly in the middle of the line and perpendicular to it. Adjust the MIRA until the red (reflected) endpoint coincides with the other endpoint.

c. Draw along the MIRA edge.

d. What have you drawn?

Construction 2:

a. Draw an angle with a vertex and two noticeable endpoints.

b. Hold the MIRA over one vertex and adjust until the endpoints match.

c. Draw along the MIRA edge.

d. What have you drawn?

Construction 3:

a. Draw a triangle.

b. Hold the MIRA perpendicular to one side so that the red (reflected) portion of the line lines up with the reflecting portion.

c. Move the perpendicular MIRA until it goes through the opposite vertex.

d. Draw along the MIRA edge.

e. What have you drawn?

Construction 4: Median

a. Draw a triangle.

b. Mark the midpoint of one side when the MIRA is bisecting the side.

c. Draw in the line between the midpoint and the opposite vertex.

d. What have you drawn?

F O R   S T U D E N T S

Activity 5.4
Alternative 2 *Geometer's Sketchpad*—A Discovery Lesson: Circumcenter, Incenter, Orthocenter, and Centroid (page 1 of 3)

PART 1 Perpendicular Bisectors of Each Side

1. On a new screen, construct a triangle as follows:
   a. Make three points with shift key down so they remain selected.
   b. Under *Display* highlight *show label* (labeling the points *A, B, C*).
   c. Under *Construct* highlight *segment* (forming a triangle).
   d. With selector (upper left arrow clicked), click mouse once to deselect segments.

2. Construct the perpendicular bisector to each side as follows (see figure).
   a. Select one side (move arrow to side and click mouse).
   b. Under *Construct* highlight *point at midpoint.*
   c. Select the midpoint and its segment.
   d. Under *Construct* highlight *perpendicular line.*
   e. Repeat steps 2(a) through 2(d) for the other two sides.

   Move one of the vertices around. Write a hypothesis for the action of the three perpendicular lines.

3. Mark the intersection point of the perpendicular lines as follows:
   a. Highlight two of the perpendicular lines.
   b. Under *Construct* highlight *point at intersection.*

4. Hide the main construction as follows:
   a. Select all three perpendicular lines. Under *Display* highlight *hide lines.* (When hiding lines, rays, or segments, be sure no points are also selected. If the menu gives "Hide Objects" as an option, you have inadvertently included a vertex or intersection point you do not wish to delete.)
   b. Select all three midpoints; under *Display* highlight *hide midpoints.*
   c. Save this sketch under a new name. If you make a mistake in the next part, you can start over from this point.

The intersection point of the perpendicular bisectors is called the **circumcenter.**

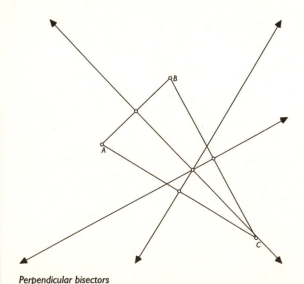

Perpendicular bisectors

FOR STUDENTS

Activity 5.4
Alternative 2 *Geometer's Sketchpad*—A Discovery Lesson: Circumcenter, Incenter, Orthocenter, and Centroid (page 2 of 3)

PART 2 Angle Bisectors

1. Using the same triangle drawing just completed in Part 1, draw the angle bisectors:
   a. Highlight three vertices.
   b. Under *Construct* highlight *angle bisector*.
   c. Repeat for each vertex. (The second vertex highlighted will be bisected.)
   Move one of the vertices around. Write a hypothesis for the action of the three angle bisector lines.

2. Mark the intersection point of the angle bisectors as follows (see figure at left):
   a. Highlight two of the lines.
   b. Under *Construct* highlight *point at intersection*.

3. Hide the main construction as follows:
   a. Select all three angle bisectors; under *Display* highlight *hide rays*.
   b. Save this sketch under a new name. If you make a mistake in the next part, you can start over from this point.
   The intersection of the angle bisectors is called the **incenter.**

PART 3 Altitude of Each Side

1. Using the same triangle drawing just completed in Part 2, construct the perpendicular of each side that intersects the opposite vertex (i.e., altitude):
   a. Select a side and the opposite vertex.
   b. Under *Construct* highlight *perpendicular line*.
   c. Repeat for each side and opposite vertex. Move one of the vertices around. Write a hypothesis for the action of the three altitude lines.

2. Mark the intersection point of the altitudes as follows (see figure below):
   a. Highlight two of the lines.
   b. Under *Construct* highlight *point at intersection*.

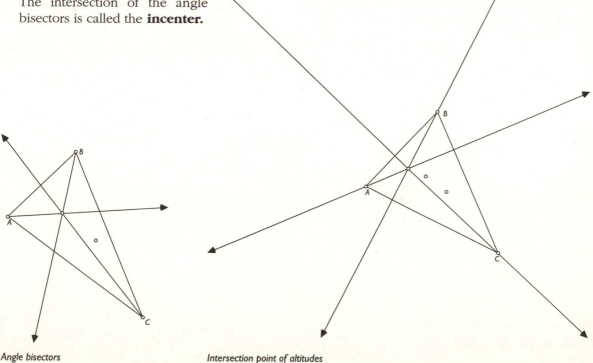

Angle bisectors   Intersection point of altitudes

F O R   S T U D E N T S

Activity 5.4
Alternative 2 *Geometer's Sketchpad*—A Discovery Lesson: Circumcenter, Incenter, Orthocenter, and Centroid (page 3 of 3)

3. Hide the main construction as follows:
  a. Select all three altitudes; under *Display* highlight *hide lines.*
  b. Save this sketch under a new name. If you make a mistake in the next part, you can start over from this point.

The intersection of the altitudes is called the **orthocenter.**

PART 4 Medians

1. Using the same triangle drawing just completed in Part 3, construct the segment from the midpoint of each side to the opposite vertex (i.e., the median):
  a. Select a side. Set the left column to segment.
  b. Under *Construct* highlight *Point at midpoint.*
  c. Select the opposite vertex. Under *Construct* highlight *segment.*
  d. Repeat for all the sides.
  Move one of the vertices around. Write a hypothesis for the action of the three medians.

2. Mark the intersection point of the medians as shown in the figure.
  a. Highlight two of the lines.
  b. Under *Construct* highlight *point at intersection.*

3. Hide the main construction as follows:
  a. Select all three lines; under *Display* highlight *hide segments.*
  b. Save this sketch under a new name. If you make a mistake in the next part, you can start over from this point.

The intersection of the medians is called the **centroid.**

PART 5 Euler's Line

1. a. Select two of the intersection points found in Parts 1, 2, 3, and 4.
  b. With line selected on the left column, under *Construct* highlight *line.*

2. Measure the sides.
  a. Select two vertices.
  b. Under *Measure* highlight *distance.*
  c. Repeat for each side.

3. Move a vertex around and answer the following questions:
  a. For what kind of triangle are all four points coincidental? (Compare the measurements only to the nearest tenth of a centimeter or inches.) Explain why this is a reasonable result.
  b. For what kind of triangle are all the four points in a straight line? Explain why this is a reasonable result.

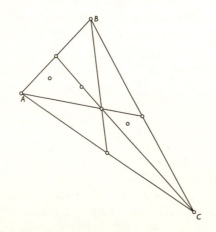

Intersection point of the medians

2. Several arrangements are represented in this table.

l	w	P	A
4	1	10	4
4	2	12	8
4	3	14	12
4	4	16	16
...	...	...	...
4	8	24	32

The equation is $A = 4w$, a direct variation.

3. The first four discrete arrangements meeting the requirements are given in this table.

l	w	P	A
3	1	8	3
6	2	16	12
12	4	32	48
24	8	64	172

The graph is exponential. One form of the equation is $A = w^{2n-2}$ where n is the month (1 for the first month, 2 for the second, and so forth). A "hollow rectangle" arrangement of 28 unit-square tables would work. Note that tables that seat 3 on one side and 1 on an end cannot be used in such an arrangement for 32 people. It would take 10 such tables, but some space would be underutilized.

4. Recognizing the common area of 120 leads to the discrete values in this table.

l	w	P	A
120	1	242	120
60	2	124	120
40	3	86	120
30	4	68	120
20	6	52	120
10	512	44	120

5. One equation for the hyperbola in Problem 4 is

$$P = (240/w) + 2w$$

Students might observe that the most efficient way of seating people seems to occur when the di- mensions of the table are long and narrow. However, rooms for long and narrow tables may have other limitations when it comes to flexibility of seating arrangements.

Activity 5.8: Kaleidoscopes

Allow the students to experiment with the mirrors first to see that differing numbers of images are formed when the angle between the mirrors is changed. Assist them in noticing that some angles produce greater symmetry than others. These are the angles that result in a whole number of images. First, a student may look in the mirrors to see reflections of his or her face. Next, the student should switch to observing an object standing in a given spot between the mirrors.

It is important that students understand that the image is the same distance behind the mirror that the object is in front of the mirror One simple way to demonstrate this is to have a student stand in front of a mirror and hold a measuring stick between his or her body and the mirror.

If you use small glass mirrors found in some hobby stores, tape the edges for safety reasons. Cheap mirrors can be made by gluing Mylar on cardboard and cutting it in pieces. Mylar mirrors can be purchased from supply catalogs for about $1 each.

The upper-left drawing in Figure D shows the positions of the three images when the angle between the mirrors is 90 degrees. Some students might believe there are four images because the back one is along the mirror hinge. Whether they look through one mirror or the other, there is only one image in the middle, and it is not a reversed image. Show the students how they can divide the plane into three sections for mirrors at 120 degrees, four sections for mirrors at 90 degrees, and so on to better visualize the different patterns.

$$\text{number of images} = \frac{\text{angle between mirrors} - 1}{360 \text{ degrees}}$$

Alternating images are reversed or not reversed.

As an extension, show some ready-made kaleidoscopes to the students, and ask them to figure out the angle measure between the mirrors. Patterns vary from threefold to tenfold. Most are sixfold, with 60 degrees between the mirrors.

See Figure E on p. 495 for a response to the Marshal problem.

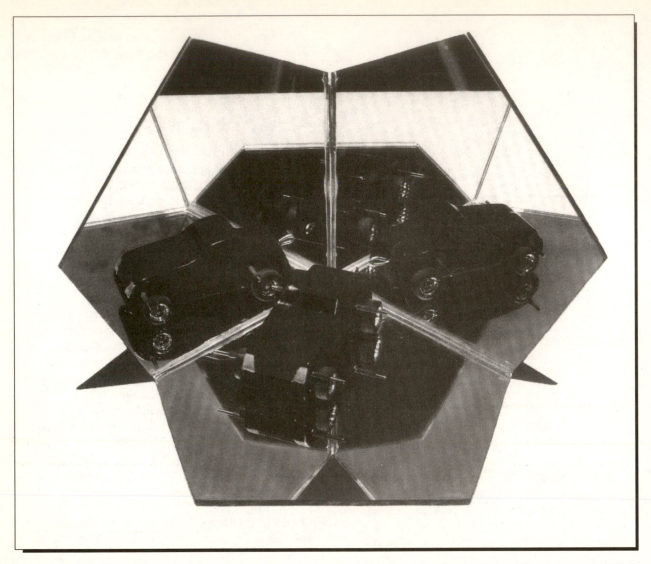

This picture shows the three images formed when the two mirrors are at right angles. The first order reflections are on the left and right. The third image, in back, is composed of images of the first two images.

Activity 5.9: See It Geometrically, Confirm It Algebraically

This activity assumes that students have had experience working with graphing calculators. They will need to know how to enter equations and adjust the range and domain before succeeding in this activity. A similar activity based on the parent function $y = x$ to explore the general equation $y = mx + b$ could be done sometime before this activity in preparation for the more complicated conic section.

Most students readily see that the coefficient a in the general vertex form, $f(x) = a(x - h)^2 + k$, affects the shape of the curve and also determines whether the curve opens up or down. The role of

the constant k is also persuasively illustrated as shifting the curve vertically. Some skeptical students may debate the role of h in shifting the curve horizontally while *not* simultaneously changing the shape of the curve. Even a graphing calculator that dynamically changes the curve from one equation to the next may not be entirely convincing. Of course, this discussion is an excellent subject for mathematical discourse. If the students do not question whether the shape changes, you might ask how they could show whether the shape changes under the different translations.

One way of demonstrating that the shape does not change is to draw a pattern and superimpose the pattern over another curve identical to the original

Figure D   Effects of Changing Mirror Angle in Activity 5.8

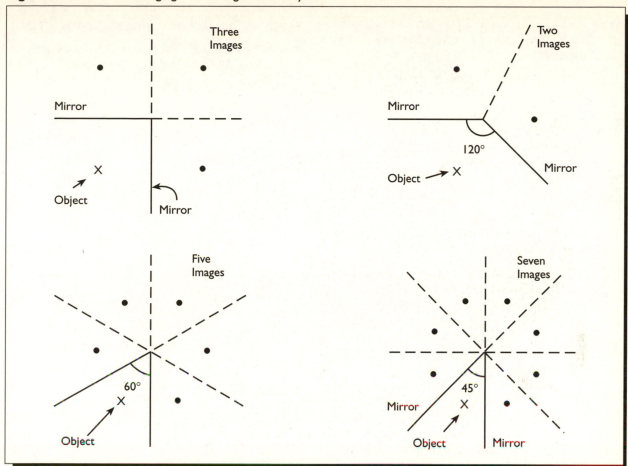

Figure E   Sample Response to Marshal Problem in Activity 5.8

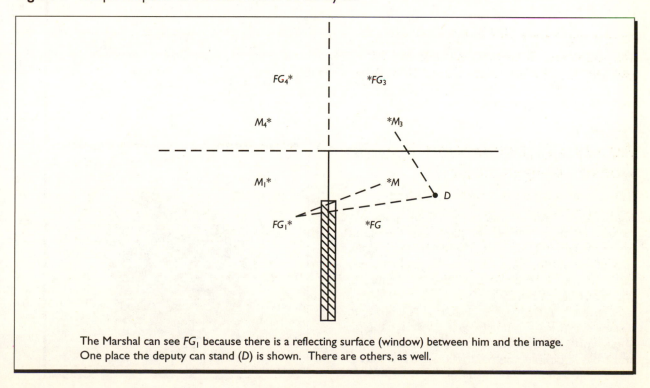

The Marshal can see FG_1 because there is a reflecting surface (window) between him and the image. One place the deputy can stand (D) is shown. There are others, as well.

except for a given constant in the general equation. For example, follow this procedure in checking the role of the constant b:

1. Ask the students to accurately graph

$$y = \frac{1}{2}x^2$$

   on centimeter graph paper by selecting five appropriate values for x, calculating y for each x, and then plotting the points.
2. Use the same procedure to graph a curve such as

$$y = \frac{1}{2}(x + 2)^2$$

3. Cut out the first pattern with scissors, and see if it fits over the original curve.

If you have access to one computer and function graphing software (or Green Globs), a demonstration in front of the class is more dramatic. Enter one curve, and outline it on tracing paper taped over the computer screen. Cut out the parabolic shape. Then enter an appropriate comparison curve, and check the fit with the paper pattern.

Importance of Parentheses

This is an important topic that frequently arises in these exercises with the graphing calculator. After students have experimented on their own, you might then ask students to graph the curve

$$y_1 = \frac{1}{2}(x - 3)^2 + 3$$

and then the curve

$$y_2 = .5\,(x - 3)^2 + 3.$$

What happens to the shape? Why is it so drastically different? This will remind students of the order of operations and alert them to the importance of effectively including parentheses.

Extension

This activity emphasizes the role of the constants a and c in the general quadratic:

$$y = ax^2 + bx + c,$$

which are of importance in graphing parabolas. However, this activity says little about the significance of the coefficient of x, which is the constant b. A visual interpretation of b in the geometric representation of a parabola can offer insight into the characteristics of parabolas.

When $x = 1$, then $y = a + b + c$. Therefore, the distance on the $x = 1$ line from the x-axis to the parabolic curve is the vector sum of the constants a, b, and c. For example, the parabola $y = 2x^2 + 3x + 4$ passes through the coordinate (1, 9).

Activity 5.10: The Oldest Living Proof

Possible calculations for the third figure in this activity are as follows (The first illustration in Figure F is unshaded to show the basic construction):

   Area (Polygon 1) = 1.78 square inches
   Area (Circle Interior 1) = 2.80 square inches
   Area (Circle Interior 2) = 1.40 square inches

   $\frac{1}{4} \times$ Area (Circle Interior 1) $- \frac{1}{4} \times$ Area (Polygon 1) = 0.25 square inch = common area

   $\frac{1}{2} \times$ Area (Circle Interior 2) $- .25 = 0.45$ square inch = area of 1 lune

   $\frac{1}{4} \times$ Area (Polygon 1) = 0.45 square inch

Thus, the area of one lune equals 1/4 the area of the square.

The areas in the second illustration in Figure F are shaded differently to facilitate discussion of a formal proof.

Figure F
Drawings for Solution to Activity 5.10

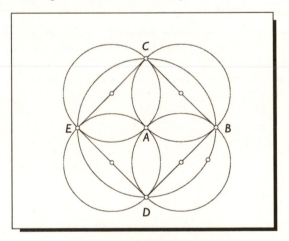

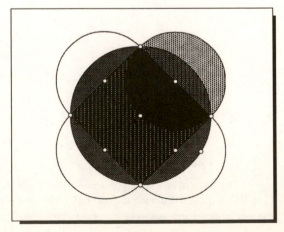

A Formal Proof

See the following simplified drawing.

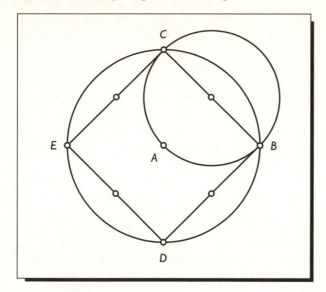

1. Consider the right triangle *ABC*.
2. By the Pythagorean theorem, $(BC)^2 = (AC)^2 + (AB)^2 = 2(AC)^2$.
3. The area of the circle with diameter *BC* is $\pi\left(\dfrac{BC}{2}\right)^2$. The area of the large circle with diameter *CD* and radius *AC* is πAC^2. Since $BC^2 = 2AC^2$ by Statement 2, the area of the small circle is the same as half the area of the larger circle. Or one fourth of the area of the large circle is equal to half of the area of the small circle. Thus, quadrant *ABC* of the large circle equals the area of the small semicircle.

4. Subtracting the doubly shaded area that is common to both the quadrant of the large circle and equal to the area of the small semicircle leaves the lune equal in area to one fourth of the square. (*Note:* This area of a portion of a circle cannot be shaded by the computer with the Geometer's Sketchpad.)
5. Therefore, the total area of the square equals that of the four lunes. Q.E.D.

This activity can be done by students using rulers, good compasses, and calculators to find the areas.

Activity 5.11: Probing Pentominoes

1. A polyomino comprising two squares is called a domino.

An example of what is *not* a triomino might be helpful. For example, squares joined at corners do not constitute a triomino.
2. There are only two possible triominoes.

Continue to have students share their favorite pentominoes, either by drawing their pentominoes on the board or by using transparencies on the overhead projector. Discuss any discrepancies. Altogether, there are 12 distinct pentominoes. As shown in the drawing below, there are standard names relating the pentomino shapes to capital letters F, I, L, N, P, T, U, V, W, X, Y, Z.
3. The approach we have seen most students take to verify that all possible pentominoes have been made is showing all possible combinations of five squares in a row plus all combinations of four squares in a row with the fifth attached at right angles and so on.

Figure G
Naming Pentomino Shapes With Capital Letters

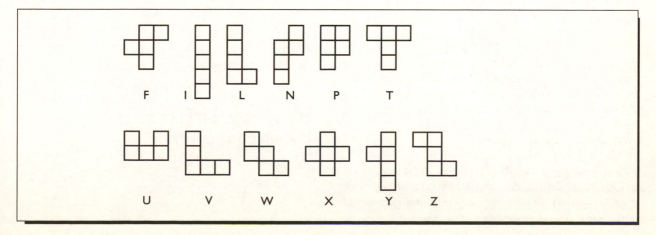

4. **a.** The following pentominoes can be folded into open-ended boxes: F, L, N, T, W, X, Y, Z.
    b. The pentominoes that tessellate the plane are F, I, L, N, T, V, W, X, Z.
5. Four spaces would be left uncovered. Since there are 12 pentominoes, each with an area of 5, they cover 60 units of area out of the 64 unit squares in a checkerboard. Yes, it can be done.
6. Based on the factors of 60, some possible rectangles are 5 × 12, 6 × 10, 4 × 15.
7. The I, F, U, and Z pentominoes make a large P pentomino. The new perimeter is 20. The new area is 20. An example is shown:

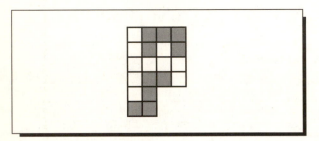

CHAPTER 6

Sample Lesson 6.2: Inventing an Algebra: Meadows or Malls?

The discussion in the teacher's text for Interactive Mathematics Program for Day 19 and 20 of this chapter is quite extensive. An abbreviated portion of the notes follows.

The variables represent the number of students from a given school who live on a given side of the river. The capital letter represents the school; the subscript represents the side of the river.

Equation I: $E_e + W_e = 300$

Equation II: $E_w + W_w = 250$

Equation III: $E_e + E_w \leq 350$

Equation IV: $W_e + W_w \leq 225$

Equation V: $E_w \geq E_e$

Equation VI: $E_e \geq 0$

Equation VII: $W_e \geq 0$

Equation VIII: $E_w \geq 0$

Equation IX: $W_w \geq 0$

There are potentially 21 sets of four equations that must be checked: namely, all combinations of the first two with any two of the remaining seven. If you didn't do so previously, you should have the class create this list. As noted previously, some cases can easily be ruled out as impossible, and students may choose to do this. You will want to get the linear expression that expresses the cost to the city (namely, $1.2E_e + 2W_e + 3E_w + 1.5W_w$) and compute the cost in each case.

For your convenience, the table in Figure H lists all 21 combinations. The table gives the common solution or states that the system is inconsistent (i.e., that there is not a common solution). For combinations with a common solution, the table then gives the cost or the constraint(s) that the common solution violates.

There are only four corner points for the feasible region for this problem. The apparent best solution is $E_e = 162.5$, $W_e = 137.5$, $E_w = 162.5$, and $W_w = 87.5$, which gives a cost of \$1,088.75.

Of course, you can't send half a student to one school and the other half of that student to another, so this isn't really the answer. It makes sense that we should round off the values one way or another. But it is not at all obvious what the best way is to do this rounding. Compare the two rounding cases that fit the constraints. You should point out that the difference in cost is trivial.

Sample Lesson 6.4: Secret Codes and the Power of Algebra

This series of exercises illustrates how matrices assist in altering the frequency of letters used in the English language, which makes codes more difficult to crack. The keyword exercise is an excellent way to have students practice operations on matrices, avoiding the boredom of multiple problems without a context. This unit is strategically placed in the second chapter of the ninth grade to excite students about the possibilities of mathematics.

The first step in solving these equations is to list the letters of the alphabet and to write the numbers 1 through 26 beside the letters, assigning 1 to A and 26 to Z. Then follow the exercises. The exercises are self-checking to some extent and encourage group work.

    4. b. PREPARE FOR THE TEST
       c. MUSIC IS MATHEMATICS

Sample Lesson Plan 6.5: Manufacturing Toys

5. 1240

6. $\begin{bmatrix} 1300 \\ 1800 \\ 1240 \end{bmatrix}$

Figure H
Possible Common Solutions for Sample Lesson 6.2

Combination of Equations	Common Solution				Constraint(s) Violated or Cost
	E_e	W_e	E_w	W_w	
I, II, III, IV	Inconsistent				
I, II, III, V	175	125	175	75	$1,097.50
I, II, III, VI	0	300	350	−100	Violates IX
I, II, III, VII	300	0	50	200	Violates V
I, II, III, VIII	350	−50	0	250	Violates V, VII
I, II, III, IX	100	200	250	0	$1,270.00
I, II, IV, V	162.5	137.5	162.5	87.5	$1,088.75
I, II, IV, VI	0	300	−75	325	Violates IV, V, VIII
I, II, IV, VII	300	0	25	225	Violates V
I, II, IV, VIII	325	−25	0	250	Violates V, VII
I, II, IV, IX	75	225	250	0	$1,290.00
I, II, V, VI	0	300	0	250	Violates IV
I, II, V, VII	300	0	300	−50	Violates III, IX
I, II, V, VIII	0	300	0	250	Violates IV
I, II, V, IX	250	50	250	0	Violates III
I, II, VI, VII	Inconsistent				
I, II, VI, VIII	0	300	0	250	Violates IV
I, II, VI, IX	0	300	250	0	Violates IV
I, II, VII, VIII	300	0	0	250	Violates IV, V
I, II, VII, IX	300	0	250	0	Violates III, V
I, II, VIII, IX	Inconsistent				

Source: Interactive Mathematics Program, Course 3, Key Curriculum Press, 1150 65th Street, Emeryville, CA 94608, 1-800-995-MATH. Reprinted with permisison.

7. $\begin{bmatrix} 1300 & 1520 \\ 1800 & 2092.5 \\ 1240 & 1362.5 \end{bmatrix}$

Sample Lesson Plan 6. 6: Spinning Flags

Through progressive questions, students discover the matrices that transform a simple flag figure through:

- a 180-degree rotation about the origin [Problem 2(a)];
- a 90-degree counterclockwise rotation centered at the origin [Problem 3(c)].

3. One advantage of a matrix representation of a transformation is that you can use it to quickly transform an entire polygon. Consider

$$\Delta ABC = \begin{bmatrix} 2 & 6 & 4 \\ 2 & 0 & -3 \end{bmatrix}$$

- Sketch this triangle in a coordinate plane.
- Multiply the matrix representation of ΔABC by the 90-degree transformation matrix to find the image of ΔABC under a 90-degree counterclockwise rotation centered at the origin. When multiplying the two matrices, put the matrix representation of ABC on the right of the rotation matrix.
- Sketch the image triangle $\Delta A'B'C'$.

Problem 4 investigates the matrix

$$A = \begin{bmatrix} 0.707 & -0.707 \\ 0.707 & 0.707 \end{bmatrix}$$

Problem 5 presents, requests discussion, and enhances discovery of the characteristics of FLAG MOVE, a 10-step program to be entered in a graphing calculator that rotates a flag about the origin using steps of 45 degrees.

Sample Lesson Plan 6.7: What Does $F(S) = KS$ Do to the Area of the Unit Square S?

1. **a.** 15
   b. Area A = 1.5, Area B = 2, Area C = 2, Area D = 1.5
   c. Area of S' = 8
   d. Area of Ss' is the absolute value of the determinant of K.
2. If R is a rectangle, then the area of R' is the value of the determinant of K times the area of R. For example, if the area of R is 3, then the area of R' is three times the absolute value of the determinant of K.
3. If P is a parallelogram, the result will be the same as that in questions 2.
4. The area of KQ will be the area of Q times the absolute value of the determinant of K.

Sample Lesson Plan 6.8: Matrices and Trigonometry

The discussion of this activity from the book follows:

$$\begin{bmatrix} \cos(\alpha - \beta) \\ \sin(\alpha - \beta) \end{bmatrix} = \begin{bmatrix} \cos \alpha & -\sin \alpha \\ \sin \alpha & \cos \alpha \end{bmatrix} \cdot \begin{bmatrix} \cos \beta \\ \sin \beta \end{bmatrix}$$

$$= \begin{bmatrix} \cos \alpha \cos \beta - \sin \alpha \sin \beta \\ \sin \alpha \cos \beta + \cos \alpha \sin \beta \end{bmatrix}.$$

For the matrices to be equal,

$\cos(\alpha - \beta) = \cos \alpha \cos \beta - \sin \alpha \sin \beta.$
$\sin(\alpha - \beta) = \sin \alpha \cos \beta - \cos \alpha \sin \beta.$

The desired identities for $\cos(\alpha - \beta)$ and $\sin(\alpha + \beta)$ are obtained.

CHAPTER 7

Activity 7.1: Graphs, Games, and Generalizations

7. The graph can be traversed only if it has either zero or two odd vertices. If there are no odd vertices, it does not matter where the traverse begins or ends. If there are two odd vertices, the traverse must begin at one odd vertex and end at the other or vice versa.
9. With vertices in the center of each room, this problem is identical to Problem 8. Note that these bridges are not all the traditional Koenig bridge problem.

Activity 7.2: From Graphs to Matrices*

1.

To	Aspen Grove	Birch Grove	Clancy's Corner	Devil's Den
From				
Aspen Grove	2	2	0	0
Birch Grove	2	0	1	1
Clancy's Corner	0	1	0	3
Devil's Den	0	1	3	4

2. $\begin{bmatrix} 2 & 2 & 0 & 0 \\ 2 & 0 & 1 & 1 \\ 0 & 1 & 0 & 3 \\ 0 & 1 & 3 & 4 \end{bmatrix}$

3. **a.** The sum of the elements in the third row is 4. This number corresponds to the number of trails (edges) by which someone can leave Clancy's Corner. The sum of the elements in the third column also is 4. This number corresponds to the number of trails (edges) by which someone can arrive at Clancy's Corner. It is also equal to the sum along the third row because all edges can be traversed in both directions.
   b. The sums of the rows are 4, 4, 4, and 8, and the total of these is 20, which is twice the number of edges. Each edge has been counted twice.
   c. The elements along the major axis in the matrix representation of this type of graph (undirected) are even. In an undirected graph, each edge connecting a vertex to itself can be traversed in two directions.
   d. Yes. In an undirected graph, the number of paths from P to Q is equal to the number of paths from Q to P.

4. **a.** $\begin{bmatrix} 2 & 1 & 2 & 0 \\ 1 & 2 & 1 & 0 \\ 2 & 1 & 0 & 1 \\ 0 & 0 & 1 & 0 \end{bmatrix}$ **b.** $\begin{bmatrix} 0 & 3 & 0 & 1 & 1 \\ 3 & 0 & 1 & 2 & 1 \\ 0 & 1 & 2 & 1 & 0 \\ 1 & 2 & 1 & 0 & 0 \\ 1 & 1 & 0 & 0 & 0 \end{bmatrix}$

Yes, the same properties hold.

5. More than one answer to these problems is possible.

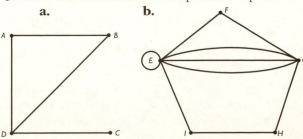
    a.   **b.**

*Glidden, P. L. (February 1990). From graphs to matrices. *The Mathematics Teacher*, 127–134. Reprinted with permission.

6. $\begin{bmatrix} 1 & 1 & 0 & 0 \\ 1 & 0 & 1 & 0 \\ 0 & 1 & 0 & 2 \\ 0 & 1 & 1 & 2 \end{bmatrix}$

7. a. The sum of the elements in the third row is 3, which represents the number of ways one can leave Clancy's Corner. The sum of the elements in the third column is 2, the number of ways to get to Clancy's Corner. These sums are not necessarily equal in a directed graph.

b. The sums of the rows are 2, 2, 3, and 4, and the total of these is 11, which is the number of edges. Remember that the trail from Birch Grove to Clancy's Corner can be traversed in two directions, so it should be counted twice. Because this is a directed graph, the edges are not double-counted.

c. The elements along the major axis of a directed graph need not be even. The edges of a directed graph cannot necessarily be traversed in both directions.

d. The matrix is not symmetric across the major axis.

8. a. $\begin{bmatrix} 0 & 1 & 1 & 1 & 1 \\ 0 & 0 & 0 & 0 & 0 \\ 0 & 0 & 0 & 0 & 0 \\ 1 & 0 & 0 & 0 & 0 \\ 0 & 0 & 0 & 0 & 0 \end{bmatrix}$ **b.** $\begin{bmatrix} 1 & 1 & 0 & 1 \\ 1 & 2 & 1 & 0 \\ 0 & 1 & 0 & 1 \\ 0 & 0 & 2 & 0 \end{bmatrix}$

9. More than one answer to these problems is possible.

a.

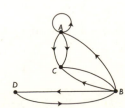

b.

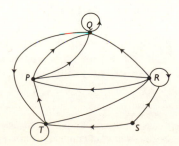

10. a.

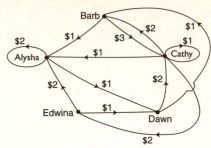

$\begin{bmatrix} 2 & 0 & 0 & 1 & 0 \\ 1 & 0 & 3 & 0 & 0 \\ 1 & 2 & 1 & 0 & 2 \\ 0 & 1 & 2 & 0 & 0 \\ 2 & 0 & 0 & 1 & 0 \end{bmatrix}$

The row totals 3, 4, 6, 3, 3 are the fines levied by each player. The column totals 6, 3, 6, 2, 2 are the fines levied against each player. Cathy fined the most, and Alysha and Cathy were fined the most.

b.

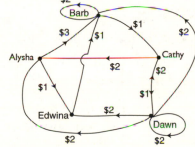

$\begin{bmatrix} 0 & 3 & 0 & 0 & 1 \\ 0 & 2 & 1 & 0 & 0 \\ 2 & 0 & 0 & 1 & 0 \\ 2 & 2 & 2 & 2 & 2 \\ 0 & 1 & 0 & 0 & 0 \end{bmatrix}$

Dawn fined the most, and Barb was fined the most.

c.

$\begin{bmatrix} 2 & 0 & 0 & 1 & 0 \\ 1 & 0 & 3 & 0 & 0 \\ 1 & 2 & 1 & 0 & 2 \\ 0 & 1 & 2 & 0 & 0 \\ 2 & 0 & 0 & 1 & 0 \end{bmatrix} + \begin{bmatrix} 0 & 3 & 0 & 0 & 1 \\ 0 & 2 & 1 & 0 & 0 \\ 2 & 0 & 0 & 1 & 0 \\ 2 & 2 & 2 & 2 & 2 \\ 0 & 1 & 0 & 0 & 0 \end{bmatrix}$

$= \begin{bmatrix} 2 & 3 & 0 & 1 & 1 \\ 1 & 2 & 4 & 0 & 0 \\ 3 & 2 & 1 & 1 & 2 \\ 2 & 3 & 4 & 2 & 2 \\ 2 & 1 & 0 & 1 & 0 \end{bmatrix}$

References

Campbell, H. C. *Linear Algebra with Applications,* 2nd ed. Englewood Cliffs. N.J.: Prentice-Hall, 1980.

Hirsch, C. R. "Graphs, Games, and Generalizations." *Mathematics Teacher,* 81, (December 1988): 741–45.

National Council of Teachers of Mathematics, Commission on Standards for School Mathematics. *Curriculum and Evaluation Standards for School Mathematics.* Reston, VA: The Council, 1989.

Activity 7.4: Graphs, Colors, and Chromatic Numbers*

1. 5

2. 4

3. yes, no

4. no

5. a. To find another way of using three colors, we must interchange the colors of the example.

b.

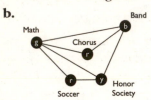

b = blue
r = red
g = green
y = yellow
p = purple

c.

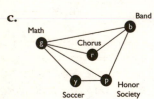

6. a. 2

b. 3

c. 5

7. The smallest number is 3. Drawings will vary An example:

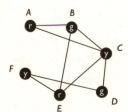

8. a. 3

b. 3

c. 3

NCTM Student Math Notes, National Council of Teachers of Mathematics, January 1998, Reston, VA. Reprinted with permission.

9. The chromatic number is 2. It indicates that two timing periods are needed.

10. The chromatic number is 3. It indicates that three timing periods are needed.

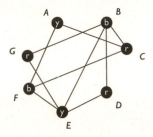

11. Some plants cross-pollinate, and some can inhibit the growth of other species. Soil requirements and the height and growth patterns of the plant sometimes affect planting locations.

12.

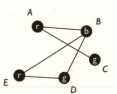

Activity 7.6: Applying Matrices to Networks

b. A B C   A B C

d. M + M

e. There are 2 pathways from C to B that use no more than 2 paths.

f. B to D

h. Yes

i. C has a weaker communication system than B.

Activity 7.7: It's a SNAP†

After students have identified there are six elements (possible patterns), have all students label them the following way so everyone is using the same definitions.

†*Mathematics Teacher,* National Council of Teachers of Mathematics, April 1996, Reston, VA. Reprinted with permission.

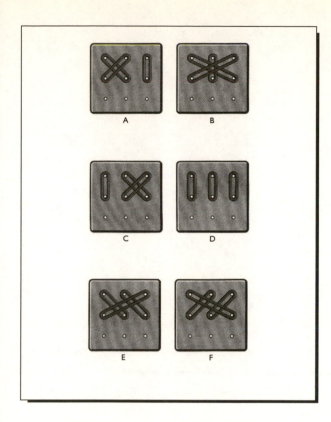

Illustrate to the students how to set up the board for the "SNAP" operation.

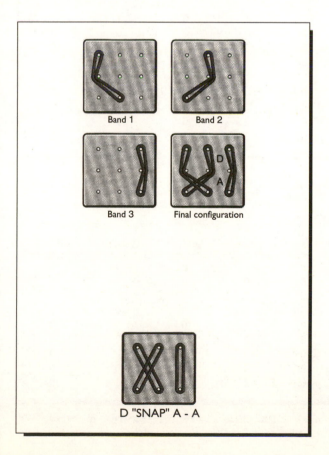

Band 1   Band 2

Band 3   Final configuration

D "SNAP" A - A

The resulting table is as follows:

		A	B	C	D	E	F
				Bottom Two Rows			
Top Two Rows	A	D	E	F	A	B	C
	B	F	D	E	B	C	A
	C	E	F	D	C	A	B
	D	A	B	C	D	E	F
	E	C	A	B	E	F	D
	F	B	C	A	F	D	E

It is best to have each group of two students responsible for filling in one of the columns of the chart. Then each group enters its findings in the master chart on the overhead projector. The several different groups of students responsible for the same column check each other.

Answers for the other questions follow.

Problem 1

The symmetries for the illustrated geometric figure are as follows, where the rotations are around the center of the figure:

R_1 = rotation of 72 degrees
R_2 = rotation of 144 degrees
R_3 = rotation of 216 degrees
R_4 = rotation of 288 degrees
I = rotation of 360 degrees

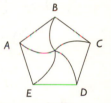

Owing to the shape of the curves in the pentagon, the figure cannot be reflected about an axis. The results are shown in the following table. Again, all the conditions of the group are met, yet this group is also commutative and, therefore, Abelian.

	I	R_1	R_2	R_3	R_4
I	I	R_1	R_2	R_3	R_4
R_1	R_1	R_2	R_3	R_4	I
R_2	R_2	R_3	R_4	I	R_1
R_3	R_3	R_4	I	R_1	R_2
R_4	R_4	I	R_1	R_2	R_3

Problem 2

Does this table 3 define a group? The answer is no for two reasons.

Problem 3

The figures can be used for additional practice in finding symmetry operations and developing the corresponding tables. Students might discover that for any geometric figure, the rotation symmetries always form a group.

Activity 7.8: The Power of a Matrix*

The tables in Figure I show the solutions for Problems 3 to 5.

Figure I
Solution to Food Web Problems in Activity 7.8

Problem 3

	Beetle	Frog	Grackle	Sawfly	Snail	Snake	Spider	Warbler	Willow
Beetle	0	1	0	0	0	0	1	1	0
Frog	0	0	0	0	0	1	0	0	0
Grackle	0	0	0	0	0	0	0	0	0
Sawfly	0	1	1	0	0	0	1	0	0
Snail	0	1	0	0	0	0	0	0	0
Snake	0	0	0	0	0	0	0	0	0
Spider	0	1	1	0	0	0	0	1	0
Warbler	0	0	0	0	0	0	0	0	0
Willow	1	0	0	1	0	0	0	0	0

Problem 4

	Beetle	Frog	Grackle	Sawfly	Snail	Snake	Spider	Warbler	Willow
Beetle	0	1	1	0	0	1	0	1	0
Frog	0	0	0	0	0	0	0	0	0
Grackle	0	0	0	0	0	0	0	0	0
Sawfly	0	1	1	0	0	1	0	1	0
Snail	0	0	0	0	0	1	0	0	0
Snake	0	0	0	0	0	0	0	0	0
Spider	0	0	0	0	0	1	0	0	0
Warbler	0	0	0	0	0	0	0	0	0
Willow	0	2	1	0	0	0	2	1	0

Problem 5

	Beetle	Frog	Grackle	Sawfly	Snail	Snake	Spider	Warbler	Willow
Beetle	0	0	0	0	0	1	0	0	0
Frog	0	0	0	0	0	0	0	0	0
Grackle	0	0	0	0	0	0	0	0	0
Sawfly	0	0	0	0	0	1	0	0	0
Snail	0	0	0	0	0	0	0	0	0
Snake	0	0	0	0	0	0	0	0	0
Spider	0	0	0	0	0	0	0	0	0
Warbler	0	0	0	0	0	0	0	0	0
Willow	0	2	2	0	0	2	0	2	0

*Coxford, A. F., and Others (1997). Core-Plus/*Contemporary Mathematics in Context*. Chicago, IL: Everyday Learning Corp. Reprinted with permission.

Figure J
Solution for Tennis Tournament Rankings in Activity 7.8

		A	C	E	J	K	M	Row Sums	
$A^2 =$	A	0	0	1	0	0	1	2 ⟶	Anne &
	C	1	0	0	2	1	0	4 ← Catherine is 2nd.	Emily
	E	1	0	0	1	0	0	2 ⟶	are 5th
	J	1	1	1	0	1	0	4 ← Julie is 3rd (beat Maria).	or 6th.
	K	0	0	1	1	0	1	3 ← Keadra is 4th.	
	M	1	0	1	1	2	0	5 ← Maria is 1st (beat Catherine).	

		A	C	E	J	K	M	Row Sums	
$A^3 =$	A	1	1	1	0	1	0	4 ⎫	
	C	1	0	2	2	0	2	7 ⎬ Ann is 5th (beat Julie).	
	E	0	0	1	1	0	1	3 ⎭ Emily is 6th (beat Keadra).	
	J	2	0	1	2	2	0	7	
	K	1	1	2	0	1	1	6	
	M	2	0	1	3	1	1	8	

6. Only snail and snake—zero in 1-way and 2-way matrices.

7. a. In this matrix, a 1 means the player in the row beat the player in the column.

	A	C	E	J	K	M
A	0	0	0	1	0	0
C	1	0	1	0	1	0
E	0	0	0	0	1	0
J	0	0	1	0	0	1
K	1	0	0	1	0	0
M	1	1	1	0	0	0

b.

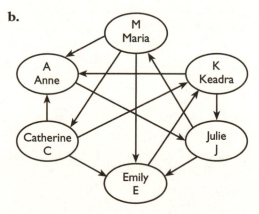

8. The row sums in matrix A (Problem 7) give the number of wins for each player:

Anne = 1
Catherine = 3
Emily = 1
Julie = 2
Keadra = 2
Maria = 3

9. Marie and Catherine each won 3 times, so each is in first or second place. Julie and Keadra won 2 times, so each is in third or fourth place.

10. By squaring and then cubing matrix A, as shown in Figure J, we can rank the six players: Maria is first, Catherine second, Julie third, Keadra fourth, Anne fifth, and Emily sixth.

CHAPTER 8

Investigation 8.1: Iteration All Over Again

The first procedure results in an arithmetic sequence beginning with 5 and increasing by 3 each time (5, 8, 11, 14, . . .). The second procedure results in a geometric sequence beginning with 3 and having a common ratio of 5 (3, 15, 75, 375, . . .).

1. The most direct iterative way is to "seed" the calculator with 100 and then multiply by 1.1 as the common ratio and add 100 using only the enter key.

100 (enter) × 1.1 + 100

(enter) (enter) (enter) . . .

100, 210, 331, 464.1 . . . , 4,559.92

There would be $4,559.92 in the account on the 18th birthday.

2. Use a similar procedure:

258,670 (enter) × 1.046 (enter) (enter) . . .

The population would be more than 400,000 in 2000. (The exact calculator amount, to the nearest whole number, is 405,567.)

3. This procedure can be one on any calculator with a key to recall a previous answer. With the given values of 40 and 5, the calculator screen shows the following values:

5, 6.5, 6.326923077, 6.324555763, 6.32455532, 6.32455532, . . .

4. The screen shows the values of .6180371353 and .6180327869 after 12 and 13 iterations, respectively.

Teacher Extension

There is a way to use the sequence capabilities of graphics calculators to do "home-screen programming" that results in a "counter" for iterations. For example, if we start with a population of 50,000 and an annual growth rate of 3%, braces can be typed in to trigger the sequence capabilities of the calculator. Procedure:

{0,50000} (enter) {Ans(1) + 1, 1.03 Ans (2)}

(enter) (enter) . . .

The first three results are {1 51500}, {2 53045}, {3 54636.35}. The first separate digit is the counter, and the others represent the population values for each successive time period.

Investigation 8.2: Painted Cubes

Possible responses to the initial questions referring to a 3 × 3 × 3 cube follow:

6 cubes have only one face painted, and 12 cubes have exactly two faces painted.
8 cubes have exactly three faces painted, and 1 cube has zero faces painted.

The completed chart looks like this:

Size	Number of Cubes	Number of Unit Cubes With Paint on Exactly ...			
		0 Faces	1 Face	2 Faces	3 Faces
2 × 2 × 2	8	0	0	0	8
3 × 3 × 3	27	1	6	12	8
4 × 4 × 4	64	8	24	24	8
5 × 5 × 5	125	27	54	36	8

Some possible patterns students generalize from the table are given below in a combination of verbal and algebraic forms. The degree of formalism expected in student answers should vary, depending on the background and experience of the class.

In an $n \times n \times n$ cube,

- the number of cubes with paint on exactly 0 sides is the same as the number of cubes two sizes smaller, or $(n - 2)^3$;
- the number of cubes with paint on exactly one side is 6 times the consecutive square numbers, beginning with 0, or $6(n - 1)^2$;
- the number of cubes with paint on exactly two sides is 12 times the consecutive whole numbers, beginning with 0, or $12(n - 1)$;
- the number of cubes with paint on exactly 3 sides always is 8.

To extend the investigations, have students try to explain, justify, or prove their conjectures.

Investigation 8.3: Consecutive Sums

One issue that frequently arises is whether to use 0 or negative numbers. Be open to discussing these options with your students. The results below assume only consecutive counting numbers.

Some of the conjectures our students have come up with are as follows:

- No powers of 2 can be expressed as consecutive sums.
- All odd numbers can be expressed as the sum of two consecutive numbers.
- Numbers divisible by 3 can be expressed as the sum of three consecutive numbers.
- Numbers divisible by 5 can be expressed as the sum of five consecutive numbers.
- Others, especially relating to multiple representations of sums.

To extend the investigations, have students try to explain, justify, or prove their conjectures.

Investigation 8.4: Fibonacci Fauna and Flora

1. The rabbit pattern follows the Fibonacci sequence. Its 12th term is 144.

2. The mouse pattern has the numbers 2, 2, 10, 18, 26, 66, 138 until there are 506 after 24 weeks. The mouse pattern stated recursively, where M_n is the nth term in the series, is $M_n = M_{n-3} + 4(M_{n-9})$. In other words, the number at the end of the nth period is the number at the end of the

Figure K
Fibonacci Square Spiral

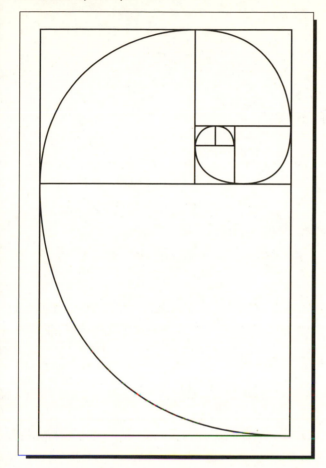

previous period (3 weeks ago) plus 4 times the number of pairs of mice at least 9 weeks old.

3–4. Answers may vary. Some known relationships are daisies with 13, 21, or 34 petals (and spiral patterns in the center), a bell pepper with 3 chambers, pears with a five-point cross-section, the star jasmine with five petals, the two opposite spirals in pinecones (usually 5 and 8 or 8 and 13), pineapples (13, 21, and 24), and sunflowers (34 and 55 or 55 and 89).

5. Fibonacci square spiral—Squares of 1, 1, 2, 3, 5, 8, 13 are shown in Figure K. Diagonals of adjoining squares are connected with a curved line to show the spiral.

Investigation 8.5: Pascal Patterns

Sum Patterns

1. a.

Row	0	1	2	3	4	5	6
Row Sum	1	2	4	8	16	32	64

b. The sums double each time.

c. The sum of a row equals 2 to the power of the row.

d. 2^{20}, 2^{100}, 2^n

2. a. the fourth element of the second diagonal; the fifth element of the second diagonal
  b. the fourth element of the third diagonal
  c. the nth in the $(r + 1)$ diagonal, where r is the number of the diagonal containing the summed elements

3. a.

Row	0	1	2	3	4	5
Triangular Sum	1	3	7	15	31	63

b.

Row	6	7	8	9	10
Triangular Sum	2^7-1	2^8-1	2^9-1	$2^{10}-1$	$2^{11}-1$

c. Raise 2 to the power 1 greater than the row, then subtract 1: $2^n + 1$ where n is the number of the row.

Additional Exploration Questions

1. Look for an "alternate diagonal" pattern on the level 8 Pascal's triangle in Figure L. Alternate diagonals are shown with circle(s) around the first sum that is a Fibonacci number, then with diamonds around the next sum, and so on.

2. The product of the numbers in a Pascal's triangle "ring" always is a square number. The proof is left to the reader.

3. The best way to discover these patterns is to give students completed Pascal triangles to shade or color to see the patterns. Once again, we see a pattern of sums of numbers along a diagonal. Sometimes these sums involve a "thick" diagonal.

Once the triangular and square numbers are found, recall that pentagonal numbers are themselves the sum of a square and a triangular number and hexagonal numbers the sum of a square and two triangular numbers.

4. In the set $\{a, b, c, d, e\}$, there is 1 empty set, $\emptyset$ and there are 5 unique subsets contain one element: $\{a\}$, $\{b\}$, $\{c\}$, $\{d\}$, $\{e\}$; 10 unique subsets containing two elements: $\{a, b\}$, $\{a, c\}$, $\{a, d\}$, $\{a, e\}$, $\{b, c\}$, $\{b, d\}$, $\{b, e\}$, $\{c, d\}$, $\{c, e\}$, $\{d, e\}$; 10 unique subsets containing three elements: $\{a, b, c\}$, $\{a, b, d\}$, $\{a, b, e\}$, $\{a, c, d\}$, $\{a, c, e\}$, $\{a, d, e\}$, $\{b, c, d\}$, $\{b, c, e\}$, $\{b, d, e\}$, $\{c, d, e\}$; 5 unique subsets containing four elements: $\{a, b, c, d\}$, $\{a, b, c, e\}$, $\{a, c, d, e\}$, $\{b, c, d, e\}$, $\{a, b, d, e\}$; and 1 subset containing all five elements: $\{a, b, c, d, e\}$. These numbers are the exact numbers in row 5 of Pascal's triangle.

Figure L
Patterns in Pascal's Triangle

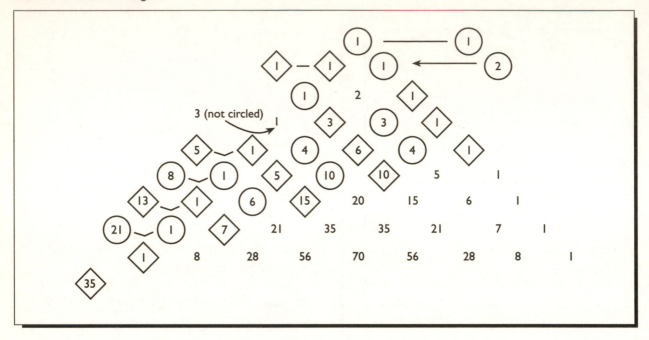

5. Most second-year algebra textbooks have some of this information, but many do not provide copies of Pascal's triangle. It is better to first give students specific examples of basic binomial expansions and let them see how the coefficients are related to the rows of Pascal's triangle. Eventually, they can see how combinatorics also are connected to Pascal's triangle and why.

Investigation 8.6: Palindromic Numbers/Numberdromes

1. Answers-to-the Palindromes worksheet are yes, yes, and yes. Any acceptable answers for four- and five-digit palindromes are fine, but this could be made more challenging by asking students to find actual palindromic numbers in real-life situations. For example, one of the authors has a hometown zip code of 47974, a five-digit numberdrome.

2. Some numbers take many steps to get to a palindrome. One such number is 89.

3. The digits are palindromes even though they are split and multiplied to get a common answer. Since three different numerals are involved, call them *a*, *b*, and *c*. Expressed in algebraic form, the problems become:

$(10a + b)(10c + b) = (10b + c)(10b + a)$
$100ac + 10ab + 10bc + b^2$
$\qquad\qquad = 100b^2 + 10bc + 10ab + ac$
$\quad 99ac = 99b^2$
$\quad\ \ ac = b^2$

This is the condition for which this type of palindrome can be formed.

Note: A similar argument follows when 0s are inserted; see Problem 5(b).

4. Since these palindromes use four different numerals, the algebraic form becomes:

$(10a + b)(10d + c) = (10c + d)(10b + a)$

You can verify that this simplifies to the condition $ad = bc$.

Note: The same argument works when the values are squared; see Problem 5(c).

5. The algebraic simplification shows that, if the digits in order are *a, b, c, d, e, f*, then:

$$\frac{a}{f} = \frac{b}{e} = \frac{c}{d}$$

Investigation 8.7: Mathematical "Black Holes"

1. The sequence should always come down to 1 eventually. For example, if the beginning num-

ber is 7, students should get the following sequence: 7, 22, 11, 34, 17, 52, 26, 13, 40, 20, 10, 5, 16, 8, 4, 2, 1.

From then on, the cycle 4, 2, 1 repeats endlessly, hence the appropriateness of the "Black Hole" designation—there is no escape!

Note that after this number, students have a shortcut for any numbers in the sequence produced beginning with 7, such as 26.

2. **a.** For example, select 7.

$$7 + 12 = 19$$
$$19 \times 2 = 38$$
$$38 - 4 = 34$$
$$34/4 = 8.5$$
$$8.5 - 3.5 = 5$$

b. Select n.

$$n + 12$$
$$(n + 12)2 = 2n + 24$$
$$2n + 24 - 4 = 2n + 20$$
$$(2n + 20)/4 = n/2 + 5$$
$$n/2 + 5 - n/2 = 5$$

3. **a.** We will use 6 and 3 for our example of this process.
   - $(-1)(6) + 3 = -3$ (third number in the sequence)
   - $(-1)(3) + (-3) = -6$ (fourth number in the sequence)
   - $(-1)(-3) + (-6) = -3$ (fifth number in the sequence)
   - $(-1)(-6) + (-3) = 3$ (sixth number in the sequence)
   - $(-1)(-3) + 3 = 6$

   b. 6, 3, −3, −6, −3, 3, 6 Here the sequence begins to repeat. The repeated pattern consists of the original two digits and their additive inverses.

4. The iterative procedure should always approach 1.

Investigation 8.8: Trains

The smallest Cuisenaire rod is a 1-unit cube. The other rods are made in unit increments. Each length of rod also has a different color, which students frequently use to describe their work. In this investigation, since a train has a front and a back, a train consisting of a 1-unit car followed by a 2-unit car is considered different from a train with the cars in reverse order.

Problems 1 and 2 help students clearly understand these counting rules by going through several examples. Students are expected to draw the trains to answer the questions in Problem 3. This is a good time for pairs or small-group work so that students can check each other's work for completeness. In Problem 4 they summarize their findings. They should get 8 trains of length 4, 16 of length 5, and 32 of length 6.

5. Possible answers: by number of cars of each length (color), by total number of cars
6. Students' choice—also a good place to end the first day or to assign as homework if not complete.
7. For Trains, Part 2, a completed table is shown below. See how the number patterns are related to Pascal's triangle.
8. Students should describe a pattern related to Pascal's triangle.
9. By continuing the pattern, or by using combinations, you get 126.

Length of Train	Number of Cars					
	1 Car	2 Cars	3 Cars	4 Cars	5 Cars	6 Cars
Length 1	1	0	0	0	0	0
Length 2	1	1	0	0	0	0
Length 3	1	2	1	0	0	0
Length 4	1	3	3	1	0	0
Length 5	1	4	6	4	1	0
Length 6	1	5	10	10	5	1

Investigation 8.9: Rod Staircases

A nice extension is to generalize the formulas as part of a bigger system of equations as shown in Figure M.

Investigation 8.10: Guatemalan Weaving Patterns

The table in Figure N indicates possible ultimate values for each number of crosses. We have just begun to scratch the surface of this investigation. We hope you play around with it before seeing what your students can come up with. Here are some patterns we have seen so far (see details in Figure O):

- All ultimate values from 1 to 9 can be found using a one-cross pattern.
- With two crosses, when starting with 1 at the upper left of the pattern and continuing with consecutive integers for each new calculation of the pattern, we can only find ultimate values of 3, 9, and 6 recycling in that order.

Figure M
Solutions for Investigation 8.9

<table>
<tr><th colspan="3">3 UNITS</th></tr>
<tr><th>No. in Staircase</th><th>Volume</th><th>Surface Area</th></tr>
<tr><td>1</td><td>3</td><td>14</td></tr>
<tr><td>2</td><td>6</td><td>24</td></tr>
<tr><td>3</td><td>9</td><td>34</td></tr>
<tr><td>4</td><td>12</td><td>44</td></tr>
<tr><td>5</td><td>15</td><td>54</td></tr>
<tr><td>6</td><td>18</td><td>64</td></tr>
<tr><td>…</td><td>…</td><td>…</td></tr>
<tr><td>n</td><td>$3n$</td><td>$10n + 4$</td></tr>
</table>

<table>
<tr><th colspan="3">4 UNITS</th></tr>
<tr><th>No. in Staircase</th><th>Volume</th><th>Surface Area</th></tr>
<tr><td>1</td><td>4</td><td>18</td></tr>
<tr><td>2</td><td>8</td><td>30</td></tr>
<tr><td>3</td><td>12</td><td>42</td></tr>
<tr><td>4</td><td>16</td><td>54</td></tr>
<tr><td>5</td><td>20</td><td>66</td></tr>
<tr><td>6</td><td>24</td><td>78</td></tr>
<tr><td>…</td><td>…</td><td>…</td></tr>
<tr><td>n</td><td>$4n$</td><td>$12n + 6$</td></tr>
</table>

<table>
<tr><th colspan="3">5 UNITS</th></tr>
<tr><th>No. in Staircase</th><th>Volume</th><th>Surface Area</th></tr>
<tr><td>1</td><td>5</td><td>22</td></tr>
<tr><td>2</td><td>10</td><td>36</td></tr>
<tr><td>3</td><td>15</td><td>50</td></tr>
<tr><td>4</td><td>20</td><td>64</td></tr>
<tr><td>5</td><td>25</td><td>78</td></tr>
<tr><td>6</td><td>30</td><td>92</td></tr>
<tr><td>…</td><td>…</td><td>…</td></tr>
<tr><td>n</td><td>$5n$</td><td>$14n + 8$</td></tr>
</table>

<table>
<tr><th colspan="3">6 UNITS</th></tr>
<tr><th>No. in Staircase</th><th>Volume</th><th>Surface Area</th></tr>
<tr><td>1</td><td>6</td><td>26</td></tr>
<tr><td>2</td><td>12</td><td>42</td></tr>
<tr><td>3</td><td>18</td><td>58</td></tr>
<tr><td>4</td><td>24</td><td>74</td></tr>
<tr><td>5</td><td>30</td><td>90</td></tr>
<tr><td>6</td><td>36</td><td>106</td></tr>
<tr><td>…</td><td>…</td><td>…</td></tr>
<tr><td>n</td><td>$6n$</td><td>$16n + 10$</td></tr>
</table>

Source: "Algebra for Everyone," National Concil of Teachers of Mathematics.

Figure N
Ultimate Value Table for Investigation 8.10

Pattern	1	2	3	4	5	6	7	8	9
(single X)	✓	✓	✓	✓	✓	✓	✓	✓	✓
(double X)			✓			✓			✓
(triple X)	✓	✓	✓	✓	✓	✓	✓	✓	✓
(quadruple X)	✓	✓	✓						✓
(quintuple X)			✓			✓			✓

510

Figure O
Examples of Guatemalan Weaving Patterns

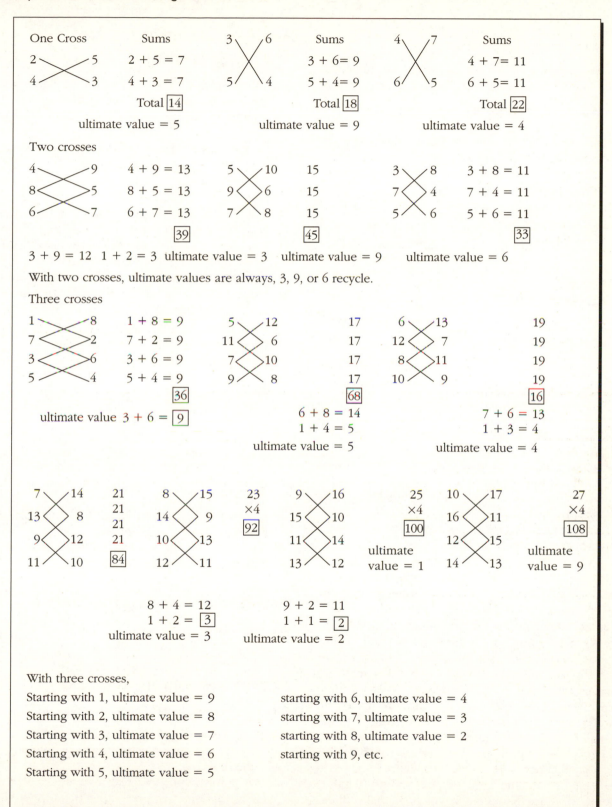

One Cross   Sums
2   5   2 + 5 = 7
4   3   4 + 3 = 7
        Total 14
    ultimate value = 5

3   6   Sums
              3 + 6 = 9
5   4   5 + 4 = 9
        Total 18
    ultimate value = 9

4   7   Sums
              4 + 7 = 11
6   5   6 + 5 = 11
        Total 22
    ultimate value = 4

Two crosses
4   9   4 + 9 = 13
8   5   8 + 5 = 13
6   7   6 + 7 = 13
        39

5   10   15
9   6   15
7   8   15
        45

3   8   3 + 8 = 11
7   4   7 + 4 = 11
5   6   5 + 6 = 11
        33

3 + 9 = 12   1 + 2 = 3   ultimate value = 3   ultimate value = 9   ultimate value = 6

With two crosses, ultimate values are always, 3, 9, or 6 recycle.

Three crosses
1   8   1 + 8 = 9
7   2   7 + 2 = 9
3   6   3 + 6 = 9
5   4   5 + 4 = 9
        36
ultimate value 3 + 6 = 9

5   12   17
11   6   17
7   10   17
9   8   17
        68
6 + 8 = 14
1 + 4 = 5
ultimate value = 5

6   13   19
12   7   19
8   11   19
10   9   19
        16
7 + 6 = 13
1 + 3 = 4
ultimate value = 4

7   14   21
13   8   21
9   12   21
11   10   21
        84

8   15   23
              ×4
14   9   92
10   13
12   11

8 + 4 = 12
1 + 2 = 3
ultimate value = 3

9   16   25
              ×4
15   10   100
11   14
13   12   ultimate
              value = 1

9 + 2 = 11
1 + 1 = 2
ultimate value = 2

10   17   27
              ×4
16   11   108
12   15
14   13   ultimate
              value = 9

With three crosses,
Starting with 1, ultimate value = 9
Starting with 2, ultimate value = 8
Starting with 3, ultimate value = 7
Starting with 4, ultimate value = 6
Starting with 5, ultimate value = 5

starting with 6, ultimate value = 4
starting with 7, ultimate value = 3
starting with 8, ultimate value = 2
starting with 9, etc.

- With three crosses, when we start with 1, we get an ultimate value of 9. With 2 we get an ultimate value of 8, and so on, so that all ultimate values can be found.
- With four crosses, once again we get only ultimate values of 3, 6, and 9.

We leave the rest up to you and your students. Here are some possible questions to pursue.

1. Can you predict what will happen with six crosses?
2. Explain why only three ultimate values are possible with two crosses and four crosses. Are there any other amounts of crosses with only three possible ultimate values?
3. What calculation shortcut can you use to find ultimate values?

CHAPTER 9

Activity 9.1: Mini-Camel

The first reaction to this problem usually is that the camel cannot get to the market with any bananas. The second thought is that Mini-Camel can walk partway, deposit some bananas, and then return for more. This suggestion usually elicits the question, "Does Mini-Camel eat a banana for each mile on the return trip?" The answer is yes. Many students begin with simply trying values such as 5 miles, 2 miles, or 1 mile for the first deposit point, using trial and error.

A more sophisticated approach is to develop a system so that when Mini-Camel starts out from a deposit point, she will always have a full load. For example, if Mini-Camel carries 15 bananas 5 miles from the beginning point (A) and saves enough to get home on each return trip, she will have deposited 20 bananas at the first deposit point (B) after traveling from A to B three times. Then, when she starts out again, she can carry 15 bananas the first trip but will return to carry only 5 bananas the second trip, i.e., not a full load. Since five total trips (two round trips and one 1-way trip) are made between A and B, it is most efficient to carry the bananas 3 miles for the first leg of the journey. Thus she will have eaten 15 bananas and have 30 bananas deposited at point B. Now it is desirable to have 15 bananas when she reaches the second deposit point, C. Since Mini-Camel will now make three trips (one round trip and one 1-way trip), she should travel 5 miles from B to C. At C with 15 ba-

nanas, she should make a run for it to the fair. Thus, she arrives at the fair with 7 bananas if she must eat 1 when arriving at the fair or during the last mile.

Activity 9.2: Finding the Area of a Triangular Region

1. Middle-school students can fold the paper and estimate the area by counting the number of squares in $\triangle DEF$. Assign each group different values of x to investigate, and then display all the values on a class set of values for discussion. Thus, students do not get bogged down in the arithmetic and can concentrate on the concept of a maximum.
2. Middle-school students familiar with the equation of the area of a triangle can estimate or measure lengths to approximate the areas of different DEF triangles for comparison.
3. Algebra students can use the Pythagorean theorem and equation of the area of a triangle to find an equation for y and use a graphing calculator to assist analysis. Since DEF is a right triangle and the distance AD is known,

$$(AD - DF)^2 = (DE)^2 + (DF)^2$$

and

$$DF = \frac{(DE)^2 - (AD)^2}{-2(AD)}$$

Thus, the area of $\triangle EDF$ is (1/2) (base) (height) or (1/2) (DE) (DF). Let $DE = x$, substitute the height of the rectangle for AD, substitute DF into the area equation (area = y), and plot on a graphing calculator to locate the value of DE when the area of DEF is a maximum.

4. Calculus students can find the derivative of the equation developed in Method 3.

Activity 9.3: Crossing the River

The equation for x adults and 2 children is T = $4x$ + 1, where T is the number of trips.

Activity 9.4: Cutting the Cake

Give the students hints such as the following:

1. Make a set of rules for cutting a round cake into seven equal pieces, and then follow the same rules.
2. Use graph paper to make a square of 7 × 7 (why this size?) representing the top of the cake. Find the perimeter, and try different cake-cutting schemes on the figure.

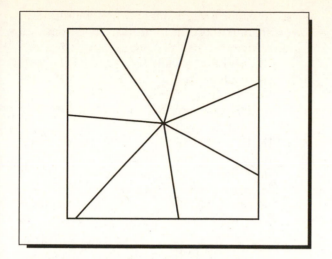

One possible configuration is shown in the figure above.

Activity 9.5: Guess My Number if You Can

The answer is 2,519. Students will explore the factors of the numbers 2 through 8 and deduce that the number is the product of 5, 7, 8, and 9 minus 1. They are finding the lowest common multiple of numbers 2 through 9 and then subtracting 1, i.e., $2 \times 2 \times 2 \times 3 \times 3 \times 5 \times 6 - 1 = 2,519$.

Activity 9.6: The Locker Problem

Begin with the pattern for 10 students and 10 lockers. Ask students how many factors are in each perfect square. The obvious answer is 2. Then ask how many prime factors are there in each perfect square? From the table you can see that the number of lockers of perfect squares have been changed an odd number of times and therefore they are the only ones left open.

Lockers	1	2	3	4	5	6	7	8	9	10
Student	c	c	c	c	c	c	c	c	c	c
1	o	o	o	o	o	o	o	o	o	o
2		c	o	c	o	c	o	c	o	c
3			c	c	o	o	o	c	c	c
4				o	o	o	o	o	c	c
5					c					o
6						c				
7							c			
8								c		
9									o	
10										c

In the original problem, only the lockers whose numbers are perfect squares are left open.

Activity 9.7: Diophantus

One method is to use the following equation:

$$(1/6)x + (1/12)x + (1/7)x + 5 + 4 = x/2,$$

where x represents the age of Diophantus. The left side is the age of Diophantus, and the right side is his son's age. The answer is 84 years.

Another method is to assume his age is a whole number. Then it must be the lowest common denominator of 6, 12, and 7. This number is $2^2 \times 3 \times 7 = 84$, a method that does not require algebra.

Activity 9.8: The Checkerboard Problem

By one method the student recognizes a series of perfect squares. There are 64 unit squares, 49 squares are 2×2, 36 squares are 3×3, and so forth. Therefore, add the number of perfect squares between 1 and 64 for a total of 204 squares.

Another student may make a table like the following:

Dimensions of Square	1 × 1	2 × 2	3 × 3	4 × 4
Number of Small Squares	64	49	36	25
Decrease in Number of Small Squares		15	13	11

After completing the table by successive subtraction, the student adds the values in the second row.

Activity 9.9: The Popcorn Problem*

Activities for all Students, Including General Math, Pre-algebra, and Algebra Students (Calculator use assumed)

1. If squares of side length 2 inches are removed from the piece of cardboard, what are the height, length, width, and volume of the box? If the side length of the removed squares is 0.25 inch, what are the height, length, width, and volume of the box?
2. Use ordinary 8 1/2" × 11" construction paper, a ruler, scissors, and tape to actually make boxes

*Waits, Bert K. and Franklin Demana, "The Popcorn Problem," The Ohio State University, Copyright 1992. Used with permission.

by cutting out squares of side length 0.25″, 0.5″, 0.75″, 1.0″, 1.25″, 1.5″, and so forth until no box can be made. Assign each student a different side length value.

a. How many *actual* boxes will be constructed if we start by removing a square of side length 0.25″ and continue by increasing the length of the cut by 0.25″ each time?

b. Use a ruler to compute the volume of each box constructed in Problem 2(a) by *measuring* height (H), length (L), and width (W) and using the formula $V = LWH$. Make a table of values as shown for the boxes constructed using the side lengths given earlier.

Side Length x	Volume V
0.25 in.	about 21 cu. in.
0.50 in.	
0.75 in.	
.	
.	
.	

3. Let the side length of the removed square be represented by x (inches).
a. What is the height of the box?
b. What is the length of the box?
c. What is the width of the box?
d. What is the volume V of the box in terms of x?

4. Use the formula in Problem 3(d) for V in terms of x to make a table of values for x and V beginning with $x = 0.25$ and increasing x by increments of 0.25 up to $x = 5$.

x	V
0.25	21
0.50	
0.75	
⋮	
4.75	
5.00	

a. Compare this table of values with the table of measured volume values found in Problem 2(b). Which table has more rows? Why?

b. What are the largest and smallest values of x possible if x *represents the side length of the removed square?* Explain your answer.

c. In either table, is there a box with greatest volume? If so, what are its dimensions and volume?

d. Can you find a value of x **not** *in the table* (i.e., different from a multiple of 0.25 inch) that results in a box with greater volume than the one identified in Problem 4(c)? How many such xs can you find?

e. Explain how the table method could be refined so you would find fewer boxes of volume greater than the box of maximum volume identified in the revised table.

f. Is there a box of greatest volume? Is there more than one such box? What size square must be removed to produce a box of greatest volume? What is the greatest possible volume?

Activities for Advanced Algebra Students (Use of a graphing calculator assumed)

5. Express the volume V of the box in terms of x, and draw a **complete** graph of the algebraic model V. That is, draw a graph that shows **all** of the important behavior of the model. What is the domain of the function $y = V(x)$?

6. Which portion of the graph in Problem 5 represents the box-volume problem situation? Draw a complete graph of the box-volume problem situation—that is, a graph showing only those values of x that make sense in the problem situation.

7. Use graphing calculator zoom-in to determine x so that the resulting box has maximum possible volume. Find the dimensions of this box and this maximum volume. State the answers with error at most 0.01 inch.

Activities for Calculus Students

8. Find the **exact** dimensions of the box of maximum volume. What is the **exact** maximum volume? Use analytic method of calculus. Support with graphing calculator visualization.

Related Problems and Extensions

9. Determine the side length x so that the volume of the resulting box is 50 cubic inches. Write an algebraic representation (equation) of the problem situation. Solve both the model (equation) and the problem situation. Why are the solutions different? Do you need technology?

10. Determine the side length x so that the resulting volume of the box is less than 50 cubic inches. Write an algebraic representation (inequality) of the problem situation. Solve both the model (inequality) and the problem situation. Why are the solutions different?

Solutions to Activities 1–4

1. $H = 0.25$ inch, $L = 11 - 2(0.25) = 10.5$ inches, $W = 8.5 - 2(0.25) = 8$ inches, and $V = 0.25(10.5)(8) = 21$ inches; $H = 2$ inches, $L = 11 - 2(2) = 7$ inches, $W = 8.5 - 2(2) = 4.5$ cubic inches, $V = 2(7)(4.5) = 63$ cubic inches.

2. **a.** 16
   b.

x	V
0.25	21
0.50	37.5
0.75	49.875
1.00	58.5
1.25	63.75
1.50	66
1.75	65.625
2.00	63
2.25	58.50
2.50	52.5
2.75	45.375
3.00	37.5
3.25	29.25
3.50	21.00
3.75	13.125
4.00	6

(*Note:* These are exact values; your students' estimates from measuring and applying the formula $V = LWH$ will vary.)

3. **a.** $H = x$
   b. $L = 11 - 2x$
   c. $W = 8.5 - 2x$
   d. $V = WLH = (8.5 - 2x)(11 - 2x)x$. This is the algebraic representation of the problem situation.

4. The table will be the same as the table in Problem 2(b), with the addition of four rows as shown.
   a.

x	V
0.25	21
.	.
.	.
.	.
4.00	6
4.25	0
4.50	− 4.50
4.75	− 7.125
5.00	− 7.50

b. If x represents a side length in inches of the removed square in the box problem situation, then $0 < x < 4.25$. Thus there are **bounds** for x, namely 0 and 4.25, but there is no "smallest" or "largest" value of x. This is subtle and will have to be carefully explained. First, you must agree that values of $x \le 0$ and $x \ge 4.25$ do not result in real boxes and thus are not candidate values. Next, students should realize that, for example, if they say $x = 0.0001$ is *the* smallest value of x, then $x = 0.00001$ is a legitimate smaller value, etc. Of course, you will get into a very interesting discussion if you admit that perhaps $x = 0.001$ is the smallest possible **practical** value. This is an opportunity to discuss what is *possible mathematically* versus what is practical. This is *real* applied mathematics!

c. Yes. It is the box with dimensions $H = 1.5''$, $L = 8''$, and $W = 5.5''$ and volume 66 cubic inches.

d. Yes, $x = 1.55$ inches results in a box with volume 66.123 cubic inches. There are *infinitely* many possible values of x not shown in the table that produce boxes of volume greater than 66. Again, you can have the *possible*-versus-*practical* discussion.

e. Make the increments between successive x values smaller, say, 0.1 inch or 0.01 inch. This discussion could lead to a practical numerical solution method (admittedly somewhat laborious) and a good discussion of error. Of course, using calculators is essential.

f. Yes. No. Guess and check with $x = 1.35$, $1.51, 1.52 \ldots 1.64, 1.65$ establishes that $x = 1.59$ produces a box of maximum volume $1.59 (11 - 3.18)(8.5 - 3.18) = 66.147816$. Determining the **exact** solution requires the theory and tools of *calculus*.

Discussion of the Solution to Problems 5–7

The formula $V = LWH$ can be applied to obtain the volume V in terms of x. If the height is x, then the length of the box is $11 - 2x$, and its width is $8.5 - 2x$. Thus, $V = x(11 - 2x)(8.5 - 2x)$ is an *algebraic* representation of the volume in terms of x.

Activity 9.10: 12 Bags of Gold

Begin by numbering all the bags as 1 through 12. Next, weigh bags numbered 1 to 4 on each side and 5 to 8 on the other side.

If these are equal, then weigh 9 to 11 against 1 to 3. If they are again equal, 12 must be different. Weigh it against any of the others to determine if it is light or heavy.

The case discussed is the simplest one: When bags do not balance, keep track of which side is lightest and which is heaviest in subsequent weighings. The rest of the solution is left to the reader (just like in a college mathematics book!).

Activity 9.11: The Boat Problem*

Following are some possible methods for solving the Boat Problem. The teacher may wish to direct the students in using particular methods based on the level of the mathematics class. There is also the possibility of allowing students to explore and determine their own solution method. The teacher may wish to share with students alternative methods of solving the problem, including methods above the current curriculum level of the class.

Solution Method 1

Give each student two pieces of centimeter grid paper and a centimeter ruler.

To get a clear picture of the problem and explore possible solutions, students should:

- Transfer the diagram to grid paper using an appropriate scale.
- Measure the total distance the victim would travel, based on the location of the ambulance.
- Solve for both the boat and ambulance times and find the total time based on their sketch.
- Repeat this process several times by selecting possible solutions on either side of their first estimated solution.
- Compare the solutions found for the various positions chosen.

Discuss the results. What location for the ambulance appears to give the shortest total time for the trip to the hospital?

Once students have reached what appears to be an optimal solution (shortest total time), they can attempt to find a more accurate solution. Students can do this on the centimeter grid paper by focusing on a limited range about their solution, using a finer scale. The students should discuss the similarities and differences in their solutions. This discussion can be extended to the class.

Solution Method 2

The teacher might want the class to see how the Pythagorean theorem could be utilized in this problem when the unknown leg of the triangle is repre-

*University of Northern Iowa (1994). Lessons in Mathematics for the Classroom and for Inservice Sessions with Alternative Assessment Procedures. Cedar Falls, IA.

sented by x. The length of the hypotenuse = $\sqrt{30^2+x^2}$. The solution for total time can be represented algebraically as follows:

$$Time = \sqrt{30^2 + x^2}/20 + (60 - x)/50$$

This formula can be used with a calculator to test some of the students' conjectures.

Solution Method 3

The problem can be illustrated on the Geometer's Sketchpad®. If students are familiar with the Sketchpad (constructing line segments and perpendicular lines, measuring lengths of segments, and doing calculations with measurements), have the students set up the situation on the computer. Otherwise either demonstrate or walk the students through the following solution.

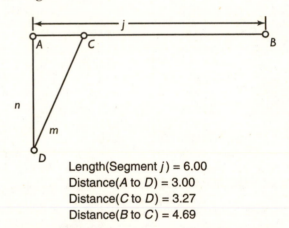

Length(Segment j) = 6.00
Distance(A to D) = 3.00
Distance(C to D) = 3.27
Distance(B to C) = 4.69

(Distance(B to C)/50+Distance(C to D)/20)*10 = 2.5

Distance(C to A) = 1.31

Solution Method 4

An alternative strategy for approximating the solution is to use a Texas Instruments TI-81® graphing calculator program. The steps in setting up the following program for the TI-81® can be adapted for other graphing calculators.

```
1 → Arow
2 → Acol
Disp "START"
Input A
Disp "STOP"
Input B
Disp "STEP"
Input C
Lbl 1
A → [A](1,1)
√(A^2+30^2)/20+(60-A)/50 → [A](1,2)
Disp [A]
Pause
```

A+C → A
If A>B
End
Goto 1

If the function is typed as Y1 on the calculator's Y= screen and the 11th line is changed to Y1 → [A](1, 2), the program can be used with other functions.

Solution Method 5

A spreadsheet program can take advantage of the computer to solve the problem using Method 2. An example of a spreadsheet that closes in on the solution with progressively smaller distance steps is shown in Figure P.

Figure P

A Spreadsheet Used to Close in on the Boat Problem Solution

A SPREADSHEET USED TO CLOSE IN ON THE BOAT PROBLEM SOLUTION

Distances in Steps of 5 Miles

Distance x	Boat	Ambulance	Total
0	1.5000000000	1.2	2.7000000000
5	1.5206906326	1.1	2.6206906326
10	1.5811388301	1.0	2.5811388301
15	1.6770509831	0.9	2.5770509831
20	1.8027756377	0.8	2.6027756377
25	1.9525624190	0.7	2.6525624190
30	2.1213203436	0.6	2.7213203436
35	2.3048861143	0.5	2.8048861143
40	2.5000000000	0.4	2.9000000000
45	2.7041634566	0.3	3.0041634566
50	2.9154759474	0.2	3.1154759474
55	3.1324910215	0.1	3.2324910215
60	3.3541019662	0	3.3541019662

Distances in Steps of 1 Mile

Distance x	Boat	Ambulance	Total
10	1.5811388301	1.00	2.5811388301
11	1.5976545309	0.98	2.5776545309
12	1.6155494421	0.96	2.5755494421
13	1.6347782724	0.94	2.5747782724
14	1.6552945357	0.92	2.5752945357
15	1.6770509831	0.90	2.5770509831

Distances in Steps of .1 Mile

Distance x	Boat	Ambulance	Total
12.0	1.6155494421	0.960	2.5755494421
12.1	1.6174130579	0.958	2.5754130579
12.2	1.6192899679	0.956	2.5752899679
12.3	1.6211801257	0.954	2.5751801257
12.4	1.6230834852	0.952	2.5750834852
12.5	1.6250000000	0.950	2.5750000000
12.6	1.6269296236	0.948	2.5749296236
12.7	1.6288723093	0.946	2.5748723093
12.8	1.6308280106	0.944	2.5748280106
12.9	1.6327966805	0.942	2.5747966805
13.0	1.6347782724	0.940	2.5747782724
13.1	1.6367727393	0.938	2.5747727393
13.2	1.6387800340	0.936	2.5747800340
13.3	1.6408001097	0.934	2.5748001097
13.4	1.6428329191	0.932	2.5748329191
13.5	1.6448784150	0.930	2.5748784150
13.6	1.6469365501	0.928	2.5749365501
13.7	1.6490072771	0.926	2.5750072771
13.8	1.6510905487	0.924	2.5750905487
13.9	1.6531863174	0.922	2.5751863174
14.0	1.6552945357	0.920	2.5752945357

Distances in Steps of .01 Mile

Distance x	Boat	Ambulance	Total
13.00	1.6347782724	0.9400	2.5747782724
13.01	1.6349771405	0.9398	2.5747771405
13.02	1.6351761373	0.9396	2.5747761373
13.03	1.6353752627	0.9394	2.5747752627
13.04	1.6355745168	0.9392	2.5747745168
13.05	1.6357738994	0.9390	2.5747738994
13.06	1.6359734105	0.9388	2.5747734105
13.07	1.6361730501	0.9386	2.5747730501
13.08	1.6363728182	0.9384	2.5747728182
13.09	1.6365727145	0.9382	2.5747727145
13.10	1.6367727393	0.9380	2.5747727393
13.11	1.6369728923	0.9378	2.5747728923
13.12	1.6371731735	0.9376	2.5747731735
13.13	1.6373735829	0.9374	2.5747735829
13.14	1.6375741205	0.9372	2.5747741205
13.15	1.6377747861	0.9370	2.5747747861
13.16	1.6379755798	0.9368	2.5747755798
13.17	1.6381765015	0.9366	2.5747765015
13.18	1.6383775511	0.9364	2.5747775511
13.19	1.6385787287	0.9362	2.5747787287
13.20	1.6387800340	0.9360	2.5747800340

Solution Method 6

Calculus students will be able to solve this as a maximum-minimum problem. The problem is to minimize T in the equation

$$T = \sqrt{30^2 + x^2}/20 + (60 - x)/50$$

A solution to this calculus problem is as follows:

$$T = \sqrt{30^2 + x^2}/20 + (60 - x)/50$$

$$dT/dx = (1/20)(1/2)(2x)/\sqrt{30^2 + x^2} + (1/50)(-1)$$

$$= x/(20\sqrt{30^2 + x^2}) - 1/50$$

$$0 = (5x - 2\sqrt{30^2 + x^2})/(100\sqrt{30^2 + x^2})$$

$$5x = 2\sqrt{30^2 + x^2}$$

$$25x^2 = 4(900 + x^2)$$

$$25x^2 = 3{,}600 + 4x^2$$

$$21x^2 = 3{,}600$$

$$x^2 = 3{,}600/21$$

$$x = 60/\sqrt{21}$$

$$x = 13.1$$

The ambulance should meet the boat approximately 13.1 miles toward the hospital from a point on shore directly in from the initial location of the boat.

CHAPTER 10

Activity 10.1: Big Numbers

Even though students may work out these problems correctly using different approaches, these problems offer an excellent opportunity to develop or review the process of dimensional analysis.

1. 60,000,000 computations in 30 seconds
2. approximately 414 gallons per year
3. 253,400,000 years
4. $4,282.47 per person

Activity 10.2: Path of a Rocket

The graph of time versus height shows a possible sketch. Here is an algebraic approach based on the assumptions of the graph.
    The general formula is:

$$d = at^2 + bt + c,$$

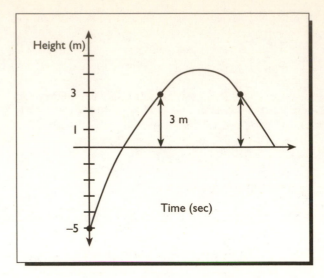

where a, b, and c are general coefficients, i.e., $a \neq 0$. When $t = 0$, $d = -5$. Substituting in the general formula from the given information, we have:

$$3 = 16a + 4b - 5$$

and:

$$3 = 64a + 8b - 5.$$

The solution to this system is $(-\frac{1}{4}, 3)$, so the specific equation that models this solution is:

$$d = -\frac{1}{4}t^2 + 3t - 5.$$

Solving this equation, we get {2, 10}.
    From the given situation, we conclude that the rocket is at ground level 2 seconds after being fired and again at 10 seconds.

Activity 10.3: Bear Flag Written-Response Item*

The task is to estimate the percent of a flag that is covered by a bear icon. This requires the solution of subproblems for which work should be clearly shown. To fully accomplish the task, student work will be evaluated on the presentation of the solution as well as its accuracy.

- To begin the problem, student work in Problem 1 will demonstrate a conceptual understanding of area by providing a reasonable strategy for estimating the area of the bear. This might include counting grid units (and fractional portions thereof) covered, adding the covered parts of columns or rows, or using inscribed or circumscribed rectan-

*MDTP Written Response Items, Copyright 1996 by The Regents of the University of California and the Trustees of the California State University. Reprinted with permission.

gles. It is essential that a thorough explanation be given for the process that determines the estimate.
- To complete the task, student work in Problem 2 will demonstrate that the area of the flag is 88, either by counting squares or by multiplying the number of rows by the number of columns. In

addition, student work will show that the percent of the flag covered by the bear is obtained by dividing the bear area estimate (from Problem 1) by 88 and multiplying the result by 100.

Figure Q shows a sample response.

Figure Q
Sample Response to Activity 10.3

1. Estimate the area of the bear in square units. Explain how you arrived at your estimate.

I drew a polygon that enclosed most of the bear. By counting, I found the number of squares in the polygon to be 32. Since some parts of squares were outside of the bear's body, I subtracted 2 from 32 and got 30 square units as my estimate.

2. Use your estimate to find the percent of the flag covered by the bear. Explain.

the area of the flag is 11 × 8 = 88

$$\frac{30}{88} = \begin{array}{r} .34 \\ 88\overline{)30.00} \\ \underline{26\ 4} \\ 3\ 6\ 0 \\ \underline{3\ 5\ 2} \\ 8 \end{array}$$

Approximately 34% of the flag is covered by the bear.

Rubric

1	Describe method of counting squares inside or outside bear or circumscribing or inscribing rectangle OR Explain how to compute percentage but fail to perform computation with a reasonable estimate of the bear's area.
2	Estimate area of bear consistently with described method OR Use numbers to correctly compute percentage with reasonable estimate of bear's area.
3	Describe method of counting squares inside or outside bear or circumscribing or inscribing rectangle AND use numbers to correctly compute percentage with reasonable estimate of bear's area (incorrect but explained areas such as 8 × 10, 9 × 11, or 7 × 11 are acceptable for a score of 3) OR Estimate area of bear consistently with described method AND explain how to compute percentage but fail to perform computation with a reasonable estimate of the bear's area.
4	Estimate area of bear consistently with described method AND use numbers to correctly compute percentage with reasonable estimate of bear's area.

Note: For further guidelines, see General Scoring Rubric for Written Response Items.

Activity 10.4: Music Company

Answers will vary, according to the responses provided by the students. See the rubric provided in Figure R..

Activity 10.5: Dream House Project

Creation of the rubric is left to the teacher.

Activity 10.6: Spirolaterals

The key to getting the deepest insights from the students is asking them questions about what they are doing, how they might extend their explorations, and how that could prove that what they see in several concrete situations is true for all situations. One school started a Spirolateral Web site so that different patterns could be shared from school to school. We have used this task with many groups of students and teachers and will report a few of the generalizations that usually are made. However, it has never failed that a new approach or recognition of a pattern arises in every group.

Figure R
Scoring Guide for Activity 10.4

	Level 1	Level 2	Level 3	Level 4
Design of Survey Instrument	Questions very limited; will not serve to obtain necessary information	Questions will elicit almost all information required for the task	Questions will elicit all information required	In addition, questions asked in a manner to ease later data analysis
Analysis of Data	Data poorly organized; hard to read and interpret	Data organization is uneven	Data organized but difficult to use for making a graph	Data well organized and neatly presented
Quality of Graph	Graph seriously flawed: inappropriate type, inaccurate, or error in execution	Graph has one serious error	Graph appropriate to the data and accurate	In addition, graph well presented with all details well executed
Mathematical Projections	Mathematical projections inaccurate, with no apparent method used	Although inaccurate, projections show evidence of a method being used	Mathematical projections essentially accurate	In addition, the mathematical projections are imaginative in their methodology
"Case" Made to Producer	Ideas not accurately summarized; a producer could not act on the findings	Minor errors in the interpretation of findings	Interpretation of data essentially accurate; data support findings	In addition, the findings are presented in an imaginative manner

Source: Danielson, Charlotte. (1997). *A Collection of Performance Tasks and Rubrics: Middle School Mathematics*. Larchmont, NY: Eye on Education.

Using this as a POW allows time for student ideas to percolate and for students to play off of each other's discoveries. One class period is too short a time for most students to have the experience of true inquiry by delving into many ideas and questioning each other's conclusions. Some common generalizations follow:

- All paths with three different lengths return to the starting point after three repeats (when square graph paper is used). *Questions:* How is the pattern affected by changes in the order of the numbers? How does the relative size of the three numbers affect the pattern, i.e., what if two of the numbers add up to the third? What if isometric graph paper were used? Do the same patterns occur?

- Paths with four different lengths spiral off infinitely. *Questions:* Why would this be a good path for a worm? What might a problem be for a worm with this type of path?

Activity 10.7: Tiling With Triangles*†

1. tessellation

2. not a tessellation
3. tessellation

4. tessellation

5. not possible
6. Check students' drawings.
7. twice
8. 180°
9. 360°
10. Answers will vary. Possible answer: Since the sum of the angle measures of any triangle is 180°, the three angles of a triangle can always be arranged twice around a point, giving an angle sum of 2(180°) = 360°. Therefore, any triangle can be used to make a tessellation.
11. **a.** translation
    b. rotation
    c. translation
12. Responses will vary; steps should parallel steps in lesson and be written in students' own words.

Mathscape (1999). Chicago, IL: Creative Publications. Reprinted with permission.

Activity 10.8: Miles of Words*†
Sample SoFlution

1. There are about 60 words in the paragraph from the novel. Reading that excerpt aloud takes about 20 seconds, or 20 ÷ 60 = 0.33 minutes. This is a rate of 60 ÷ 0.33 = 180 words per minute. Any reasonable estimate close to this is acceptable.
2. Trains go fast (greater than 70 mi./hr.) but also make stops. An estimate of 60 mi./hr. as an average seems reasonable.
3. At a rate of 60 mi./hr. traveling 200 miles takes:

$$200 \div 60 = 3\frac{1}{3} \text{ hours} = (3\frac{1}{3}) \text{ minutes} = 200 \text{ minutes}$$

A quicker solution is 60 mi./hr. = 1 mi./min., so 200 miles requires 200 minutes.

At a rate of 180 words per minute, the number of words in 200 minutes is (180)(200) = 36,000 words, assuming the person talked all the time. This is not quite 40,000 words. Either the person talked faster, or the train went slower or had multiple stops. Or perhaps the author exaggerated.

Using This Task

The figuring in Problem 1 gives $T = D/s$, while the figuring in Problem 2 gives $N = rT$. Combining these gives the result $N = r(D/s)$. This expresses the number of words in terms of the rate of speed s, the rate of speech r, and the distance D. The equation can be used to see if the number of words (40,000) mentioned in the article is reasonable.

If it were presented in this straightforward way, the task would be simple and mechanical. But it is not presented in this way. To get to the heart of this task, students have to do some meaningful work. They need to make sense of a given written passage where the context is set, and they need to make reasonable estimates of the rate of speed of a train and the rate of normal speech. These estimates will become the given rates in the next stage of the task. In carrying out the heart of the task, students need to know (and know how to use) rate relationships such as "distance equals rate times time." They also need to make appropriate unit conversions: the time T they find in Problem 1 will be in hours, and they will have to convert this to minutes before they can use it in Problem 2, where the rate is in words per minute.

†This task comes from High School Assessment Package I, developed by the project Balanced Assessment for the Mathematics Curriculum. Balanced Assessment packages, comprising additional tasks and instructional support, are published by Dale Seymour Publications. Further information can be obtained from the publisher or the project Web site: http://www.educ.msu.edu/MARS. Reprinted with permission.

Activity 10.9: Get a Clue

A Venn diagram is shown in Figure S, and the scoring rubric provided in the program is shown in Figure T. An activity to be added is badminton—it is moderately active and includes aspects of other favorite activities.

Activity 10.10: Planning a Bookcase

One possible solution is to make a bookcase that is 4 feet high and 6 feet wide, using the advertised shelving, making a four-shelf bookcase similar to the one in the ad that cost $59.87. One 8-foot board costs $5.25. It could be cut into two 4-foot pieces to be used as the sides of the bookcase. Three 12-foot boards could each be cut into 6-foot lengths, resulting in five shelves, as in the bookcase illustrated, and one 6-foot length left over. The total cost of this bookcase is:

One 8' board @ $5.25	$ 5.25
Three 12' boards @ $7.30	21.90
Total Cost	$27.15

This is a savings of $32.72.

There are other solutions.

Activity 10.11: Effective Tax Rates

Either by trial and error or by the equation $.06(x - 10{,}000) = .05x$, when x represents a person's total income, we find that someone earning $60,000 would have an effective tax rate of 5%. It is impossible to have an effective tax rate of 6%, as $10,000 would always be subtracted from the income before the tax calculation.

Figure S
Venn Diagram for Activity 10.9

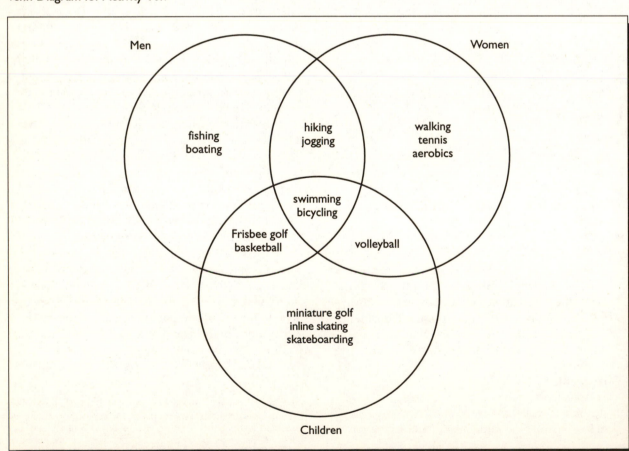

Figure T
Scoring Rubric for Activity 10.9

Level	Criteria
3 Superior	• Shows thorough understanding of the concepts of logical reasoning • Uses appropriate strategies to evaluate and model expressions • Computations are correct • Written explanations are exemplary • Diagrams are accurate and appropriate • Goes beyond requirements of the problems
2 Satisfactory, With Minor Flaws	• Shows understanding of the concepts of logical reasoning • Uses appropriate strategies to evaluate and model expressions • Computations are mostly correct • Written explanations are effective • Diagrams are mostly accurate and appropriate • Satisfies all requirements of the problems
1 Nearly Satisfactory, With Serious Flaws	• Shows understanding of most of the concepts of logical reasoning • May not use appropriate strategies to evaluate and model expressions • Computations are mostly correct • Written explanations are satisfactory • Diagrams are mostly accurate and appropriate • Satisfies most requirements of the problems
0 Unsatisfactory	• Shows little or no understanding of the concepts of logical reasoning • May not use appropriate strategies to evaluate and model expressions • Computations are incorrect • Written explanations are not satisfactory • Diagrams are not accurate or appropriate • Does not satisfy requirements of problems

Source: Adapted from Foster, D., Gillian, S., Price, J., McClain, K, Martinez, B., and others. (1995). *Interactive Mathematics: Activities and Investigations*. Westerville, OH: Glencoe.

Activity 10.12: Insect Population

1. Students could use the repeat capabilities of almost any calculator to develop the following table:

Year	Insect Pop.
0	15
1	60
2	240
3	960
4	3,840
5	15,360
6	61,440

2. By continuing to use the calculator or by a formula, they will find that the insect population at the end of 10 years is 15,728,640.
3. The recursive form is $a_1 = 15$; $(a_n = (a_{n-1}) 4)$; The explicit form is $15(4^x)$.
4. Yes, assuming no predator or other environmental or human factors caused a decrease in the insect population.

Activity 10.13: Wall Posters

One solution is shown below, using graph paper as a tool. We have seen many middle-school students take this approach to similar problems, if graph paper is available. The solution shown is our choice, to give some variety to the wall.

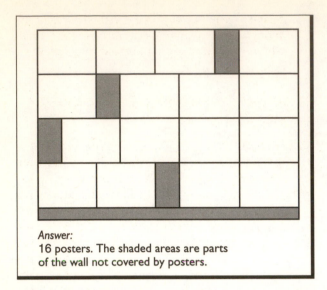

Answer:
16 posters. The shaded areas are parts of the wall not covered by posters.

CHAPTER 11

Activity 11.1: Census Data Line Graph

1. Answers will vary.
2. doctoral degree group—about $60,000 per annum
3. professional degrees—Since people may be older when they attain these degrees, the initial earnings may be below those of their peers with doctoral degrees. However, as they become established in their professions, there is a greater opportunity for growth by becoming leaders and administrators in their chosen field.
4. In general, the lower the educational attainment, the flatter the earning curve. Having a limited income seems to limit opportunities for advancement.
5. The period of time from the early 50s to the late 50s shows a decrease in earnings of people with a doctoral degree. Perhaps they are retiring from university positions during this decade of their age.

Activity 11.2: Operations on Fractions

Note: In the book from which this activity was taken (NCTM Middle School Addenda Series, *Developing Number Sense*), there is a sample of discourse (pp. 11–12) between students and teacher that was used for evaluation purposes.

Answers
1. *C*
2. *B*
3. *C*
4. ≈17
5. ≈23

Activity 11.3: Exploring Equivalent Expressions With Decimals

Expressions 1, 4, 5, 6, 7, and 8 are equivalent to 12.8 × 48. Student explanations will vary. Three different students verified the equivalence 64 × 9.6 = 12.8 × 48 in these ways:

Student 1: 64 = 4/3 of 48, so use 3/4 of 12.8 (which is 9.6) to get the other factor.
Student 2: By factoring and using number properties, 64 × 9.6 = 6.4 × 96 = 6.4 × 2 × 6 × 8 = (6.4 × 2) × (6 × 8).
Student 3: Divide the first factor by 5, and multiply the second factor by 5: (64 ÷ 5) × (9.6 × 5) = 12.8 × 48.

Activity 11.4: Numerical Horse Sense

Most of these problems have solutions that vary with different circumstances. However, to find out how old a person would be a million minutes from today would have a standard approach. Using dimensional analysis, we have:

1,000,000 × 1 hr/60 min × 1 da/24 hr × 1 yr/365 day ≈ 1.9 years more than the current age.

Activity 11.6: MATHCOUNTS Sample Item: Back to School

1. Since the ratio is 4:5, we can set up the following equation: $4x + 5x = 27$. The solution to that equation is 3. That means that there are 4(3) = 12 girls and 5(3) = 15 boys, so there are 3 more boys than girls. Many students will solve this by setting up tables, which is an acceptable solution strategy.
2. Since there are four sixth-grade classes, there are (4)(3)(2)(1) = 24 different orders in which they could have been called into the auditorium. There are only (3)(2)(1) = 6 orders for the seventh-grade class and 24 for the eighth-grade class. Together, there would be a total of (24)(6)(24) = 3,456 different orders in which the 11 classes could have been called to the auditorium.

Activity 11.7: AMC Sample Item: Exponents

Because $64 = 2^6$, we see that 64 is a sixth power, a cube, a square, and a first power. Therefore, $z = 6$, 3, 2, or 1. For $z = 6$, we have only $(x, y) = (2, 1)$; for $z = 3$, we have $(x, y) = (4, 1)$ and $(2, 2)$; for $z = 2$, we have $(x, y) = (8, 1)$ and $(2, 3)$; and for $z = 1$, we have $(x, y) = (64, 1)$, $(8, 2)$, and $(2, 6)$. There are 8 solutions in all.

Activity 11.8: Estimation Contest

1. depends on the circumstances
2. ≈30 million
3. Answers will vary.
4. about 2.75 years
5. 100,000
6. There were close to 225,000 in 1982.

Activity 11.11: Advanced Number Sense

1. **a.** m **e.** n
   b. l **f.** q
   c. m **g.** h
   d. p **h.** p

2. **a.** T   **e.** T
   b. F   **f.** T
   c. T   **g.** F
   d. T

CHAPTER 12

Exemplary Lesson 12.1: Voting

1. UCLA (7) vs. USC (1); UCLA (5) vs. Stanford (3); UCLA (5) vs. Harvard (3). UCLA is the winner in all two-way votes, but there is not always one that can win over all others. Then you could use Duncan Black's method of counting the number of wins each has in two-way votes.
2. UCLA: $3(4) + 2(4) + 2(2) + 1(1) = 25$
   USC: $3(3) + 2(3) + 2(1) + 1(2) = 19$
   Stanford: $3(2) + 2(2) + 2(3) + 1(3) = 19$
   Harvard: $3(1) + 2(1) + 2(4) + 1(4) = 17$
3. USC (5) vs. Stanford (3); USC (5) vs. Harvard (3); USC (1) vs. UCLA (7). It would not matter which order the offers came in because UCLA can win over all three.

4. Answers will vary. Some examples might be about which elective to take next semester, with whom to go to the prom, where to go on vacation, and what job to take.

Exemplary Lesson 12.4: Dr. Pepper on the Ramp

Richard Sisley, the source of this lesson, writes, "The lessons and assignments summarized have also been experienced by teachers in workshops given on the MAC [Mathematical Analysis of Change] course. My experience is that they constitute a very effective technology based introduction to a central idea— there are patterns in changing rates of change whose description can be discovered and related to the descriptions of patterns in other data sets arising from the same event. The students come to see this as one of the goals of calculus."

Step 1

Have the students speculate on the type of function whose graph might at least come very close to passing through the data point. Because of their experience with motion data, the students suggest trying a quadratic model. You can guide the students to select a representative sample of three data points and use the coordinates of these points to write a system of three linear equations whose solution they expect will be the coefficients of a quadratic model function for all the data points expressed in a standard form. Even though students choose different trips and the coordinates of their solutions differ depending on this choice, the quadratic graphs generated using these various solutions should visually seem to fit the data points. (If you prefer, students can use their calculator's Quadratic Regression command rather than using a sample of three data points.)

Step 2

The students are asked how fast the can was moving as it crossed the upper edge of the tape. Recall that the upper edge of the tape is 6 feet from the front of the motion sensor. At first students discuss dividing 6 by the time it took to reach a position closest to 6 feet. This would be the time for data point $(1.375, 6.0534)$. However, this suggestion eventually gets replaced when they recall that in order for the motion sensor to function properly, the can had been started from a position about 1.5 feet in front of the sensor.

Students come to suggest computing an average speed based on the two data points $(1.350, 5.9273)$ and $(1.375, 6.0534)$. They think this is the best number to use as the speed as the can crossed the front edge of the tape, which can be computed from the available data points.

Step 3

When students are asked whether there might be a pattern in their data triples, they draw on their experience to suggest looking at a scatter plot. Richard Shepley, this activity's author, notes, "It is always a pleasure to note the surprise some openly express when they see that these data points appear to be at least nearly collinear. When we use our calculators' Linear Regression commands on our data sets, the results usually show a correlation coefficient impressively close to 1. In doing this I have seen correlations greater than 0.999."

Students may comment on the fact that the y-intercept of their linear model for the (time, average speed) data points is fairly close to the linear coefficient of their quadratic model for the (time, position) data points. Students may also notice that the slope of the model line for the (time, average speed) data points is about twice the quadratic coefficient of their quadratic model. You can simply note that these comments are "interesting."

Step 4

Computing average speeds indirectly from the quadratic models rather than directly from the data points is a very crucial change. A program is provided. The quadratic model should be entered in a way that uses the greatest number of digits possible in the coefficients. If QuadReg is used, the regression equation can be transferred to the $Y1$ position.

The students find that the (time, average speed) data points generated with this program are always so close to perfectly collinear that their calculators invariably give a correlation coefficient of 1. This happens regardless of their choices for the middle times they enter as they run the program. This also happens regardless of the particular quadratic expression they have entered as $Y1$ in the function list before running Program Veldata.

References

Advanced placement program® mathematics vertical teams toolkit. (1998). Austin, TX: College Board.

Aichele, D. B., & Coxford, A. F. (1994). *Professional development for teachers of mathematics.* Reston, VA: National Council of Teachers of Mathematics.

American Association of University Women. (1992). *How schools shortchange girls.* Washington, DC: AAUW Education Foundation.

Andreasen, C. (1998). Fibonacci and Pascal together again: Pattern exploration in the Fibonacci sequence. *Mathematics Teacher, 91(3),* 250–253.

Arithmetic Teacher. (1986, February).

Armstrong, D. G., & Savage, T. V. (1998). *Teaching in the secondary school: An introduction.* Upper Saddle River, NJ: Prentice-Hall.

Armstrong, T. (1994). *Multiple intelligences in the classroom.* Alexandria, VA: Association for Supervision and Curriculum Development.

Artz, A., & Newman, C. (1990). *How to use cooperative learning in the mathematics classroom.* Reston, VA: National Council of Teachers of Mathematics.

Ashlock, R. B. (1976). *Error patterns in computation: A semi-programmed approach.* Upper Saddle River, NJ: Merrill/Prentice Hall Publishing.

Association for Supervision and Curriculum Development. (1990). Cooperative learning [focus issue]. *Educational Leadership, 47,* 4.

Asturias, H. (1994). Using students' portfolios to assess mathematical understanding. *Mathematics Teacher, 87(9).*

Banchoff, T. (1990). Dimension: In L. A. Steen (Ed.), *On the shoulders of giants* (pp. 11–59). Washington, DC: National Academy Press.

Bandura, A. (1977). *Social learning theory.* Englewood Cliffs, NJ: Prentice-Hall, Inc.

Bandura, A. (1986). *Social foundations of thought and action.* Englewood Cliffs, NJ: Prentice-Hall, Inc.

Barnes, S. J. (1993). Involve the community. *Mathematics Teacher, 86(6),* 442–448.

Barnett, C., Goldenstein, D., & Jackson, B. (Eds.). (1994a). *Facilitators' guide to mathematics teaching cases: Fractions, decimals, ratios and percents, hard to teach and hard to learn.* Far West Laboratory for Educational Research and Development. Portsmouth, NH: Heinemann.

Barnett, C., Goldenstein, D., & Jackson, B. (Eds.). (1994b). *Mathematics teaching cases: Fractions, decimals, ratios and percents, hard to teach and hard to learn.* Far West Laboratory for Educational Research and Development. Portsmouth, NH: Heinemann.

Baroody, A. J. (1993, Fall). Introducing number and arithmetic concepts with number sticks. *Teaching Exceptional Children, 7–11.*

Barr, R. (1987). Content coverage. In M. Dunkin (Ed.). *The International Encyclopedia of Teaching and Teacher Education* (pp. 364–368). New York: Pergamon Press.

Barrett, G. B., Bartkovich, K. G., Compton, H. L., Davis, S., Doyle, D., Goebel, J. A., Gould, L. D., Graves, J. L., Lutz, J. A., & Teague, D. J. (1992). *Contemporary precalculus through applications.* Dedham, MA: Janson Publications, Inc.

Begley, S. (1998, March 30). Homework doesn't help. *Newsweek* 50.

Benson, J., Dodge, S., Dodge, W., Hamberg, C., Milauskas, G., & Rukin, R. (1994). *Gateways to algebra and geometry.* Evanston, IL: McDougal Littell.

Berkman, R. M. (1994, February). Teacher as "kimp." *Arithmetic Teacher,* 326–328.

Berlinghoff, W. P., Sloyer, C., & Hayden, R. (1998). *MATH connections: A secondary mathematics core curriculum.* Armonk, NY: It's About Time, Inc.

Berzenyi, G., & Maurer, S. B. (1997). *The contest problem book V (Mathematical Association of America) 1983–88*. Reston, VA: National Council of Teachers of Mathematics.

Billstein, R. (1998). *Mathematics*. Evanston, IL: McDougal Littell.

Blais, D. M. (1988). Constructivism—a theoretical revolution for algebra. *Mathematics Teacher, 81,* 624–631.

Bloomer, A. M., & Carlson, P. A. T. (1993). *Activity math: Using manipulatives in the classroom*. Menlo Park, CA: Addison-Wesley.

Bohan, H. (1990). Mathematical connections: Free rides for kids. *Arithmetic Teacher, 38(3),* 10–14.

Borenson, H. (1986). Teaching students to think in mathematics and to make conjectures. In M. Driscoll & J. Confrey (Eds.), *Teaching Mathematics: Strategies That Work K–12* (Teachers Writing to Teachers Series, pp. 63–70). Northeast Regional Exchange, Inc.

Bradley, E. H. (1997). Is algebra in the cards? *Mathematics Teaching in the Middle School, 2(6),* 398–403.

Brandt, R. S. (Ed.). (1992). *Educational Leadership. 50(2).*

Bright, G. W. (1998). Classroom assessment: Translating information about students into instruction. In G. Bright & J. Joyner (Eds.), *Classroom Assessment in Mathematics*. Lanham, MD: University Press of America.

Bright, G. W., & Joyner, J. M. (1998). *Classroom assessment in mathematics: Views from a National Science Foundation working conference*. Lanham, MD: University Press of America.

Brooks, N. R. (1996, September 2). The science of auto body repair. *Los Angeles Times,* p. D-1.

Brown, A. L., Campione, & Day. (1981). Learning to learn: On training students to learn from texts. *Educational Researcher, 10(2),* 14–21.

Brown, C. A., & Borko, H. (1992). Becoming a mathematics teacher. In D. A. Grouws (Ed.), *Handbook of Research on Mathematics Teaching and Learning* (pp. 209–239). New York: Macmillan Publishing Company.

Brueningsen, C., Bower, B., Antinone, L., & Brueningsen, E. (1994). *Real world math with the CBL™ system*. Lubbock, TX: Texas Instruments.

Bruner, J. S. (1966). Some elements of discovery. In L. S. Shulman & E. R. Keislar (Eds.), *Learning by Discovery: A Critical Appraisal*. New York: Rand McNally.

Burden, P. R. (1995). *Classroom management and discipline: Methods to facilitate cooperation and instruction*. White Plains, NY: Longman Publishers USA.

Burns, M. (1982). *Mathematics for smarty pants*. Boston: Little, Brown.

Burrill, G. (Ed.). (1994). *From home runs to housing costs: Data resource for teaching statistics*. Palo Alto, CA: Dale Seymour Publications.

Burrill, G., Burrill, J. C., Coffield, P., Davis, G., de Lange, J., Resnick, D., & Siegel, M. (1992). *Data analysis and statistics* (Addenda Series, Grades 9–12). Reston, VA: National Council of Teachers of Mathematics.

Caldwell, J. H., & Masat, F. E. (1991). A knapsack problem, critical-path analysis, and expression trees. In M. J. Kenney & C. R. Hirsch (Eds.), *Discrete Mathematics Across the Curriculum K–12* (1991 Yearbook, pp. 228–234). Reston, VA: National Council of Teachers of Mathematics.

California Assessment Program. (1989). *A question of thinking: A first look at students' performance on open-ended questions in mathematics*. Sacramento: California State Department of Education.

California Mathematics Council. (1994). *Constructivist assessment in mathematics,* p. 55. Clayton, CA: California Mathematics Council.

California Mathematics Council. (1995). *They're counting on us: A parent's guide to mathematics education/Cuentan con nostoros: Unad gu´a de matemáticas para los padres de familia*. P.O. Box 880, Clayton, CA.

California Mathematics Council & EQUALS. (1989). *Assessment alternatives in mathematics*. Sacramento: California State Department of Education.

Callahan, W. (1994). Teaching middle-school students with diverse cultural backgrounds. *Mathematics Teacher, 87(2),* 122–126.

Callis, R. (1997). *Teaching style and students' attitudes toward mathematics*. Unpublished master's thesis, California State University at Northridge.

Campbell, D. E., & Davis, C. L. (1988). *Improving learning by combining critical thinking skills with psychological type*. (ERIC Document Reproduction Service No. 306 250)

Campbell, P. F., & Fey, J. T. (1988). New goals for school mathematics. In R. S. Brandt (Ed.), *Content of the Curriculum* (1988 ASCD Yearbook, pp. 53–73). Alexandria, VA: Association for Supervision and Curriculum Development.

Carlson, R. J., & Winter, M. J. (1998). *Transforming functions to fit data: Mathematical explorations using probes, electronic data-collection devices, and graphing, calculators*. Berkeley, CA: Key Curriculum Press.

Carnine, D. (1997). Instructional design in mathematics for students with learning disabilities. *Journal of Learning Disabilities, 30(2),* 130–141.

Catterall, J. S. (1987). *Standards and school dropouts: A national study of the minimum competency test.* Unpublished document, Center for the Study of Evaluation. Los Angeles: Graduate School of Education, University of California.

Charles, C. M. (1996). *Building classroom discipline*. White Plains, NY: Longman Publishers USA.

Clark, D. (1997). *Constructive assessment in mathematics*. Berkeley, CA: Key Curriculum Press.

Clark, H. C., & Nelson, M. N. (1991, May). Evaluation: Be more than a scorekeeper. *Arithmetic Teacher, 38(8)* 15–17.

Clarke, J., Wideman, R., & Cadie, S. (1990). *Together we learn*. Scarborough, Ontario: Prentice-Hall, Inc.

Clements, D. N., & McMillen, S. (1996, January). Concrete manipulatives. *Teaching Children Mathematics,* 270–279.

Cobb, P. (1994). Where is the mind? Constructivist and sociocultural perspectives on mathematical development. *Educational Researcher, 23(7)* 13–20.

Cohen, E. (1994). *Designing groupwork: Strategies for the heterogeneous classroom* (2nd ed.). New York: Teachers College Press.

College Board. (1997). *Advanced placement mathematics vertical teams toolkit*. Austin, TX: Charles A. Dana Center, University of Texas.

Confrey, J. What constructivism implies for teaching. In R. B. Davis, C. A. Maher, & N. Noddings (Eds.), Constructivist views on the teaching and learning of mathematics. *Journal for Research in Mathematics Education* (Monograph 4), 107–122.

Cooney, T., Davis, E., & Henderson, K. B. (1975). *Dynamics of teaching secondary school mathematics*. Prospect Heights, IL: Waveland Press.

Cooney, T. J., & Hirsch, C. R. (Eds.). (1990). *Teaching and learning mathematics in the 1990s* (1990 Yearbook). Reston, VA: National Council of Teachers of Mathematics.

Cooper, H. (1989, November). Synthesis of research on homework. *Educational Leadership, 47(3),* 85–91.

Countryman, L. L., & Schroeder, M. (1996). When students lead parent-teacher conferences. *Educational Leadership,* 64–68.

Coxford, A. F., Burks, L., Giamati, D., & Jonik, J. (1991). *Geometry from multiple perspectives* (Addenda Series Grades 9–12). Reston, VA: National Council of Teachers of Mathematics.

Coxford, A. F., Fey, J. T., Hirsch, C. R., Schoen, H. L., Burrill, G., et al. (1998). *Contemporary mathematics in context: A unified approach*. Chicago: Everyday Learning Corp.

Coxford, A. F., & Schulte, A. P. (Eds.). (1988). *The ideas of algebra, K–12* (1988 Yearbook). Reston, VA: National Council of Teachers of Mathematics.

Cozzens, M., & Porteer, R. (1989). *Recurrence relations—counting backwards* (High School Mathematics and Its Applications [HiMAP]). Arlington, MA: Consortium for Mathematics and Its Applications (COMAP), Inc.

Cuban, L. (1990). Reforming again, again, and again. *Educational Researcher, 48(4),* 3–13.

Cummins, J. (1991). The role of primary language development in promoting educational success for language minority students. In *Schooling and Language Minority Students: A Theoretical Framework* (pp. 3–35). Los Angeles: Evaluation, Dissemination and Assessment Center, California State University.

Dalton, L. C., & Snyder, H. D. (Eds.). (1983). *Topics for mathematics clubs*. Reston, VA: Mu Alpha Theta and the National Council of Teachers of Mathematics.

Danielson, C. (1997). *A collection of performance tasks and rubrics: Middle school mathematics*. Larchmont, NY: Eye on Education.

Data insights. (1989). [Computer software.] Pleasantville, NY: Sunburst Communications.

Data models. (1991). [Computer software.] Pleasantville, NY: Sunburst Communications.

Davidson, N. (1990). *Cooperative learning in mathematics: A handbook for teachers*. Menlo Park, CA: Addison-Wesley Publishing Company.

Davidson, N., & Kroll, D. L. (1991). An overview of research on cooperative learning related to mathematics. *Journal for Research in Mathematics Education, 22(5),* 362–365.

Davis, B. (1996). *Teaching mathematics: Toward a sound alternative*. New York: Garland Publishing.

Davis, R. B. (1966). Discovery in the teaching of mathematics. In L. S. Shulman & E. R. Keislar (Eds.),

Learning by Discovery: A Critical Appraisal. New York: Rand McNally.

Davis, R. B., Maher, C. A., & Noddings, N. (1990). Introduction: Constructivist views on the teaching and learning of mathematics. *Journal for Research in Mathematics Education* (Monograph 4), 1–7.

Dees, R. (1991). The role of cooperative learning in increasing problem-solving ability in a college remedial course. *Journal for Research in Mathematics Education, 22(5),* 409–421.

DeMeulemeester, Katie. (1995). *Math projects: Organization, implementation, and assessment*. Palo Alto, CA: Dale Seymour Publications.

Department of Mathematics and Computer Science, North Carolina School of Science and Mathematics. (1988). *New topics for secondary school mathematics: Matrices*. Reston, VA: National Council of Teachers of Mathematics.

Devlin, K. (1994). *Mathematics: The science of patterns—the search for order in life, mind, and the universe* (Scientific American Library). New York: W. H. Freeman and Company.

Devlin, K. D. (1997). Why we should reduce skills teaching in the mathematics class. *FOCUS (Mathematics Association of America,* www.maa.org).

Dick, T., & Kubiak, E. (1998). Issues and aids for teaching mathematics to the blind. *Mathematics Teacher, 90(5),* 344–349.

Dixon, J. K., & Falba, C. J. (1998). Graphing in the information age: Using data from the World Wide Web. *Mathematics Teaching in the Middle School, 2(5),* 298–304.

Doczi, György. (1981). *The power of limits: Proportional harmonies in nature, art, and architecture*. Boulder, CO: Shambala Publications, Inc.

Dossey, J. (1991). Discrete mathematics: The math for our time. In M. J. Kenney & C. R. Hirsch (Eds.), *Discrete Mathematics Across the Curriculum K–12* (*1991 Yearbook*, pp. 1–9). Reston, VA: National Council of Teachers of Mathematics.

Dossey, J. A. (1992). The nature of mathematics: Its role and its influence. In *Handbook of Research on Mathematics Teaching and Learning* (pp. 39–48). Reston, VA: National Council of Teachers of Mathematics.

Drake, R., & Quesada, S. (1993). *Modeling lab*. Presentation for Viz-Math Project, California State University, Northridge, CA.

Driscoll, M. J. (1981). *Research within research: Elementary school mathematics*. Reston, VA: National Council of Teachers of Mathematics.

Duckworth, E. (1964). Piaget rediscovered. *Journal of Research in Science Teaching, 2,* 172–175.

Dunham, P. H. (1991, November). *Teaching with the graphing calculator: A survey of research on graphing technology*. Paper delivered at the Fourth International Conference on Technology in Collegiate Mathematics, Bloomington, IN.

Duren, P. E., & Cherrington, A. (1992). The effects of cooperative group work versus independent practice on the learning of some problem-solving strategies *School Science and Mathematics, 92(2),* 80–83.

Dyke, F. V. (1995). A concrete approach to mathematical induction. *Mathematics Teacher, 88(4),* 302–306, 314–318.

Edwards, C. H. (1997). *Classroom discipline and management*. Upper Saddle River, NJ: Merrill/ Prentice Hall.

Ehrich, P. (1994). Writing and cognition: Implications for mathematics instruction. In *Empowering Students by Promoting Active Learning in Mathematics: Teachers Speak to Teachers* (pp. 31–36). Reston, VA: National Council of Teachers of Mathematics.

Eisner, E. W. (1983, January). The art and craft of teaching. *Educational Leadership, 40,* 4–13.

Elliott, P. C., & Kenney, M. J. (Eds.). (1996). *Communication in Mathematics K–12 and Beyond* (1996 Yearbook). Reston, VA: National Council of Teachers of Mathematics.

Emmer, E. T., Evertson, C. M., Clements, B. S., & Worsham, M. E. (1997). *Classroom management for secondary teachers*. Needham Heights, MA: Allyn & Bacon.

English, L. D., & Warren, E. A. (1998). Introducing the variable through pattern exploration. *Mathematics Teacher, 91(2),* 166–170.

Erickson, T. (1986). *Off and running* (EQUALS Program). Berkeley, CA: Lawrence Hall of Science.

Erickson, T. (1989). *Get it together: Math problems for groups, grades 4–12* (EQUALS Program). Berkeley, CA: Lawrence Hall of Science.

Erickson, T. (1996). *United we solve: Math problems for groups, grades 5–10*. Oakland, CA: eeps media.

Fairbairn, D. M. (1993, November). Creating story problems. *Arithmetic Teacher,* 140–142.

Fendel, D., Resick, D., Fraser, S., & Alper, L. (1997). *Interactive mathematics program 1, 2, 3*. Berkeley, CA: Key Curriculum Press.

Fennema, E., & Leder, G. C. (Eds.). (1990). *Mathematics and gender*. New York: Teachers College, Columbia University.

Flanders, J. R. (1987, September). How much of the content in mathematics textbooks is new? *Arithmetic Teacher, 35(1),* 18–23.

Flener, F. O. (1990). *Mathematics contests: A guide for involving students and schools*. Reston, VA: National Council of Teachers of Mathematics.

Flinders, D. J. (1989). Does the "art of teaching" have a future? *Educational Leadership, 47(8),* 16–20.

Foley, G. D. (1994, April). *Organizing, processing, and analyzing data using tables and lists on the TI-82*. Presentation at the NCTM Annual Meeting, Indianapolis, IN.

Fraser, R., Burkhardt, H., Coupland, J., Phillips, R., Pimm, D., & Ridgeway, J. (1988). Learning activities and classroom roles with and without computers. *Journal of Mathematical Behavior,* 305–338.

Fraser, S., Gilliland, K., Kreinber, N., Stenmark, J., & Thompson, V. (1986). *The EQUALS book of scripts* (for trainers only, EQUALS Program). Berkeley, CA: Lawrence Hall of Science.

Friedlander, A., & Tabach, M. Promoting multiple representations in algebra. In A. A. Cuoco & F. R. Curcio (Eds.), *The Roles of Representation in School Mathematics* (2001 Yearbook, pp. 173–185). Reston, VA: National Council of Teachers of Mathematics.

Froelich, G. W. (1991). *Connecting mathematics* (Addenda series). Reston, VA: National Council of Teachers of Mathematics.

Gallagher, A. M., & De Lisi, R. (1994). Gender differences in scholastic aptitude tests: Mathematics problem solving among high-ability students. *Journal of Educational Psychology, 86(2),* 204–211.

Gamoran, A. (1992). Is ability grouping equitable? *Educational leadership, 50(2),* 11–17.

Gardner, H. (1983). *Frames of mind*. New York: Basic Books.

Gardner, H. (1995). Reflection on multiple intelligences: Myths and messages. *Phi Delta Kappan, 77,* 200–210.

Gardner, M. (1973). Mathematical games. *Scientific American, 229,* 116–123.

Garfunkel, S., Godbold, L., & Pollack, H. (project leaders). (1998). *Applications reform in secondary education (ARISE)/Mathematics: Modeling our world*. Cincinnati, OH: South-Western Educational Publishing.

Geddes, D. (1992). *Geometry in the middle grades* (Addenda series grades 5–8). Reston, VA: National Council of Teachers of Mathematics.

Geddes, D. (1994). *Measurement in the middle grades* (Addenda series grades 5–8). Reston, VA: National Council of Teachers of Mathematics.

Geometer's Sketchpad. [Computer software.] Berkeley, CA: Key Curriculum Press.

Glaser, R. (1966). Variables in discovery learning. In L. S. Shulman & E. R. Keislar (Eds.), *Learning by Discovery: A Critical Appraisal*. New York: Rand McNally.

Glidden, P. L. (1990, February). From graph to matrices. *Mathematics Teacher,* 127–134.

Gnandesikan, M., Scheaffer, R. L., & Swift, J. (1987). *The art and techniques of simulation*. Palo Alto, CA: Dale Seymour Publications.

Goldman, S., McDermott, R., Greeno, J., & Pake, P. (principal investigators). (1998). *Middle-school mathematics through applications*. Palo Alto, CA: Institute for Research on Learning.

Good, T. L., & Brody, J. E. (1997). *Looking in classrooms*. White Plains, NY: Longman Publishers USA.

Goodlad, J. I. (1984). *A place called school: Prospects for the future*. New York: McGraw-Hill Book Company.

Goodnow, J. (1992). *Junior high cooperative problem solving with geoboards*. Mountain View, CA: Creative Publications.

Gregorc, A. F. (1985). *Inside styles: Beyond the basics*. Maynard, MA: Gabriel Systems.

Grouws, D. A., & Lembke, L. O. (1996). Influential factors in student motivation to learn mathematics: The teacher and classroom culture. In M. Carr (Ed.), *Motivation in Mathematics* (pp. 39–62). Cresskill, NJ: Hampton Press, Inc.

Groves, J. (1997). *Attitudes and perceptions of teachers on block schedules*. Unpublished master's thesis, California State University at Northridge, Northridge, CA.

Guilford, J. P. (1967). *The nature of human intelligence*. New York: McGraw-Hill.

Guskey, T. R. (1994). Making the grade: What benefits students? *Educational Leadership, 51(7),* 14–19.

Halpern, P. A. (1996). Communicating the mathematics in children's trade books using mathematical annotations. In P. C. Elliott & M. J. Kenney (Eds.), *Communication in Mathematics K–12 and Beyond* (1996 Yearbook, pp. 54–60). Reston, VA: National Council of Teachers of Mathematics.

Hanf, M. B. (1971, January). Mapping a technique for translating reading into thinking. *Journal of reading, 14,* 223–230.

Hart, D. (1994). *Authentic assessment: A handbook for educators.* Menlo Park, CA: Addison-Wesley Publishing Co.

Hart, E. W. (1991). Discrete mathematics: An exciting and necessity addition to the secondary school curriculum. In M. J. Kenney, M. J. Hirsch, & C. R. Hirsch, *Discrete Mathematics Across the Curriculum K–12* (1991 Yearbook, pp. 67–77). Reston, VA: National Council of Teachers of Mathematics.

Hart, L. C., Schultz, K., Majee-ullah, D., and Nash, L. (1992, September). The role of reflection in teaching. *Arithmetic Teacher, 40(1),* 40–42.

Heid, M. K. (1995). *Algebra in a technological world* (Addenda series grades 9–12). Reston, VA: National Council of Teachers of Mathematics.

Hembree, R., & Dessart, D. J. (1986). Effects of hand-held calculators in precollege mathematics education: A meta-analysis. *Journal for Research in Mathematics Education, 17(2),* 83–99.

Henderson, K. B., & Pingry, R. E. (1995). Problem-solving in mathematics. *The Learning of Mathematics: Its Theory and Practice* (21st Yearbook, pp. 228–270). Reston, VA: National Council of Teachers of Mathematics.

Hirschhorn, D. B., & Thompson, D. R. (1996). Technology and reasoning in algebra and geometry. *Mathematics Teacher, 90(2),* 138–142.

Hirschhorn, D. B., Thompson, D. R., Usiskin, Z., & Senk, S. (1995). Rethinking the first two years of high school mathematics with the UCSMP. *Mathematics Teacher, 88(8),* 640–647.

Hodgson, T., & Harpster, D. (1997). Looking back in mathematical modeling: Classroom observations and instructional strategies. *School Science and Mathematics, 97,* 260–267.

Hoey, B. (1997). *College preparatory mathematics: Change from within, assessment handbook.* Sacramento, CA: CMP Educational Program.

Hoffer, A. (1981). Geometry is more than proof. *Mathematics Teacher, 74(1),* 11–18.

Hofstadter, D. R. (1985). On number numbness. In *Metamagical Themes: Questing for the Essence of Mind and Pattern* (pp. 115–135). New York: Basic Books, Inc.

Holmes, E. E. (1990). Motivation: An essential component of mathematics instruction. *Teaching and Learning Mathematics in the 1990s* (1990 Yearbook). Reston, VA: National Council of Teachers of Mathematics.

House, P. (1996). Try a little of the write stuff. In P. C. Elliott & M. J. Kenney (Eds.), *Communication in Mathematics K–12 and Beyond* (1996 Yearbook, pp. 89–94). Reston, VA: National Council of Teachers of Mathematics.

House, P. A. (1988). Reshaping school algebra: Why and how? In A. F. Coxford & A. P. Shulte (Eds.), *The Ideas of Algebra, K–12* (1988 Yearbook). Reston, VA: National Council of Teachers of Mathematics.

House, P. A. (Ed.). (1987). *Providing opportunities for the mathematically gifted.* Reston, VA: National Council of Teachers of Mathematics.

Huetinck, L. (1990). *Gender differences on science exams with respect to item type, format, student interest, and experience.* Unpublished doctoral dissertation, University of California, Los Angeles.

Huinker, D., & Laughlin, C. (1996). Talk your way into writing. In P. C. Elliott & M. J. Kenney (Eds.), *Communication in Mathematics K–12 and Beyond* (1996 Yearbook, pp. 81–89). Reston, VA: National Council of Teachers of Mathematics.

Hunt, W. J. (1995, December). Spreadsheets—a tool for the mathematics classroom. *Mathematics Teacher, 88(9),* 774–777.

Hunter, J. (1994). *Enhancing teaching.* New York: Macmillan.

Hunter, M. (1987). *Mastery Teaching.* El Segundo, CA: TIP Publications.

Hynd, G. W. (Ed.). (1997, January–February; March–April). *Journal of Learning Disabilities.*

Introduction to TIMSS, the third international mathematics and science study. (1997, September). Washington, DC: U.S. Department of Education.

Jacobs, H. (1974). *Geometry.* San Francisco, CA: Freeman and Co.

Jamski, W. D. (Ed.). (1990). *Mathematical challenges for the middle grades from* The Arithmetic Teacher.

Reston, VA: National Council of Teachers of Mathematics.

Janes, N. S. (Ed.). *Wonderful ideas*. P.O. Box 64961, Burlington, VT.

Jennings, R. (1993). *Overview of ARISE*. Presentation for Viz-Math Project, California State University, Northridge, CA.

Jitenda, A., & Xin, Y. P. (1997). Mathematics work—problem solving instruction for students with mild disabilities and students at risk for math failure: A research synthesis. *Journal of Special Education, 30(4)*, 412–437.

Johnson, D. (1982). *Every minute counts: Making your math class work*. Palto Alto, CA: Dale Seymour Publications.

Johnson, D., Johnson, R., & Holbec, E. (1988). *Cooperation in the classroom* (Rev. ed.). Edina, MN: Interaction Book Co.

Johnson, R. S. (1996). *Setting our sights: Measuring equity in school change*. Los Angeles: Achievement Council.

Johnson, R. W. (1993, October). Where can teacher research lead? One teacher's daydream. *Educational Leadership, 51(2)*.

Johnson, W. B., & Packer, A. E. (Eds.). (1987). *Workforce 2000: Work and workers for the twenty-first century*. Indianapolis, IN: Hudson Institute.

Joyner, J. M., & Bright, G. W. (1998). *Focusing on classroom assessment*. Greensboro, NC: University of North Carolina, Center for School Accountability and Staff Development.

Kagan, S. (1992). *Cooperative learning*. San Juan Capistrano, CA: Resources for Teachers, Inc.

Kaput, A. (1992). Technology and mathematics education. In D. A. Grouws (Ed.), *Handbook of Research on Mathematics Teaching and Learning*. (pp. 515–556). New York: National Council of Teachers of Mathematics, Macmillan Publishing Company.

Keirsey, D., & Bates, J. (1984). *Please understand me: Character temperament types*. Del Mar, CA: Prometheus Nemesis.

Kelemanik, G. (with Janssen, S., Miller, B., & Ransick, K). (1997). *Structured exploration: New perspectives on mathematics professional development*. Newton, MA: Educational Development Center, Inc.

Kennedy, L. M. (1986). A rationale. *Arithmetic Teacher, 33(2)*, 6, 7, 32.

Kenney, M. J., & Hirsch, C. R. (1991). *Discrete mathematics across the curriculum* (*1991 Yearbook*).

Reston, VA: National Council of Teachers of Mathematics.

Khisty, L. L. (1995). Making inequality: Issues of language and meanings in mathematics teaching with Hispanic students. In W. G. Secada, E. Fennema, & L. B. Adajian (Eds.), *New Directions for Equity in Mathematics Education* (pp. 126–145). Cambridge, MA: Cambridge University Press, in collaboration with the National Council of Teachers of Mathematics.

Kieran, C. *The changing face of school algebra* (1996, July). Paper presented at the 8th International Congress of Mathematics Education, Seville, Spain.

Kinach, B. (1993). Solving linear equations physically. In C. R. Hirsch & R. A. Laing (Eds.), *Activities for Active Learning and Teaching—Selections from* The Mathematics Teacher. Reston, VA: National Council of Teachers of Mathematics.

Kleiman, G., & Bjork, E. (principal investigators). (1998). *MathScape: Seeing and thinking mathematically*. Mountain View, CA: Creative Publications.

Kloosterman, P. (1996). Students' beliefs about knowing and learning mathematics: Implications for motivation. In M. Carr (Ed.), *Motivation in Mathematics* (pp. 131–156). Cresskill, NJ: Hampton Press, Inc.

Kohn, A. (1994). Grading: The issue is not how but why. *Educational Leadership, 51(7)*, 38–41.

Kohn, A. (1996). *Beyond discipline from compliance to community*. Alexandria, VA: Association for Supervision and Curriculum Development.

Kolpas, S. (1992). David Copperfield's Orient Express card trick. *Mathematics Teacher, 85(7)*, 568–570.

Koontz, T. (1997). Know thyself, the evolution of an intervention gender-equity program. In J. Trentacosta & M. J. Kenney (Eds.), *Multicultural and Gender Equity in the Mathematics Classroom: The Gift of Diversity* (1997 Yearbook). Reston, VA: National Council of Teachers of Mathematics.

Kounin, J. S. (1970). *Discipline and group management in classrooms*. New York: Holt, Rinehart and Winston.

Kramer, S. L. (1996). Block scheduling and high school mathematics instruction. *Mathematics Teacher, 89(9)*, 758–768.

Kroll, D. L., Masingila, J. O., & Mau, S. T. (1992). Grading cooperative problem solving. *Mathematics Teacher, 85(8)*, 619–627.

Kysh, J. M. (1995). College preparatory mathematics: Change from within. *Mathematics Teacher, 88(8)*, 660–666.

Ladson-Billings, G. (1995). Making mathematics meaningful in multicultural contexts. In W. G. Secada, E. Fennema, & L. B. Adajian (Eds.), *New Directions for Equity in Mathematics Education* (pp. 126–145). Cambridge, MA: Cambridge University Press in collaboration with the National Council of Teachers of Mathematics.

Landfried, S. E. (1989, November). "Enabling" undermines responsibility in students. *Educational Leadership, 7,* 80–83.

Lappan, G. (1996). *Connected mathematics.* Palo Alto, CA: Dale Seymour Publications.

Lappan, G., & Briars, D. (1995). How should mathematics be taught? In *Prospects for School Mathematics, Seventy-Five Years of Progress* (pp. 131–156). Reston, VA: National Council of Teachers of Mathematics.

Larkin, S. (1986). Word problems for kids by kids. In M. Driscoll & J. Confrey (Eds.), *Teaching Mathematics: Strategies That Work* (Teachers Writing to Teachers Series, pp. 51–61). Northeast Regional Exchange, Inc.

Laycock, M., & Schadler, R. A. (1973). *Algebra in the concrete.* Hayward, CA: Activity Resources Co., Inc.

Lénárt, I. (1996). *Non-Euclidean adventures on the Lénárt sphere.* Emeryville, CA: Key Curriculum Press.

Lessons in mathematics for the classroom and for inservice sessions with alternative assessment procedures (1990–1994). Cedar Falls, IA: University of Northern Iowa, Leadership Development and Enabling Change Project.

Levin, J., & Nolan, J. F. (1996). *Principles of classroom management: A professional decision making model.* Boston: Allyn & Bacon.

Lewis, S. (1998, October). Presentation at the Math Mini-Morsels Conference, California State University, Northridge, CA.

Lindquist, M. M., & Schulte, A. P. (Eds.). (1987). *Learning and teaching geometry, K–12* (*1987 Yearbook*). Reston, VA: National Council of Teachers of Mathematics.

Lott, J. W., & Burke, M. J. (Co-directors). (1996). *Systemic initiative for Montana mathematics and science (SIMMS)/Integrated mathematics: A modeling approach using technology.* New York: Simon & Schuster Custom Publishing.

Lutkin, D. (1996). The incredible three-by-five card! *Mathematics Teacher, 89(2),* 96–98.

MacPherson, E. D. (1985). The themes of geometry: Design of the nonformal geometry curriculum. In

C. R. Hirsch & M. J. Zweng (Eds.), *The secondary school mathematics curriculum* (1985 Yearbook, pp. 65–80). Reston, VA: National Council of Teachers of Mathematics.

Malcom, S. (1997). Making mathematics the great equalizer. In L. A. Steen (Ed.), *Why Numbers Count: Quantitative Literacy for Tomorrow's America* (pp. 30–35). New York: College Entrance Examination Board.

Margenau, J., & Sentiowitz, M. (1977). *How to study mathematics.* Reston, VA: National Council of Teachers of Mathematics.

Marquis, J. (1989). What can we do about the high D and F rate in first-year algebra? *Mathematics Teacher, 82(6),* 421–425.

Marshall, S. (1984). Sex differences in children's mathematics achievement: Solving, computations and story problems. *Journal of Educational Psychology, 76(2),* 194–204.

Martin, T. S., Hunt, C. A., Lannin, J., Leonard, W. Jr., Marshall, G. L., & Wares, A. (2001). How reform secondary mathematics textbooks stack up against NCTM's *Principles and Standards. Mathematics Teacher, 94(7),* 540–545, 589.

Math matters: Kids are counting on you. (1989). [Planning kit plus videotapes]. Chicago: The National PTA.

Mathematical Association of America. (1991). *A call for change: Recommendations for the mathematical preparation of teachers of mathematics.* Washington, DC: Author.

Mathematical Sciences Education Board. (1989). *Everybody counts: A report to the nation on the future of mathematics education.* Washington, DC: National Academy Press.

Mathematical Sciences Education Board. (1991). *Moving beyond myths: Revitalizing undergraduate mathematics.* Washington, DC: National Academy Press.

Mathematical Sciences Education Board, National Research Council. (1990). *Reshaping school mathematics: A philosophy and framework for curriculum.* Washington, DC: National Academy Press.

Mathematical Sciences Education Board, National Research Council (1991). *Counting on you: Actions supporting mathematics teaching standards.* Washington, DC: National Academy Press.

Mathematics in context: A connected curriculum for grades 5–8, sampler. (1996). Chicago: Encyclopaedia Britannica Educational Corporation.

Mathematics Teacher, 91(8).

MathScape: Getting in shape. (1998). Mountain View, CA: Creative Publications.

McCoy, S., & Reinke, K. S. (1997). MATHCOUNTS: It really works! *Mathematics Teaching in the Middle School, 3(1),* 32–38.

McKnight, C. C. (1987). *The underachieving curriculum: Assessing U.S. school mathematics from an international perspective.* Champaign, IL: Stipes Publishing Company.

Meiring, S. P., Rubenstein, R. N., Schultz, J. E., de Lange, J., & Chambers, D. L. (1992). *A core curriculum: Making mathematics count for everyone* (Addenda series grades 9–12). Reston, VA: National Council of Teachers of Mathematics.

Metz, J. (1994). Seeing the b in $y = ax^2 + by + c$. *Mathematics Teacher, 87(1),* 23–24.

Michael, J., & Meyerson, L. (1962). A behavioral approach to counseling and guidance. *Harvard Educational Review, 32(4),* 382–402.

Miller, S. P., & Mercer, C. D. (1997). Educational aspects of mathematics disabilities. *Journal of Learning Disabilities, 30(1),* 47–56.

Moore, D. (1989). *Against all odds: Inside statistics* [Video series]. S. Burlington, VT: The Annenberg/CPB Collection.

Murdock, J., Kamischke, E., & Kamischke, E. (1996). *Advanced algebra through data exploration: A graphing calculator approach.* Berkeley, CA: Key Curriculum Press.

Mussack, S. M. (1996). *A descriptive study of interaction between mathematics students with differing personality types, one "judging," one "perceiving," engaged in collaborative problem-solving situations.* Unpublished master's thesis, California State University, Northridge, California.

Muthukrishna, N., & Borkowski, J. G. (1996). Constructivism and the motivated transfer of skills. In M. Carr (Ed.), *Motivation in Mathematics* (pp. 63–88). Cresskill, NJ: Hampton Press, Inc.

Nahrgang, C. L., & Petersen, B. T. (1986, September). Using writing to learn mathematics. *Mathematics Teacher,* 461–465.

Narode, R. (1996). Communicating mathematics through literature. In P. C. Elliott & M. J. Kenney (Eds.), *Communication in Mathematics K–12 and Beyond* (1996 Yearbook, pp. 76–80). Reston, VA: National Council of Teachers of Mathematics.

National Board for Professional Teaching Standards. (1966). *Mathematics adolescence and young adulthood portfolio.* Washington, DC: Educational Testing Service.

National Board for Professional Teaching Standards. (1996). *Adolescence and young adulthood mathematics: Standards for national board certification.* Washington, DC: Educational Testing Service.

National Council of Teachers of Mathematics. (1980). *Agenda for action: Recommendations for school mathematics of the 1980's.* Reston, VA: Author.

National Council of Teachers of Mathematics. (1989). *Curriculum and evaluation standards for school mathematics.* Reston, VA: Author.

National Council of Teachers of Mathematics. (1991). *Professional standards for teaching mathematics.* Reston, VA: Author.

National Council of Teachers of Mathematics. (1992, August). *Algebra for the twenty-first century* (Proceedings of the Conference). Reston, VA: Author.

National Council of Teachers of Mathematics. (1994, May). Board approves statement on algebra. *NCTM News Bulletin, 30,* 1.

National Council of Teachers of Mathematics. (1995). *Assessment standards for school mathematics, 88(8),* 630–666. Reston, VA: Author.

National Council of Teachers of Mathematics. (1995). (Focus issue: Emerging programs). *Mathematics Teacher, 8.*

National Council of Teachers of Mathematics. *Principles and standards for school mathematics: Discussion draft* (1998). Reston, VA: Author.

National Council of Teachers of Mathematics. (2000). *Principles and standards for school mathematics (PSSM).* Reston, VA: Author.

National Information Center for Children and Youth with Disabilities. (1997, August). The IDEA amendments of 1997. *News Digest, 26,* 1–39.

National Research Council (1989). *Everybody counts: A report to the nation on the future of mathematics education.* Washington, DC: National Academy Press.

National Research Council. (1996). *National science education standards.* Washington, DC: National Academy Press.

National Research Council, Committee on Research in Mathematics, Science, and Technology Education (1985). *Mathematics, science, and technology education: A research agenda.* Washington, DC: National Academy Press.

NCTM student math notes. Reston, VA: National Council of Teachers of Mathematics, June, 1996.

New standards performance standards. (1997). (Vol. 2, Middle School; Vol. 3, High School.) Rochester, NY: National Center on Education and the Economy and the University of Pittsburgh.

Newman, C. M., Obremski, T. E., & Scheaffer, R. L. (1987). *Exploring probability (Quantitative literacy series).* Palo Alto, CA: Dale Seymour Publications.

Nielsen, L. J., & de Villiers, M. (1997). *Is democracy fair? The mathematics of voting and apportionment.* Berkeley, CA: Key Curriculum Press.

Noddings, N. (1990). Constructivism in mathematics education. In R. B. Davis, C. A. Maher, & N. Noddings (Eds.), Constructivist views on the teaching and learning of mathematics. *Journal for Research in Mathematics Education* (Monograph 4), 7–18.

Oakes, J. (1985). *Keeping track: How schools structure inequality.* New Haven, CT: Yale University Press.

Oakes, J. (1996). Detracking for high student achievement. *Educational Leadership, 55(6),* 38–41.

Okolica, S., & Macrina, G. (1992). Integrating transformational geometry into traditional high school geometry. *Mathematics Teacher, 85(9),* 716–719.

O'Neil, J. (1995). On technology schools: A conversation with Chris Dede. *Educational Leadership.*

Ormrod, J. E. (1995). *Educational psychology: Principles and applications:* Upper Saddle River, NJ: Merrill/Prentice Hall.

Osborne, A. (1992). Mathematical literacy and teacher education. *Journal of Research and Development in Education, 15(4),* 19–29.

Pandey, T. (1991). *A sampler of mathematics assessment.* Sacramento: California Department of Education.

Pavlov, I. P. (1928). *Lectures on conditioned reflexes* (W. H. Gantt with G. Volborth, Trans.) New York: Liveright Publishing Corporation.

Pavlov, I. P. (1941). *Conditioned reflexes and psychiatry* (4th ed., W. H. Gantt, Trans. and Ed., 1967). New York: International Publishers.

Pereira-Mendoza, L. (1993). What is a quadrilateral? *Mathematics Teacher, 86(9),* 774–776.

Peressini, D. (1997). Parental involvement in the reform of mathematics education. *Mathematics Teacher, 90(6),* 421–426.

Perfect, V. (1997). *Gender differences in using calculators in the mathematics classroom.* Unpublished master's thesis, California State University, Northridge, California.

Peterson, L. L. (1990, April). Seven ways to find the area of a trapezoid. In Sharing ideas from *Mathematics Teacher,* 283–286.

Phillips, E. (with Gardella, T., Kelly, C., & Stewart, J.). (1991). *Patterns and functions* (Addenda series grades 5–8). Reston, VA: National Council of Teachers of Mathematics.

Pirie, S. E. B. (1996). Is anybody listening? In P. C. Elliott & M. J. Kenney (Eds.), *Communication in Mathematics K–12 and Beyond* (1996 Yearbook, pp. 105–115). Reston, VA: National Council of Teachers of Mathematics.

Polya, G. (1967). *Mathematical discovery: On understanding, learning, and teaching problem solving.* New York: John Wiley & Sons, Inc.

Polya, G. (1988). *How to solve it.* Princeton, NJ: Princeton University Press.

Popham, W. J. (1998). *A message to parents: Don't judge your child's school by its standardized test scores.* Los Angeles: University of California.

Posner, G. (1987). Pacing and sequencing. In M. Dunkin (Ed.), *The International Encyclopedia of Teaching and Teacher Education* (pp. 266–272). New York: Pergamon Press.

Pressey, S. L. (1963). Teaching machine (and learning theory) crisis. *Journal of Applied Psychology, 47(1),* 1–6.

Pressley, M., & McCormack, C. B. (1995). *Cognition, teaching and assessment.* New York: Harper Co. College Publishers.

Qin, Z., Johnson, D. W., & Johnson, R. T. (1995). Cooperative versus competitive efforts and problem solving. *Review of Educational Research, 65(2),* 129–143.

Rafferty, Y. (1997). Meeting the educational needs of homeless children. *Educational Leadership, 56(4),* 48–53.

Redirecting assessment. (1989). (Focus Issue.) *Educational Leadership, 46(7).*

Reis, S. M., & Renzuilli, J. S. (1992). Using curriculum compacting to challenge the above-average. *Educational Leadership, 50(2),* 51–57.

Rescorla, R. A. (1988). Pavlovian conditioning: It's not what you think it is. *American Psychologist, 43(3),* 151–160.

Resnick, L. B., & Klopfer, L. E. (Eds.). (1989). Toward the thinking curriculum: Current cognitive research. *1989 Yearbook of the Association for Supervision and Curriculum Development*. Alexandria, VA: Association for Supervision and Curriculum Development.

Reys, B. J. (1996). *Developing number sense in the middle grades* (Addenda series grades 5–8). Reston, VA: National Council of Teachers of Mathematics.

Reys, B. J., & Wasman, D. G. (1998). Math is FUNctional: A math fair for kids. *Mathematics Teaching in the Middle School, 3(4),* 260–266.

Rideout, C. A., & Richardson, S. A. (1989). A team building model: Appreciating differences using the Myers-Briggs type indicator with developmental theory. *Journal of Counseling and Development, 67,* 529–533.

Ridgway, J. (1998). From barrier to lever: Revising roles for assessment in mathematics education. *National Institute for Science Education (NISE) Brief* (University of Wisconsin–Madison), *2(1),* 7.

Rigol, G. (1990, April). *New possibilities and the SAT.* Presentation to the National Council of Supervisors of Mathematics, Chicago, IL.

Rockinger, N. R. (1980). *Joining hands: Using learning and teaching styles.* Presentation to the Alternative Schools Conference, Bloomington, IN. (ERIC Document Reproduction Service No. 285 275).

Rogers, K. B., & Kimpston, R. D. (1992). Acceleration: What we do vs. what we know. *Educational Leadership, 50(2),* 58–61.

Romagnano, L. (1980). *Data analysis: Integrating applications and statistics into algebra, a computer workshop.* Presentation at the NCTM Northeast Regional Conference, Philadelphia, PA.

Rosemond, J. (1989, September 12). The seven hidden values of self-motivated homework. *Los Angeles Daily News.*

Rosenthal, T. L. (1978). *Social learning and cognition.* New York: Academic Press, Inc.

Rosenthal, T. L., Alford, G. S., & Rasp, L. M. (1972). Concept attainment, generalization and retention through observation and verbal coding. *Journal of Experimental Child Psychology, 13,* 183–194.

Rubenstein, R. N., Craine, T. V., Butts, T. R., Cantrell, K., Dritsas, L., et al. (1995). *Integrated mathematics 1, 2, 3.* Evanston, IL: McDougal Littell/Houghton Mifflin.

Rubenstein, R. N., Schultz, J. E., Senk, S. L., Hackworth, M., McConnell, J. W., Viktora, S. S., Aksoy, D., Flanders, J., Kissane, B., & Usiskin, Z.
(1992). *University of Chicago School Mathematics Project: Functions, statistics and trigonometry.* Glenview, IL: Scott-Foresman Publications.

Ryder, R. J., & Hughes, T. (1997). *Internet for educators.* (2nd ed.). Upper Saddle River, NJ: Merrill/Prentice Hall.

Sandera, M. (1994). Listening to students through writing. In *Empowering Students by Promoting Active Learning in Mathematics: Teachers Speak to Teachers* (pp. 25–30). Reston, VA: National Council of Teachers of Mathematics.

Santamaria, P. (1996). *A descriptive study of secondary students' attitudes toward cooperative long-term projects in mathematics.* Unpublished master's thesis, California State University, Northridge.

Scheaffer, R. L. (1990). Why data analysis? *Mathematics Teacher, 83(2),* 90–93.

Scherer, M. M. (Ed.). (1997/1998, December–January). *Educational Leadership: Reaching for Equity, 55(4).*

Schulte, A. P., & Choate, S. A. (1977). *What are my chances?* Mountain View, CA: Creative Publications.

Schulte, A. P., & Smart, J. (Eds.). (1981). *Teaching statistics and probability* (1981 Yearbook). Reston, VA: National Council of Teachers of Mathematics.

Schunk, D. H. (1982). Effects of effort attributional feedback on children's perceived self-efficacy and achievements. *Journal of Educational Psychology, 74(4),* 548–556.

Schwartz, S. L. (1996, March). Hidden messages in teacher talk: Praise and empowerment. *Teaching Children Mathematics,* 396–401.

Senechal, M. (1990). Shape. In L. A. Steen (Ed.), *On the shoulders of giants,* 139–181. Washington, DC: National Academy Press.

Senk, S. L. (1985). How well do students write geometry proofs? *Mathematics Teacher, 78(6),* 448–456.

Senk, S. L., Beckmann, C. E., & Thompson, D. R. (1997). Assessment and grading in high school mathematics classrooms. *Journal for Research in Mathematics Education, 28(2),* 187–215.

Seymour, D. (1986). *Visual patterns in Pascal's triangle.* White Plains, NY: Dale Seymour Publications.

Seymour, D. (Compiler). (1996). *Encyclopedia of math topics and references: A resource for projects and explorations.* Palo Alto, CA: Dale Seymour Publications.

Shannon, A. (1996). *What is the new standards math exam?* (New Standards, University of Pittsburgh and the National Center on Education and the Economy). San Antonio, TX: Harcourt Brace Educational Measurement.

Shannon, A. (Ed.). (1998a). *High school assessment: Balanced assessment for the mathematics curriculum*. White Plains, NY: Dale Seymour Publications.

Shaughnessy, J. M., & Dick, T. (1991). Monty's dilemma: Should you stick or switch? *Mathematics Teacher, 84*, 252–256.

Shavelson, R. J., Baxter, G. P., & Pine, J. (1992). Performance assessments: Political rhetoric and measurement reality. *Educational Researcher, 21(4)*, 22–27.

Shaver, A. V., & Walls, R. T. (1998). Effect of Title I parent involvement on reading and mathematics achievement. *Journal of Research and Development in Education, 31(2)*, 90–97.

Shell Centre for Mathematical Education, University of Nottingham, England. (1982). *The language of functions, and graphs: An examination module for secondary schools*. Manchester, England: Joint Matriculation Board.

Shell Centre for Mathematical Education, University of Nottingham, England. (1984). *Problems with patterns and numbers*. Manchester, England: Joint Matriculation Board.

Siegel, M., Borasi, R., Fonzi, J. M., Sanridge, L. G., & Smith, C. (1996). Using reading to construct mathematical meaning. In P. C. Elliott & M. J. Kenney (Eds.), *Communication in Mathematics K–12 and Beyond* (1996 Yearbook, pp. 66–75). Reston, VA: National Council of Teachers of Mathematics.

Silent squares. (1986). In *EQUALS Book of Scripts* (pp. 11–12). Berkeley: University of California Regents, Lawrence Hall of Science.

Silver, E. A., Smith, M. S., & Nelson, B. S. (1995). The QUASAR project: Equity concerns meet mathematics education reform in the middle school. In W. G. Secada, E. Fennema, & L. B. Adajian (Eds.), *New Directions for Equity in Mathematics Education* (pp. 9–56). Cambridge, MA: Cambridge University Press in collaboration with the National Council of Teachers of Mathematics.

Simmons, J. H., Perkins, D. E., & Colburn, T. R. (1986). If you don't ask the right questions, you don't get the right answers. *Teaching Mathematics: Strategies That Work* (Teachers Writing to Teachers Series, pp. 173–179). Portsmouth, NH: Heineman.

Skemp, R. R. (1971). *The psychology of learning mathematics*. Middlesex, England: Penguin Books.

Skinner, B. F. (1954). The science of learning and the art of teaching. *Harvard Educational Review, 24(2)*, 86–97.

Skinner, B. F. (1968). *The technology of teaching*. New York: Meredith Corporation.

Slavin, R. (1980). Cooperative learning. *Review of Educational Research, 50(2)*, 315–342.

Slavin, R. (1988). Cooperative learning and student achievement. *Educational Leadership, 47(3)*, 31–33.

Smith, J. P. III. (1996, July). Efficacy and teaching mathematics by telling: A challenge for reform. *Journal for Research in Mathematics Education, 27(4)*, 387–402.

Smith, L. (1993). Multiple solutions involving geoboard problems. *Mathematics Teacher, 86(1)*, 25–29.

Sobel, M. A. (1988). *Reading for enrichment in secondary school mathematics*. Reston, VA: National Council of Teachers of Mathematics.

Sotto, E. (1994). *When teaching becomes learning: A theory and practice of teaching*. New York: Cassell.

Stallings, V., & Tascione, C. (1996). Student self-assessment and self-evaluation. *Mathematics Teacher, 89(7)*, 548–554.

Standera, M. (1994). Listening to students through writing. In *Empowering Students by Promoting Active Learning in Mathematics: Teachers Speak to Teachers* (pp. 25–30). Reston, VA: National Council of Teachers of Mathematics.

Steen, L. A. (Ed.). (1990). *On the shoulders of giants*. Washington, DC: National Academy Press.

Stein, M. K., & Smith, M. S. (1998). Mathematical tasks as a framework for reflection: From research to practice. *Mathematics Teaching in the Middle School, 3(4)*, 268–275.

Stein, M. K., Smith, M. S., Henningsen, M. A., & Silver, E. A. (2000). *Implementing Standards-based mathematics instruction: A casebook for professional development*. New York: Teachers College Press.

Stenmark, J. K. (Ed.). (1991). *Mathematics assessment: Myths, models, good questions and practical suggestions*. Reston, VA: National Council of Teachers of Mathematics.

Stenmark, J. K., Thompson, V., & Cossey, R. (1986). *Family math/Matemática para la familia*. Berkeley, CA: Lawrence Hall of Science, EQUALS.

Sternberg, R. J. (1994). Allowing for thinking styles. *Educational Leadership, 52(3)*, 36–40.

Stevenson, H. C., & Fantuzzo, J. W. (1986). The generality and social validity of competency-based self-control training intervention for underachieving students. *Journal of Applied Behavior Analysis, 19(3)*, 269–276.

Struik, D. J. (1969). *A source book in mathematics, 1200–1800*. Cambridge, MA: Harvard University Press.

Suydam, M. N. (1986). Manipulative materials and achievement. *Arithmetic Teacher, 33(6)*, 10.

Suydam, M. N., & Higgins, J. L. (1977). *Activity-based learning in elementary school mathematics: Recommendations from research*. Reston, VA: National Council of Teachers of Mathematics.

Tate, W. F. (1994). Race, retrenchment, and the reform of school mathematics. *Phi Delta Kappan, 75(6)*, 477–485.

Third International Mathematics and Science Study Report. (1996a). *Many visions, many aims: A cross-national exploration of curricular intentions in school mathematics*. Dordrecht, The Netherlands: Kluwer Academic Publishers Group.

Third International Mathematics and Science Study Report. (1996b). *Pursuing excellence: U.S. eighth-grade mathematics and science achievement in international perspective*. Washington, DC: National Library of Education.

Third International Mathematics and Science Study Report. (1996c). *Splintered vision: An investigation of U.S. mathematics and science education executive summary*. Washington, DC: National Library of Education.

Thompson, D. R., Senk, S. L., & Viktora, S. S. (1991). Matrices in the secondary school level. In *Discrete Mathematics Across the Curriculum K–12* (*1991 Yearbook*). Reston, VA: National Council of Teachers of Mathematics.

Thornton, C. A., & Biey, N. S. (Eds.). (1994). *Windows of opportunity: Mathematics for students with special needs*. Reston, VA: National Council of Teachers of Mathematics.

Thornton, D. A., & Wilmot, B. (1986, February). Special learners. *Arithmetic Teacher*, 38–40.

Tibbs, P., & Jordan, J. (1994). Sharing teaching ideas: Career posters. *Mathematics Teacher, 87(6)*, 410–411.

Trentacosta, J. (1993). Using the what-if machine. *CMC ComMuniCator, 18(2)*, 2.

Trentacosta, J., & Kenney, M. J. (Eds.). (1997). *Multicultural and gender equity in the mathematics classroom: The gift of diversity* (*1997 Yearbook*). Reston, VA: National Council of Teachers of Mathematics.

Tufte, E. R. (1983). *The visual display of quantitative information*. Cheshire, CO: Graphics Press.

Turik, D., & Blum, D. (1993). Ladders and saws. *Mathematics Teacher, 86(6)*, 510–513.

UCLA Mathematics Diagnostic Testing Program. (1996). *Written response items*. University of California, Los Angeles.

University of Northern Iowa. (1994). *Lessons in mathematics for the classroom and for inservice sessions with alternative assessment procedures*. Cedar Falls, IA: Author.

Useem, E. L. (1990, Fall). You're good but not good enough. *American Educator*, 24–27, 43–45.

Usiskin, Z. (1987). Resolving the continuing dilemmas in school geometry. In *Learning and Teaching Geometry, K–12* (1987 Yearbook, pp. 17–31). Reston, VA: National Council of Teachers of Mathematics.

Usnick, V., Lamphere, P. M., & Bright, G. W. (1992). A generalized area formula. *Mathematics Teacher, 85(9)*, 752–754.

VanLeuvan, P., Smith, B., Dion, G. S., Simon, D. S., & Kaplan, C. (1996). Math options: Exploring career possibilities. *Mathematics Teaching in the Middle School, 1(8)*, 654–660.

Vygotsky, L. S. (1962). *Thought and language* (E. Haufman & G. Vakar, Ed. and Trans.). Cambridge, MA: MIT Press.

Vygotsky, L. S. (1978). *Mind in society: The development of higher psychological processes*. Cambridge, MA: Harvard University Press.

Waits, B., & Demanna, F. (1994, July). *The popcorn problem*. Presentation at the Viz-Math Summer Institute, California State University, Northridge, CA.

Waits, B. K., & Demanna, F. (preprint). *What have we learned in ten years?* Columbus: The Ohio State University.

Wallace, E. C. (1993). Exploring regression with a graphing calculator. *Mathematics Teacher, 86(9)*.

Walter, M. I. (1995). *Boxes, squares, and other things: A teacher's guide for a unit in informal geometry*. Reston, VA: National Council of Teachers of Mathematics.

Watanabe, T., Hanson, R., & Nowosielski, F. D. (1996). Morgan's theorem. *Mathematics Teacher, 89(5)*, 420–423.

Webb, N. M. (1980). An analysis of group interaction and mathematical errors in heterogeneous ability groups. *British Journal of Educational Psychology, 50,* 266–276.

Webb, N. M. (1992a). Assessment of students' knowledge of mathematics: Steps toward a theory. In D. A. Grouws (Ed.), *Handbook of Research on Mathematics Teaching and Learning.* Reston, VA: National Council of Teachers of Mathematics.

Webb, N. M. (1992b). *Collaborative group versus individual assessment in mathematics: Group processes and outcomes* [Report]. Los Angeles: National Center for Research on Evaluation, Standards, and Student Testing.

Weissglass, J. (1998, April 3). *The SAT: Public spirited or elitist?* Handout provided at a presentation in Los Angeles, CA, for the Los Angeles Urban Systematic Initiative.

Welchons, A. M., Krickenberger, W. R., & Pearson, H. R. (1963). *Algebra Book Two* (Modern Ed). Boston: Ginn and Company.

Widdel, M. E. (1996). *Patterns of interactions between boy-girl pairs in a mathematical problem-solving activity.* Unpublished master's thesis, California State University, Northridge, California.

Wiggins, G. (1993). Assessment: Authenticity, context, and validity. *Phi Delta Kappan, 75(3),* 200–214.

Index